AN HISTORICAL GEOGRAPHY OF EUROPE

'*For as Geography without History seemeth a carkasse without motion, so History without Geography wandreth as a Vagrant without a certaine habitation*' JOHN SMITH, Generall Historie of Virginia

AN HISTORICAL GEOGRAPHY OF EUROPE

by

GORDON EAST
Professor of Geography in the University of London

with 64 maps

METHUEN & CO. LTD LONDON
E. P. DUTTON & CO. INC. NEW YORK

First published 5 September 1935
Second edition, Revised, July 1943
Third edition, Revised, August 1948
Fourth edition, 1950
Reprinted with minor corrections 1956
Reprinted with a new epilogue 1962
Fifth edition, 1966

Printed in Great Britain by
Jarrold and Sons Limited, Norwich
5·1

PREFACE

IT is significant of the unimportant and ill-defined part played by historical geography among academic studies in England, not many years ago, that Professor Haverfield should have described it as an 'up-to-date' study which 'somehow concerns history and maps', whilst another professor of history disposed of it even more succinctly as an illegitimate form of history. It must be admitted that the content and purpose of historical geography long remained and still remains in this country, except among specialists, little understood or variously interpreted. It is pertinent, however, to recall by way of explanation that modern geography is scarcely more than a generation old in Britain and that it is only in recent years that British geographers have become increasingly clear as to the methods and goal of their study. Further, it was only when the study of contemporary geography had made progress that the need arose to inquire into the conditions which obtained in the historical past. Historical geography thus arose as a separate field of investigation subsidiary to the study of present-day geography: as such it has much to do with maps, but it makes no claim to parade as an interpretation of history. It is clearly a frontier study in which the researches of historians, archaeologists and geographers are brought into close relationship; it is no less clear that its function and *raison d'être*, as Professor Rodwell Jones urged not long ago,[1] are the discovery of correlations between human societies and their geographical settings.

The present work has been written as an attempt to apply in a particular case the modern conception of historical geography. The historical geography of Europe in this sense remains still in large measure an unexplored field for research, or rather a forest of tangled undergrowth in which the explorer only with difficulty makes his way. There seemed some justification for the attempt to survey in broad outline the whole of Europe, although the result is admittedly introductory in character and selective in treatment. The lack of text-books on this subject

[1] *Economica*, Nov., 1925.

may be explained, though hardly excused, by academic caution. The few English books which bear the title Historical Geography of Europe do not treat this subject as it is now interpreted by geographers. Freeman's *The Historical Geography of Europe*, which Professor Bury revised in 1903, has long proved an invaluable handbook to historians, but despite the definite article, its content is limited to the changing areas and names of states and is thus concerned with only one part of the historical geography of Europe.

The limits of space have necessitated a great deal of selection and omission, and no attempt has been made to deal comprehensively, even in outline, with every part of Europe or with the whole of historical time. Further, it was thought expedient not to include the British Isles, since it was clearly impossible to deal adequately with this region in a book of these proportions. Again, the book begins quite arbitrarily with the Roman Empire: it was scarcely possible to do justice to the abundant findings of modern archaeology in the light of which the earliest phases of the geography of Europe must be conceived, and further, the period of Greek and early Roman civilization has received relatively fuller treatment from the geographical standpoint. Similarly, if it does not cover the most recent period of European history, it does at least reach in the 1870's the threshold of our present civilization. Moreover, the complexities of European culture, in the past as in the present, make it virtually impossible to treat the human geography of Europe as a united whole. Thus different regions have been selected for treatment at successive periods, in the hope that some of the major geographical contrasts in time and place may be depicted. A number of cross-sections or 'period-pictures' have been presented, therefore, alike in ancient, medieval and modern times. Finally, it seemed desirable to avoid the grouping of chapters on a purely chronological basis, since this was in any case scarcely practicable, but rather to arrange them under the three general headings The Geography of Settlement, Political Geography and Economic Geography. Even so, although each of these headings indicates the main emphasis of the chapters included under each, the writer has had continually in mind the regional conception of geography, which focuses attention on all the many inter-relationships between human societies and their physical environments.

The preparation of this book has been spread over several years and it has been written primarily to serve the needs of students. The writer is of the opinion that historical geography, as it is now interpreted, provides one of the more fruitful studies in the relationship between geography and history, but that, in view of the infancy of this subject, it is necessary to substitute for the pursuit of wide generalization the careful study of particular illustrative cases. The following chapters, therefore, which are sufficiently self-contained, seek, so far as is possible within a general survey, to focus attention on concrete instances of the activity of human societies in relation to their habitats, which at the same time offer them opportunities and set them limitations.

The spelling of geographical names has raised many difficulties. No attempt has been made consistently to use the spellings current at particular periods; nor, on the other hand, have the present-day forms been invariably used. Where familiar English forms existed they have been adopted; in cases where modern names have two or more linguistic forms, one form, past or present, has been used throughout. Further, this difficulty has been met to some extent in the index where the alternative forms of certain names have been given.

The writer thanks those publishers and authors who kindly allowed him to produce in this book a number of maps which contain material in published maps.

Finally, he wishes to record his gratitude for help given: by his wife, by Dr. H. Ormsby and Mr. L. G. Robinson, M.A., who, from time to time, have given him both encouragement and suggestions, and by Professor E. G. R. Taylor and Dr. S. W. Wooldridge, who kindly, yet critically, read the proofs. He wishes to thank, also, for their courteous help, the staff of the British Library of Political Science.

W. G. EAST

THE LONDON SCHOOL OF ECONOMICS
AND POLITICAL SCIENCE, *February*, 1935

PREFACE TO THE THIRD EDITION

The opportunity has been taken in this edition to revise, in the light of recent advances in palæobotany, outmoded ideas about 'open' or forest-free lands in their relation to early settlement (see Chapter III). Revisions have been made throughout the book, especially in Chapter XVIII and in the Epilogue. A number of new items has been added to the Bibliography and Fig. 21 improved.

September, 1947. W. G. E.

PREFACE

It is gratifying that historical geography, as a study of the relationship of man and land, has established itself so effectively in this country during the last thirty years or so, so much so, that a proper training in geography cannot dispense with the light which it sheds on the contemporary world.

The passing of the years has not weakened the premise on which this book was built, namely that a geographical view of the continent of Europe must take account of the continuing processes of history which have moulded, and continue to mould it. With ' infinite riches in a little room ', Europe presents a remarkably variegated surface for its size, coupled with a complexity of social relationships which, as they ever change, are rooted nevertheless in its past. While this book remains fundamentally unchanged as it was first conceived and as it grew out of the teaching of undergraduates, the chance of a reprinting for this edition has made it possible to correct a few errors of fact (e.g. on pages 19–20), to bring up to date a few references to present conditions (e.g. on pages ix and 391), and to rewrite the Epilogue, which attempts a brief review of Europe today as it appears alike in its demographic, economic and political relationships.

BIRKBECK COLLEGE, *September*, 1965. W. G. E.

CONTENTS

MAPS AND PLANS

INTRODUCTION

THE historical geography of Europe is its human geography at the successive stages of civilization through which it has passed, and its human geography in turn is the expression on the face of Europe of the efforts of human societies to mould and adapt the countryside to their use. The European peninsula, as the home of man, presented at all times a changing panorama, the elements of which were both natural and man-made, and the human geography of present-day Europe is the product of some thousands of years during which men have occupied and modified this environment. A full analysis and synthesis of European geography throughout the ages which has never been, and can scarcely ever be, written, involves penetration into the dim recesses of historical time, a time which must now be conceived to include the thousands of years illuminated by archaeological discoveries. At many points of time and in many regions the picture of European geography in the past is obscure, and its detail can never be seen as clearly as that of those new countries, the present culture of which has its roots in recent centuries. Even so, a great deal is known about the earliest stages of European civilization—too much, in fact, to be treated adequately in a short survey—and it is possible in this book only to allude to the prehistoric distributions and activities of human groups which settled on European soil from the days of the Palaeolithic Age onwards.

The impact of human groups on any region expresses itself in a number of characteristic ways. In the first place, intrusion and settlement provide one of the most striking reactions to, and modifications of, geographical environments. Men, moving in groups along lines of least resistance, intrude into and take possession of those lands which offer them, according to their cultural conditions and aspirations, optimum opportunities for the satisfaction of their needs. If they were purely wandering pasturalists, i.e., nomads, they continued for some time at least to live a life of continual movement from pasture to pasture, a life which precluded the establishment of fixed settlements. If they were able to till the land, as was characteristically the case in Europe from the Neolithic Age onwards, the requirements of agriculture enforced an entirely, or almost entirely, sedentary life. In short, their occupation of the land was marked by the establishment of settlements—social and economic groupings the distribution of which conformed with the conditions of physical geography and of natural vegetation. Thus the process of settlement, associated with the adaptation of the soil to the needs of sedentary agriculturists, forms one of the central themes of human geography. The varied types of settlements, the way in which they were distributed, the peculiar selection of the sites, which were certainly not chosen haphazard—all these aspects of settlement are of outstanding geographical interest. Moreover, the colonization of Europe was not a simple unitary process which was completed at one particular period : it was operative throughout broad periods of time from the prehistoric onwards, first in one and then in another part of the European peninsula. Even so, it is true to say that immigration and settlement occupy chronologically an early stage, as they mark geographically an initial stage, in the historical geography of Europe.

The first part of this book, covering Chapters I to VI, has been called *The Geography of Settlement in Europe*. It provides, even in outline, only a partial treatment of this vast theme : it ignores or assumes much relevant material for the period which precedes the creation of the Roman Empire in 27 B.C. Moreover, it does not deal exclusively with settlement alone, although the main emphasis of its chapters is on settlement structure—the evolution of towns and villages up to the end of the Middle Ages, that is until about A.D. 1500. In many respects the Roman Empire provides a good starting-point, since it embraced within its borders the whole of Mediterranean, and a large part of continental, Europe and since, moreover, it is a period about which a great deal of detailed information is available. It is possible to move with assurance along the Roman roads and the Mediterranean seaways, to note in passing Roman ports, towns and farms, to halt in the many well-built, and often wall-girt, cities, and to examine the organization of the frontier regions. Further, many cities of to-day, whatever their peculiar functions and relative importance, occupy the sites of Roman cities ; what is more—and it is a remarkable illustration of what may be called geographical inertia—some of these sites had been settled in prehistoric times. The Roman Empire, although it included so much of continental Europe, left outside its frontiers broad regions which became known, because of their non-Roman and relatively backward culture, as the 'barbarian world'. These regions, which embraced much of Middle Europe, Russia and Scandinavia, have been described hitherto mainly in the light of Roman literature, but thanks to the revelations of scientific archaeology it is now possible to envisage them more clearly. It was from the barbarian world, superior in the vigour of its peoples if inferior in its command over nature, that emigrants moved out and slowly penetrated the Roman Empire. This immigration resulted in further settlement in western and southern Europe. Thus again, although much remained unchanged, new features of a permanent character were impressed on the countryside. The medieval period, which began with the Germanic settlement and lasted until the geographical discoveries at the end of the fifteenth century, witnessed a great colonizing movement. It had its mainspring in the increase of population in western Europe chiefly in the twelfth and thirteenth centuries, which, with varying force according to time and place, led to the creation of villages and towns in lands hitherto scantily settled, if at all. This process of colonization was indissolubly linked up with the practice of agriculture, and it was the need for arable lands which stimulated the attack on the 'negative' lands—lands which, hitherto, owing to their natural character, had been largely avoided by settlers.

The utilization of the soil, together with other economic activities, all of which in different degrees are related to the geographical setting, develops subsequently to settlement. The characteristics of settled lands in respect of soils, climate, drainage and natural vegetation present varied possibilities which, according to their level of technical skill and knowledge, settlers attempt to exploit. Agriculture remained the predominant feature in European economy from the Roman period until the mid-nineteenth century everywhere, including Britain. It was conducted from rural settlements for the most part and underwent little change throughout the ages until in the seventeenth and eighteenth centuries new methods and new crops began to be introduced, first in the Low Countries and then in England. From the geographical standpoint many features of this agricultural economy are of interest: the field systems, the varieties and distribution of crops, and the conquest by the plough of woodland, marsh and heath. Some of these aspects have been examined in this book, notably for the medieval period in Chapters IV and V, and again for a later period in Chapters XIX and XX. But if agriculture was the widespread and characteristic economic activity in Europe, industry and commerce played important parts in almost every age. Industry was centred largely, but not entirely and invariably, in towns, which came to be essentially the resort of economic specialists, *mercatores*, who were both artisans and traders. Moreover, industries tended to a considerable extent to be localized in certain regions of Europe, and a great deal of commercial traffic in raw materials, natural products and finished goods was carried along the roads, the seaways and the rivers. The network of engineered roads which was laid out by the Roman legions, to some extent persisted and was in a small degree modified to meet the needs of trade. Seaports were selected and sea routes established, whilst mountain passes and navigable rivers were utilized. Again, as in industry, so in commerce and transport, some degree of localization is apparent at all times. It is significant of the great value of the waterways that, in proximity to them, stood the chief industrial and trading regions. The inland seas became the first nurseries of seamanship and commerce; later, in the sixteenth century, with the beginning of the Oceanic phase of European history, certain countries with Atlantic seaboards won the lead in maritime trade. The great rivers of Europe, too, above all the Rhine, carried in the past a considerable share of inland traffic. It is easy, however, in the absence of precise information, to under-exaggerate the use of roads and to exaggerate the function of rivers in historical geography, since, as a study of the Danube route-way shows in Chapter XVIII, the usefulness of rivers was restricted continually by political factors as well as by the conditions of physical geography. Finally, although the economic order of Europe retained many of its medieval characteristics even in the eighteenth and nineteenth centuries, drastic changes rapidly took place, first in Britain and then on the continent, in the course of the latter century. Chapter XX reviews broadly the economic geography of continental Europe about the year 1870, by which time railroads had been generally established. But although Britain at this time had become the workshop of the world and a land of urbanized life and large-scale industry based on coal and iron, the rest of Europe was only just beginning to bear the impress of the new economic order.

It has been seen therefore that, subsequently to their occupation of the soil, human societies establish settlements of several kinds and engage in various kinds of economic activity. The distribution and localization of industry—whether this consists of agriculture, horticulture, pastoral farming, manufacture, trade or transport—have close relationships with physical geography. But it is important not to over-simplify this relationship. Although it is true that economic activities are inspired and localized to a considerable extent by the immediate possibilities of the countryside—by its ability to produce foodstuffs and raw materials, by its wealth in metals, in wild animals, in fish and in timber, by its advantageous location in relation to easy routes and to other countries of contrasted products—nevertheless, these activities are not a little governed by the peculiar aptitude of the people themselves and by the way in which they themselves and their neighbours are politically organized. The effect of changing political conditions on the human geography of a country has been examined in a particular instance in Chapter XIV, since Sicily provides a remarkable illustration in miniature of ever-changing political conditions within a small but well-endowed geographical region. Moreover, political conditions, apart from their influence on economic activities, constitute an important aspect of the human geography of Europe. Europe, twice re-organized after each of the two Great Wars, now contains thirty-four independent states: that is to say, about a quarter of the states of the world are concentrated within a twelfth of its inhabited area. The peculiar political organization of Europe could be explained only in terms of its large number of distinct and self-conscious nationalities. Certainly the chief lines of political division were provided not by race either in the anthropological or linguistic sense of the term, but by nationalities, and in a lesser degree by language. In other words Europe was differentiated in respect of its nationalities and its languages no less than in respect of its physique and climate. These distinctions of nationality and language originated from the processes of immigration, conquest and settlement, which were for the most part effected, at least in western Europe, by the time of Charles the Great. Whereas the great imperial states of the past, like the Roman Empire, the Byzantine Empire—its surviving eastern part—and the Arab Caliphate, comprised territories in which numerous groups of varied nationalities and languages lived side by side, in contrast other states later arose which came to approximate, but only to approximate, to the concept of the nation state. Typical of such states were the French Kingdom, and the German Empire founded in 1871, in each of which one nation group and one language were predominant, although minorities of other peoples of distinct language and nationality were comprised within them.

In Part II of this book attention is given to the territorial evolution of a number of modern states. Further, it includes studies of the geography of some of the more outstanding imperial states of the past, notably the Roman Empire (Chapters I and II), the Byzantine Empire (Chapter VIII), and finally the Arab Empire (Chapter IX), in so far as that lay within continental Europe and the Mediterranean world.

In the Epilogue to this book, under the title 'Europe in the Twentieth Century', the attempt is made to assess the changed position of Europe in the world after the two wars of 1914–19 and of 1939–45 in which it took the leading part. Here interest naturally focuses on the way the Continent is now divided—politically, economically and socially—and on the efforts which are being made towards some degree of integration.

PART I

THE GEOGRAPHY OF SETTLEMENT IN EUROPE

'La Nature prépare le site et l'homme l'organise pour lui permettre de répondre à ses besoins et ses désirs' VIDAL DE LA BLACHE

CHAPTER I

THE MEDITERRANEAN LANDS OF THE ROMAN EMPIRE

THE Roman Empire, for the first and the last time in history, imposed a common political authority on the peninsulas and bordering lands of the Mediterranean Sea. Moreover, it extended its civilization through the northern mountainous rim of the Mediterranean basin into the hitherto remote and less civilized regions of continental Europe. Mediterranean civilization before the rise of Rome, whether Phoenician, Etruscan or Greek, had been mainly marginal and maritime, especially in the western part of the basin. Both the Phoenicians and the Greeks in turn had established colonies which engaged in industry, fishing, commerce, and agriculture around the coastlands, as Plato put it, ' like ants and frogs around a pool '. Prior to the rise of Rome the Mediterranean was divided into two spheres of interest. The Phoenicians commanded the western basin of the sea, since they held the Strait of Gibraltar and the approach between western Sicily and Carthage, whilst in the east they held their original bases along the north Syrian coast. The Greeks, in contrast, were above all pivoted around the Aegean Sea, whence they had penetrated north-eastwards, through the Hellespont into the Sea of Marmora and the Black Sea, and westwards into the Ionian Sea, which they controlled from their settlements in Magna Graecia, that is, in southern Italy and eastern Sicily. Finally, around the Ligurian and Lion Gulfs Greeks, Carthaginians, and Etruscans met in trade competition, and Marseilles was a distant outpost of Greek civilization. Rome, however, overcame all these maritime powers, and from a landward base built up maritime supremacy throughout the whole basin. Further, its arms were carried north-westwards and northwards to the Rhine and the Danube, into lands which contrasted in their climate, vegetation, and civilization with the geographically favoured and precociously civilized Mediterranean world. Rome thus imposed a common rule and a common culture on the heterogeneous parts of its Empire : it built cities, ports, and roads; it established frontier defences and exploited agricultural and mineral resources. Some of this work had permanent effects on the human geography of Europe, for many of the cities of to-day occupy Roman (and even pre-Roman) sites, whilst the alinement of some modern roads still follows that selected by the Roman road-builders. Moreover, it is not without importance to the human geography of Europe that the Roman Empire marked the extension north-westwards of empire-building. In common with all the great empires which preceded it—those of China, Assyria, Persia, Athens, and Alexander—its territories were located mainly in the sub-tropical belt of the

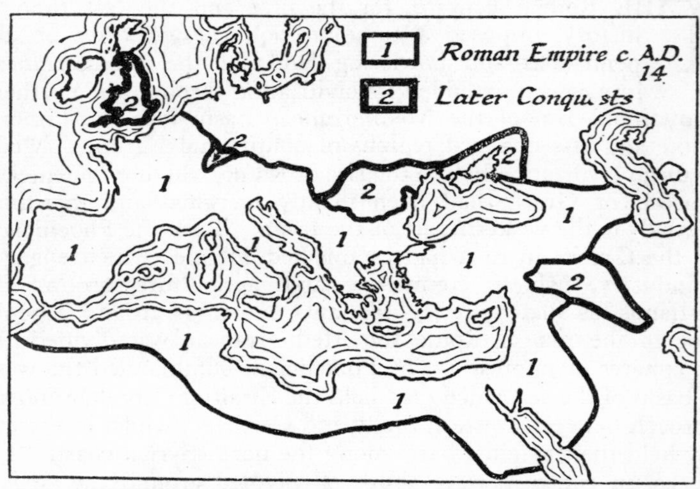

FIG. 1.—The Territorial Extent of the Roman Empire

northern hemisphere.[1] It differed, however, from its predecessors not only in its westerly location along this belt but also in its intrusion northwards into the temperate and forested lands of continental Europe.

The Mediterranean Sea formed the axis of the Empire and around its shores—particularly in the east—were grouped its most populous and civilized lands (Figs. 1 and 2). On a number of grounds—position, climate, configuration, elevation, and cultural level—these lands were geographically differentiated. The abundance of record, both literary and archaeological, makes it possible to describe with considerable detail the geography of these regions. It is attempted here to sketch broadly the human

[1] Cp. Sten de Geer, 'The Sub-Tropical Belt of Old Empires', *Geog. Ann.*, No. 3, 1928.

geography of the lands which comprised the Mediterranean base of the Empire during the first four centuries A.D., with an eye to their own distinctive characteristics and also to their relations within the Mediterranean world as a whole.

Italy

The historical geography of Italy does not begin with Rome or even with Latium in which Rome stood; nevertheless it emphasizes the superior importance of the western half of the peninsula. The country between the Apennines and the western coast had certain geographical advantages, the utilization of which is

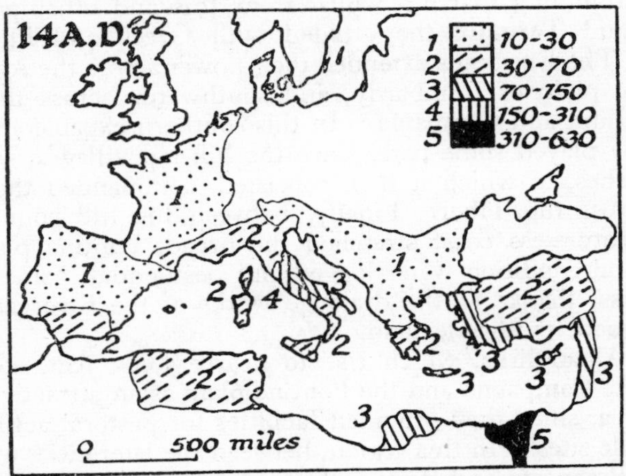

FIG. 2.—Population densities per square mile within the Roman Empire *c.* A.D. 14 (after Usher). Cp. *infra* Figs. 15 and 50. Courtesy of the *Geographical Review*, published by the American Geographical Society of New York

evidenced by the civilization of the Etruscans, of the Greek cities, and finally, later of Rome. Below the backbone of the Apennines the country consists of plateaux, rounded hills, upland basins, and coastal, marsh-fringed plains. These varied areas are brought into close relation with one another largely by the valleys of rivers, which though unnavigable, open up land routes. Rivers, like the Arno, the Tiber and the Liri, pursue at first longitudinal courses in the mountains, and then by right-angular bends flow westwards to the sea. The broken hilly country of western Italy is further diversified by the spread, particularly in Latium and in southern Etruria, of volcanic soils derived from pumice and basalt, which at their best are very fertile. Finally, their westward orientation and the mountain girdle landwards exposed these regions to the moist westerly winds ; whilst further, small port sites offered access to the sea highways. Into Etruria, where the zone of hill and plain between the Apennines and the sea is widest, the Etruscans came, it would seem from Asia Minor, and established themselves about 1000 B.C. They developed a high civilization based on industry, agriculture and trade ; built numerous walled towns on hill-top sites ; drained, partially at least, the *maremma* or coastal marshes ; quarried marble from the Apuan Hills near Massa and Carrara ; brought iron from Elba and worked it at their near-by town and chief port of Populonium, which stood on a hill above the surrounding marsh ; whilst from this and other ports like Caere and Tarquini they traded with Greek and Phoenician cities. The Etruscans extended their power across the Apennines into the plain of Lombardy, and southwards across the Tiber into Latium and Campania. In this southern expansion the site of Rome played some part, since the hill-top villages, separated by marshes, of which it then consisted, commanded the lowest ford across the Tiber. Finally, between the hill country and a low featureless coast stretched the broad, Pontine plain : in its natural condition water-logged and pestilential, some of this plain was, thanks to the drainage works of the Etruscans, rendered good, cultivable land.

The Alban hills, which rise to nearly 3,000 feet, stood out above the Campagna and the Pontine plain as an attractive settlement area, since they provided facilities for pastoral activity and defensible sites. In this region, between the later cities of Rome, Tibur, Praeneste and Ardea, the earliest settlements in Latium were made by Iron Age ancestors of the Latins. Transhumance was practised between the summer pasturage of the hills and the winter pasturage of the Campagna, and arising out of this seasonal movement the first settlement was made about the year 1000 B.C. on the Palatine hill, one of the volcanic hills of Rome, which stood on the left bank of the Tiber. Settlement later pushed southward to the seaward flank of the Lepini hills : under Etruscan rule walled cities of refuge, e.g. near Cora, Norba, Setia, were built ; they were provided with water cisterns and connected by a hill road ; and their inhabitants cultivated part of the Pontine plain. On the coast Satricum was the earliest seaport : it exported wool and timber before 700 B.C.

Latium, like southern Etruria, was originally a region of volcanic activity. The undulating Campagna plain around Rome was a tract composed of volcanic rocks ; it was dissected by many little ravines and well supplied with springs. Towards the sea an alluvial lowland marked the limit of the Campagna. To the east of the Alban hills Latium included a belt of broken hill country which lies below the high ranges of the central Apennines and is bounded southwards by the upper course of the Liri river. Streams from these hills drain to the Sacco river which flows south-east through a broad plain to reach the Liri : the two valleys formed a natural route between Campania, the Alban hills and Rome, and was guarded in the north by the ancient Latin stronghold of Praeneste (Palestrina). To the south of the Sacco river the Lepini hills, a rugged and lofty limestone spur of the Apennines, stood higher than the Alban hills and approached the sea near Terracino, where a narrow gap was left through which the Via Appia was later carried into Campania.

Latium presented in ancient times a more productive agricultural area than it does to-day, and was thus able to produce adequate food supplies and to support the large population of yeoman farmers who fought the wars of Rome. The growth of jungle over the volcanic ash had produced a cover of humus soil. Beech trees and other species, which grew on plains now treeless, provided food for pigs ; tree roots held up water to some extent and dams were built to check the wastage of soil by swift winter torrents. In the Campagna a system of underground tunnels (*cuniculi*) existed long before the rise of Rome for the purpose of draining and irrigating the soil, and despite its many vicissitudes during the Roman period the Campagna remained well cultivated and well populated (Fig. 3). The desolation of the Campagna began only after the fall of Rome in the early medieval period and reached its worst phase in the seventeenth and eighteenth centuries.[1] Wheat, barley and spelt were cultivated ; there was ample timber ; and pigs, sheep and oxen were reared. Figs were grown, the vine at first on a very small scale, whilst the olive was later introduced from the Greek cities of Campania. Salt was produced from the estuarine marshes of the Tiber, but the country lacked mineral wealth and industries. Maritime traffic rested in the hands of its more civilized neighbours, especially the Greeks. The rapid current of the Tiber and its estuarine marshes were uninviting to early commercial enterprise ; Ostia was not founded until the fourth century B.C.,

[1] The Campagna suffered badly in the sixth century when Rome was several times besieged. Aqueducts were cut, drainage works were neglected, and in consequence the swampy plain became malarial. In contrast, in the Roman and pre-Roman period, the Campagna seems to have been little or not at all afflicted by this disease. Cp. Almagia, ' The Repopulation of the Roman Campagna ', *G.R.*, Oct. 1929. Quite recently the Campagna has been reclaimed and populated.

and although the river at Rome usually had a navigable depth,[1] navigation was not an early Roman activity. The site of Rome occupied at first a frontier position between Etruria and Latium which masked its potentialities : but old routes from Etruria and Campania converged on the ford which it controlled, whilst the Via Salaria (salt road) ran up the Tiber valley from Rome. The city of Rome was created, as a single-walled town, *c.* 600 B.C.,

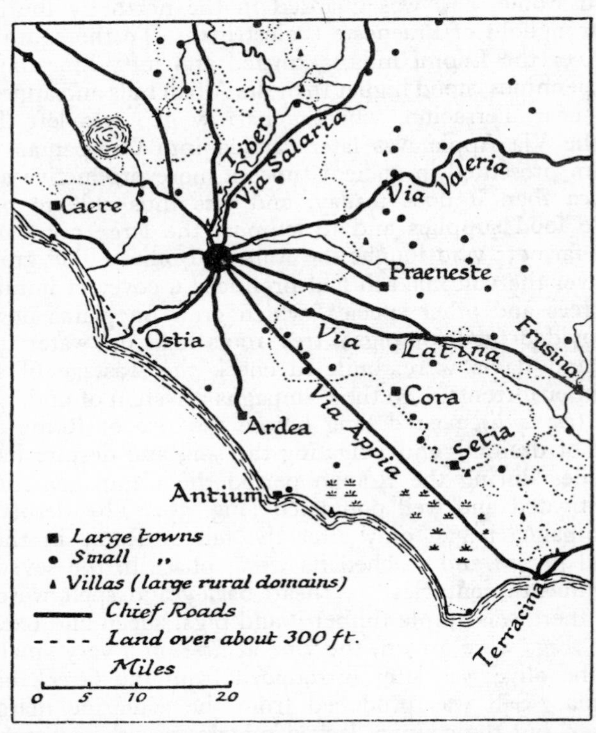

FIG. 3.—Settlements around Rome under the Empire (based upon the International 1 : 1,000,000 map of the Roman Empire, provisional edition)

out of the union of hill-top villages ; the Palatine hill, the earliest hill occupied, consisted—as did the site of Roman London—of twin hills which were steep-sided and further protected by marsh, whilst just below it lay the ford. The growth of the

[1] The Tiber, as Pardé has shown, is not a typical Mediterranean river with marked extremes of high and low water. Moreover, its floods have been much exaggerated. See the summary in the *G.J.*, Sept. 1933.

city was marked by the building of new walls (the one which was begun in A.D. 282 enclosed a population of half a million): whilst numerous aqueducts carried water into the city. Rome came to enjoy the advantages of a central position, but, never a manufacturing centre, it had little to send down to its port. In fact, the harbours which were successively excavated at Ostia and stand to-day silted up some two or three miles from the sea, served primarily for the import of foodstuffs.

Campania, the northern outpost of Greek civilization in Italy, is structurally an ancient sea-gulf which has been elevated and filled in with volcanic tufa. An extensive plain, ringed around by broken hill masses, it was covered with a soil, decomposed from the tufa, which was so rich that it never suffered—as did that of Latium—from exhaustion. Further, its coastline well suited it to maritime activity. The Gulfs of Naples and Salerno offered to Greek colonists sheltered ports and hill sites, of which the chief were Neapolis (Naples), Paestum and Cumae. Behind these ports colonies were founded in which industries developed; notable among these was Capua, a route-centre, which lay to the south-east of the present Capua on the Volturno river. The Greeks introduced the olive and vine; corn and cattle also were great elements in the wealth of Campania; and metal, pottery, glass and woollen industries were active in its towns. The Roman conquest of Campania was marked by the construction of the Via Appia in 312 B.C. When later on Roman Italy became the economic centre of the Mediterranean world and the Greek cities in southern Italy had been ruined, Campania became very prosperous, and its prosperity was reflected in the activity of the ports of Neapolis and, more particularly, of Puteoli, which outdistanced Cumae as the chief outlet on the Bay of Naples. Until the second century A.D., by which time Ostia had become its successful rival, Puteoli remained the busiest port of western Italy: more productive than Latium, Campania had always wine, oil and manufactures to send as return cargoes in the ships which brought oriental commodities from Alexandria and Seleucia. The smaller ports of Herculaneum and Pompeii stood also on the Bay of Naples in the shadow of Mount Vesuvius, which buried them in its lava during the eruption of A.D. 79; numerous elegant villas also were strung out along the Campanian coast.

In the coastlands of southern Italy and in eastern Sicily—in Magna Graecia—Greek colonies formed the western outposts of the Greek world and were orientated towards the Ionian and Aegean seas. Under Roman rule these lands exploited new opportunities. In the hands of Rome southern Italy and Sicily possessed a strategically central position within Mediterranean waters, and challenged Carthage for the maritime supremacy of the sea. They controlled the Straits of Messina, the narrow channel through which, despite its winds and currents,[1] lay the ship-way between the eastern Mediterranean and the Tyrrhenian Sea ; they partially controlled the Ionian Sea and the approach therefrom into the Adriatic ; whilst Sicily shared with Carthage the command of the 'waist' of the Mediterranean Sea between its eastern and western basins.

In general, southern Italy and Sicily consisted of coastal plains or terraces, backed by highlands of granite or limestone, which were thickly forested and trenched by deep torrential rivers. The uplands provided in their valleys and clearings habitats for pastoral peoples who practised transhumance between the lowlands and the uplands. The seaward spurs of the interior highlands broke up the coastal plains into a number of separate sectors which formed convenient frame-works for the Greek city-states. In proportion to its length the coastline of Magna Graecia offered few natural harbours, but the best of these, Tarentum and Syracuse, were cities of first-rate importance, although under Roman rule they relatively declined. The nature of their hinterland—a dry, clay plain and a wooded limestone plateau—limited the Apulian ports, despite their favourable position, to secondary importance. Brindisi had, however, strategical value, in that it stood at the end of the Via Appia from Rome and was the ferry port for Dyrrhachium (Durazzo): it was thus an important station on the shortest route between Rome and Byzantium, and thence to the Euphrates frontier. In southern Italy the dense forests of the Basilicata, now largely destroyed, helped to prevent inundation by checking the run-off of water, so that better conditions were provided for agriculture in the coastal plain. Cereals, olives, and vines were grown, and wool from the uplands was used in the woollen industry of Tarentum. To the west the wild forests of the Sila and Aspromonte mountains were an important source of ships' timber [2] in turn to Greek and Roman cities on the coast. Finally, the port of Messina in Sicily provided the best harbour of refuge for ships making the passage

[1] The terrors of this passage were exaggerated, perhaps even deliberately, by the Carthaginians. The chief difficulties were rapid and irregular currents and heavy gusts of wind blowing down valleys and gorges.

[2] The islands of Sicily, Sardinia and Corsica also provided timber, and the loss of these islands was for this reason a hard blow to the maritime power of Carthage. On the Mediterranean forests see Semple, *The Mediterranean Region*, Chapter XI.

through the Messina Straits. In Sicily, which became a battlefield between the Romans and Carthaginians for maritime ascendancy in the western basin of the Mediterranean, Syracuse with its double harbour was the richest and most populous of the Greek cities, whilst settlement was dense on the rich lava soils which were spread around the flanks of Mount Etna. Under Roman rule Sicily was exploited mainly as a grain-producing land ; its vine and olive cultivation was largely and deliberately curtailed ; and it exported to Rome not only cereals but also manufactures, sulphur, marble and salt. Similarly, southern Italy was converted into great estates engaged primarily in sheep and cattle rearing for the Roman market. In short, Magna Graecia, as a result of policy and of wars, became a provincial region subordinate to Rome : where Syracuse and Tarentum had formerly reigned, Puteoli and Ostia ruled.

Just as Roman expansion into Magna Graecia made Rome a maritime power in the Mediterranean, so also the conquest of Gallia Cisalpina encouraged political ambitions in continental Europe. The original frontier of Italy was marked by the folded ranges of the Apennines and the small Rubicon river, now identified with the Fiumicino, which enters the Adriatic to the north of Rimini. Gallia Cisalpina, or the Po basin, thus lay outside Italy, and this distinction is confirmed by modern geographers who emphasize the continental, as distinct from the peninsular or Mediterranean, characteristics of the northern plain of present-day Italy. Gallia Cisalpina formed the largest lowland area in Italy and was limited, as it was well watered by, the Alpine arc which presented a steep wall to the north. In its geological origin a gulf of the Adriatic Sea, which has been elevated and filled in by marine and glacial materials, it is fringed to the north and south, below both the Alps and the Apennines, by a belt of well-watered productive hill country. The plain itself is furrowed by the Po and its many right- and left-bank tributaries, and is floored by glacial deposits which provide varied soils. Its climate, which combines features of both the Mediterranean and continental régimes, favoured varied cultivation ; and when, under Roman initiative, drainage and irrigation works were carried out, it became very productive alike of cereals and fruits. Owing to its many passes, the Alpine girdle served as much to unite as to separate the plain from continental Europe ; the physique of the Alps is such as to make access from the north, from the basins of the Rhône, the Rhine and the Danube, relatively easier than movement northwards from Italy ; whilst the climate and economic possibilities of the north Italian plain formed in themselves a strong attraction to invaders from the north. Moreover, a well-graded route, frequented in the Iron Age, crossed the Apennines where they narrow between the modern Bologna and Pistoia, by way of the Reno valley and the Futa pass, and led thence into Tuscany.

Already in the Iron Age, the Villanovans who peopled Latium had crossed the Alps into Italy. So also, about 400 B.C., came the Celtic Gauls, by way of the Great St. Bernard and Brenner passes. Their ingress into Italy challenged the power of the Etruscans who had already established certain cities in the northern plains, which became in turn great Roman and modern towns. In the north Melpun (near Milan) and Verona stood at the terminals of Alpine routes on the fertile zone above the plain ; in the south along the similar fertile belt at the foot of the Apennines stood Parma, Modena and Bologna ; Piacenza and Cremona, which guarded crossings of the Po, and Mantua were Etruscan cities ; whilst they held also the ports of Ravenna, Rimini and Pisaurum. The Etruscans, however, were unable to hold the northern plain from these well-placed cities ; the Gauls occupied in turn Milan, Verona, Bologna and (by 350 B.C.) the coast towns, and as early as about 390 B.C. they reached the Tiber and burnt Rome. The Gauls were semi-nomadic and pastoral in their economy ; cattle, pigs, and sheep were reared, whilst they established small hill-top villages, and a few tribal centres. Rome advanced towards the north by way of Umbria, and reached the coastlands of the Adriatic, where colonies were founded at Hadria (Atri) in 289 B.C. and at Rimini—the first colony outside Italy —in 268 B.C. Rimini, accessible from the sea, was made a strongly fortified base ; it was linked with Rome by the Flaminian Way in 220 B.C., by means of which Gallia Cisalpina could be held. The eventual conquest of these lands was accompanied by the creation of strong towns, ports and roads, whilst industry, agriculture and commerce were developed. The Via Aemilia, built in 187 B.C., ran along the fertile belt below the Apennines and connected Rimini with Cremona and Piacenza.

In 181 B.C. Aquileia was founded at the head of the Adriatic ; it stood well to the north-east of the Po delta and had a deep water channel through the Grado lagoon ; its site now lies inland owing to the accumulation of river alluvium. Aquileia became, like Puteoli, one of the greatest ports of Italy. It was the predecessor of Venice, and its importance illustrates the permanence of certain favourable factors of geographical position. It became a focus of land routes ; the Via Popilia linked it with Rimini, and thence with Rome ; a road ran westwards to Verona,

Milan and Turin ; another ran around the head of the Adriatic and into the Dalmatian coastlands as far south as Durazzo ; whilst highways over the Julian Alps, which provide the lowest, shortest and easiest routes over the Alpine girdle, connected it with the middle Danube and by way of the Save valley with the Balkan peninsula and the lower Danubian lands. The full prosperity of the port was reached in the first century A.D. when city life in Gallia Cisalpina had developed and when the Danubian frontier provinces of Noricum, Pannonia and Moesia had been created and incorporated into the Empire. At this time Gallia Cisalpina, formerly given over to sheep, cattle and corn, became a land of flourishing vineyards and olive groves, whilst cities, girt by walls, supplied with aqueducts and beautified with triumphal arches, fostered many crafts. Aquileia became a market for the iron, lead and timber of Noricum ; for amber brought from Samland in the Baltic ; for oil, wine, cloth, glass and tiles ; moreover, it was essentially a market from which supplies were carried to the army stationed on the Danube. To its port came ships from the Dalmatian and Italian ports, and from Alexandria, Seleucia, Carthage and Marseilles.

Iberian Peninsula

Spain at first included only 'Nearer' and 'Further' Spain, which had their capitals respectively at New Carthage and Cordova, whilst garrisons were stationed along the coast at Tarraco (Tarragona), Valencia and Cadiz, which were already connected by a pre-Roman road. Later on Spain comprised as many as five or even seven provinces, two of which lay outside the peninsula—the Balearic islands and Tingitana or western Mauretania, which was closely linked by ferry with southern Spain. The peninsula itself was finally divided into three provinces, which may be briefly noticed : Baetica, Lusitania and Tarraconensis.

Baetica occupied the middle and lower basin of the Guadalquivir, and stretched coastally between the lower Guadiana and Murcia, and northwards to include the Sierra Morena ascent to the Meseta. This region in the past always proved the richest, most civilized and the most densely peopled region of Spain (cp. pp. 203–7). The high well-watered plain of the Guadalquivir between Seville and Cordova, and the south-facing hill slopes westwards of Seville, afforded good soils and slopes for the cultivation of the vine, the olive and the fig, as well as cereals. The high Sierra Nevada mass, between the Guadalquivir and the sea, was a reservoir of water and was also rich in metals ; moreover, though lofty, it was crossed by routes to the port of Malaga. Gold, silver, copper and lead were mined by shaft workings in the Sierra Morena and at the foot of the Sierra Nevada. The town of Cadiz stood on an island site, away from the estuarine alluvium of the Guadalquivir, some ten days' sailing distance from Italy, and in the early Roman period it became one of the greatest ports of the Empire. Roads focused on Seville, to which ships and boats came up on the tide from Cadiz. Oil, wine, fruits and corn, minerals and metal goods, esparto grass and flax, high-quality wool from sheep crossed with north African rams, pickled fish, especially the tunny—these were the many products of Baetica which were exported to Rome, chiefly from Cadiz and Malaga.

The territory of Lusitania, which lay broadly between the middle Guadiana and the middle Douro and stretched some distance eastwards up into the meseta, was occupied by Celto-Iberian peoples who were less civilized than the mixed inhabitants of Baetica and had fallen outside the sphere of Carthaginian rule. Lusitania at first formed a frontier region and was reduced from the fortress of Emerita Augustus (Merida), a bridge-head on the Guadiana, on the road from Baetica to Galicia which crossed the Tagus at the still-existing bridge at Alcantara (= 'the bridge'). This westerly province fell under the modifying climatic influences of the ocean: it had more rain, especially in the north-west, and less extremes of temperature than Baetica—a climatic contrast which was mirrored in its use of butter instead of olive oil, of beer and cider instead of wine, whilst even ground acorns were used in bread. Towns stood within the alluvial basins of the Tagus and the Guadiana; minerals were extracted from the Algarve, where ancient rocks of the meseta are exposed near the coast; and fishing was an active pursuit. Each of the great rivers had its port near the estuary: Lisbon, on the Tagus, Oporto on the Douro and Aesuris on the Guadiana.

Finally, the remaining large area of Spain formed the province of Tarraconensis. Its Mediterranean coastlands in Catalonia were very productive of olive and vine; fishing was very important; the Via Augusta connected the plain with Baetica, and by the Perthus pass over the Pyrenees with Provincia Narbonensis. Tarraco (Tarragona), although badly endowed as a port, displaced Carthagena as the first port of eastern Spain, since it had an advantage in its nearness to Rome, just as Carthagena had had in its nearness to Carthage. Tarraco gave entry into the Ebro basin by means of a road to Illerda (Lerida): the Ebro itself was unnavigable in its lowest reaches. Saragossa, situated on the upper Ebro, was an early Roman station and military base which became an important route-centre, since upon its crossing of the Ebro converged roads from the Pyrenean passes of Roncevalles, Somport and Puigcerda. Well watered, well wooded and cultivated, the Ebro basin, with its wealth of cities, was a storehouse of food supplies. Industries were not lacking in the towns: e.g. arms were made at Bibilis on the Jalon river. On the meseta a few towns were built in the Tertiary basins of the upper Tagus and the Douro (the later Old and New Castiles), but elsewhere village tribal settlements were typical and cattle, horse and sheep rearing formed the chief source of wealth.

Finally, in the wet, forested plateau of Galicia, gold, copper, lead and iron were won mainly from river-side workings and either shipped from the ports of Corunna and Oporto, or carried in wagons by road to the metal-working centres—e.g. to Toledo on the Tagus, or to Bibilis. The oak and beech forests provided good mast for pigs and deer, and there was off-shore fishing. Galicia and Cantabria proved difficult to conquer; hence many roads were built and fortress centres at Astorga, Leon and Pisorca, were strategically placed to command convenient routes over the Cantabrian mountains, e.g. by the Pajares pass, or into the Minho basin of Galicia.

In short, under the stimulus of Roman colonization and road-building, Roman Spain became very productive alike of metals, oil, wine, wool and flax. Despite its difficult relief it had an excellent system of routes (Fig. 4). Its trade depended largely on the Roman market and it prospered as Italy became more densely populated and less self-supporting. Spain was an early conquest of Rome (201 B.C.), and romanization had a permanent effect on the development of the Spanish tongue; only in the north-west astride the Pyrenees did the Iberi, the ancestors of the modern Basques, preserve intact their peculiar speech.

Provence

Roman Provence—Provincia Narbonensis—the first Roman conquest in Gaul beyond the Alps, was annexed in 121 B.C. and gave the Romans political control of the important land link between Italy and Spain. It included the whole of that part of Gaul which was Mediterranean both in climate and outlook, and lay between the western Alps and the eastern Pyrenees, and between the sea on the one hand and the Massif Central and the upper Rhône on the other. Provincia thus controlled the greater part of the Rhône valley, and the rivers Durance and Isère, the valleys of which offered access towards convenient Alpine passes—e.g. Mont Genèvre and the Little St. Bernard;

to the west it had a colony at Toulouse, a fort at Carcassonne, whilst it held also the Perthus pass across the eastern Pyrenees. The Rhône itself below Lyons is a fast-moving river; it entered the sea by three meandering channels, whilst about its mouth large quantities of alluvium were deposited, some of which was carried westwards by the 'anti-clockwise' Mediterranean current

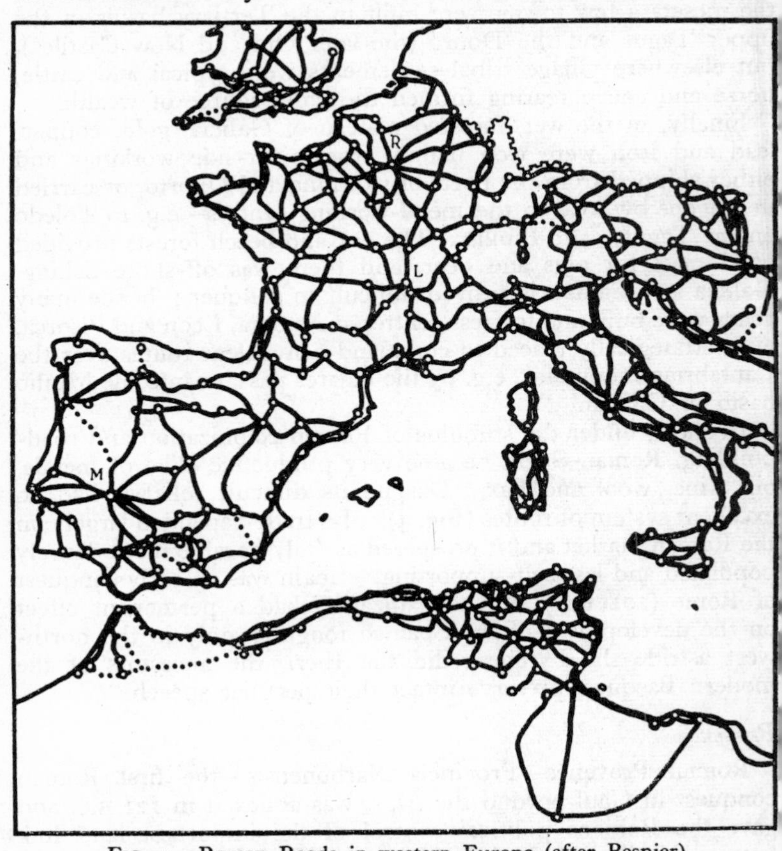

FIG. 4.—Roman Roads in western Europe (after Besnier)
R stands for Rheims, L for Lyons and M for Merida

to form sand-dunes and to enclose lagoons along the coast of Bas Languedoc. Owing to the accumulating sands the Rhône was very difficult and dangerous to enter from the sea, whilst the rapidity of the river's current restricted *up*-stream transport: towers were erected to mark the approaches to, and the channel through, the delta, whilst Marius constructed a canal between the small harbour of Fos (Martigues) which stands to the east of the delta and Arles, which was situated on a hill site at the head of the delta. More Roman than Rome, Provincia was a land of Roman cities such as Aix, Vienne, Arles and Nîmes, but its activities were largely maritime, and the possibilities offered by the physical character and position of its coast had long been exploited by Greek and Phoenician traders. East of the River Var, in Gallia Cisalpina, high Alpine spurs trending north-south reach the sea and present a steep, rocky coast, which —as Strabo noted—afforded roadsteads but not harbourage. West of the Var, however, in Provincia, although the dry limestone Provence mountains run east-westwards and impede movement northwards, the coastlands were essentially favourable to colonization and commercial ambitions, since although this coast is rocky there are also many small rounded bays or basins, to-day partly silted up, which formerly provided sheltered havens; moreover, there were small coastal plains, where the vine, olive and cereals could be grown. Hence Greeks, but not Phoenicians, it would seem, selected sites on this coast, which were defensible hills or peninsulas commanding a port and a small food-producing area.

The great commercial city of Marseilles, which was in turn allied to, and largely destroyed by, Rome, illustrates the location and activities of these coast settlements. Its site, first occupied about 650 B.C. by Greek colonists from Phocaea in north-west Asia Minor, was a small peninsula which presented steep sides to the sea; it overlooked a sheltered basin, which was adequate then for shipping although it has now partly silted up, since into it drains the small River Jarret. It had little local water; a small Tertiary basin behind the town provided some vine and olive, but not much corn; whilst, despite the hill ranges which somewhat isolated it landwards, Marseilles traded with Gaul, from which were imported iron and tin—the latter derived from Brittany and Cornwall. The selection of Marseilles as a site for a Greek colony, it should be noted, offers a useful commentary on the extent to which physical features and advantages define the sites of urban settlements. If it offered real advantages it was also ill-favoured in some respects; moreover, why was it chosen in preference to the analogous site of St. Tropez a few miles farther east?

West of the Rhône the low, lagoon-fringed coast of Bas Languedoc contrasts with that to the east, but in Graeco-Roman times it offered better commercial possibilities, since it lay then more open and ships were small. Thus Narbo (Narbonne), which stood at the head of an open bay where the Aude river enters, became together with Marseilles and Corbilo at the mouth of the Loire one of the three chief ports of Gaul. Finally should be noted the road constructed by the Romans to connect Italy and Spain : it ran along a ledge or cornice overlooking the Ligurian Gulf to Fréjus ; thence, in order to reach the colony of Aquae Sextiae (Aix), it utilized the depressed belt of sandstone drained by the Argens river ; it crossed the Rhône at Tarascon, not Arles ; and finally from Nîmes it followed the coastal plain to Narbonne and entered Spain by the Perthus pass.

Africa

The first and most important Roman conquest in Africa was the peninsula of Tunis—known to the Romans successively as Carthage and ' Africa '—which projects north-eastwards towards Sicily and occupies a commanding position between the eastern and western basins of the Mediterranean Sea. The converging ranges of the folded Atlas mountains run south-west to north-east across Tunis and reach the sea between Cape Blanc and Cape Bon, where a well-embayed coast afforded good access from the sea. Thanks to its elevation and latitude Tunis received a moderate winter rainfall, greater certainly than that in arid Tripoli to the south-east ; but in the south-eastern plain behind the Sahel hills rain was scanty and steppe conditions prevailed. In contrast with the Atlas lands to the west Roman Africa was hilly rather than mountainous and cultivable land was more extensive. The longitudinal Mejerda valley, which empties its waters into the Bay of Tunis, was very closely settled ; it produced under Carthaginian rule much olive oil, wine and cereals, whilst it opened up a route inland towards the Aurès massif. Elsewhere the best cultivable lands lay in the north behind the coast, and along the Sahel hills of the east coast.

Carthage was founded about 800 B.C. by the Phoenician city of Sidon, as a rival to Utica near by, the trade station of Tyre, and it became not only the chief outlet for the rich produce of Tunis but also the undisputed mistress of the commerce of the western Mediterranean. It occupied a triangular walled site in the coastal plain and had two ports on the Bay of Tunis aloof from the Mejerda delta ; whilst inland the hill of Myrsa (= ' fortress ') formed the fortified citadel and cradle of the town. The site of Carthage lacked convenient water-supply, for water could be got only by deep wells, some 80 feet below the surface : the houses therefore had rain-water cisterns, and engineering works, carried out by the Carthaginians and later by the Romans, brought an ample supply to the town from the Zaghuan hill, 56 miles away. Destroyed in 146 B.C. to satisfy the vengeance of its Roman conquerors, Carthage gradually revived under the Empire, and formed a military base from which Roman rule was extended in northern Africa. In order to safeguard the vine and olive cultivation of Italy and to supply Rome with foodstuffs, 'Africa' was cut up into large estates and the cultivation of wheat was substituted for the intensive vine and olive culture for which it had proved itself excellently suited. It proved equally well suited to wheat growing, for in Byzacium and especially in the Mejerda valley, thanks to soils rich in natural phosphates, were harvested the heaviest wheat crops of the ancient world.[1] Well placed in relation to Ostia and Puteoli, 'Africa' supplied in the fourth century A.D. one-third of the corn supplies which reached Italy, whilst cattle, wool, dried fish and marble were exported. In the south of 'Africa' and the conquered Numidian lands immediately to the west, the Aurès massif formed an obstacle between the Tell highlands and the desert, and outflanking it on both sides lay routes by which nomads from the desert raided the settled lands in the north. On the northern slopes of the Aurès the Romans established the two fortresses of Tebessa, at its eastern, and Lambaesis at its western end, both of which exploited their natural nodality by converging route systems. Further, in the shadow of Lambaesis was established the colony of Timgad—the well-preserved remains of which illustrate many typical features of Roman towns in Africa: the hilly site, the use of aqueducts, the rectangular 'lay-out', the public buildings including baths. To the south of the Aurès and of the road which connected the outpost of Biskra with Gabes on the coast, lay a depressed zone occupied by a line of shotts, and there desert conditions prevailed. Roman civilization made no permanent penetration across this climatic frontier into the vast Saharan wastes.

The limestone plateau of Cyrenaïca projects northwards towards Crete and Greece and is ringed in landwards by desert or steppe. Its elevation and projection seawards gave it a relatively high rainfall, and made Mediterranean cultivation possible. The plateau provided some pasture lands and cedar and cypress forest, whilst there were arable zones in the deep *wadis*, and above all within the terraces which descend from the African plateau to the Mediterranean. The most westerly Greek colonies in northern Africa had been established within these cultivable

[1] Albertini, *L'Afrique romaine*, p. 28.

lands: notably Hesperides (Berenice) on the coast, the ruins of which lie north-east of Benghazi, and Cyrene and Barca which stood inland. Cyrene, founded *c.* 620 B.C., was the chief city of Cyrenaïca, as indeed of Hellenic Africa. In full view of the sea, only ten miles to the north, and sheltered by high ground to the south, it stood on the upper edge of two terraces and commanded copious springs. A road led from Cyrene to the harbour of Apollonia, which has been destroyed by silting. Barca also occupied a well-watered terrace site, about 60 miles west of Cyrene and somewhat farther from Hesperides. This seaport stood where the coast lay nearest to Sicily and had for its hinterland the most extensive cultivable area in Cyrenaïca; it superseded Cyrene as the chief city and exported wine, olive oil, fish, the purple dye, and wool derived from sheep pastured on the plateau. To the west of Cyrenaïca, Tripoli offered fewer possibilities of settlement and economic development, since it forms a low level plain behind the unbroken coastline of the shallow Great Syrtis bay and is mainly steppe owing to its low elevation and aridity. Behind the coastal sand-dunes, however, runs a belt of country well supplied with springs; there stood Roman, and formerly Carthaginian, cities, and there, also, cereals, olives, and dates were grown. To the south the plain rose to the Jebel plateau, from which in winter a few streams flowed northwards to the sea, and provided patches of cultivation in their valleys. Farther south, remote from the civilized shorelands, large oases dotted the Fezzan basin and the Ghadames plateau. An old trade route from Lake Chad in central Africa passed via the Fezzan oases to Oea (Tripoli) on the coast, along which ivory and slaves were brought. In 18 B.C. Rome actually conquered the Fezzan and Ghadames oases by a punitive expedition, the object of which was to protect the trade route and the coastlands from the attacks of nomad tribesmen. The chief cities of Tripoli were the ports of Oea, Sabrata and Leptis Magna; they exported some corn, oil, cattle, horses, wool and leather; the long exposed desert frontier behind the coastlands proved difficult to protect, and towards the end of the fourth century Tripoli and Leptis suffered severely from the attacks of Berber tribes.

To the west of 'Africa' Mauretania with its rocky coast and the broad, high Atlas zone behind, was entered only late and conquered only partially by the Romans. Rome, like Carthage, occupied certain coastal sites but attempted little penetration inland: the wide belt of steppe enclosed between the chains of Mediterranean and Saharan Atlas was left largely in the occupation of independent Berber pastoralists. Communication was difficult even in the coastlands: the Roman road from Carthage stopped at Melilla, and thence to Tingi (Tangier) the journey had to be completed coastwise by ship. Mauretania had some importance to Rome since it was a coast notoriously suited to piracy, and its possession afforded some security to the neighbouring lands of Spain and 'Africa'.

The Aegean Coastlands

In the Aegean basin, as in the eastern Mediterranean basin generally, Greek civilization was predominant, and the short-lived empire of Alexander the Great had sought to give realization in the political sense to the extension of Greek or Hellenistic culture. Roman conquests in these regions of old and highly developed civilization were very important, in that they included the most wealthy and densely peopled lands of the Mediterranean world: in particular, Egypt, Syria and the sea-board of Asia Minor. Further, in the ports of Syria and Egypt, Rome won the keys to commercial intercourse with the Far Eastern countries, which could offer products unavailable in the Mediterranean, such as spices, silks, dye-woods, gems, &c.; whilst the Greek cities, although they had declined, had long traditions of industry and trade, and Egypt was a storehouse of food-supplies.

Macedonia and Greece were conquered by Rome in the course of four 'Macedonian' wars between the years 205 and 146 B.C. by means of advances landwards from the Illyrian coast where Rome had secured the alliance of the Greek maritime cities of Epidamnos and Apollonia. Macedonia, which had formed the original kingdom of Alexander, extended broadly astride the Vardar, and combined in position and outlook both continental and maritime characteristics. Unlike Greece it had wide stretches of pasture and cultivable land; its climate had distinct continental, rather than Mediterranean, features; and its original Illyrian inhabitants had been largely Hellenized. It was famed for its horses, whilst flax and hemp were grown, crops which through lack of moisture were precluded in the Mediterranean region proper. The Roman road system, in linking up the chief Macedonian city and port of Thessalonika with Italy and with Asia, extended Macedonian relations landwards: roads were built westward to Durazzo—the Via Egnatia, eastwards to Constantinople and northwards to Nish and Belgrade.[1] The Via Egnatia, which connected Rome with Durazzo by a short sea passage to Brundisium, offered the shortest route to the frontier in eastern Asia Minor by way of Byzantium.

To the south of Macedonia the heart of Greece lay in the islands and eastern mainland of the Aegean Sea, within which area uniform geographical conditions obtained and Greek cities

[1] Cp. *infra*, Chapter VIII. For maps of this and other imperial roads, see K. Miller, *Itineraria Romana* (1916).

and culture were well established. Greece proper was a world of mountains and small enclosed plains, deeply penetrated by the sea: climate and soils and hill slopes fitted it to produce mainly the olive and vine, whilst in its towns industry supplemented these products with other articles of commerce. In its hey-day Greece had occupied a very central position within the Greek world which was centred in the Aegean, with colonial 'outliers' in the Black Sea, in the Ionian Sea and at distant Marseilles, and it had been essentially the purveyor of oil, wine and manufactures. But at the time of its conquest by Rome the commerce and city life of Greece was in decline: civil wars arrested its economic development and the wars of Alexander had drained it of men; the commercial centre of the Mediterranean was shifting to its political centre, which was Italy under Roman rule; whilst the Greek cities suffered the competition not only of old ports like Rhodes and Ephesus but also of the new foundations of Alexander, namely Alexandria and Antioch, which became the two chief ports of the Roman east. Rome conquered Greece by an advance up the Aous river into Thessaly, and the great commercial city of Corinth was in 146 B.C. like Carthage destroyed, but only to rise again. Greece was held at first by the 'three fetters of Greece', the fortresses of Corinth, Chalcis (in Euboea) and Demetrias (in Thessaly), all of which occupied strategical positions in eastern Greece, and were accessible from the sea. The position of Corinth was such as to ensure some revival in its fortunes, since the narrow isthmus which it controlled possessed 'rollers' by means of which ships could pass between the Ionian and Aegean seas; it thus commanded an important military and commercial route.[1] Ships using this route avoided the gusty winds off Cape Malea, and Nero contemplated cutting a canal through the isthmus. In fact, the only two towns in Greece and Macedonia which were at all comparable with the other great cities of the Empire were Thessalonika and Corinth.

The peninsula of Asia Minor presents a marked contrast between the interior and the western and north-western sea-board: inland stretches a high plateau containing desert, salt lakes, grain lands and rough pasture; below this, fronting the Aegean and the Sea of Marmora, lies a zone of plains divided off from each other by hill spurs, which is watered by long rivers, and presents a well-embayed coastline and is Mediterranean in climate. By 100 B.C. Rome held Gallipoli and in Asia Minor the western plains and their approaches to the plateau: the land

[1] Cp. also *infra*, pp. 174–5.

of Greek cities, which was watered by the streams which enter the Sea of Marmora east of Cyzicus, and by the Hermes and the Meander, near the mouth of which was the capital city and port of Ephesus. A hundred years later Roman dominion extended to and beyond the Halys river in the north, and in the south to the Taurus mountains, across which, by the pass of the Cilician Gates, Rome had access into Syria, which became a province in 64 B.C. The incorporation of Asia Minor gave to Rome lands along the coast with surplus Mediterranean produce —oil and wine, a frontage on the southern coast of the Black Sea, with the ports of Sinope and Trebizond, and a region along the course of the upper Euphrates which was organized in turn against the Parthian and Persian empires.

Syria and Palestine

Syria consists of a series of north-south belts running parallel to the coast. The coastal plain is narrow in the north, where in Phoenicia it is confined landwards by the Lebanon mountains (10,000 feet), but broadens in Palestine to the south, where the plateaux of Judaea and Samaria stand back from the sea. The narrow northern plain between the Taurus mountains and Mount Carmel was well watered, since the Lebanon caused westerly winds from the sea to drop their moisture and, further, its snow-cap stored up and distributed water. In the south, e.g. about Gaza, the southern plain is practically desert, and the ancient city of Gaza, built in an oasis, was a 'port,' frequented by tribes from the Arabian desert. The northern coastal belt was therefore very productive country and was important, too, since its coast was somewhat indented. There stood the old Phoenician ports of Tyre and Sidon; farther north the river Orontes breaks through the inner mountain zone to reach the sea; on its lower valley stood Antioch, the chief city of Syria, and near its mouth stood Seleucia, its port. Further, the Lebanon ranges were well wooded, thus providing timber for ships and for building. Antioch occupied a striking position which largely explains its importance. It commanded a relatively easy route eastwards by way of the Orontes gorge through the north-south mountain obstacle, and further—since the Anti Lebanon mountains do not extend northwards to the latitude of Antioch—the way lay open to the Euphrates, either to its northern frontier sector or to its ports, like Rakka. Moreover, Antioch controlled the routes into Asia Minor either coastally around the Amanus range by the Gulf of Alexandretta or across that range by the Bailan pass, whilst the Orontes valley—partially irrigated by water-wheels along the river—was well settled and very productive. Finally, the town of Seleucia occupied a strongly defensible hill site in the Bay of Seleucia away from the Orontes mouth, but even so it was inconvenienced by the silt deposited by a torrent which entered the haven and by the alluvium carried by marine currents which move northwards along the Syrian coast from the Nile delta. Hence to improve the port a remarkable engineering feat, carried out by Vespasian in the first century A.D., diverted the water of the stream into a tunnel over 1,000 yards long which was burrowed through a mountain on the flanks of the stream. Antioch had both military and commercial importance. Its out-port was the most convenient port for landing troops destined for the Euphrates frontier—the most critical frontier of the Empire ; further, it was an entrepôt city connected with Rakka and Balis near the head of the Euphrates navigation, to which boats and caravans carried oriental commodities destined for the Roman world. In the north of Syria the limestone country between the Orontes and the Euphrates which is now largely desert, was then occupied by oases with some trees and terraced vine and olive cultivation, and Palmyra between Damascus and the Euphrates was a frequented trade station. Similarly, farther south Bostra and Petra were caravan cities flourishing in what is now desert.[1] A condition of greater rainfall has been postulated [2] to explain the presence of cities like Palmyra in lands now arid, but part of the explanation lies in the great organizing skill and care exercised in storing and distributing water.

In Syria, as in the more thoroughly Greek lands, Rome ruled a land of ancient culture. Many cities had become Greek since the time of Alexander ; but the population was very mixed : Arameans in the north, Jews in the south, and Arabs on its eastern margins. The Syrians (Arameans) and Jews formed the chief traders of the Roman world : they had their colonies in all its trading cities.

Syria was a land rich in agricultural and manufactured commodities, which together with oriental goods were exported to the Italian markets from its ports of Seleucia, Berytus, Tyre and Byblus. The cedars and firs of the Lebanons were used for Roman shipbuilding ; these forests have been long extinct, although to-day scientific afforestation is being undertaken ; pine wood from the Lebanon was also used in the glass industry at Sidon, which utilized the siliceous sand about the Naaman

[1] Rostovtzev's *Caravan Cities*, 1932, examines the archaeology of these cities.

[2] See H. C. Butler, ' Desert Syria ', *G.R.*, Feb. 1920.

river. Metal industries were well developed; copper was imported from Asia Minor and the iron used at Damascus was brought by Persian merchants from India. Raw silk was brought from the Far East, especially from China, either via Persia or the Euphrates, and used especially at Tyre and Berytus in the manufacture of rich fabrics; the famous purple dye was prepared at Tyre from the *murex* and *buccinum* shell-fish which were caught in baskets off the coast. The interior hill country produced abundant supplies of wool, which together with locally grown flax, supplied material for woollen and linen industries in the towns. The lower slopes of Lebanon, the river valleys—e.g. the Orontes, and cultivable oases—e.g. around Gaza and Damascus, were used for the cultivation of the olive, vine, wheat, figs and flax; and canals and water-wheels were used to irrigate the fields. The rich volcanic soils about Damascus and the plain of Palestine produced wheat as well as fruits. With the security afforded by Roman rule and the improvement and extension of land routes much oriental and Arabian trade, which formerly was directed to the Red Sea and Egypt, was brought via the Persian Gulf and the Euphrates to the Syrian ports. The cities of Palmyra, Bostra and Petra, which stood on the eastern plateau of Syria on the margins of the desert, were connected with Damascus and with the Euphrates and the ports of the coast. In the second century A.D. silk, spices, cotton goods, myrrh, ivory and slaves were brought to these inland cities and exported from the Syrian ports.

Egypt

Egypt, thanks to its own productivity and to its position, had a twofold importance to the Roman world. It was not only a great storehouse of cereal foodstuffs which were carried largely to Ostia, but it also controlled the shortest route-way between the Mediterranean and the tropical monsoon lands of the Far East. The products of the Far East and Arabia—silks, cottons, spices, gems, &c.—as well as those of the Sudan, notably ivory and slaves—reached the Mediterranean seaports of Egypt by several routes. One was by way of a canal which ran from Arsinoe at the head of the Gulf of Suez to Bilbeis on the Pelusiac branch of the Nile, and thence down to Pelusium on the coast. Other routes involved a camel portage from the Red Sea ports of Berenice (lat. 24°), Kosseir and Myos Hormos across the desert to Coptos on the Nile, and so down-stream by boat. It is significant that routes from the Nile across the highland desert of Egypt to the Red Sea ports radiated from the river north of Thebes, where the Nile makes a large horseshoe bend towards the east (Fig. 5). The canal from Arsinoe followed a natural depression but was not very serviceable : it was navigable only when filled by the Nile in flood and required continual dredging. It was, in fact, temporarily abandoned. The desert

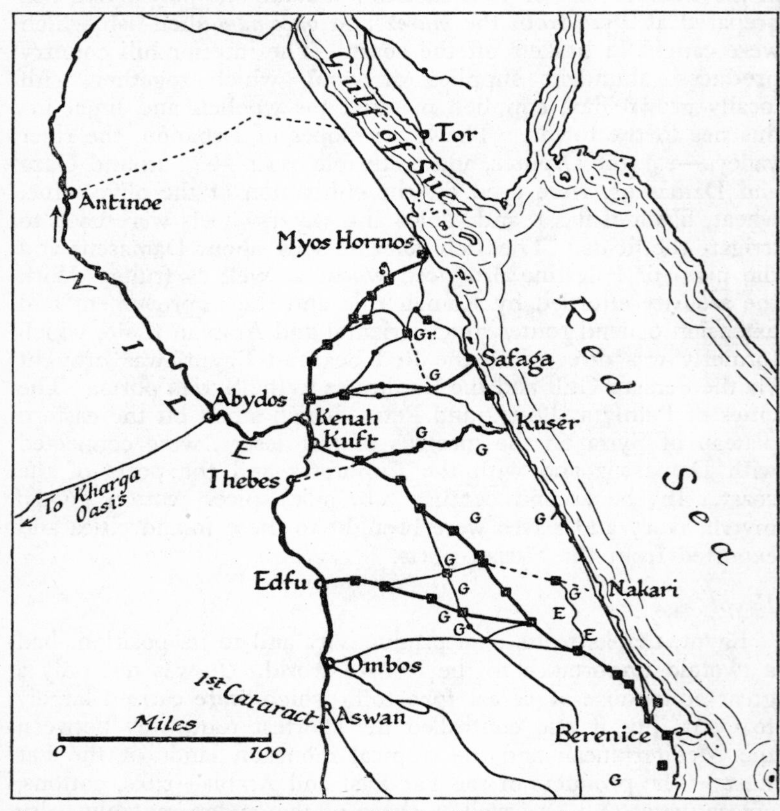

FIG. 5.—Roman Routes across the Highland Desert of eastern Egypt (after G. W. Murray in the *Journal of Egyptian Archaeology*, Oct. 1925)

G stands for Gold, Gr. for Granite, and E for Emerald, workings. 'Kuft' occupies the site of the ancient Coptos. The most important routes are shown by the thick lines

routes were provided with wells and rest-houses at convenient stages ; these transits, occupying between one and two weeks, had the advantage of shortening the navigation of the Red Sea, which was difficult owing to its many islands, its northerly winds and its inhospitable coasts.

The chief seaports of Egypt in Roman times were Pelusium and Alexandria which stood respectively at the eastern and western ends of the Nile delta, and of these the latter became easily the more important. Alexandria, founded in 331 B.C., was situated opposite the island of Pharos between the sea and Lake Mariut, which was connected by a waterway with the

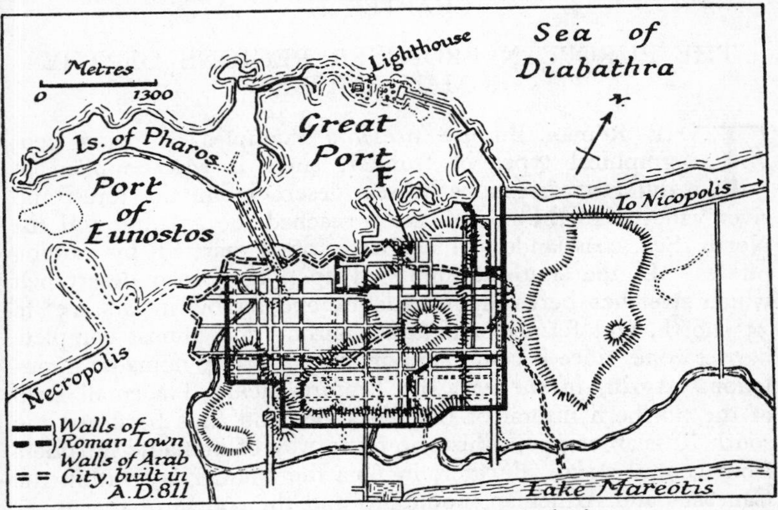

FIG. 6.—Alexandria in Roman and Arab times

Note the hilly site, the causeway built from the mainland to Pharos island, the lighthouse and the reduced area of the Arab town. (See *infra*, p. 199.) F marks the Roman Forum

Canopic branch of the delta (Fig. 6). A lighthouse stood on Pharos island from which an embankment was built to the shore. The two harbours of Alexandria lay on either side of the breakwater; and in actual area as well as in economic importance they formed the greatest seaport of the Roman world.[1]

[1] The port of Alexandria could hold 1,200 ships; its area was 368 hectares, compared with 27 at Marseilles and 24 at Puteoli. The lighthouse was built by the Ptolemies *c.* 270 B.C. and fell as a result of earthquakes only in the fourteenth century. The recent discovery of a twelfth-century MS. has made it possible to reconstruct the scale and proportions of the lighthouse: see the account in *The Illustrated London News*, 27 Jan. 1934.

CHAPTER II

THE EUROPEAN FRONTIER REGIONS OF THE ROMAN EMPIRE

THE Roman Empire presents examples of many geographical types of frontier, since it was bounded in different directions by sea, desert, mountain, forest and river valley. In the north-west it reached the Atlantic and the North Sea coastlands, which were often harried by raiding pirates. In the south it impinged upon the broad desert belt which stretches between the Atlantic and Arabia in lats. 15° to 35° north, and formed a naturally strong and almost complete barrier zone, since it could support only a scanty nomadic population. Again, in the east the Empire included a small strip of the northern littoral of the Black Sea and thus bordered the south Russian steppe, a historic route-way of nomadic intruders from central Asia. Further, in Asia the frontier lay within the Caucasus and Armenian mountains and the course of the upper Euphrates: this region where the Empire made contact with the highly organized Persian state became a zone of continual conflict and proved for a time the most critical frontier of the whole Empire.[1] Finally, in continental Europe, parts of the Rhine and Danube valleys were selected as frontiers, and there again were presented conditions of dis-equilibrium, owing to the persistent pressure of Germanic peoples.

The alinement of the Roman military frontier for the most part along the valleys of the Rhine and Danube, was a purely arbitrary political measure. The military frontier line or *limes* underwent continual change, and was definitely established only after a policy of trial and error. Thus Roman armies campaigned across the Rhine and Danube and between the years A.D. 6 and A.D. 9 it was hoped, by means of a joint advance from these two rivers, to extend the frontier to the Elbe. Although to the Romans the frontier or *finis* was an essentially fluctuating or

[1] On this frontier see Chapot, *La Frontière de L'Euphrate de Pompée à la Conquête arabe*, 1907.

rather expanding borderland,[1] an attempt was made to stabilize it under the Emperor Augustus. The unsuccessful policy of extension across the lower Rhine was, temporarily at least, abandoned, and the Rhine was adopted as a convenient military line from the falls of Schaffhausen (above Basle) down to the sea. Roman arms and settlement were subsequently extended across the middle Rhine and the upper and lower Danube, so that in the second century A.D., in the hey-day of the Empire, the rivers themselves provided only a short and discontinuous boundary.

The Roman military system until its partial collapse in the third century A.D. depended on the fortification of frontier districts, where garrisons were permanently stationed and behind which, in lands thus secured from external attacks, stood unwalled towns and villae (farms). The Romans, it should be noted, distinguished between fortresses (castra) at which legions were stationed, and smaller forts (castella) which were garrisoned only with auxiliary troops. The legionary centres were the essential strongholds from which, by means of military roads, forts and bridges, wide areas were controlled and defended. With certain notable exceptions, e.g., Rome, Nîmes, Fréjus and London, camps were the only walled settlements in the first century A.D., and the building of walls around towns, alike in Gaul, Italy and Moesia on the lower Danube, was a later and largely third-century phenomenon, which is explained by the failure of the Empire to prevent or control the ingress of barbarians through the frontier regions. These regions along the Rhine and the Danube had thus a predominantly military character, which was soon modified however, since trade, personified by Italian and Syrian merchants, invariably followed the Roman eagle. Under the protection of walled fortresses these immigrant merchants formed small *canabae* or bazaars, which satisfied the needs of the garrisons and formed the nuclei of trading towns, the population of which consisted mainly of local inhabitants, veteran soldiers, Roman immigrants and slaves. The troops themselves were drawn from the diverse racial stock of the Empire; Illyria, Armenia, Spain and Belgica in north-eastern Gaul produced particularly vigorous recruits; but the legions became essentially Roman, both in language and culture, so that their demands in backward frontier lands stimulated trade, the more so since certain products such as wine and oil, which were essential to them as Romans yet unobtainable on the frontier owing either to unsuitable climate (in the case of

[1] For the distinction in Roman law between the *finis* and the *limes*, see Lapradelle, *La Frontière*, Chapter I.

the olive) or to local ignorance of their cultivation (in the case of the vine), had at first to be brought long distances from Italy or Provincia or Spain.

The Rhine Frontier[1]

Near Basle the Rhine issues from a deep, confined valley between the folded Jura and the Black Forest massif and makes a right-angular bend to the north, a direction which it then consistently keeps. Much of the human significance of the Rhine valley below Basle springs from its relation to the forested Hercynian mountains, which extend in a wide but broken belt between the Bohemian 'quadrilateral' to the east and the Massif Central and Breton plateau to the west. Actually the Rhine occupies a north-south breach through the breadth of this upland zone: it passes through the wide rift valley between the Vosges and Black Forest, and then again lower down continues its passage through the Hercynian system by etching its valley in a narrow gorge between Bingen and Bonn, which separates the two halves of the Rhine Massif. At Bonn the river leaves the gorge confined between steep-sided river cliffs and enters the north European plain, whence it makes its way through the alluvial lands of modern Holland, to enter the sea by three channels.

In the Rhineland between Basle and Bonn high forested lands formed a characteristic feature, and imposed some obstacle to settlement and communication. The Rhine slate and sandstone plateau, comprising on the western side the Ardennes, the Eifel and the Hunsrück uplands, consists of folded rocks which have been peneplaned and re-dissected by steep-sided valleys; further, high rainfall and brown forest soils favoured the growth of dense oak, ash and fir forest. In consequence, this formed a 'repulsive' region from which settlers and routes were largely diverted. Within it, however, the rivers Moselle and Lahn flow respectively from the west and the east along clay-filled depressions and mark out lines of movement to the Rhine. The entrenched and tortuous Moselle valley provided a small area of flats and a greater area of slopes; viticulture was introduced in the second century A.D. and the country was developed as a supply area for garrisons stationed on the Rhine. The Moselle was navigable below Metz down to the fortress of Confluentes (Coblenz), but the valley bottom was too restricted to allow space for a road. The colony of Trèves, an early walled city which, like Cologne and Mainz, became essentially German in population, was a supply centre standing at the junction of the Sarre with the

[1] For Roman roads in the Rhineland, see Fig. 10.

Moselle; routes radiated from Trèves to Coblenz, to Rheims, to Bavay across the Ardennes via Dinant, and to Bingen and Mainz across the Hunsrück; whilst owing to its strategical position in relation to the Rhine frontier it was at times selected as the imperial capital. To the south of the Rhine plateau and westwards of the plain of Alsace, a forest belt, still fairly continuous but more extensive at this time, stretched north-southwards over the sandstones of the Low Vosges and the gneiss, schists and granites of the High Vosges. This high forested curtain to the Alsatian plain was not an entire barrier to communication: prior to the Roman occupation a Celtic road crossed the High Vosges by way of the Meurthe valley to its junction with the Moselle. Nevertheless, it diverted settlement to the foothills and the plain along which ran the north-south Roman highway. On the eastern side of the rift valley similar conditions of relief and vegetation presented themselves within the region of the lower Main and Neckar basins, which was called the Agri Decumates: the ancient blocks of the Spessart, the Odenwald and the Black Forest formed 'negative' forested areas above the hills and plains.

The two military districts and later provinces of Lower and Upper Germany, both of which were well settled by German peoples, were carved out on the left bank of the Rhine during the first half of the first century A.D. Lower Germany fronted the river below Coblenz and was guarded by fortresses at Bonn, Cologne, Neuss and Xanten; in Upper Germany, which was bounded by the river from Coblenz up to a point below Basle, stood the fortresses of Coblenz, Mainz and Strasbourg. Above this province and situated near the confluence of the Aar, Reuss and Limmat rivers, the legionary fortress of Vindonissa (Windisch) guarded the Rhine between Basle and Lake Constance and commanded routes between Alpine passes and Upper Germany. In the second century A.D. Lower Germany was held by only two fortresses, namely those of Cologne and Xanten, together with subsidiary forts; in Upper Germany the existing fortresses remained, but Vindonissa was abandoned before 100 A.D. when the military frontier line as well as the province itself was extended across the Rhine up the Main and the Neckar by the incorporation of the Decumates lands (Fig. 7).

The military stations of the frontier and their connecting highways lay along the Rhine valley and its tributary streams and along certain depressions which offered convenient access across the wooded uplands. Two areas within this region stand out as particularly important: Alsace, together with the

Sundgau plateau to the south, and the triangle of lowland between the Taunus ridge and the Rhine. The rift valley, in which Alsace and the Sundgau lie, is floored with Tertiary deposits, over which light, porous ' loess ' soils are spread to the west and north-west of Strasbourg, in the Sundgau and generally at the foot of the Vosges. Historically these loess areas played a distinctive rôle. That they were free of heavy woodland and continuously settled is evidenced by the discovery of prehistoric objects of many periods ; further, they were sheltered, adequately watered and fertile. They thus formed optimum settlement areas within somewhat forbidding lands around, for elsewhere in Alsace sand and gravel soils bore light woodland, for example, in the Hardt forest to the south and in the Hagenau to the north, whilst the Rhine itself was bordered by a broad marshy fringe. The river formed an indistinct zone of separation, but was in no sense a barrier and scarcely indeed a serious obstacle. It flowed through an intricate network of meandering channels within flood plain marshes which were themselves contained within wooded gravel terraces. In Alsace, therefore, settlement stood well back from the river. Owing to the natural conditions of the river channels and the rapidity of the current, navigation above Strasbourg—except for ferry crossings—must have been difficult. The great north-south highway ran along the gravel terrace of the left bank, and the chief Roman stations stood well back from the Rhine. The hill fortress of Argentoratum (Strasbourg) affords a good illustration. It stood on the navigable Ill near its junction with the Rhine ; its walls were built of stone brought from the volcanic hill of the Kaiserstühl, which stands across the Rhine to the south-east ; its position at the intersection of routes gave Strasbourg then, as it does still to-day, great strategical importance. Westwards a road led to the fort of Tres Tabernae (Saverne) which commanded a low, short and easy passage across the narrow northern end of the High Vosges, to the Moselle cities of Toul and Metz. Eastwards from Strasbourg roads led across the Rhine, one to the Neckar via the plain of Baden, and another up the Schütter valley and across the Black Forest to the Danube. North and south from Strasbourg ran the route from the Rhine estuary to Vindonissa and the Alps. Finally, a line of Romanized villas was strung out along the loess-covered foot-hills below the Vosges, and was connected by a pre-Roman road which ran from the present site of Belfort, via Horburg to Brumath and Saverne. This is to-day essentially a vineyard zone : viticulture originated there in the second century A.D., and the Roman soldiery ceased to be dependent on wine imported from southern lands, notably from Italy and Seville.

The rift valley of the Rhine, since it offered some good settlement land and agricultural possibilities, attracted German tribes, and hence between Bingen and Basle the frontier was exposed to their continual penetration. The position of the Black Forest, which provided in itself little open land and relatively difficult routes, tended to deflect German invaders to the north and to the south, where, in consequence, they exerted most pressure. In the south a depression between the Vosges, the Black Forest and the Jura opened a way to the Rhine and to Gaul from the Swiss plateau and from the upper Danube. In later days this gateway was called the Gate of Burgundy: it was defended in the Middle Ages by the fortress of Montbéliard and later by that of Belfort. In the first century A.D. before the extension of the frontier beyond the Rhine it was guarded by a fort at Augst, near Basle, from which roads led in all directions: to Horburg and Strasbourg; to Besancon on the Saône; to Iverdun and thence by Caesar's road over the Jura to Pontarlier; and finally, to Vindonissa, from which one route led across the Alps by Chur and the Splügen pass to Milan, and another eastwards to Augsburg, itself a route centre. To the north of the Black Forest, the frontier was particularly exposed in the neighbourhood of the Main confluence. Between the Taunus and the Odenwald two natural routes converge. The one from the north occupies the north-south Hessean depression, which is interposed between the ancient Rhine-slate massif and the forested massif east of the Weser: it afforded a zone of access to the Rhine between Mainz and Coblenz to German invaders from the northern plains either by the lower Main or else by the Lahn valley. The other is defined by the valley of the lower Main which flows through a wide loess-covered plain towards the Rhine. These routes therefore converge on a depressed triangular area between Manheim, Mainz and Frankfurt, which had good agricultural soils and a dry, warm, sheltered climate. It was guarded by the legionary fortress of Mainz, at which a bridge was built across the Rhine to the fort of Castel, and from which a road led westwards to Trèves by way of Bingen and across the Hunsrück. In view of the strategical importance of the country round Mainz, and when it is recalled that by A.D. 100 the Roman legions had advanced northwards to the upper Danube, it is easy to grasp the military value of acquiring the Agri Decumates. By this acquisition the frontier was extended to include a large part of south-western Germany between the

Taunus and the upper Danube, and moreover it was fortified by the construction of walls and entrenchments known as the Pfahlgraben, which left the Rhine just below Coblenz and reached the Danube near Kelheim, above the fortress of Ratisbon (Fig. 7). It will be more convenient to note the geography of this area, with its military and village settlements, when considering the evolution of the Danube frontier.

The historical facts of this extension into the Agri Decumates so called, which began about A.D. 73–74, may be briefly summarized. The Romans annexed the Neckar basin and the Black Forest, which, formerly occupied by Celts and Germans, had

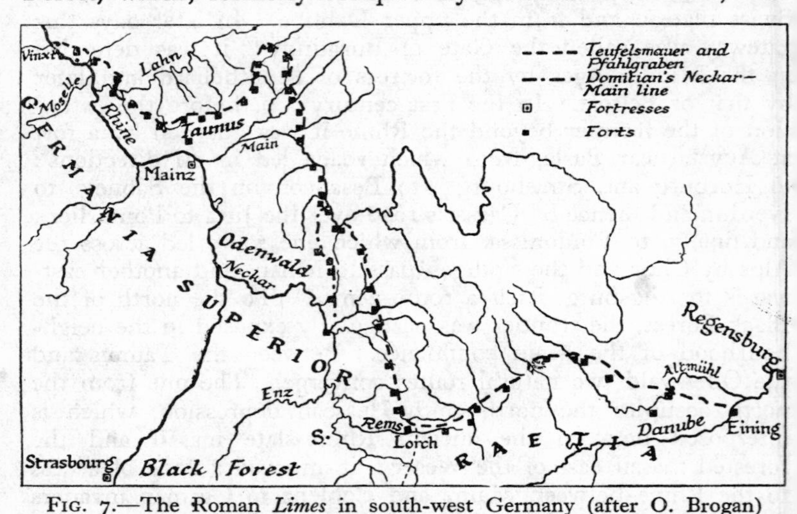

FIG. 7.—The Roman *Limes* in south-west Germany (after O. Brogan)

Forts far to the rear of the *Limes* are not shown. S marks the site of the present-day Stuttgart. Note the use made of the Taunus summits and of part of the Main valley in the alinement of forts. The scale is approximately 56 miles to the inch.

become a debatable land almost devoid of settlers. The province of Raetia on the upper Danube had been already created under the Emperor Augustus (15 B.C.) and a road made to connect the Rhine and Danube between Strasbourg and Tutlingen: it ran across the Black Forest by way of the Kinzig valley and Rottweil on the Neckar. Much of this scarcely settled country in and around the Black Forest became imperial demesne land, and the same is probably true of the Ardennes. Further, the Romans conquered the country south of the Taunus which is watered by the lower Main and its tributaries the Wetter and Nidda. They had already, early in the first century A.D., occupied much of this favoured region with its hot springs at Wiesbaden and its silver and iron mines in the Taunus: the raids of the Chatti, in fact, induced them to incorporate districts which were both economically productive and strategically important. In A.D. 83 Domitian established a new frontier: it ran from Kesselstadt on the Main northwards to include the Wetterau, thence it continued along the Taunus ridge, from which it struck north-west across the lower Lahn to reach the Rhine just below Coblenz, where the left-bank tributary the Vinxt enters. A route connected the fortress and permanent bridge at Mainz with the Wetter river; earthen forts were built along the frontier line, and stone forts along the roads between it and the Rhine, whilst forts were constructed along the Main from Kesselstadt to Worth, and thence along the ridge of the high, forested Odenwald massif to Schlossau; finally they were continued from Schlossau to Wimpfen and along the Neckar to Kongen (Fig. 7). Another road ran along the Baden plain, well back from the Rhine, to Offenburg on the Kinzig river and to Cannstadt on the Neckar, whence it was continued to Faimingen on the Danube. The completion of this route, attributed in part at least to Trajan, provided a continuous imperial highway between the estuary of the Rhine and the delta of the Danube. Finally, the Emperor Hadrian and his successor Antoninus straightened out the military line between the Main and the Danube by constructing the Teufelsmauer or Limes Raetiae, a continuous and straight stone wall between Heinheim (above Ratisbon) by way of the Altmühl valley to Lorch; from this point the reconstructed Pfahlgraben, an earthen rampart and ditch, continued to the confluence of the river Vinxt with the Rhine.

In the second century A.D. the frontier coincided with the Rhine, therefore, only from a point below Coblenz, that is, within the province of Lower Germany. In this sector Cologne was the outstanding stronghold, consisting of a legionary fortress on the left bank, connected by a permanent bridge with a fortress at Deutz. Its position fostered both its commercial and its strategical importance. The town stood below the Rhine gorge towards the southern limits of the northern plain; it commanded means of communication by river and by road along the Rhine, whilst it lay abreast of a natural zonal route which ran east-westwards across Europe along (for the most part) loess-covered foothills from the Galician plateau to the plains of Brabant and Flanders. Moreover, westwards from Cologne ran 'the vital route of northern Europe' via Tongres and Bavay to Boulogne (Figs. 12 and 23). Below Cologne the river makes its way through lowland which is at times sandy heath like the Campine, or inundated plain, like the Peel marshes. The three channels by which it entered the sea have undergone certain physical changes since Roman times.[1] The Old Rhine (Rhenus Medius), the most northerly of the channels, usually formed the frontier line : already in Roman times it carried only a very small share of the Rhine's water as it does to-day. Southwards of this the Lek diverged at Dürstede and flowed through a canalized channel—the Fossa Civilis—which was connected with the Old Rhine by the Fossa Corbulonis and with the Yssel river by the Fossa Drusiana. On the Waal, the most southerly channel, stood Nijmegen. The Meuse then entered the sea independently of the Rhine by two channels, whilst the Yssel flowed into the Lacus Flevo. The Lacus Flevo, which was enlarged by marine inundation to form the Zuider Zee only in the twelfth and thirteenth centuries, then lay open to the sea and was connected also to a smaller lake, the sea of Haarlem, which was drained in the nineteenth century. A Roman fleet, the Classis Germanica, patrolled the Rhine and ships were built, notably at Mainz. It might be thought that the estuarine channels of the Rhine with their adjacent marshes would have formed a physical obstacle to the German peoples, but in fact the latter are found at different times settled alike on both banks : for example, the Batavii and later the Salian Franks settled astride the river. Between Cologne and the sea Xanten, on a hill site above the Rhine, was a legionary station (Fig. 20) and Neuss, Utrecht, and Leiden were walled cities and ports. Fectio which stood on the Old Rhine channel near Utrecht was an active entrepôt port : it traded with London, the chief port of Britain, whilst by way of the rivers Scheldt and Moselle and thence to the Rhine the peoples of Belgic Gaul sent foodstuffs from the plains of Hesbaye and Hainaut, wine from the Moselle valley, iron from the western Ardennes between the Sambre and Meuse, and salt from the marshes of maritime Flanders.

The Danubian Frontier

At its fullest extent in the second century A.D. the Empire incorporated the whole of the Danube valley from its sources in the Black Forest down to the Black Sea, and established frontier provinces along or astride the river. The full story of this frontier evolution and of the causes which governed it are not relevant here, but it may be noted here the conditions which led the Emperor Augustus to advance northwards towards

[1] See the note in the *A. de G.*, May, 1927, p. 273.

the Danube. The extension of Roman power beyond Italy—which was bounded by the Apennines and the river Rubicon (the present Fiumincino)—to the Alps, left the northern plains—Gallia Cisalpina—exposed to attacks, especially from the north-east where the Alpine girdle afforded little protection. The conquest of Gaul by Caesar (58–51 B.C.) made it necessary to command certain passes of the western Alps in order to maintain communication with the Rhineland, whilst the conquest of Greece, Macedonia and Thrace left Rome with a frontier open to invaders from the lands of the lower Danube and the Save. Early invasions into Italy of Germans and Gauls had demonstrated the weakness of the Alpine system as a barrier frontier, and even in the time of Caesar the hostile activities of Burebista, king of Dacia, threatened both Italy and Thrace. The need for a stronger frontier together with political ambition dictated a forward or expansionist policy, which would advance the frontier of conflict farther away from the Mediterranean centres of the Empire. In result the provinces of Raetia, Noricum, Pannonia, Moesia and Dacia were added to the Empire, each of which formed a well-defined physical entity, and, except for Dacia, was bounded by the Danube.

In order adequately to hold Gaul and to secure the Rhine frontier against barbarian incursions, Augustus subdued the many peoples established in the Alpine valleys, and won control of essential passes. The organization of the Rhineland for frontier defence may well have diverted wandering German tribes to the south and increased the dangers of invasion across the central or eastern Alps. Certainly the Alps, that 'splendid traitor', are deceptive in the natural protection which they afford. In particular, at their eastern end the Alps are weakest and most easily accessible to the invader. In this region the Alps splay out fanwise into a number of ranges which fall greatly in elevation, whilst the rivers Save and Drave, tributaries of the Danube, have so cut back into the limestone rocks of the Julian Alps that the headstreams of the Isonzo and the Eisack which drain to the Adriatic may be quickly reached across easy passes. This watershed, then, between the Danube draining to the Black Sea and rivers draining to the Adriatic imposed few difficulties to movement, and actually stimulated intercourse, since it coincided with a well-defined climatic frontier zone which differentiated the produce of the contiguous regions. Towards the sea the Alps present a dry, high, stony plateau which is Mediterranean in its climate and products, but very soon to the north, across what are in fact the lowest passes of the Alps, are reached the well-watered valley lands of the navigable Save and Drave, rich in timber and in pasture. In this eastern section of the Alps behind the Adriatic Sea lies, therefore, one of the crucial geographically defined gates from the Mediterranean world to Danubian Europe and from Italy to the Balkan peninsula. Further, to the west, the Brenner pass, which had long lain open to prehistoric migrations, gave access by one low well-graded pass from the Inn tributary of the Danube to the rivers Adige and Eisack which led down into the plains of Venetia.

The river Danube may be conveniently divided on physical grounds into some four sections, each of which formed roughly and, at least for a time, the boundary of a frontier province. The first stretches from the Black Forest head-waters down to Passau, where the river receives the waters of its great Alpine affluent, the Inn, and is accordingly doubled in volume; the second, between Passau and Vienna, occupies a series of gorges; in its third section the river flows from the Vienna gorge through a generally low open plain to the series of defiles and rapids between Moldava and Turnu Severin; finally, the last stretch of river from the Iron Gate cataract to the channels of the delta flows between the high Bulgarian and low Rumanian banks.

Raetia, enclosed between Lake Constance, the upper Rhine, and the lower Inn, fronted the Danube above Passau and was constituted by the Bavarian Alps and sub-Alpine plateau. The latter region is made up of many fluvio-glacial terraces; there are areas of sandstone covered with gravel, as well as pebbled plains called *feld*, and marshy belts, especially along the Danube, described as *moos* and *ried*. Although, in contrast to the Alps, the plateau is dry, it was extensively forested with larch and maple, and generally lacked agricultural possibilities, except on the loess patches east of the Iller river and along the sheltered, warm rim of Lake Constance. In Raetia the Danube was only partially navigable by boats; its swift Alpine tributaries ran due north or north-eastwards in deeply trenched valleys, and were as useless for navigation as their valleys were obstacles to east-west communication. In short, Raetia was less important economically than strategically as a *pays de passage* between the Alps and the middle Rhine and Main.

The conquest of Raetia by the Emperor Augustus (15 B.C.) was followed by the opening up of new routes across the Alps. From Milan, by way of Lake Como, a road was built across the Raetian Alps via the Splügen pass to the upper Rhine and thence to Lake Constance and to the fortress of Vindonissa. Further, the Brenner pass, approached by the Adige valley from the wealthy Augustan colony of Verona, carried a road of easy gradients to the Inn and thence to the Danube at Passau. On this route the colony Augusta Vindelicorum (Augsburg) was founded at the junction of the Wertach and the Lech: it became a focus of routes between the Alps, on the one hand, and the upper Rhine on the other. Originally a market village, Roman Augsburg collected the trade of its essentially rural region—Raetic timber, cattle and wine; it developed industries, notably cloth and pottery, and became a resort of merchants. Here, as elsewhere in Raetia and in barbarian territory across the Danube, there was active trade intercourse between Romans and Germans from the second century A.D. onwards.

The frontier defences in Raetia were later developed by Claudius who built a line of forts, some few miles away from the marshes and moors of the Danube on its southern side, from Mengen down to Regensburg (Ratisbon). This latter site, to become the only legionary station in Raetia, had obvious strategical importance: it occupied a limestone bluff where the Danube, in reaching its northernmost latitude, cuts through the edge of the Franconian Jura, at a point near the junction of the rivers Regen and Naab, both of which came down from the Bohemian Forest. Above Regensburg a stretch of river marsh impeded passage of the Danube, whilst below it the steep, forested wall of Bavarian Forest formed the northern valley side of the river and made access to the river by armies impossible. Further, passes through the Bohemian Forest gave access to the Regen and Naab rivers from the Bohemian plateau, the home in turn of Celts (the Boii) and Germans (the Marcomanni and Quadi). Around the fortress were arable fields, which produced supplies for the garrison. In A.D. 160 after a war with the Marcomanni the Emperor Antoninus completed the Limes Raetica, the outer wall of which together with its road reached the Danube near the confluence of the Altmühl, some twenty miles above Regensburg, and it was at this time the fort at Regensburg was converted into a legionary fortress.

In contrast to Raetia, Noricum and Pannonia, which fronted the Danube between Passau and Belgrade, were much more valuable economically whilst the latter was strategically much more important. Both provinces stood nearer to Italy, since the Alps there formed a link whereas between Italy and Raetia they formed a broad, high and more complex dividing zone. The minerals of Noricum and the agricultural wealth of Pannonia stimulated the growth of towns, and trade with Italy was fostered. Finally, Pannonia, which was enclosed by the Danube both to the north and to the east, constituted an area of frontier tension.

Roman traders and civilization had intruded over the passes of the eastern Alps, long before Roman arms, into the mountainous province of Noricum—' the foreland of Italy ', Mommsen called it—which lay eastwards of the lower Inn and southwards of the Danube between Passau and the Wiener Wald above Vienna. Noricum was essentially an Alpine province: the Black Sea-Adriatic watershed formed by the crystalline range of the Hohe and Nieder Tauern, in which lay metalliferous seams, runs obliquely across it, whilst northwards stood the limestone belt of the Alps, cut through by the rivers Salzach, Mur, Enns, Drave and Save, in the valleys of which Romanized city life was fostered. Farther north, below the mountains, stretched a plateau, the narrowing continuation of the Bavarian plateau, edged on the north by the Danube and limited eastwards by the Wiener Wald. Noricum, like Raetia, was relatively a safe and naturally guarded section of the frontier since the Danube passes through a deep and steep-sided valley to which access from the north was impeded by the Bohemian and Weinsberger forests. Hence only ' secondary ' troops were normally stationed there before A.D. 200, and only later was a legionary camp established at Lauriacum (Lorch) at the junction of the Enns with the Danube. The country was most valued for its timber, its salt, and its iron mines and for the manufacture of implements and weapons, e.g. at Noreia in the Styrian Alps, reached by a somewhat difficult road from Aquileia over the Julian Alps via Virunum (Muriasaal).

Nowhere on the whole Danube frontier was the tension more acute and the danger more serious than in the province of Pannonia. It is significant that, whereas the Rhine frontier was guarded by as few as six or even four legions, some eight, ten and even twelve legions were required at successive periods on the Danube, of which about a half were stationed in Pannonia alone. This province formed only a part of the Pannonian or Hungarian basin, as modern geographers define it. A broad plain diversified by hills, delimited both to the north and east by the Danube, it stood below the Austrian Alps and stretched southwards and south-westwards towards the *karst* uplands of Istria and Dalmatia. Its strategical importance sprang from its position and from its ability to support a large nomad or sedentary population. Pannonia was the ante-room to Italy. On it converged easy, natural routes from central Europe and from the Near East: the March or Morava river on the one hand, which leads down from the Oder and Vistula headstreams, and the Drave and Save valleys, on the other, which afford access towards the Balkan peninsula. These routes converged, it will be recalled, just where the Alpine girdle of Italy was weakest. Furthermore, Pannonia provided a highly attractive settlement area: the wide cover of loess soils, together with the high summer temperatures, minimized forest growth, and the 'open' character of the country may likewise be inferred from the abundant artefacts of many prehistoric cultures. Pasture was plentiful, water-supply adequate, and arable cultivation easy and productive; the vine could be grown, whilst the rivers, notably the Save and Drave, were navigable. Both position and lack of obstacles to movement favoured trade, and an ancient, pre-Roman 'amber route' from the lower Vistula via the Morava valley, crossed Pannonia *en route* for the valley of the Po. On economic ground—to secure a potential storehouse of supplies—and even more so, on strategical ground—to protect Italy and to control the easiest land route to the Near East—it was desirable that Rome should hold Pannonia and hold it strongly. The Danube, however, ceased to be in Pannonia the natural shield which it had been in Noricum, and much greater military defences were therefore required. Below Carnuntum (Petronell, west of Bratislava) the Danube flows through a low-lying plain until it cuts a way just above Budapest between the Bakony mountains, a detached ridge of the Alps, and the Visegrad mountains, a protruding spur of the Tatra massif. The only natural obstacles presented by the river were its breadth, its interlacing channels, and broad flood plain marshes: e.g., in the Grand Schutt and along parts of the north-south course of the river below Budapest. Even so, the Danube presented a long weak exposed line: the simplest boats, such as the hollowed tree trunk canoes, could cross it, and its winter freezing further facilitated raiding.

Augustus's conquest and colonization of the Istrian peninsula and of Dalmatia formed the prelude to the subjugation of the Celto-Illyrian peoples to the north, whose country constituted the natural hinterland of the northern Adriatic ports, particularly of Aquileia. Trieste, and Emona (Laibach) near the upper Save, were founded in 35–34 B.C., whilst Nauportus (Ober Laibach), which stood near the head of the Save navigation, had long been occupied by Roman merchants trading with the peoples on the Save. The Save valley was first annexed, but the whole of Pannonia was not fully subdued until A.D. 9, that is after conquests had been made on both its left and right flanks, namely in Raetia and Noricum and in Moesia. Pannonia was rapidly and thoroughly Romanized, both in a military and civil sense. Towns and fortresses were established and under their protection agriculture was introduced, whilst roads were built to link it up effectively with the Roman world. Trade was in consequence stimulated; merchants frequented its towns from Gaul and from the East; the old amber route was not only utilized but carefully explored; and with the German Marcomanni of Bohemia the Romans engaged in profitable trade when they were not involved in the sterner business of war. Transversely across Pannonia, forming the main thoroughfares for armies and merchants, was built the road from Aquileia to Vindobona (Vienna) and Carnuntum (Petronell), along which urban settlements flourished as market centres for the produce of scattered villae: Nauportus, Emona, Poetovio—from which a road was carried down the Save to Belgrade, and Scarbantia and Savaria, which served the farms of the Arrabo (Raab) valley. Many of these towns were originally tribal centres; others began as military stations, around which civil settlements grew, and had been used by the legions in their progress from the Save to the Drave and thence to the Danube. Siscia (Sisak) on the upper Save was used as a military headquarters in wars directed against the Dacians. Lower down-stream Sirmium (Mitrovitsa) guarded the approaches from the Tisza and the lower Danube, whilst Poetovio (Pettau) standing near the Drave was an early fortress site and road centre. Near the confluence of the Drave with the Danube stood Mursa (Eszek), the headquarters of the middle Danube fleet.

During the first century A.D. the Pannonian Danube was strongly fortified as the military frontier of the Empire; permanent garrisons of legionary and auxiliary troops were stationed at camps, to which cultivable land was assigned for the provision of supplies. Vindobona (Vienna), Carnuntum (built A.D. 73) and, beyond the Grand Schutt marsh, Brigetio (O. Szöny) held the river against the Marcomanni and their dependants, the Quadi, to whom the March valley afforded a tempting southward route. Below Brigetio the Danube makes a complete right-angled bend, and except for the gorge above Budapest flows through the low-lying Hungarian plain. This region, owing to its relief and soils, its hot summers with light rains and its extensive prairies, has been often called an outlier of the steppe of central Asia, and it is an historical fact that it continually attracted nomad horsemen from the eastern steppe. From the first century A.D. the Jazyges horsemen occupied the

Alföld, the sandy east Hungarian plain. On the Danube itself the forts of Aquincum (Alt Ofen) and facing it on the left bank, Trans Aquincum—the Roman equivalents of the later Buda and Pest which stood a little down-stream—occupied hill sites so placed to control river passage through the gorge above, at a point where the Danube is relatively narrow. There were other fortified camps lower down-stream, whilst both the northern and eastern sections of the Danube were linked up with Pettau, a convenient headquarters and route-centre behind the lines.

The Danubian frontier system of the Empire was finally completed by the conquest and organization of Moesia and Dacia on the lowest reaches of the river. Roman conquests in Dalmatia, Greece, Macedonia and Thrace had early made Rome a Balkan power, with a frontier in the north exposed to the lower Danubian lands. This frontier was critical since the kingdom of Dacia—which consisted of the Wallachian plain, Moldavian plateau and the Transylvanian basin—developed precociously a strong political and military organization and was early characterized as a breeding-ground of invasions. Furthermore, an essential geographical unity linked the middle Danube in Pannonia with both the Balkan and Dacian lands. The Drave and Save rivers formed a physical link with the lower Danube of which merchants from Italy and Pannonia had long availed themselves, whilst the salt and gold of Transylvania had attracted merchants across the Danube and the Tisza. On the Danube itself passage down-stream was checked by the gorges and cataracts below Belgrade.[1] Entry into the Balkan peninsula could be made from the Danube above the gorges by way of the Mlava and Morava valleys, whilst with difficulty passage could be made across the Dinaric Alps which shut off the Dalmatian coastlands from the interior. Actually the conquest of Upper Moesia, which was annexed in 29 B.C., was carried out from bases in Macedonia and Thrace. It stretched eastwards from Belgrade to the River Vid, and was bounded northwards by the Danube. Politically and economically this conquest brought under Roman control the land route which left the Danube at Kostolač (Viminacium) below Belgrade and proceeded up the Mlava and Morava valleys to Nish, the chief city of Upper Moesia, and thence to both Thessalonica and Byzantium. The new province, which had long stood aloof from the Greek culture of Dalmatia, Macedonia and Thrace, remained resistant to Romanization. Its mountainous character, involving difficult communication and precluding extensive agri-

[1] Cp. *infra*, Chapter XVIII, and Figs. 7*a*, 53 and 55.

culture, supported hardy peoples of mixed Thracian, Illyrian and Celtic stock who, together with the Illyrians to the west, were intensively recruited in the Roman armies. Cattle raising formed the chief occupation, and there was little urban development. Under the Emperor Claudius, in A.D. 46, the frontier was carried down to the Danube delta by the incorporation of the Bulgarian platform, lands which later formed the province of Lower Moesia, eastwards of the River Vid. This province consisted of the hilly Dobrudja 'corridor' which leads southwards from the Danube delta, and a broad plateau which lies below the Balkan mountains and presents a steep face to the Danube. Climate, relief and soils alike favoured arable cultivation, and as early as A.D. 50 Lower Moesia became important as a source of grain supplies both for Rome and for troops serving on the Danube. There was, particularly in the second century, a steady down-stream flow of Roman colonists, to cities like Scupi (Uskub) and Ratiaria (Artchar) in Upper Moesia, and to the more numerous military and civil centres in the lower province. Later in the first century A.D. the lower Danube was fortified by the construction on its high southern side of fortresses at Novae (Sistov), Durostorum (Silistra), and Troesmis (Igliţa). In Upper Moesia fortresses were built at Drobeta (Turnu-Severin) and Tsierna (Orşova), both of which stood on the north bank of the Danube, whilst below Orşova stood the fortress of Ratiaria (Artchar) (Fig. 7*a*).

Across the lower Danube below Belgrade, as across the upper Danube and the upper Rhine, the Roman frontier was extended, so that it enclosed a broad salient of territory between Transylvania and the Black Sea. In the west extension beyond the upper Danube was easily effected by the occupation and fortification of lands lightly settled by loosely organized German tribes, but on the lower Danube extension was the hard-won result of three campaigns waged by Trajan[1] against the powerful Dacian kingdom of Decebalus, the reduction of which was necessary if Pannonia, Italy and the Balkan provinces were to be adequately defended. Culturally, as well as politically, Dacia contrasted with the Balkan lands from which it was divided by the Danube. The Dacians were well organized politically; they were settled agriculturists; whilst their country was rich in minerals, in pasture and in timber. From their ports just above the Danube delta Greek merchants had long traded with the Dacians on both sides of the Carpathian passes, whilst Celtic civilization

[1] On Trajan's campaigns, see B. W. Henderson, *Five Roman Emperors* (1927).

had established itself and linked Dacia racially and culturally with Gallia Cisalpina and even Gaul. In the Balkans, in contrast, in the mountains and forests of Illyria and Upper Moesia, a Thracian and Illyrian population of shepherds, horse-breeders and miners were relatively uncivilized and scarcely affected by Roman influences, whereas in Dacia, for some two centuries before its conquest by Trajan, the Roman merchant had established contact with Rome.

The kingdom of Decebalus was enclosed by the Danube, the Tisza, the Pruth and the Carpathians, and lay across the main thoroughfare of nomad horsemen moving westwards from the steppe north of the Black and Caspian Seas. Dacia was thus a European outpost against the steppe ; but to the Romans it was rather a Danubian power which continually threatened (especially when the river was frozen) the lands across the long, exposed river frontier line. The heart of the Dacian kingdom lay in Transylvania, in the basin of the navigable Maros, where gold, silver, copper, iron and salt mines supplemented pastoral, timber and agricultural resources and where settlements were abundant from prehistoric times onwards. Its capital, Sarmizegetusa (Gradistea) stood in the south-west corner of the basin, well placed to command the rich hills and plains of the Banat of Temesvar and of Wallachia which lay below the Transylvanian bastion. Sarmizegetusa was fortified by a series of terraces surrounding a central hill-top palace, the road approaches to which were guarded by the forts of Muncel Cetatea and Tapae.

Three valley routes led from the Danube to the Dacian capital and were all used by Trajan—as indeed earlier by Domitian—in his efforts to strike at the centre of the Dacian power. One ran from Kostolač above the defiles to Temesvar, thence via Tapae and the Iron Gate *pass*.[1] The second left Turnu-Severin, just below the Iron Gate rapids, and continued by way of Orşova to Temesvar where it joined the first road. Finally, farther to the east, in Wallachia, a road ascended the river Oltu, twice bridged the river and reached the Red Tower pass ; thence by Sibiu (Hermannstadt) and along the river Maros. In his first campaign in A.D. 101, Trajan used the first route from the Danube and fought an indecisive battle at Tapae : in A.D. 89 Domitian, using the same route, had fought a battle likewise at Tapae. In 102 Trajan chose the third or Wallachian route, as Domitian had done in A.D. 87 : this time the invasion was successful, for Muncel Cetatea was captured and Dacia became a dependent state. In Trajan's last campaign (A.D. 105), as a

[1] See Fig. 7*a*.

result of which Dacia was annexed as a Roman province, one of the first two routes was used. In this year Trajan reached Turnu-Severin from Italy: his much-debated itinerary lay, it would seem, by ship from Ancona to Zara, by the Dalmatian coast road to Salona, thence by ship to Lissus, and from Lissus overland via Nish to the Danube. In his earlier campaigns he had moved more directly down the Danube from Pannonia: ships and boats on the river provided transport for stores, and pontoon bridges were built across the river to effect its passage. In Trajan's last campaign (A.D. 105) the legions crossed the Danube at Turnu-Severin by Trajan's newly-built bridge which was supported by twenty stone piers, the bases of which remain to this day.

Roman Dacia, thus united to the Roman Empire, consisted only of a part of the original Dacian kingdom, namely, the south-western half of the Transylvanian basin, the south-eastern part of the Banat, and the Little Wallachian plain, westwards of the river Oltu. Northwards it fell short of the Carpathians and the upper Tisza; near the Somes, a tributary of the Tisza, stood Mograd, the northernmost Roman station. From Mograd a road ran south to Apulum, which commanded the crossing of the Maros and routes into Wallachia by the Oltu, and into Pannonia and Moesia by way of the Banat. From its annexation in A.D. 106 until the withdrawal of its garrisons in 272 Dacia served Rome both as a source of metals and as a bulwark against the steppe. A legion was established at Apulum and another, in the third century, was moved forward from Troesmis on the Danube to Potaissa.[1] The Oltu river was fortified, whilst above its confluence with the Danube Oescus and Ratiaria, deprived of their legions, became purely civil settlements. Below the Oltu confluence the Danube remained the military frontier. In eastern Wallachia and in Moldavia and Bessarabia Roman military and civil occupation scarcely extended: this region formed a no-man's-land in which Roman power was more or less exercised. Trajan established a fort at Barboși, the old Greek commercial station on the Sereth near its junction with the Danube, and a detachment of the Moesian fleet navigated the Sereth. What is probably a Roman fortification ran between Tyras (Cetatea Alba) on the Dniester estuary and a point near Tabac on the Pruth: this may be conceived as a subsidiary defence to the wall, probably built in the first place by Domitian, which runs across the upland Dobruja 'cor-

[1] Apulum, Troesmis and Potaissa occupied the present sites of Alba Iulia, Iglița and Turda respectively.

ridor' between Constanţa on the Black Sea and Rachova on the Danube. Further, in the steppe borderlands between the Roman and the nomad worlds a road was made to connect certain Black Sea ports, such as Nikolayev and Cetatea Alba, with the Danube, whilst another passed up the Sereth valley from Barboşi en route for Transylvania by way of the Oituz pass.[1]

By the work of Trajan the Roman frontier achieved for a time a condition of equilibrium along or beyond the Danube. The middle Danube above Belgrade ceased thus to fulfil its age-long function as a corridor of migration from the east; thrusts against the frontier were now from the north; whilst along sections of the valley the river became a thoroughfare for armies and traders.

[1] V. Pârvan, *Dacia*, p. 193.

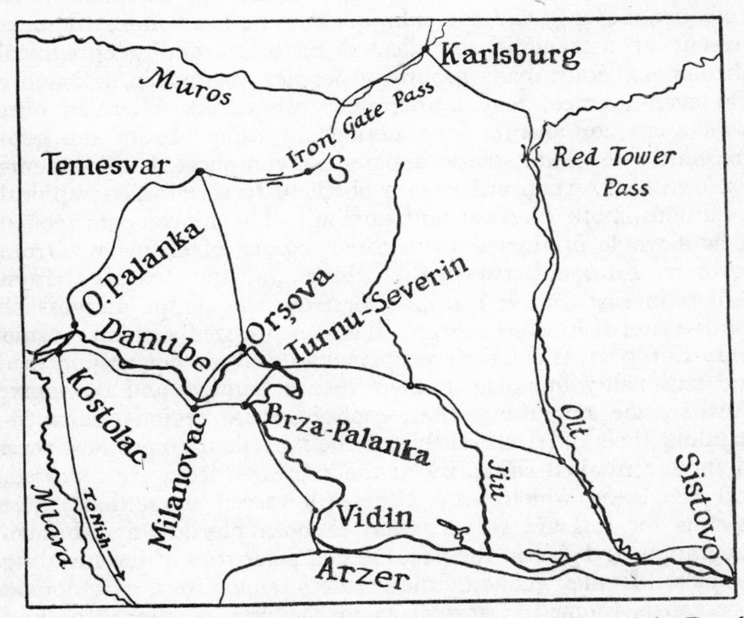

FIG. 7*a*. Roman Roads along the Gorge and cataract section of the Danube and into Dacia. The modern names are given

CHAPTER III

THE BARBARIAN INVASIONS AND SETTLEMENT

THE highly organized frontier zone of the Roman Empire, which had been created from the North Sea to the Black Sea in order to stem the persistent pressure of ' barbarian ' (i.e. non-Roman) [1] peoples and to safeguard Roman provincial civilization, broke down during the third and fourth centuries A.D. and made possible on an extended scale the process of colonization which had already peaceably begun under the sanction of the Emperors. The ' barbarian invasions ', or Völkerwanderung, and the subsequent conquests and settlement present at first sight complicated historical and geographical phenomena, since many groups of peoples, distinct in nationality and even in race, raided, migrated, conquered or settled over wide areas and during long periods of time. From the geographical viewpoint these apparently complicated movements conform to a certain order, as if obedient to certain geographical conditions, both physical and human. The movements looked at as a whole originated from three regions of diffusion : from northern Europe between the Rhine and the Vistula ; from Galicia in east-central Europe ; or from the steppe margins of south-eastern Europe. From these contrasted habitats came Indo-European and Asiatic peoples who differed not only in race and nationality but also in their speech, culture and economy. Further, the migrations from each of these regions, notwithstanding their different dates and their particular episodes, tend to show a marked similarity in the routes which were followed, and the areas which were either plundered or settled. The reasons for this are to be found in both physical and human geography, and also in the peculiar characteristics of the invading peoples. In their economy the invaders ranged from pure nomad pastoralists (nomad = grazer) as in the case of the Huns and

[1] Historians and philologists emphasize that the term ' barbarian ' as applied to the German peoples in these times did not mean ' savages ' or even ' enemies of culture '. The latter terms apply only to certain Asiatic peoples, e.g. the Huns.

the Magyars, to the economy of the German peoples who combined agriculture with the rearing of horses, cattle and sheep. The ambition of the invaders was to secure new lands, either to ravage, or, as was more often the case, for settlement.

The geographical possibilities of different types of country were thus, from this point of view, an important factor in conditioning their movements. The new immigrants tended above all to follow the line of least resistance, that is to say, to follow lines of communication which had already been long explored, and to occupy lands which had already been long exploited. In this way various geographical factors appear to have operated as attractive or deterrent forces. It now appears that forests were by no means such obstacles to movement as was formerly believed. Many of them, like the Weald in England, the Ardennes in France, and the *Carbonnière* in Belgium, were already crossed by Roman routes. Nor can Hoop's view, stated over forty years ago, be now accepted. 'Primeval forest,' he wrote,[1] 'is the enemy and not the friend of man; primitive man may make expeditions into the forest but will not settle permanently there.' But if, as we shall note below, forests were by no means wholly negative areas avoided by early settlers, it is right to believe that fields and pastures had a superior attraction to the Germanic intruders. Marshy areas, although their island sites might eventually be occupied—as in the English Fenlands—were for similar reasons at first avoided. Mountainous regions again formed areas of minimal penetration, since movement was relatively difficult owing to gradients, forests and even bogs—as in the Ardennes and Vosges—which restricted the areas open to settlement. Soils, again, either directly or indirectly had a very important effect on the goal sought for conquest or colonization. The soils which proved most attractive to the immigrants were not necessarily those which were potentially the best for cultivation: certainly areas of loam soils figured prominently in these movements, but so also did those which were covered with inferior sandy soils and were, as a result, well drained and easy to work. Further, the existing system of engineered Roman roads, and, as in eastern England and the Low Countries, navigable river valleys, exerted a guiding influence on the routes of invasion. Finally, it should be noted that the general direction of the invasions, which was to the west and also to the south, was, it is clear, directly conditioned by the lay-out of the Romanized lands; the advance therefore was directed towards the Mediter-

[1] *Waldbäume und Kulturpflanzen im germanischen Altertum* (1905), p. 91.

ranean climatic region within which a large part of these lands lay.

The region originally occupied by the German peoples in the second millennium B.C. included the coastlands between the lower Rhine and the Oder, the Schleswig peninsula and islands, together with southern Sweden. The homelands of the Germans —who formed one branch of the peoples of Indo-European language—had a broad geographical similarity. They had alike undergone glaciation; they consisted largely of level plains, covered with wide stretches of sandy soils; they included considerable areas of marsh, peat bog, lakes, and moor, and were extensively covered with deciduous forest and undergrowth. Scania and the coast west of the Oder estuary were alike well embayed and offered river access inland; proximity—for the Baltic narrows in the extreme west—the disposition of islands, the many convenient havens and, occasionally, the freezing over of the sea, all served to unite Scania, the Schleswig peninsula and the north German plain in close relationship. Jutland, or the Schleswig peninsula, together with Frisia stretching westwards to the Rhine, presented also broken coastlines to the North Sea. By about 200 B.C. the Germans had moved south as far as the Main into country then occupied by Celts, whilst at the same time they had reached the broad plains between the Oder and the Vistula. It is possible that some stimulus was given to this movement owing to a wet climatic period which conditioned an extension of forest and peat bog.[1] This movement brought them up against the Hercynian mountain system between the middle Rhine and Oder, and against the Carpathian ranges eastwards of the headwaters of the Oder and Vistula. In this central highland zone of Europe gradients were steep, deciduous and coniferous forests were dense, 'open' lands for pasture and tillage were relatively scanty, and the natural lines of movement were restricted to valley routes and mountain passes. If, however, these elevated lands were essentially unattractive areas for colonization, they were by no means barriers to movement. Some time before the establishment and organization of the frontier of the Roman Empire, in fact as early as 114 B.C., Germanic tribes had reached and crossed the Alps and the Rhine, carrying their devastations into the territories of Rome. That the German peoples should have pressed towards the south, south-east and south-west rather than eastwards is not difficult to explain, once the necessity or desire

[1] See Huntington, 'The Evolution of Climate in North-Western Europe', *G. R.*, Jan. 1922.

to move had arisen. The alternative was to push into the well-wooded plains of Poland or Russia, where there was no highly developed civilization to plunder or inherit, where the winters were long and hard, where naturally defensive 'frameworks' for state-building were lacking and, finally, where nomad populations then roamed. On the other hand, advance southwards from the Baltic shore brought the Germans to areas covered with loess soils, along the northern foothills of the Hercynian mountains and in the Galician plateau, which had attracted agriculturists even in prehistoric times. Moreover, to the south of the Hercynian mountains stretched lands which enjoyed warmer temperatures and river basins and plains which had long been occupied and cultivated: the Main, Neckar and upper Elbe basins, the Transylvanian basin, and even the south Russian steppe.

Knowledge of the culture and economy of the German peoples and of their habitat, especially in the western part of Middle Europe, has been greatly advanced in recent decades thanks to the results of geographical study of soils and vegetation and above all to those of scientific archaeology. The conception of Montesquieu, which long held the field, portrayed the Germans at the time of their first contact with the Romans as nomad pastoralists without fixed abodes, who occupied oases of pasture or temporary clearings made by burning, within a land consisting essentially of all-pervading primeval forest and marsh. It is true, of course, that a greater part of Middle Europe was covered at this time by forest, moor and marsh vegetation than to-day. Even so, the references of Caesar and Tacitus afford literary evidence that settled and cultivated areas alternated with wide forested regions. Tacitus' description of interior Germany as 'silvis horrida et paludibus foeda' probably exaggerates, as a Mediterranean observer would be prone to do, those physical and vegetational conditions which were unfamiliar in the Mediterranean world. Moreover, the Hercynian forest, as Caesar [1] described it, could be crossed in nine days by a fast runner, although its eastern end lay more than a sixty-days' march distant. It is no less clear that throughout the wide sweep of prehistoric times, from the Neolithic to the Iron Age, measurable areas at both low and high levels were settled and cultivated. Many of these early settled areas coincide with tracts of 'loess', a fine wind-borne dust which was carried and deposited during intervals of the Great Ice Age, and to-day affords optimum arable land. It used to be asserted that loess areas were, as now, forest-free and that because they were always naturally 'open'

[1] *De Bello Gallico*, VI, 25.

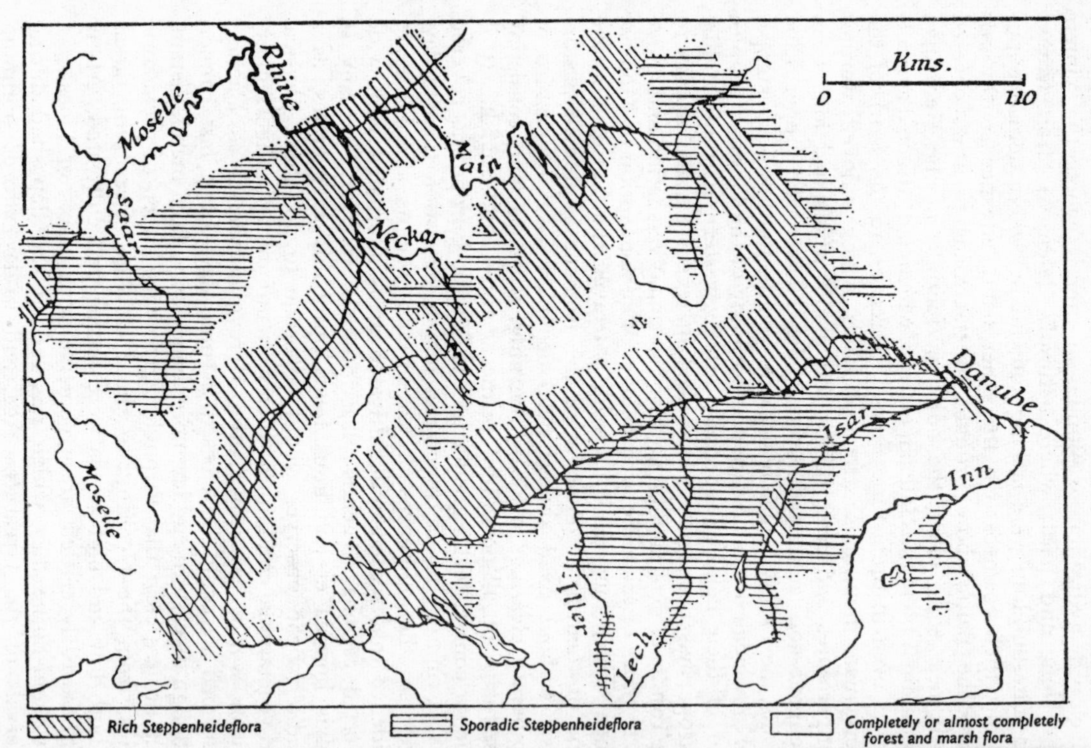

FIG. 8.—The Distribution of Steppenheideflora in south-west Germany and the Rhineland (after Gradmann's

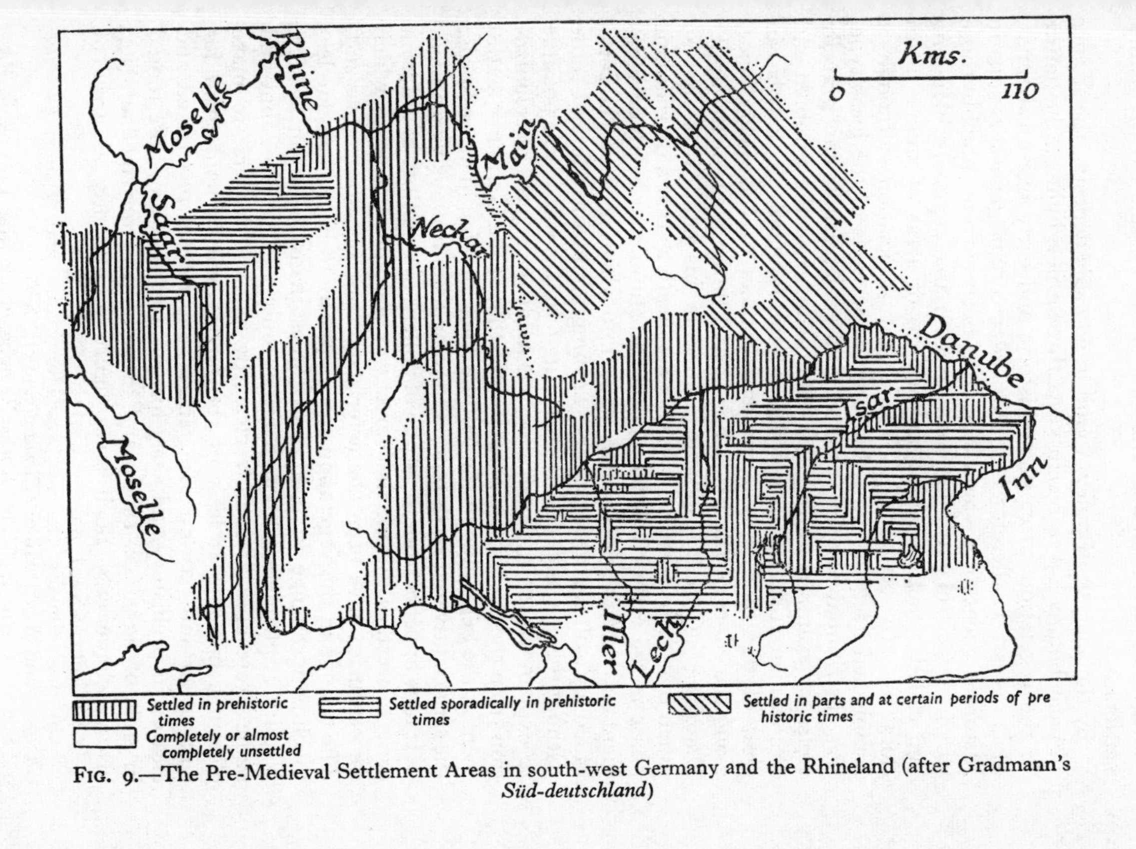

FIG. 9.—The Pre-Medieval Settlement Areas in south-west Germany and the Rhineland (after Gradmann's *Süd-deutschland*)

lands, they were among the first areas chosen by prehistoric settlers.

By the analysis of pollen found in dateable deposits, the science of palæobotany has in recent years thrown new light on the nature of the vegetation cover in prehistoric and early historical times. It is necessary, therefore, to reconsider certain generalizations in historical geography which have long been current, notably those of which Gradmann in Germany was an able exponent. He long ago called attention to the importance of areas of steppe-heath flora to early settlement. This plant association, although it established itself on some, but only some, soils of the loess type, was distributed also in regions of infertile, sandy and gravelly soils, for example, on the limestone plateaux of the Swabian and Franconian Jura, in parts of the Alpine foreland, in the plateau west of the Iller, on the western borders of Lake Constance, along the edges of the Black Forest and in the plain of the upper Danube (Fig. 8). Gradmann argued in his later work[1] not so much that these areas had always been heath as that a dry climatic phase in the early Neolithic period had stimulated heath development and thus provided 'open' areas into which peoples who combined agriculture with pastoral farming could intrude and settle without the necessity of forest clearing.[2] In this way it was possible to explain why so little advance was made in the area of colonization from the prehistoric period up to that of the Germanic settlement at the beginning of the Middle Ages, or why, in other words, the same cultivated lands tended to remain continuously occupied.

It now appears from the study of pollen[3] in a number of different areas of western Europe that forest was widespread in areas which for centuries have been characterized as open heath or grassland. The change in the vegetation cover appears to have been due less to climatic change in prehistoric times than to human agency. Neolithic intruders, although armed only with axes of flint and stone, were able, it is now clear, by axe and by fire, to make clearings in some at least of the forests and to hold them for cultivation and pasture. In general, the forests penetrated and cleared in prehistory and early historical times were those rooted in soils of light (i.e. sandy and gravelly) and intermediate (i.e. loamy) character.[4] Such areas figure prominently as areas of

[1] *Süd-deutschland*, I, 86.

[2] On past climatic changes, see Huntington and Visher, *Climatic Changes*, and A. A. Miller, *Climatology*, ch. XV.

[3] See A. Garnett, "The Loess Regions of Central Europe in Prehistoric Times", *G. J.* (1945) CVI, 132–43, and G. Clark, "Forest Clearance and Prehistoric Farming, *Econ. Hist. Rev.* (1947), XVII.

[4] Cp. the article by Wooldridge and Linton in *Ant.*, Sept. 1933.

early or ' primary ' settlement ; others covered with wet and heavy clay soils, more densely wooded, more difficult to drain and also to plough, were long avoided : colonized only in later times, these have been called areas of ' secondary ' settlement.

Archaeological distributions of prehistoric cultures show clearly that wide areas of plain, plateau, river valley and terrace, mantled by light and intermediate soils, were exploited by successive settled peoples. It is equally evident that for several millennia before Christ, in fact from the Neolithic Age, agriculture had been widely practised in these regions by peoples who occupied for the most part fixed settlements.[1] Thus the Rhine plains of Hesse, Baden, and Alsace, parts of which were once conceived to have been largely impassable marsh, were, as Schumacher has shown, successively settled and cultivated at least from the Bronze Age (Fig. 10). Similar conditions are known to have obtained in many other parts of Middle Europe, some of which in south-west Germany have already been noted above. Further, in Thuringia a belt of loess land, watered by the Unstrut and Helme rivers, lay open between the border of the Hercynian forest to the south and that of the marshland to the north, and there, too, prehistoric settlement associated with agriculture is well attested. Again, in north-western Germany settlement was made in the broader valleys, at the foot of the mountains, and generally in both high and low regions which were free of forest or marsh. Even the low North Sea plains were occupied, although they were liable to marine inundations, since in order to engage in fishing people built dwellings on artificially made earthen hills.[2] In fact, as the distribution maps in the studies of Professor Childe[3] abundantly show, prehistoric cultures were widely extended and interrelated throughout Middle Europe. In particular it should be noted how the distribution of successive cultures is related to the disposition of loess soils which lie in an almost continuous zone within the basin of the middle Danube and along the northern edge of the Hercynian mountain zone from the plateau of Galicia to the plains of Hainaut and Hesbaye in Belgium.

Hence in the first centuries A.D., when they came increasingly into contact with the superior civilization of Rome, the Germans

[1] Dopsch, *Wirtschaftliche und Soziale Grundlagen der europäischen Kulturentwicklung*, 2nd ed., 1928, I, ch. 2.

[2] For a detailed study of early settlement in north-west Germany, see Knüll, *Historische Geographie Deutschlands im Mittelalter*, pp. 65–8.

[3] E.g. *The Danube in Prehistory*, 1928 ; *Dawn of European Civilisation*, 1925. See also the learned study of Prof. J. L. Myres in the *Cam. Anc. Hist.*, vol. I, ch. II (with maps).

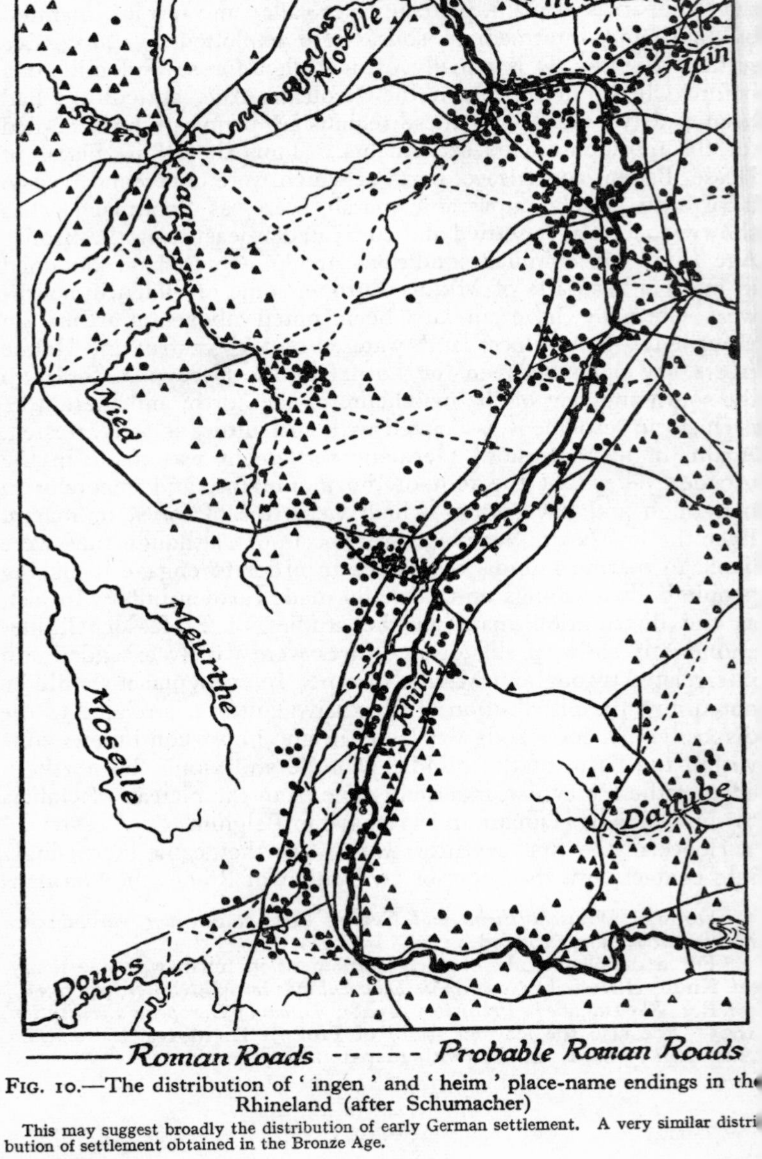

FIG. 10.—The distribution of 'ingen' and 'heim' place-name endings in the Rhineland (after Schumacher)

This may suggest broadly the distribution of early German settlement. A very similar distribution of settlement obtained in the Bronze Age.

in the west were by no means 'barbarians' who wandered through their endless forests engaged in hunting wild animals or in purely pastoral pursuits.[1] It seems clear that west of the Oder both agriculture and the habit of settled life were characteristic. Indeed, it is not easy in the light of archaeological discoveries throughout Middle Europe to feel certain that the picture of the wandering pastoralist fully described the cultural condition of the German tribes living *eastwards* of the Oder in the time of Caesar or even that of the German tribes as a whole in the days before the rise of Rome. Even so, although it is true enough that by the time the Roman frontier system was collapsing agriculture and fixed settlement had become more typical among the west Germans than among their kinsmen beyond the Oder, it is equally clear that the west Germans had not lost their habit of long-distance migration. There is good evidence also to show that they had a keen eye to the qualities of arable soils and that these afforded sufficient ground for the movement of large groups made up of federated tribes, together with their flocks and herds.

It seems true that, except in a rudimentary form, urban concentrations of population were lacking among the Germans, but it is no less true that permanent rural settlements were typically established. The older conceptions of German village and agrarian life have been greatly modified in recent years. It is no longer believed that the compact or nucleated village was the only or even the characteristic German settlement; nor is it now held that the villagers were all freemen, who, moreover, possessed equal shares in the arable fields and cultivated these in common. It is evident that Germans had settlements of both the recognized types, i.e. nucleated villages and scattered homesteads, and that they shared the arable land unequally, and proportionately to social status. The agrarian system of the Germans in the western part of Middle Europe is not too clearly and certainly known, since the writings of Caesar and Tacitus, despite the close critical scrutiny to which they have been subjected, are by no means unambiguous. There seems, however, to be agreement on the primitive and 'extensive' character of German agriculture, the common practice of which involved the ploughing up of grassland which, after cultivation, was allowed to revert to grass. But this practice did not involve the shifting of settlements, any more than did the similar 'run-rig' system long prevalent in Scotland and elsewhere. It simply meant the ploughing up of different parts of suitable land within the 'mark',

[1] J. B. Bury, *The Invasion of Europe by the Barbarians*, pp. 5–11.

and the working of this land from permanent settlements.

At the time of the barbarian invasions the German tribes had become federated into larger groups or 'peoples', e.g. Alamanns and Franks, and their originally scattered settlement areas had been loosely thrown together to form considerable territories. The territory of a German people consisted of an aggregation of small regions, originally the 'agri' of a tribe, and comprised land of varied kinds, in particular open cultivated fields ('arvi') and pasture, woodland and waste ('ager inutilis'). The settlements stood scattered throughout the islands of cultivation within the territory, and the settlement area, like the territory itself, was surrounded by 'marks'. The term 'mark', which came to be applied by historians to a highly conjectural conception of the village and agrarian system of these times, was originally in essence a geographical expression. It applied to the 'waste' frontier zone or 'negative' lands around villages and territories, that is, to lands which were characterized by their lack of settlement and cultivation. The mark served a dual economic and strategical purpose: on the one hand, it provided ample pasturage and timber, and on the other it constituted a natural 'insulation' or protection for the cultivated and settled lands. The mark varied in its geographical character from region to region; it must have consisted to a large extent of woodland; but it was never composed of cultivated land—with which, in effect, it was essentially contrasted—and was peopled not by men but by birds and beasts. Finally, the mark was undivided land, owned and utilized in common; the arable fields, on the other hand, were divided into shares which were severally owned and worked.

Finally, it may be noted that the underlying cause of the barbarian invasions or, to use a fitter term, the folk migrations, is believed to have been over-population, although it is obvious that the political weakness of the Empire afforded a stimulus to movements and also that the westward advance of Asiatic immigrants exerted an impulsive force. This explanation savours somewhat of the paradoxical when it is considered in the light of recent estimates of the population numbers of the German peoples.[1] A large nation or people like the West Goths or Vandals numbered some 80,000 to 120,000; a small nation, like the Burgundians, some 25,000 to 50,000. The Empire itself with a total population of about 70 millions in A.D. 300, was certainly more densely populated than the German lands. The Empire was not, however, over-populated, owing partly to its geographical character and more particularly to its highly-

[1] These are the figures given by Bury, op. cit., pp. 42–3.

developed civilization and hence great productivity. The hypothesis that the German lands became over-populated rests on the nature of the economy of the Germans in relation to the geographical conditions of their habitat. This economy which combined stock-raising with a primitive agriculture of the 'extensive' type, required considerable areas of open land, which were, in fact, much restricted by forest, marsh and sterile heath and moor. The Germans were faced with the choice of reclaiming new lands for utilization by organized social effort or of migrating into Roman lands which had already become serviceable to settlement. In moving forward towards the Mediterranean world where geographical conditions had long favoured precocious cultural development, the German peoples followed the line of least resistance which had been frequently taken in earlier times : by the Achaians, for example, who moved into Greece, and by the Celts, who entered the Balkans, Italy and Spain.

So much for the habitat of the German immigrants. Outside Europe on the steppes of Asia nomad herdsmen lived in continual seasonal movement, moving northwards for summer and southwards for winter pasture. The conditions of climate, which controlled the seasonal distribution of grass, governed this movement, since in the south summer drought curtailed pasture whilst in the north during winter fallen snow largely reduced supplies of grass. Further, it is possible that periodical decreases in rainfall may have reduced the pasture, and have thus reduced the means of subsistence for a population which had grown during wetter periods.[1] At any rate, from the fifth century steppe horsemen of Turki-Mongol race—Huns, Avars, Bulgars and Magyars—moved westwards to enter Europe by the steppe route of the Ural-Caspian gate.

Finally, there remain two distinct groups of invaders of, and settlers within, the Roman Empire : one was the Arabs,[2] a non-Indo-European Semitic people, the other was the Slavs who were Indo-European and constituted a 'race' only on the basis of language. The original habitat of the Slavs and the routes of their dispersion are not too clearly revealed by history. The evidence derived from their language and from geography gives some ground for identifying their original prehistoric home with the marshes and islands which lie to the north and south of the Pripet river ; later they seem to have moved thence to the Galician platform and it is from this region, it would seem, that in the fifth, sixth and seventh centuries they dispersed in

[1] Peake and Fleure, *The Steppe and the Sown*, p. 17.
[2] See *infra*, Chapter IX.

all directions.

The immigration of the German peoples, which was a slow and often peaceful penetration into the heart of the Romanized lands of Europe tended to follow definite geographical lines. Certain physically well-marked routes, 'gates' and mountain passes appear to have been continually used, whilst certain pivotal areas seemed at all times to have tempted the intruder. The reasons for this are found in the combination of many factors of varying significance which collectively characterized the geography of these strategical lines or regions: soil, vegetation, relief, proximity and, above all, the 'humanized' or cultural features of the landscape—roads, cities, cultivated fields and vineyards. It remains to sketch briefly some of these continually frequented routes and occupied lands: to show, as far as possible, their contemporary geographical physiognomy, and the impress made thereon by the invaders. Further, it can be shown by detailed illustrations how in their ingress and in their first settlement the invaders reacted to, and modified, the geographical stage.

The Routes of the Barbarian Invaders

A broad zonal route lay across Europe from the Baltic to the Black Sea, which was marked by the valleys of the Vistula and its tributaries and the Dniester. This route had long been utilized, since it has been identified as one of the trans-European routes along which amber, collected on the Samland coast to the east of the Vistula estuary, was carried to the Black Sea and the Aegean world. The route outflanks the mountain zone of central Europe, which terminates eastwards with the N.W.–S.E. folded ranges of the Carpathians; it has only to cross the low watersheds of the Galician or Podolian plateaux, which were covered with light, porous loess soils, and were hence relatively forest-free pasture lands. This zonal route was confined eastwards by the broad belt of marshes, which lay to the north and south of the Pripet river and set a barrier to north-south passage. Further, the seasonal migrations of the East German tribes in their search for good pasture must have served to make this route partially at least familiar, for it was well frequented by them. In the period of the invasions the Goths, for instance, passed along it down to the Black Sea coastlands, and established themselves in the south Russian plain first to the east, and later also to the west, of the river Don. Thence along the southern margin of steppe an open way led westwards to the frontiers of the Empire: invaders in turn sought ingress into either Moldavia and Wallachia, or across the Danube above the delta into the Dobruja, or over the Carpathian passes—especially the Oituz pass—into Transylvania. At times when the frontiers were too well guarded the movement of invaders was deflected north-westwards, via Galicia to the upper Vistula and Oder.

The Vistula–Dniester route brought German peoples to the threshold of the Empire in the east. The 'Moravian Gate', so called, offered ingress towards the heart of the Empire. The Moravian Gate is the depression between the Sudetes mountains and the Carpathians, which gives access by the valley of the upper Oder to the March or Morava river, which, in turn, leads directiy south to reach the Danube just above Bratislava. The Moravian Gate could be reached not only along the line of the Oder but also from the upper waters of the Vistula, and it affords one of the most marked breaks through the Hercynian mountain system of Europe: only a narrow upland neck separates the plain of Silesia from that of Moravia. This route was one of the most ancient trans-continental thoroughfares: Baltic amber *en route* for Italy is known to have been carried along it in prehistoric times; whilst in the reign of the Emperor Nero the route was explored from the March valley to the Vistula estuary (Fig. 11). The Morava plain was occupied successively by Celtic and by German peoples (the Boii and Quadi respectively) with whom the Romans traded and fought. The fortress of Carnuntum (now Petronell) on the south bank of the Danube just above the March confluence, with its legionary garrison and its fleet, guarded the Danube against assaults by way of the March valley. The great importance of this approach can be gauged from its position in relation to Pannonia, the broad plain to the south of the Danube, since this region on which invading movements converged was the ante-room to Italy itself. Carnuntum was destroyed by invading barbarians about A.D. 374; in consequence, the Roman military head-quarters were transferred for a time to Vindobona (now Vienna), which, in turn, fell into the hands of the barbarians. The fall of the Danubian strongholds left way open into Pannonia and thence across the passes of the eastern Alps into Italy. This was the route followed in turn by the Huns, Ostrogoths and Lombards.

Farther west, so long as the Agri Decumates were held, barbarian movement was deflected to the Naab valley and so converged on Ratisbon which stood near its junction with the Danube. Towards this fortress on the Danube led routes from the passes of the Bohemian forest and from the upper Main and Saale.

The Romans were, however, unable to prevent infiltration into the Main, Neckar and middle Rhine lands, where good soils, bearing vineyards, and cultivation offered attractive settlement lands and easy movement towards the Rhine. The plains of

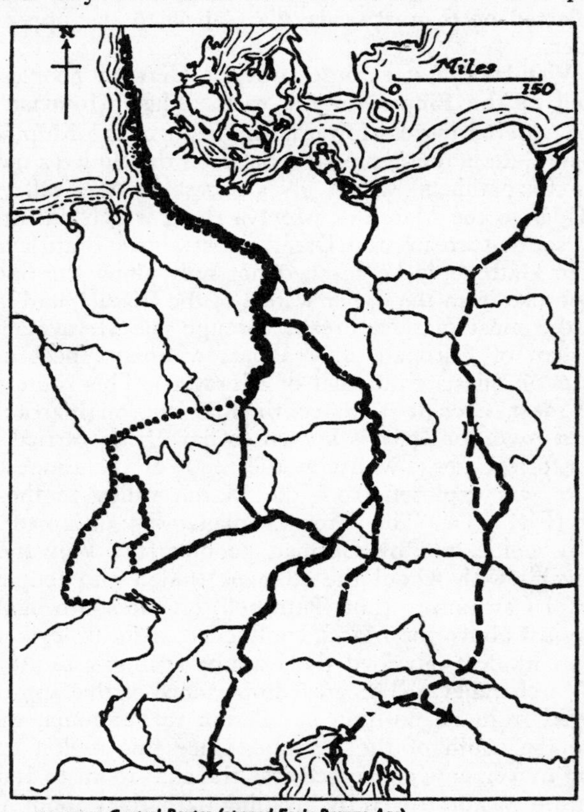

Central Routes (opened Early Bronze Age)
Western Routes (opened Middle Bronze Age)
Eastern Routes (opened Early Iron Age)

FIG. 11.—Prehistoric 'Amber Routes' between northern Europe and Italy (after J. M. de Novarro, *G. J.*, Dec., 1925)

Mr. Novarro informs me that since publishing his map in 1925 he has made some modification of his views. The Western Route shown above followed an independent course between a point near Kelheim on the Danube and the Inn valley. Again, he now believes that the routes shown above were opened up respectively as follows: the Central Route *c.* 1800 B.C., the Western Route *c.* 1600 B.C., and the Eastern Route in the eighth century B.C.

Baden and Alsace and their continuations northwards to the Main and the hill-slopes of the Hunsrück-Taunus ranges, were already, long before the legions abandoned the Agri and the Rhine, colonized by German peoples. In A.D. 213 the Alamanns made a great attack on the Roman frontier districts beyond the middle Rhine, and by 260 they had established a hold on all this territory.

The Ural-Caspian Gate, so called, was a broad lowland gap which extends between the southern end of the wooded Ural mountains and the Caspian Sea. In this region the climatic conditions fostered steppe vegetation, essentially grassland, tending to park land on its northern borders. It connected the broad Asiatic steppe regions with a narrowing steppe belt westwards along south Russia, Wallachia and the Dobruja. The route of the steppe nomads was confined between the Black Sea and the northern forests, to a zone where tillage had long been practised, despite its exposure to ravaging hordes. Pressure from newcomers into the steppe drove peoples established there onwards to the thresholds of the Empire. Through the Caspian gate came in turn Huns, Avars, Bulgars and Magyars: destructive, swift-moving horsemen, patriarchally organized, who dwelt in tents, lived on meat and mares' milk, and despised agriculture. Of these peoples the Magyars and the Bulgars eventually became settlers in Europe, and occupied lands which offered marked similarities to their original steppe habitats.

Dacia, which lay to the north of the lower Danube, formed an exposed outpost of the Empire in the east. The incursions of the Goths, the first to threaten this frontier region, may be taken as illustrative of the geography of the invasions on this sector of the frontier. The Goths came from the north German plain by the Vistula-Dniester route and settled to the east of the lower Don; driven across that river in the early third century,[1] they pressed forward to the borderlands of the Empire. They entered Bessarabia and Moldavia, the Wallachian plain, and by the Oituz pass advanced into the Transylvanian basin. Their ravages in Dacia began about A.D. 255; the province was wholly abandoned by Aurelian during the years 270–275. Viminacium (Kostolač), a fortress and road centre on the Danube just above the cataracts and gorges, was lost in 256, and the old fortified cities on the south side of the lower Danube were re-garrisoned. This military frontier proved unable to withstand the Goths: the line was long and although a broad belt of marsh stretched along the north bank and in the delta, and although the Roman fortresses occupied the higher southern bank, invaders passed easily across the river either in rafts, in hollowed tree-trunk canoes, or over the ice during the winter months when the river usually freezes over. In A.D. 330 the Emperor Constantine in

[1] Bury, *History of the Later Roman Empire*, I, 97.

his campaigns against the Goths actually built a bridge across the Danube at Oescus near the modern Bulgarian town of Nikopoli, in order to improve his communications. The bridge linked up the road from Serdica (Sofia) by way of the Isker with the road up the Oltu valley to the Red Tower Pass (Fig. 7*a*). The Dobruja, in particular, formed a corridor of invasion : just above the swamps and channels of the delta a ridge of high dry land reached the river, and thence across to the steppe plateau of the Dobruja which was confined between the Danube and the Black Sea. The fortifications attributed to Domitian and Trajan which had been built across this land bridge proved an insufficient defence. The Emperors used Marcianopolis (to the east of the modern Šumla) as a military base : the capital of Lower Moesia, it was an arsenal and fortified stronghold which commanded passes over the Balkans to the south. At Abrittus in the marshes of the Danube delta the Emperor Decius was defeated and killed in A.D. 251, whilst the defeat of the Roman army outside Adrianople in 377 cost the Emperor Valens his life. Both events shook the Roman world : by land and also by sea the Goths were ravaging the countryside and often they actually sacked walled towns. The best Balkan lands of the Empire—the Moesias, Thrace, Macedonia and Thessaly—were continually wasted, and the defences at the Gate of Thermopylae failed to protect Greece. Marcianopolis was taken in 245 and Philippopolis was sacked in 250 ; Adrianople escaped capture and Thessalonika, often threatened both by land and sea, remained safe within its walls ; but Athens, Corinth and Sparta were all sacked. Attacks launched from the Black Sea ports by means of the fleets of captured imperial cities were no less successful : Pityus and Trebizond were sacked in 258 ; the rich cities of Bithynia—Nicomedia, Chalcedon and Nicaea were captured ; even Byzantium itself was captured by sea, but only temporarily, in 267. Nevertheless, in the end the Empire survived. The three strategically placed cities of Byzantium, Thessalonika and Adrianople, the first two of which had access from the sea, escaped capture and gave the Emperors military bases within their European territory. From their capital established either at Byzantium, Thessalonika or Antioch the Emperors fought the Goths by diplomacy and by war. In 380 they allowed them to settle in the plateau country between the Danube and the Balkan mountains. The political geography of the Empire in the east, however, was not changed. It was later intruders, the Slavs and Bulgars, who actually established kingdoms for themselves.[1]

[1] See *infra*, Chapter VIII.

The Settlement of the Barbarians within the Empire

Thus far attention has been centred on the geography of the invasions of peoples into Roman lands. It must now be asked: 'What effect had the immigrants on the human and economic geography of the Roman lands?' The German immigrants essentially sought new lands for settlement; and even some of the Asiatic nomads, notably the Magyars and the Bulgars, although their original motive was as much plunder as new pastures and although they had no practical knowledge of agriculture and no tradition of sedentary life, eventually formed fixed settlements. In other words, the barbarian invaders were essentially colonists, and it is thus important to inquire to what extent their colonization within the Empire modified the 'cultural landscape'. This question is one of the most baffling, as it is one of the most relevant, to historical geography. It is true that of late the researches of historians have done much to illuminate the obscurity of the so-called 'Dark Ages' of European history, ages which are dark as much through lack of record as through their deficiencies in intellectual and technical achievement. Nevertheless, the appellation 'dark' applies with undoubted force to the dimly seen processes of post-Roman settlement and culture. Even so, despite the scarcity and piecemeal character of contemporary literary sources, some reconstruction of past conditions is possible with the aid of the important discoveries and hypotheses which have been made by archaeologists, philologists and geographers.

The questions, and they are many, may at least be raised, although they can scarcely be answered here. To what extent did the Roman patterns on the soil, made by its cities, villages, route networks, boundaries and field systems, survive undefaced in the western part of the Empire which fell under the rule of 'barbarian' victors? To what extent, again, did the distribution of settlements after the invasions had ended compare and contrast with that which obtained earlier? What became the characteristic types of settlement, and to what extent were settlements extended into hitherto unsettled land? What kind of sites were selected? Were new field systems and agricultural practices introduced? And finally, it is important to ask whether the changes in these man-made features of the countryside indicated either the drastic transformation, or the essential continuity, of Roman civilization.

The archaeological evidence which throws light on these questions is by no means as abundant as in the case of the Roman period, and consists mainly of graveyards and various artefacts. Where available, it is very apposite, since it provides datable and geographical information on Germanic settlement. The help derived from philology comes from the study of the earliest forms of place-names, and although the conclusions made are often hypothetical, they deserve careful examination, the more so since they can be considered in relation to geographical facts and speculations.

Place-name experts suggest that certain suffixes can be dated back to the earliest phase of Germanic settlement, say between A.D. 400 and 600, and moreover, that, when interpreted, they help to illuminate the process of settlement. Certainly some of the interpretations originally made have had to be abandoned with increasing knowledge, but even so the residuum left after criticism has been made possesses distinct value. Thus place-names containing the element ' -ingen ' (in German), ' -ange ' (in French) and ' -ing ' (in English) are believed to represent many of the earliest German settlements. Kemble in 1849 interpreted ' -ing ' names as indicating the settlement of a clan or family, but this meaning has now been extended to include the ' comitatus ' group of a leader and his followers. Moreover, ' -ing ' names are commonly Germanic, not merely Frankish as was once thought. The distribution of ' -ing ' names in many parts of the imperial lands affords very suggestive results. Thus in Bavaria their distribution suggests three important conclusions. First, ' -ingen ' names occur alike in nucleated villages, especially in the western part of Upper Bavaria, and in scattered homesteads which are found particularly in the eastern part of upper, and also in lower, Bavaria. Second, the distribution of ' -ingens ' is closely related to that of Roman and prehistoric cultivation and settlement. Third, these names are related above all to areas of cultivable land and tend to disappear where the arable land ends, where pasture and forest predominate, and where other names occur. Similar conclusions have been reached elsewhere. In the Agri Decumates Germanic settlement began under Roman rule in the second century A.D. and was continued by the Alamanns, who took possession of the region in the third century, and later by the Franks, who conquered it in 496. ' Ingen ' names are very common in modern Baden, Würtemberg and Lorraine (Fig. 10), and there again, as a study of individual sites shows, they occur in the areas cultivated, and sometimes even on the sites occupied, in Roman and pre-Roman times. The theory that German place-names ending in ' -weiler ' (*sc.* Roman 'villa') indicate early Germanic settlements on Roman sites, has but partial truth: in some cases these are definitely late Germanic settlements and in many cases, too, they lie in regions unsettled by the Romans.[1]

German Settlement in Belgium

The colonization of Belgium by the Franks, which can be followed in considerable detail,[2] may be examined as a good illustration of the way in which immigration and settlement were related to, and modified, contemporary geographical conditions. In the third century A.D. a group of peoples known as the Salian Franks had established themselves as masters of the country between the Yssel and the lower Meuse rivers. They formed part of the tribes collectively called the Franks, who occupied the whole of the Rhinelands from the lower Main to the mouths of the Rhine and Meuse. The Salian Franks, it appears, took their name from their habitat, although it is not certain whether 'Salian' described their maritime position ('sal' = 'sea-water') or was derived from the Yssel river, which was known as the 'Isala' or 'Salas'. At the end of the third century they had taken possession of the large and fertile island, now known as Betawe, which was enclosed between the Lek and Waal channels of the Rhine. In the fourth century they crossed the Waal, were defeated by the Emperor Julian, but were allowed (in A.D. 358) to settle in Toxandria, which corresponds with the modern North Brabant. Toxandria was not an attractive settlement area to sedentary agriculturists: characterized for the most part by sandy, heather-clad moorland, it was separated from the Meuse in the east by the wide belt of the Peel marshes, whilst in the north-west lay lands along the coast and around the estuary of the Scheldt which were then submerged. From their new base in Toxandria the Salian Franks gradually extended the area of their settlement by a process of slow infiltration and usurpation, carried out by groups of families. The movement was essentially slow and piecemeal, and in no sense the violent or devastating onrush of hordes of peoples. What is of particular geographical interest is the way in which the lines of movement and the distribution of settlement, which have been discovered by a close study of data derived from history, physical geography, place-names and early legal systems, suggest a

[1] Gradmann, op. cit., 1, 87

[2] Des Marez, *Le Problème de la Colonization Franque . . . en Belgique*, *passim*. The above account is based on this study, one of the ablest in this difficult field

deliberate avoidance of forests, marshes and heath in favour of plains and valleys which were devoid of thick woods and undergrowth, were more productive agriculturally and, moreover, were already partly cultivated.

In the first stage of their expansion and settlement, which occupied the years *c.* A.D. 358–450, the Salian Franks moved southwards from Toxandria along the higher ground which lies above the estuarine marshes of the Scheldt, crossed the Scheldt above and below Ruppelmonde and thence penetrated westwards up the valleys of the Scheldt and Lys. Three geographical factors were operative in defining the lines of this movement and the distribution of settlements within the Lys and Scheldt valleys. The first was the broad belt of inundated coastland which stretched along the coast of Flanders from the mouth of the Meuse; the second was the hilly Campine country to the south of Toxandria, a repellent country of barren, sandy heath and lakes through which rivers, subject to much flooding, drained into the Scheldt; whilst finally, the forests of Flanders, of which the most important was the Carbonnière, constituted a region of repulsion. This great forest, the Silva Carbonnaria of the Romans, is an excellent instance of a forest which has now largely disappeared, the approximate limits of which in the fourth and fifth centuries are sufficiently well known. The greater part of this forest was rooted in soils of sand and mixed sands and clays in the plain which is defined by the Dyle, the Sambre and the Scheldt between Valenciennes and Ghent; northwards it thinned out towards the Ruppel, whilst it continued westwards in a narrowing belt as far as the Boulonnais. In its northern parts where it advanced towards the lower Scheldt and the Ruppel the Carbonnière became more open since it had long been settled; moreover, despite its character of genuine forest, it was by no means a complete obstacle, since a few Romanized settlements stood in clearings within it and Roman roads, which were guarded by forts, ran boldly across it: roads connected a station near the junction of the Ruppel and the Scheldt with both Bavay and Namur; another linked up Bavay and Tournai, whilst, most important of all, the historic east-west route, which joined Cologne and Boulogne by way of Tongres and Bavay, cut its way through the southern area of the forest. The soils which supported this forest were mainly Tertiary sands and clays, but it should be noted that it flourished, too, on certain *limon* or loam soils, which were once thought to have remained forest-free. That the Salian Franks avoided passage through the Carbonnière forest was due, in fact, not

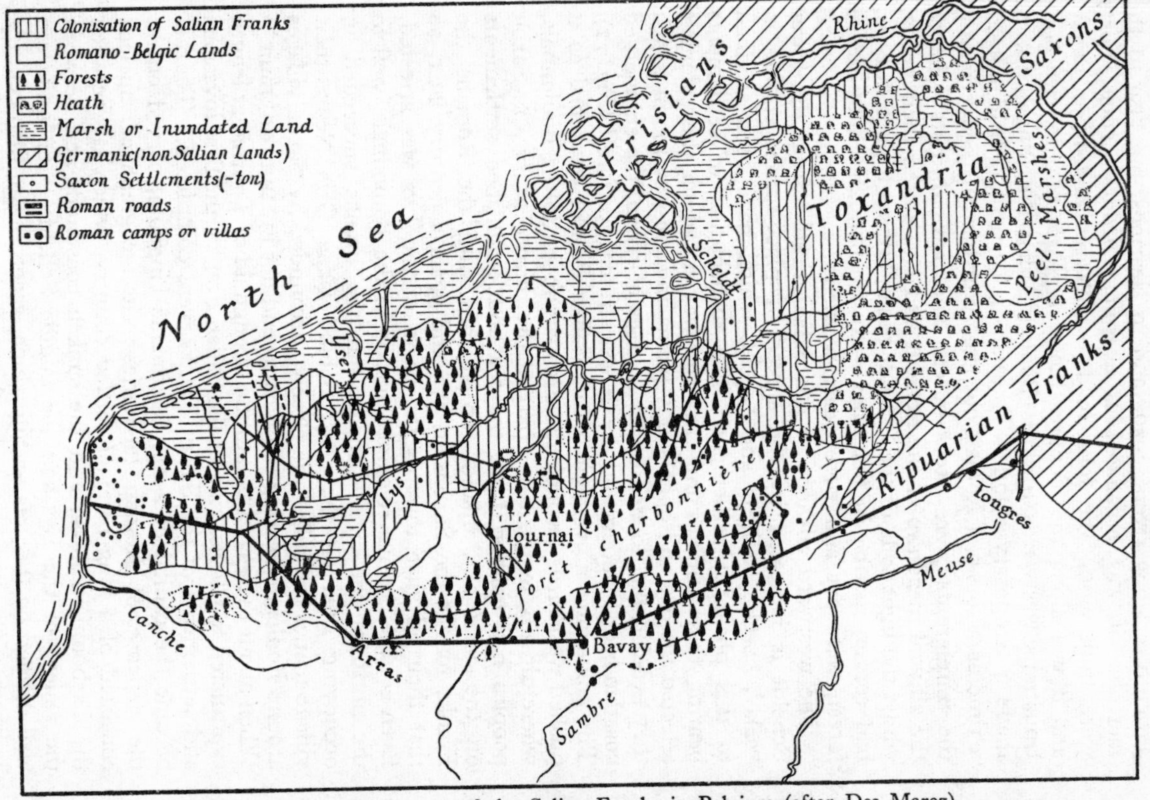

FIG. 12.—The Settlement of the Salian Franks in Belgium (after Des Marez)

The small black dots indicate Salian settlements which have place-names ending in -zel, -sel, or their variants

merely to its wooded character and its scanty opportunities for agriculture along rivers, roads and in clearings, but also to the fact that it was organized as a Roman frontier zone. Forts were built along the four roads which radiated from Bavay, and it was along the Tongres-Bavay highway and its two continuations westwards towards Boulogne that the Roman troops made a temporary stand: Tournai, in particular, held out for a time as a fortified Roman outpost. Further, in their economy the immigrants were stock-raisers and agriculturists: hence the alluvial meadows of the Scheldt and Lys suited their needs, whilst the light soils of the Scheldt basin, although poor in type, had certain merits, in that they were unencumbered by dense forest, were dry and were easily worked.

The westward advance of the Salian Franks from the lower Scheldt is indicated by the spread of place-names ending in 'sala', 'zeel', 'zel(e)' and 'seel', which have been ascribed to this phase of settlement. The distribution of settlements bearing these suffixes indicates the way in which the colonists selected the dry and open sandy plains and the way too in which they avoided the flooded upper courses of rivers, the submerged coastlands of Flanders and the denser stretches of forest (Fig. 12). The colonizing movement of the Salian Franks weakened as it pushed westwards through the Flanders forest to the Boulonnais, where already in the latter part of the third century A.D. Saxon peoples had entered from the sea and established settlements on the coast and inland. In alliance with the Romans the Franks fought the Saxons in 373 and again a century later, so that their advance towards the basin of the Lys was arrested. Even so, the Saxons remained settled in the Boulonnais, well to the north of the river Canche, but the Franks succeeded in occupying sites on the coast behind Cape Gris Nez: their village names in 'selle' are closely surrounded by Saxon villages around Boulogne bearing place-name endings in 'tun' or 'thun'.[1] When about the year A.D. 446 the stronghold of Tournai at length capitulated to Clovis, king of the Salian Franks, the first invasions and settlements of the Salian Franks were completed. Tournai became the capital of a new Germanic kingdom, carved out at the expense of Roman territories: its geographical nucleus consisted of a long band of settled country, which lay between the Carbonnière forest and the sunken coastlands and between the valleys of the Lys and the middle Scheldt. Its limits are well defined by the area within which, according to fifth-century codifiers, Salic law operated; this area formed also the cradle in which Flemish speech developed and from which it extended.

[1] See Fig. 12, p. 69.

CHAPTER IV

RURAL SETTLEMENT AND AGRICULTURE IN WESTERN AND CENTRAL EUROPE IN THE MIDDLE AGES

THE human geography of medieval Europe is concerned to a large extent with problems of rural settlement and agricultural economy. It is true that the beginnings of village settlement and agriculture can be traced back into the prehistoric past, and it is no less evident that the civilization developed under Roman rule left surviving features in the landscape of western and southern Europe. Even so, the Middle Ages witnessed a great colonizing movement which began with the barbarian invasions and continued, under the stimulus of lay, ecclesiastical and monastic authorities, with intermittent force and varying effect from century to century and from region to region until about 1500, which marks the conventional end of the medieval period. The pressure of a growing population, the economic ambitions of feudal lords, the zeal of monks and proselytizing bishops—all served in various ways to organize a widespread attack on those 'negative' lands of continental Europe, which settlement and agriculture had hitherto largely avoided. West of the Rhine village life and tillage had already at the fall of Rome in A.D. 476 advanced far within this well-forested land; eastwards of the Rhine, although some colonization in Roman times had been effected in the Agri Decumates and in the lower Main region, and although patches of naturally open terrains had been tilled from prehistoric times, the country presented largely the characteristics of a natural landscape in which mixed forests, marsh, moor and heath predominated over small insular areas of cultivated field and meadow. Colonization, thanks to the firing and cutting of the woodlands, and to the dyking and embanking of ill-drained areas, was extended, above all beyond the Rhine, but also to a considerable extent in western Europe. The peoples of Europe, although very limited in respect of technical equipment, thus adapted the countryside to their use. They established themselves in settlement groups, large and small, which varied alike in their types and in their geographical distribution, whilst they no less organized the lands of their villages—the fields, meadow and woodlands—to serve their essential needs. Thus the Middle Ages constitute an important formative period in the fashioning of what may be conveniently called ' the cultural landscape '. Field systems were engraved, as it were, on the soil, and these, together with their associated agricultural practices, lasted continuously and with little change, right down to the early nineteenth century. Similarly, the location and distribution of present-day settlement was largely ' fixed ' during the medieval period. The Middle Ages have been called many things—dark, dangerous, spiritual and what not ; geographically their fundamental characteristic derives from their work of colonization.

Rural Settlement in France

Roman Gaul, compared with Italy or with Egypt, was scantily peopled, especially in the north, but it was nevertheless a land of villages and farms. Romano-Gallic villae occupied naturally open country and also scattered clearings amidst the woodlands and organized cultivation and the rearing of live stock. The decline of Roman power and the consequent anarchy, war and social disintegration led to the abandonment of many farms and to the relapse of cultivated land into rough waste, *lande* or woodland. The immigration of the German peoples—Franks north of the Loire, Alamanns, Burgundians and Visigoths elsewhere—modified the settlement geography of Gaul, since the new-comers remained and settled down in groups among the existing population. The settlement group seems to have been, sometimes at least, a large patriarchal family or even a clan, which is suggested in France (as in Lombardy) in those place-names which include the patronymic ' fère ' (' fara ' in Lombardy) : e.g. La Fère. The nature of this German colonization, the character and location of their early settlements, can be only partially visualized in the light of archaeology, fragmentary records, place-name study [1] and the modern topographical map. It seems clear that the invaders were not very numerous and were distributed unequally throughout Gaul : at any rate it was only

[1] On the contribution of place-name study to the problems of early settlement see Mawer and Stenton, *Introduction to the Survey of English Place-Names*, I, (1) ; Des Marez, op. cit. ; Tourneur-Aumont, *Etudes de Cartographie Historique sur l'Alemanie* ; and Dopsch, *Wirtschaftliche und Soziale Grundlagen der europäischen Kulturentwicklung*, vol. I, chapter I.

in certain peripheral regions, namely in Flanders, Alsace and eastern Lorraine, that they were able to impose their language. French, as it developed north of the Loire, was but slightly affected by the speech of the Franks, and it is significant that in general the Gallo-Roman language prevailed : in the same way German immigration failed to impose its speech on Italy and Spain, but in lowland Britain, which was much less thoroughly Romanized than the continental lands, the speech of its Anglo-Saxon colonists formed the basis of the English language.

Nevertheless, the large number of Germanic place-names of French villages, although they provide somewhat baffling clues to the history of settlement, testifies at least to the importance of the Germanic colonization. The Germanic name does not necessarily indicate a newly chosen site, for it is clear that Romano-Gallic villages were often occupied and re-named by the immigrants ; nor does it, as a rule, define clearly the period of settlement. Certain place-name endings, however, are believed to indicate the first stage of Germanic settlement ; thus the endings in ' zelle ', ' selle ' and their variants mark the early settlements of the Salian Franks in Belgium ; place-name endings in ' ing ', and ' ingham ', Eckwall has shown, in many cases mark the earliest Anglo-Saxon settlements in the English plain. In Lorraine and Würtemberg, as Tourneur-Aumont pointed out, ' ingen ' names are very numerous as are ' heim ' names in Alsace, but it is not clear what bearing this has on the sequence of settlement. In short, the Germans in Gaul grouped themselves on new and old sites, and occupied both fields which were then under cultivation and other land, *agri desertes*, which had been allowed to revert to natural vegetation. Thus the place-name ' Bouzonville ' suggests the occupation of a Romano-Gallic villa or farm and its re-naming after its German chief ' Boson ' ; whilst, on the other hand, abandoned lands were selected for new settlements, for example, in the dry, loam-covered plain of Beauce. Almost the whole of Gaul fell under the influence of German colonization : only Brittany, in its remote maritime position, appears to have escaped this impress. It received contemporaneously with the Germanic invasions—in the fourth and fifth centuries—Celtic-speaking immigrants from Britain, and its typically Celtic place-names testify, as in Wales, to its aloofness from Germanic penetration. Even under Charles the Great it formed a march land on the confines of the Empire.

The geography of rural settlement in the Middle Ages, alike in France and in the territories of the Holy Roman Empire, presents an ever-changing pattern. The stability of medieval rural life, as Professor Power recently suggested,[1] can be and has been exaggerated, and such a view finds little support in the continual changes which occurred both in the areas of cultivation and in the distribution of settlement. Unstable political conditions in the latter part of the ninth, and during the tenth, centuries militated against the extension of cultivation and the spread of small defenceless village groups, but when government was relatively firm—as under the rule of Charles the Great—efforts were initiated by kings and nobles to bring old or new lands into productive use. Thus already in the sixth century Gregory of Tours records the creation of new farms, the planting of vines, the building of houses and the clearing of waste, whilst Charles the Great ordered his officials to make clearings in the forests and to prevent their reversion to woodland. Generally, between about A.D. 500 and 1050 colonization and cultivation made little headway; probably much of the land cultivated was formerly tilled land which had been abandoned; land reclaimed was balanced by land lost; the ravages of the Northmen along the riverine lands and of the Saracens in Corbière and Languedoc destroyed cultivated lands; whilst the break-up of the Carolingian Empire brought disorders and depopulation. Cultivated land reverted in part to heath or forest 'waste', and an extension of forest seems to have occurred. Only in Flanders had the attack on marsh and forest achieved much success by this time; and in some parts of France a few settlements actually disappeared from the map. In short, the country was still much occupied by its natural cover of forest, gorse, heath and, in the south, garrigue and maquis scrub, within which stood scattered settlements with their small patches of tilled fields, water meadows and vineyard slopes. It is significant of their scanty settlement in the early Middle Ages that the great wooded massifs escaped the parochial organization established elsewhere.

During the period between 1050 and 1300 a successful attack was launched on wide forest and marshy areas of France.[2] The area of cultivated land was considerably extended; forests, formerly continuous, were largely broken up into detached fragments; and hand in hand with the exploitation of new lands, whether drained or cleared, went as a rule the extension of settlements and an increase of population. These changes were not peculiarly French phenomena, but rather characteristic

[1] 'Peasant Life and Rural Conditions (*c.* 1100–*c.* 1500)', *Cam. Med. Hist.*, VII.

[2] Bloch, *Les Caractères Originaux de l'Histoire Rurale Française*, pp. 5–14.

generally of the temperate lands of western and middle Europe. In England reclamation and colonization occurred together, for example in the marshes of Holderness and in the forests of the Weald ; similarly in the wide march lands of the Empire German (and even Flemish) colonists formed settlement groups among the Slavs and the Magyars, no less than within their own forests and marshes to the west of the Elbe. Both in France, and more especially in Germany, the all-pervading forest formed the chief objective of this advance, the leadership of which was taken by kings, lords and monks. It must be emphasized that the forests in past periods, although they are conveniently described as 'negative' regions, i.e. regions which deterred settlers and impeded communications, constituted in fact an important and essential element in medieval rural economy ; nor had they ever been entirely void of some nomadic or sedentary population.[1] Men hunted or trapped beasts and game ; made charcoal and forged iron ; collected fuel and timber and wild honey and wax ; but above all the forests provided village communities with pasture lands for their cattle, horses and pigs. It is significant of the human value of the north temperate forests in medieval times that they were often measured in terms not of crude area but of their food supply (pannage)—acorns, beech mast, &c.—for so many pigs. In the destruction of the forests man and beast both took part, for grazing animals by eating young shoots retarded plant and tree growth, whilst man cleared land for cultivation.

The conquest of the forest did not necessarily involve new village groups : thus in Beauce newly reclaimed land was added to existing villages.[2] Often, and probably this was the typical condition, the forest was broken up by the settlement of small hamlet or homestead groups within it. The modern topographical map continually suggests how small hamlets were diffused throughout the forest in patches which were cleared, and evidence derived from history and from place-name study often determines the dating of this process. Thus the forest which covered the wet, clayey soil of the Argonne massif was broken up and settled at different times during the Middle Ages, whereas at an earlier date, since it was thickly wooded and largely lacking in population, it had been selected as a convenient frontier between the dioceses of Châlons and Rheims to the west, and those of Verdun and Toul to the east. Similarly,

[1] Cp. Bloch, op. cit., p. 7, and Tourneur-Aumont, op. cit., pp. 91–3.

[2] Cp. Bloch, 'La Vie Rurale', in *A.H.E. & S.*, Jan. 1930.

throughout the whole of Champagne 'humide' medieval clearings were made for rural settlement.[1] In the high, wet, forested massifs of the Ardennes and the Vosges, as also in the western Alps, monastic zeal was directed against the dominant forest. The Cistercian monks in particular, in their desire to escape from the world and to live by their own hands, sought the wooded solitudes and became proficient agriculturists. Their scattered granges or farmsteads organized clearing and became eventually the nuclei of villages. In contrast to the small hamlets which occupied forest clearings and drained areas in the marsh large compact and defensible villages were also built, often in direct response to the recurrent need for defence against attack. In the *Midi* this tendency was clearly operative. In south-western France, which was a frontier region of conflict between the English in Gascony and French territories in Languedoc and Toulouse, and also in Provence which was equally open to attack from Saracens in the western Alps and to pirates from the sea, new fortified villages or towns called *bastides* were built on carefully selected sites.[2] And even in Provence, where climate restricted the species and density of the woodlands, trees, bushes and maquis scrub were destroyed mainly by human agency.

The destruction of forest with a view to increasing the area of cultivable land in some cases produced physical reactions to the detriment of man. In her studies of the Alps of Dauphiné and of Provence Mlle. Sclafert has shown [3] that settlements were clearly fixed in the valleys by the eleventh century and that the valley sides and mountain heights seem then to have been amply forested. In the southern part of the French Alps grew not only *garrigues* suited to the summer drought of the Mediterranean climate, but also vineyards and forests; but in the northern and wetter part of this region no *garrigues* or viticulture intruded into the woodland. Medieval records refer to '*terres gâtés*', which consisted of uncultivated lands with scattered trees, whilst the practice of letting these and more wooded lands in return for a payment known as a 'tâche' became common. The 'tâche' consisted of a share of the annual produce of lands which were cleared and cultivated, and cultivation consisted usually of cereals and vines. This practice, which was adopted particularly between the thirteenth to the sixteenth centuries, led to widespread destruction of forest on valley slopes and high-

[1] Chantriot, *La Champagne*, p. 49.

[2] Cp. *infra*, Chapter VI, pp. 112–119.

[3] *La Haut-Dauphiné au Moyen Âge*, and articles in the *A. de G.*, May and June 1933.

lands even up to levels above 3,500 feet. The woods were destroyed by burning; the land was then worked, but although it proved fertile for a few years it was quickly exhausted. More woodland and even young bushes and trees were then burnt in order to provide ash fertilizer for crops and vineyards. This human effort brought only temporary reward, whilst at the same time it caused indirectly permanent losses—not only of the forests themselves but also of the thin soil cover which, no longer held *in situ* by the tree roots, was removed by the torrential rains of winter.

The marshy areas of plain in France, which had been largely left untouched by the Romans, were in some measure reclaimed during the eleventh, twelfth and thirteenth centuries, although the effective continuation of this work was left to Dutch engineers in the seventeenth century. In Poitou, areas to the north of Rochefort and of La Rochelle were partially drained in the twelfth and thirteenth centuries [1] by abbeys, by the building of dams and cutting of ditches. In Flanders, where this task was successfully undertaken at this time, scattered hamlets arose along the dykes within the drained 'polder' lands. In some measure, too, land occupied by wild grasses, heather and gorse and scrub was brought under the plough. It is significant that here as elsewhere along the European coastlands between the Elbe and Gascony where early drainage works were effected, free colonists were settled, and thus 'a belt of freedom', as it were, was created in response to the peculiar geographical conditions.

In short, some tentative generalizations emerge. The period between 1050 and 1300 witnessed an extension of cultivation and of settlement in France, particularly north of the Loire. In Gascony, in contrast, this economic development seems to have been checked, since people were encouraged to migrate into the Christian kingdoms of northern Spain. Again, population increased in step with these advances, especially north of the Loire, although it should be noted that there was an overflow of population from Provence into Italy. In northern France, therefore, about A.D. 1300, population was denser than in the south, and this distribution marked a change from that which obtained in Roman Gaul, when the south, best adapted by climate and by position to Roman civilization, became the wealthier and more populous part of Gaul. It should be noted, however, that this population increase reflects also commercial and urban development in northern France (cp. pp. 112–119).

[1] Clouzot, *Les Marais de la Sèvre Niortaise et du Lay, du Xe à la fin du XVe Siècle.*

The advance in cultivation, colonization and population, which has been noted above, suffered retrogression between 1300 and 1500, as a result primarily of political conditions. Thus the Hundred Years War (1338–1453) left its mark on the face of rural France. 'De fixe qu'elle était', writes Flach [1] 'la population redevient nomade.' The ravages of war and the plague, together with the collapse of central government, caused depopulation in the countryside and the abandonment and even disappearance of some settlements. The larger and more compact villages, no less than the towns, prepared themselves for defence: sometimes they were girt around with walls, and often churches were fortified. Much marshland which had been drained, e.g. in Poitou, reverted to its natural condition; many fairs were either suspended, as in the case of that of Lendit in Paris, or removed to more favourable spots, as in the case of those of Lyons which were transferred to Geneva. The ravages of organized war and of military bands were particularly severe in certain districts: thus the lands between the Loire, the Seine and the Somme suffered, mainly at the hands of lawless bands in the fifteenth century. On the other hand, regions like Brittany and Languedoc, which then stood away from the theatres of war, were much less affected, so that St. Malo and Nantes remained relatively prosperous and Languedoc continued to trade with the Levant.

A good illustration of geographical changes brought about under these conditions of war and lack of governance is provided by the history of the Dombes region, which lies to the south of Bresse between the Saône and the Upper Rhône. It consists of a gently sloping plateau covered with impermeable clay of glacial origin. Prior to the fifteenth century it appears to have been well settled and sufficiently prosperous; certainly it had lakes occupying the depressions and the badly drained slopes of the plateau, but these were then few in number. In fact, great forests absorbed the humidity of the Dombes; there was a good network of routes; and even the vine was grown in many parts. Continual wars, however, transformed the face of the region: population and settlements rapidly decreased; towns declined, to become mere villages, whilst roads were neglected or destroyed and even parishes disappeared.[2] Moreover, the dwindling and impoverished population resorted to a new kind of economy which intensified the desolation of the Dombes: lakes were artificially formed so as to create fisheries, and then

[1] Flach in Foville's *Enquête sur l'Habitation en France*, vol. II, p. 87.
[2] Gallois, 'La Dombes', *A. de G.*, Jan. 1892.

were sometimes drained in order to allow of cultivation. In result, the area of standing water was much extended, and fevers spread to weaken the physique of the population. Only in the later decades of the nineteenth century, as a result of drainage works, of liming the soil and of improved agricultural technique, did the region recover its former prosperity.

The population of France is estimated [1] to have diminished by about one-third during the Hundred Years War period which includes the years of the Great Plague in 1348–9. Critical studies of population numbers and changes at this time can arrive at only very rough estimates, but these are worth some attention. The French historian Lot [2] has estimated that on the eve of the Hundred Years War (i.e. in 1338) the population reached some 19 millions, of which over 90 per cent. were rural dwellers. Further, he suggests that the rural population of 1338 exceeded the 20 millions which it numbered in 1846—so great was the set-back to population inflicted during the fourteenth and fifteenth centuries. Moreover, he estimates that the number of *lieux-dits* in 1338 was in excess of the number to-day, and this hypothesis, which is difficult to interpret (for what exactly is a 'lieu-dit'?) does at least emphasize the degree to which the countryside of France had become settled and 'humanized' by the fourteenth century, in contrast to a country like Spain where inhabited areas were separated off from each other by arid, almost deserted, lands. It should be noted, however, that the conclusions or hypotheses of Lot have been subjected to close criticism by Professor Sée,[3] who would suggest some scaling down of these figures for population in medieval times. Only in the late fifteenth and sixteenth centuries did political circumstances favour the recovery of rural life. Italians emigrated into Provence —a reversal of the thirteenth-century flow of population, and in Provence also villagers began to leave their strong upland sites and to distribute themselves in smaller villages in the valleys and lowlands. Again, the organization of a system of *Postes* by Louis XI in 1464 fostered re-settlement: relay stations were selected at intervals of four leagues and became the nuclei of new villages. Similarly, a renewed attack with improved Dutch technique on the marshlands of France fostered new settlement in the seventeenth century. By this time it would be tempting but rash to believe that the spread of villages in France was largely 'fixed', and that subsequently only minor

[1] Flach, op. cit., p. 89.
[2] *Bul. Int. Com. Hist. Sc.*, July 1933.
[3] *Rev. d'Econ. Pol.*, July–Aug., 1924.

changes were effected in their distribution, as when in 1703 a royal army destroyed some 460 rebel hamlets in the Cevennes.[1] But it must be remembered that in the nineteenth century additional clearing of forest and *lande* sometimes, as in the Ségalas,[2] led to a spread of dispersed farms.

Rural Settlement in Central Europe

Of the lands which comprised imperial Germany and Austria in 1914 only a small part lay within the Empire of Charles the Great, whilst the rest were then occupied by Slav and Avar peoples. The wanderings of the Germanic peoples of the fourth and fifth centuries—in particular their thrust southwards and westwards into the Roman Empire—were doubtless in part caused, and certainly followed, by the advance westwards of both Slavs and Avars into the lands which they had vacated. Slavs established themselves in the north German plain and highlands to the east of the lower Elbe and Saale and within the Bohemian 'quadrilateral', whilst farther south the Avars advanced from Transylvania into the middle Danubian plain of Pannonia and, despite the checks which Charles the Great inflicted on them at the Raab river, advanced along the line of the Danube into the Bavarian plateau. Charles the Great exerted vigorous and persistent efforts to establish a frontier of equilibrium against both Slav and Avars, and he succeeded in creating military districts or march-lands as buffer territories against them, as he did also in Holstein against the Danes. Even so, these advanced frontier territories constituted only military zones into which Germanic settlement had only just begun to penetrate. The Saale and lower Elbe rivers defined roughly this military boundary in the north, but German settlement and civilization as yet scarcely extended eastwards from the Rhine and lower Main; similarly in the south the East Mark (to become Austria) and the marches of Carinthia and Carniola were merely buffer lands, held by the Empire but occupied by Slav and Avar. In the northern frontier region the foundation, usually on existing Slav sites, of German 'burgs' or fortified trading posts, e.g., Magdeburg, Erfurt and Halberstadt, characterized the beginnings of German colonization in Slav lands east of the Rhine. Nevertheless, it should be noted that the eastern region of the Carolingian Empire consisted of territories which, for the most part,

[1] Flach, op. cit., p. 90.

[2] Ségalas provides an instance of 'intercalated dispersion', that is, of homesteads being founded amidst original nucleated villages and hamlets.

had been included within the Roman Empire: only Frisia, Saxony and the march-districts, of which the former were Germanic in population, marked an advance beyond the old Roman frontier. In short, it was only in the later Middle Ages, in particular between the years A.D. 900 and 1300, that German colonization and culture were successfully and permanently extended eastwards to the Baltic, significantly known to the Germans as the Ostsee, to 'Slavia' beyond the Elbe, and thus to the Oder, middle Danube and even beyond.

The advance of the frontier of German colonization and Roman Catholicism—for the Church co-operated closely in this movement—was largely organized and stimulated by kings, together with lay and ecclesiastical lords, who desired to secure and to exploit cheap land, since, under conditions of growing population and trade activity, the price of land in the settled parts of the Empire—e.g., the Rhine and Meuse lands—increased rapidly between 900 and 1300. Undoubtedly the shift of the frontier registered the introduction of a higher culture into relatively backward lands. The Germans were Christians, they were agriculturists, whilst they were reviving in their own lands city life and trade. The pagan Slavs, like the Avars and Magyars on the south-eastern border of the Empire, were largely pastoralists, though unlike these nomadic tent-dwellers they lived in fixed settlements. Their villages, which lay thinly scattered in the clearings of forests and within marshy areas, were typically round or 'ring fence' in ground plan, and consisted of a circle of dwellings enclosing a field in which grazed the stock of the village. Many of their settlements bearing place-names ending in 'in' and 'zig' were destined to become German towns which preserve these suffixes—e.g., Berlin, Leipzig; whilst the excellent sites of some of their fishing settlements, such as those at the estuaries of the Oder and Trave, provided, in embryo, urban and trading stations. In general, however, the economy of the Slavs was of a rudimentary type, which reflects their feeble hold on a world as yet but slightly adapted to human use: agriculture and trade had little place in their economy; their typical products, which the Germans sought in trade, were derived from forest, fen, river and sea, namely furs, honey and wax, fish and amber; whilst rye, hemp and flax were grown, and strips of linen were used as media of exchange. The penetration of German settlers within the lands occupied by Slav and Avar produced, under the stimulus of more effective and organized human effort, a transformation in their human and economic geography. A vigorous attack, first initiated by Charles the

Great and then renewed later, was launched on much virgin forest, whilst marsh and moorland were reclaimed. Towns were founded which came to combine some or all of the functions of ecclesiastical, monastic, military, administrative and trading centres. Villages, both of the hamlet and nucleated types, were formed, and agriculture and viticulture were developed. Further, the rich mineral resources of the Harz and Erzgebirge mountains were exploited by colonists who formed the nuclei of new urban groups. New and old tracks were beaten out to provide routes for soldier, priest and merchant, whilst it is clear that the river ways, e.g., the Saale, Elbe and Havel, were well utilized. Finally, the expansion of the Germans effected a new and largely permanent distribution of Germanic population throughout central Europe, a distribution which, though compact over broad areas, became more scattered and discontinuous in the broadening lands beyond the Oder.

Already in the eighth and ninth centuries new monastic, ecclesiastical and military settlements were established in that Germanic non-Roman part of the Empire of Charles the Great which lay to the east of the Rhine and to the north of the Main. Right-bank tributaries of the Rhine, e.g., the Lippe, Ruhr, Sieg, Lahn and Main, which led towards the Fulda, Weser, Saale and lower Elbe, marked out valley routes into Franconia, Thuringia and Saxony. Monasteries at Fulda, Hersfeld and Amoeneburg, and bishoprics at Erfurt, Fritzlar and Freising were founded in the eighth century, either within or on the margins of lands which were essentially German in population. Farther afield, beyond the eastern limit of German population but within the military frontier of his Empire, Charles the Great established a series of fortified trading posts amongst the Slavs. These posts lay in proximity to the frontier which was aligned along the lower Elbe, Saale and Itz rivers, and along the edge of the Bohemian forest: among them were Bardowick and Schesel (both near Hamburg); Magdeburg; Halstat near Bamberg; Pfreimt on the Naab; and Forcheim, Lorch and Regensburg on the Danube. These settlements were rather villages than towns, although at the frontier posts some trading developed with the Slavs who offered wax and honey, hemp and flax and furs. Towards the end of the tenth century settlers moved forward in the wake of German conquests along all sectors of the frontier, and formed what were at first islands of Germanic population in and around fortified ‘burgs’, which often served both as ecclesiastical and military centres. They moved first from the Saale boundary towards and beyond the upper Elbe: the foundation of Merseburg on the Saale, Meissen on the Elbe, and Leipzig on a tributary of the Saale, marked this progress. The preference for sites on the banks and at convenient crossing points of navigable rivers is apparent, but in most cases existing Slavic sites were occupied. Similarly, colonies were founded farther afield, e.g., at Breslau which stood in loess country on the Oder, and at Brandenburg in the Middle March, which was reached from the Elbe by the Havel river, whilst at Prague, Gnesen and Posen outlying bishops' sees were established. Meanwhile, in the northern plain, to the east and west of the lower Elbe, a line of German strongholds were set along the border against the Danes and Slavs, namely, Oldenburg, Bremen, Hamburg, Schwerin, and Wismar on the Mecklenburg coast; whilst, already in the tenth century, village settlements were spreading out in Saxony and in the forests of Schleswig. Some real checks to settlement beyond the lower Elbe were imposed, however, by the determined resistance of the Slavic Wagri from their stronghold on the Trave, which was to achieve fame later as the German city of Lübeck. Moreover, the broad marshes of the lower Elbe and Weser, as well as the poor heath country of the Lüneburg Heath westwards of the Elbe, were at first avoided by colonists. Nevertheless, by 1142 the Wagri were conquered, and new attempts were made to repair the destruction which they had inflicted on German settlements, and in particular, Dutch and Flemish immigrants were brought in as colonists to use their technical skill in draining marshlands around Bremen, Hamburg and even Berlin. Farther south, German colonization pushed up the Main valley: forests were cut into and marshes drained, and *pari passu* military outposts and bishoprics were founded in turn at Würzburg and later (in 1107) at Bamberg. In the valley of the Danube the Germans were faced by the advancing Magyars, who just before A.D. 900 had poured into the plain of the Tisza from Transylvania and were extending their ravaging attacks far up the Danube and even to the Rhine and into Saxony. Nomad pastoralists, horsemen and tent-dwellers, the Magyars represented an antithesis to the German sedentary agriculturist; but in 955 owing to their defeat at the battle of the Lech in Bavaria the Magyars were driven back along the Danube valley, and German colonists, monks and traders, especially from Bavaria, were able to follow them and to settle in the Ostmark (Austria). For a time the Alpine spur of the Wiener Wald which reaches the Danube above Vienna marked the frontier between the Ostmark and the Magyars, but later German settlement pushed eastwards beyond it and in 1055 the Margrave of the Ostmark founded the city of Vienna on the site of the Roman Vindobona. Moreover, monks and bishops selected sites not only in the Ostmark but also in the more remote and mountainous march-lands of Styria and Carinthia. The relative strength of Germanic colonization in these south-eastern lands is reflected in the complete Germanization of the Ostmark, whereas in Styria and Carinthia the Germans formed only the dominant class amidst the Slav peasantry.

The force of Germanic colonization tended to weaken as it advanced eastwards. In the Baltic coastlands, at least in Mecklenburg and in Pomerania, Slavic resistance to German conquests was stubborn, and German settlement was relatively slow and restricted largely to the towns. Slav historians challenge the view that German influence was strong in these parts, as also in Bohemia, and Egorov has shown, on the basis of detailed researches, that colonization and reclamation in Mecklenburg were the result of activity directed from within by Slav lords and peasants. Nevertheless, Germanic language and nationality did eventually impose itself on the Slav peasantry there, as also in Pomerania. In Bohemia, on the other hand, German immigration was small in scale, and some of it came much later, e.g., in the eighteenth century, so that the Slav population largely escaped Germanization. The forested, mountain framework of the Böhmer Wald, the Erzgebirge and the Sudetes, in some measure defended the Slavs of Bohemia from large waves of German immigration, since they formed wide, 'insulating' areas of scanty population and of difficult communication. Even so, Germans pressed into, and subsequently over, the Erzgebirge from the north-west, so that this range fails to-day to define a frontier of nationality and language. Similarly, they entered Bohemia over the Böhmer Wald by way of the Eger river from the Naab, and over the Bavarian forest from Linz by way of the Moldau (Vltava) valley.

In one direction, however, the German thrust towards the east was by no means weakened, namely in the coastlands to the east of the Vistula. The country between the lower Vistula and the Narva was occupied by non-Slavic peoples, in particular, by Balts (or Letto-Lithuanians) and Finns. Its geography presented uniform features : wide, low-lying plains with extensive tracts of marsh and endless stretches of coniferous forest, through which rivers wound their way into sea-gulfs and afforded ingress from the sea and inland navigation. Between the lower Vistula and the Niemen the Prussians, a Balt people, were settled ; in

Kurland, beyond the Niemen, mainly Lithuanians predominated, whilst in Livland, north of the Dwina, were settled (among others) the Letts. Moreover, both in Kurland and in Livonia, as well as in Estonia, which fronted the Gulf of Finland, Finns, an Asiatic people, had intruded from north Russia. The character of these northern plains fostered the disunity of tribes and tribal areas ; settlements, some of which grew up around castles, were scattered along the sandy coast, in forest clearings or at the margins of lakes and swamps ; some agriculture, apiculture [1] and horse-rearing were engaged in ; whilst the difficult communications in this country, except perhaps by water, together with its remoteness and poor resources, may help to explain its escape from conquest by its more powerful Russian, Polish and Lithuanian neighbours. In fact, German conquest and colonization came mainly seawards. The foundation of Lübeck, permanently effected by 1158, gave the Germans their first effective foothold on the Baltic and stimulated the exodus of priests, warriors, traders and even artisans, e.g., masons, who set out for the east Baltic lands already known to the Danes, who had established a bishopric at Reval on the Gulf of Finland. The first immigrants entered by the Gulf of Riga and the Dwina river, along which a trade route from the Black Sea and the Dnieper had run, especially in the eighth and ninth centuries ; a church was built at Ukhüll in 1184 ; Riga—a port and bishop's see—was founded in 1201 ; the Cistercians built an abbey at Dünamunde ; whilst the foundation of castles at Kokenhusen (Dwina), Wenden and Fellin and bishoprics at Dorpat and Pernau, marked the conquest of Livonia. The Order of Teutonic Knights similarly undertook and effected in fifty years the conquest and partial extermination of the Estes or Prussians. They began by building castles at Torun (1231), Kulm (1232) and Marienwerder (1233) on existing sites on the right bank terrace above the Vistula. They operated both land- and sea-wards, where sites were occupied at Elbing, Balga (on the Frisches Haff), and at Königsberg. The conquest involved fierce wars and some destruction : thus in Sambia land formerly settled reverted to forest and waste, but generally the conquest was followed up by intensive German settlement. The proximity of Prussia to the march-lands of Germany made it, both by land and by sea, more accessible than Livonia to German immi-

[1] 'There is so much honey in the land of the Estes (Prussia) that the king and rich persons leave all the mead to the poor, themselves drinking the milk of mares' : so wrote Wulfstan in the late ninth century.

grants : the frequented land route in the thirteenth century along which settlers moved ran from the Elbe at Meissen via Kottbus and Posen to Torun, whilst Elbing and Königsberg afforded sea entries. On the southern confines of Prussia stretched ' the Wilderness ' so called, known now as the Mazurian Lake region, the fen-like character of which was preserved as a protective frontier against the Lithuanians and Poles. Only in the fifteenth century was the colonization of this land of mere and marsh actively, although partially, undertaken. In short, Germans constituted in Prussia the basis of the rural and urban population, although farther afield in Livonia they remained only an upper social stratum. The impress of this colonization, which had the effect of cutting off from the sea both Polish and Lithuanian peoples, was left permanently on the map ; and a problem was bequeathed to vex the present world.

It was the achievement of the German people, therefore, by their colonizing activity, to conquer wide areas of formerly ' negative ' land for agriculture and settlement.[1]

Many village names of central Europe attest to this day the pioneering conditions under which they were formed, and some of them at least can be dated to the later Middle Ages : such common German place-name elements suggestive of village origins are *roth* and *rode* (= ' rooting up '), ' *ried* ' (= ' marsh '), *au* (= ' meadow '), *schlag* (= ' filling '), *metz* and *hau* (= ' hewing '), *schwand* and *brand* (= ' burning '), *hagen* (= 'fence '). The effect of this colonial enterprise on the forests of Middle Europe was striking. In particular deciduous forests were cleared, since they were established on the better soils, and in consequence the region became chiefly one of coniferous forests and only a few deciduous species, notably birches and alders, survived in any numbers. Thus whereas early place-names often suggest the original presence of many deciduous species—ashes, elms and limes—these trees have almost disappeared.

[1] For a full account of German settlement see Knüll, *Historische Geographie Deutschlands im Mittelalter*, ch. III. See also J. W. Thompson, *Feudal Germany*.

CHAPTER V

RURAL SETTLEMENT AND AGRICULTURE IN WESTERN AND CENTRAL EUROPE IN THE MIDDLE AGES (Continued)

WESTERN and Central Europe were thus lands characterized above all by rural settlement, since urban groups, even in the later centuries of the Middle Ages, were few and scattered and, except in one or two areas, accounted for only a very small proportion of the population, as was still true as late as 1800. The rural settlement of Europe as it was extended during the Middle Ages imprinted a distinctive pattern on the landscape, a pattern which contrasted somewhat from region to region in response to different sociological, agrarian, and physical conditions. It is no easy task accurately to reconstruct the distribution of settlement as it obtained in medieval Europe. In England, except for the four northern counties, the unique Domesday record of 1086 provides reliable data for the contemporary distribution of rural settlements, and suggests the generalization that in their actual sites and distribution villages have not drastically changed since then. It would be rash, however, to infer that continental settlement history follows analogous lines. The researches of Lamprecht [1] on the settlements of the Moselle lands seem to suggest very marked changes in the actual number of villages within the medieval period alone, and it is well known how foreign and civil wars, like the Hundred Years' War in France and the Thirty Years' War in Germany, produced depopulation and destruction of villages in many parts of the countryside. The modern large-scale topographical map is, as Maitland noted [2] some time ago, a veritable 'palimpsest' of rural history: even so, although it offers numerous suggestions as to the course and cause of settlement types and distributions, it raises perhaps more problems than it solves. Clearly, fuller understanding of the facts of medieval rural settlement awaits

[1] *Deutsches Wirtschaftsleben*, vol. I (1), pp. 140–65.

[2] 'The most wonderful of all palimpsests', he wrote, 'is the map of England, could we but decipher it.'

the findings of detailed regional studies which will utilize above all the collections of early place-name forms. All that can be attempted here is broadly to review and account for the main types of rural settlement and their distributions.

It was Meitzen [1] in Germany and subsequently Maitland in England who directed attention to the two major village types which were, as they still are, widely spread throughout Europe. Briefly the two types of Meitzen were the *dorf* or nucleated village, and the *einzelhof*, which is, strictly speaking, a single homestead. The basis of this classification is the way in which habitations are arranged ; in the one case they are grouped closely together into single large villages, in the other they are scattered widely, occupying separate sites. It has been emphasized recently that a threefold classification of village types is required,[2] since intermediate between the two noted above stand hamlets which possess features of both : typically they are smaller than nucleated villages, they are essentially groups of habitations on one site, but, like the homestead, they are characteristically scattered. Nevertheless, it must suffice here to note the two main types : the large compact village in which the rural population is concentrated, and the scattered type of settlement, whether hamlet or homestead. It must be emphasized that these types, whether two or three are selected, are not always well differentiated : one tends to shade into another, just as the nucleated village is not always easily distinguishable from the small country town.

The distinction between the nucleation and diffusion of habitations can be easily grasped by a particular instance : thus if the rural settlements of the two French *départements* of La Manche in Cotentin and Marne in Champagne, which are not very unequal in area, be examined, it is found that whereas in the former they number 18,930, in the latter they number only 1,580.[3] This disparity in numbers reflects, not the relative density of population, but the contrasted grouping of habitations. To the geographer the distribution of the two settlement types presents an interesting and intricate problem, towards the solution of which he can suggest much that is strictly geographical. It may well be that the two types to some extent mirror on the soil the different psychological and social ideas of different European groups,

[1] *Siedelungen und Agrarwesen der Westgermanen und Ostgermanen*, &c., 1895.

[2] M. A. Lefèvre, *L'habitat rural en Belgique*, 1925.

[3] Demangeon, 'La Géographie de l'Habitat Rural', published in the 1st *Report on Rural Settlement*, 1928.

'racial', national or even religious. Thus invaders may bring with them their own peculiar habits of social grouping or their own agrarian systems, or conditions of insecurity may foster nucleation and the abandonment of small defenceless scattered sites. There can be no doubt, however, that the distribution of village types registers man's adaptation of varied geographical regions, but the differential conditions of these regions in respect

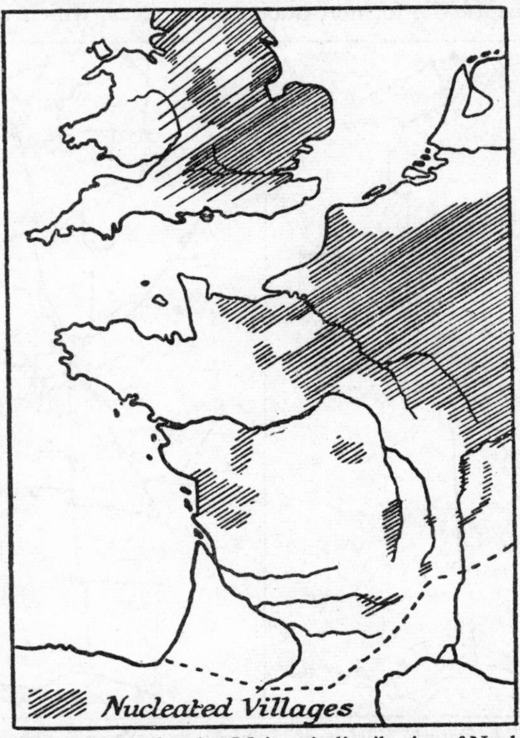

FIG. 13.—Generalized Map showing Meitzen's distribution of Nucleated Villages (Dörfer) and Single Farms (Einzelhöfe). (After S. Harris)
No distribution is shown for the area south of the broken line

of water supply, soils, vegetation cover, land forms and climate, afford one of the chief explanatory factors.

It is scarcely possible to produce a map which shows accurately the distribution of nucleated and scattered settlements in the later Middle Ages. The present-day distribution of these types is, in broad outline, known,[1] and is shown for western Europe on Meitzen's map (Fig. 13), which, however, is open to criticism

[1] Cp. Demangeon, art. cit.

in detail. But it must be remembered that the present-day distributions represent a considerable modification of earlier conditions, and do not provide a safe basis from which to reconstruct the past distributions. Thus it is known that in some cases, alike in the Middle Ages and in later times, originally nucleated settlements broke up into smaller diffused groups: in Denmark and southern Sweden, for example, as Professor Vahl pointed out for the former, nucleated villages, which were typical

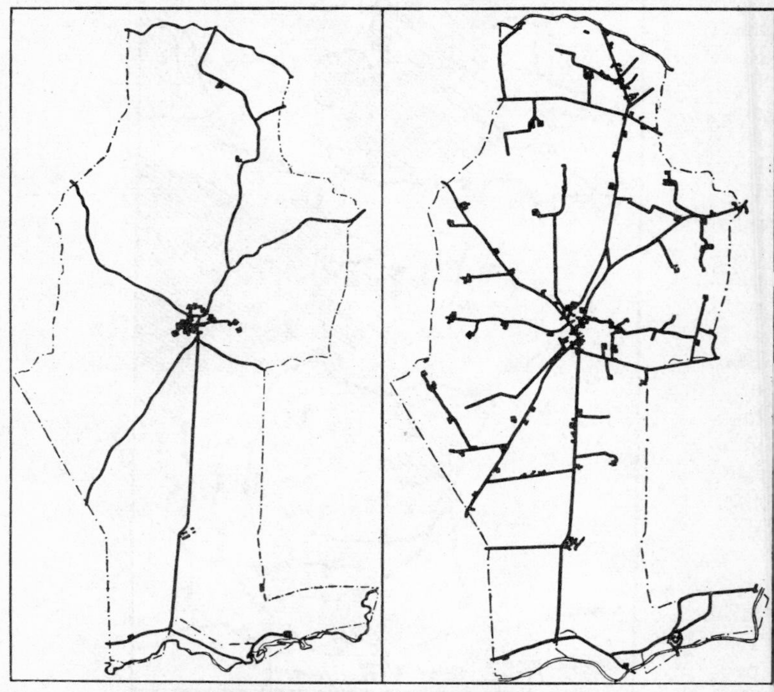

FIG. 14.—The Danish Village of Solbjerg in 1782 and 1909 (after Vahl)

as late as 1800, gave place to scattered farms which moved out to the fields [1] (Fig. 14). Again, the creation of hamlets around an original nucleated settlement has often occurred in the past, being often associated with the process of reclamation of land for agriculture: thus 'secondary dispersion' of settlements, to use the expert's term, occurred in eastern Normandy, in southern Flanders, and in Perchois, where settlers from Beauce cleared the woods and *landes* and established hamlets in the later Middle Ages. In contrast, original homesteads and hamlets sometimes

[1] In *Comtes Rendus du Congrès International de Géographie*, Paris, 1931, vol. III.

grew into nucleated villages, as, for example, in maritime Flanders where dispersed settlements were originally typical, and it is a familiar fact how in recent times, when water can be made more available, country houses have been spread out in country formerly unsettled. Nevertheless, it is probable that in Europe generally, as would seem to be the case in England, the conditions of rural settlement have not drastically changed since the later Middle Ages.

Broadly speaking, in lowland England, in southern Sweden and in the north European plain eastwards into Poland and Russia the nucleated village was the common form of settlement. Even so, within this extensive region, above all where woodlands and marshes had been reclaimed and colonized, homesteads and hamlets were characteristic, as was the case in the drained polder-lands from Flanders to the Elbe estuary and also in the English Weald and in formerly wooded parts of East Anglia. Again, it is the dispersed types of settlement which were most common in those mountainous and plateau areas where forests and rough pasture were naturally abundant: in northern England, Wales, interior Brittany, in the Massif Central, the Pyrenees, the Alps and, generally, within the Hercynian mountain zone of central Europe. It is significant, too, that in the wet, wooded highlands of Norway dispersed farms were, as they still are, typical; in fact, the Norwegian language has no word to describe the nucle-ated village proper.[1] Finally, in southern France and in the Mediterranean region both types of settlement occurred, although the scarcity of water-supplies and the need for defence in coastal districts conditioned much nucleation of dwellings.

What were the conditions of rural settlement in the vast region of eastern Europe, where it seems clear, although reliable data are lacking, that population was relatively scanty (Fig. 15)? In Estonia, north Livonia and the island of Ösel, which were peopled chiefly by the Estes speaking a Finnish language, it is probable that small nucleated villages were typical: certainly the small farms which generally obtain to-day date to a large extent from the nineteenth century and were the result of the deliberate policy of the German landowning nobility.[2] Farther south in southern Livonia and Kurland, which were occupied by Letto-Lithuanian peoples, small dispersed farms were prob-ably characteristic in the late Middle Ages, as maps and plans certainly show as early as the seventeenth century. In the Russian plain settlement conditions varied broadly along latitu-

[1] F. Klute (ed.), *Die ländlichen Siedlungen in verschiedenen Klimazonen*, p. 16.

[2] Woeikof, 'Le Groupement de la Population Rurale en Russie', *A. de G.*, Jan. 1909.

dinal lines. In the north, where 'podzol' or 'forest' soils were characteristic, hamlets and farms were founded in the clearings of the forests, and settlements such as these were typical in the region around Novgorod in the fifteenth century. To the south of the Oka river permanent settlement made little or no advance in the Middle Ages, owing to the insecurity of the steppe lands occupied by successive semi-nomad, semi-agricultural peoples. In fact, south of the Oka extended a political frontier belt which was also a frontier of settlement, and settlement from the north was achieved only hand in hand with measures of military organi-

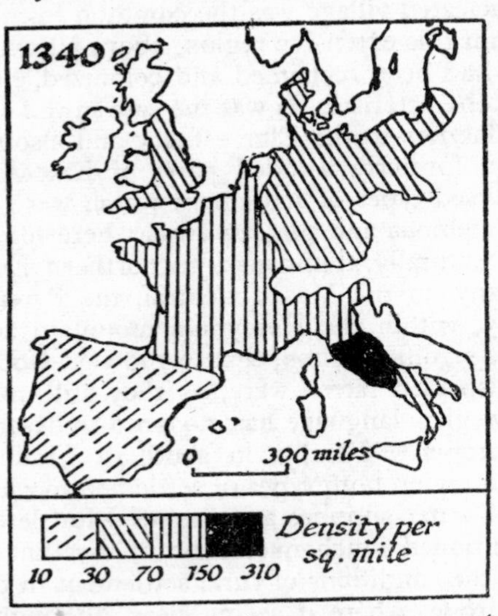

FIG. 15.—Population densities in Europe, *c.* A.D. 1340 (after Usher)
(Cp. with Fig. 2 and Fig. 50)

It is important to emphasize that a map of this kind, owing to the inadequacy of the evidence, can claim only a hypothetical value. No density is shown for the area left white.

zation from the sixteenth century onwards. Nor is it surprising that owing to the need for defence compact villages were formed. These villages, in common with those of western and middle Europe, were associated with the open field system, which lasted on in Russia down to the present century.

Given this broad distribution of settlement types, what are the chief explanatory factors? Clearly the complexity of the problem precludes sweeping generalization. The explanation offered by Meitzen certainly fails to be convincing in the light of detailed regional study. It may be recalled that he regarded the nucleated village, together with the open field system which usually accompanied it, as a Germanic institution, whilst he conceived the scattered homestead, which stood usually near its enclosed arable holding, to represent a Celtic type of settlement. A simple so-called 'racial' interpretation of this kind invites numerous inescapable objections. Thus in the heart of the English plain, where Anglo-Saxon colonization was thoroughly established, dispersed settlements commonly occur, as in Suffolk, side by side with nucleated villages (Fig. 16). Again, the nucleated village was a well-attested fact in Romano-Celtic Gaul long before the invasions of the Germans. Similarly, in essentially Celtic lands which stood remote from German penetration, as in some at least of the Channel Islands, the nucleated village was not untypical. Finally, in a wide lowland area of north-western Europe between the Weser and the Channel in which German colonization began early, the scattered type of settlement is typical. Thus the 'racial' factor does not afford a complete explanation, although it does suggest the important fact that the immigrant German peoples may have established in the lands of the Roman Empire their own agricultural and sociological practices. Do geographical factors, on the other hand—considerations of regional diversity in relief, elevation, climate, soils, water-supply and vegetation cover—provide a more convincing solution of the problem? Certainly they suggest many correlations, although for the present these must be rather tentatively advanced.

It may be suggested that western and central Europe comprised broadly two types of landscape which, on the ground of physical geography, were best suited respectively to arable and pastoral farming. There were, on the one hand, stretches of level plain, the drainage and soils of which fitted them essentially for cultivation; there were, on the other hand, wide areas of land, which for reasons of elevation, relief, drainage, climate or poorness of soils, were equipped above all for woodland and the pasturage of stock. Now it may be suggested further that the nucleated village is best adapted to an agrarian system in which cultivation prominently figures, whereas scattered settlements find their *raison d'être* in an economic scheme where the emphasis is on pasture. For a large rural community of the nucleated type postulated agriculture in order to produce its food supply, and moreover, only a small area of land was necessary to sustain a large group on the basis of cultivation. On the other hand, stock-raising under past conditions implied wide spaces of natural pasturage in woodland or moorland; moreover, where cultivation was possible only on a small scale, smaller groupings only

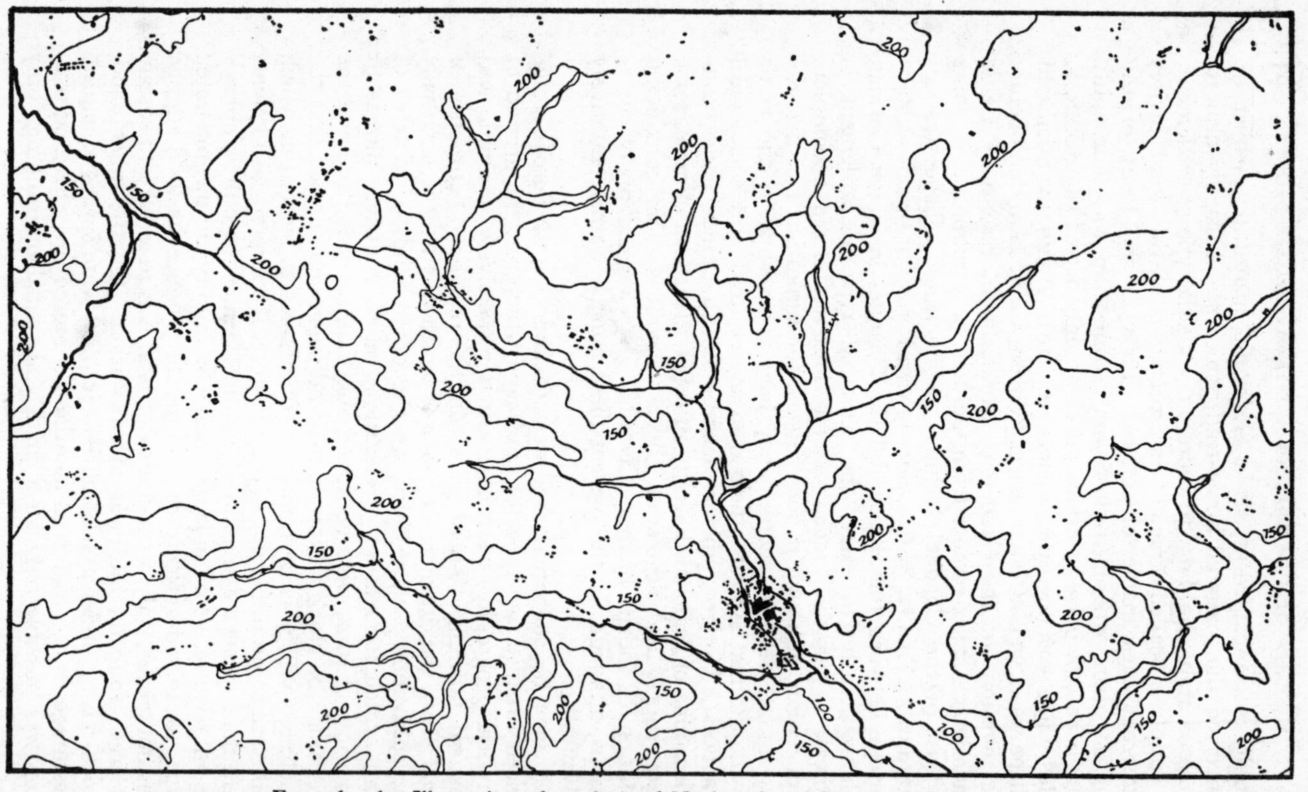

FIG. 16.—An Illustration of an Area of Nucleated and Dispersed Settlements

Note that there are shown one town (Stowmarket, Suffolk), a few nucleated villages, together with many small hamlets and scattered farms. Contours are shown in feet; based upon the Ordnance Survey Map

could be supported. Thus the distances involved in pastoral farming, coupled with the scarcity of cereal foodstuffs, would seem an argument for a diffusion of small hamlets or homesteads in country geographically fitted for pastoral farming. Hence, if this argument is valid, an explanation is provided for some at least of the distributions of nucleated and scattered settlements. In the light of it, there is no difficulty in understanding the predominance of scattered settlement in Norway, in Wales and in Northumberland, or for that matter in the ill-drained and formerly wooded clay lands of the Weald in south-eastern England, or on the high, wet plateaux of the French Massif Central, where additionally soils were often thin and poor. Nor does the historian's suggestion[1] that dispersion of hamlets represented a tenurial arrangement necessarily exclude a geographical explanation: tenurial systems may well have been adapted, in some measure, to environmental conditions.

Similarly, the availability of water, since it was essential to man and beast, may have played a part in defining the distribution patterns on the landscape. It must be admitted that Mediterranean Europe affords little support for this view, since the large compact village, which is very typical in the region, occupies as a rule an elevated site away from river and springs; this seems to indicate not only an original need for security but also the fact that cultivation could be carried on at high levels. In western and central Europe, however, this preoccupation, although it was expressed in Gallic cities, does not appear very evident, nor in fact did topography always afford sites easy of defence. It is noteworthy how scattered settlements often occur, as in Brittany, where water is plentiful and ubiquitous. On the other hand, in country where the sub-soil is porous and the availability of water in medieval times was rigidly restricted, as in Champagne and in the chalk lands of England, nucleated villages are the rule and are situated along rivers or 'stream lines' where water occurs at the surface. Again, below the 'Côtes' of the Meuse, where water was plentiful, villages were strung out and the lands of the village were so arranged as to include three distinct elements—pasture, forests and slopes for vines. Similarly, where water could be got only by wells, the organized effort and capital cost required implied a concentration of villagers.

Then again, the peculiar conditions of woodland and marshland, considered in relation to the technical and capital equip-

[1] See the article on 'Northumberland Institutions', by Joliffe in the *E.H.R.*, Jan. 1926, and his study *Pre-Feudal England: The Jutes* (1933).

ment of medieval times, help to explain the dissemination of small settlements in such lands which were reclaimed. Thus small-scale piecemeal colonization within forest and moor was usually effected by small groups of the hamlet or homestead type; similarly, in the course of marsh reclamation small enclosed parcels were drained in turn and, as in Flanders, were cultivated by pioneer free-holders who dwelt in homesteads situated on the raised embankments and close by their enclosed holding.

The study of rural settlement in medieval Europe raises other problems, apart from those discussed above, which may at least be alluded to here. There is first the distribution of population throughout the countryside; but since this involves a consideration also of urban conditions, it may best be reviewed later; second, the detailed siting of villages, and third, the peculiar ground plans which they presented.

The siting of medieval villages invites interesting analysis and classification for which space does not allow here. One point may be noted. The contrasting characteristics of rivers in the Mediterranean region and western and central Europe are reflected in man's selection of village sites. In the Mediterranean the rivers are normally torrential and dry according to the season; they seldom afforded easy routes either by water or along the valley sides; whilst the valley bottoms were often ill-drained and even malarial. But if settlements for good reason show much avoidance of rivers in the south, their siting is different in the north. Under the 'oceanic' and 'continental' conditions of climate which obtain in Europe outside the Mediterranean world, rivers offered waterways and valleys routes, often too, well-drained terraces standing above the area of flood plain. Thus villages are typically found there situated on terraces or bluffs along the line of rivers. Clearly, again, elevated sites are characteristic in ill-drained lands, as in the villages on Fen islands in England and Brandenburg. In upland areas the rims of sheltered basins often provided settlement sites; so also did the edges of lakes, marshes or lagoons, and the raised dyke in reclaimed marshland, whilst 'spring lines', or, more strictly, zones along which springs occurred, attracted village settlers.

Finally, upon examination villages may be found to adopt one of a number of 'lay-out' patterns, the forms of which have been adapted to the particular topographical conditions of the sites. It is possible, too, that certain 'lay-outs' may be associated with certain peoples: thus, the 'round' or 'ring fence' village has been called a Slavic type, since it was, and is still, very common in Slav Europe, e.g. Poland ; but it is by no means exclusively found in Slav lands. Other common types are the 'roadside' village, the 'cross road' village, and the 'grid-iron' village and the 'nebular' village (Fig. 17).

(i) Round Village (ii) Roadside Village

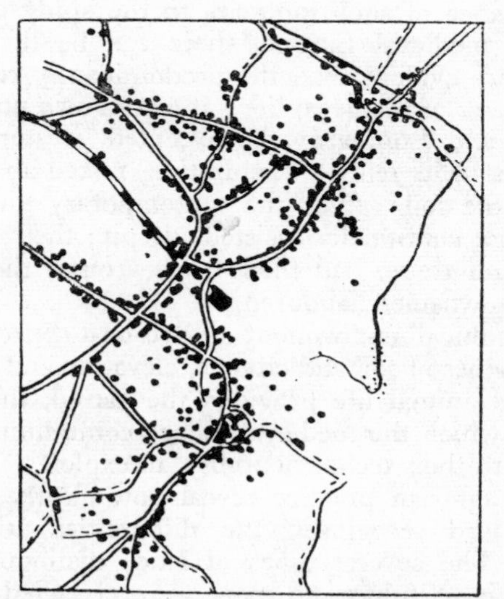

(iii) Nebular Village. Note the lack of any dominant centre

FIG. 17.—Types of Village Plans

The Utilization of the Soil

It has been noted above how in the course of the Middle Ages village communities gained an increasing hold on the soil of western Europe, establishing themselves widely in settlements, the sites, types and distribution of which, far from being fortuitous, reflected to a considerable degree human selectivity from varied natural possibilities. Despite their many differences in different parts of western Europe, the rural settlements were alike in their close dependence on the utilization of the soil amidst which they stood, and whatever else they may have represented —social groupings, legal entities and economic units—they were emphatically also geographical phenomena, alike in the patterns which they produced on the landscape and in the relationship which they embodied to the soil. It falls to the economic and social historian—unenviably enough—fully to analyse the agrarian conditions of medieval rural life and to explain the many baffling problems which surround the origins of the village community and their associated field systems. It is a sufficient task for the historical geographer to indicate the peculiar patterns which medieval rural life impressed upon the soil, and further, to discover what relationship existed between the village groups and the environment within which they were distributed. As to the importance of such inquiries to the study of the human geography of medieval Europe, there can be little doubt, for nothing is more evident than the predominantly rural and agricultural character of medieval life : if one or two notable regions, like Flanders and Lombardy, be excepted, western Europe, in its economy as in its feudal organization, rested above all on the utilization of the soil. Even the contemporary towns, as Maitland and others continually insisted, despite their concentration on industry and trade, had their fields around them, in which some of the townsmen laboured.

The geographical endowment of western Europe in all its regional diversities of soil and climate, elevation and slope, natural vegetation and animal life provided the varied, though limited, opportunities which the medieval village communities sought, in accordance with their technical ability, to exploit. Legal records of customary agrarian practice reveal how clearly the medieval villager and lord recognized the differential utilities of the countryside. The several types of land, distinguished on the ground of their usefulness to man, were classified in a manner which was actually as geographical as it was in intention economic ; and these various types of land, attached to a village and organized for exploitation according to certain systems and to customary practices, were combined together in a certain proportion, so as best to satisfy human needs. There was first the arable land : its physical requirements were a soil which was both sufficiently drained for cereal cultivation and stripped of its natural vegetation cover. The arable land, situated desirably but by no means necessarily in gently graded plain or sheltered river valley or upland basin, served the village primarily as provision for food and drink : to wit, cereals for bread and also for ale, a few vegetables and the vine, and certain 'industrial' plants, like hemp, flax, woad and madder. Second, there was the natural meadow-land, which provided not only pasture for stock, but also small and valued supplies of hay for winter feeding. It is important to note that meadow land had, because of the hay and rich pasture which it yielded, a very great value in medieval Europe out of all proportion to that which it possesses to-day. In fact, Thorold Rogers estimated that in the fifteenth century the price of a unit area of meadow compared with that of arable was five times that which obtained in the nineteenth.[1] The high price of meadow-land reflected the relative scarcity of winter food for cattle, since in its almost, but not quite complete, ignorance of fodder root crops and cultivated grasses, the medieval village suffered from a continual lack of foodstuffs with which cattle could be fed throughout the winter season. For meadow land in these days of primitive agricultural knowledge and practice was rigidly limited by geography: above all it was the natural vegetation of the rich, alluvial soils spread throughout the flood plains of rivers or lakes. Hence the situation of villages on the banks of streams, so typical of the greater part of France, although in no sense typical in the Mediterranean south where the devastating river floods introduced a condition repellent to settlement, was of service, not only in providing water but also in providing winter hay. Further, it may be suggested that the alinement of parishes at right angles to a river axis, is significant rather of the way in which it shares the meadow crop than in sharing a frontage to the river. In addition to the arable and the meadow another category of land was equally essential to the village community, namely that which, misleadingly and even paradoxically, was called the 'waste'. For the waste, whether it comprised woodland, sandy heath (*lande*), peaty moor (*bruyère*), ill-drained fen or coastal marsh (*marais*) was valuable in respect of its offerings as it was extensive in actual area. The waste yielded much rough pasture; flesh and fowl; fuel in the form of wood or peat; timber for constructional purposes; reeds, salt and fish. Nor indeed did water, indispensable to human life, the distribution of which in these days was for the most part geographically controlled, escape classification in medieval economic texts, since it could be turned to productive service—to provide fisheries or to turn mill-wheels. The windmill marks a technical discovery and was not commonly employed until the twelfth century. Incidentally it may be noted that the use of the windmill did not so much displace as supplement the watermill: the former

[1] Cited by Simkhovitch, 'Hay and History', *Pol. Sc. Qu.*, Sept. 1913.

was distributed especially in exposed positions especially towards the coast; the watermill remained to a large extent along the upper reaches of rivers.[1]

The organized and in some measure collective effort of village communities adapted these varied lands of the village with a view primarily to providing their own subsistence. The village was to a very large extent a self-sufficing unit; moreover it sought quite normally, and increasingly in the later centuries when towns were developing as mercantile centres, to produce a surplus.[2] A medieval traveller throughout western and middle Europe, had he possessed the eye of an Arthur Young, would have been struck perhaps more by the uniformity of agricultural conditions as far as these were visibly marked on the soil than by the broad diversities which could also be detected by the intelligent observer. The similarities, in fact, between the agriculture in England, France and the lands across the Rhine are a striking fact, and justify the conception of a 'Northern Civilization' type.[3] The same type of field system—the open field system—with as a rule three unhedged arable fields, *tended* to be typical throughout the north European lowland eastwards across most of the English plain, across what was Gaul north of the Loire, thence eastwards across the Rhine as far as the great Polish plains and hills of the Vistula basin. Admittedly there were regional exceptions to this generalization, alike in the field systems and in agricultural emphasis, especially where drained marshland—as in maritime Flanders—or plateau or mountainous country—as in the Ardennes, High Vosges or interior Brittany—revealed a different and distinctive response to the local geographical conditions. Even so, the three-field system, in association with the nucleated village, typically occurred and with markedly common features throughout the north European plain (Fig. 18). The village itself formed a group of timbered and thatched dwellings with the manor house and church, together with some enclosed demesne land and garden plots; the alluvial meadow lay about the village stream, beyond which stretched the unhedged arable fields, which, in turn, were surrounded by the 'waste'. Around the manor house was a compact 'home-farm' consisting of gardens for fruit, vegetables and arable cultivation. The arable fields were divided by balks into narrow, elongated 'quarters', or 'virgates' as they were called in the English

[1] Cp. the distribution maps of mills in the past as shown in the case of Kent by W. C. Finch, *Watermills and Windmills*, 1933.

[2] Cp. Eileen Power, art. cit.

[3] Bloch, *Les Caractères Originaux de l'Histoire Rurale Française*, p. 35.

midlands, and these were subdivided into small parcels, which were so allotted as to give each land-holder in the village plots scattered throughout the three fields. This peculiar arrangement, if, as seems very probable, it arose out of some attempt to give equality of holdings, is easily explicable in terms of the relative values of different soils in medieval days. In recent days it has become easy greatly to modify the chemical constituents of soil, so that, as Mackinder noted [1] in Belgium, the best soils of to-day are not necessarily those which were naturally the best. In the absence of means of effective fertilization of soils the

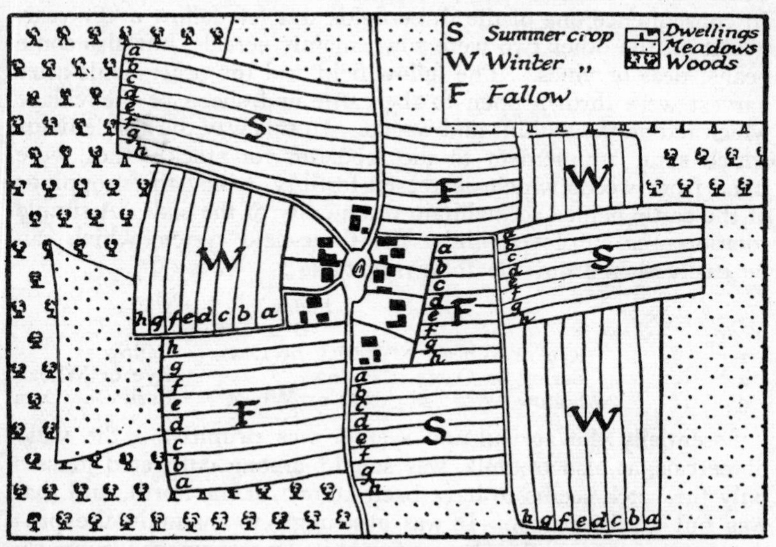

FIG. 18.—Schematic Plan of a Nucleated Village with Open Fields

Note the association of the three types of land—arable, meadow and woodland. Note also the strip holdings of the open fields, the letters *a*, *b*, *c*, &c., represent the landholders of the village, and it will be seen how each held a strip in each of the fields (after Putzgers' *Schul-Atlas*)

qualities of land, as defined by their physical characteristics—soil, slope, drainage, &c.—were almost entirely constant, and arable land of different qualities was regarded as constituting different, and *permanently* different, kinds of property. Then again, difficult though it is to distinguish cause and effect in medieval agrarian conditions, it is evident, on the assumption that land holdings had to be scattered through the open fields, that a compact or nucleated settlement was almost inevitably implied, since it would scarcely have been convenient to have resided at one of many isolated small plots.

[1] *The Rhine*, p. 180.

In the absence of scientific rotation of crops and the sufficient fertilization of land the medieval village resorted to the practice of the fallow field. Europe was lacking in areas which were naturally and regularly fertilized, like the Nile plain, and it was only in suitable places, as in Alderney,[1] where, thanks to the tidal sea, seaweed could be gathered easily from the foreshore and used as a fertilizer, that the same land could be cultivated continuously without fallowing. The root and grass-crops of to-day were lacking, and fertilizers—wood-ash, manure and seaweed—were available only in small and insufficient quantities. In consequence one of the three fields was left fallow every year, whilst on the other two were sown mainly cereals, but also some beans, peas or vines. The fallow field and the other fields after harvest were thrown open to the cattle and sheep of the village which fed on the stubble and weeds. In this way the arable fields added some supplement to the foodstuff for stock; they were freed from weeds which decreased fertility, whilst the droppings of the cattle helped to maintain the quality of the soil. A simple rotation was employed under the three-field system which can be easily seen from the following table:

		Fields	
Year	A	B	C
1 . . .	Rye or Wheat	Barley or Oats	Fallow
2 . . .	Barley or Oats	Fallow	Rye or Wheat
3 . . .	Fallow	Rye or Wheat	Barley or Oats

Essentially the agricultural system was primitive: the yield of cereals, as also of milk, was small; among cultivated grasses only the vetch seems to have been known in the north, and that was but rarely grown. It was a struggle to maintain the productivity of the soil, let alone attempt its improvement; similarly it was far from easy to keep stock through the winter immune from disease or decease. Even so, it is probable that the killing off of cattle on the approach of winter varied considerably according to the local opportunities of fodder production, and not only hay but other feeds, such as dried leaves, were utilized.

The hay and pasturage of the meadow was shared by the village in common, and the fact that it was not parcelled up into separate individual holdings as was done with the arable fields may well be geographically explained: the meanderings of streams, their floods and changes of course, introduced a set of variable factors which prevented any satisfactory and permanent allotment of the meadow through which the waters flowed.

[1] Harris, 'The Village Community of Alderney', *S.R.*, Oct. 1926.

In the north European plain, therefore, the agricultural system of the later Middle Ages presents certain correlated features which express the human adaptation of similar physical conditions. The region is primarily plain, whilst the climate and soils, though they vary regionally and include wide stretches of sand as well as clays, were in varying degrees suited to arable cultivation. The three-field system was typical, but stock-raising was relatively more important than agriculture. There was much pasture land around the numerous glacial lakes. Horse-rearing was important, native stock being crossed with Arabian horses, to produce stronger animals suitable to draw the plough and to carry armoured knights. The village type, as has been noted, was predominantly nucleated. A distinct type of plough was utilized in the north, different from that commonly used in southern and Mediterranean Europe. It was the *charure*, a plough which, as its name suggests, was mounted on wheels, the use of which in northern Gaul was remarked on by Roman writers, and it appears to have been an invention of the north European plain.[1] The great length of the ' quarters ' into which the arable fields were divided seems to have been an adaptation to this type of plough, whereas in the south of France and in the Mediterranean broadly the hand-worked plough, the *araire*, more flexible in use, may be correlated with a different field pattern and different topographical conditions. Then again, to return, the crops cultivated in the north European lowland show a marked homogeneity : it is probable that rye, a hardy and inferior cereal, less exacting than wheat in its climatic and soil requirements, was the chief cereal grown and the chief bread-stuff, alike in England[2] and in the continental plain. Sometimes wheat and rye mixed (*méteil*), were sown as well as millet, barley and oats ; and sowings, whether of these or of oats or barley, were made successively in autumn and in spring. A few vegetables, notably peas and beans, were grown, but many staple crops of to-day were entirely lacking, e.g., potatoes, maize and buckwheat. Flax and hemp, together with woad and madder, were cultivated : flax, in particular, flourished luxuriantly in the damp plains of northern Europe in the new land rich in humus which was cleared of deciduous forest. Again, many fruit trees, like the apple, pear, plum and cherry, the better varieties of which had been introduced into continental Europe by the Romans, were grown within enclosed plots. Specialization of crops and monoculture which are typical to-day had only a small

[1] Cp. Bloch, op. cit., pp. 52–3.
[2] Cp. Ashley, *The Bread of our Forefathers*, *passim*.

place in the medieval scheme. In fact, owing to the difficulties of communication and to the rudimentary organization of internal trade, varied cultivation was practised even in places badly suited to it; corn was grown on Alpine slopes and on wet clay soils regarded to-day essentially as pasture lands, whilst the vine was grown far beyond the northern limit to which it extends at the present day. Even so, in Germany as in the Slav lands, beer, flavoured with hops, was the common drink, certainly from the ninth century onwards.

Outside the north European plain other field systems with certain variants in agricultural practice were observable. There was first the run-rig system which was characteristic in western and northern Britain, and in certain mountainous or plateau areas of France and Germany. This system has been styled 'Celtic',[1] a designation which is open to criticism, since there is no proof of its exclusive association with Celtic-speaking peoples either in its origin—which may be prehistoric—or in its medieval practice. Certainly in Britain it remained the dominant system in those parts of the country where Celtic-speaking peoples preserved their own peculiar culture from the waves of Teutonic conquest and settlement which overwhelmed, or rather infiltrated, the English and Scottish lowlands. Similarly, run-rig was widely, though incompletely, extended in Brittany, which had very marked Celtic traditions. Even so, what seems much more fundamental than its apparent association with the Celts is its correlation with a certain type of country: upland country, characterized by heavy rainfall, by abundant natural wood and pasture land, by relative scarcity of plain and arable soils, and by the dispersion of hamlets and homesteads. In France the run-rig system prevailed throughout interior Brittany, Maine, the Ardennes plateau, the High Vosges, the Jura and in Alpine and Pyrenean areas. The poorness of the soils in these regions, together with their wetness and exposure, the extent of forest cover and even boggy tracts—supply a set of geographical factors, which may well explain the distribution of a common agricultural system.

Broadly, the run-rig system involved an enclosed arable area around the hamlet, the ('infield',) and the temporary enclosure, for the purposes of cultivation, of areas within the waste. Forest or moorland plants were destroyed by burning, the cleared land was cropped for the few years during which it remained productive, and it was then abandoned for a new clearing in the waste. The custom of common pasturage within the arable fields

[1] Gray, H. L., *English Field Systems*, ch. V.

—a typical and important feature of the open field system—had no place under the run-rig system, for the good reason that natural pasturage was abundant in highland country. In the middle Garonne region a variant on the run-rig system occurred : land was cleared of forest for ploughing and then kept productive without fallowing by the use of rotted undergrowth and manure.[1]

Finally, in the south of France and generally throughout much of southern and Mediterranean Europe, the field systems and agricultural practices introduced distinctive features which justify a generalized conception of a common southern type of civilization.[2] The open-field system, as it occurred widely in southern France, was two-field in character, a system which was employed generally throughout the Mediterranean world from the dawn of history.[3] This implied that one-half of the arable area was left fallow for one or more years according to the quality of the soil. The two-field system was thus less productive than the three-field system applied to the same area, since a greater fallow area was left ; but it was better suited to poor soils, as to those of the chalk downlands in England. Even so, the prevalence of the two-field system in southern France was probably due rather more to economic reasons : whereas in northern France the pressure of increasing population favoured the adoption of the more efficient form of the open-field system, the same pressure of population does not seem to have been operative in the south. Again, the field shapes and field divisions were different in the south from those in the north : the fields tended to be rather square, as also did the parcels into which the fields were divided up. The explanation of this may be found in the type of plough, the *araire*, which, introduced from the Mediterranean, was typically in use. The *araire* had no wheeled under-carriage, and it was thus more flexible in use and better adapted to hilly country. Further, enclosure was more common in the south : compact, individual holdings reclaimed from the waste, were often found outside the limits of the arable fields, whilst in the purely Mediterranean parts of France climate and topography favoured horticulture. In Low Languedoc, the lower Rhône and in Provence the vine, the olive, the orange, almond and fig were thus grown largely within enclosures. Many slopes were terraced for cultivation, and some irrigation, e.g., for oranges, was practised to

[1] Deffontaines, *Les Hommes et leurs Travaux dans le pays de la Moyenne Garonne*, 1932, p. 250.

[2] Cp. Bloch, op. cit., p. 35.

[3] Cp. Jardé, *Les Céréales dans l'Antiquité Grecque*, 1925, and Harris, article in the *S. R.*, July 1928.

overcome the difficulties of summer drought. The corn was sown in autumn (i.e. ' winter corn '), and spring corn was sown only if the winter crop failed, since drought in summer militated against the spring sowing. In general, the two-field system extended throughout the Garonne basin, northwards as far as Poitou, and throughout the Mediterranean south. In south-eastern England compactness of holdings instead of scattered parcels was typical, and this somewhat superior system perhaps represented the survival of Roman field system in lowlands which included some of the best loam soils of England.

In the Mediterranean south, as also in the Pyrenean, Alpine and High Vosges regions, seasonal contrasts in climate between land at high and low levels conditioned contrasts in vegetation, which in turn explain the practice of transhumance. Thus in Provence and in Low Languedoc and the lower Rhône valley flocks of sheep were led up in spring to the pastures of the plateaux, to be led down again in autumn to the pasture of the lowland.

In short, despite the variation in field patterns, in settlement types and in agricultural emphasis, medieval village folk engaged in essentially unspecialized farming. The potentialities of different regions on the basis of their peculiar conditions of soil, climate, aspect and relief, remained to a large extent unexploited in an age of small-scale internal trade. Nevertheless, the relative qualities of soil are in some measure reflected in the length of the fallow period and in the prevalence of either the two- or three-field system. The village derived from its fields, its meadows and its wastes the main essentials of food, drink and clothing. Only a few articles, like millstones, salt, pepper and fine vestments, the production of which was geographically restricted, had to be brought in from outside. The limited degree to which specialization in agriculture had taken place is well illustrated by the case of a plant which in recent times became markedly localized. The vine had been introduced into central and northern Gaul by the Romans, and its cultivation owed much also to the establishment of Christianity—a Mediterranean religion, in certain sacraments of which the use of wine was indispensable. Thus a widespread demand for wine was created, and it is doubtless a comment on the restricted facilities for internal trade and transport that wine, a commodity relatively easy to transport, was so widely produced, even in areas little suited to viticulture, such as Flanders, Mecklenburg, Pomerania and Brandenburg. Thus it was an exceptional circumstance that villagers on the upper Yonne river around Auxerre neither sowed nor reaped :[1] the reason was geographical, namely that the Yonne provided convenient transport for wine down to a good market, Paris. Similarly, along the foothills of the Taunus range and of the High Vosges viticulture was certainly well and early established : it is suggestive of this that the Treaty of Verdun in 843 so defined the frontier between the eastern and middle kingdoms, as to include in the former wine-producing country across the Rhine, around Spires, Worms and Mainz. Again, in the later Middle Ages British Gascony became an outstanding area of wine production, and Roussillon, Toulouse and Foix made wine which competed with that of the Gironde. The wine trade was served by roads which converged on Bordeaux, whilst the rivers Garonne, Dordogne and Adour also carried wine, which was exported largely from Bordeaux. The rivers were not always serviceable to navigation, and wine could not be carried down the Garonne, for instance, until about 11th November. So marked was the specialization in viticulture around Bordeaux that corn—in part from England—had to be shipped to Bordeaux to support the population of the vineyard country. It is evident that the relative ease of maritime communication and the stimulus of demand from England, a country ill adapted to the cultivation of the vine, explain this remarkable instance of specialization in the use of the soil. According to Edrisi, the vine was grown in the twelfth century in Brittany and around Bruges, Bremen and Cracow : his translator Jaubert [2] was frankly, but wrongly, sceptical of this, but he had better ground for doubting the validity of the statement that the olive was grown in Poland.

[1] Bloch, op. cit., p. 23, who, however, underestimates the amount of medieval specialization in viticulture.

[2] He writes ' (*sic*) ' after each statement in his translation !

CHAPTER VI

MEDIEVAL TOWNS AND ROUTES IN WESTERN AND CENTRAL EUROPE

THE sites and distribution of present-day towns in Europe reflect to a considerable extent conditions which have long existed, so that a review of the urban geography of the Middle Ages is a matter of more than antiquarian interest. The nice problem as to just what constitutes a town cannot be fully explored here. It may be suggested that at all periods a town, as distinct from a rural settlement, is characterized by special functions and distinctive geographical features. On the one hand, although it is not necessarily divorced from agricultural activity, the town tends to serve some or all of a wide variety of functions, commercial, industrial, political, ecclesiastical, judicial and military. On the other hand, it tends to occupy a site and position of such a geographical character that it can be utilized as a ' node ' or centre of routes by land or by water. It is true that a town might well have, as it often did in the Middle Ages, cultivated fields within and around it, and that part of its population might be engaged in purely agricultural pursuits, but, even so, this aspect of its life is less typical than its many wider and regional functions, which find expression in its markets and fairs, its cathedral and fortifications, its workshops and harbours, its palace and its court. Therefore, it may be suggested that, apart from marginal cases where the distinction between the large village and the small town is very fine, the town is geographically a definite and recognizable form of settlement, the more so since its particular functions are associated with visible spacial features, such as walls, harbours, fortresses and markets. In other words, to the geographer the town is a phenomenon of the cultural landscape, the manifestation of a peculiar kind of inter-relation between a human group and its physical and regional setting.

The antiquity of urban settlement is now well attested, but the origins of medieval towns are not very clearly ascertained. Certainly it seems necessary to speak with caution of the creation of towns in the Middle Ages, since, although the town may be newly created in some legal sense, e.g. as a corporate borough, as a staple town or as a port, the site itself may have been long occupied by a settlement. The results of modern archaeological study suggest the presence of fixed points of production and the practice of exchanging commodities as early as the Neolithic Age, and in some cases it is known that such a prehistoric site was also the site of a town in successive historical periods. The 'towns' of the prehistoric period already show marked local and positional characteristics: they stand often on sites which are easily defensible and are so placed, e.g., at river crossings, on the sea coast, or at the convergence of natural routes, as to suggest that they were route centres and were related thus to a wide area. The discovery that in certain cases the same site or a near-by site was occupied not only in the prehistoric but also in Roman and post-Roman times suggests the remoteness of some urban origins. In fact, the origin of medieval towns raises many difficult problems and evokes conflicting theories. On the one hand are theories which visualize the creation of towns of the early Middle Ages under the stimulus of new sets of conditions, and on the other, those which emphasize the idea of continuity of settlements—in their sites, though not in their municipal institutions—throughout pre-Roman, Roman and post-Roman times. In the first case it is argued that towns are largely 'seignorial' creations which arose in places which were selected by the great landowners of the early Middle Ages for the marketing of the surplus produce of their lands (Figs. 19 and 20). Or again it is suggested that towns typically arose in association with a palace, a monastery, a castle or a bishop's see, which all afforded nuclei around which population might gather with a view to satisfying by industry and trade the economic demand thereby created. Both of these theories rest on the assumption, which is now much challenged, that early medieval conditions were almost exclusively agricultural, and they regard the town therefore as in origin a village which has become transformed under the influence of special economic forces. To whatever extent these theories are valid it is certain they fail adequately to interpret all the relevant known facts, and it is probable that industrial and mercantile populations, however small, occupied settlements which were distinctively urban continuously from the Roman period, and that, despite a marked agricultural element in their economy, towns even in the early Middle Ages were recognizably distinct from village settlements.

These rival theories of town origins are by no means irreconcilable. In fact, urban development reveals different features from region to region. In some areas, as Pirenne has shown for Belgium, only a very few of the medieval cities were Roman

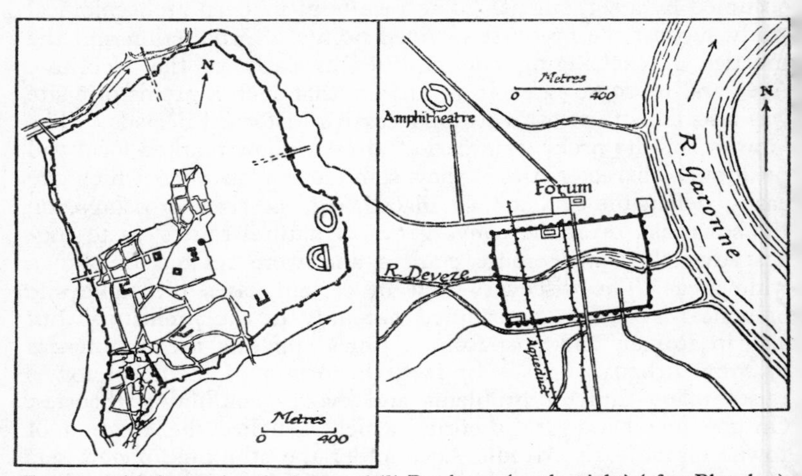

FIG. 19.—(*a*) Autun (on the left) and (*b*) Bordeaux (on the right) (after Blanchet)

The heavy lines show the limits of the Roman towns. Note, in the case of Autun, how the post-Roman settlement occupied only part of the Roman 'enceinte'. At first this consisted of the small, walled, southern corner of the site, around the church. At Bordeaux the cathedral was built on the site of a Roman temple (at the S.W. corner of the 'enceinte'), the latter serving the town until the twelfth century

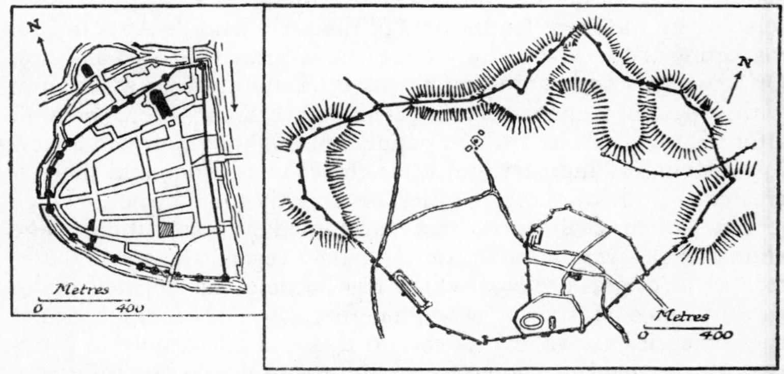

FIG. 19.—(*c*) Chalon-sur-Saône (on the left) and (*d*) Nîmes (on the right) (after Blanchet)

Note, in the case of Nîmes, the small post-Roman 'enceinte', occupying a small part of the Roman town. Note also, as the four plans show, the various shapes of Roman towns, these shapes being in some measure dictated by topographical features

foundations, and much the greater number occupied newly selected sites, where the castle of a lord or a monastery established a settlement, within or outside of the walls of which

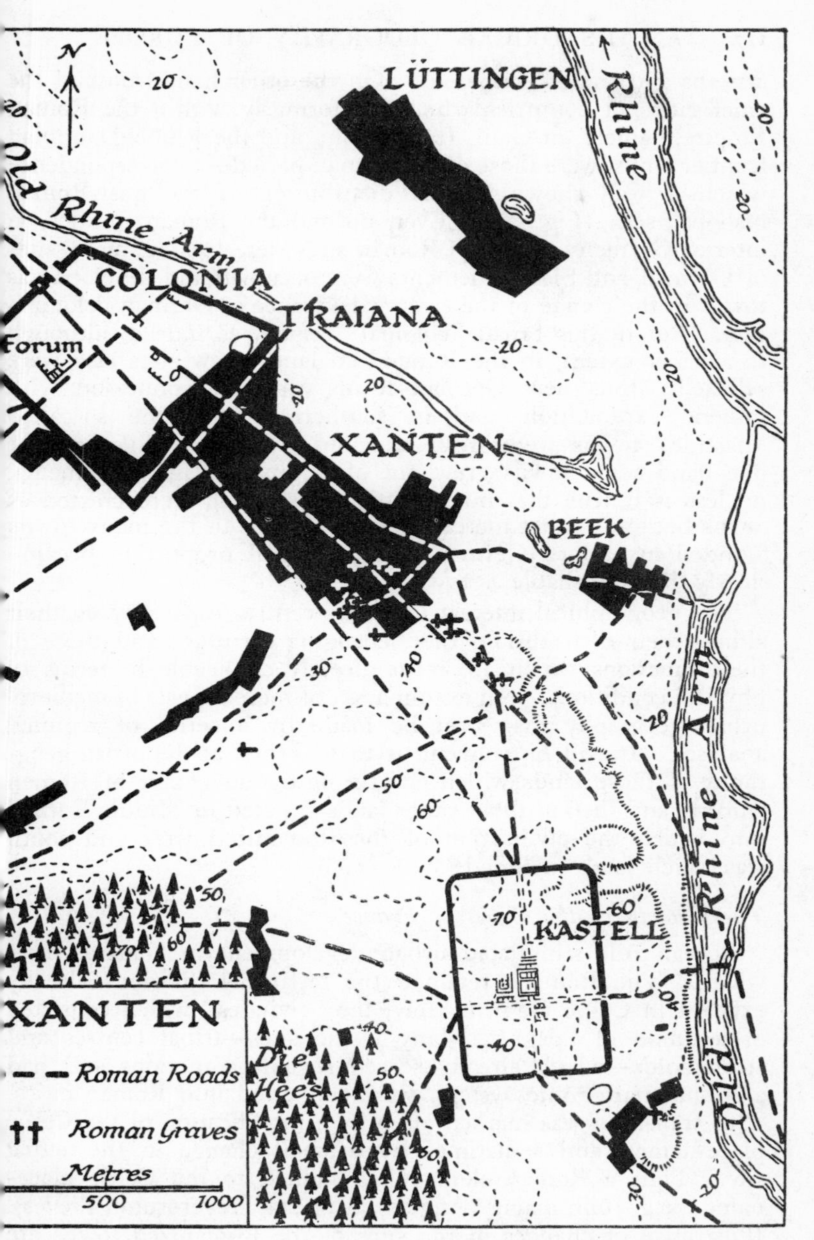

FIG. 20.—Roman and Post-Roman Xanten (after Schumacher)

Contours are shown in metres. The heavy lines show the fortified Roman sites ; the solid black areas, the present settlements

artisans and traders gathered.[1] On the other hand, most of the chief cities of countries which lay formerly within the Roman Empire, namely, in Gaul, Italy, Spain, and the Rhine–Danubian frontier lands, were those of the Roman period—a correspondence which is well shown by the distribution of the post-Roman bishops' sees (Fig. 21). Even beyond the Roman frontier, in interior Germany, although Roman sites were lacking, many sites of German and Slav settlements were occupied and developed as towns in the course of the eastward advance of German colonization. But in this broad ' colonial ' region, as indeed, although to a lesser extent, in the Romanized lands, new sites also were selected ; thus new German towns arose in connexion with mineral exploitation, and in southern France the so-called ' bastide ' towns were fresh creations. Finally, whilst on the one hand some towns grew out of original village settlements, no less is it true that many settlements which were created as towns became in fact merely villages. Thus of the many towns founded in eastern Germany, only a small proportion became clearly distinguishable as towns.

The geographical interest in towns centres especially on their siting, their distribution, their changing fortunes, and those of their functions which are most directly explicable in terms of physical conditions. An examination of these aspects of medieval urban geography may best be made by a series of regional analyses. It will be convenient to look first at the urban geography of those lands which had the initial advantage of Roman culture, and then at those other lands situated in Middle Europe into which the civilization of the Romanized west and south was much later extended.

The Growth of the Cities of France

Roman rule stimulated urban development in Gaul as elsewhere. The Romans retained the territorial divisions already existent in Celtic Gaul, namely, the ' civitates ' which consisted of a union of ' pagi '. Many Celtic sites—tribal centres and strongholds—which already served regional functions and had a rudimentary route system, were converted into Roman cities. This transition was marked often by a modification of the Celtic place-names, and sometimes by a small change in the actual site. Thus a Roman element was added to the Celtic place-name : e.g. Julio-magus (Angers), Augusta Treverorum (Trèves). Illustrative of changes in the sites of the Romanized towns are Autun and Clermont-Ferrand, where—since the need for a

[1] Cp. *infra*, pp. 333–6.

defensive upland oppidum no longer obtained—the new towns occupied valley sites below the Gallic strongholds, respectively, of Bibracte and Gergovia. The ' chefs-lieux ' of Gallic civitates often became the regional centres of medieval and modern times, and in place of the Romanized names they came to take names deriving from the people of the civitas : in this way ' Lutetia ' became ' Paris ' after the Parisii ; ' Limonum ' became ' Poitiers ' after the Pictones ; ' Augustobona ' became ' Troyes ' after the Tricasses. A great number of these Romanized towns have successors on the same site to-day, and it is probable that, despite the collapse of the Roman order and some destruction, the Roman towns of Gaul were for the most part continuously settled. This common phenomenon illustrates what may be called geographical inertia, the tendency for people to remain in places which have been long adapted to their needs ; it nevertheless suggests the skill with which the Gauls chose their original sites, and the ability of the Romans, by means of engineering works, such as roads, aqueducts, walls, &c., to improve site values.

The spread of Christianity into Gaul was one important factor in the preservation of its Roman cities. It made its entry into Roman Provence and penetrated northwards up the Rhône and Saône valleys. Lyons is believed to have become the first bishop's see, and a little later, by *c.* A.D. 200, the Christian faith was making converts in the cities of the south : Arles, Narbonne, Toulouse, Limoges, Clermont-Ferrand, Bourges and Tours, and even as far afield as the Rhine and Moselle, where it was carried by soldiers and traders. More certain light on the spread of Christianity is afforded in the year 314, when sixteen dioceses are recorded. Seven of these lay in the south, in Provincia Narbonensis ; three in the south-west, namely, Bordeaux, Eauze and Mende ; three in the centre, namely, Autun, Lyons and Rouen ; finally, the three in the north-east were Rheims, Trèves and Cologne. During the succeeding centuries a few dioceses disappeared, whilst others were created or recast. The disappearance of bishops' sees was sometimes due to the destruction of the episcopal town during the storms of the invasions. Thus Augst (near Basle), Port-sur-Saône, St. Paulien (near Le Puy, its successor), and Iverdun ceased, owing to the effects of the invasions, to remain episcopal cities. In the Merovingian period (e.g. during the seventh century) Gaul was divided into twelve ecclesiastical provinces which comprised a hundred and six bishops' sees (Fig. 21). Under the Carolingian dynasty some more metropolitan cities were selected, so that in the tenth century there were seventeen archbishopric centres. What is so remarkable about this scheme is its essential correspondence with the administrative division of Roman Gaul into civitates, and moreover the fact that it persisted without any drastic modification down to the eve of the French revolution. From the present standpoint the ecclesiastical organization of

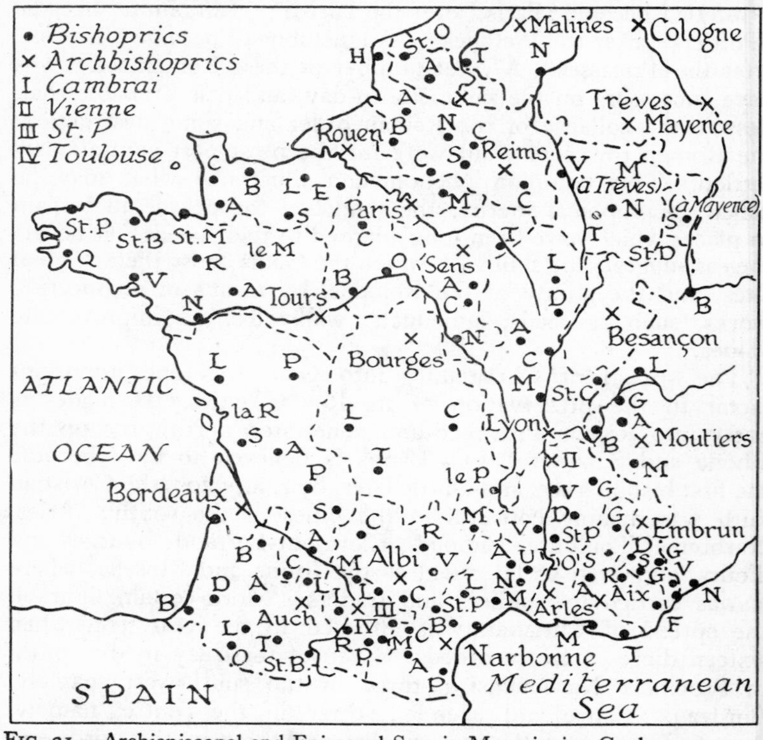

FIG. 21.—Archiepiscopal and Episcopal Sees in Merovingian Gaul, *c.* A.D. 700 (after Mirot, *Manuel de Géographie Historique de la France*)

The limits of the archbishoprics are shown by the broken lines. Note the concentration of bishops' sees in the south and in the Rhône basin, i.e. in the most Romanized part of Gaul

Gaul is interesting as showing the existence in the early Middle Ages of cities of Roman or pre-Roman foundation. It must not be inferred, however, that these towns were necessarily either very industrial or commercial ; but there is some evidence to suggest, as Dopsch argues, that the presence of an episcopal residence indicates relatively important centres of population, since bishops did not establish themselves in deserted places.

If it be admitted, therefore, that many French towns may

have preserved certain features, e.g. of site and activities, from the Roman period, it is nevertheless true that they were primarily centres of refuge, guarded by walls and moats, and that they did not become important centres of trade and industry until the later Middle Ages, say after A.D. 1000. It is doubtless relevant to point [1] to the presence of castles, monastic houses, and the residences of kings, bishops and lords as factors in their mercantile development, since merchants and artisans tended to collect around these fortified centres, grouping themselves usually in contiguous suburbs. The towns of Chateauroux, and Niort, which had castles in the tenth century, and Alençon, Beaucaire and Mirepoix, which had them in the eleventh, may be cited as instances of the growth of towns around strongholds, although it may be noticed that in the case of Beaucaire, situated at a passage point on the lower Rhône, the medieval city is largely the analogue of the Roman city. Similarly, many instances can be adduced of towns which grouped themselves around abbeys and monasteries. Thus the abbey town of Sens on the Yonne river is known to have been very prosperous in the year 1008 as the resort of numerous pilgrims from France, Italy and oversea, since it possessed—in common, it must be admitted with many other places—a piece of the rod of Moses, and merchants settled there to exploit its possibilities as a market. In the same way the famous abbey of Cluny proved to be the nucleus of a town. The ruins of Roman towns were often plundered to supply building stone for medieval cities. At Narbonne a mercantile burg grew up around the Abbey of St. Paul and was joined by a Roman bridge across the river Aude to the city within the Roman ' enceinte '. Similarly at Metz and Verdun trading suburbs developed across the river connected by bridges with towns occupying Roman sites. Royal residences (cp. Fig. 22) originally stood in rural sites, but these sometimes grew later into towns, as was the case with Charlemagne's capital at Aachen.

One of the most interesting aspects of the urban geography of medieval France is the creation of *bastides* in the south and particularly in the south-west. The recent study [2] by Dr. Deffontaines of the historical geography of the middle Garonne region, where the building of *bastides* in the thirteenth and fourteenth centuries was most actively undertaken, illustrates effectively this phase of French urban development. The middle Garonne

[1] See Flach in vol. 2 of *Enquête sur . . . l'Habitation en France*, chapter VI.

[2] Op. cit., pp. 146–56 (with plans).

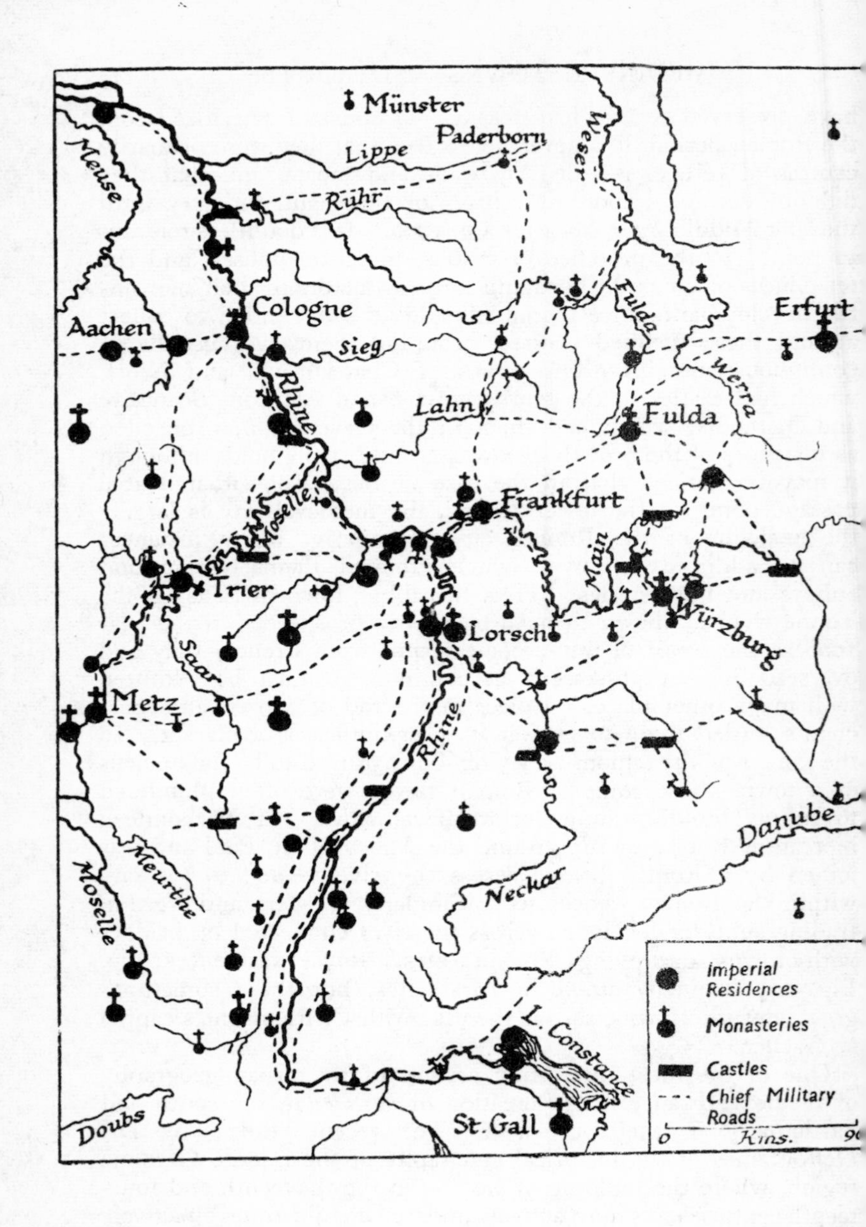

FIG. 22.—Imperial Residences, Monasteries and Castles in the Rhineland in the Carolingian Period, *c.* A.D. 800 (after Schumacher)

The map helps to illustrate the importance of the Rhineland as the political and cultural heartland of Medieval Germany

region was a frontier district which included lands of the French king, of his vassal the count of Toulouse and of the English king in Aquitaine, and it had suffered much depopulation in the course of Anglo-French wars and in the Albigensian religious war. The *bastides* were usually (though not invariably) newly created settlements, and what is more, as in the case of Roman cities, they were laid out according to a definite geometric plan. The plans were very often rectangular, but other shapes were adopted in conformity with the topography of the site, where, for example, the town was strung out along a valley or seated on the top of a spur of a plateau. Many of the *bastides* marked the advance of agriculture at the expense of the forest, as was the case in the *molasse* [1] country south of the middle Garonne. In fact, the economy of the *bastides* was essentially agricultural, but in other ways their urban character was evident, since not only were they well-fortified centres but their inhabitants were freemen—one of the distinguishing features of urban society. Actually the royal or noble founder of the towns recruited their populations from neighbouring rural settlements. For the most part the *bastides* persisted, but tended to become in modern days purely rural centres; in contrast Villeneuve, in the lower valley of the Lot, remains to-day a sizable town.

The Fairs of Champagne

It will be suggested later [2] that the lands of northern Europe underwent a marked change in geographical values in and subsequently to the time of Charlemagne (d. 814). An excellent illustration of this is provided by the Champagne fairs which flourished as the most important international marts of Europe during the twelfth and thirteenth centuries. Already at this time Flanders had long become the seat of industrial and mercantile cities which specialized in the manufacture of linens and woollens and imported English wool; similarly, the maritime and commercial cities of the Mediterranean, notably Venice, Pisa, Genoa and a number of ports in southern France and Provence, had become entrepôts and distributors of Oriental commodities and other goods, especially high-grade manufactures, produced in the towns of Italy and at Constantinople. Moreover, when it is remembered that the direct sea route between the Mediterranean and the Channel was not widely used until the fourteenth century, it is evident that the towns of Champagne and Brie were well placed in relation to the land routes between

[1] *Molasse* is a soft sandstone.
[2] Cp. *infra*, pp. 299–300.

Flanders and the Mediterranean cities. That the towns of Champagne—Châlons, Troyes, Bar-sur-Aube, &c.—enjoyed this advantageous position is attributable in some measure to the original alignment of Roman roads in Gaul, since the thirteenth-century network of routes shows some correspondence with the Roman road pattern, e.g., convergence of routes at Rheims and Troyes (Fig. 4). The Roman road system in Gaul, it should be noted, had especially in view, as political and strategical ends, the connexion of Italy with the Rhine frontier and with the Channel, but it may be inferred that some at least of the Champagne towns inherited from the Romans advantages in relation to communication which served them well under the economic conditions of the later Middle Ages.

Commercial activity of an international character in the region of Champagne and Brie is evidenced as early as the ninth century. At this time the town of Chappes, now a small village, situated near Troyes, on the river Aube, was the resort of Syrian, Jewish and Italian merchants, who brought there Antioch leather, Tyrian purple cloth, rich fabrics, and gems. Meaux, which stood on the Marne above Paris, was also a mercantile centre. Paris itself, which was described in this century as a well-populated place standing in the midst of fertile country, had suburbs on both banks of the Seine and a fair at St. Denis from the seventh century, to which Italians, Spaniards and others came. The fairs which became famous in the twelfth century were held at the towns of Bar-sur-Aube, of Châlons and Lagny on the Marne, of Troyes on the Seine, and of Provins. Of these cities all except the last stood at crossing points of rivers and had the advantage of waterway communication with Paris. Merchants from Flanders reached the fairs by a choice of land routes ; those from Normandy came by water up the Seine and Oise as far as the bridge at Verberie Rouanne, and continued thence by road. Italian merchants crossed the Alps mainly by the Great St. Bernard pass and passed via Dijon or Langres, which (as Edrisi describes it) was remarkable for its buildings, its commerce, and the facilities available both for business and travel. The road along the left bank of the Rhône and that via the Mont Cenis pass, which met at Lyons, were also used by the Italians. The Rhône–Saône road, together with another which, lying entirely within France, crossed the Massif Central by way of Le Puy and Clermont-Ferrand, led northwards from the French and Provence ports. Merchants from Spain used either these routes or others northwards from Bordeaux, whilst they commonly came by sea to the lower Rhône. German merchants from the

Rhine cities and British merchants also frequented the Champagne fairs.

The fairs were held at fixed dates which fell within all seasons of the year. Not a little reason for their success was the administrative efficiency of the Counts who ruled jointly Champagne and Brie ; they protected merchants and lightened tolls, canalized the Seine at Troyes so that its waters should serve the local cloth industry, and no less cleared forests and extended viticulture and tillage. Under their firm and enlightened régime the fairs became entrepôts for a wide variety of commodities of diverse origin ; woollen and linen textiles from Flanders ; finer woollen fabrics from Syria, Persia and Egypt ; rich silks woven in Lucca, Genoa, Florence and Venice ; furs, skins and leather ; gold and silver work ; raw materials, such as wool and iron ; cattle ; foodstuffs ; and finally, slaves. Even before 1300, however, the fairs began to lose their European pre-eminence largely because merchants refused to pay the very onerous dues demanded : war between the French king and the Count of Flanders, together with the opening up (in 1317) of organized sailings between the Italian ports and those of the Channel, hastened their decline. Owing to these adverse conditions, merchants carried their wares instead to the fairs of Flanders : to Thourout, Bruges, Ypres, Lille, Ghent and Antwerp, where in consequence trade greatly flourished.

The Routes of France

Not only to traders but also to pilgrims France was a ' pays de passage ', for travellers from the north bound for Rome and Santiago. The ' Great Route of Spain and of St. James ' is referred to elsewhere ;[1] it must suffice here to describe the pilgrim routes between London and Rome as they are clearly revealed in an itinerary, pictorial rather than cartographical in form, which is dated 1253 and is associated with, though not ascribed to, Matthew Paris.[2] The road from London follows the Roman road via Rochester and Canterbury to the castle town and port of Dover, which is described as ' the entry and the key of the rich island of England '. The Channel crossing was made either to Calais, Boulogne or Wissant, from each of which routes continued south-eastwards across France. It will suffice here to note some of the principal stages on these routes. That from Wissant reached Paris by way of Beauvais ; thence

[1] See *infra*, p. 234.

[2] The itinerary and maps are published in K. Miller, *Mappaemundi*, pt. III, pp. 84–90.

it passed through the Seine towns of Nogent, Troyes, Bar and Châtillon. At Troyes it was joined by the road which left the coast at Calais and continued via St. Omer, Arras, St. Quentin, Rheims and Châlons-sur-Marne. From Châtillon pilgrims made their way over the Côte d'Or to Beaune, where the road from Boulogne joined, having passed by way of Abbéville, Luzarches, St. Maur(?) on the Marne, Sens, Auxerre and Vezélay. From Beaune the route led to Chalon-sur-Saône and down the Saône valley ; Lyons was entered by crossing its bridge over the Saône, and was left, *en route* for Chambéry and the Mont Cenis, by way of its Rhône bridge. At the Mont Cenis, which was one of the most-frequented passes between Italy and France, a monastery was founded in 726, and a hospice and church were established a century later.[1] Moreover, it possessed its holy shrines of St. Waltharius and of Bertha, wife of Charlemagne—notwithstanding that the latter never had a wife so called, nor did his wife die at Mont Cenis, as legend avowed. From the Mont Cenis pass Italy lay open, by way of Susa to Turin ; thence the pilgrim bound for Rome passed along the old Via Aemilia to Bologna, crossed the Apennines through Abruzzi, and entered Rome by way of Viterbo and Sutri. Alternatively, he could leave the Via Aemilia some few miles short of Parma, cross the Apennines by the Cisa pass, and thence by Pontremoli, Luna, Lucca, Siena and Viterbo to Rome, ' terminus itineris multorum et laborum initium '.

The Rhine Towns

One of the most outstanding regions of urban development in medieval Europe lay within the Rhineland, which formed part of the kingdom of the Germans, itself part of the Holy Roman Empire. Within this region, for example the rift valley of the Rhine in Hesse, Baden and Alsace, lay one of the most anciently settled lands of Europe. Moreover, since it stood for three or four centuries within the Roman Empire, the Rhineland was highly urbanized, the more so on account of its frontier position, for the needs of the frontier made the building of fortified stations necessary, whilst the position of these at the meeting-place of Roman and Germanic culture was advantageous to trading activity. In fact, as Schumacher's remarkable studies have shown, the lands of the middle Rhine and the lower Main, which on account of their soil and vegetation cover were attractive to early settlement, present a whole succession of settlement distributions and routeways at successive periods from the Neolithic Age onwards. The towns of the medieval period,

[1] Bédier, *Les Légendes épiques*, III, 8.

as indeed those of to-day, occupy in several cases Roman sites, which in turn had been occupied by Celtic or pre-Celtic settlements. The Austrian historian Dopsch, who emphasizes the theory of continuity of settlement sites in the Rhineland, has pointed further to the fact, which in a number of cases can be proved, that the same hill-top bore successively a pagan temple, a Roman fort, and a Christian cathedral or church.

It seems probable that, despite the collapse of the Roman frontier before the pressure of the Alamanns, Franks and other 'barbarian' invaders, the Roman cities of the Rhineland were continuously occupied down to the early Middle Ages. Contemporary literary record, it is true, often relates the destruction of the Rhine cities: thus Cologne was said to have been destroyed in A.D. 355 by the Alamanns, and Mainz was described as both 'excisa' and 'deleta' in the fifth century. But it is clear, thanks largely to archaeology, that these statements are not to be taken literally. Doubtless the towns suffered considerably from sacking; they were partially destroyed and burnt; and their institutions failed to survive the barbarian invasions. Even so, many of the elements of the Roman towns did survive. The immigrants settled usually within or close by the actual Roman site, utilizing often the Roman walls, streets and bridges. The position of the early grave-yards of the invaders often proves the presence of barbarian settlement within the Roman town. Thus the following Roman cities were reoccupied by German immigrants: Neuss, Düren, Cologne, Coblenz, Andernach, Mainz, Frankfurt-on-Main, Worms, Trèves, Strasbourg, Basle, Constance and Chur. Similarly, farther west in Lorraine, Metz, Verdun and Trèves were reoccupied. In some cases it can be shown that a part of the Roman street plan remained in use, that Christian churches were placed in relation to the Roman street pattern, and that cathedrals came to be built on the highest point within the town which was formerly crowned by fortifications. Thus some Roman street lines survive at Frankfurt, Mainz, Cologne and Worms; walls survived, at least in part, at Cologne, Neuss, Mainz and Strasbourg; whilst cathedrals replaced forts on eminences at Frankfurt, Strasbourg and Cologne. Even the Roman cemeteries were sometimes used by the newcomers, as at Worms. The permanent bridges at Mainz and Cologne, although the date of their eventual destruction is not clearly known, appear to have lasted for several centuries.[1]

[1] Cp. Keussen, *Köln im Mittelalter*, p. 40. There is some evidence that Charlemagne crossed the Rhine by the Roman bridge, and its ruins were noted in the late fifteenth century. Cologne had a bridge of boats in 1643

Moreover, the main highways linking up the Roman towns of the Rhineland with the Danube, the Alps and with Gaul remained largely intact. Finally, already in later years of the Empire Christianity had spread into the Rhineland from southern Gaul by way of the Rhône–Saône valleys, and many of the cities were selected between the fourth and the sixth centuries for bishops' sees, a fact which may be taken as evidence of their importance as centres of population, since only the more important settlements were chosen for this purpose.

Cologne, the Colonia Agrippina of the Roman Empire, stood out as one of the most active and populous cities of medieval Europe, and its development may be taken as typical of urban life in the Rhineland. The original Roman city consisted of a legionary fortress on the left bank of the Rhine, which was connected by a permanent bridge with a fort at Deutz. If Cologne was thus primarily important as a legionary headquarters, nevertheless it included a civil population and engaged in trade, both within and without Roman territories. The town became a focus of Roman trade routes, and was equally well placed to serve as a sea and river port. It has been proved that the so-called 'destruction' of Cologne in A.D. 355 after its siege and capture by the Alamanns is not to be taken literally; recaptured in 356 by Roman forces, it fell later and without resistance into the hands of the Franks, and thus continued to be, what it had already long been, a town of largely German population. In fact, Cologne is an excellent instance of a Roman town site the continuance of which into the medieval period is well attested. Its selection in the Merovingian period as an archiepiscopal see suggests that it was then of some importance. Its Roman walls remained, and needed only to be repaired after the ravaging attacks of the Norsemen in the ninth century. The Roman bridge appears to have remained several centuries after the fall of Rome. The route system converging on the town continued in use; moreover, the Roman street plan of the town is still recognizable in its present streets, and early Christian churches were located in relation to the Roman street pattern. The geographical position of Cologne was much improved after *c.* A.D. 800 as a result of German colonization beyond the Rhine and of the development of maritime trade in the North and Baltic seas. Cologne prospered as the greatest Rhine seaport and as a Hanseatic city, and it had no down-stream rival during the medieval period. It largely controlled traffic on the Rhine and enjoyed both 'staple' and 'transfer' rights: that is, it could exact that certain goods were landed and exposed for sale in the town, and also that goods which were bound for ports above or below the town were transhipped into its own vessels. The importance of Cologne is well illustrated by its areal extension in the course of the Middle Ages. The eastern half of the Roman town shows the best evidence of early post-Roman occupation, which spread thence beyond the walls down to the river bank. This riverside area, called the Rheinvorstadt, contained the markets and landing-places, and was joined by walls to the Roman town by the tenth century. On the eastern side of the Roman town stood the Jewish quarter, and in its south-east corner the cathedral was built on the site of a Roman temple. The town continued to expand during the eleventh and twelfth centuries, new walls were accordingly built in 1106 and 1180 (Fig. 23), and it became the largest city of the Empire.[1] The subsequent history of Cologne contrasts with this phase of rapid growth, for the 'enceinte' of 1180 proved adequate right down to the late nineteenth century, when, in response to the economic development of Westphalia and the expansion of Rhine traffic, the town began again to grow. Cologne developed varied industries, notably the manufacture of iron goods from iron brought from the Harz.

Farther up-stream, and occupying a position at the confluence of the Main with the Rhine stood the city of Mainz, 'aureum regni caput', which was outstripped in commercial importance by Cologne only in the twelfth century. A legionary fortress commanding a permanent bridge which linked it with its right-bank suburb, Mainz benefited greatly by the extension of the Roman frontier into the lower Main and Neckar basin, and the opening of routes directly from the upper Danube. Already in the Roman period, in A.D. 368, Mainz had become a bishop's see. Its position at a point where routes from Germany converged on the Rhine exposed it to continual attack in the course of the Germanic migrations, but it appears some centuries later to have recovered its old functions as a place of trade and a diocesan centre. In the sixth and seventh centuries Jewish and Syrian merchants came to the town, as also to Worms, with silks, pepper and other spices. In the ninth and tenth centuries merchants came from afar and established colonies in the towns, e.g., Frisians who brought cloth, and Italians who brought spices, silks and precious stuffs. Like Cologne, Coblenz and Strasbourg, it had its guild of keelmen who controlled water transport on

[1] It may be noted that, as Püschel has shown for western Germany generally, towns grew rapidly and extended their walls often during the eleventh, twelfth and thirteenth centuries.

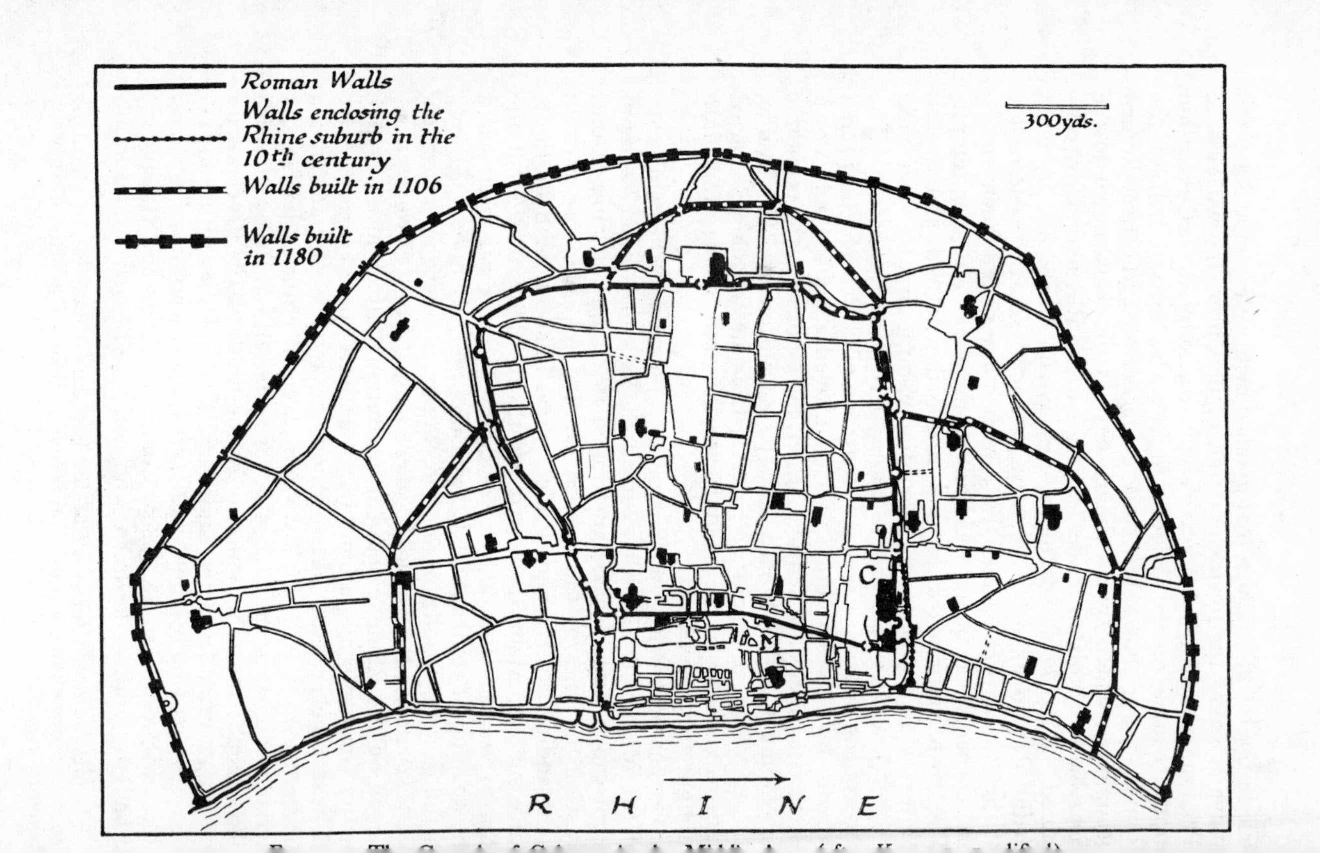
Roman Walls
Walls enclosing the Rhine suburb in the 10th century
Walls built in 1106
Walls built in 1180
300yds.
C
RHINE

the Rhine and Main. Similarly, it had a variety of industrial guilds.

South-west Germany

Upper or south-west Germany, which, like the Rhineland, developed urban life and trade under the Roman Empire, also stands out in the Middle Ages in respect of its towns and trade routes. In the Rhineland the cities stood closely related to the main highway which followed the Rhine, particularly on its left bank, and also to the subsidiary routes which approached this axis by way of a number of lateral affluents, like the Neckar, Main, Moselle, Ruhr, &c. In south-west Germany cities stood at convenient stages on the north-south roads from Italy to north-western Europe. In the west Constance lay at the junction of roads from Milan, Strasbourg and Ulm. A Roman site, Constance succeeded the old fortress town of Vindonissa as a bishop's see about the year 550. It stood in the midst of the fertile, favoured lakeside country and was a port for ships which plied on the lake. A number of former Roman cities along the southern bank of the upper Danube, such as Ulm, Donauworth, Regensburg and Passau, developed into important trading cities in the later centuries of the Middle Ages. Ulm stood at a point where the Danube became navigable, at least for part of the year, and was reached by roads from both the Septimer and Brenner passes of the Alps. The Roman fortress-city of Regensburg, which had already in the last centuries of the Roman Empire a considerable Germanic population, was probably never destroyed during the barbarian invasions. Its Roman walls remained in part, and in the eighth century it was described as 'an impregnable fortress, built of hewn stone and guarded by towers'. Like Ulm, Donauworth and Passau, it commanded a crossing of the Danube, and was a river port, but it is suggestive of the late development of the upper Danube towns that in the tenth century it was best known for its cattle market. Lower down the Danube and situated on a hill site commanding the confluence of the great Alpine river Inn, lay Passau, the Roman fortress of Batava. On the highest ground between the Danube and the Inn, formerly occupied by Roman fortifications, was built the medieval cathedral; across the Inn and outside the line of the Roman walls, grew up the mercantile suburb of Innstadt. Below Passau the Roman station of Lauriacum (now Ennsburg), standing at the junction of the Enns with the Danube, was reoccupied about the year 800, when it became the residence of a 'marcher count and a frontier station for trade with the Avars. In the

Bavarian plateau three of the more important towns may be noted. Augsburg, the old Roman colony, was situated at a crossing point on the Lech and on the highroad which ran north from the Brenner via Donauworth to Nuremberg. The bishopric town of Salzburg stood on the Salzach tributary of the Inn where, having left the mountains, it flows through a broadening valley, and occupied a site which seems to have been settled from pre-historic times onwards. It had a hill fort on the site of the Roman oppidum and an urban settlement at its foot. The deposits of salt near by at Halle and Reichenhall (' hall ', Celtic, = salt) were exploited during the Middle Ages and distributed widely within the Empire by way of the Salzach and the Danube river system. In general, therefore, the cities of south-west Germany stood on Roman sites, although sometimes, as at Kempten on the Iller, the medieval settlement occupied a site across the river from the Roman city, as was the case with medieval St. Albans in England. Kempten was a station on the Roman road between Augsburg and Chur (Coire) on the upper Rhine. The town of Munich, which was selected for a city by Henry the Lion, Duke of Saxony and Bavaria, in the second half of the twelfth century, affords a contrast to those cities which occupied Roman sites. His action was inspired by mercantile ambitions. He destroyed the bridge over the Isar at Föhring in the territory of the bishop of Freising, and built a bridge and a stronghold higher up at Munich. He hoped thus to profit from the salt trade which flowed westwards from Salzburg to Augsburg and had formerly passed via Föhring, and he was able, moreover, to deflect some of the trade which passed by way of the Brenner pass from Italy *en route* for the old-established towns like Augsburg, Regensburg and Passau. It shouid be noted that the growth of an industrial suburb outside the walls of the Roman city was a characteristic of the towns of south-western Germany, as elsewhere, and this occurred equally at Regensburg, Augsburg, Passau and Salzburg.

Inner Germany

Urban life in that part of central Europe which lay beyond the Roman frontier was belated in its development, but nevertheless it had some roots in the Roman period. Caesar and Tacitus referred to ' oppida ' which were established in Inner Germany, and Ptolemy, whose map of Germany was prepared in the mid-second century A.D., records πόλεις, which were probably ' gau ' centres and stations on the long-distance amber and salt routes which then passed through the country. It must be noted that the currents of Roman trade flowed with some strength into the barbarian lands beyond the frontier. There is good literary evidence for the first century A.D. of the amber route which joined up the Po delta with Carnuntum on the Danube, thence by way of Moravia, upper Silesia and Posen to the Vistula estuary.[1] Moreover, considerable finds of Roman coins and other objects attest the extension of Roman trade relations: e.g. into Hanover, up the Main valley, to the islands of the Netherlands, and even to those of the Baltic, where in the island of Gothland alone over 4,000 Roman coins have been found. A much-frequented trade route occupied the depressed zone from Thuringia southwards through Hesse to the lower Main and middle Rhine; and the spread of Roman coins extends as far east as the Vistula, which, it may be added, was the limit to 'Germania' given by Ptolemy. Such tokens of trade activity suggest the presence of trading settlements at fixed points. Moreover, the gau organization of the German people involved within each gau a number of settlements or 'vici' which played a definitely regional rôle as centres of military defence, of worship, of government, of communications and trade. In the Merovingian period coins reveal the presence of numerous vici within a single gau; and it is known that some of the vici at least were early fortified by rude timber stockades and ditches. It is probable that many of these early settlements, some of which were occupied by the Slavs as they pressed westwards towards the Elbe, became later the sites of medieval towns.

Thus settlements with faintly urban characteristics existed in Inner Germany in the Roman period and exercised a considerable influence on the choice of sites made later during the centuries when Germanization and Catholicism were carried eastwards from the Rhine. The selection of a number of central stations was dictated by military, ecclesiastical and administrative needs. The opportunities of frontier trade provided these stations with a trading function, whilst the insecure political conditions—e.g., dangers from the conquered population, from Northmen and from Magyars—were met by the fortification of some of the more important towns. A brief account of the foundation of German cities from the eighth century onwards has already been given.[2] It should be noted here that it was only in the later centuries of the Middle Ages that towns east of the Rhine sprang into real importance, because it was only then that the northern lands of Middle Europe were thoroughly colonized and that in

[1] Cp. Tozer, *A History of Ancient Geography*, p. 32.
[2] *Supra*, pp. 82–4.

consequence, their agricultural and natural resources were more fully exploited. The rule of those Emperors who were dukes of Saxony between 911 and 1002, did much to develop this northern part of the Empire—a region never incorporated in the former Roman Empire. Similarly with the eastward extension of the frontier to the Elbe, and thence to the Oder and even beyond, great colonial areas were brought into relation with the life of western and Mediterranean Europe. It must suffice here merely to note some representative town sites of Inner Germany and to examine the broad distribution of cities as it obtained towards the end of the Middle Ages.

The distribution of towns in north central Europe is closely related to the contrasted geographical zones which characterize the Germano-Polish lowlands east of the Lüneburger Heide. Along the southern coastlands of the North and Baltic seas stood a number of towns within a belt which is floored with good light glacial soils and includes stretches of alluvial *marschen*, which, when drained, proved productive land. The development of these maritime cities, some of which became 'Free' cities of the Empire and prospered towards the end of the Middle Ages, will be discussed later.[1] It is sufficient to note here that the cities on the Baltic coast stood on or near former Slav sites at points convenient for sea access: e.g., at the estuaries or estuary heads of rivers, at the heads of bays, and in the shelter of lagoons. Southwards of the Baltic coastal belt the country rises to the Baltic Heights, which form an undulating plateau rising in places to 1,000 feet and are covered by thick deposits of a variety of glacial materials. Much of this region is sandy, gravelly and strewn with boulders, like the Lüneburger Heide itself and the low level plain which extends westwards thereof towards the Rhine and the Frisian marshes; it is described as 'geest' and consisted to a large extent of heath (*heide*) and peat bog (*moor*). In this forbidding zone therefore urban settlement was scanty and occurred for the most part on sites along the great north-flowing rivers or at gaps. Farther south succeeds a depressed zone through which small rivers occupying broad, marshy valleys drain to the east and west, and in which again lies much sandy heath. A few towns grew up there in relation to the east-west water-routes, notably Havelberg and Brandenburg (on the Havel), Berlin, and Posen (on the Warta). Finally, still farther south, forming a bordering zone at the foot of the Hercynian mountain system, extended a belt of hilly country mantled with good loess soils. The importance of these

[1] See *infra*, pp. 339–46.

loess lands in relation to early settlement and agriculture has been noted already, and it is no less significant that in medieval Europe they were outstanding areas of urban development. The loess country often came to be distinguished by regional names, as in the case of the Hellweg in Westphalia and the Börde in Saxony, and it extended not only up the Saale valley but also west of the upper Oder in Silesia, along the upper Vistula and thence into the Galician plateaux watered by the upper Dniester system. Parts of the loess country, e.g. in Westphalia and Saxony, were noted for their agricultural prosperity, and the function of market centre to rural areas was one of the chief elements in the economy of its towns. Among these may be noted Dortmund, Soest and Paderborn in Westphalia ; Hanover, Brunswick, Leipzig, Dresden in Saxony ; Breslau and Cracow. Many of these cities occupied riverside sites and served thus as river ports and passage points. The disposition of routes running eastwards from Cologne testifies, as it added, to the importance of these new cities. Moreover, several of them, notably Brunswick and Leipzig, became focal points of routes leading northwards from the Alps and eastwards from the Rhine. Cracow, the capital and university city of the Polish kingdom, occupied a similar position at the intersection of routes, and it was reached both by Venetian traders and Armenians, who made their way up the Dniester or Pruth valleys.

Résumé

In short, towards the end of the Middle Ages, the Holy Roman Empire was studded with some 3,000 towns, which showed a varied regional distribution and conformed broadly to two types. There were, on the one hand, as Bücher noted [1]metropolitan cities, such as the bigger sea ports and political and regional capitals, which enjoyed long distance relationships and, on the other, market towns with very restricted local relationships. The former group included in 1500 about 12–15 towns with more than 10,000 inhabitants, and 150 with between 1,000 and 2,000.[2] The latter, numbering about 2,800, had populations ranging only between 100 and 1,000, and are comparable with nucleated villages of to-day. These towns each had their local area of influence which varied from 40–50 square miles in south-western

[1] *Bücher's Industrial Evolution*, trans. Wickett, pp. 119–21.

[2] See R. E. Dickinson *The Development and Distribution of the Medieval German Town*, G., vol. 27 (1942) and *The Morphology of the Medieval German Town*, G. R., vol. 35 (1945). The ground plans of these medieval towns, which assumed various forms, is usually still recognizable and provided the nucleus around which the towns grew, notably after 1870 with the advent of the Industrial Age.

Germany to 60–85 square miles in the centre and north-east and to 100–170 square miles in the east, where town development had less advanced and population density was relatively low. In each case the area served by these towns was such that a peasant living on the periphery of the region could reach the town and return by nightfall. The peasants brought in their produce for exchange for the manufactured goods made in the towns.

It is possible, thanks to the advance which was made in the art of cartography in the sixteenth and seventeenth centuries, to define and to classify the 'lay-outs' or ground plans of the chief cities of Europe at the end of the Middle Ages. The early seventeenth-century plans of cities in the Rhineland collected by Werdenhagen and an excellent atlas[1] of sixteenth-century Belgian towns, reveal a state of things which had not drastically changed since the end of the Middle Ages. Towns were always girt around by walls or water or both, and in Belgium, for example, a broad water girdle was sometimes the sole defence. The disposition of the town is often closely related with certain features of the geographical setting. Thus in Belgium there are towns strung out along a highway, as at Leuze; towns confined to the high ground within a loop of a river, as at Limbourg; aligned along the sea-coast, as at Ostend; or seated astride an important river, at the head of the estuary, as at Antwerp, or at passage points up-stream, as at Tournai. Sometimes, as at Lille and Lierre in Belgium, the *enceinte* of the town was a watercourse. Broadly speaking, the walls of Belgian towns in the sixteenth century were the walls of the late medieval period, and in some cases, as at Poperinghe, the built-up area appears to have shrunk by the sixteenth century, the economic activity of these towns having been diminished under the stress of civil wars.

The Alpine Passes

Already before the road building of the Roman Empire the Alpine passes had permitted entry into Italy, as was well illustrated by the advent of the Celts into Lombardy *c.* 350 B.C. and by Hannibal's famous march in 220 B.C. 'There is no need of Gods or heroes to help in crossing the Alps', wrote Polybius, and Hannibal's achievement showed that the difficulties were less those presented by geography than the inexperience of guides, the bad season and the hostility of the inhabitants of the valleys. From the time of the Emperor Augustus road construction was effected across the Alps at several points in order to serve above all military and political needs. In the western Alps the roads

[1] *Atlas des Villes de la Belgique au XVIe siècle*, 2 vols., n.d.

by the two St. Bernard passes, by the Mont Genevre and along the Provence coast were the most used. In the central Alps there were routes via the Septimer and Splügen, whilst in the eastern Alps, where passages were lowest, the Brenner, the Pontebba and the Birnbaumer (Pear Tree) passes were the chief. There is no valid ground for believing that after the fall of Rome trans-Alpine communication was interrupted: in fact, it is clear that barbarian immigrants and conquerors in Italy, Ostrogoths, Huns and Lombards, utilized roads through the Alpine passes. The Roman state post between Italy and Spain was continued by the Ostrogothic rulers of Italy in the sixth century; Lombard merchants are known to have been present in the seventh century at the fairs of St. Denis near Paris; Roman provincials from Noricum sought safety from the advancing Baioarii by crossing into Venetia by way of the Pontebba pass in 488; and there is evidence to show that the Brenner was used in the sixth century. In other words, the Alpine route system in the Middle Ages followed to a large extent that elaborated by Rome, although there is some evidence of medieval road-making, bridge building and the founding of hospices. Incentives to travel in the Middle Ages came with the opening up of interior Germany, the ecclesiastical organization of the Catholic Church from its centre at Rome, the commercial enterprise of the Italian cities, and the political union, within the Holy Roman Empire, of northern Italy and Germany in 962.

The relative utility of the many Alpine routes and the way in which the traffic of traders, pilgrims and armies was distributed between the various passes, were the resultants of a number of factors, geographical, historical and political. Certainly the position of the passes in relation to important termini of travel, together with conditions of physical geography, differentiated fairly sharply the possible routes. On the other hand, the Alpine roads bequeathed by Rome, although doubtless they deteriorated in the course of the early Middle Ages, must have served to a considerable extent to determine the flow of traffic. Finally, a whole set of politico-economic conditions, which varied continually according to time and place, must have exerted a marked influence on the choice of routes. Such conditions related to the state of political relations, the security afforded, the amount in dues demanded, and the extent to which roads and bridges were maintained and hospices provided.

The passes of the Alps may be grouped under three heads: those in the west, the centre and the east. In the western Alps the Mont Genèvre, the Great St. Bernard and the Mont Cenis passes were the most frequented in the Middle Ages. The physical factors which favoured these passes were less considerations of elevation [1] than those of position and convenience. Thus the relatively low Argentière and Tenda passes were not important because they stood too far south to serve international traffic between Italy and north-west Europe ; moreover, the Argentière route, which led via the Durance valley to Aix and Avignon, was outflanked by the sea route to St. Gilles on the western arm of the Rhône delta and also by the littoral route through the Genoese Riviera and Provence. The Mont Genèvre, Great St. Bernard and Mont Cenis passes, on the other hand, had important positional advantages in relation to valley routes which permitted passage at right angles to the direction of the mountain chain and, moreover, they stood in a more or less direct line between Piedmont and those regions of north-western Europe, like Champagne, Flanders and the Rhineland, in which industry and trade were concentrated. These three passes were thus essentially fitted to serve international, as distinct from merely local, needs. They were approached from the Piedmont city of Turin by divergent routes which were controlled by the towns of Susa and Aosta, which stood respectively in the upper Dora Riparia and Dora Baltea valleys and were analogous in position and function. The first commanded the approach up to both the Mont Genèvre and Mont Cenis passes, and the second was the key to both the Great and Little St. Bernard. The Mont Genèvre carried travellers *en route* not only for the lower Rhône by way of the Durance but also for Lyons by way of Grenoble—a traverse, however, which involved the negotiation of another pass. The Mont Cenis, which stood near the heads of the Susa-Arc valleys, offered a choice of routes to Valence, Lyons and Lake Geneva. It had, moreover, a physical advantage over the Great St. Bernard in that it provided a route towards central France which was not only direct but avoided a long and rather difficult passage across the Jura ranges. Even so, it was the Great St. Bernard which carried the greatest share of traffic—of pilgrims, armies and traders—in the western Alps, on journeys between Basle and Lombardy, notwithstanding certain physical difficulties which it presented. The Little St. Bernard, so much used in the Roman period, e.g. by Julius Caesar, became relatively little frequented ; whilst the Mont Cenis pass became important for the first time in the Middle Ages. Similarly, the Simplon route, although it involved diffi-

[1] The elevations of the chief passes (in feet) are as follows : Argentière, 6,545 ; Tenda, 6,145 ; Mont Genèvre, 6,083 ; Great St. Bernard, 8,111 ; Mont Cenis, 6,893 ; Simplon, 6,892.

culties, came into use mainly after 1250; it connected Milan with Dijon and crossed the Jura by the Jougne pass to Pontarlier. It was during the later centuries of the Middle Ages, particularly after the year 1000, that the traffic on the western passes of the Alps assumed large proportions. In fact, for some two centuries prior to 972, travel was much interrupted and endangered by the presence of Arab raiders, who had their base at La Garde Fresnet on the Provence coast and ravaged throughout the Alpine valleys as far inland as Lake Geneva.

Among a number of routes across the central Alps the Septimer and St. Gotthard became the most important. Their chief value lay in their position in relation to central Lombardy and Basle, whence routes continued northwards by road and by river through the Rhineland or north-westwards towards Champagne and Flanders. In Lombardy Milan became the greatest mercantile city and focus of routes diverging into the central Alps, whilst Piacenza on the Po was a centre for roads across the Apennines into Tuscany. The chief routes northwards from Milan reached Como, whence travellers continued either across the lake to Riva and thence to Chiavenna, or by road via the Mont Cenere passage to Bellinzona at the head of Lake Maggiore. Both Chiavenna and Bellinzona had great strategical importance as essential route foci: from the first the way lay open to the Septimer, Splügen and Julier-Maloja passes, and from the second to those of St. Gotthard, Lukmanier, Bernardino. The Septimer, which was held by the Abbey of Chur, was at first the most frequented, although in common with all the other passes except the St. Gotthard it involved a considerable détour on the route to Basle, by way of Chur on the upper Rhine; the route thence ran via Sargans, the Walen See and Lake Zürich, the navigation of which formed an essential part of the journey. The use of the Bernardino, Splügen and Septimer passes involved a difficult passage through the Via Mala on the 'posterior' Rhine to the north, and this passage was not improved until the fifteenth century. Moreover, the use of the St. Gotthard awaited the construction on its northern side of a bridge at the Schöllenen gorge and a valley road along the Urserenthal into the Reuss valley. Thus the so-called 'opening' of the St. Gotthard at a much-debated date in the early decades of the thirteenth century,[1] refers not to the actual pass-way but to the removal of physical obstacles presented on its northern approach. When this had been done the St. Gotthard route sprang into first-rate importance, inasmuch as it stood on the direct line between Milan and Basle, and, unlike

[1] See J. E. Tyler, *The Alpine Passes, 962–1250*, ch. IX.

the Septimer, avoided the détour via Chur and also the passages across the lakes of Como, Walen and Zürich. It is not surprising therefore that the St. Gotthard route served above all for merchants and their wares: the name Val Levantina, which attaches to the Ticino valley, testifies to the origin of perhaps the chief commodities carried northwards towards this pass. In general, notwithstanding their centrality of position, which made them potentially useful to Italian cities between Genoa on the one hand and Venice on the other, the passes of the central Alps did not achieve outstanding importance in the last centuries of the Middle Ages. The reasons for this were largely of a political order: the fact that the Emperors had sufficient control over the western passes and over the Brenner system to the east, and that after 1176, their antagonism towards the Lombard cities rendered the central passes unsafe.

Finally, in the eastern Alps the passes of the Brenner system completely overshadowed in importance other frequented passways, e.g., the Pontebba, Plöcken and Birnbaumer. The Brenner itself was a bottle-neck from which were offered a wide choice of routes both northwards and southwards. Its geographical position was much improved by the thirteenth century when the German cities of the Baltic were developing fast and when the frontier of the Empire reached to the Oder and beyond. From the Brenner northwards the road ran to the Inn bridge at Innsbruck, whence routes diverged to many passage points on the Danube, from which they continued in direct lines towards the cities of the upper Main, or across the accessible Fichtel Gebirge to those of the northern plains and coastlands. In the south Verona, situated astride the Adige where it has left the mountains and debouched into the Italian plain, held the main approach to the Brenner, but alternate approaches did exist, both from the east and the west, notably that which led from Venice up the Brenta to Trent on the Adige. In short, it was the Brenner which was most used by Imperial armies and Emperors *en route* for Italy and also in trade relations between south Germany and Venice. It had a number of physical advantages: above all its low elevation—4,495 feet—and consequent escape from heavy winter snows; the ample food supplies from its productive country-side; and finally the wide choice of routes which it commanded.

In sum, the Alpine system, despite the real difficulties which it placed in the way of travel—stiff gradients, avalanches, winter snows, long détours, &c.—played a part of first-rate importance in the system of communications of medieval Europe. The ecclesiastical organization of Catholic Christendom, the political unity of the Holy Roman Empire and the scope of international trade, and pilgrim traffic even from as far afield as Iceland, showed alike an essential dependence on the Alpine pass-ways. Hence some efforts, though small-scale and piece-meal, were made to construct or improve roads, to build and maintain bridges, and to establish hospices for the convenience of travellers and beasts of burden. The latter consisted chiefly of mules and asses, laden with packs. Even the rigours of winter did not cause that cessation of trade characteristic of the sea-ways, for, as Mlle. Sclafert indicates [1] in the case of the Mont Cenis, roads were to some extent cleared of snow and considerable traffic actually passed through in the height of winter. As is well known, the products carried northwards across the Alps consisted largely of Oriental goods—silks and cottons, spices, dye woods and drugs; Levant goods, e.g., alum; and fine textiles and metal wares made in the Italian cities. In return wool, cloth and linen were brought into Italy from the north. It is above all after the 1st Crusade of 1096 that this traffic grew in volume, but there is some evidence to suggest that already in the tenth century Italian merchants carried these products into France, and that German merchants came to Venice to buy them. In any case the political circumstances of the tenth century were everywhere adverse to extensive trade: the Moslems still ruled the Mediterranean and harassed the western passes; the Magyars ravaged throughout Bavaria until they were permanently expelled in 955; the Northmen were still troublesome in the north in the early decades of the century; and finally the Italian cities, e.g. Amalfi, Pisa and Venice, were only just springing into real importance as distributors of wares brought from the Levant. To a small extent it should be noted that the passes were outflanked by the sea route, e.g. from Genoa and Pisa to the Rhône delta, whence traffic was carried either up the Rhône waterway, which was by no means easy, or by road.

[1] See the note in the *G.J.*, March 1934, p. 253.

PART II

THE POLITICAL GEOGRAPHY OF EUROPE

' Il n'y a plus rien de " donné tout fait " à l'homme par la nature, d'imposé à la politique par la géographie. Il y a adaptation de l'homme à des possibilités seulement. . . .
Qui dit limite naturelle dit limite prédestinée—idéal à conquérir et à réaliser ' L. FEBVRE

CHAPTER VII

EARLY STATE-BUILDING IN WESTERN AND CENTRAL EUROPE

IN the eastern half of the Roman Empire the immigration of 'barbarian' peoples—German, Slav, and Bulgar—was effected without immediate changes in the political geography, since the Empire succeeded there, temporarily at least, in preserving its political organization and in absorbing or controlling these new settlers.[1] In the west, however, the Roman political organization was slowly undermined as a result of 'the wandering of the peoples', although it is true that the new barbarian rulers were often granted Roman titles and that in theory some semblance of imperial power lingered on. Nevertheless, in the place of a single political structure there emerged a set of Germanic kingdoms. The seeds of these new state units were sown by the barbarian conquests and settlement not only in the existing Romanized territories but also in the non-Roman lands beyond the Rhine and Danube frontiers. The emergent states were continually changing in area and often short-lived, and a study of their transformation has only slight links with geography, since it was conditioned by human factors, above all by the relative military strength of different peoples and the Germanic policy of partition among the sons of rulers. Even so, one thing stands out clearly. The former Roman scheme of administrative division into provinces within the western part of the Empire was considerably modified though not effaced, and new political patterns were formed some of which have remained remarkably stable throughout subsequent historical time. Further, the nomenclature of the state and state divisions in western and middle Europe was largely established during the centuries which immediately followed the fall of Rome. It is not necessary here to review fully the tangled political geography of the early Middle Ages, and it must suffice to examine the processes which led to the creation of the Empire of Charles the Great, the subsequent partitions of which had permanent effects on the political geography of Europe.

[1] See *infra*, pp. 173 and 176.

The Germanic state-builders of western Europe were collections of tribes which had federated together to form nations or peoples. Thus the tribal names of the Germans as recorded by Tacitus in the first century A.D. had almost entirely disappeared from the map by the third and fourth centuries, since tribes which occupied adjacent territories had merged together into larger groups, occupying wider and continuous areas. Of these new nations the Franks, the Alamanns, the Burgundians and the Goths may be cited as typical, and it is with their settlement and conquests that the re-shaping of the political map is mainly concerned. By the end of the fifth century these new patterns had achieved a certain fixity on the soil, which it is

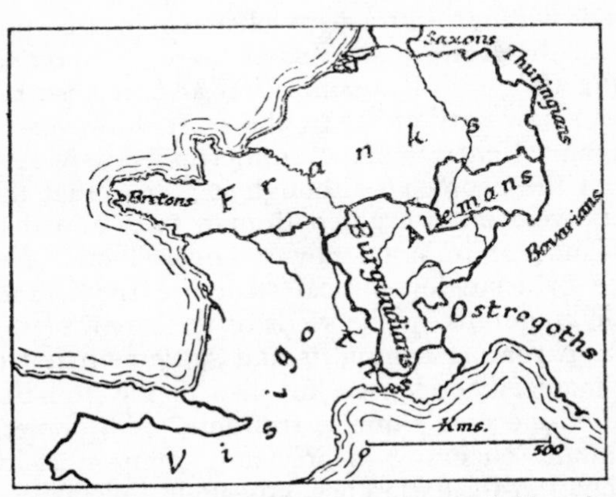

FIG. 24.—Gaul and Neighbouring Lands, *c.* A.D. 506 (data from Longnon)

possible to analyse geographically (Fig. 24). Their significance can best be grasped if the separate nations concerned are dealt with in turn, and if attention is centred on two geographical aspects; first, the nuclear areas of the respective states, and second, their maximum territorial extent.

The Franks

Of all the German peoples in western Europe the Franks were destined to play the most striking part on the political stage. The first historical mention of the Franks records their establishment in the neighbourhood of Mainz: moreover, the so-called Peutinger map,[1] the original of which can be attributed to the third century A.D., describes the land on the right bank of the

[1] The Peutinger map so called is a thirteenth-century copy, preserved at the Imperial Library in Vienna.

Rhine down even to its estuary as 'Francia'. At a somewhat later stage the Franks are divided into three groups: the Salians, the Ripuarians, and the Chatti—the two latter being sometimes regarded as one group. The Salians, whose immigration into the Low Countries has already been examined in some detail,[1] occupied at first the low country on the right bank of the lowest channels of the Rhine, whence by the year 431 they had extended and settled in northern Gaul as far west as the Somme. The Ripuarian Franks, who dwelt to the south of the Salians, captured the Roman town of Cologne *c.* A.D. 463 and made it their chief head-quarters. The area of their original habitat extended northwards to the Rhine town of Neuss, and southwards beyond the Ahr, a left-bank tributary of the Rhine which came down from the Eifel plateau: whilst westwards it included the districts around Malmedy and Aachen. Finally, the Chatti dwelt to the east of the Ripuarians and had their earliest homes in the region of Hesse. Their territories came to stretch across the middle Rhine from the line of the Moselle valley and the Diemel tributary of the Weser in the north to the rivers Murg and Enz, which drain down from the northern edge of the Black Forest, in the south. To the east the Chatti branch of the Franks pushed across the Werra river and even through the Thuringian Forest; they pushed also through the Franconian Forest to the upper waters of the Main, and southwards thence into the basin of its affluent the Regnitz. In other words, the Franks held the dominant offensive position on the threshold of Roman Gaul. Above all they had in their possession the lower Rhine plain in the north, and in the south a broad region in which wooded upland plateau alternated with river valleys and lowlands of great agricultural potentialities: notably, the basins of the Main and Neckar, and the Rhine plain above Mainz.

The advance of the Franks into Roman Gaul and the area of their settlement there is indicated broadly by their capture of Roman towns. In the north Tournai on the middle Scheldt was made the capital of the Salians about the year 431, and the area in which their settlements were made extended across the lower Rhine from the Zuider Zee to beyond the great Roman highway between Cologne and Boulogne. The Ripuarians, who adjoined the Salians to the south, occupied the cities of the Rhine, like Neuss and Cologne, whilst the Chatti occupied Mainz and Coblenz, as well as Trèves and Metz on the Moselle. It was Clovis, king of the Salian Franks, who brought to an end Roman power in Gaul. The territorial remnant of that power was the

[1] Cp. *supra*, Chapter III, pp. 66–70.

central part of the Paris basin—the region between the Somme, the Seine and the Loire—a region favoured by converging routes and food-producing plains. The victory of Clovis over the Roman forces at Soissons in 486 enabled the Franks widely to extend their territories in northern Gaul; in fact, their power was extended to the Loire. The broad belt of flooded land around the junction of the Cher and the Loire formed part of the frontier zone between the Franks and the Visigoths, as it had done earlier between Visigothic and Roman territory.[1] Moreover, a union between the three branches of the Franks was effected in the year 507, and in consequence a great Frankish state was constituted stretching across the Rhine and reaching to the Channel. The capital city of this state was Paris, to which Clovis moved from Tours in 508. Within this region the Franks were not only rulers but settlers. But it must be noted that within Gaul they settled down amongst a Romano-Gallic population who were both numerically stronger and better civilized than themselves, and where in consequence a Romance language, not their own Germanic tongue, came to prevail. In contrast, in the eastern portion of their state, along both sides of the Rhine, where Germanic peoples had been long established, their German speech persisted.

The Alamanns

The Alamanns, who are first heard of in the year A.D. 213 when they came into contact with the Romans, were, like the Franks, a confederation of German tribes. Their original homeland was in the basin of the upper Main, whence they moved gradually westwards into the Agri Decumates, the Roman frontier region beyond the Rhine and the upper Danube.[2] After about A.D. 282 they established themselves there permanently, and in the fourth century the land of their settlement, called 'Alamannia', stretched eastwards from the Rhine bridge at Mainz to the Güns tributary of the Danube and reached in the south as far as Lake Constance. In the course of the fifth century they crossed the Rhine and occupied the Palatinate, Alsace and the eastern valleys of the Vosges; further, they occupied the plain of the lower Main, the country south of the Neckar, and pushed into north Switzerland westwards to the Jura. The town of Worms and others in the Main valley are described in the fifth century as Alamannic: they were captured in 496, however, by Clovis, king of the Franks, who inflicted a crushing defeat on the Alamanns

[1] Longnon, *Géographie de la Gaule au VIe Siècle*, p. 159.
[2] Cp. *supra*, Chapter II, pp. 31–4.

near Toul. In result the boundaries of the Alamannic kingdom were moved back southwards to the Murg and Enz rivers. Somewhat later the Alamanns made settlements in Bavaria between the rivers Iller and Lech. At their greatest extent their territories stretched eastwards to the Lech and northwards from the Alps to the Saarne and Aar rivers of Switzerland, across the Jura to the Vosges, and to the line of Murg-Enz and the Altmühl-Wernitz. The conquering Franks under Clovis shattered and absorbed the Alamannic kingdom; the name 'Alamannia' survived, however, since it was used in the twelfth century, together with 'Terra Teutonica' and 'Teutonia', to describe the whole German kingdom, and it persists in the French 'Allemagne' to this day.

The Goths

The Goths, one of the more numerous German peoples, moved south-eastwards from the north German plain to the lowlands north of the Black Sea. Advancing westwards from this region to the lower Danube, some of them settled within the Balkan lands of the Byzantine Empire, whilst others moved up the valleys of the Drave and Save and thence into Italy. The Ostrogoths, as they were called, established a kingdom in Italy, which they ruled from the old Roman capital of Ravenna. Another branch of the Goths, who became known as the West or Visigoths, crossed the western Alps and conquered a large part of southern Gaul, which they governed from Toulouse. In the year 413 they took possession of the cities of Valence on the lower Rhône, the 'gap town' of Toulouse and the seaport of Narbonne. In its initial stage, about the year A.D. 410, the kingdom of the Visigoths extended between the Atlantic, the Garonne and the Pyrenees. From this base they conquered in a few years the whole of Aquitaine, and also the town of Poitiers, which commanded the Roman route northwards to the Loire. Further, they crossed the Pyrenees and succeeded by the year 457 in conquering almost the whole of Spain. Shortly after this they captured definitively the town of Narbonne and also Nîmes, Marseilles and Arles, and consolidated their rule over Low Languedoc, the lower Rhône and even Provence south of the Durance. At its greatest extent, at the end of the fifth century, the Visigothic state embraced southern Gaul between the Loire, the lower Rhône, the Atlantic, the Gulf of Lion and the Pyrenees, whilst only a part of Spain withstood their advance. In the northwest from the lower Tagus to Galicia earlier German immigrants, the Suevi, escaped conquest, whilst in the western Pyrenees and the Cantabrian mountains the Basques preserved their independence. It was as an advance post against these sturdy mountaineers, descendants of the Iberi of Caesar, that the Visigoths built in the year 581 their only town in Spain, namely Vitoria, which stands above the Zadorra river, the valley of which carried the coast road from Gaul down to the upper Ebro. The advance of the Visigoths to the Loire brought them to the southern frontier of the Frankish kingdom, and in the warfare that ensued between the two peoples the Visigothic forces suffered decisive defeats. In particular, they were defeated by Clovis in the year 507: having forded the Vienne river, though it was in flood, he fought them at Vouillé, which stands to the north-west of Poitiers on the broad gap which unites the basins of Paris and of Aquitaine. Not only did this prevent the progress of the Visigoths into the Paris basin, but it marked the recession of the Visigothic kingdom. It shrank back towards the south, and by about the middle of the sixth century contained in Gaul only the region known as Septimania or Gothia, which lies between the Cevennes, the lower Rhône, the Pyrenees and the Mediterranean. It is significant that in the writings of Gregory of Tours this region is also called 'Spain': thus the division of Gaul and Spain by the water-parting of the Pyrenees was not clearly defined in the sixth century as it was during the Roman Empire, but was analogous to that which obtained in pre-Roman times, when, as Strabo records,[1] Iberia began at the Rhône. Nor did the advance of the Arabs and Moors into Spain and Gaul and the consequent overthrow of the Visigothic kingdom on both sides of the Pyrenees, re-establish a political frontier along that mountain zone. The swift success of the Moslems wiped the Visigothic state from the political map in the second decade of the eighth century.[2] Nor did the Visigothic settlement in Gaul and Spain leave any impression on the language, since, relatively few in number, the Visigoths were absorbed into the existing Romanized population.

The Burgundians

The Burgundians, another German people, established themselves in south-eastern Gaul, and gave their name to a number of distinct territories during the Middle Ages. At the beginning of the fifth century they occupied the Rhine plain around Worms, but they suffered defeats in turn at the hands of the Romano-Gallic forces and of the Huns led by Attila. After this latter

[1] *Geography*, Bk. III, ch. IV, sect. 19.
[2] See *infra*, Chapter IX, p. 202.

disaster the Roman authorities granted the surviving remnant of the Burgundian people lands in what are now the départements of Haute-Savoie and of the Ain, the bulk of which consisted of the 'civitas' of Geneva. From this base astride the Rhône between lake Geneva and its junction with the Saône the Burgundians moved down the Rhône and occupied Lyons about the year 470; thence they pushed farther down the Rhône and up the Saône, where they captured Chalon and Langres. The Burgundian kingdom reached its greatest extent at the end of the fifth century by which time it included almost the whole of the Rhône basin southwards to the Durance river, whilst it extended northwards to the Doubs and the upper waters of the Saône and Seine and westwards to the upper Loire. Further, the kingdom stretched at this time across the wooded solitudes of the Jura, which formerly separated the settlements of the Burgundians from those of the Alamanns, and included the whole of the Swiss plateau. That the valley of the Rhône formed the essential axis of the Burgundian state is indicated by the location of its capital cities along the banks of that river—at Geneva, Lyons and Vienne. As in the case of the Visigoths, so in that of the Burgundians, their territories were conquered and absorbed into the Frankish state. If the Burgundian state thus disappeared by the year 534, it was nevertheless later re-constituted in the ninth century, although it did not survive the Middle Ages. The Burgundian name remained attached, however, to two parts of the original kingdom: to the duchy of Burgundy, a fief of the French crown, which lay for the most part west of the Saône, and to the county of Burgundy, a fief of the Holy Roman Empire, which lay between the Saône and the Jura. The so-called Burgundian state of the fifteenth and sixteenth centuries, the territorial basis of which lay on the Scheldt, Meuse, Rhine and Saône, is an interesting instance of the vagaries of geographical nomenclature.[1]

The Bretons

In one part of Gaul, namely in the peninsular region of Brittany, the German invaders of Gaul scarcely succeeded in establishing their rule. In this remote province, where Roman influences were much weaker than in southern Gaul, Celtic-speaking immigrants from oversea came in the fourth and fifth centuries to strengthen the Celtic element of its Romano-Celtic population. These immigrants came from western Britain, their

[1] See *infra*, Chapter XII, pp. 254–5.

migration being stimulated in some measure by the entry of the Anglo-Saxons into the English lowlands. In the course of their settlement in Brittany, a country which had very much in common geographically with the maritime regions of western Britain, the Britons founded four kingdoms. One was the kingdom of Cornouailles around Quimper in the south-west; another was built up around Léon in the north-west, whilst the other two stood farther east. The Bretons waged wars in turn with the Visigoths and the Franks, and recognized the suzerainty of the latter in the sixth century. Subsequently they regained their independence within territories defined by the sea-coasts on three sides and the Vilaine river in the east.

The Danes

The original home of the Danes seems to have been southern Sweden whence they moved west and south into the islands of Zealand, Falster and Laaland, the latter forming at an early stage the heart of their kingdom. When the Angles had migrated from Jutland to the English lowlands the Danes moved into the peninsula and also into the island of Fünen. They settled in Jutland as far south as the broad belt of forest which lay astride the Eider valley, whilst they retained control of several districts in what is now southern Sweden, namely, Scania, Halland and Blekinge, as well as the island of Bornholm. Moreover, the fact that the Danish kingdom maintained its hold on these lands helps to explain its political importance in the Middle Ages, since the territories in Sweden were valuable both on account of their location along the Baltic and the Sound, and also on account of their lowland character and agricultural potentialities. Incidentally, the name Jutland recalls the Jutes, who according to literary tradition were established in the peninsula. Even so, recent archaeological research [1] suggests that the Jutes who moved into southern Britain had their homes in country astride the lower Rhine.

The Saxons, Bavarians and others

The term 'Saxony', like that of 'Burgundy', has had many geographical interpretations throughout history. At the time of Ptolemy the Saxons, whose name is derived from the word *sachs*, a sword, were settled in Holstein and across the lower Elbe. In the late third century, together with the Franks, they made themselves feared as sea robbers along the North Sea coastlands

[1] Joliffe, *Pre-Feudal England : the Jutes*, p. 100.

and along the coasts of western Gaul. At this time the Saxon people comprised a confederation of German tribes which occupied the hilly country north of the Harz and between the Saale and the Rhine : those to the west of the Weser were known as the Westphalians (' falah '—a field or plain), those to the east of it, the Eastphalians. On their northern flank stood the Frisians, who were settled along the coastlands between the Weser and the Rhine, and at a later stage, in the ninth century, along the western coast of, and in the islands off, Schleswig between Husum and Tondern. To the south of the Saxon territory stood the Franks along the Rhine and Thuringians, whose lands lay between the Saale and the Werra and extended southwards to the upper Main. Finally, in the south beyond the Danube and kingdom of the Alamanns the Roman province of Raetia was settled by Germanic peoples. The German immigrants into Raetia were the Marcomanni who had long been settled in Bohemia. In the sixth century they are referred to as the Baioarii, a name which was derived from the Celtic Boii, who preceded them as settlers in Bohemia. They moved out from Bohemia into the Nordgau ; this region lies to the west of the Bohemian mountains and is drained by the River Naab, which enters the Danube at Regensburg. Thence they crossed the Danube and settled the Bavarian plateau southwards to the Alps and eastwards to the Enns. Later, from the eighth century onwards they pushed farther eastwards and settled in the Alpine march-lands of Austria, Carinthia and Styria. Finally, it may be noted that Bavaria took its name from these German immigrants, a name which is etymologically akin to that of Bohemia (' the home of the Boii ').

Gaul and Germany about the year A.D. 500

An examination of the political map of Gaul in the year 506 (Fig. 24) shows the disposition of the German kingdoms before the important changes brought about by the battle of Vouillé and the consequent predominance of the Franks. At the accession in the year 481 of Clovis, the first Merovingian king of the Franks, German kingdoms covered the whole of Gaul except Brittany, and extended farther across the Alps, the Pyrenees and the Rhine. Even when the Franks had overthrown all the neighbouring states, Gaul tended to remain a politically divided land, owing to the Germanic practice of dividing lands equally amongst all the male heirs. It is both unnecessary and unprofitable to discuss in turn the many successive partitions of the Frankish kingdom after the death of Clovis in 511, since they afford little of geographical interest.[1] It is worthy of note that during the Merovingian period, which lasted on until the latter half of the eighth century, Gaul was often divided into three or four kingdoms without any attempt being made to respect the distribution of nationalities and languages, administrative limits or even geographical convenience. Thus the several kingdoms were often discontinuous territorially, consisting of scattered blocks of land which in the aggregate made up roughly equal shares. The attempt to secure equality in the value of all lands including conquered territories involved on many occasions the division of the truly Frankish lands north of the Loire. Thus in 511, on the death of Clovis, and again in 561, these northern lands where Frankish settlement and power were strongest, were shared between four heirs, but it was in these parts of their respective kingdoms that the four rulers established their capitals, the four cities being Soissons, Paris, Orleans and Rheims.

It is important, further, to note that the term 'Germany' has come to acquire a new geographical content. Whether this term is held to include all the country of German settlement or of German conquest, or whether it is restricted to those lands where German cultural influences were in the ascendant, it is clear that the term applies to a region different from that designated by the Romans as 'Germania'. To the Roman geographers this term had two distinct meanings: the broader concept, as expressed in the maps of Ptolemy, defined the region between the Rhine, the Danube and the Vistula; the narrower concept, however, denoted the two provinces on the left bank of the Rhine, Germania Prima and Germania Secunda, which had their chief cities respectively at Mainz and Cologne. In any case, however it may be conceived retrospectively, Germany was still in the sixth century a geographical and not a political expression. Moreover, it had pushed its bounds well to the west of the Rhine and to the south of the Danube, although in the east, as will be seen later, its bounds had receded from the Vistula to the line of the Elbe-Saale rivers.

The Slavs

The migrations and settlement of the Slavs in middle and eastern Europe were no less important in their effect on the political map than those of the German peoples. History is silent on the early location and movements of the Slavs, who,

[1] The authoritative maps for this period are those of Longnon in his *Atlas Historique de la France* and his *Géographie de la Gaule au VIe Siècle*.

on the basis of language, form a unit but not a race. There is some ground for placing their original homeland in Polesia, the broad region of the Pripet marshes,[1] and in the early centuries A.D. they seem to have occupied the Galician plateau. It is clear, however, that they moved westwards [2] into those parts of central Europe which were vacated by the German peoples in the course of the Völkerwanderung. Prior to this latter movement the Germans were established between the Rhine and the Vistula, beyond which the Slavs dwelt. By the end of the fifth century, however, when the Germans had founded kingdoms in Spain, Italy, Gaul and even beyond the eastern frontier of Gaul, the Slavs had penetrated westwards as far as the lower Elbe and its tributary the Saale, whilst large and small Slav groups had settled even west of this line. It is not certainly known to what extent, if at all, German peoples may have remained in this region after the Völkerwanderung, but the Slavs appear to have formed at least the bulk of the population. Those who colonized the country between the Elbe and the line of the Oder-Bober rivers were called Polaben ('Po'—on, 'Labe'—Elbe); they were known too as Wends, a name which was applied to them by the Germans to the west and is derived from the word Venedi, applied formerly by Tacitus to their predecessors in this region. The Slavs who dwelt to the east of the Oder-Bober line formed the Polish group, and settled broadly throughout the Vistula basin between the Baltic in the north and the Sudetes mountains in the south. (The name 'Pole' is derived from the Slav word 'polje', which means a plain or field.) There were two main branches of the Polish Slavs: the Pomeranians, who were settled between the lower Oder and the lower Vistula southwards to the River Netze, the name of whom indicates their maritime location: 'Po'—on, 'morje'—sea; the other was the Masurians, who occupied land on both sides of the middle Vistula. Finally, a third major division of the Slav peoples was formed by the Czechs, the Moravians, the Slovakians and the Slovenes. Peoples of this group moved southwards across the passes of the Carpathians into Bohemia and Moravia when these lands had been vacated by the Baioarii and the Lombards. The Slovaks and Moravians settled respectively in the western

[1] For the eastward movement of the Slavs and their colonization in Russia, see *infra*, Chapter X, pp. 215–18. Similarly their movement into the Balkan peninsula is discussed in Chapter VIII, p. 178.

[2] Cp. Chapter XIV by Dr. Peisker, in the *Cam. Med. Hist.*, vol. II. The evidence derived from the study of their early language is consistent with their having occupied a region of this geographical character.

Carpathians and the basin of the March or Morava, from which the former took their name. The Czechs established themselves in various groups farther west in Bohemia, their most important group occupying the valley of the Vltava (Moldau). These immigrations and colonial movements were still proceeding in the sixth century. Meanwhile, about the year 568, when the Lombards had moved south from Pannonia on the middle Danube across the Alps into Italy, the eastern Alpine valleys stood open to the Avars, a Uralo-Altaic people, whose advance drove forward and brought in its train large numbers of Slavs who settled within the mountains as far west as the Inn.

In general, the Slav peoples occupied scattered agricultural settlements and were at first loosely organized. Since their territories adjoined those of the German peoples in the west and since, further, they were but scantily settled, they provided an inviting field at a later stage for German colonization. Although they did not found states for some centuries the Slavs were divided up into a number of groups and regions within which national consciousness and political organization were able eventually to develop. Even by the year A.D. 600, however, the Slavs had made a permanent modification of the map. They occupied a broad and continuous belt across central Europe from the Elbe to the Vistula and between the Baltic, Black and Adriatic Seas, since—as will be noted later [1]—they had extended their settlements south of the Save and Drave and south of the lower Danube into the Balkan lands of the Byzantine or East Roman Empire. It should be observed, nevertheless, that the geographical continuity of the Slav lands was broken in two places. To the north of the lower Danube, in the plain of Wallachia, in the plateaux of Moldavia and in the Transylvanian basin, despite some Slavic settlement, the Romano-Dacians, the forbears of the present Rumanians, preserved their individuality and their Romance tongue, which was to become the symbol of their national development.[2] Again, to the west of Transylvania, in the basin of Hungary, first the Avars, and then later another Asiatic people, the Magyars, established themselves and thus drove farther westward the wedge which divided the Slav peoples to the north and the south.

The Carolingian Empire

The political power of the Franks, despite the temporary effects of partitions and foreign and civil wars, reached its zenith under

[1] See *infra*, Chapter VIII, p. 178.

[2] See Seton-Watson, *A History of the Roumanians* (1934), chapter I.

the able leadership of the Carolingian dynasty. At the end of the eighth century Charles the Great united under his sole rule the whole of the Frankish inheritance, which, moreover, he greatly enlarged through successful war. It is not necessary here to indicate the stages by which he extended his territories and the many wars in which he engaged, the chief of which were fought against the Moslems beyond the Pyrenees, against the Saxons in the Westphalian region, against the Avars on the upper and middle Danube, and finally against the Lombards in north Italy. In the year 800, Charles assumed at Rome the title of Roman Emperor (Imperator Romanorum), but the empire which he had created offered many contrasts with the Roman Empire as it was formerly constituted. Even so, it is a striking fact that the whole of his Empire had been either included in, or at least influenced in some degree by, the Roman Empire. In the first place it should be remembered that the Roman Empire still existed, though in a reduced form, in eastern Europe; moreover, the empire of Charles the Great was not in any strict sense identical with the western part of the Roman Empire which had disrupted in the fifth century. In any case the territorial fabric of the Carolingian Empire did not last long as an unbroken whole, but since its break-up produced many lasting changes on the political map, it is important to examine its geographical extent and character.

The Carolingian Empire (Fig. 25) had been built up from a base in northern Europe between the Loire and the Rhineland, and was essentially continental in character and, unlike the Roman Empire, had little contact with the Mediterranean region where it held only a small area, in northern Italy, in north-eastern Spain and in southern Gaul. Moreover, the dominance of the Arabs in the Mediterranean Sea and its restrictive effect on maritime commerce emphasized the continentality of the Frankish state. Like the Roman Empire, it reached the coast-lands of Gaul, except those of the Breton peninsula, but it included additionally the North Sea coastlands between the Rhine and the Eider estuary. On the other hand, towards the east the empire of Charles the Great extended considerably beyond the Roman *limes*. In this direction it included lands of two kinds: lands which were fully incorporated within the Empire, and others over which it held only a nominal power. In the first category were the territories which were largely Germanic in population between the Rhine and the rivers Saale and lower Elbe, together with those which lay east of the Agri Decumates and north of the Danube, which were to a large extent Slav in population. In the second category stood lands, geographically more extensive, which had never been fully conquered and united with the Frankish Empire, but were tributary to the emperor. These regions were essentially non-Germanic, for they comprised the Slav countries between the Elbe–Saale line and the Vistula, the Avar kingdom which had its base in Pannonia, and the southern Slavs beyond the Save, in what is now Croatia and Bosnia. Similarly in Italy the imperial power was directly

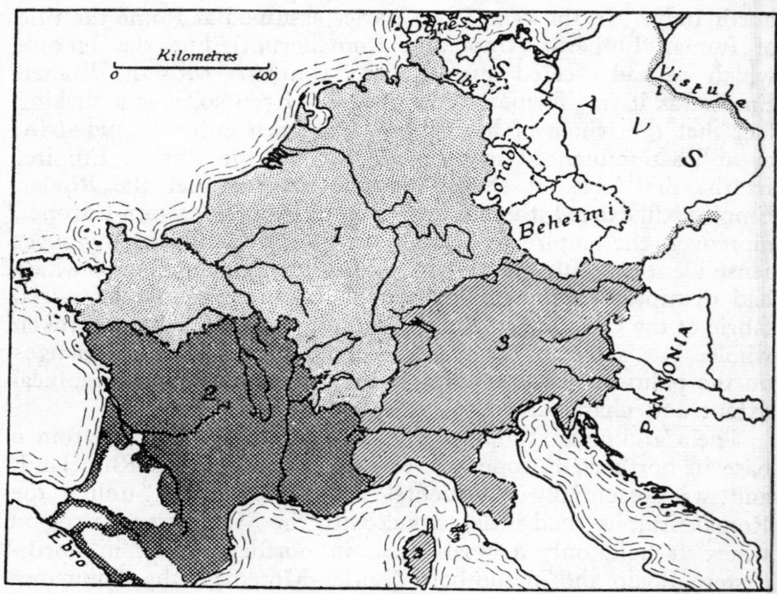

FIG. 25.—The Projected Partition of the Carolingian Empire in A.D. 806 (data from Longnon)

Note the complete absence in this scheme of any suggestion of a future French kingdom, and note also that the truly Frankish lands in the north are left undivided.

effective only in the northern plain and in Tuscany, whilst south of these regions of Romance culture the Papal states and the duchies of Spoleto and Beneventum were largely, though not legally, independent of the emperor.

The Carolingian Empire was thus an essentially continental state established astride the valley of the Rhine. It extended farthest in the east along the Danube, where it reached as far as the confluence of the March river ; whilst in the south it stretched across the ranges of the Pyrenees and the Alps. The most original feature in the geographical framework of this state

vas its eastern borderland. Like the Roman *finis* along and
eyond the Rhine and Danube, this eastern frontier represented
fluctuating zone in which the imperial Germanic state sought
o extend its rule and its culture. This frontier, again, divided
he Christian from the pagan world, whilst that beyond the
'yrenees divided the Christian from the Mohammedan dominions.
'urther, the eastern frontier defined, though not very sharply,
n ethnic division between the German and non-German peoples,
nd finally, it separated regions of somewhat contrasted levels
f culture.

It is worth examining more closely the eastern frontier of the
Carolingian Empire, since it afforded the first stage, both in time
nd in place, for the expansion of German colonization in Middle
Europe, for what has been called in fact the greatest achieve-
nent of the Germans in the Middle Ages. The reign of Charles
he Great witnessed the beginning of the ' mark ' system, i.e.
he establishment of borderland territories on the threshold of
he non-German world. The mark was in its original sense a
vaste district surrounding settled areas, but the term came to
e applied to territories organized along or beyond the frontier
f the Empire. No mark was established in the time of Charles
long the Danish frontier. In the year 808 the Danes built the
Danewirk ', a boundary wall between the Baltic and the North
Sea, which was recognized as a boundary by both the Danes
nd the Empire, and ran along the north bank of the Treene
iver, a right-bank tributary of the Eider. Farther south, where
he Germans and Slav peoples dwelt side by side, two marks
vere created by Charles the Great. The first was in the north
nd stretched from the Trave river across the Elbe estuary:
vith its forts, its garrisons and German colonies, it was designed
o withstand the attacks of the Slavic Obotrites. No mark was
s yet created against the Sorabes who dwelt beyond the Saale,
ut two fortresses were built about the year 806 on the banks
f the Elbe and Saale opposite the sites of Magdeburg and
Halle. The second, the mark of Bohemia, was established
eyond the upper Main, in the Nordgau, as a defence against
he Czechs. Further, after the defeat of the Avars in the year
803, the south-eastern frontier of the empire was strengthened
y the creation of the Ostmark, which occupied lands on both
ides of the Danube between the March and the Rötel rivers in
he east and the Wienerwald in the west. Finally, on the western
rontiers of the Empire also marks were organized against the
Bretons and against the Moslems The one consisted of a belt of
erritory east of the Vilaine river, whilst the other, the Spanish

March, which lay on the southern side of the eastern Pyrenees, embraced the lands around the cities of Urgel, Bergadan and Barcelona.

These early mark territories, like those which were subsequently created, were to a large extent peopled by non-Germans. Thus Slav peoples, as place-names testify, occupied many districts west of the Saale–Elbe line, whilst in the Danubian lands of the Ostmark, dwelt both Slav and Avar peoples. Nevertheless, in these borderland districts German forts were established and German colonists settled, and they were destined, in fact, to become thoroughly Germanized and to serve as bases from which German conquest, colonization and Christianization were extended among the relatively backward and pagan peoples of Middle Europe.

It may well be asked to what extent the empire of Charles the Great constituted a compact and organized whole, and from what capital cities it was governed. Actually, three cities in particular stand out as capitals at this time. The capital of the Empire was in theory Rome itself, although in fact that city greatly decreased in population and importance since the early centuries A.D., had fallen into the control of the Popes, as bishops of Rome. The most important city from the political standpoint was Aachen, the capital of the kingdom of Germany, which stood between the Meuse and Rhine in the heart of the lands of original Frankish settlement on the old Roman road which connected Cologne and Boulogne. Moreover, near Aachen lay the chief royal estates between the Rhine, Moselle and Meuse ; nearby also were the forest of the Ardennes, which was a famous hunting-ground for deer and boars, and the Moselle valley, which supplied the Court with wine. Finally, as king of Lombardy Charles had a capital city at Milan. In fact, coronation ceremonies were staged at all three capitals : Charles was crowned emperor at Rome (with a golden crown) ; king of the Lombards at Milan ; and king of the Germans at Aachen. But it should be recognized that, in days when transport by horse or by river craft was slow, the capital moved with the ruler. It is indeed a remarkable fact that Charles himself, who travelled continually for the purposes of war or government, is said to have covered 12,000 miles on horseback.[1]

The difficulties of government were met by a scheme of administrative division, which is of particular interest since in many respects it proved permanent. The empire was broken up into a number of provinces which were themselves composed

[1] Pinnow, *History of Germany*, English trans., 1933, p. 28.

of a number of smaller entities which in Gaul were called ' pagi '. In origin the pagus goes back to Celtic and Roman Gaul : in the former it indicated the country occupied by part of a Celtic people or federation of tribes, the whole territory of the people being called a ' civitas '. Under the Romans both the civitas and the pagus were retained as administrative entities, whilst in German lands beyond the Rhine the equivalent of the civitas was called a ' gau '. In the Merovingian period these terms were retained but their significance changed. The civitates in many cases formed the territorial bases of the dioceses which were formed by the Church, but the pagus lost its former precision of meaning. In some cases it defined a former civitas ; occasionally it was used to cover what is to-day called a natural region ; very often, too, especially in those parts of Gaul settled by the Franks, the old city territory or civitas was much broken up in the course of colonization and the pagi were merely parts of former civitates. Many of the pagi, again, became the counties of a later period when the feudal system of government established itself from the ninth century onwards. What, however, is of most interest to the geographer is the fact that many of the original pagi of Celtic Gaul still persist as geographical entities or natural regions with their distinctive names, a fact noted by Chéruhel [1] as early as 1858. The reason for this correspondence is that Celtic pagi were often contained within tracts of country of a particular geological character which tended to give them a certain uniformity in natural vegetation and in economic possibilities. It must suffice merely to indicate a few of the natural regions of present-day France which originally formed pagi in Celtic Gaul : thus the Lyonnais was the pagus Lugdunensis, Barrois was the pagus Barrensis, Limousin was the pagus Lemoviscus.[2] Similarly, some of the gaus in Roman territory beyond the Rhine persist to-day as geographical entities, e.g. Niddagau and Rheingau in the basin of the lower Main. Finally, it may be recalled that the French ' pays ' derives from the Latin ' pagus ' and is commonly employed to indicate natural regions.

The provincial divisions of Gaul under the Franks have also in some cases direct connexion with Roman geography. This is true of those two southern regions in which Roman influences, despite Germanic settlement, remained predominant, namely Aquitaine and Provence. The Aquitaine of the Carolingian Empire occupied broadly the country between the Loire and

[1] Cited by Jacobs, *Géographie de Grégoire de Tours*, 2nd ed., p. 54.
[2] See Mirot, *Manuel de Géographie Historique de la France*, p. 80.

the Pyrenees, together with the borderland cities of Tours and Toulouse. But if the name Aquitaine survived from Roman geography, it nevertheless acquired an extended meaning, since it included not only the imperial provinces of Aquitania Prima and Secunda but also Provincia Novempopulana, the Aquitaine of Caesar which was enclosed between the Garonne and the Pyrenees. The word Wasconia, which was applied for a time by the Franks to Aquitaine in their sense of the term owing to its temporary subjection to the Gascons or Basques, came to be restricted to the area between the Garonne and the Pyrenees into which the Basques had extended from their mountain homes in the sixth century, and it reappeared later in the duchy of Gascony. The other province of Roman Gaul which retained its Roman name was Provence. In the sixth century Frankish Provence was only a small part of Roman Provincia Narbonensis : it stretched from the Mediterranean to the Durance with an extension across the lower Rhône to include the district around Uzès. Later the Burgundian territory between the Rhône and the Alps was added, so that Provence recovered its original northern limit. In the west the Provence of the Franks and of later times remained curtailed : the region of Low Languedoc, formerly part of Provincia, fell under the rule of the Visigoths between *c.* 507 and 711, when it passed in turn into the power of the Arabs and the Franks. It derived from its political vicissitudes a distinctive name, ' Gothia ', and was also called, for reasons that are not very clear, ' Septimania '.

Elsewhere in Gaul, as also in those parts of the Carolingian Empire which had never been subject to the Romans, provincial units, new both in name and in geographical framework, came into being. Of these Francia is of particular interest in that it eventually gave its name to the kingdom of France. This province, which underwent many territorial modifications and divisions, consisted essentially of those lands ruled by Clovis or his relatives, which stretched from the sea in the north to the Loire and the Main in the south. It was divided *c.* 550 into two parts—Neustria and Austrasia—but later under the Carolingians a third part, Media Francia, appeared between these two. In result, Neustria was restricted between the Seine and the Loire, Austrasia to its lands beyond the Rhine, whilst Media Francia, which came to be known simply as ' France ', occupied lands astride the Meuse and Moselle and included the dioceses of Laon, Rheims, Verdun, Metz and Trèves. Its position, it will be observed, was intermediate and transitional between the regions in which French and German speech were developing.

Further, adjacent to Francia, Aquitaine and Provence, the province of Burgundy embraced part of the land originally settled by the Burgundians, together with Frankish land in the upper Seine basin. In the south-east the Jura divided Burgundy from Alamannia; in the south, after the loss of land to Provence, the Rhône from Lake Geneva to a point a little below Lyons marked the limit of Burgundy. Its losses in the south were more than made good in the early ninth century, when Burgundy extended in the north-west to include districts around Paris, Etampes, the Gâtinais between the Seine and the Loire, and other districts around Toul, Bar, and Perthes across the upper Marne.

On the eastern borderlands of Gaul and beyond the Rhine the provincial divisions of the Carolingian Empire underwent modification in the ninth century when that empire was subjected to continual partition. These partitions and their consequent effect on political geography will be noted later, but it may be noted here how they affected the provincial division of the east German lands. In the ninth and tenth centuries a number of territorial frameworks were created which became feudal duchies or counties and persisted down to the eighteenth and nineteenth centuries. In the north the province of Lothringen or Lorraine took its name from its ruler Lothaire II, being part of the kingdom assigned to him in the year 855. Lorraine was an extensive area, situated for the most part to the west of the Rhine below St. Goar, which had been settled largely by the Franks. In the south it reached the southern Vosges, but it did not include the plain of Alsace and that around Worms; in the north it extended across the lower Rhine, but was cut off from the sea by the maritime province and county of Frisia, which stretched from the Meuse to the Weser. Finally, its western limit lay along the Scheldt and a little beyond the upper Meuse. About the middle of the tenth century Lorraine was divided into two separate duchies, and it was with upper Lorraine, which was essentially the basin of the Moselle, that the name became identified. It should be noted that in respect of language and nationality this duchy was a transitional region, where Germanic and Romano-Gallic influences were rather equally balanced. Farther to the south the Burgundian kingdom of Arles as it was reconstituted in the ninth century between the southern Vosges and the sea contained a number of counties: e.g. the county of Provence, from the sea to beyond the Durance, and the county of Burgundy. Beyond the lower Rhine the duchy of Saxony coincided broadly with the limits of the early Saxon kingdom. It included not only a broad stretch of plain from the Bourtanger marshes to the Slav country, now Holstein, beyond the lower Elbe, but also the highland country of West- and East-phalia. This duchy was an essentially Germanic land, in which colonization made its beginnings under Charles the Great, and its importance among the duchies of eastern Germany is suggested by the fact that its dukes founded the Saxon dynasty which ruled Germany from 918 until 1002. Southwards of Saxony were the three other great duchies of medieval Germany : Franconia, Swabia and Bavaria. The name Franconia or Frankia, which was originally applied to all the lands of Frankish settlement, survived not only in the kingdom of France but also in the region, settled in part by the Franks and in part by the Alamanns, which had its axis in the valley of the Main and included also part of the basin of the Neckar and the lowlands around Worms and Spires on the left bank of the Rhine. Franconia became the heartland of medieval Germany ; the banks of the Main and the Rhine were studded with important cities of which the chief, Mainz and Frankfort, became commercial centres and imperial capitals. The duchy of Swabia, which adjoined Franconia to the south, stretched across the upper Danube, and like Franconia, extended across the Rhine, thus including Alsace. Eastwards it reached beyond the Lech and southwards to the Alps beyond the upper Rhine. Swabia took its name from the Suevi, an alternative name for the Alamanns, and covered the greater part of the region of early Alamannic settlement. Finally, eastwards of Swabia, the duchy of Bavaria lay likewise astride the Danube. Northwards of the Danube it included the Nordgau ; north-eastwards the Nordwald or Bohemian Forest marked its limit ; westwards it advanced towards the Lech and eastwards towards the Enns, although until about the year 1000 it included the Alpine march-land of Styria. In the south Bavaria advanced into the Tyrolese Alps, beyond the Brenner pass, Bozen being one of its frontier towns. It may be noticed that Swabia and Bavaria corresponded roughly with the Roman provinces of Raetia and Noricum.

Western Europe about A.D. 1000

In conclusion, it may be emphasized that the appropriation and colonization of the soil in western Europe by the Germanic peoples initiated a process of state-building which entirely re-cast the political map. Where formerly western and southern Europe had constituted part of a single political structure, the Roman Empire, beyond which stretched the politically disorganized 'barbarian' world, there came into being a number of smaller states, the territorial frameworks of which had their origin in the settlement of the several immigrant peoples. What is more, in many respects the outlines of the present states system of western Europe were already perceptible in the ninth and tenth centuries. The tripartite division of the Empire of Charles the Great by the Treaty of Verdun in 843,[1] a division which survived subsequent partitions, has been called 'la charte constitutive de la France'. It did, in fact, define for the first time the limits not only of the kingdom of France, but also that of Germany. Moreover, it created a broad elongated middle kingdom between the two, which stretched from the North Sea to the Apennines, and this kingdom, since it essentially lacked the cohesive elements of a state, broke up eventually into many fragments, some of which, notably Holland and Switzerland,[2] became the states of to-day. Similarly, on the eastern borderlands of the German kingdom, the mark system originated by Charles the Great, proved to be the first stage in the development of other modern states, above all, Austria and Brandenburg.[3]

[1] See *infra*, pp. 230–1. [2] See *infra*, Chapter XII.
[3] See *infra*, Chapter XIII.

CHAPTER VIII

THE BYZANTINE EMPIRE

HISTORIANS emphasize the fact that the division of the Roman Empire into two parts in A.D. 395 was purely a matter of military and administrative convenience, which left the unity of the empire unimpaired. Where one emperor had formerly ruled at Rome now two imperial colleagues, ruling jointly, shared the burdens of government: in the west one emperor resided at Rome, Milan, Ravenna or Trèves, whilst in the east Antioch, but above all Constantinople, became the capital of the other. Under the assaults of the barbarian invaders only the western part of the empire collapsed; the eastern part, in which Greek culture was dominant although Roman and oriental ideals prevailed in its organization, not only survived these attacks and held the critical Euphrates frontier, but lasted in some form or other until it was destroyed by the Ottoman Turks in the fifteenth century. During this long period, from the fall of Rome in 476 until that of Constantinople in 1453, the Roman Empire in the east, or as it is alternatively called, the Byzantine Empire, preserved some political unity and much of classical culture. From the geographical standpoint this empire was a continually changing expression. At one time it succeeded in winning back a large part of the former Roman lands in the west, but despite periods of vitality and reconquest its frontiers tended to recede; new states were created out of its territories, and it came, like the present Turkish Republic, to rest largely on an Asiatic base. It is worth while therefore to note first the fluctuating frontiers of the Byzantine Empire before turning to other aspects of its geography.

The dividing line adopted in A.D. 395 to mark off the empire in the west which was assigned to Arcadius from the empire in the east which was assigned to Honorius coincided with the existing boundary between the 'prefectures' of Italy and Illyricum (Fig. 26). To Arcadius, who ruled mainly from Ravenna, was given the government of the prefectures of Gaul and Italy, whilst to Honorius fell the rule of the prefectures of Illyricum and the East. The line, or more strictly the zone, which delimited their respective territories is geographically significant, and moreover remained after the fall of the empire in the west to mark the frontier of the East Roman Empire. It ran north-south from the Save near Sirmium (Mitroviţa) to the Adriatic near Dyrrhachium (Durazzo), and was continued in northern Africa behind the Great Syrtis Bay. The geographical significance of this zonal frontier resided in the fact that it passed through country which tended naturally to exert a separating influence: namely

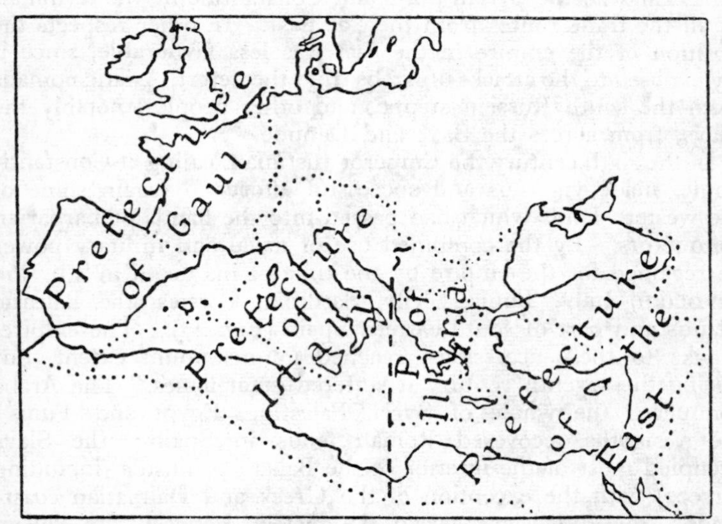

FIG. 26.—The Division of the Roman Empire in A.D. 395 (indicated by the broken line)

The dotted lines show the limits of the dioceses of which each prefecture was composed

the wooded and scantily settled mountains of Serbia, the alternately rocky and marshy coast of Albania, and the steppe country south of the Great Syrtis Bay. Moreover, the empire in the west was predominantly Latinized in culture, that in the east was essentially a Greek or Hellenistic world.

The lands of the eastern half of the empire, although roughly comparable in area with those in the west, had in some respects a greater importance. They had certainly the greater share of the population of the whole empire, which may have reached a total of about seventy millions.[1] Moreover, the empire in the east included the anciently civilized lands of Greece, the

[1] Bury, *The Later Roman Empire*, I, 62.

Aegean islands, Asia Minor, Syria, Cyprus, Egypt and Cyrenaïca, as well as Dacia, Thrace to the south of the Danube, and the Chersonesus in the Crimean peninsula. It had command of the corn lands of Egypt and of the northern coastlands of the Black Sea; of the silver, copper and some other metals of Bosnia, Cappadocia, Cilicia and Cyprus; of the Mediterranean produce—olive oil, corn and wine—of the islands and mainlands of the Aegean, together with the manufactures of Constantinople and the Syrian, Egyptian and Greek cities. It controlled also at Alexandria, the Syrian ports and Constantinople the terminals of all the trade routes from the Far East. In other respects the position of the empire in the east was less favourable, since it lay exposed to the attacks of Arabs from the desert, Asiatic nomads from the south Russian steppe, and other peoples, notably the Slavs, from across the Save and Danube.

In the sixth century the Emperor Justinian, ruling at Constantinople, made vigorous and successful efforts to regain some of the western lands which had passed into the hands of barbarian conquerors. By the combined use of naval and military power he regained for the empire by the time of his death in A.D. 565 Illyricum, Italy, Tunis, Sicily, Sardinia, Corsica, the Balearic islands and part of south-eastern Spain (Fig. 27). The empire, thanks to these accessions, reached its maximum extent, but during the seventh century it suffered great losses. The Arabs conquered the whole of Syria, Palestine, Egypt and Tunis; the Visigoths recovered Roman lands in Spain; the Slavs occupied most of the interior of the Balkan peninsula (including Greece) with the exception of the Greek and Dalmatian coastlands; the Bulgarians seized the plateau between the Balkan mountains and the Danube; whilst in Italy only a small part of imperial territory, mainly in the south, escaped conquest by the Lombards. In fact, what remained of the empire *c.* 700 consisted of a number of scattered lands and islands, together with what may be called its base or nuclear region. The first consisted of Sardinia, Corsica, Sicily, the lagoon islands at the head of the Adriatic, and coastal strips around Ravenna, Bari, Amalfi and elsewhere in Italy. The nuclear region comprised those lands which bordered the Sea of Marmora, the Aegean and the Black Sea, the whole of Asia Minor, Cyprus, and the Aegean islands including Crete. Within this reduced empire and an important source of its strength the city of Constantinople stood at the intersection of arterial routes, by land from Thrace and Asia Minor and by sea between the Aegean and Black Seas. Moreover, in its reduced form the Empire exhibited its

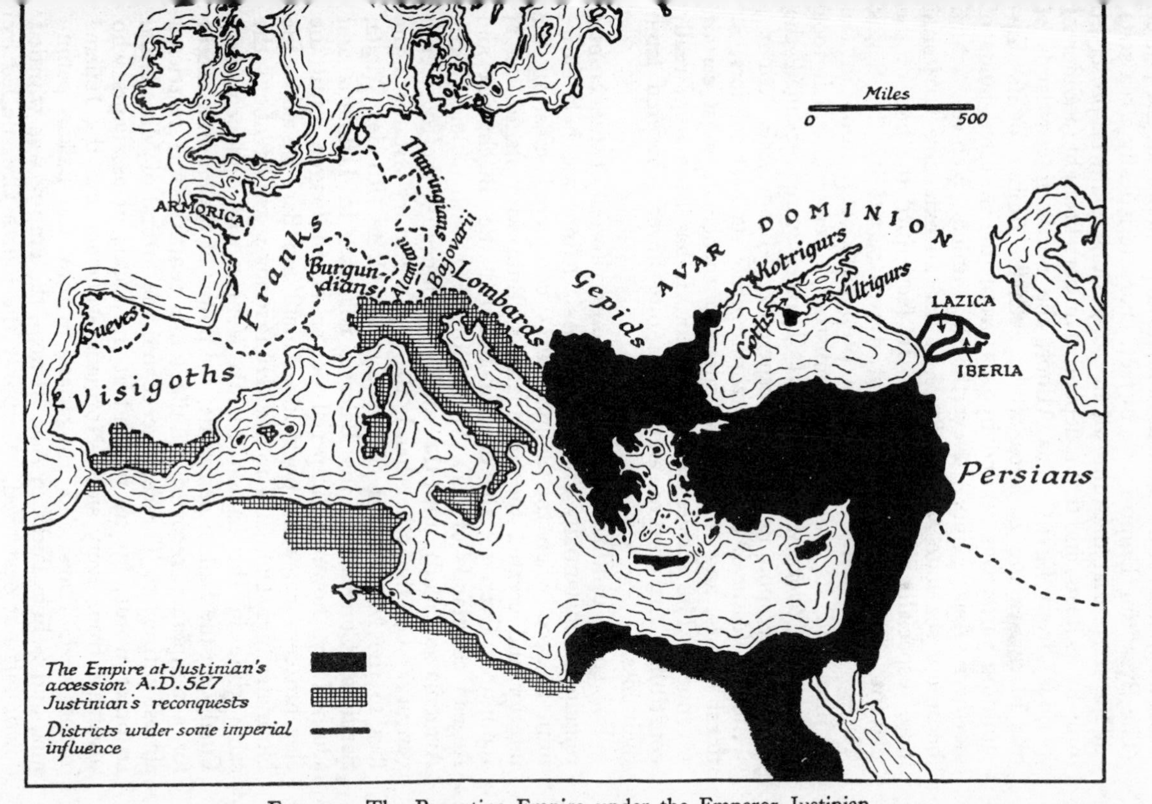

FIG. 27.—The Byzantine Empire under the Emperor Justinian

Note the dependence of Justinian's conquests on sea power. His hold on Italy was largely limited to the coastlands

essentially maritime character and its dependence on sea-power. The Byzantine Empire was, in fact, characteristically a sea-state, in the sense that the unity of its possessions could be preserved only by its fleets, and that it depended on corn brought (at different periods) from Egypt, Asia Minor, the northern coastlands of the Black Sea and Lemnos, whilst even the timber for its shipbuilding yards was carried by sea from the forested lands of northern Asia Minor. Nevertheless, unlike Venice, which became a sea-state *par excellence*, it had an extensive territorial base, especially in Asia Minor. In fact, until the end of the eleventh century when much of it was seized by the Seljuk Turks, Asia Minor occupied a preponderant position in the empire, and its *themes* or administrative regions, which took precedence over Macedonia and Thrace, were reckoned the most fertile, populous and prosperous. 'From Asia Minor', writes Professor Diehl,[1] 'the empire drew its best soldiers, its finest sailors, and the treasury derived thence its most certain revenue.' The *themes* of Asia Minor, it has been said, really constituted the empire, and the empire never recovered from their loss.

For some centuries after 700 the territories of the empire remained substantially unchanged. Asia Minor was held entire until *c.* 1100 when the Seljuk Turks conquered most of the interior and created the Sultanate of Rum with its capital at Iconium. Even so, the empire retained the Black Sea and Aegean coastlands of Asia Minor, together with Cilicia (Little Armenia so-called), until the Turkish conquest in the fourteenth century. On the other hand, the ninth century witnessed the loss to the Moslems of Sicily, Cyprus, Crete, Rhodes, Malta, Sardinia, Corsica and the Balearic islands. In Dalmatia and south Italy, however, imperial power lasted longer, until the eleventh century, when ports like Amalfi and Bari passed to the Normans and Dalmatia to the Hungarians; whilst about the same time in the lagoon islands Venice won independence. Finally, in the Balkan peninsula, the power of the empire, except for a temporary recovery in the tenth century, was restricted almost entirely to Thrace, Greece and the littoral of Macedonia. In other words, bit by bit and at the hands of assailants who advanced from every side—Normans, Magyars and the Italians in the west, Slavs and Bulgarians within the Balkan peninsula, and Seljuk Turks in Asia Minor—the empire was whittled down, but not destroyed. Certainly the fourth Crusade led by Venice in 1201 resulted in the capture of Constantinople and

[1] *Cam. Med. Hist.*, IV, 733.

the parcelling out of imperial lands, but the empire survived, though weakened, from this depredation, and succumbed finally to the Ottoman Turks, only in the mid-fifteenth century. It is significant that Constantinople itself, in the Middle Ages an almost impregnable city, was the last remnant of imperial territory in the Balkan peninsula to disappear. The Turks used cannon and took the city in 1453 : these proved as effective in attack as the terrifying ' Greek fire ' had earlier proved to the Byzantine city efficacious in defence.

Vegetation

The vegetation of countries in which human societies have established themselves is never constant and unchanging throughout history, and it is an important though difficult task for the historical geographer to reconstruct its characteristic features at successive periods of time. It is easy to describe in general terms the salient characteristics of the vegetation cover of the Balkan peninsula and of Asia Minor as it obtains to-day, and moreover to indicate the sharp contrasts which it manifests in relation to regional differences in climate and soil. Alike in the cultivated plants and in the remnants (if any) of natural vegetation unmodified by man, the vegetation cover of these countries at the present day reflects the climatic contrast between the Mediterranean climate which prevails in the coastlands of Dalmatia, Greece and Asia Minor and the varied ' continental ' conditions of climate which occur in the interior of the Balkan peninsula and in the Anatolian plateau. Again, it is easy to sketch broadly the present-day distribution of forests, scrub, steppe, pasture and cultivated lands, and to enumerate the chief cultivated trees and crops and to show their broad distributions. When this has been done, how much light has been shed on the vegetation conditions of these regions in the Middle Ages? Certainly in many respects the account given would be inaccurate and irrelevant. Some present-day crops, like tobacco, had no place in medieval agriculture ; some areas now under cultivation —for example, the coastal plain to the west of the Vardar estuary —have only recently been reclaimed ; moreover, the forest and scrub vegetation of to-day has been much modified since medieval times, and again land that was formerly mantled with humus soil and forest in some cases lies to-day destitute alike of forest and soil. In short, the main differences between the vegetation of the present and of the Middle Ages are fairly evident : they concern the character and distribution of forest and the human utilization of the soil.

The study of meagre yet suggestive evidence derived from archaeology and history indicates clearly enough that much woodland has disappeared in the Balkan peninsula since prehistoric times, and further that in the Middle Ages, although they had been and were being destroyed, forests were more extensive than they are to-day.[1] Under 'continental' conditions of climate, which provided a sufficiency of heat and rainfall, almost the whole of the peninsula was originally extensively wooded, with the exception of marshy tracts and parts of the north-east where the summer heat is scorching and semi-steppe conditions prevail. Even in the 'karstic' highlands of the north-west, where to-day soil and forests are largely lacking, e.g., in northern Istria, Croatia and Dalmatia, thick and valuable forests existed in the Middle Ages which were exploited by the Venetians and the Ragusans for ships and the building of houses. Again, medieval travellers refer often to the 'Bulgarian Forest', which stretched broadly across the Morava basin and was particularly dense, where the highway passed between Belgrade and Nish. It took Crusaders eight days to traverse the forest between these towns in 1096–7, but to-day the country lies fairly open and has little but deciduous brushwood on the slopes. These instances are probably typical of the destructive exploitation of woodland which went on during and since the Middle Ages. In this change men have been directly or indirectly the principal agents of change. Timber has been sought for numerous purposes: for ships, houses, mineral smelting, the manufacture of lime and for cooking. Shipbuilding must have taken considerable toll of the forests for Greeks, Romans, Byzantines, Venetians and Turks in turn were great maritime peoples and nothing appears to have been done to re-afforest. Moreover, the process of natural seeding was checked continually by the voracity of goats to whose discriminating palates new shoots and young seedlings proved irresistible. To the Slavs who settled throughout the central Balkans and the interior of Greece is attributed a great increase in the rearing of sheep and goats. Finally, forest fires—as at Ragusa in the thirteenth century—and the firing of forests for military and political reasons added to their destruction. In result, much humus soil which covered the hard rocks of the peninsula and had been held by the roots of trees was swept away by winds and heavy rains; and in the place of forest at best scrub or rough pasture, or at the worst bare rock, was substituted. The Balkan mountains and the Rhodope massif have, on the other hand, preserved considerable

[1] Turrill, *The Plant Life of the Balkan Peninsula*, ch. X.

forests, although large areas of the latter forest have degraded into scrub.

In what ways, other than by supporting forests, was the soil utilized in the Middle Ages? It is clear that stock-raising—cattle, goats, pigs and sheep—formed the chief use to which the land was put. Transhumance between the winter pastures of the Mediterranean coastlands, e.g., small lowland patches in Dalmatia, and the summer highland pastures of the interior was then as now a characteristic feature. The olive was cultivated along the littoral within limits restricted by the Mediterranean climate; the vine was grown in Greece, Dalmatia and the Aegean coastlands of Macedonia and Asia Minor, but it was not grown in Egypt. Cereal cultivation was widespread, although it is significant that Constantinople drew her supplies less from Thrace and Macedonia than from the northern coastlands of the Black Sea. The introduction of silk cultivation in the sixth century by the Emperor Justinian led to an increase in the growth of the mulberry tree, especially in Syria and the Morea, in order to provide the large quantities of leaf for the rearing of silkworms. The mulberry tree, the original habitat of which was Medo-Persia, had been introduced into classical Greece, where it was prized for its fruit, the juice of which was even used by comic actors and ladies to colour the face.[1] It had already in Roman times spread to Italy, Spain and Gaul, whilst the new use of the tree in medieval times stimulated its cultivation—the more so since it could be grown even in north-western Europe. Two cultivated products now very important in the southern parts of the Balkan peninsula, had no place in its medieval cultivation: tobacco, which was introduced in the sixteenth century, and currants, 'probably a variety of grape produced by degeneration', which appeared first at Naxos and later—in the seventeenth century—in the Morea.

Industry and Trade

Even when the empire lost its flourishing industrial cities in Syria and Egypt, it still possessed in Asia Minor and the southern parts of the Balkan peninsula towns in which manufacture and trade were actively carried on. The chief towns of Asia Minor included ports like Ephesus, Smyrna and Trebizond, and inland cities, like Nikaia and Phokaia. Of the ports, Trebizond was a busy entrepôt of trade between the Greeks and the Moslems: it could be reached from Constantinople in nine and a half days by sea, but the journey by land took twenty-eight days. Thebes,

[1] Hehn and Stallybrass, *The Wanderings of Plants and Animals*, p. 292.

Corinth and Patras, after the loss of Syria, grew famous for their silk working, and recovered something of the prosperity which they had enjoyed in the days of classical Greece. Salonika had important smelting and metal works, whilst Constantinople was the greatest industrial city of the empire. The silk industry is worth particular notice in view of its spread from the Eastern Empire into many other parts of Europe. At first dependent on the importation of raw silk from China and Ceylon the industry began in the sixth century to utilize silk which had been produced within the empire. The trade in silk brought overland from China was in the hands of the Persians, and that brought by sea was controlled by the kingdom of Axum (Abyssinia). The high prices for silk maintained by the Persian and Abyssinian merchants made it very desirable to produce local supplies of silk, but this was at first impossible since the Chinese preserved with care the secrets of its cultivation. Between the years A.D. 552 and 554, however, either monks or a Persian succeeded in smuggling some silk-worm eggs past the Chinese frontier, and brought them to Constantinople hidden in a hollow cane.[1] In the course of a few decades the rearing of the worm in Syria and Greece provided adequate supplies of raw silk and the old trade with China ceased. Factories for the manufacture of silk fabrics were set up at Constantinople, Berytus, Tyre and Antioch, and in certain cities of Greece. It was from Syria and by the Arabs that the cultivation and manufacture of silk was carried westwards into Sicily and Spain; whilst the Normans, who succeeded the Arabs as rulers of Sicily, further stimulated the industry by introducing silk operatives from Thebes and Corinth. From Sicily the silk industry passed into Italy, and thence by way of the Ligurian coastlands into southern France.

Routes

The military and trade routes which Rome constructed in the Balkan peninsula survived under the Byzantine Empire as the essential links between urban settlements, and they played a part continually throughout the Middle Ages in migration, warfare, pilgrimage and trade. Their lay-out was closely related to the configuration of the country: they utilized the great river valleys, belts of depression and mountain passes. The Via Egnatia afforded the shortest route between Rome and Constantinople, and thence, to Asia Minor. It ran from the ports of Durazzo and Apollonia by the Skumba valley, via the

[1] Cp. Hudson, *Europe and China*, ch. IV, and Vasil'ev (Eng. trans.), *History of the Byzantine Empire*, I, 204.

cities of Pella, Heraclea, Ochrid, Prespa and Voden to Salonika; thence it ran along the southern plain below the Rhodope massif, and passed along the Ergene valley to enter Constantinople by the Golden Gate. This route from Rome involved a short sea passage from Brindisi, and Constantinople could be reached in between twenty-three and twenty-six days, or less if haste was necessary; from Salonika to Constantinople was a full twelve long days' journey. An alternative and entirely overland route between the two capitals ran via Ravenna, Aquileia, Poetovio (Pettau) on the Save, and Belgrade. From Belgrade the road followed the Danube to Kostolač, then via the Mlava valley reached the Morava valley and Nish; from Nish a valley draining from the south-east carried the road into the basin of Sofia; thence the Maritza valley was reached by the Succi pass, and the road followed that valley by Philippopolis and Adrianople, below which it joined the road from Salonika to Constantinople. The journey from Belgrade to Constantinople occupied about twenty-one days.[1] From Nish another road climbed the southern Morava valley to Skoplje, and thence reached Salonika by the Vardar valley. The journey from Belgrade to Salonika took twenty-four days. A difficult road made its way along the hilly plains and mountain spurs of the Adriatic coastlands from Aquileia to Spalato, Cattaro, Antivari, Alessio and thence to Durazzo and Apollonia. Two other transverse east-west routes supplemented the Via Egnatia. One ran from the cities of Scutari, Alessio and Antivari by way of the Drin valley, and thus into the intramontane basin or *polje* of Kossovo, where *Ulpiana*, the modern Lipljan, commanded routes north-east to Nish and south-east to *Scupi* (Skoplje) and Salonika. The other connected Avlona (Valona) with Armirion on the Gulf of Volos via Janina, Castoria and Larissa. In addition should be noted the route along the high southern bank of the Danube which connected a line of fortresses from Vidin to Sistova and Silistra, from which ran off routes to the north and south of the river. Three of these gave access to the south over Balkan passes: the most westerly led from *Oescus* (near Nicopolis), via the Osma valley to the pass of Trajan, and thus to Philippopolis; another from *Novae* (Sistov) by way of the Jantra valley led up to the Sipka pass, thence to the Maritza towns; and finally, to the east from Marcianopolis, which stood at Pravadi, twenty-five miles east of Sumla, a road led via the Gylorski pass into Thrace. It is easy to see that certain fortified cities on these routes developed a controlling strategical importance: thus the pass

[1] Bury, op. cit., I, ch. IX, section 1.

of Succi was the key to Thrace, as that of Thermopylae was the key to Greece; Durazzo was a gateway into the eastern part of the peninsula, even from Constantinople by means of a fleet. Constantinople, Salonika, Durazzo, Sofia, Nish and Belgrade formed the essential strongholds from which the peninsula might be controlled; the loss of the last three, when it occurred, left the empire restricted to the lands with which communication by sea was available, namely Greece, southern Macedonia, Thrace and the Dalmatian coastlands. Constantinople, Salonika and Durazzo had a great advantage in occupying maritime positions. The traffic of the roads was that of armies, pilgrims and merchants passing between the old Roman cities. Distinct from this type of traffic but no less characteristic of the life of the peninsula were the movements of shepherds and their flocks between the winter pastures of valley and plain and the summer pastures of the mountains.

In Asia Minor the Romans completed a network of trade and military roads which were designed above all to provide direct communication between Rome and the critical frontier along the upper Euphrates.[1] The most important Roman highway started from Ephesus, which was the chief port and capital city of Asia Minor in the early centuries A.D., although its harbour began to silt up even during the Roman period and the town is now several miles inland. It passed up to the Anatolian plateau by way of the Meander valley, 'the one easy path that nature has made between the Aegean coast and the high grounds of the plateau'; it reached the flourishing town and route-centre of Apameia, and thence, keeping to the south of the great Salt Desert, crossed the Taurus mountains by the historic pass of the Cilician Gate to Tarsus and thence into Syria. Other roads diverged from this arterial highway in order to reach the fortress cities of the Euphrates, of which the chief was Melitene. The selection of imperial capitals in the east, at Nikomedeia in A.D. 292 and then permanently at Constantinople in 330, caused a new orientation of the route system of Asia Minor. New routes were created which specifically served the political and economic needs of Byzantine rulers at Constantinople, whilst the chief roads of the Roman period declined in importance. In the Roman period southern Asia Minor, through which ran the trunk highway noted above, exceeded in population and wealth the northern part of the peninsula. In the Byzantine Empire, however, cities, like Apameia, which stood in the south

[1] Ramsay, *The Historical Geography of Asia Minor*, G.J. Suplt Papers, vol. 4, 1890.

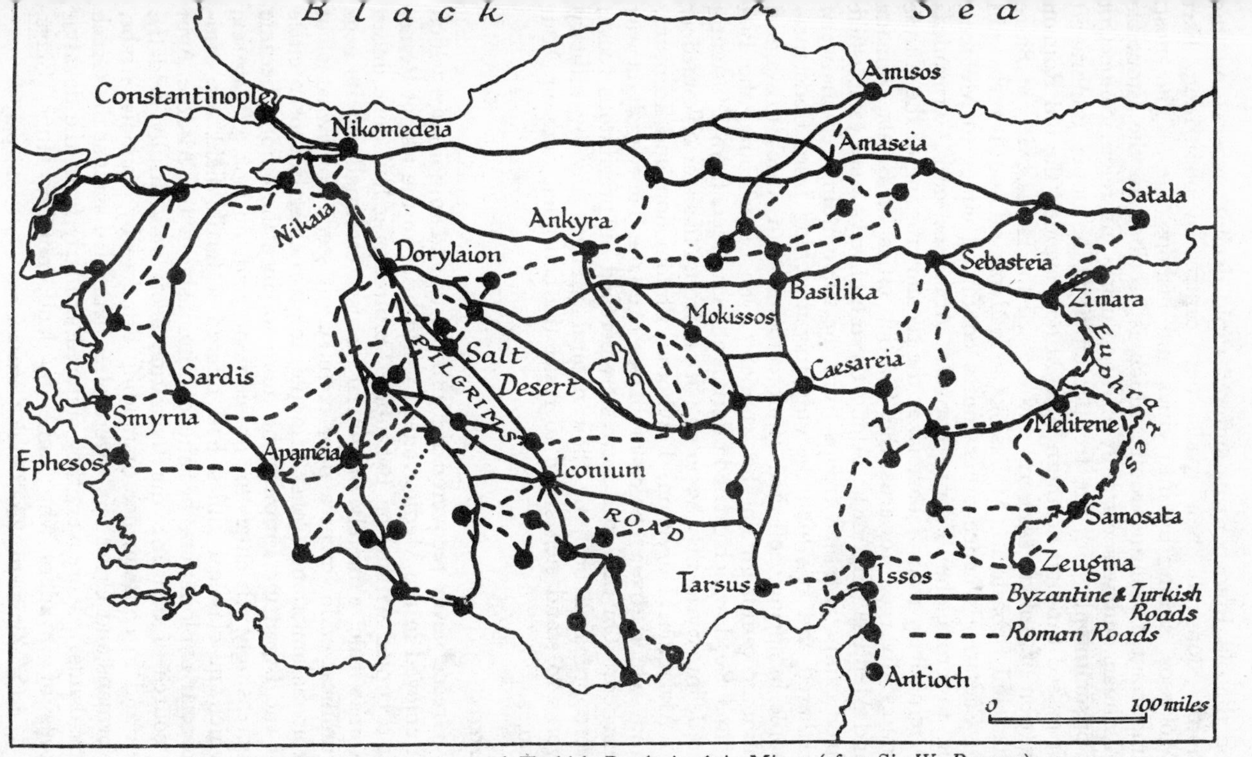

FIG. 28.—Roman, Byzantine and Turkish Roads in Asia Minor (after Sir W. Ramsay)

Note the effect on the alinement of roads of the position of Constantinople as capital in the Byzantine period

on the old Roman roads suffered rapid decline, whereas in the north, along the new roads, new centres of population, like Mokissos, sprang up into cities and bishops' sees. The most important Byzantine route, which is ascribed to the Emperor Justinian and was certainly in use during his reign, connected Constantinople with the frontier cities of the upper Euphrates. It passed through northern Asia Minor, avoided the old Roman station of Ankyra (Angora) and crossed the Halys twice, at Basilika and Sebasteia. At Basilika a road ran off south-westwards to Caesareia whence other routes continued either to Melitene or to cross the Taurus between Arabissos and Germanica. Alternatively from Sebasteia, at the second crossing of the Halys, routes diverged towards the frontier cities of Satala, Zimara and Melitene (Fig. 28). Along these highways were established fixed camps at which troops from the surrounding regions were gathered and at which the emperor, marching from Constantinople in spring, collected reinforcements with which to wage a summer campaign on the frontier. One other route, the Pilgrims' Road, which carried pilgrims and crusaders from Constantinople into Syria, may be noted : it ran from Nikaia or Nikomedeia to Malagina, Dorylaion, Polybotos, Philomelion and Iconium, from which, by a choice of passes over the Taurus, Syria was reached. On this road fortresses, perched on precipitous rocks, were prepared both by their natural strength and by military works to stand sieges and to resist the continual raids of Arab forces.

Greece

Greece never recovered the prosperity and importance which it enjoyed in the Mediterranean world prior to the rise of Rome. It occupied within the Byzantine Empire, as it had done under Roman rule, a merely provincial status : essentially in its geographical endowment a poor country,[1] it stood somewhat aloof from Salonika and Constantinople, the two chief European cities of the Byzantine Empire, the more so since the empire became increasingly Oriental in its content and outlook. The sea, which in classical times had offered a fertile field for commercial exploitation, became continuously in the Middle Ages a source of danger : the Byzantine fleets only fitfully held the sea and in consequence marauding attacks—by Vandals, Arabs, Normans and Crusaders—were often launched against the Greek coastlands. Moreover, they suffered similarly from the devastations of invaders who came by land, notably Huns, Slavs,

[1] Cp. Zimmern, *The Greek Commonwealth*, 5th ed., part I.

Bulgarians and Avars, whilst Greece was afflicted more than once by earthquakes and by the bubonic plague.[1] It is significant that the six *themes* into which Greece [2] was divided ranked below those of Asia Minor, Thrace and Macedonia, and that Byzantine officials regarded Greece as an ' utter hole ' and service there as virtual exile. The Emperor Justinian strengthened the defences of the country by rebuilding fortresses at the cities of Thessaly of Corinth, and Athens, and by securing the pass of Thermopylae. His work, although it did not safeguard Greece from further invasions, e.g., of Slavs in A.D. 576 and 746 and of Avars in 589, may well have saved it from complete conquest. The Slav immigrants who entered Greece in 746 occupied the countryside widely outside the walled towns, as their place-names still testify, but they became absorbed into the existing Greek population. In one respect Greece advanced under Byzantine rule, since the silk industry, based on the local production of raw silk, was established in the sixth century in the cities of central Greece and the Morea. It is probably for this reason that Thebes, where the silk industry was important, and not Athens, despite its ancient glory, became the capital of the *theme* of central Greece and Euboea. A plain around Thebes which is now destitute of mulberry trees is significantly called *Morokampos*, after the ' morus ', the mulberry tree.[3]

The predominance of Slavs in the country districts of Greece was offset by the foundation of Greek military settlements and monasteries in their midst. The defeat of the Slavs at Patras in 807 prevented the Morea from becoming a Slav principality : Patras was a small port and the chief city of the Morea, which formed a separate *theme* and was one of the most prosperous parts of Greece. Its many small towns engaged in the preparation of silk, the purple dye and parchment, as well as in short-distance maritime commerce which was aided by the recovery of Crete from its Arab conquerors in the ninth century. The rearing of sheep and goats, and the cultivation of the olive, vine, fig and wheat, all played a part in the economy of Greece. That southern Greece (including the Morea) enjoyed a certain though fluctuating measure of economic activity is suggested by the fact that during a famine at Constantinople in 1037 it was able to supply the capital with wheat. Moreover, Jews were settled, and Venetians had trade depôts, in its cities. If Athens had little importance, except as a university centre,

[1] Miller, *Essays on the Latin Orient*, ch. II.
[2] That is Greece within the limits which obtained in 1912.
[3] Miller, op. cit., p. 52.

Corinth became for a while a busy town. Even when the Norman king Roger II of Sicily sacked Thebes in 1146 and carried thence its best silk weavers and dyers the silk industry did not disappear from Greece, although that country ceased thenceforth to hold the monopoly of silk-making in Christian lands. In fact, during the last centuries of the Middle Ages Greece, cut up though it was into a number of small principalities, was relatively prosperous.

The fortunes of Corinth typify the alternation of decline and prosperity in the larger cities of medieval Greece. Its remarkable geographical position exposed it to the full brunt of invasions both by land and by sea, but it provided also, when political conditions became more settled, the basis of its economic success. Through the narrow rocky isthmus of Corinth passed of necessity the highway into the Morea, and the walls built across this waist, although restored by Justinian, were unable to bar the way to immigrants from the north. Again, in the Middle Ages as in classical times, the two ports of Corinth—' one for ships from Asia, the other for those from Italy '—had a strategical importance, in that small ships could be carried across from one sea to the other, thereby shortening considerably their sailing distance and also avoiding the difficult passage around the Morea. But this signal geographical advantage, although it promised great wealth to the city, no less attracted the naval attacks of seamen bent on plunder ; and despite the great natural strength of Acrocorinth, its citadel which frowned down from an almost unscalable hill, Corinth fell into the hands of invaders, e.g., the Normans in 1146 and the Turks in 1458. Until *c.* A.D. 800 Corinth's history is largely a record of disaster and decline : it suffered not only at the hands of invaders but also from earthquakes, e.g., in A.D. 395, and from plagues, e.g., in 542. In the ninth century, with the revival of imperial power, trade and industry markedly developed, and it is clear, too, that at this time the ordinary route of travel between Italy and Constantinople lay via Patras, across the isthmus of Corinth, and thence by sea.[1]

Towards the end of this century a Byzantine admiral had his ships transported across the isthmus in order to chastise Saracens

[1] Finley, ' Corinth in the Middle Ages ', *Speculum*, Oct. 1932 ; Bury, *The Later Roman Empire*, I, p. 378, n. 1. The canal through the isthmus was completed only in 1892, although the idea goes back to the Emperor Nero. In classical times there were ' rollers ' at Corinth over which ships were hauled : Charlesworth, *Trade-Routes and Commerce of the Roman Empire*, p. 117.

who had seized Patras. The practice of hauling small ships across the isthmus was still adopted—as Edrisi notes [1]—in the twelfth century. When Corinth fell into the hands of Roger II in 1146 it was clearly a wealthy city; the silk industry was flourishing and the town was the emporium for the Levant trade in Greece. In the remaining centuries of the Middle Ages, however, it again declined, and its poverty and many deserted homes are recorded in 1395; nor did it later under Turkish rule witness again the transient prosperity of its best medieval period, still less that of its classical days.

The First Bulgarian Empire

The original framework of the Bulgarian state built up in the seventh century at the expense of the empire was the well-defined geographical region which lies between the Black Sea, the Balkans and the Danube. The high central chain of the Balkan mountains trends north-westwards to reach the Danube at and above the Iron Gate; eastwards it sends lower spurs towards the Black Sea; to the south it presents an abrupt faulted edge, east of the Strednja Gora; whilst to the north extend first a belt of folded hills and then a broad platform which overlooks the Danube and its low northern bank. The Balkan chains constituted an obstacle to north-south passage: their massive summits were well watered and thickly forested; passage could be effected only by way of certain transverse valleys and high passes. The ascent was more gradual from the north than from the south. Two routes were of outstanding importance: one via the Šipka pass which was reached by way of a tributary valley of the Jantra river, and farther to the west the route offered by the river Isker, the rocky valley of which leads up into the basin of Sofia. The lower Danubian or Bulgarian platform in the north is covered extensively with light, porous, loam soils, in which rivers flowing northwards are entrenched. The climate has the characteristics of the central European type, modified by steppe influences which become dominant farther east in Deli Orman and the Dobruja. The hot scorching summers and the character of the soils were inimical to forest development; the natural conditions were above all suited to agriculture; under the summer heat meadow and pasture became scanty, but in the hills and mountains to the south summer pasture could be and was continually sought. Further, the lower Danubian platform stood open to invaders from the north and north-east, many of whom entered Europe from the steppes of Asia by way of the Caspian Gate.

[1] *La Géographie d'Edrisi*, trans. Jaubert, II, 123.

The lower Danubian platform (east of the river Timok) had formed the Roman province of Moesia. The Dobruja coast, south of the Danube delta, was in early times well embayed and afforded sites for maritime stations, where the Greeks in the sixth century B.C. established the colonies of Istria, Tomi (Constanţa) and Mangalia, which engaged in fishing and traded across the Dobruja with stations like Axiopolis and Harsova, situated on the high Dobruja bank of the Danube. Under the empire fortified cities were built along the south bank of the Danube, represented to-day by such towns as Vidin, Nicopolis, Sistov and Ruschuk, and further, colonists from Italy and elsewhere came and established *villae* (farms) from which to exploit the agricultural possibilities of the province.[1] It is described early, e.g., about the year A.D. 50, as a grain-producing area, which provided supplies to the riverside garrisons, and later, when Trajan constructed a riverside route above the Iron Gate, grain-supplies could be towed up-stream. The West Goths were later allowed to settle in Moesia, and when the Bulgar horsemen entered in A.D. 679 groups of Slav pastoralists already occupied the land. The Bulgars had been established between the Caucasus and the lower Don; they were driven westwards before the advance of the Khazars and later the Magyars. One group of them entered Bessarabia, crossed the Danube above the delta and advanced into the Dobruja; Salonika was besieged—unsuccessfully—between the years 675 and 677; others took possession of the lower Danubian platform, and Sofia was left as an island of imperial authority, until eventually it was sacked *c.* 800. The emperors tried at first with some success to defend the Maritza basin by holding a frontier along the Balkan mountains; the Bulgars attempted to move across the eastern Balkans and to capture the group of Greek ports—Develtus, Anchialus and Messembria—situated around the Gulf of Burgas, and if possible to capture Constantinople itself. About the year 716 they demarcated their frontier against Thrace by constructing 'the Great Fence', a ditch and earthen rampart, between Macrolivada on the Maritza and a point to the north of the imperial fortress of Develtus on the Bay of Burgas. A century later they had pushed farther south and west; and they won supremacy over Serbia and controlled the great highway from Adrianople to Belgrade. The empire had to abandon the cities of the Bay of Burgas as well as Adrianople, Philippopolis, Sofia and Ochrida. In the tenth century Bulgaria lost the territories which it had held to the north of the Danube, except Wallachia, but ruled

[1] Pârvan, *Dacia*, p. 176.

as far west as the Adriatic by way of the Via Egnatia and the route from Ulpiana to Dulcigno. It thus held the ports of Durazzo and Dulcigno, and dominated the whole peninsula, with the exception of Dalmatia, the Greek lands of southern Macedonia (around Salonika), Greece and southern Thrace (around Constantinople). The ninth century thus witnessed the creation of the powerful first Bulgarian Empire, which was crushed in turn by Russians and the Byzantines a century later; a second Bulgarian kingdom based on Macedonia and with a capital at Ochrida was also crushed in 1018 by the Emperor Basil, 'the Bulgar Slayer'.

The capital cities of the first Bulgarian Empire lay in the north-east between the Balkans and the Danube, and with the extension to the Adriatic additional cities to the west were used. The first capital was at Pliska; in the ninth century it was moved to Preslav near by. Great Preslav, now in ruins, stood on the Gt. Kamtchik river, which drains eastwards from the Balkans to the Black Sea, near Marcianopolis (the modern Pravadi), and was so placed as to control the pass of Kazan through the Balkans, whilst it commanded a route across the Danube into Wallachia by crossings at Silistra or Ruschuk. In the tenth century Sofia, and the three old Roman cities of Vodena, Prespa and Ochrida which stood on the Via Egnatia, were used as capitals. Nevertheless, the base of the first Bulgarian state lay in the north-east, not only in a political but also in an economic sense. Ships entered the lower Danube to trade and glowing accounts testify to the importance in the tenth century of commercial activity on the Danube delta. The chief port was Little Preslav, to-day represented by a village on the south side of the St. George channel of the delta, near where it enters the Sulina channel. To this port were brought silver, fabrics, wine and fruit from Greece, silver and horses from Bohemia and Hungary—via Transylvania and the lower Danube—and skins, wax, slaves and honey from Kievan Russia. Great Preslav itself before its destruction by the Byzantine Empire in 972 was described (though with some exaggeration) as second in size and wealth only to Constantinople itself. In their culture the Bulgarians were markedly influenced by their new habitat and its proximity to Constantinople: their language died out and was replaced by that of the Slavs, into which had been introduced the Cyrillic (Greek) alphabet. Byzantine influences were similarly expressed through the Greek Church, of which Bulgaria formed a patriarchate, with its see at Great Preslav and later (in 927) at Silistra; whilst in architecture, town life and commerce the same influences were paramount. The highway from Constantinople to Belgrade remained open as an avenue—but a relatively unimportant one—by which exports from Constantinople were moved into central Europe. Develtus and Anchialis were trading towns ; and Sofia had a fair. The fact that taxes were payable in corn and wine testifies to the practice of cultivation.

The Serbian Empire

In the north, where the Balkan peninsula is broadest and is welded to continental Europe, it lay open across the lower Danube and the Drave to the great plains of Dacia and Pannonia, both of which had long formed thoroughfares and reservoirs of immigrant peoples. From these regions whence access into the peninsula is unimpeded by physical obstacles the Slavs entered during the sixth century and by way of the great longitudinal routes—along the Adriatic coast, the Morava–Vardar and Morava–Maritza highways—overran the peninsula, which the emperors were powerless to defend. The Slavs penetrated as far south as the Peloponnesus and settled in inland Greece which they invaded ten times between A.D. 584 and 589. The great Roman colony of Salona on the Dalmatian coast was destroyed, but generally the strong walled cities of the coastlands survived capture and remained outposts of imperial authority : Durazzo was besieged in the year A.D. 547, Adrianople in 550, Constantinople in 558 and Thessalonika in 597. The empire succeeded in preserving from conquest the Greek lands to the south of Epirus and the Balkans ; but in the seventh century the Emperor Heraclius could claim only suzerainty over the Slav lands of the north-west. In fact, throughout the Middle Ages imperial authority in this part of the peninsula, except for fitful recoveries, was limited at best to roadside fortresses such as Nish and Belgrade, and ports such as Durazzo, the key to the west Balkans, at which on occasions armies conveyed by sea were disembarked in campaigns against the Serbs. The Slavs who had established themselves between the Balkan mountains and the Danube were, as it has already been noted, themselves conquered by Bulgar immigrants from the north-east in the seventh century. Between the Adriatic coastlands and the Morava highway, in the region of mountain, valley and upland basins, the Slavs were, however, free to build up independent kingdoms and to nourish political ambitions which are vital to-day.

Two Slav states were created during the Middle Ages at the expense of the Byzantine Empire. One was Croatia, with its core in the middle Save and Drave lands and a frontage on the Dalmatian coast. It lay mainly outside the peninsula; its contacts were with the west, as is illustrated by its absorption into the Roman Church; and in 1102 it was annexed to the Hungarian kingdom. The other was Serbia, to the south, which developed from a nucleus of river sources and upland basins.

Medieval Serbia, known variously as Sclavonia or Raška, affords an interesting study of what may be called the 'nuclear area' of a state. In sharp contrast with medieval France it had its political centres and its base in a region not of confluents but of river sources. The physical geography of the western half of the Balkan peninsula offered many difficulties and few aids to state-building. This country is occupied by the Dinaric mountain system, which consists of parallel mountain 'spines' running N.W.–S.E. (north of latitude 42° N.), from which are thrown off to the east and to the west curving lateral spurs. Thus to the west of the Morava river, if the Mediterranean coastlands be excepted, highland country clad with thick forests and pasture formed the typical landscape. In one respect, however, the physique of the land afforded possibilities in an area of relatively level country where communication was not too difficult, where pasture was available and productive cultivation was possible. This region consisted of a series of *polja*, tectonic basins or depressions, formerly occupied by lakes, through which the headstreams of four important rivers drained *en route* to the three neighbouring seas. The region was, in short, a hydrographic area of dispersion, and consisted of centrally placed basins which were ringed around by steep slopes (Fig. 29). Four basins stood in close relationship: the basin of Kossovo, along the upper Ibar head-streams; that of Metohija, along the upper Drin; that of Tetovo, along the upper Vardar; and finally, the basin which lay between the southern Morava and the upper Vardar valleys, with the cities of Kumanovo and Skoplje. These divergent valleys led in three directions: the waters of the Ibar flowed northwards to the Morava, thence by way of the Danube to the Black Sea; the Drin cut a transverse passage to the Adriatic below Scutari; the Vardar reached the Aegean west of Salonika, whilst the southern Morava was tributary to the Morava which entered the Danube below Belgrade. The essential artery of this region, within which stood successive residences or capitals of the Serbian rulers, was the almost continuous longitudinal furrow between the town of Skoplje (the old Usküb) on the Vardar, and the Serbian fortress of Maglic, where the Ibar swings round from a northerly to an easterly course. On or near this line stood as capitals of Raška, Novi Pazar, Pŗiština, Prizren, and the old Roman city of Skoplje. The first capital of Serbia, an entirely inland state until the twelfth century, was Raš or Raška on the Ibar. The state attempted with success to expand seawards both to the south along the Vardar and to the west along the Drin. Towards the end of the twelfth century Serbian territories included north Albania and Herzegovina;

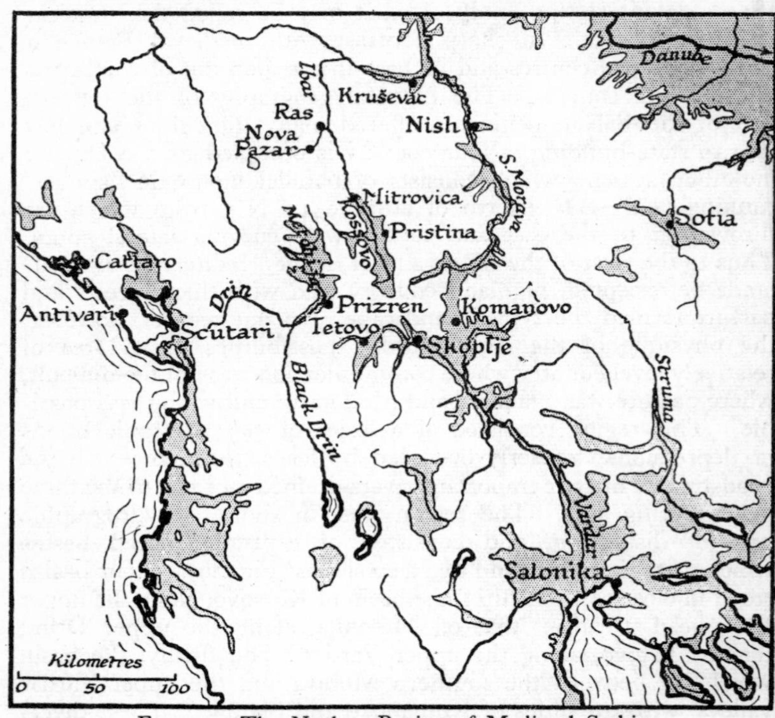

FIG. 29.—The Nuclear Region of Medieval Serbia
The stippled areas indicate the lowland regions (below 200 metres)

they fell short of the Morava valley to the east and were limited by the Ban or Kingdom of Bosnia to the north; whilst at the Bay of Cattaro they included an outlet on the Adriatic. A century later Skoplje was the Serbian capital, and remained so in the much-extended kingdom of Stephen Dushan. Stephen won Scutari and Antivari; Epirus and Thessaly; Macedonia to the Gulf of Salonika, but failed, as modern Jugo-Slavia has failed, to capture the Aegean outlet, Salonika. The frontiers of the Serbian kingdom receded only with the advance of the Ottoman

Turks: the latter in 1386 captured Nish, a route-centre with a bridge across the Morava; the kingdom was shattered at the memorable battle of Kossovo in 1389; a temporary capital was fixed at Kruševač on the lower Ibar; but in 1459 the remnant of Serbia was absorbed into the Ottoman Empire.

The economy of medieval Serbia reflected the varied though restricted opportunities offered by its geography. In 1168 the Serbs were described as uncivilized dwellers in mountains and forests, who did not practise agriculture but possessed many cattle; later, however, particularly in the fourteenth century, agriculture made some advance. The central basins, or *polja*, were floored with a rich, black humus soil, which was both well watered and sheltered, and cereals, hemp, flax and beans were all cultivated there. In the Metohija basin between Pec and Prizren—with its fortress and its fair—and also in that of Kossovo, nucleated villages were very numerous and population was abundant—greater in the fourteenth century than it is to-day.[1] Cultivation was in some measure increased by deforestation, which was allowed in 1168 to settlers in the Serb republic of Ragusa, and also later (*c.* 1300) to 'Saxon' colonists in mining centres. But in the late fourteenth century it was in some cases forbidden 'to plough up the pastures of the mountain'. Cattle, pigs and horses were the chief source of wealth; transhumance was practised, cattle were led up from the winter pastures of the Mediterranean coastlands, e.g., from Cattaro and Ragusa, to the summer pastures of the interior mountains. Pigs were fed on the mast of the oak and beech forests, and salt pork was marketed to ships in the Adriatic ports. Other features of Serbian economy were trapping, hunting, and fishing in lake and river, whilst apiculture, for honey, wax and mead, was deliberately extended. In the small hollows of the coastland, which were favoured by Mediterranean climate near to the cities like Scutari, Dulcigno, Antivari and Cattaro, the vine, olive, wheat, fig, almond and citrus fruits were cultivated. The old Roman cities within the Serbian kingdom continued their old occupations—commerce, shipbuilding, manufacture, fishing and piracy. The Roman east-west transverse routes from the Adriatic into the interior carried an exchange of commodities which was to some extent stimulated by the contrasted character of these geographical regions: from the coast, oil, wine, manufactured and Oriental goods; from the highlands timber—for ships and wine casks—cattle, gold and silver, honey, wool, skins and leather. The industries of the coast towns were based on

[1] Jireček, *La Civilisation Serbe au Moyen Âge*, p. 48.

the raw materials derived from their mountainous hinterland: thus Cattaro worked gold and silver, tanned leather, prepared wax, made shoes and armour, and built ships.

In the interior towns were few. Apart from the old imperial cities like Skoplje, Nish and Belgrade, there were a few trading towns which grew up around mineral workings. The Kapaonik mountain, which lies eastwards of the upper Ibar, was rich in metals, especially gold and silver, and in consequence mining towns and villages grew up around it. German colonists from Hungary—called Saxons—were allowed to found new settlements and to exploit mineral seams. Such towns were Brescoa (Brskovo) near Kolasin on the Tara river, frequented by the Ragusans; Novo Brdo, now a ruin, near the source of the eastern Morava, as well as Janjevo and Kratovo, which lies to the east of Skoplje.

Salonika (*Thessalonika*)

Salonika, the second European city of the Byzantine Empire and one of the best ports of the Mediterranean, described equally with Constantinople as 'l'oeil de l'Europe et la parure de l'Hellade', has, thanks to its excellent geographical position, tended from the time of St. Paul to be a great city as it has also continually been a goal of political ambitions. Founded by Macedonia in the fourth century B.C. it stood at the head of the Gulf of Salonika to the east of the delta of the Vardar river, the valley of which from prehistoric times,[1] has afforded a route-way from the Aegean through Macedonia to the Morava valley, and thence to the Danube just below the site of Belgrade. Salonika (or alternatively Thessalonika) possessed a good natural harbour; only the accumulation of silt carried in by marine currents, by narrowing and shallowing the channel which gives access from the Aegean, has in modern times threatened it adversely. Already under the Roman Empire it had developed the functions of a provincial capital (of Macedonia), of a fortress, a seaport and a road focus. In the early Middle Ages its walls defended it against the repeated landward assaults by Goths, Avars, Slavs and Bulgars. The immediate hinterland of the town, the basin of the lower Vardar, was continually ravaged, so that agriculture, viticulture and cattle raising, for all of which it was well adapted, suffered. Even so, it functioned as the natural outlet for the surplus produce of Serbia, Macedonia, Bulgaria and Thessaly; even the plains of Moldavia and Wallachia across the lower Danube had trade relations with it, whilst mule and horse caravans from Constantinople brought to its fairs the

[1] Cp. *infra*, pp. 373–4.

products of that city and also those of Russia and the Far East. The Via Egnatia connected the town with Durazzo and Appollonia on the Adriatic, via Monastir and Ochrida. Surviving roads of the Roman Empire equally linked it with Belgrade, Sofia, Larissa and Constantinople. Seawards its own Greek sailors, as well as the Genoese and Venetians, brought it into commercial contact with the whole of the Mediterranean and with Constantinople. Economically, its annual fair held outside the walls on the banks of the Vardar attracted merchants and products from the Mediterranean lands and even from Flanders and France, and the importance of its fair is testified from the tenth to the fourteenth century.[1] Culturally, Thessalonika was a fortified island of Hellenic and Christian culture in the Balkan peninsula, and from it Christianity—it was an archbishopric of the Greek Church—the Cyrillic alphabet, and other cultural influences spread northwards into the southern Slav lands. Politically, its fortress provided a strategic base for the Emperors in their campaigns against the Bulgarians and the Normans. Within its walls a population of the order of 40,000 was concentrated—that is, of about the size of Bruges, and of the size of a first-grade medieval city. It further boasted industries and fine buildings. The naval power of the Byzantine Empire was not always strong enough to defend from the sea its chief Aegean port. The Arabs sacked the town in 904; the Normans from Sicily took it by military assault in 1185; it fell into the hands of Latin princes during the 4th Crusade from 1204 to 1246; it surrendered to the Venetians in 1423; and to the Turks in 1430. It might be noted here how its more recent history has merely repeated that of its past, and emphasized its great geographical value as a sea gateway and an essentially cosmopolitan city. Greeks, Serbs, Bulgarians and the Austro-Hungarian Empire alike sought to possess it during the Balkan Wars of 1912–13, and it was occupied to serve as a military base by the Allied Powers in 1915.

Constantinople

In Constantinople was expressed all the life and culture of the Byzantine Empire. The city combined all the activities of an urban settlement. It was not only a capital, but also a fortress, an industrial centre, a naval, trading and fishing port, and the ecclesiastical capital of the Greek Church. It was a rare instance in the Middle Ages of a great concentration of population, when it is believed to have numbered nearly a million inhabi-

[1] Tafrali, *Thessalonique au XIVe Siècle*, pp. 117–29.

tants [1]: only Baghdad in its hey-day could be at all compared with it in this respect, and medieval Rome in contrast had only some 50,000 inhabitants. The site of Constantinople (Fig. 30) consisted of a steeply edged peninsula which stood at the southern outlet of the Bosporus and was washed by the Sea of Marmora to the south and by the long arm of the Golden Horn to the north. On the hills at the eastern end of this peninsula Greeks from Megaris first established the colony of Byzantium

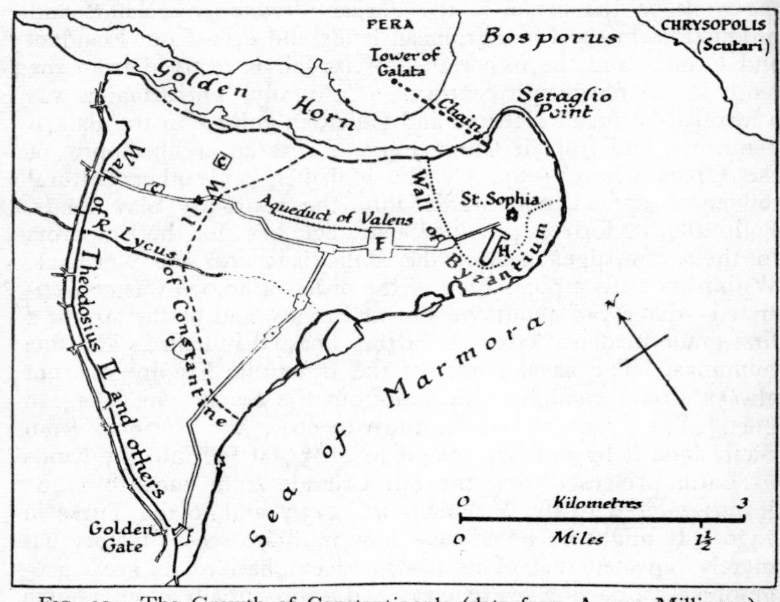

FIG. 30.—The Growth of Constantinople (data from A. van Millingen)

F indicates Forum, H Hippodrome, C cistern. North of the Lycus river an undulating ridge, rising to 250 feet, runs west-east to reach the sea about Seraglio Point. To the south of the river runs a lower parallel ridge. The ground rises steeply from the coasts on every side, but a strip of alluvium along the Marmora coast permitted the construction of harbours which are now silted up

in the year 657 B.C. It was then a small station well placed to assist ships which undertook the difficult voyage from the Aegean into the Black Sea. A rapid surface current flows continually from the Black Sea to the Aegean, the prevailing winds blow from the north and north-east, but in summer a south-west wind favoured the navigation through the winding Dardanelles and Bosporus channels. The Golden Horn may have owed its name to the rich shoals of fish, notably the huge tunny, which

[1] Cp. Andréadès, 'De la Population de Constantinople', *Metron*, vol. I, No. 2, 1920. The population declined to about 100,000 by the year 1453.

moved along with the current from the Black Sea and constituted in the early days of the town its chief revenue ; it was difficult of entry because of the north-east winds but afforded a deep sheltered roadstead which was navigable for seven miles inland. The selection of Constantinople as a joint capital with Rome was conditioned by the need for defending the Euphrates frontier and gave recognition to its geographical advantages as a gateway into Asia. Nikomedeia (now Iṣmid) at the head of the Gulf of Ismid on the Asiatic side and other cities were also considered as possible capitals. Constantinople, like Nikomedeia, not only commanded a route up to the Anatolian plateau along the Gulf of Ismid and the upper Sakaria valley, but it had in addition continuous land communications with Rome and held also the gateway into the Black Sea and to the ports of Sinope and Trebizond, which lay conveniently near the Euphrates.

The town within the walls of Constantine in 330 A.D. spread across the little Lycus river ; Theodosius extended the city in 413, and built ramparts even on its seaward sides. Within this large area, enclosed by walls some nineteen miles in length, were many crowded urban and village settlements interspersed between orchards, meadows and parks. The town had harbourage on both the Sea of Marmora and the Golden Horn, where ships unloaded directly on to the quays. Large supplies of food were kept in the city and underground water was collected in two large cisterns. Suburbs of the town grew up at Galata and Pera across the Golden Horn, over which Justinian built a stone bridge at a narrow point just above the town. The medieval city proved almost impregnable to assaults by land and by sea : attack by sea was made difficult by the rapid south-west flow of the current, and on the landward side the triangular site exposed only one side. In fact, the Roman city, although it has been the goal of countless invaders by land and sea, has only twice been taken—by the Crusaders in 1204 and in 1453 by the Turks, who attacked with both military and naval forces.[1]

The medieval trade of Constantinople will be noticed later.[2] An entrepôt city, it usually controlled the Aegean and the Black Seas ; it had trade relations with Kievan Russia in the ninth and tenth centuries, and with China, by overland routes. It specialized in rich silks and brocades, and in working gold and silver and precious metals. It depended on imported foodstuffs. From the thirteenth century onwards Genoese, Venetian and Florentine merchants largely monopolized its trade.

[1] Cp. Pears, *The Destruction of the Greek Empire* (1903), *passim.*
[2] See *infra,* Chapter XV, pp. 301–2.

CHAPTER IX

ARAB EUROPE IN THE MIDDLE AGES

IF, as is now generally agreed, the geographical conception of Europe includes the islands and marginal lands of the Mediterranean Sea, the Arabs may be said to have made substantial European conquests in the course of the seventh, eighth and ninth centuries. Although few in numbers, the immigrant conquerors revived and re-fashioned a civilization markedly different from that of contemporary Christian Europe, no less in its outward manifestations than in its basic ideas. The economic and political geography of medieval Europe, and to a lesser degree the geography of settlement, were transformed, and these changes can be the more readily assessed, since Mohammedan geographers and travellers have described the Arab countries with a scientific grasp and precision which are remarkable in medieval literature. The lands of the Caliphate comprised the whole of the former Persian Empire and part of the Byzantine (or East Roman) Empire, and at their greatest extent in the eighth century formed a long, sub-tropical belt from the Indus to the Atlantic, and included those favoured regions of ancient culture which were based on the Tigris, Euphrates, Indus and Nile valleys (Fig. 31). In continental Europe the advance of the Arabs was arrested by two decisive defeats : they were defeated in A.D. 732 between Poitiers and Tours, whilst in 718 they finally failed, after a combined attack by land and by sea, to capture Constantinople. Even so, the Iberian peninsula, Syria, Egypt, northern Africa and the chief Mediterranean islands fell into their hands, and the Mediterranean became for a time, in consequence, a political, religious and economic frontier zone between the mutually hostile Christian and Mohammedan worlds.

The Arab Empire, during its short life as an undivided state, constituted above all, despite its extensive maritime frontage, a vast land power. At its maximum extent in the early eighth century it was remarkable for both its sheer length and its territorial continuity, broken only by the Strait of Gibraltar, and it thus contrasted with the relatively compact Byzantine Empire, which was pivoted around, and held together by, the Aegean and Marmora Seas. The Caliphate consisted, as empires are bound to consist, of a number of distinct 'nuclear' regions, which, in area, population and productivity were suitable bases for separate states. Dense populations were concentrated, as Edrisi's twelfth-century map illustrates,[1] in the Euphrates–Tigris region, in the Nile valley and delta, and in parts of Syria, Sicily, Tunis and southern Spain. Each of these nuclear regions was insulated either by sea or by wide stretches of scantily occupied steppe or desert. In other words, physical and climatic geo-

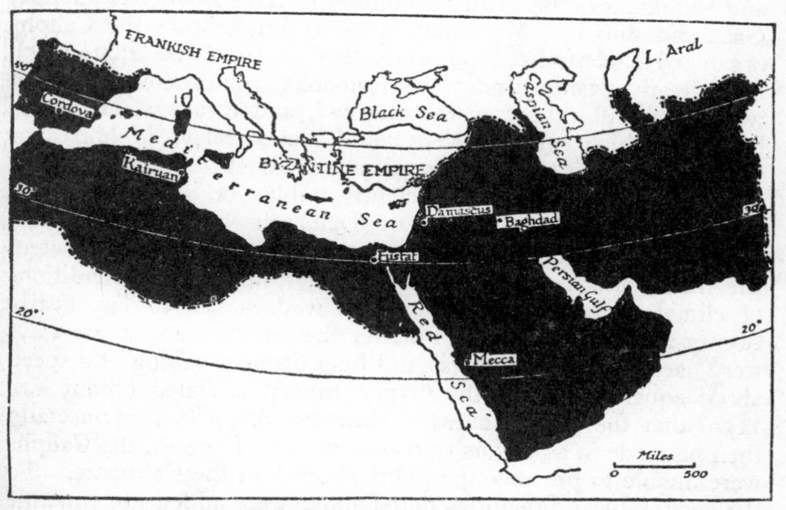

FIG. 31.—The Conquests of Islam, A.D. 632–945

The region shown in black includes all the territories conquered by the Arabs. Note that the frontiers were continually shifting and that Arab territories remained only for a short time politically united. Note the island conquests in the Mediterranean. Note also the compactness of the Byzantine Empire, pivoted around the Aegean Sea, in contrast to the territorial diffuseness of the Arab lands. Capital cities are shown.

graphy differentiated the Arab Empire into a number of constituent parts, and this division proved a real source of weakness owing to the peculiar shape of that empire. Its great length in relation to its breadth deprived it of any geometric centre from which political power could be exercised. Medina, Damascus, Baghdad and Fustât were successively chosen as capital cities,

[1] Edrisi's map of the world, completed in A.D. 1154, was an attempt scientifically to present the *contemporary* distribution of towns within a framework which was based on Ptolemy's world map. Edrisi's map is reproduced on a reduced scale in two sheets, together with explanatory text, by K. Miller, 1927.

and the Caliphs did all in their power, by the creation of rapid means of communication, to overcome the disruptive forces exerted by distance and by regional separatism. Their speediest means of communication were afforded by signals of fire (at night) and of smoke (by day), which could be transmitted over long distances from stations set on hill-tops or on towers: thus the news of a threatened invasion, for example, could be conveyed from the Euphrates at Rahba or Bira to Cairo in a day *or* a night.[1] Similarly, pigeons were used to provide the fastest transit for written messages between important cities: e.g., between Cairo and Damascus or Basra and from intermediate towns like Aleppo, Gaza and Bilbeis. Moreover, in the eighth century the Caliphs organized a centralized postal system or *barid* like that which had already existed under the Romans: route-books, some of which are still extant, were compiled, and caravanserais established at which royal couriers could secure relays of horses or camels. In this way, urgent public business could—when political conditions were sufficiently stable—be quickly effected. The journey between Cairo and Damascus by *barid* took four days, which represents a rate of travel some three times that of the trade caravan, since the latter under sub-tropical conditions of climate, covered then, much as it does still to-day, nearly twenty-five miles a day. Finally, the Mediterranean sea-ways were used for both coastwise and long-distance sailing at a speed about equal to that of the *barid*: thus it is stated (about A.D. 1150) that the voyage between southern Spain and Syria could then be made in as few as thirty-six days.[2] Even so, the Caliphs were unable to preserve the political unity of the Caliphate. To the geographical difficulties noted above were added the endemic disorders which arose out of national, religious and dynastic differences. As might well be expected, the provinces most distant from Baghdad were the first to achieve independence, and it was the highly productive district of southern Mesopotamia, in which Baghdad stood, which remained longest under Arab rule.[3]

The Arab Empire, if it formed essentially a much-distended land power, was nevertheless so placed geographically as to command nearly all the chief maritime routes of the medieval world.

[1] Cp. Gaudefroy-Demombynes, *La Syrie . . . d'après les Auteurs Arabes* (1923), p. 258.

[2] Edrisi, *Description de l'Afrique et de l'Espagne*, trans. Dozy and Goeje (1866), p. 266.

[3] Cp. the 'duration map' of the Arab Empire made by Sten de Geer in 'The Sub-Tropical Belt of Old Empires', *Geog. Ann.*, No. 3, 1928.

At first the Arabs, who were destined to make considerable advances in shipbuilding and the art of navigation,[1] were both unfamiliar with the Mediterranean and somewhat incredulous as to its usefulness, as is shown by the reply of the Governor of Egypt to an inquiry about the Mediterranean made by the Caliph Omar I (about A.D. 650): 'The sea', replied the Governor, 'is a huge beast which silly folk ride like worms on logs.'[2] But suitable land bases, the indispensable condition of sea-power, frequently if not inevitably encourage maritime ambitions. In these the Arab lands were exceptionally favoured, since they enclosed the Strait of Gibraltar and the wider passage between Sicily and Tunis; the ports of Syria, Egypt, northern Africa and Spain, and the islands of the Mediterranean; the southern shores of the Aral, Caspian and Black Seas; the coastlands of southern Arabia and Persia; whilst the Red Sea and the Persian Gulf were inland waters which controlled the shortest and easiest route-ways between the Far East and Europe. The Arabs had, in fact, inherited from the Persian and Byzantine Empires the commanding position which they had shared in the geography of commerce. In Egypt and Syria the Arabs held the European terminals of the trade routes which led respectively from the Red Sea and the Persian Gulf. Egypt remained under Moslem rule throughout the Middle Ages as also did Syria except for the two centuries—the twelfth and thirteenth—when it fell partially under the rule of Crusading states. Only religious and political enmity with the Christian world prevented for a time the full exploitation of these commercial opportunities.

Finally, by their settlement and their utilization of the land within the Mediterranean basin the Arabs not only revived much that was typically Roman but also stamped on the soil the distinctive pattern of their own civilization. They extended the area of garden and terrace cultivation; they directed the submersion of riverside fields and gardens, and even by means of water-wheels, reservoirs and canals effected a certain amount of irrigation proper; they introduced new exotic plants, notably the sugar-cane, rice, the cotton and saffron plants, and the orange and lemon trees; they opened up new caravan routes for merchants and for pilgrims, and built or rebuilt fortified cities, which were divided into tribal quarters, each with its own mosque, bazaar and burial ground.

[1] On Arab achievement in navigation, see Carra de Vaux, *Les Penseurs de l'Islam* (1921), vol. I, ch. I, and Ferrand, G., *Introduction à l'astronomie nautique arabe* (1928).

[2] Cited by S. Lane-Poole, *The Barbary Corsairs* (1890), p. 7.

Syria and Palestine

Prior to their conquest by the Arabs, Syria and Palestine, which they called *Ash Shâm* (= 'the left' or 'the North'), formed a part of the Byzantine Empire and served to link up by land Byzantine Egypt and Asia Minor. They were conquered by a twofold advance; one army advanced from Mesopotamia, and another moved northwards from the Hejaz by the old 'Spice Road' which had long connected Yemen and Syria. It will be recalled that by its position, its configuration and its climate Ash Shâm is sharply differentiated from the steppe and desert of the Arabian peninsula, and further, that it consists broadly of four parallel, north-south belts, a regional analysis based on physiography which the Arab geographers themselves adopted.[1] There is first the maritime plain narrow in the north (i.e., in Phoenicia) and broad in the south (i.e., in Palestine); second, the central highlands, which consists of the high Lebanon chain, to the north and south of which highland country extends; third, the depressed zone, which is occupied by the Sea of Galilee, the Jordan valley, the Dead Sea and the valley of Akaba; and finally, to the east, the Anti Lebanon mountains, south of which extends a series of limestone and basalt plateaux, which constitute a desert border with a small and irregular rainfall. The Arab armies attacked and captured the chief cities which controlled these varied regions. The army from Mesopotamia secured Palmyra and Bostra which were outlying and thriving trade stations situated on the eastern plateau of Syria on the Roman routes between Syria and the Euphrates. Damascus, thanks to its irrigated oasis a garden of fertility, and owing to its position a 'port' from the desert, was taken in A.D. 635; it was evacuated, however, in 636, only to be recovered in the same year after the decisive victory won at the Yarmuk (Hieromax) river, which drains westwards to the Jordan just below the Sea of Galilee.[2] The Battle of Yarmuk allowed the Arabs to enter the Jordan valley, whilst at the same time an army from the Hejaz captured Gaza and overran the maritime plain of Palestine. Judaea was thus encircled, and Jerusalem, the chief city of Byzantine Palestine, fell in A.D. 637. The conquest of Ash Shâm was completed by the occupation of Emessa, Aleppo and Antioch, the capital of Byzantine Syria. Antioch controlled the best route-ways between Syria and Asia Minor, either along the coast from the Orontes estuary or—what was the frequented caravan

[1] Le Strange, *Palestine under the Moslems* (1890), p. 15. (This is an invaluable study based on Arab sources, which are freely quoted.)

[2] Dussaud, *Topographie historique de la Syrie*, p. 319.

route[1]—across the Amanus range by the Beilan (or Baghras) pass. In their movement northwards from Syria the Arabs were confronted by the line of strongly organized Greek cities notably Tarsus, Adana and Mopsuestia, standing between the Taurus and the sea, and Melitene, Mansur, Samosata and Balis, situated on or near the Euphrates.[2] The Arabs captured these cities and held them for about two centuries; they failed entirely to wrest Asia Minor from the Byzantine Empire; they succeeded, however, in conquering Armenia, and thus opened up a caravan route between the Persian Gulf and Trebizond on the Black Sea.

The Arab geographers from the ninth century onwards provide abundant data on the human geography of Syria and Palestine, which appeared to them above all 'a land of blessing'. The Arabs occupied the many cities along the well-indented coast of Syria which then offered, with or without artificial improvements, convenient ports. The old Roman port of Seleucia, which served Antioch, had silted up and the town was abandoned by the time of the Crusades: in its place was built a little to the south, at the mouth of the Orontes, the town of Suedia, known to the Crusaders as Port St. Simon. Tyre, Acre, Tripoli, Laodicea and Beirut had good harbours which in the case of Tyre and Acre were improved by engineering works. Jaffa and Ascalon were the chief ports of Filastan, the Arab province of Palestine, the coast of which was guarded by watch-towers. The maritime cities of Ash Shâm were markets for both local and oriental produce. They were connected by trade routes with Khorasan, Persia and Irak: one route from Balis or Rakka on the Euphrates ran to Aleppo and thence either to Antioch and its port or to Laodicea; another left the Euphrates at cities lower down, ran via Palmyra to Damascus, and thence either to Tripoli, Beirut, Sidon or Tyre.[3] The Arab geographers noted the contrasts in temperature and rainfall along the maritime plain. In Syria, where the highlands stand close to the sea, it was cooler and wetter than in Palestine, and there was abundant water for cities and for irrigation. The sugar-cane was grown around Tyre, Tripoli and Sidon, as well as figs, olives, vines, oranges and bananas. The mulberry tree had already been introduced into Syria by Justinian, and silk was produced in Phoenicia and around

[1] Ibid., p. 434.

[2] Le Strange, *The Lands of the Eastern Caliphate*, 2nd ed., 1931, ch. IX.

[3] Dussaud, op. cit., pp. 432–3. There is also (p. 472) a map of Roman and Arab routes in Syria.

Ascalon in Palestine. In the plain of Palestine rainfall was low, the palm tree was more typical than in Phoenicia, there were stretches of barren sands, but cultivation of fruit was carried on without irrigation. The newly created city of Ar Ramlah (= 'the sandy'), which became the Arab capital of Filastan, typifies the geographical conditions of the Palestinian plain. It stood between the coast and the plateau of Judaea; it derived some water from a river, collected rain-water in cisterns and brackish water from deep wells; it was thickly girdled with trees which provided abundant fruit, especially olives and grapes, whilst beyond this oasis of cultivation stretched sandy wastes.

In interior Syria the Lebanon and Anti Lebanon mountains, although they stand in the same latitude as the arid country around Gabes in Tunis, received thanks to their elevation a high rainfall and, further, were snow-clad in winter.[1] As a result, water was provided for rivers, such as the Jordan and the Abana, for irrigation at the foot of the mountains, and also for the growth of timber trees. The Lebanons were historically an important source of timber for building and for ships; ancient Egypt, the Phoenician and the Roman cities in Syria in turn derived supplies therefrom; the forests have to-day largely disappeared, and there are suggestions that even in Roman times supplies were decreasing. Arab writers, however, refer to 'summer shade' which the Lebanons afforded and speak, although not very precisely or fully, of its forests. The vine and olive pushed up their slopes, and villages based on cultivation were well distributed within the mountains.[2] In the uplands of Filastan, that is to say, of ancient Samaria and Judaea, fruit trees—the olive, vine, fig and sycamore—formed the only tree species, and the natural vegetation was mainly copse and scrub. The rainfall was moderate, but owing to the porous limestone rocks there were no springs available for irrigation. Arab geographers, however, noted the fact (which modern knowledge confirms) that

[1] The Arabs had always a keen eye for water, and an Arab poet noted the chief geographical significance of the Lebanon, which he said, 'carried winter on its head, spring on its shoulders, whilst summer slumbers at its feet'. Cited by Dussaud and others in *La Syrie antique et mediévale*, p. 2. Moreover, to satisfy the caprice of Mamluk Sultans of Egypt, snow was actually carried from Syria to Cairo both by camel and by sea. Cp. Gaudefroy-Demombynes, op. cit., p. 255.

[2] On the Lebanon forests in Roman times, see Bouchier, *Syria as a Roman Province* (1914), pp. 1 and 159. The woods behind Beirut appear to have been largely used up in Roman times. Cp. Dussaud, *Topographie historique de la Syrie*, p. 68. On the woodlands in Arab times, cp. Le Strange, *Palestine under the Moslems*, e.g. pp. 77–9.

in summer, when rainfall is lacking, dew is deposited at night and thus assists cultivation. Sheep and cattle were reared, and both agricultural and manufactured products were abundant: raisins, oil, honey, bananas; cotton and silk goods; cheese; whilst good building stone and even marble were near at hand.

The narrow, deeply sunken zone between the Sea of Galilee and the Gulf of Akaba was called by the Arabs the *Ghaur* or *Ghor*, a word which signifies ' a cleft between mountains '. The temperature was hot and the rainfall rather less than 20 inches a year; the inundation of the river Jordan in winter supplied, however, water for cultivation, and irrigation was practised. Rice and cotton were typical crops, e.g., around the Waters of Merom in the north and around Baisan farther south; the date palm and the indigo trees were even more characteristic; wheat was grown, and in the thirteenth century the sugar-cane was extensively cultivated. The Dead Sea produced asphalt from which bitumen was produced and used to protect the fruit trees from insects. Small ships sailed the Dead Sea and the Sea of Galilee; the Jordan was not navigable, and across it, just below the Sea of Galilee, a bridge carried the road from Damascus to Ar Ramlah and Egypt.

Finally, high up above the *Ghaur* the eastern plateaux of Syria and Palestine formed a broad transitional region of scanty and irregular rainfall (less than 10 inches a year), which was exposed to the encroachment of Beduins from the desert. In the tenth century there were many villages with springs and even forest trees along this belt.[1] The chief towns were Aleppo, Damascus, Palmyra, Bostra, Moab and Amman. The volcanic soils of the Moab and Hauran plateaux were well settled and fertile: olives, figs, grapes, almonds and wheat were grown. The caravan route from Yemen and the Hejaz passed along the eastern plateaux *en route* for Damascus, whilst in the north many routes both Roman and Arab in origin linked up Syria with the Euphrates and with Baghdad. There exist to-day in north-eastern Syria, in what is now largely desert, abundant ruins of large and flourishing Roman cities together with evidences of former forests and of the cultivation of the vine and the olive.[2] The destruction and abandonment of most of these cities may have resulted from the conquering attacks of both Persians and Arabs in the early

[1] Le Strange, *Palestine under the Moslems*, Chapter I.

[2] Cp. Butler, ' Desert Syria ', *G.R.*, Feb. 1920. This article contains important criticisms of the views on the past climate of Syria advanced by Huntington in *Palestine and its Transformation* (1914).

seventh century. Already in the early centuries A.D. they suffered from the increased use of the Egyptian trade routes. Certainly the Arabs do not appear to have restored the walls, public buildings and above all the indispensable organization of water-supply on which these cities depended. This decay of settlement and of cultivation may be explained in terms of human neglect; an explanation cannot be found in terms of decreasing rainfall, since the evidence seems to indicate a high rainfall during the Arab period.[1] Moreover, it may be recalled that many routes crossed the semi-desert country between Ash Shâm and the Euphrates, and that certain outlying cities, although much less prosperous than in Roman times, continued to exist as caravan stations, notably Palmyra and Bostra, where the vine was still cultivated in the thirteenth century.

Under the Omayyad Caliphs, between the years A.D. 661 and 762, Syria provided in Damascus the capital of an empire which (by A.D. 711) stretched from the Atlantic to the Indus river. Damascus enjoyed certain geographical advantages which marked it out even by this time as an enduring city of outstanding importance. Situated in plateau country between the snow-clad Anti Lebanon to the west and what has become to-day almost desert to the east, it commanded routes to the Mediterranean ports, Armenia, Mesopotamia, Egypt, the Hejaz and Yemen. The waters of the Abana river were its greatest asset, since it received only about 10 inches of rain a year. The Abana passes through a gorge in the Anti Lebanon, flows throughout the year, and pours out its wealth of water by means of numerous channels over the broad oasis of *Ghutah* around the city, where in consequence flourished fields, gardens, orchards and meadows. Sugar, cotton, corn, olives, roses, grapes and other fruits were produced in abundance. The industries of Damascus included arms, silks, brocades, carpets, glass, perfumes and paper, probably made from cotton. In the Arab Empire Damascus no longer occupied the ex-centric position which it had held in the Byzantine Empire, but became centrally placed in relation to Baghdad, Mecca and Cairo. In contrast, Antioch came to occupy a marginal position whereas in the Byzantine Empire it commanded a junction of land and sea routes. In consequence, Damascus assumed the primacy formerly held by Antioch; it flourished as a political, economic and religious centre; above all, its agricultural wealth

[1] Evidence of a few large Arab baths in cities where the country to-day is practically desert suggest that rainfall was ample in Arab times. For one instance see Dussaud, *Topographie historique de la Syrie*, p. 259.

mpressed the Arab mind, and the city was acclaimed a veritable aradise on earth.

gypt

The desert of Tih, which occupies the lower northern half f the mountainous Sinai peninsula, imposed no obstacle to the rab advance into Egypt: oases with springs and palm trees xisted here and there, and the desert could be crossed in six ays. The Arab army from Palestine reached El Arish—then s now the frontier town of Egypt; it then crossed the Tih esert, keeping behind the lagoons of the coast and captured he old Roman port of Pelusium. The army entered Lower (or eltaic) Egypt by way of the narrow isthmus between the lagoon f Lake Manzala and the Balah Lakes, the isthmus through which he historic route between Egypt and Palestine has always run. t won a victory at Heliopolis, and in A.D. 641 captured the egionary fortress of Babylon, which stood near the later city of airo at the head of the delta. Alexandria itself, despite help rom the sea, fell to the conquerors in 642, and finally in 646.[1])n the site now known as Old Cairo just outside the stronghold f Babylon, the victorious leader Amrou pitched camp and built ustât (= 'the tent'), the first Arab capital of Egypt. Fustât tood on the right bank of the Nile, above the delta and opposite he ancient capital city of Memphis; the island of Roda facilitated bridging by two chains of boats—some ninety in all, whilst here, also, was rebuilt a Nilometer for measuring the flood. In hus placing their capital city the Arabs abandoned, as capital, he city of Alexandria which had served in turn Ptolemaic, Roman nd Byzantine rulers of Egypt. Alike to the emperors at Rome nd at Constantinople, who held the sea routes, Alexandria had bvious advantages as a capital. To the Arabs, who lacked seaower at this time, it lay too exposed to attack from the sea, vhilst moreover during the summer inundation of the delta ommunications between Alexandria and the Caliph's capital at Medina were interrupted. Cairo (= 'the victorious'), which vas built in 969 a little to the north of Fustât, succeeded the atter as capital. A bridgehead and river station, Cairo became wealthy and populous city surrounded with orchards, plantaions of sugar-cane, vineyards and gardens. It was, moreover, onnected with Suez by an old canal, which the Arabs reopened n order to provide a continuous water route for the carriage of orn to Medina. The origin of the canal is ascribed to the 'tolemaic rulers of Egypt; it was available only during the

[1] A. J Butler, *The Arab Conquest of Egypt* (1902).

summer flood season and needed continual dredging ; for politica
reasons it was temporarily filled in about 761, but reopened i
780. Three other canal projects were considered in the reig
of Harun ar Rashid (A.D. 763–809) only to be abandoned fo
geographical or political reasons. One was to link up the Mediterranean and Red Seas between Pelusium and Suez, but it wa
dropped owing to the erroneous view that the Red Sea stood a
a higher level than the Mediterranean and might therefore drai
away.[1] Another scheme was to cut a canal between the uppe
Nile and the Red Sea in the latitude of Jidda, but this was tech
nically out of the question. Finally, the idea of a canal alon
the delta between Alexandria, Lake Tinnis and Pelusium wa
opposed on the ground that it would facilitate the Byzantin
fleets in any advance that might be made against Mecca.

Except for its maritime cities Egypt lies outside Mediterranea
Europe, but in two respects it was very important to Europ
in the Middle Ages. In the first place it stood astride the mai
route-way between Europe and the Far East—lands of contraste
climates and products. In the second, it was in itself a grea
producing area of agricultural, industrial, and—to a much smalle
extent—mineral wealth. The great solitary and perennial rive
with its gentle current provided a waterway for boats below th
first cataract at Aswan : it took twenty-five days to go up rive
from Fustât to Aswan. The régime of the Nile, characterize
by a regular seasonal rise but an inconstant volume of floo
water, as ever, conditioned the agricultural activity and settle
ment distribution of Egypt, and a government department care
fully measured the rise of the flood and maintained the mor
essential dikes, dams and irrigation channels. The Nilomete
at Roda island (near Fustât) registered the rise of the river be
tween July and October : the optimum level was 16 cubits ; i
the rise exceeded 18 cubits, trees and houses were flooded an
destroyed, whilst a rise of less than 12 involved the country i
drought and consequent sterility.[2] The cultivated lands o
Egypt formed an unbroken ribbon of fields from Aswan to Fustâ
varying from half to a day's journey (about thirty miles) i
breadth, together with the whole of the delta and the Faiyu
oasis. The varied products of Egypt included cereals, especiall
wheat and millet, which were sown in autumn after the floods
flax, hemp, indigo and cotton, which was an ancient native crop
whilst the sugar cane, introduced by the Arabs, was grow
particularly in the delta and in the Faiyum oasis, where the juic

[1] Carra de Vaux, op. cit., I, pp. 6–7.
[2] Édrisi, op. cit., p. 59. Edrisi wrote in the mid-twelfth century.

was extracted by mills worked by oxen.[1] The chief deficiencies of Egypt, which were made up by imports from Europe, were timber, pitch, iron and steel; its minerals were chiefly precious stones, e.g., the much-prized emeralds from the Kharbar mines worked in the distant granitic highlands of the south-east and the rubies from Thara to the south of Cairo.[2] Roads followed along both banks of the Nile, aloof from the flood plain and connecting up numerous settlements, whilst a lateral channel—the Joseph canal which is shown on Edrisi's map—left the Nile at Sol, whence via a line of cities it reached and watered the highly productive Faiyum oasis, to the south-west of Cairo. The Byzantine industries of Egypt were maintained and extended under Moslem rule: high-grade silk, cotton, linen and woollen fabrics; sugar-refining; flour-milling; shipbuilding; the working of precious stones and metals; paper, glass and pottery. Thanks to its agriculture, industry and transit trade, Nilotic Egypt, a great oasis within a desert, was filled with towns never more than a day's journey apart,[3] and was one of the most densely settled areas of the medieval world. It is significant that the population of Egypt at the Arab conquest is estimated broadly on the basis of poll-tax returns, at between 10 and 20 millions[4]; about the year 1800, after centuries of Turkish rule and under changed conditions of world trade routes, it had fallen to little more than 2½ millions, and it is remarkable that certain crops, e.g., cotton, which were introduced into Egypt in the mid-nineteenth century, should be to-day referred to as new crops.[5]

Egypt provided passage-ways for merchants and for pilgrims bound for the Holy City of Mecca, and—particularly in the later Middle Ages—for oriental products destined for Europe. Pilgrims usually went overland from the Nile delta to Suez, and thence by ship to Jidda, the port for Mecca. Arabian and Far Eastern merchandise—silks, spices, gems, perfumes, gums—which were destined for the Mediterranean seaports of Egypt, were at first carried by the Red Sea to Suez, thence by canal

[1] The particular requirements—aspect, water, manure, &c.—for the cultivation of the sugar-cane are noted by Arab writers on agriculture. It was planted in March; the cane was cut in January and after the extraction of juice given to the horses. See Ibn-Al-Awam's *Livre d'Agriculture*, pp. 365–7, trans. Clément-Mullet (1864).

[2] Quatremère, *Mémoires géographiques et historiques sur l'Egypte* (1811).

[3] Cp. Edrisi, op. cit., p. 59.

[4] Cp. the facts cited by Dr. M. Awad in the publication of the International Geography Congress, Cambridge, 1927, p. 330, and an article by El-Darwish, in *Population*, vol. I, no. 2.

[5] Brunhes, *L'Irrigation* (1902), p. 327.

to Fustât and by the Nile channels to the ports. The great entrepôt for the products of India, China and southern Arabia was Aden, situated on the coast of Yemen near to the entrance of the Red Sea. It was exceptional, prior to the fifteenth century, for those ships which were engaged in the Far Eastern trade to enter the Red Sea, since, owing to its coral reefs, its many islands, its northerly winds and its inhospitable coasts, that sea was very dangerous for the large vessels of the ocean unless they were skilfully piloted.[1] In the late tenth century the decline of Baghdad and piracy in the Persian Gulf served to deflect traffic to the Red Sea and Egypt, the more so since the Gulf–Euphrates–Syria route was less direct and more expensive owing to the long land portage. Aden prospered as the port of transhipment between the two seas, and the Red Sea–Egyptian route was well frequented. In the Red Sea boats were employed which were easy to handle and specially adapted to its conditions: they were built without nails, and the timber was secured by coco-nut fibre and made water-tight with gum Arabic. At the end of the eleventh century when Christian armies in Palestine made Suez unsafe, merchants and pilgrims used alternative overland routes through Egypt. The most frequented route ran up the Nile to Kuft near the ancient Coptos and continued thence for some seventeen to twenty days by camel across the desert to Aidab, situated in latitude 22° on the scorching, barren Red Sea coast, whence Jidda could be reached by a day and night's crossing. The town of Aidab has now completely disappeared, but it is the only Egyptian port on the Red Sea which is marked on Edrisi's map. Dependent on the outside world for both water and food supplies, Aidab owed its existence and its importance to fishing and pearl diving and more especially to the ferry traffic with Jidda and to the 'break of freight' necessary at the junction of the sea-way from Aden and the camel-way from the Nile. It declined rapidly after about 1378, when the Egyptian custom-house was transferred from Aidab to Tor, which stands on the south-west coast of the Sinai peninsula (cp. Fig. 5, p. 26).

Commercial intercourse between Egypt and Christian Europe was at first interrupted owing to the hostility which reigned over the Mediterranean sea; in the twelfth century, however, despite Papal prohibitions on the export to Egypt of arms and iron, trade relations were established between Italian cities and the ports of the Nile delta, and in the following century Venice

[1] See A. Kammerer, 'La Mer Rouge, l'Abyssinie et l'Arabie depuis l'antiquité', vol. I, 1929.

asserted supremacy in the markets of Egypt. Alexandria, which had a population of some 600,000 under Byzantine rule, since it ceased to be the capital city under the Moslems, suffered some decline [1] both in population and in commerce, but even so it tended to remain a great cosmopolitan city and entrepôt port, where the merchandise of India, China and Arabia was collected for distribution mainly by sea to the ports of Arab and Christian Europe. Alexandria had a canal-way which linked it with Rosetta on the Rosetta arm of the Nile delta, and possessed two large harbours on either side of the embankment which joined up the island of Pharos with the mainland (Fig. 6). The great lighthouse, which had been built as early as *c.* 270 B.C. on the eastern end of Pharos island, served until its collapse in the fourteenth century both to warn the town of the approach of hostile fleets and to guide vessels into the port by flashing sunlight by day and lights by night.[2] During the Middle Ages other and newer maritime cities, notably Damietta, Rosetta and Tinnis, shared with Alexandria the commerce of Egypt. Both Rosetta and Damietta were flourishing medieval cities ; the Rosetta and Damietta channels provided them with better waterways to Cairo than Alexandria enjoyed ; whilst, further, at this time, their river estuarine harbours stood nearer to, and were more accessible from the sea—a fact which served not only to foster their trade but also to facilitate the attacks of the fleets of the Crusaders.

Cyrenaïca and Tunis

The bordering steppe and desert to the west of Egypt proved no barrier to the Arab advance, and Barca (Cyrenaïca), reached from Alexandria by a journey of twenty-one days along the littoral, was conquered and incorporated in Egypt. The Barca plateau, thanks to its elevation and its projection northwards, received a moderate rainfall which made possible the location of towns along the maritime slopes and plains and in the internal depressions. Hence in these favoured areas the Arabs were able to cultivate olives and even cotton, whilst sheep were pastured on the plateau. Westwards of Barca steppe conditions prevail behind the Great Syrtis Bay, but there was a narrow strip of cultivated land around Tripoli, which the Arabs

[1] The Arab walls built in A.D. 811 enclosed only about half of the city area in the time of Hadrian. The population estimate given above is that given by Prof. Diehl, in vol. III of the *Histoire de la Nation Egyptienne*, p. 480.

[2] Cp. *The Travels of Benjamin of Tudela*, ed. M. Komroff (1928), p. 317. These travels covered the period 1160–73.

captured in A.D. 643. The best lands of northern Africa are situated in northern Tunis, which had formed the base in turn of Carthaginian power and of the Roman province of 'Africa' and was to become the Arab Afriqiya. The conquest of Tunis presented difficulties to the Arabs. The heart of Tunis consists of the basin of the Mejerda river to which access can be made directly from the sea-coast around Carthage. The Carthaginians and Romans had conquered Tunis by an advance from the sea; the Arabs had only land forces. Furthermore, although Tunis was largely under the control of Berbers, it was nominally Byzantine territory, and it was, in fact, studded with fortresses and maritime strongholds through which help by sea was obtained.[1] The difficulties involved in reducing Tunis by a landward advance from Tripoli explain the selection of the site of Kairuan, the future Arab capital of Afriqiya. The site of Kairuan, like that of Mecca itself, cannot be explained in terms of physical and climatic geography.[2] The chief cities of Tunis then stood near its coasts in the midst of cultivable country. Kairuan (= 'the tent'), in contrast, stood about thirty miles from the strip of cultivated land along the Sahel coast; it has no navigable river, nor was it a crossing-point of land routes; whilst the surrounding country, which receives a low and irregular rainfall (about 12 inches), is mainly steppe in character. In short, only the historical circumstances at the time of the foundation of Kairuan serve to explain the selection of its site: the Arabs in their landward advance were attacked on the flank by Byzantine sea-power which held the coastlands and the ports, e.g., Carthage and Susa, and Kairuan was a convenient military base, situated midway between the enemy coast and eastern edge of the Atlas plateau, from which they might advance towards the better-watered and well-settled lands in the north. It is interesting to note how the selection as capital cities of Damascus, Cairo and Kairuan in place of the Byzantine seaward capitals of Antioch, Alexandria and Carthage illustrates in each case how the early Caliphate rested solely on military power.

The Islands

The Arab conquest of the Mediterranean islands illustrates the efforts of a land power to dominate a sea and its trade by securing its insular bases. In Egypt, Tunis and Spain the Arabs held excellent land bases from which to launch attacks against the neighbouring islands, which were almost all outlying posses-

[1] Diehl, *L'Afrique Byzantine* (1896).
[2] Cp. Despoir, 'Kairouan', in the *A. de G.*, XXXIX, Mar. 1930.

sions of the Byzantine Empire. Rhodes, Crete and Cyprus lay temptingly near to Egypt and Syria; Sicily, Malta and Sardinia formed obvious objectives to the rulers of Afriqiya; whilst the Balearic islands could easily be reached from Spain. The islands had long served, under their Byzantine rulers, as in earlier times under the predominance of the Carthaginians, Greeks or Romans, as control points on the sea-ways along which local and oriental commodities were exchanged, whilst some of the larger islands, notably Sicily and Cyprus, were themselves important producing areas. To the Arabs, possession of the sea promised not only an alternative means of communication between Spain, Africa and the Near Eastern ports which was quicker and easier than by caravan, but it enabled them to harass the routes of Byzantine commerce and to aspire to an important share in Mediterranean trade. Their conquest of the islands, in striking contrast to their rapid movement by land, was slow, and their hold on them was short-lived: their efforts were ill-organized; at first they were inexperienced sailors and weak in sea-power, and the rich, walled Byzantine cities, protected by their fleets, made a long resistance. Until they had learnt from the Syrians and Egyptians, the Arabs showed little inclination to venture on the unfamiliar sea[1]; later they raided islands by expeditions from near-by coasts and established pirate strongholds; finally definite conquest took place. Thus Cyprus was reached from Syria and held almost continuously between A.D. 708 and 966; Malta was taken (869) and Sicily was eventually conquered bit by bit between *c.* A.D. 800 and 965; whilst Crete and the Balearic islands—both occupied by adventurers from Spain—were similarly seized and held. Arab attacks by sea were launched also at the maritime cities of the mainland: Genoa was sacked by pirates in 935; Salonika in 904; whilst Garde Fresnet on the Provence coast was captured and held. In result between the seventh and the tenth centuries, Constantinople alone of the Christian cities maintained a precarious and localized trade by sea; but the main currents of trade between the Near East and western Europe were practically stopped, as is suggested by the disuse of Egyptian papyrus in Gaul about A.D. 677, the decline of Marseilles and the extreme poverty of Provence.[2]

[1] It should be remembered that in the Indian Ocean Arab seamen were well known, but it does not seem clear whether this sea-faring population of southern Arabia took any part in Mediterranean navigation.

[2] This is the thesis enunciated by Pirenne in *Medieval Cities*, pp. 28–30. It has, however, been recently challenged by Patzelt in *Die Fränkische Kultur und der Islam* (1932).

Moreover, the stoppage of the Mediterranean trade is not unconnected with the opening up of the overland routes across Russia from the Black and Caspian Seas to the Baltic. The recovery of the Mediterranean islands by the Christian powers from the eleventh century onwards marks the revival of maritime commerce under the leadership of the Italian cities.

In the larger islands, e.g., Sicily, Arab rule stimulated agricultural development and the growth of population. (See Chapter XIV.)

The Iberian Peninsula

The Moslem lands in Spain bore the name Andalos [1] and were first conquered by Taric the Moor. He landed with 12,000 Moors at Algeciras in the year A.D. 711 and won a decisive victory near Medina Sidonia on the Barbate river where the road crosses from Algeciras to Seville. The conquest was rapid and reached up to, and beyond, the Pyrenees. Andalos was a continually changing geographical expression, for the northern frontier of Moslem rule was never stable. The conquests of Galicia, Leon, Old Castile, Navarre and Aragon, were not permanently held; Asturias, between the Cantabrian mountains and the sea, was never conquered; and the Pyrenees, although they were crossed, never formed part of the frontier system. At its greatest extent in the tenth century Arab Spain extended northwards to the Douro whilst in the north-east it included most of the Ebro basin. Even so, the frontier fluctuated continually with the fortunes of war and gradually receded (Fig. 32); and the fortress cities of Saragossa, Medinaceli and Toledo formed the fixed points in the Arab marches. It is significant that Arab rule was never permanently established beyond the limit of Mediterranean climate, or, as Edrisi puts it, 'the climate of the olive' (Fig. 32).

Spain, a land of sharp physical and climatic contrasts, has, like northern Africa, large areas of steppe on the meseta, in the Ebro basin and in Murcia. The highest Arab civilization in Spain, as in Arabia itself, was developed not on the steppe but

[1] *Andalos* took its name, though indirectly, from the Vandals who crossed from Spain into Africa in the fifth century, and the word is preserved in Andalusia, in which lay the last remnants of Moslem rule. It appears that the Vandals embarked for Spain at the port now known as Tarifa, which was named after them Andalos. It was here that Tarifa landed with a small band in 711 and discovered the weaknesses of Visigothic rule in Spain. The port of Andalos was re-named Tarifa after the invader, but its old name was transferred to the whole of Moslem Spain. Cp. Dozy, *Recherches sur l'histoire politique et littéraire de l'Espagne*, 3rd ed., I, 301–3.

in the valleys, hills and plains, where either rainfall or irrigation permitted sub-tropical cultivation. The bulk of the Moslem immigrants into Spain were Moors, not Arabs, and these uncouth mountaineers were settled generally throughout Andalos in mountainous or plateau country where pastoral activity was typical: e.g., in the steppes of Estremadura and La Mancha, and in the Guadarrama and Nevada mountains. The Arabs proper, although they were relatively few in number, became the leaders in Spain. They came not from an original desert habitat but from the settled lands of Yemen and the Hejaz, and by secondary dispersions from Egypt, Syria and southern Persia. This fact

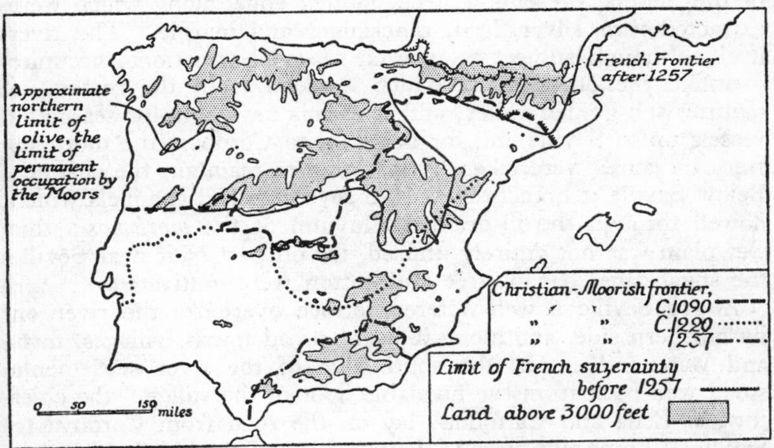

FIG. 32.—The Recession of the Frontier of Moslem Spain (data from map 62 of the *Cam. Med. Hist.*)

Note that the northern limit of permanent occupation of the Moors coincides roughly with the northern limit of the culture of the olive. The significant control on their settlement in the north was rather the severe winters of northern Spain.

helps to explain their preference for, and localization within, villages and towns of Andalusia, Valencia and Murcia,[1] the remarkable skill with which they exploited the agricultural potentialities of southern Spain, and finally the ease with which they rebuilt and revived its Roman cities. Arab culture, industry and trade were expressed in the cities, and these were concentrated above all in Andalusia, Murcia and Valencia, that is to say, in those basins and plains which lay around and below the meseta and were favoured both in climate and in their proximity to the sea.

The valley of the Guadalquivir (= 'the Great River') forms

[1] Cp. Stokes, *Spanish Islam*, p. 139, and Lévi-Provençal, *L'Espagne Mussulmane au Xème siècle*, p. 23.

a triangular, alluvial floored depression, the base of which fronts the Atlantic and lies directly open to the moist south-westerly winds. The winds precipitate their moisture on the high slopes which enclose the valley on the north, south and east, and the rainfall is fairly high for the latitude, so that cultivation could largely dispense with irrigation. Even so, some of the soil is salty; there are patches of steppe with esparto grass; whilst for the intensive garden and orchard cultivation along the river it was necessary to supply additional water either by water-wheels or by means of conduits from the mountain streams to the north. On this side of the valley the Sierra Morena, part of the meseta, presents a steep, faulted edge, along which were extracted iron, silver, lead, quicksilver and marble. The river itself, although subject to marked seasonal variations, occupies—unlike the other rivers which descend from the meseta—a mature well-graded valley, and was thus navigable for sea-going vessels up to Seville and for boats up to Cordova, the more so, since measures were taken by dredging to maintain the channel. Below Seville it branches out into several broad channels which flowed through the ill-drained alluvium of the *marismas*: this wet plain was not entirely unused, for on part of it near Seville the sugar-cane, banana-tree and cotton were cultivated.

Above Seville a well-watered terrace overlooks the river on its northern side, and along it were spread towns, villages, forts and water-mills. On the south side of the river settlements stood well back from the floodable floor of the valley: the chief towns—Ecija and Carmona—lay on the road from Cordova to Seville. Three sub-areas of dense settlement within the Guadalquivir basin were outstanding: the plain of the Campiña, to the south-west of Cordova; the country of which Jaen was the centre, to the east of Cordova; and the Ajaraf plateau to the north of Seville. Jaen stood in the midst of cornfields, orchards and meadows, but it was famous for the working of silk produced in numerous villages around. The wealthy and populous city of Seville commanded by its bridge of boats the lowest crossing over the Guadalquivir; standing a few miles below the tidal head of the river, it was a port to which ships, venturing through the Straits, often came; it was a fortress and also a great market. It built ships and worked silk, whilst it prepared and marketed oil, wine and figs. The figs, olives and vines came mainly from the fertile Ajaraf slopes which stretched westwards to Niebla and lay between the coastal flats and the meseta.

Cordova, which served the Omayyad rulers of Spain as a capital from A.D. 756 until 1002, is a remarkable medieval instance of the concentration of population, as it was remarkable also for its material splendour and its intellectual pre-eminence. It stood on the north bank of the river in the midst of varied and productive country: the Cordova plateau to the north yielded timber, pasture, vine and olive, as well as abundant streams; the Sierra Morena was mined, above all for iron, mercury and silver; whilst the Campiña was a rich agricultural plain. Cordova controlled the natural route of Andalusia towards the Atlantic, whilst upon its bridge—the first bridge above Seville—converged routes from the Mediterranean and Atlantic coastlands and the Pyrenees. The site of Cordova in the tenth century occupied several times the area of the present town; its population in the former period is estimated at about half a million, but to-day it is about a hundred thousand. The Arabs rebuilt the Roman bridge, which after many restorations still survives,[1] and a dam was built across the river just above the town along which a dozen mills were erected. Water was carried in leaden pipes from the Sierra Cordova to supply the numerous gardens, mosques, baths and houses as well as the great palace of the city; pomegranate and date, together with orange, fig and almond trees, flourished in its gardens; whilst silk-weaving, pottery-making, leather- and metal-working were actively carried on. The great mosque, part of which survives, was built immediately to the north of the bridge, on a site formerly occupied in turn by a Roman temple and a Visigothic cathedral. Red marble for its columns—they numbered over a thousand—was brought from Cabra, to the south-west of the town, although much was also brought long distances—from Africa, Sicily, Greece and Constantinople. Pine-wood from the distant Sierra de Guda, which was excellent alike for building and for ships' masts, was brought by sea from Tortosa on the Ebro. No less important than its sheer size and beauty was the intellectual ascendancy of Cordova at a time when Christian Europe, with the exception of Constantinople, had lost the art of scientific and philosophical speculation. And it was from Cordova, which was renowned for its university and its royal library, that western Europe became reacquainted with the thought and learning of ancient Greece, through the medium of translations of Arab translations of Greek texts.

At the southern extremity of the Guadalquivir basin and at the foot of the Sierra Nevada stood the successor to Cordova, Granada, from which during the years 1248 and 1491 the Moslems

[1] It has sixteen arches and is about 240 yards long. Cp. Lévi-Provençal, op. cit., p. 202.

ruled their surviving territories in Spain, namely a narrow state encircling the Sierra Nevada between Gibraltar and Almeria. This town grew up at the junction of the Darro and the Jenil rivers and below its twin palace fortresses of the Alhambra and the Generalife. The luxuriant Vega, of which Granada was the natural centre, was abundantly watered, above all by the Jenil itself which descends from the snow-clad Sierra Nevada, and was filled with irrigated gardens, fields and orchards. In the town itself, which is said to have had a population of about 400,000, silk-, flax- and metal-working industries prospered. Farther south, on the seaward side of the Sierra Nevada, was the district of Alpujarras, which was divided up by spurs of the Sierra into a number of high, narrow, enclosed glens, where the rich soils of the valley bottoms and all the suitable slopes were irrigated as vineyards, olive and mulberry groves and orchards, whilst sheep and cattle were kept on the rocky uplands. It was in this self-contained world, where their industry was extracting the utmost from the soil, that the Moors in the years 1569–70 made their last stand against the Christians and were finally either wiped out or deported. Farther away, the great ports of Lisbon and Barcelona lay somewhat aloof from the centres of Arab culture, and Barcelona was never long held by the Moslems. The ports best placed for relations with the other Arab lands in the Mediterranean were Malaga, Almeria, Carthagena, Denia and Valencia. Malaga and Almeria stood within small coastal plains, but the mountains pressed closely on the neighbouring coastlands, so that it took seven days to travel between the two towns by land as against two days by sea. Nevertheless, this restricted coastland produced sugar, figs, bananas and palms. Malaga was noted for its export of figs and straw, whilst Almeria (= the 'Watch Tower') became the chief port of commerce and naval stronghold of Moslem Spain. It was the only town in Spain newly created by the Arabs [1]; it had large-scale industries: shipbuilding, silk-spinning, and the manufacture of glass, copper and iron goods; it produced fruits in the Andorax valley, and was visited by ships from Syria, Egypt and the Italian cities. Carthagena was a convenient port of refuge at the head of a bay, and also served the dry plains of Murcia, parts of which at least were irrigated for agriculture. In Valencia, with its two ports of Valencia and Denia, the rainfall though irregular is slightly

[1] R. Dozy, *Recherches*, &c., I, pp. 295–6. The town of Az-Zahra, 'City of the Fairest', near Cordova, occupied a new site but was soon destroyed. Except for Almeria, the Arabic forms of Spanish place-names are simply translations of the pre-Arab names.

higher than in Murcia, and water from its torrential rivers was collected in reservoirs and distributed by means of conduits so as to supply flower gardens and orchards as well as houses in the towns. Its wealth of flowers won for it the description 'the scent bottle of Andalos'. Figs, raisins, grain and esparto were grown, and even some sugar-cane. Denia, which became a naval station, was important for its shipbuilding. It used pine-wood timber from the Sierra de Cuenca, which was drifted down the River Cabriel into the Jucar, thence to Cullera and so by sea to Denia.[1]

Towns, associated with Mediterranean cultivation, were likewise spread throughout the south-western provinces of the peninsula. Edrisi describes the cultivation of the vine along the western plains, for example, up the Mondego valley from Coimbre. The southern slopes of the Algarve massif were richly productive of figs and vines; the silk-worm was reared and timber from the Algarve was used for shipbuilding, e.g., at Silves. It is of interest that the lower Tagus plain between Lisbon and Santarem was so fertile that wheat was said to grow there in forty days.[2] In the wetter lands towards the west of Andalos dairy farming was relatively more important than in the south-east; thus Alcacer do Sal, which ships could reach from the sea, produced much milk, butter and meat. On the meseta generally many sheep and horses were reared; the higher, wetter mountains, like the Guadarrama, afforded the best pastures, and Toledo was noted for its fat cattle and sheep; whilst new breeds of sheep from north Africa were introduced by the Moors. The olive was cultivated throughout most of Arab Spain; its most northerly extension was in the Ebro basin where it was grown to the south of Jaca and around Lerida.

The political and cultural base of Moslem Spain lay in the more southerly lands of Mediterranean climate, but almost all of the rest of the peninsula felt the impress, though less markedly, of Moslem rule. In the far north the young folded Cantabrian mountains form a high edge to the meseta with which they are welded, whilst between them and the sea lies a narrow belt of broken country, which is called Asturias in the west (where it is widest) and forms the Basque provinces in the east, at its

[1] Edrisi, op. cit., pp. 237–8. This practice long persisted and is described by Reclus in the late nineteenth century.

[2] This statement is not incredible. There were many varieties of wheat, and spring wheat is known to have grown with great rapidity, in as few as thirty days at Milos in the Aegean. Cp. Jardé, *Les Céréales dans l'Antiquité Grecque*, pp. 11, 75, 77.

tapering end. These lands were never conquered by the Arabs, and it was Asturias, the last refuge of Visigothic power in Spain, which eventually led the Christian advance against the Moslems. Galicia in the north-west was overrun but not permanently held: hence Santiago was able to grow famous as a place of pilgrimage.[1] In the early days of the conquest the Arabs pushed across the Pyrenees, and through the Poitou gap and up the Rhône–Saône valleys. Although they were driven back after their defeat between Poitiers and Tours in A.D. 732 they retained control of Languedoc for nearly a century and from Garde Fresnet in Provence raided in the passes of the western Alps. Then in 814 the Franks created the Spanish March, which occupied the southern Pyrenean slopes of Aragon and Catalonia and had its capital at Barcelona. Saragossa became the frontier stronghold of Arab Spain in the north-east. The rise of the Christian states on the northern borderlands of Arab rule, and the slow, eventual regression of Moslem power before their advance, cannot be noted here (Fig. 32). These states were the country of Portugal on the lower Douro and Tagus, with its capital at Coimbre in 1128; the united territories of Asturias, Galicia and Old Castile, with a capital at Leon; Navarre, with its capital at Pampeluna; and finally, Aragon, with its capital at Saragossa, which in 1157 absorbed Catalonia with its great seaport Barcelona. The Christian advance can be measured by the fall of the great Arab cities. The frontier fortress of Toledo, with its copper and iron mines, its metal industries, and its irrigated gardens, fell permanently into Christian hands in 1086, and by 1100 the frontier was withdrawn from the Douro to the Tagus. Lisbon, Seville, Valencia and Cordova were all captured by 1260. The decisive defeat of the Moslems took place at Navas de Tolosa, near Linares, in 1212: the Christian armies had secured the important defile of Despeñaperros which leads down from the meseta to the Guadalquivir, and their victory led to the fall of Cordova itself.

In short, southern Spain, favoured in position and climate and aloof from the northern frontier of conflict, enjoyed again under the stimulus of Moslem rule the economic and intellectual vitality that had characterized it in the days of Rome. It is rather important to emphasize that in many respects Arab rule revived rather than created prosperity in Spain. Irrigation had certainly been practised in Spain by the Romans, but the Arabs seem to have considerably extended its use and improved its methods. It is suggestive of this that the nomenclature of irrigation in

[1] On the supposition, for which there is no scientific justification, that the bones of St. James rested there.

nodern Spanish is essentially Arabic,[1] whilst some of the new
lants introduced by the Arabs into the hot dry plains of Valencia
ınd Murcia, e.g., rice, the sugar-cane and the orange, could not
e grown there without irrigation. The many flourishing cities
f Andalos were all, with the exception of Almeria, formerly
Roman sites, and many of the fruit trees and plants, in the culti-
ation of which the Arabs excelled, had already been cultivated

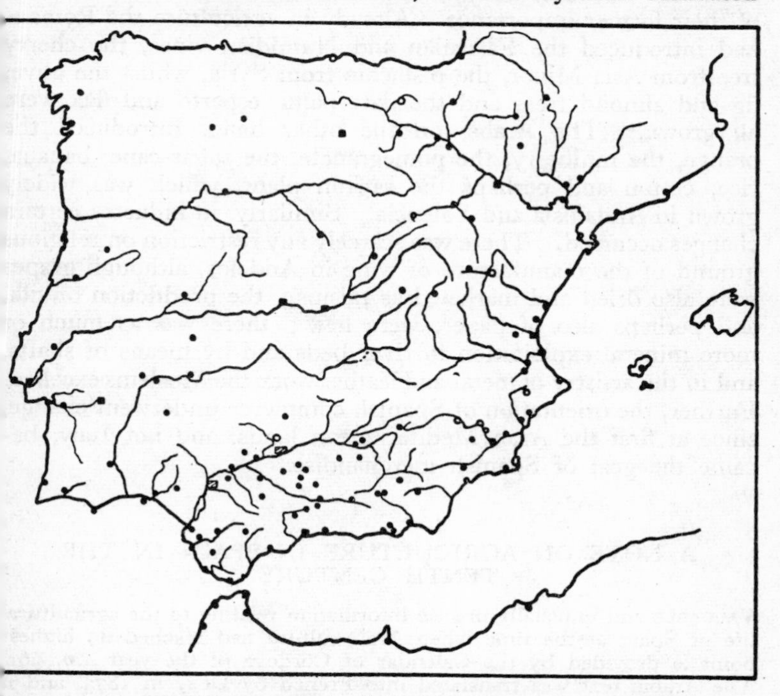

FIG. 33.—The Chief Towns of the Iberian Peninsula in the twelfth century
(The *Geography* of Edrisi has been used as the basis of this map)

ome attempt has been made to grade the towns according to their contemporary importance. Cordova and Seville are shown by rectangles. The order of decreasing importance of the other owns is shown by squares, open dots and black dots. Note the concentration of towns in the south-east

r introduced by the Romans. The road system of Moslem
Spain, which is described clearly by contemporary geographers,
vas based largely on the old Roman network.[2] The relative

[1] Cp. Lévi-Provençal, op. cit., p. 166.

[2] The Arab geographers noted the centrality of Toledo from which
ll chief towns around the *meseta* could be reached in nine days: Cor-
lova, Valencia, Lisbon, Almeria, Santiago and Jaca. Routes from
very direction focused, too, on Cordova.

importance of Spanish towns underwent some change of geographical ' values ', just as they had changed during the centuries of Carthaginian and Roman rule. Cordova was more important than Seville in the tenth century ; Christian Barcelona surpassed Tarragona, which was the chief Roman city in Spain ; Malaga and Denia were greater in the Arab period, whilst Carthagena and more especially Cadiz—then noted for its goats !—had little of their former importance. Already in agriculture the Romans had introduced the Falernian and Numidian vines, the cherry tree from Asia Minor, the pistachio from Syria, whilst the olive, fig and almond trees and the date palm, esparto and flax were all grown.[1] The Arabs, on the other hand, introduced the orange, the mulberry, the pomegranate, the sugar-cane, banana, rice, cotton and perhaps the saffron plant, which was widely grown in Andalusia and Valencia. Similarly, in industry certain changes occurred. There was scarcely any restriction on religious ground of the manufacture of wine in Andalos, although grapes were also dried and marketed as raisins ; the production of silk, and perhaps also of paper, were new ; there was as much or more mineral exploitation in river beds and by means of shafts, and in the artistry of metal and leather work the Moslems excelled. Further, the orientation of Spanish commerce underwent change, since at first the Arab Mediterranean lands, and not Italy, became the goal of Spanish merchandise.

A NOTE ON AGRICULTURE IN SPAIN IN THE TENTH CENTURY

VALUABLE and unusually precise information relating to the agricultural life of Spain at the time when Arab culture had reached its highest point is provided by the Calendar of Cordova of the year A.D. 961. The Arabic text was translated into French by Dozy in 1873, and it has been summarized recently by Lévi-Provençal in his *L'Espagne Mussulmane au Xe Siècle*, pp. 170–3. The Calendar describes month by month the activities of the agriculturist, and indicates how richly varied was the sub-tropical cultivation of Spain in the tenth century. It invites comparison and contrast with the agricultural conditions of present-day Spain. Below is given in bald summary of its instructions to farmers.

January : prop up the olive and pomegranate trees, prune the vines, and gather the sugar canes.

February : graft the pear and apple trees, and incubate the silk-worm eggs.

---

[1] Cp. L. C. West, *Imperial Roman Spain : The Objects of Trade* (1929), pp. 21–8, Table II, and pp. 59–62, Table VII.

March : plant sugar canes and make 'shield graftings' on the fig trees.
April : plant jasmine cuttings, sow henna, basil, rice and beans.
May : gather the oil seeds.
June, July and August : harvest and thrash the corn and gather fruit.
September and October : gather the olive, make the wine, and prepare for the ploughing.
November : gather acorns and chestnuts, and pick the flowers of the saffron.
December : respite for the farmer.

CHAPTER X

THE RUSSIAN STATE

THE earliest strictly 'Russian' states, which were built up around capitals successively at Kiev and Moscow, occupied only part of the broad Russian plain as that region is conceived by modern geographers. Nevertheless, the development of colonization and of political and economic activities in early Russia is so intimately interwoven with the geography of the East European plain, and that geography exerted such a stringent influence on human affairs, that it is essential to review briefly its salient features. That region consists strictly of a number of low plateaux and plains, is generally undulating rather than level in its relief, and is essentially lacking in mountain obstacles to movement. The Russian plain is very loosely framed by nature: in the north, the Baltic and White Seas provide a definite limit, but only a chain of lakes stand between it and Finland; in the south the Caspian and Black Seas and the Caucasus form a clear divide; but eastwards the low Ural mountains do not differentiate the Russian from the Siberian plain, for they are easily crossed, or outflanked in the south; finally, westwards where the Russian plain contracts between the Carpathians and the low Dnieper-Vistula watershed, physical conditions set no effective limit. Thus the Russian plain, situated towards the confines of Europe and Asia, imposed no physical obstacles to ingress from every side, and it was entered alike by Arctic Lapps and Finns, by steppe horsemen from central Asia, by pastoral peoples from middle Europe and by boatmen from the Baltic and Black Seas.

But if the Russian plain has indefinite frontiers, it is nevertheless clearly divided within itself into some three broad zonal regions, each of which has its particular vegetation and its distinctive human response. The zonal distribution of vegetation in the Russian plain follows roughly along latitudinal lines and is governed both directly and indirectly by variations in climate: directly, by the changes in temperature and precipitation; and indirectly by the different types of soils which have ıemselves been formed under, and differentiated by, varied limatic and vegetational conditions. In the extreme north, eyond the Arctic circle, a cover of ice or snow lies for over alf of the year ; tundra vegetation, which consists of moss, chen, dwarf scrubs and peat moor, is everywhere prevalent ; voodland proper and agriculture cannot endure the climate. The tundra belt was occupied by nomad Lapps and Samoyeds vho eked out a livelihood from reindeer breeding and summer shing. Southwards of the Arctic circle the vegetation gradually hanges from the pure tundra type to that of the broad forest one, which occupied the whole of medieval Russia. The forest one extends far to the south to a line roughly drawn between Perm, Kazan and Kiev ; the soils are broadly of the ' podzol ' or sh-coloured type, ranging from stiff clays to loams and sands ; here are large areas of marsh and peat moors especially in the north, whilst the tree species and their associated undergrowth vary with the variations in the temperature and precipitation. Thus in the north and north-east coniferous forests of spruce nd fir are the common species, the former being found mainly n clay, the latter on sandy, soils. Peat mosses and swamps occur alike in watersheds, depressions and valleys, since the gradients of the Russian plain are inadequate to drain off the nelted snows of spring or the heavy summer rains. In the outhern limits of the forest belt where it impinges on the south Russian steppe, and particularly in the warmer south-west, the oak become the typical species : the oak requires greater warmth han the spruce and does not tolerate complete podzolization of he soil, so that it found favourable conditions for extension on he borderlands between the podzol and black earth regions, and n early times before man had cut into the forest, it extended nto the black earth zone. Moreover, the oak pushed south between the Dnieper and Volga, along high river terraces where suitable soils were found. Finally, southwards of latitude 55° N. approximately, stretches the belt of chernozem or black earth steppe ; and the climate becomes drier, especially to the south-east. The black earths are a fine-grained wind-borne soil derived from the southern limits of the glaciers which covered the forest belt during the Ice Age ; rich in humus, they form excellent soils for agriculture, whilst in their natural condition they supply in spring and summer a wealth of high pasture grasses. Certain areas within the steppe belt lack the black earth soils and present other characteristics : thus, to the north of the Caspian and across the lower Volga, a depression which was occupied formerly by the Caspian was covered with chestnut and brown soils, and forms semi-desert or salt steppe; whilst a narrow rim of land along the north of the Black Sea, including the Crimea, is so situated as to enjoy a climate of a semi-Mediterranean character, which suits it for the cultivation of the vine and olive.

Of the three major zonal regions into which the Russian plain may thus be broadly divided, it was the second, the forest belt, within which, or on the margins of which, the first Russian states were built up, on the basis of settlements made in clearings and above all along river valleys. The steppe belt, distinct yet by no means entirely aloof from this truly Russian world to the north, had throughout history a life of its own: along the black earth country the nomad horsemen ('nomad' = 'grazer') freely roamed, having come in almost every case through the Caspian Gate, between the Caspian and the Urals, from their steppe habitat in central Asia. In the far south, on the Black Sea coast, in contrast, fixed cities from the time of the Greeks onwards were established, the economy of which was based on fishing, agriculture and trade. In general, although the steppe has been a zone of political instability under the rule of successive conquerors from central Asia, it has nevertheless fostered at all times from the Neolithic Age onwards some settled village life and agriculture along the great river valleys of the Dniester, Bug and Dnieper, in sheltered pockets of land, like the Kuban delta, and in the Crimea.[1]

The climatic régime to which the Russian plain was exposed rigidly controlled human activity, and also differentiated the products of the soils in different latitudes. Thus in the distant tundra regions furs, skins and salt were the typical products, and cereal cultivation was impossible. In the great forests the trapping of animals for their furs, bee-keeping and timber felling were the chief rural occupations, and agriculture was restricted to small-scale farms along river valleys and in small clearings. Similarly, in the steppe, grazing of herds was characteristic, except in winter when the nomad became a sedentary city dweller. During the long hard winter of some three to six months when the plain was covered with snow agriculture was suspended, the river-ways were frozen, but conditions for travel by land were opened up by sledging over the 'snow-ways'. With the melting of the snow in spring the rivers were opened to navigation; in the summer rainy season, on the other hand, owing to the develop-

[1] Thus Herodotus refers to Scythian husbandmen, and the northern lands of the Black Sea produced corn for export throughout the Classical Period.

ment of marsh, land routes tended to be difficult or even impassable. Similarly, agriculture was closely adapted to the seasonal conditions: rye, barley and wheat were sown in early autumn, and after a long growing period, reaped in summer: autumn frosts, when they occurred, often proved disastrous to the food crop. In the same way a warm winter was very unwelcome, since in the absence of the snow-ways movement by land was practically suspended.

The highly developed river system of Russia provided not only its chief geographical asset but also the most influential geographical factor in its history: hence it is suggested that Russian history is essentially river history. The rivers were extremely long: the precipitation provided abundant supplies of water; whilst the low gradients of the plateaux and plains, by restricting the rate of flow and the occurrence of rapids, gave the rivers a high degree of navigability. Moreover, those which drain northwards to the Baltic or the White Sea are generally separated by short, easy portages (voloks) from those which drain southwards to the Black and Caspian Seas, so that despite the great breadth of the Russian plain the ease of access by its rivers made of it, from the days of the prehistoric amber trade, a trans-European thoroughfare. River travel was possible from about April until November when freezing began. Two main transverse river routes stood out prominently in Russian history: one by the way of the Dnieper from the Black Sea, and the other by the Volga from the Caspian; in both cases by short overland journeys the merchant could proceed northwards from the head of either river to stations on river and lake waterways to the Baltic. The two most important of these led to the Gulf of Finland: the one by way of the Lovat, Lake Ilmen, the Volkhov, Lake Ladoga and the Neva; the other by way of the Velikaia, Lake Peipus and the Narva. Similarly, there were other river ways to the Baltic, i.e., by the West Dwina to the Gulf of Riga, and also a route to the White Sea by the North Dwina and its affluents.

The coming of the Slavs illustrates the entry into the Russian plain from its open western margins. In the second century A.D. the Slavs occupied lands to the north of the middle and lower Danube; in the fifth and sixth centuries some were pushing into the lands of the Eastern Empire and settling in Illyria and the Balkan peninsula generally, whilst others—to be known as the Czechs—were occupying Bohemia. In the sixth century, moreover, it is clear that Slav peoples were well established in the Carpathian region about the head-waters of the Vistula and the Dniester and on the platform of Galicia. At this time they are described as living not in towns but in scattered settlements among forests and swamps. It was from this centre of diffusion that one branch of the Slavs—the East Slavs—moved eastwards to the Dnieper valley in the seventh century and gradually settled part of the Russian plain. The area of their settlement stretched eastwards from the middle Dniester to the valleys of the Dnieper and the Don, and lay essentially within the belt of broad-leaved forest and towards its southern border. The character of this country is described by Jordanes in the sixth century as 'an immense territory, covered with forests, and almost impenetrable owing to its marshes': it was thus similar to the country from which the Slavs had migrated. They settled in scattered farmsteads, which were defended by earthern ramparts, and aligned along river valleys, e.g., the Dnieper, or in the few areas of dry, open land within the marshes and forest; their economy consisted primarily of trapping, apiculture and to a smaller extent husbandry. The valley of the Dnieper bisected the region of their settlement, whilst the river itself soon formed an avenue of colonization and trade. On its high western bank at the margin of the forest towards the steppe the town of Kiev arose, according to tradition, out of the union of separate homesteads situated on contiguous hills.

In the subsequent history of medieval Russia its great river valleys formed the fundamental conditioning factor. Colonization flowed northwards by way of the Dnieper through the forest belt and over the low watershed to the Volkhov and Lakes Ilmen and Ladoga. Settlements were made along the riverways; Scandinavian traders, called both Varangians and Rus-men, entered Russia from the Baltic by way of its rivers; moreover, the political circumstances along the steppe belt to the south and in the Volga basin were such—prior at least to about A.D. 850—to facilitate commercial relations across Russia between the Baltic and the Black and Caspian Seas. In consequence a line of great trading cities arose along the banks of the rivers of Slav Russia, essentially in those places in which the Varangian traders settled. It is significant that Ibn-Dasta, a tenth-century Arab writer, states that the Rus-men, in contrast to the Slavs, had neither hamlets nor ploughed fields, but a great number of towns. Finally, these cities, thanks to their geographical position, to their trading and military power, established control over wide surrounding regions or provinces, and thus created the administrative framework of medieval Russia.

In their expansion northwards up the Dnieper valley the Slavs made contact with Finnish tribes, an Asiatic people who inhabited the northern plains; to the south the steppe belt west of the Don was occupied in the eighth century by the Khazars to whom the Slavs became tributary; whilst the Bolgars occupied the middle and lower basin of the Volga. Farther south lay the civilized and powerful empires of the Arabs and of East Rome. The economic and political development of Slav Russia in the ninth century owed much to external stimuli exerted by the Viking or Rus boatmen from the Baltic and by the steppe horsemen to the south. The ninth century witnessed the maritime activities of the Viking raiders who from bases in Scandinavia ravaged the coasts alike of the North Sea, the Channel and the Baltic and sailed up the rivers of Britain, Gaul and Russia. The Vikings pushed up into Russia by the Neva, Volkhov and Lovat rivers, thence by way of the Narva and by short portages they reached the Dnieper itself. The Rus-men were quick to perceive the trade possibilities of the Russian rivers, and to establish trade intercourse between Russia and both the Greeks of the Byzantine Empire and the Arabs. They settled in the rural trading centres of the Slavs along the Dnieper and its affluents, and these collecting centres of local produce grew quickly, under the stimulus of river navigation, into mercantile towns. Trade across the steppe by way of the Dnieper was not impeded by the Khazars, who were semi-sedentary and civilized. This people, however, was conquered in A.D. 835 by the Uzi and Pechenegs, who pushed westwards from the Asiatic steppe. In result, the trade route across the steppe became threatened; traders had to move down the Dnieper in strongly organized and armed water 'caravans', and Varangian-Slav Russia within its forests had to organize a military frontier of defence against their enemies in the steppe.

The *gorods* or fortified centres of the Slavs in which the Rus-men settled stood on the rivers Dnieper, Volkhov and West Dwina, and had become already by A.D. 850 the centres of wide provinces for which they served as a convenient place of refuge and collecting centres. Towns like Kiev, Novgorod, Polotski, Smolensk, Tchernigov and Periaslav became the centres of provinces: this process of regional organization was largely conditioned by the river-ways which linked rural settlement areas with the main arterial waterways, and it is suggestive of the unifying influences of the Russian rivers that regions directly linked by river with the Volkov and Dnieper willingly submitted to the political control of the central cities, whereas tribes which were not so linked had to be coerced into submission. The provinces lying within the Russian forests astride the Volkhov–Dnieper axis were welded into a state under the influence of the Rus princes who, having come as raiders, traders and settlers, remained as military and political organizers. The first *Russian* state, from which the present-day Russia is historically derived, was created out of the union of Slav and Finnish tribes under the political leadership of the Rus-men. They were able to achieve a loose political association which expressed in some measure the common interest arising out of trading activity and out of the common danger from the steppe. The Northmen conquerors gave their name to the new state : *Rus* had originally connoted the Baltic homelands of the Varangians—Sweden and Denmark, but in the eleventh and twelfth centuries the terms *Rus* or 'the Russian land' denoted the region around Kiev. It is significant that the varied stock of which Russia was composed—chiefly Slavs, Finns and Varangians—were not at this time called the Russian people.

It is no accident that the capital of the first Russian state was Kiev, which had already established for itself the controlling position in the economic life of 'the Russian land'. Kiev, 'the mother of all towns', became early from both a military and a commercial standpoint indispensable. It was a 'forward' capital, an advanced stronghold with its castle and wall of brick, near to which ranged the Pechenegs of the southern steppe ; and at a distance varying from a day to two days' journey defensive frontier works were constructed. Economically, Kiev was important as a depôt at a point of convergence of routes which led from the West Dwina, the Volkhov and the upper Dnieper ; moreover, it was the starting-point of trading caravans destined for Constantinople and was the cathedral city of the metropolitan, the head of the Orthodox or Greek Church in Russia.

The trading relations between Kievan Russia and Constantinople, which began certainly as early as the ninth century, are described by a tenth-century writer. The Prince himself and his nobles took a large share in the trade, together with private merchants. In November when the snow roads lay open the Prince left Kiev for a tour of the provincial cities at which the state revenues were collected. In April when the Dnieper was open to navigation he returned to Kiev with the collected taxes which were paid principally in kind. Meanwhile in the rural districts the winter season was a time for tree-felling and boat-building : when the rivers were open the boats were brought down to Kiev and sold. In June a large fleet laden with the commodities which the prince and his retinue had collected during the winter and with the produce of private merchants set out from Kiev for Vitichev, where it was reinforced by ships from Novgorod, Smolensk, Lubiech, Tchernigov, Vishgorod, &c. Thence was begun the 'troublous voyage full of perils and mischances' towards the Black Sea and Constantinople. The cargoes consisted chiefly of furs—which formed the usual medium of exchange in Russia—honey, slaves and perhaps corn. The chief difficulty of the voyage arose from the attacks of the Pecheneg hordes, and this difficulty was increased owing to the physical character of the Dnieper between Ekaterinoslav and Alexandrosk. In this stretch of the valley for over forty miles the Dnieper cuts through the granitic plateau of Avratinski heights; its valley sides are steep and stand some 250 feet above the river-bed, while some seven cataracts obstructed passage. At certain points it was necessary actually to carry the ships overland past the rapids: this task fell to the slaves, while armed boyars and merchants protected the convoy against the Pechenegs who chose such favourable moments for their attacks. These difficulties overcome, the fleet continued down-stream until it anchored at Berezan island at the mouth of the Dnieper, where the Russians offered thanksgiving for the merciful completion of their journey and at the same time fitted out their ships with suitable tackle for the Black Sea crossing. In the final stage of their voyage to 'the Greek land' the Russians sailed closely along the Black Sea coast until at length in the autumn Constantinople was reached.

By a series of treaties made in the ninth, tenth and eleventh centuries the Rus-men were granted facilities for trading in the Imperial capital, at this time the greatest city of the European world. They were assigned a 'quarter' in the suburb of St. Mamo across the Golden Horn, and allowed to purchase in exchange for their wares rich silks, wine, fruit and gold; provision, however, was made to prevent them from raiding under the cloak of trade. Similarly, in the ninth and tenth centuries there are evidences of trade between the Russians and the Bulgarians who had built up a strong and well-organized state between Thrace and the lower Danube: Little Preslav, in particular, which is represented to-day by a small village on the St. George channel of the Danube delta near its confluence with the Sulina arm, was an active Bulgarian port and market to which the Russians resorted. The Dnieper route-way, known to contemporaries as 'the Greek road', became thus despite its physical difficulties a vital artery of Kievan Russia, and along it flowed not only the commodities of trade but Greek Christianity from Constantinople and other cultural influences, e.g., in architecture and literature. It was largely owing to the Polovtsi or Kumani of the steppe, who cut this arterial route in the early twelfth century, that Kievan Russia declined in political influence and in population, and that the political centre of Russia shifted eventually to the north-east, away from the steppe margins, into the hitherto remote forests and marshes of the country around Moscow. This shift of political power northwards in the eleventh and twelfth century is the counter-part in Russia of what occurred in eighth-century Gaul, and was in both cases the result of changed geographical values : in the one case the Dnieper river no longer afforded a route for trade, in the other the Mediterranean sea-ways had been cut by Arab conquests and pirates.

The political organization of Kievan Russia, in the same way as its town development and foreign trade, arose out of the exploitation of its geographical possibilities. The Rus princes of Kiev were able to establish themselves as the senior or suzerain princes of a number of loosely united Rus principalities. The geographical limits of Kievan Russia, the first Russian state, can be defined in the twelfth century, but only in somewhat general terms. Southwards its limit was well marked by the transition zone, park land in its vegetation, which lay between the northern oak forests and the grass steppe lands to the south : the princes of Kiev never attempted to conquer this broad, open land which was traditionally occupied by peoples who were at best sedentary only during the winter season, and they adopted an essentially defensive position behind military frontier defences which were erected at only one or two days' journey from the stronghold of Kiev.

The occupants of the steppe lands were successively the Khazars, to whom the Russian (Slav) cities paid tribute in return for which they were left to trade unimpeded by way of the Dnieper ; the Pechenegs and Uzi, who wrested control of the steppe from the Khazars in the mid-ninth century, were, as has already been noted, the continual enemies of Kiev ; the Pechenegs fell in turn before the attacks of the wild Polovtsi and Kumani, against whom Kievan Russia fought successfully until about 1132 but finally in vain. These successive peoples occupied the steppe westwards of the Bolgar territories astride the Volga, and divided their time between the life of the nomad horsemen and that of townsmen when in winter the steppe no longer afforded opportunities for pasture or for raiding. Finally, in the thirteenth century the Turks and Tartars from central Asia, known as the 'Golden Horde', swept through the Caspian Gate, overthrew the Bolgar kingdom on the Volga, ravaged the steppe, and led armies into the heart of forested Russia to the north. Kiev, the lands of which had already become largely abandoned and depopulated under the stress of the Polovtsi raids, fell to the Tartars in 1240; the new political strongholds of Russia on the middle Volga and Oka rivers were compelled to pay tribute and recognize the Tartars as overlords; and even distant Novgorod only escaped capture in 1236 thanks to its vast morasses and an unusually wet summer, since, as the Novgorod Chronicle records, 'all this summer stood with wet'. The Tartars consolidated their power and long continued to hold the principalities of Slav Russia in dependence, and to limit and control their then restricted relations with southern Europe.

In general, the lands which had recognized the leadership of Kiev lay across the axis of the Dnieper, Volkhov and West Dwina, and the plains in the far north beyond the Dnieper watershed. North-eastwards of Kiev to the Volga stretched an impenetrable forest occupied by the Slav tribe of the Vatizes through which no road ran until about 1150. The lands which lay round the Slav towns of Rostov and Suzdal near the Volga were known to Kiev as 'zalassi', that is, 'behind the forest'. Moreover, it is significant that although the lands of the Oka and upper Volga were scantily settled by Finns and Slavs, the Slav immigrants had entered not from Kiev by way of the inaccessible valley of the Desna but by way of the upper Volga from the region of Novgorod, to which town the lands were subject. In the west Kievan Russia included the outlying provinces of Galicia and Volhynia, which in the fourteenth century were absorbed in the growing kingdom of Lithuania-Poland. Finally, the broad belt of lands south of the White Sea and Baltic and westwards of the Urals owed nominal allegiance to Kiev, although they were more effectively subject to Novgorod. The settlement and organization of the northern plain was essentially the work of Novgorod, an original Slav city which enjoyed excellent geographical advantages. It stood on both banks of the Volkhov river where it issues from Lake Ilmen, and was closely related with the Baltic by the navigable waters of the Volkhov, Lake Ladoga and the Neva river. Rus-men settled in the town, promoted its trade between the Baltic and up-stream by the Volkhov and short portages to the Dnieper and Volga, and made it their first capital in Russia, until after some twenty years they left it for the rival and superior trading city of Kiev. The Slavs of Novgorod continually extended their area of colonization: northwards where they impinged on the sea-board countries occupied by the Lithuanians, Letts, &c.; and eastwards and south-eastwards to the Volga into the forests settled by the Finns; and in the north-east towards and beyond the Urals and down the North Dwina valley to the White Sea, in lands occupied by Finns and Lapps. Quite early, in the eleventh century, colonists had reached Lapland, the White Sea and the Urals. The North Dwina basin was organized as the province of Trans Volok about 1100 ('volok' = 'watershed' or 'portage'); Yugra—a market for sables and silver—was founded on the lower Ob valley beyond the Urals, and Viatka was settled as a trade station in 1174.

These distant lands of Novgorod formed tributary provinces and spheres of trade, as distinguished from the homeland territories which were under the direct control of Novgorod. Furs formed the chief product of the far north, while silver mines were early worked in the Urals in 'the lands beyond (i.e., to the north of) the Kama'. A great variety of furs collected as tribute—sables, marten, beaver, fox, mink and squirrel—were collected at Novgorod in large numbers, and its trade in furs was on a large scale and served a widely extended market. Of Novgorod itself and its surrounding lands prior to the thirteenth century its Chronicle speaks clearly. The city extended its trade relations both to the north and to the south, and exploited its position on the trans-European route-way between the Baltic and the Black Sea. Even when this route was closed in the thirteenth century owing to the devastations of the Tartars and the capture of Constantinople by the Italians and Franks,[1] Novgorod was related by way of the Volga with the Caspian and in particular silk was imported along this route. Its own products were chiefly furs and honey; cereals, especially rye, were grown, although autumn frosts which occurred from time to time killed the corn and produced scarcity or even famine. Thus in 1128 the inhabitants of Novgorod were reduced to eating the leaves of lime trees, birch bark, pounded wood pulp, husks, straw, butter-cups, moss and horse-flesh. Occasionally a rainy autumn was followed by freezing of Lake Ilmen; the ice then broke

[1] It is significant of the importance of the through routes across Russia that the fall of Constantinople bulked largely in the Novgorod Chronicle. This event meant that the western Mediterranean cities, especially the Italian, would henceforth control the trade of the eastern Mediterranean, and that the water route of the Dnieper would reach only a blind alley. Even so, Novgorod remained in relation to southern lands by way of the Volga.

up and was carried by a south wind into the Volkhov : in result part of the town was flooded and the Great Bridge which linked up to the two halves of Novgorod was periodically broken. Similarly, the effect of climatic conditions on the facilities for travel at different seasons is well exemplified in contemporary records. Winter snows and freezing produced open ‘ snow roads ’ by which princes set out in sledges on military expeditions or for the collection of tribute ; on the other hand, a warm winter without snowfalls, as for example in 1303, impeded communication by road and caused scarcity and distress. It was subsequently to the Kievan period that Novgorod reached its greatest importance, when in the thirteenth, fourteenth and fifteenth centuries it became the resort of German merchants and was made a station or depôt of the Hanseatic League.

During the latter half of the twelfth century began a series of historical events which in the course of the two succeeding centuries transferred from the region of Kiev the political and economic centre of the Russian state. The Polovtsi and Tatars in turn strangled the foreign trade of Kiev, and further ravaged widely over its southern lands. There followed about 1150, in consequence, a stream of emigrant boyars and peasantry from the Dnieper lands of Russia into lands to the west and to the north-east. One stream of emigrants went westwards along the route by which their Slav ancestors had first entered the Russian plain in the seventh century, and thus re-settled Galicia and Volhynia, about the waters of the Western Bug, and the upper Dniester and Vistula. It was the other main stream of emigration which affected so drastically the whole human and political geography of medieval Russia. By way of the valley of the Desna, a left-bank tributary of the Dnieper, the emigrants succeeded from about A.D. 1150 in opening up a direct route, a ‘ straight-running road ’, from Kiev to Murom on the lower Oka, through country which hitherto had remained impassable owing to its forests, its thickets and its robbers. The result of this movement to the north-east in search of secure, rural settlements was the colonization of the region of the *Mezdhuriechie* or land of Suzdal, which was destined to become the nucleus of the new Muscovite state of Russia.

The *Mezdhuriechie*, which has been called the Mesopotamian region of Russia,[1] lay between the upper Volga and its tributary the Oka, and was covered by wide stretches of woodland and marsh and furrowed by a complicated network of streams. The soil was a stiff, clayey loam ; the summers were short ; the

[1] See Vaughan Cornish, *The Great Capitals*, pp. 179–92.

open country available for agriculture, was small and for the most part aligned along the streams. Moreover, although it was related to Novgorod in the north, the Oka–Volga lands formed remote, undeveloped country, aloof from the main currents of trade and culture. The *Mezdhuriechie* formed a frontier region of Slav and Finnish settlement: its basic population consisted of the Finns, who—as their surviving river and place-names still testify—originally occupied the vast area between the Oka and the White Sea; but the Slavs had early entered the region from the north-west and settled in a number of small, agricultural towns along or near to the upper Volga and Oka, notably at Rostov and Suzdal. The aloofness of the *Mezdhuriechie* and the sparseness of its population and its settlements made it, however, an attractive habitat to the boyars and peasants of Kiev, since it offered ample scope for colonization and development and further provided within its forests and its marshes a much-desired protection from the dangers of the steppe. These dangers were lessened thanks to the oak forests which covered the country to the south-west of the Oka and eastwards between Tula, Tambov and Kazan.

Under the stimulus of the immigration and settlement of Kievan Russians, the Oka–Volga region became gradually studded with towns and villages. Out of the fusion of its Slav and Finnish inhabitants developed the Great Russian stock; while at the same time the region was able at length to become a great centre of converging routes, for which it was geographically well placed. The Slav peasants settled in small scattered farmsteads chiefly along river valleys which were cut off from each other by stretches of forest and marsh; and it was thanks to the efforts of the ruling princes who built towns at central points that some unity and organization were created in the *Mezdhuriechie*.

In the fourteenth century Slav Russia formed a great island divided up into numerous small principalities and ringed around by the Lithuanians to the west and the Tartars to the south. The Lithuanians from a base in the Baltic coastlands had conquered far south, and absorbed not only Volhynia and Galicia but even the region around Kiev itself. Within Slav Russia the princes of Moscow in the latter half of the thirteenth century succeeded in creating a new Russian state by securing their primacy over the other Slav princes. The town of Moscow is first heard of about A.D. 1147, at which time it was a small station in the principality of Rostov, on the boundary between Rostov and Tchernigov provinces. The prince of Suzdal in 1156 surrounded his villa there with a wooden wall; the original site of the town on the Moskva river ('va' is Finnish and means 'water') occupied a part of the present Kremlin area. The capital of Suzdal was at first shifted to Vladimir, the new town created by the princes of Vladimir, but later, and permanently from 1263, the capital was fixed at Moscow. In 1328 the Great Khan, the Tartar ruler to whom Slav Russia paid tribute, recognized the Prince of Moscow as suzerain prince of Rus, a position which was used in order to promote his political control over the other Russian princes. Moreover, about the same time, Moscow became the spiritual head of Russia, since the Metropolitan moved there from Kiev. Moscow built up a system of routes which followed or linked up the river valleys near which it stood. The Volga was reached by water and by road along the rivers Moskva, Istra, Lama and Sosh; a highway ran from Moscow along the Kliasa to the Oka; another ran to the middle Oka; and finally a north-south route connected Periaslav, Rostov and Yaroslavl on the Volga. Thanks to this intersection of routes Moscow was able to profit in dues from the flow of commerce, and to develop industries.

The subsequent history of the Russian state is marked by the efforts of the 'Great Princes' of Moscow to consolidate and extend their power. During the reign of Ivan III 'the Great' (1462–1505), the vassal principalities of Russia were forced to submit to the power of Moscow and Great Novgorod was reduced from the status of a wealthy, commercial republic to that of a provincial town. It must be emphasized, however, that Russia remained aloof from western and central Europe, and backward in its material culture. Unlike Poland and Lithuania, its western neighbours, it formed part of the Eastern Church: in fact, after the capture of Constantinople by the Turks in 1453, Russia assumed its leadership. Shut off at first from the Baltic and the Black Seas, Russia had maritime relations only with the White Sea and the Arctic Ocean. In fact, it long remained essentially Asiatic in its outlook: a great marchland against Asia, peopled by many different ethnic stocks, it defended, but did not share, the superior culture of peninsular Europe to the west.[1]

[1] The reader is referred to B. H. Sumner's *Survey of Russian History* (1944), the standard work in English, Chapter I of which provides a geographical introduction. Of particular interest, too, in stressing the rôle of rivers in Russian expansion is R. J. Kerner's *The Urge to the Sea* (1942).

CHAPTER XI

THE POLITICAL UNIFICATION OF FRANCE

'L'ÉTAT n'est jamais donné ; il est toujours forgé.' The growth of a state—the consolidation of certain territories and their populations under a single, sovereign authority—is essentially an historical process. In creating a state men simply adapt nature to their uses. The geographical frameworks which states come to occupy are certainly never predestined, as it were, by conditions of physical geography. Nevertheless, beneath the surface of historical events which mark the progress towards political unification, geographical factors, though largely masked from view, are in no small degree operative. A state, it is a truism to observe, of necessity requires a territorial basis and territorial limits, no less than a minimum density of population, and it is for these reasons, therefore, that the peculiar physical and human conditions which attach to, and distinguish, different land areas, may serve to foster or to impede political development. Moreover, the so-called ' nation state ', of which France forms a typical case, has its origin in the growth of national sentiment amongst the inhabitants of a given region. It is easy to see that certain parts of the earth's surface are so constituted geographically as to preclude the rise of states : it is no historical accident that states did not arise amidst the equatorial forests of Africa or in the Arctic lands, since the natural conditions of climate and vegetation drastically limited the settlement of people, their growth in number and their intercourse with each other. Even in the north temperate zone, where climate and vegetation were by no means inimical to human settlement, expansion and intercourse, some kinds of country were ' negative ', whilst others were ' positive ', in respect of their usefulness in fostering state-building. In France, as elsewhere in Europe, the negative lands were above all the dense forests and impassable marshes ; the positive lands were areas where the soils were well drained, easy to work and free from dense woods, and where pasture and meadow were available.

The Geographical Basis of France

The geography of France, in so far as it conditioned settlement, intercourse and the growth of national feeling, must thus be reckoned as a factor in French political unity. Gaul, of which France was merely a part, was at the dawn of history settled largely by Celtic-speaking Gauls, although at its margins other peoples were established: the Belgi, a mixed Celtic and Germanic people, spoke a distinct language and occupied the north-east; Greek colonists occupied parts of the southern coastlands and the lower Rhône; whilst, ever conscious of their ethnic differences from the Gauls, the Iberi, the ancestors of the modern Basques, were settled between the western Pyrenees and the Adour and even in Low Languedoc. Viewed as a whole, Gaul appeared to Roman geographers as a highly favoured region. Strabo [1] emphasized its varied wealth in meadow, arable and forest lands, and also its many long and navigable rivers—facts which made a special appeal to an observer familiar with the Mediterranean region, where, in contrast, rivers were torrential and irregular and summer drought limited vegetation. Wide areas of Gaul were covered by forests, particularly on the wet plateaux formed by the massifs of schists, gneiss and sandstone rocks, such as the Arduenna Silva. Caesar states that Aquitania and Provincia Narbonensis, with the exception of the Cevennes, Cahorsin and the Alps, were much less wooded than the north of Gaul; and in the light of this it is of interest that he estimates that one-third of the population of Gaul were settled in Aquitania.[2] The peoples of Gaul, prior to the Roman conquest (58–51 B.C.), formed tribal groups, and were settled mainly in scattered villages, which utilized usually a stream, pasture, woodland and arable fields, and were divided off from each other by wide stretches of unoccupied waste—forest, heath or marsh. The villages of a tribal group with their adjoining lands were known to the Romans as pagi (hence the French 'pays'), and a number of pagi organized together formed a federation of tribes known as the civitas or city, which occupied an area as large as several English counties put together. Now it would seem that as population grew, the small tribal pagi with their pastures and fields extended their area of settlement and utilization by breaking into the surrounding waste lands, and, in result, established interrelations with each other. This development depended to some extent on the ease with which routes could be established,

[1] *Geography*, Loeb ed., Book IV, I, 2.
[2] *De Bello Gallico*, III, 20.

along rivers, escarpments or hill summits. 'The land made the pagus, the route, the civitas'; 'au berceau des états, il y a une route—un premier filet de vie générale'.[1] Thus the French historian Jullian has stressed the function of route-ways among the geographical factors which fostered tribal unity in pre-Roman Gaul. The use by several villages of a common route; the convergence of routes towards the same river valley; the use in common of certain upland, tribal strongholds, well situated for defence; the exchange, e.g., between plateau and plain, of products which, owing to varied conditions of soil, elevation, climate, slope and aspect, were differentiated within the same civitas;—such factors as these helped the merging of originally detached and scattered pagi into the larger and geographically much more complex region, the civitas.

The civitas of the Gallic people, the Arverni, may be noticed by way of illustration. Their territory, which occupied part of the Massif Central, was bisected by the river Allier from its sources down to Moulins; and consisted of physically contrasted areas which were adapted to different purposes. One part of its land was wet, high plateau of schist and granite rocks, and was useful in that it afforded rough pasture and defensible sites. Another part consisted of plateau land covered with good volcanic soils; finally, the best lands of the 'city' stood in a series of basins of rich soil through which the Allier flowed, known collectively as the Limagne. In these sheltered, well-watered lands, cultivation was carried on; the plateaux provided pasture and timber; the Allier valley afforded an axial route; whilst on the volcanic Mont Dore, high above the Limagne, stood the Arverni stronghold or oppidum of Gergovia, which has recently been excavated. In short, already before the Roman conquest, Gaul had attained through its organization of tribal 'cities' a certain, though incomplete, measure of national solidarity. This national solidarity was rather foreshadowed than achieved: Gallic tribes warred with each other, and as we have seen Belgi, Iberi and Greeks formed other distinct ethnic elements.

In its degree of culture, as in its climate, products and position, Mediterranean Gaul, with its Greek cities—notably Marseilles, Nice and Hyères—stood ahead of the rest of Gaul. It had a well-developed city life, based on industry, trade, fishing and the cultivation of the olive and the vine, and its very distinctness from central and northern Gaul stimulated trade activity. Wine, oil and money found their way up the Rhône valley from the Greek cities of the coast; whilst tin from Brittany and Britain,

[1] *Histoire de la Gaule*, I, p. 103.

and other commodities, were carried overland across Gaul to Marseilles. As early as 150 B.C. Gaul had three busy seaports—Marseilles, Narbonne and Corbilo at the estuary of the Loire. Thus trade had opened up arterial routes across Gaul which might help to develop common interests among the separate tribal units established along them.

The Roman conquest and occupation of Gaul for some five hundred years served materially to knit together its many cities and peoples. The population of Gaul was only slightly modified by the settlement in small numbers of Roman civilians and veterans and by the colonization of the Rhinelands by German immigrants. Many new cities, often on Gallic sites, were established ; a network of paved roads was constructed throughout the country by Roman legionaries ; Gaul was girt around by well-defined military frontiers ; whilst the Roman *pax* stimulated industry, trade, intercourse and the growth of population. Above all, the Romans implanted their language in Gaul so thoroughly that, despite the subsequent immigration and settlement of barbarian peoples, it survived to mould French speech. As Roman power in Gaul weakened, new invaders entered and settled in the land : many German peoples, Celtic-speaking Britons in Brittany, a few Saracens in the extreme south, and last of all Northmen from Scandinavia in Normandy. New kingdoms arose in Gaul based on the conquests of these various immigrants,[1] and for a time, between A.D. 800 and 843, Gaul was absorbed in the empire created by Charles the Great. This empire in turn collapsed, and centrifugal forces were let loose in Gaul. In the political sphere the new kingdom of France took shape, but became a loosely knit aggregation of feudal fiefs. The Roman route system was allowed to fall into decay ; Gallo-Roman ' cities ' survived in some cases to form ecclesiastical divisions or dioceses, but at the same time new feudal units such as duchies and counties came into being ; in the economic sphere the almost self-sufficing village formed the typical unit ; whilst the population of different regions, as is well evident from the variety of dialects, became sharply distinguished in their outlooks, interests, loyalties and speech. Moreover, the contrasts between northern and southern Gaul which have been noted above reappeared in medieval France. To the north of the Loire the three-field system of cultivation was employed and population was denser than in the south where the two-field system was typical.[2] There were similar contrasts between the langue d'oil speech of the north and the langue d'oc of the

[1] See *supra*, Chapter VII.

[2] See *supra*, Chapter IV, p. 77.

south;[1] between Romanesque architecture of the south and the Gothic styles evolved in the north; between Roman law which persisted in the south—where Romanization had lasted longer and was more thoroughly effected—and the new royal codes of the north; whilst even in religious outlook the south challenged the orthodoxy of the north. On the other hand, certain factors stimulated the development of national and political unity. The growth of population, especially between the years A.D. 1050 and 1300 led to a continued attack on those 'negative' uplands, forests and marshes, which formed belts of separation between settled areas. International trade, as reflected in the rise of famous fairs, first in Champagne and then at Lyons, Geneva and Beaucaire, in small measure at least brought different parts of France into relations with each other. The long-continued wars between England and France evoked for the first time a strong national consciousness in France out of which political unity was forged. Finally, the French kings, in consistently seeking the extension and consolidation of their power, were no less consistently, whatever their immediate ends, moulding the nascent state.

Thus far we have noted some of the changing conditions of human geography—the spread of settlement, the growth of population, the conquest of 'barrier' regions, and the consequent development of intercourse and common interests between originally scattered and distinct tribal groups—conditions upon which the structure of a state could be founded. It is time to turn to the other aspect of the unification of France, and to examine the sequence of historical events which created France on the stage thus set and thus confined by geography.

The Emergence of the French State

As a state France is recognizable for the first time in the kingdom of the West Franks, the most westerly of the three political units into which the Empire of Charles the Great was divided in A.D. 843 by the Treaty of Verdun (Fig. 34). Charles's Empire embodied the Roman principle of undivided sovereignty, but since Frankish custom prescribed the equal division of land among male heirs this temporarily consolidated empire was involved in a series of continual and arbitrary partitions. The ninth century thus witnessed the creation of many short-lived states, the territories of which tended to ignore alike the contemporary distribution of nationalities and the physical regions

[1] Cp. Mortillet, *Formation de la Nation Française*, p. 160, and Fleure, *The Human Geography of Western Europe*, pp. 65–7.

of modern geographical analysis.[1] That the Treaty of Verdun should have defined the permanent geographical bases of modern France and Germany was certainly unforeseen and undesigned, since, like other schemes of division which proved purely ephemeral, it did not aim to perpetuate new political regions but rather to share between three ruling colleagues the government of the undivided Regnum Francorum. Not only did it in some measure defy both human and physical geography but also it differed markedly from other schemes for partition,

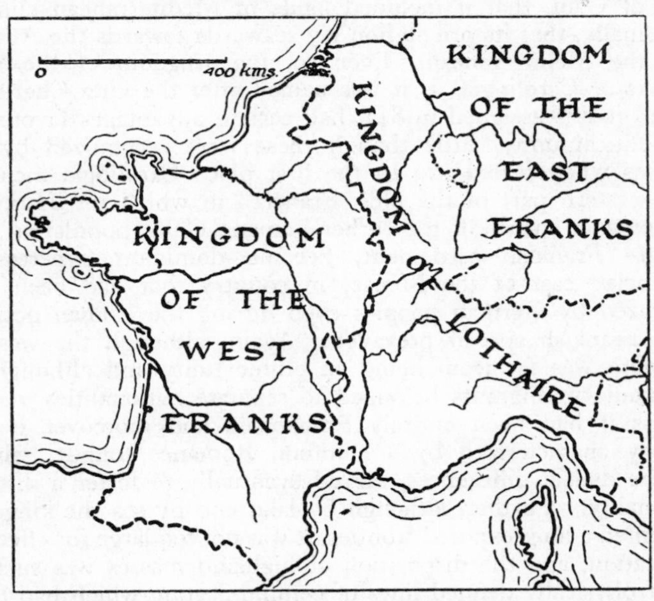

FIG. 34.—The Partition of the Carolingian Empire made by the Treaty of Verdun in A.D. 843 (data from Longnon)

notably those of the years 806 and 817. In particular, the Treaty of Verdun adopted a longitudinal line of division, whereas earlier divisions had more usually followed a latitudinal line. In the partitions of 806 (Fig. 25) and 817 'Francia', which had been settled by the Franks themselves, was treated as a single unbroken region: it lay between the Channel, the Loire and the frontiers of Brittany, and stretched eastwards across the lower Rhine and Main—in short, it represented the kingdom of Clovis, the Merovingian king of the Franks, as it existed in A.D. 506 before the rest of Gaul had been conquered. Again,

[1] Cp. the maps in Longnon's *Atlas Historique de la France*.

the partitions of A.D. 806 and 817 gave recognition to certain differences which distinguished southern from northern Gaul, not only by separating Frankish 'Francia' from the rest of Gaul but also by selecting the basin of Aquitaine, which had been made a duchy by Charles the Great, as the basis of a state. Aquitaine, with or without other southern lands in Gaul, appears also among the kingdoms created in the years 855, 863, 870 and 880, and this southern kingdom, carved out on latitudinal lines, had a certain *raison d'être* in that it comprised the most Romanized part of Gaul, that it included lands of Mediterranean climate, and finally, that its orientation lay seawards towards the Atlantic and the Mediterranean. Even so, the kingdom of the West Franks or Carolingia, as it was named after the king Charles to whom it was assigned in 843, had certain advantages favourable to political unity, little though these were recognized by the princes who created it. In the first place Carolingia included that western part of the old 'Francia' in which the Latinized or Romance speech of the earlier Romano-Gallic population had, despite Frankish settlement, become dominant, whereas in 'Francia' east of the Meuse, in country that had been well colonized by German peoples even during the Roman occupation, Frankish speech prevailed. Again, although the western kingdom was far from being an ethnic unity and although its Germanic immigrants belonged to separate nationalities, nevertheless it had been entirely Romanized and moreover it was already characterized by a common Romance tongue, which, despite dialect differences, served eventually to foster a distinct nationality. Further, although by land and by sea the kingdom presented a long-exposed frontier, it was not too large for effective unification, and the disposition of highland masses was such as allow physically defined lines of communication which had been utilized by the Roman road system. Finally, in the Paris basin, the new state possessed a central region, well provided with river routes and good agricultural land, from which political power might be extended and unification be undertaken. It was a geographical circumstance both fortuitous and fortunate that the demesne or territorial possessions of the first Capetian kings lay contiguous to, and to a small extent within, the basin of Paris.

The kingdom of the West Franks, as it was first carved out by the Treaty of Verdun, was essentially, therefore, an arbitrarily selected region which no informed observer of the ninth century would have regarded as an obvious, permanent or inevitable framework for a state. Actually the political map of A.D. 843

was several times re-made during the subsequent decades, until for a short time the dismembered fragments of the Carolingian Empire were reunited under the sole rule of the Emperor Charles the Fat. The kingdom of the West Franks, with approximately the same limits it had had in 843, reappeared however in 887, when Charles the Fat retired and the empire was finally dismembered. In one important respect the division of 887 differed from that of 843 : the middle kingdom of Lotharingia, which had been created between the eastern and western Frankish kingdoms, was by then disrupted into a number of separate kingdoms or duchies. Lotharingia, that elongated kingdom between the North Sea and Italy with its various nationalities, its many physical obstacles and its utterly indefensible frontiers, lacked geographical elements favourable to political consolidation. Even so, it contained within it the three imperial capitals—Aachen, Milan and Rome—and had for its axis the Roman highway which linked up Rome with the lower Rhine. Its consequent break-up, however, left on the eastern borders of the West Frankish kingdom a medley of feudal territories, (e.g., the duchies of Lorraine, Bar, Burgundy, and Provence) which already in 887 or soon afterwards owed allegiance to the kings of the East Franks.

What were the geographical limits and characteristics of the new western kingdom to which the name France—first used to describe the lands actually settled by the Franks—was eventually given ? It must be emphasized at once that France at its inception should be sharply distinguished from Gaul, of which it formed merely a large part.[1] It was bounded by the English Channel, the Atlantic and the Gulf of Lion ; it included territories which modern France has lost, namely Flanders, the Channel islands and Catalonia beyond the Pyrenees ; whilst towards the east it fell far short of the Rhine, Saône, Rhône and Alps, since it was limited by the Scheldt, the Meuse, the Côte d'Or and Langres plateaux, and the Cevennes summits. The lands along the Moselle, the Rhine, the Saône and the Rhône, which formed the dismembered parts of Lotharingia, lay outside the kingdom and were, or soon came to be, attached to the eastern Germanic kingdom. In the language of modern geography the new French kingdom consisted, therefore, of a number of physically well-defined regions : the basins of Flanders, Paris and Aquitaine ; the peninsular salients of Normandy and Brittany ; the plateaux and upland basins of the Massif Central ; finally, the foothills and plain of Low Languedoc, and the

[1] Cp. Freeman, ' France and Gaul ', in *Historical Essays* (3rd series)

sub-Pyrenean county of Catalonia. However differentiated geographically, these several regions were physically so related as to permit of easy routes and intercommunication. The Massif Central lay open from the north by way of the valleys of the Loire and its tributary the Allier, and along the Allier valley ran an important medieval route which connected Orleans with Nîmes and the ports of St. Gilles and Aigues-Mortes in the far south. Similarly, another road, which passed through the broad gap of Poitou, joined up Paris and Orleans with Bordeaux: this was part of 'the great road of Spain and of St. James' which connected Bruges and Santiago, where the remains of St. James were supposed to lie. The Naurouze pass, a narrow sill, carried the Roman road from Narbonne and Languedoc via Toulouse into the basin of Aquitaine. Finally, France held the Faucilles gap and the Langres 'gate', both of which led into the basin of Paris. The configuration and actual area of the French kingdom offered thus no great impediments to political unification. The skeletal road system bequeathed to Gaul by the Romans, although it was largely neglected and although it had been designed less to unify Gaul than to unite Italy with the Channel and with the Rhine frontier, was nevertheless an asset which Germany, for example, largely lacked. But the political advantages of a network of main routes were neutralized by the political conditions produced by feudalism: political authority became localized and divided among a host of feudal lords great and small, who were able to levy tolls on traffic and to block the routes along which royal power from its base on the Loire and on the Seine could make itself effective.

The French kingdom, if it formed a single legal conception and a compact territorial unit, was nevertheless divided from the standpoints of administration, nationality and language. In the county of Flanders, which stood to the north of Carbonnière forest and between the Scheldt and the Canche rivers, the Flemings spoke a Low German speech. In the duchy of Normandy, Northmen formed the ruling class, but they were rapidly assimilated to the speech and culture of the subject population. Divided from Normandy by the Cuesnon river, Brittany, by position aloof from the rest of France and maritime in outlook, was occupied especially in its western half by Celtic-speaking people. It had formed a peripheral 'march' land of the Carolingian Empire; and it was only from the tenth century onwards that French speech effectively advanced into Brittany (Fig. 35). Its ultimate absorption into the French state in 1491 came very late; and its place-names to-day attest—as also do those of Wales—its

British traditions. Finally, in the duchy of Gascony, within the basin of the Adour and on the flanks of western Pyrenees, the Basque language of the old Iberi population persisted, although over a gradually receding area ; whilst to the south of the eastern Pyrenees and to the north of it in Roussillon Catalan, a distinct language derived from Latin, was dominant. For the rest the Romance or Latinized speech of the Romano-Gallic population of Gaul prevailed with marked regional differences to the exclusion of the Germanic speech brought by 'barbarian' immigrants. In

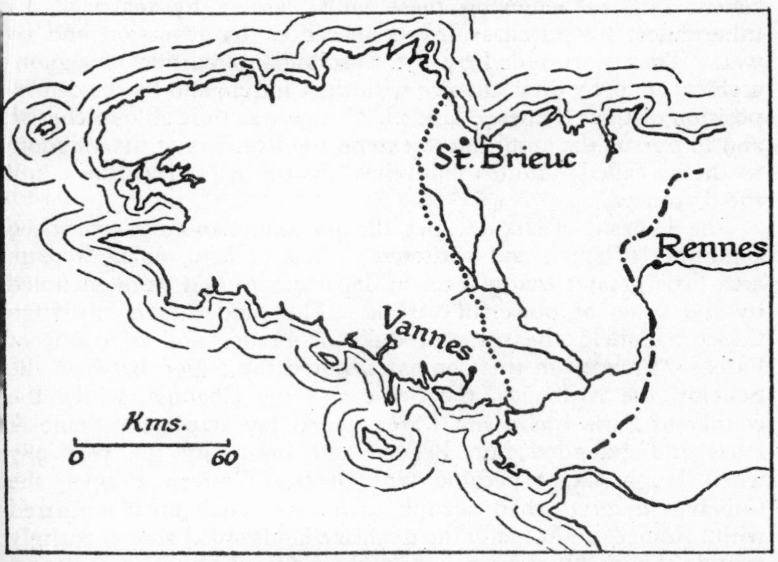

FIG. 35.—The Eastern Limit of Breton Speech in the Ninth Century (data from Mortillet)

The dotted line shows the eastern limit of Breton speech, *c.* A.D. 900, as it had receded before the advance of French speech

particular, langue d'oil and langue d'oc developed respectively to the north and south of a broad east-west belt between Belfort and Bordeaux.

Similarly, at the accession of Hugh Capet as king in A.D. 987, France was far from constituting a unit in the political sense. With the collapse of the centralized government of the Carolingian Empire feudalism had established itself as a system of government based on the tenure of land. The effective authority of the first Capetian kings was restricted to the royal estates or demesne which they directly administered. Outside this small area, which formed the geographical nucleus of the French state, the kings exercised only suzerainty or overlordship over great feudal lords who governed extensive territories and were themselves overlords of lesser vassals. The political unification of France, largely achieved by *c.* 1610, resulted from the growth of royal power, and this was effected by the extension and consolidation of the demesne lands and, further, by the establishment of royal authority over lands which originally owed allegiance outside the kingdom. Both the Capetian kings and (after 1328) their successors the Valois showed, with certain exceptions, consistent skill in achieving these ends, largely by marriage, by inheritance, by purchase, by confiscation, by reversion and by war. They were aided by the Carolingian tradition of a monarchical state, by their alliance with the Church, and by the central position of their demesne lands. France was thus able to cherish and to pursue the ambition to extend the frontiers of the kingdom to the so-called 'limites naturelles' of the Alps, the Rhine and the Pyrenees.

The demesne of Hugh Capet, the first Capetian king, comprised a number of small and scattered parcels of land which were in area little greater than a French département and were encircled by the lands of powerful vassals. The predecessors of Hugh Capet had held the titles of duke of France and of count of Paris: 'France' in this context denoted the region between the Scheldt, the Ardennes, the Seine and the Channel, whilst the county of Paris was a small area which lay across the Seine at Paris and extended into Beauce and Brie. By the year 987 when Hugh Capet became king of the Western Franks, the Capetian demesne had shrunk to a very small area compared with 'France'. Actually the demesne lands stood almost entirely outside the duchy of France, and Hugh Capet had even alienated the county of Paris itself. The largest and most compact portion of his demesne consisted of the contiguous counties of Orleans and Etampes; to these were added the county of Sollentois and Senlis, on the left bank of the Oise, an adjoining small area around Poissy on the left bank of the Seine just above Paris, the distant Montreuil-sur-Mer at the Canche estuary in Artois, and finally, Attigny, situated towards the frontier of the kingdom, on the upper Aisne (Fig. 36).

The activities of the first Capetian kings were confined to strengthening the royal demesne, and they scarcely moved outside this territorial base. Their capital city, from the accession of Hugh Capet until the end of the eleventh century, moved with their residence, and they resided either at Senlis, or Poissy or Etampes, above all at Orleans, and scarcely at all at Paris.

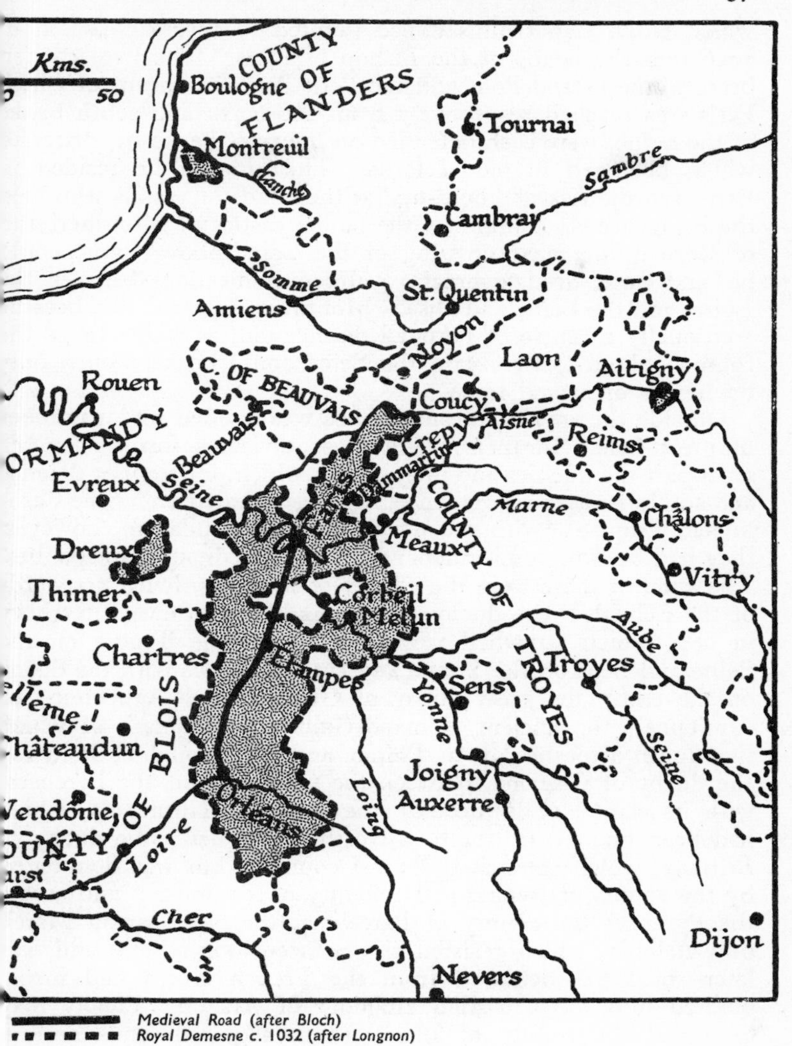

Fig. 36.—The Royal Demesne of the French King, *c.* A.D. 1032 (data from Longnon and Bloch)

Note the detached areas of the royal demesne, and the way in which it was surrounded by vassal territories, e.g. the Counties of Laon, Troyes, Nevers (to the south), and Blois

It is true that they had a palace on the island site of Paris where the Palais de Justice now stands, but it was clearly seldom visited. The reasons are not far to seek. The county of Paris, which Hugh Capet himself had granted to a vassal, passed in 1016 into the hands of the Bishop of Paris. The two wooden bridges, the Grand Pont and the Petit Pont, by means of which Paris was reached respectively from the north and south banks of the Seine, were each defended on the river banks by fortresses which belonged to feudal lords. The king, if he resided in Paris, ran the risk of 'hold-up' at the hands of vassals who held the bridgeheads. Similarly, the feudal castles of Montlhéri and of Corbeil, the next crossing of the Seine above Paris, could be, and were, used to break royal communications between the Loire, and the Seine and Oise. Montlhéri, in particular, became continually a centre of baronial disaffection, at which times the route between Orleans and the Seine could be kept open only by means of armed force.

Outside the royal demesne France was divided into a number of great fiefs. In their origin these divisions formed for the most part the duchies and marquisates which, for frontier defence and administrative convenience, had been created under the Carolingian Empire; with the development of feudalism, however, they had become semi-independent and hereditary principalities. The chief of these were the county of Flanders, lying westwards of the Scheldt; the duchy of Burgundy, an extensive territory in 987, which stretched westwards to include Troyes on the Seine and Sens on the Yonne and lay contiguous with the Saône on the east; the great duchy of Guyenne (= 'Aguyenne' or Aquitaine), the ancient Romano-Gallic 'Aquitania', of which the ducal demesne lay in Poitou and the capital at Poitiers; the duchy of Gascony, between the Garonne and the Pyrenees, with its capital at Bordeaux; the duchy of Normandy, which had been granted in 911 to a Northman prince; the duchy of Brittany, which comprised several counties, but was dominated by the counts of Rennes; the county of Toulouse; and across the Pyrenees the county of Barcelona, the old Spanish March of Catalonia, which resisted the Saracens for a time and was later—in 1181—detached from the French crown and incorporated into the Christian kingdom of Aragon. Finally may be noted the county of Blois, which acquired lands around Dreux, Melun, Troyes and Beauvais as well as around Blois, Tours, Chartres, and Châteaudun and thus surrounded the royal demesne.

Restricted within their demesne by powerful vassals, the Capetian kings nevertheless gradually increased it during the eleventh century, and even, a little later, began to make military expeditions outside it, e.g., against the insubordinate barons of the Auvergne in 1122. During the eleventh century the demesne was somewhat enlarged and consolidated. Avallon, Autun, Dijon, Melun, Dreux and Sens were acquired; the county of Vexin, which lay between the Epte and Oise and across the Seine, was won, as well as the county of Gâtinais, which united Sens and Etampes and reached the Orléanais; whilst by the purchase of the vicomté of Bourges in 1100 the king secured for the first time fortresses beyond the Loire, namely those at Bourges and at Dun. Moreover, the acquisition of Montlhéri in 1118 and of Corbeil in 1112 gave the kings control of the axial route, which partially followed the line of the old Roman road, from Orleans to Etampes, Paris, Senlis and Poissy.

The Capitals of France

Prior to about 1200 the city of Orleans served usually as the capital, and its selection for this function emphasized the importance which the middle Loire country held in the early history of France. A recent writer[1] on the present-day geography of France stresses the inferiority of the Loire as compared with the Seine as a navigable water-way, and suggests further that the middle Loire region belongs geographically to the Paris basin. In medieval times, in contrast, it would seem that the Loire equalled, and at times surpassed, the Seine in importance, and that in the Orléanais rather than in the country around Paris lay the central region of France. The unfavourable features in the régime of the Loire[2]—its well-marked seasonal changes of level, its floods, its shoals and shifting channels—were less of a hindrance to the small sailing ships and barges of the day, and the river provided cheaper and safer freight than by way of roads which were both bad and unsafe. That there were some two hundred toll stations on the Loire and its affluents in the Middle Ages testifies to the activity of the river's traffic, and in the thirteenth century all the merchants of the river formed a guild, whilst 'colleges' of boatmen were formed. The difficulty of communication east-westwards across France south of the Loire owing to the high broken Massif Central; the fact that the Rhône valley lay outside the kingdom and that its chief north-south route ran across the Massif Central by the Allier valley; and finally, the fact that Aquitaine was in English hands between 1152 and 1453—all of these circumstances favoured the importance of the Loire in the route system of France. Already at the arrival of the Romans, Gallic cities stood along that river,

[1] H. Ormsby, *France*, pp. 154 and 357.
[2] On the Loire, see *Le Val de Loire*, by R. Dion, 1934.

usually on bluffs commanding crossings from the south side. Refounded by the Romans, these cities persisted during the Middle Ages as centres of industry, trade and religion.

It is only towards the end of the Middle Ages that Paris became beyond question the political capital of France, although it is true that much earlier, for example under Clovis, it temporarily

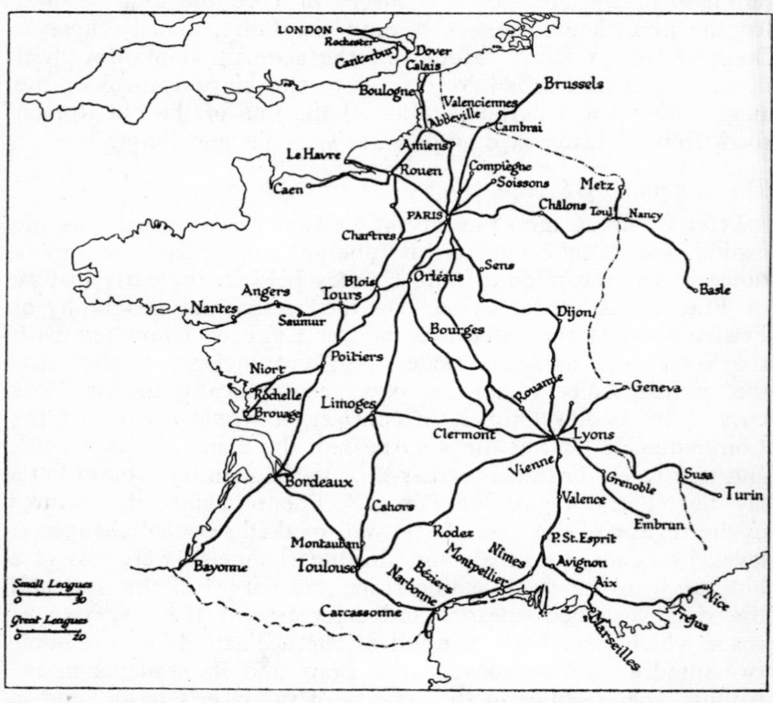

FIG. 37.—The Post Roads of France in the early seventeenth century (data from Tavernier's map, 1632)

It is significant that the eastern frontier of France was then incompletely mapped. Note that the route focus at Lyons appears then, as in Roman times. The convergence of routes on Paris does not occur, however, in the Roman period

fulfilled this rôle. As the French monarchy increased its power and centralized its government, Paris supplanted the other cities which had served as capitals, notably Orleans and Lyons, which had been the capital of Roman Gaul. Tavernier's map of the 'Post' roads of France, which was engraved in 1632, shows unmistakedly the important position of Paris as the chief route centre of France (Fig. 37). Thus at this time Paris is connected by main roads with peripheral cities like Bordeaux and

Marseilles, with the frontier fortresses of Metz and Toul, and with Italy by two routes : from Avignon to Aix and Fréjus and thence along the coasts of Provence and Genoa, and from Lyons by way of the Isère valley and Susa to Turin. Finally, it should be noted that in the latter part of the seventeenth century, although Paris remained the capital for many purposes, the Court moved to Versailles, where on the site formerly occupied by a village and a royal hunting-box in forested and marshy country was erected the royal palace of Louis XIV.

The Expansion of France and ' les Limites Naturelles '

By the year 1610 the feudal territories of the French monarchy were absorbed into the royal demesne, and the work of unification, which had been begun by the Capetian kings, may be said to be completed. The frontiers of France in 1610 represented an advance, except in the north and the south-west, beyond those which obtained at the Treaty of Verdun. In the north Flanders and Artois and in the south-west the Pyrenean counties of Roussillon and Cerdagne, which were originally part of the kingdom, had shaken off their allegiance to the French crown ; in the east, in contrast, French territories pushed beyond the Meuse and beyond the Cevennes. The bishoprics of Metz, Toul and Verdun, island territories in Lorraine, were in French hands ; so also were districts in Bresse and Bugey between the lower Saône and the Rhône ; whilst in the south the frontiers extended across the lower Rhône to include Dauphiné and Provence. The kingdom thus constituted was threatened by the power of the Habsburg rulers in the Empire and in Spain. The territories of the latter branch were so disposed as almost to encircle the French state, since apart from Spain the Spanish monarchs ruled in the southern Netherlands, in Franche-Comté —the old county of Burgundy, in Alsace and in northern Italy. It was the achievement of French policy by diplomacy and by war to break through this girdle, to extend the land frontiers of the kingdom, and so substantially to attain ' les limites naturelles '.

The doctrine of ' les limites naturelles ' is an instance of political ambition which sought its justification in physical geography.[1] The idea, which goes back to the Middle Ages, that the Alps, the Rhine [2] and the Pyrenees formed the natural

[1] L. Febvre, *La Terre et l'Evolution Humaine*, p. 361.

[2] Thus it is recorded in the Treaty of Paris (1810) : ' it was a constitutional principle in France that the *thalweg* of the Rhine was the boundary of the French Empire '. Cp. *infra*, p. 260, for the French claim to Holland at this time.

limits of France, was based on an identification of France with Gaul for which there is no historical ground. It has already been emphasized that at its inception France differed essentially from Gaul. In fact, the claim of states to natural frontiers has always cloaked their desire for territorial aggrandizement: natural frontiers which involve territorial loss have never been claimed. It should be noted that the frontiers of France in 1610, in fact right down to the post-Napoleonic settlement, suffered from the many defects which characterized frontiers before the practice of demarcation was developed and applied. Instead of a continuous defined boundary the border of the kingdom consisted of a number of islands and peninsulas of territory intermingled with the territories of neighbouring states. It is significant of this lack of territorial definition that the map of Oronce Fine, the first modern map of France, which was made in 1526, fails to show the landward boundaries of France; similarly, in Tavernier's map, in 1632, the boundaries are shown with remarkable vagueness (Fig. 37). The reasons for this lack of precision were twofold: first, the confused entanglement of political rights which varied from full sovereignty to mere overlordship, and second, the fact that the arts of surveying and cartography had not sufficiently advanced.[1] Thus, although a boundary, that between France and Flanders, was actually fixed cartographically as early as 1718,[2] the linear demarcation of French boundaries as a whole awaited the Vienna settlement in 1815 (cp. Fig. 38).

The attainment of the natural frontiers of the Rhine, the Alps and the Pyrenees was achieved for the most part in the seventeenth century and subsequently completed. Two results of this expansion may be noted: in the first place, the frontiers were pushed back farther from the capital, and strongholds were secured suitable for offence; in the second place, lands were incorporated into France which bore the transitional features of frontier regions in respect of language and nationality. In the north-west the frontier against the Spanish Netherlands lay at first along the watershed of low hills between the drainage of the Scheldt and that of the Canche and Seine. French conquests, however, won lands well beyond this line, notably Artois and parts of southern Flanders, Hainaut, and Luxemburg, and although most of these were peopled by Walloons a small part was Flemish in population. In the east were acquired Alsace,

[1] On the development of triangulation and cartography in France, see Brunhes and Deffontaines, *Géographie Politique et Géographie du Travail*, Appendix.

[2] G. N. Clark, *The Seventeenth Century*, p. 144.

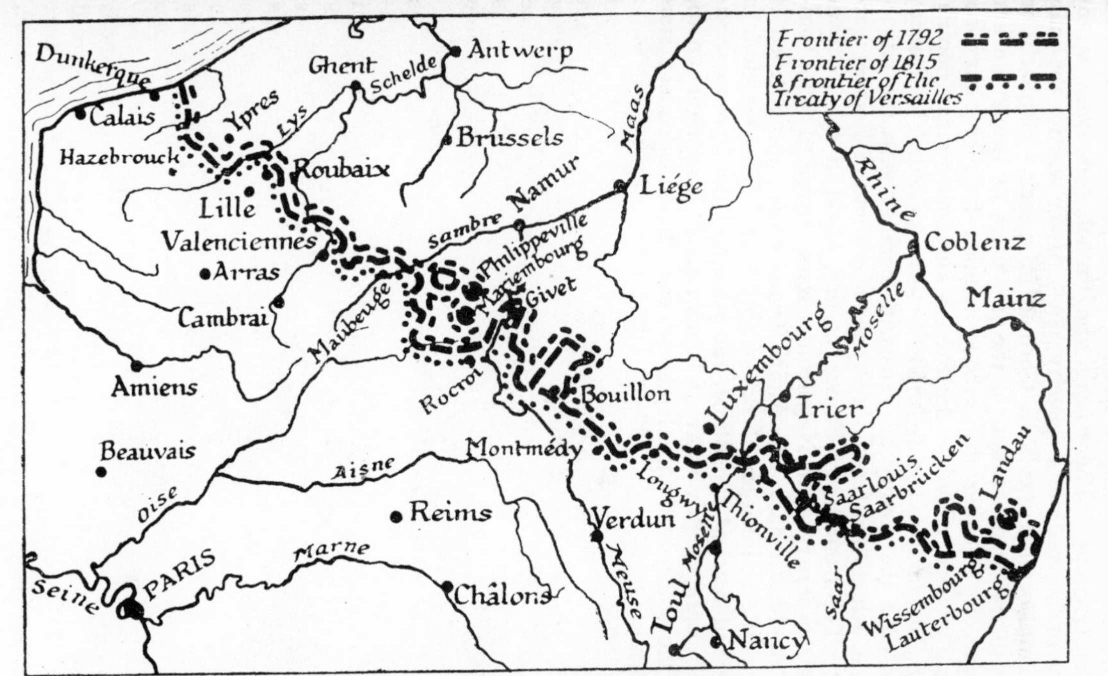

FIG. 38.—The Northern Frontier of France in 1792 and 1815 (after Brunhes and Deffontaines)
A section of the French frontier to show how a linear boundary replaced a discontinuous border with enclaves and islands

the Franche-Comté and eventually—in 1766—the duchies of Bar and Lorraine. There again the French state grew at the expense of linguistic homogeneity, since Alsace was for the most part, and Lorraine was half, German in speech. Similarly, in the south the incorporation of the provinces of Roussillon and Cerdagne, in aligning the Franco-Spanish frontier along the eastern Pyrenees, added to the French kingdom a small population of Catalan speech. In 1768 Corsica was ceded to France; and in 1792 the county of Venaissin together with the city of Avignon, which had formed a Papal *enclave* within France, were added. The frontiers of France, as they stood in 1789, despite the Revolutionary and Napoleonic wars, survived with only minor modifications. The Alpine frontier was strengthened in 1860 by the acquisition of Savoy and Nice. The kingdom of France had reached the Rhine, the Alps and the Pyrenees: its frontiers were roughly those of Roman Gaul, except that in the north the southern Netherlands became the independent state of Belgium.

CHAPTER XII

THE CREATION OF SWITZERLAND, BELGIUM AND THE NETHERLANDS

SWITZERLAND

THE emergence of the Swiss Republic as an independent political unit was an achievement of the later Middle Ages. The territories which it eventually comprised included part of the middle kingdom which was assigned to the Emperor Lothaire in 843 on the partition of the heritage of Charles the Great.[1] In common with that kingdom as a whole the Swiss lands were already marked by the transitional characteristics of a frontier region in that they fell within the zones of French, German and Italian speech. Originally, like Gaul and the north Italian plain, Switzerland was colonized, though scantily, by Celtic peoples, and subsequently conquered by the Romans. Under the Roman Empire these lands occupied a strategical position in relation to routes between northern Italy and Gaul, and the emperors were therefore zealous to build routes and cities. The Great St. Bernard, the St. Gotthard, the Septimer and the Julier passes carried Roman roads northwards across the mountains and towards the valleys of the upper Rhône and Rhine. Among the cities which grew up under the stimulus of Roman rule and became the first episcopal centres in Switzerland may be noted Geneva and Martigny on the upper Rhône; Coire on the upper Rhine; Avenches and Augst on the Rhine above the later site of Basle; and Vindisch at the junction of the Reuss and the Limmat. As they were organized under the Roman Empire the lands of Switzerland fell into two distinct provincial units: that part which stood to the west of Lake Constance and the upper Rhine and was occupied by the Celtic Helvetii, formed part of Gaul; whilst the small eastern part was included in Raetia. With the collapse of the Roman Empire in the west Germanic tribes entered Switzerland from several sides and made settlements which affected permanently the distribution of languages. Alamanns from the Agri Decumates

[1] Cp. *supra*, Chapter XI, p. 231.

pressed in from the north-east, occupied the plateau between Lake Constance and Lake Lucerne, and pushed into the mountain valleys within this region. In the west Burgundians penetrated the Jura valleys, reached the shores of Lake Geneva and the upper Rhône valley, and advanced their conquests north-eastwards to the lower Aar. Further, the Ostrogoths in Italy temporarily extended their sway across the Alps by way of the upper Ticino valley northwards to the waters of the upper Rhine, the Reuss and Limmat, and to the shores of Lake Lucerne and the Walensee. The Burgundians who settled within the Swiss lands were absorbed by the Romano-Gallic population and lost their Germanic speech, but the Alamanns, who had come from the margins of the empire, established and extended their language into the lands settled by the Burgundians in the upper Rhône and Aar. About the year A.D. 500 the Franks from Gaul conquered and absorbed into their kingdom the whole of Switzerland. During the three succeeding centuries of their rule ecclesiastical reorganization and the development of monastic foundations exerted some influence on the settlement geography. The new episcopal centres were shifted from the old Roman cities to other sites: thus Basle took the place of Augst, Constance of Windisch, and Sion of Martigny. No less important were the monastic settlements which were made not only in the valleys of the high Alps (e.g., at Dissentis on the Hither Rhine) and near the summits of passes, but also on the plateau, many of which, like the famous abbey of St. Gall, were destined to become *chefs-lieux* and even large towns.

Thus far the geographical interest of the Swiss lands centres on their character as a *pays de passage* and as a region of contact of Germanic and Romance speech. Politically they had no individuality. This latter aspect was thrown into sharp relief when, with the final break-up of the Empire of Charles the Great in 887, the Swiss lands were divided between the two neighbouring kingdoms of Burgundy and Germany. The zone of division ran northwards from the St. Gotthard pass to Lake Zurich and the Rhine. Eastwards of the dividing zone the upper Rhine lands of Switzerland were included in the German kingdom. To the west, the greater part of the Swiss plateau and the upper Rhône basin became Burgundian: it formed the province of Cisjurane Burgundy and had its capital cities on the plateau, at Thun on the lake of that name and at Payerne on the Broye river, near Lake Neuchâtel. The kingdom of Burgundy, which embraced the whole Rhône basin and had its capital at Arles, was incorporated in the year 1032 into the Holy Roman

Empire, of which the German kingdom was the chief part. It was within the confines of the Holy Roman Empire therefore that the Swiss cantons established their autonomy.

It has been stated that ' like Hellas, the Swiss land was born divided ', and also that ' political solidarity has a hard, slow birth in the mountains '. Certainly the physical geography of the Swiss lands in serving sharply to confine movement and widely to separate settled areas did not facilitate intercourse and thus political co-operation. In mountainous Switzerland, at any rate, village communes tended to occupy the narrow lateral valleys of the Alps, where they engaged in agriculture and pastoral pursuits, in a state of almost complete political and economic isolation and self-sufficiency. On the other hand, the geographical position of the Swiss lands was such as to induce a continual current of traffic *en route* for the passes of the central Alps, whilst the major valleys of the Alps, the Rhône, the Rhine and the Inn, together with the many lakes of the Alpine foreland, formed the main highways of communication. Moreover, the Swiss plateau stretching between Lakes Constance and Geneva and between the Alps and the Jura, formed a broad belt of well-watered and relatively low-lying land which was capable, on the basis of agriculture, of supporting a population very much denser than that of the mountains. Actually, however, it was not the more-favoured plateau lands but certain cantons of the mountains which provided both the leadership in the wars of independence and the nuclear region around which the state grew. The reason seems to be that in the mountain valleys the peasant and shepherd population tenaciously defended their freedom from the encroachments of feudal powers, and largely escaped being reduced to serfdom, as were the inhabitants of the plateau.

The history of the Swiss state began with the resistance of Swiss mountaineers to the encroachments of Habsburg rulers whose territories and feudal rights were widely extended throughout north-eastern Switzerland. In the thirteenth century this famous house had reached only an early stage in its remarkable career. The Counts of Habsburg took their name from their ancestral castle at Habsburg, which was situated between the Reuss and the Limmat rivers, near the Roman town of Windisch. By about 1300 they had become dukes of Austria and ruled the plateau country of Thurgau, Zurichgau and Aargau to the west of Lake Constance, whilst they secured by purchase the port and market town of Lucerne. The policy of the Habsburg house to extend its power and so to encroach on neighbouring lands was the more vigorously pursued after 1273, when its count became Emperor. In result the 'Everlasting League', the germ of the Swiss Confederation, came into existence in 1291. It consisted of a permanent alliance between the three mountain cantons of Uri, Schwyz and Unterwalden, which in 1315 inflicted a crushing defeat on the Habsburgs at the Mortgarten defile on the road from Schwyz to Zug (Fig. 39).

The 'Four Forest Cantons'—Uri, Schwyz, Unterwalden and Lucerne—whose alliance in the Everlasting League laid the basis of Swiss independence, were grouped around Lake Lucerne, the waters of which afforded their best means of intercommunication. The first three were essentially Alpine. Uri extended across its central artery the upper Reuss valley, along which passed the road to the St. Gotthard. Its cultivable land was contained in this valley and along its lateral streams; it had a port on Lake Lucerne at Flüelen, and it had abundant summer pastures and forests on the high Alps. In the south Uri had access by the St. Gotthard pass to the Ticino, which led into the Milanais, whilst in 1410 it got possession of the Unserer tributary of the Reuss, which gave it an open gate into the Valais by way of the Furka pass. The canton of Schwyz stood to the north of Uri and eastwards of Lake Lucerne on which it held a port at Brunnen. Its lands lay within the Muota basin and stretched to the north across a number of valleys which drained northwards to Lake Zurich. Unterwalden lay to the south of Lake Zurich and had its best lands in the valleys of the Aa and the Melch and around the Sarner See. The distinctive feature of these three cantons was their sturdy democratic character. In the course of the thirteenth century they secured from the Empire a status of 'immediacy', that is, they held their rights direct from the Emperor, and like the 'Free Cities' were free from feudal interference and free to govern themselves. In Uri and Schwyz, though less so in Unterwalden, serfdom was absent, and all three cantons were governed by democratic assemblies in contrast to the Free Cities of the Swiss plateau where oligarchic conditions prevailed. Finally, it is significant, in relation to the political development of the Forest Cantons, to note that a little before A.D. 1140 the St. Gotthard route across the Alps had been made practicable to traffic.[1]

The history of Swiss independence is concerned, therefore, with the fortunes of four confederated cantons which collectively occupied an area equal to that of an English county and were severally self-governing within the Empire. Their territory was almost completely set in the mountains, although the Piedmont

[1] Cp. *supra*, p. 133.

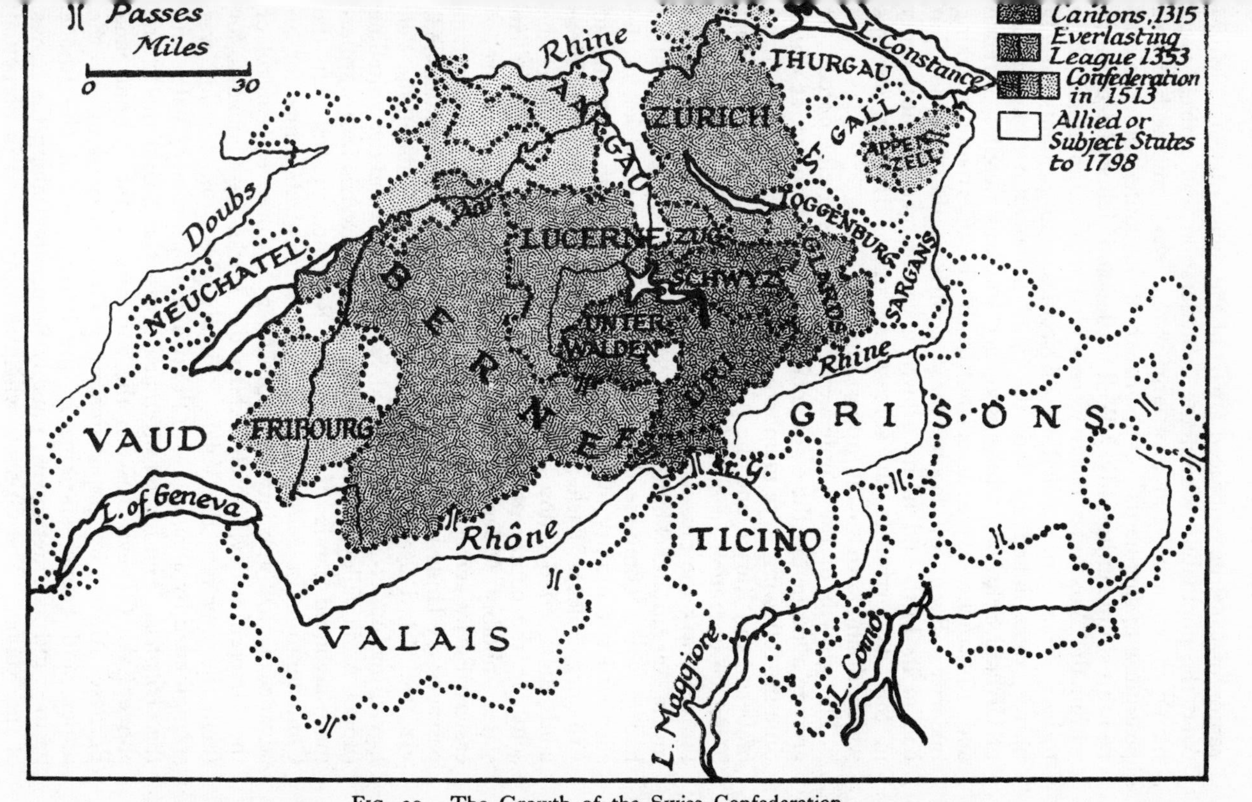

FIG. 39.—The Growth of the Swiss Confederation

St. G. is the St. Gotthard and F. the Furka Pass. Note the importance (i) of Lake Lucerne in providing a means of communication between the three original cantons, and (2) of the position of Uri in relation to the St. Gotthard and Furka passes

canton of Lucerne embraced a part of the Swiss plateau. Moreover, the population within the confederation was entirely Germanic in language, and to a large extent was composed of free peasants and shepherds. The growth of the confederation modified this simple uniformity. Well-settled and richer plateau lands within the Aar-Reuss basin were added to the mountain territories; Free Cities, ruled by oligarchies, and peasants largely unfree, were linked up with the more democratic communities of Uri and Schwyz; whilst Romance-speaking peoples—French and Romanche—were associated with the Germanic-speaking majority. Even so, despite these contrasts, the confederation had at its birth and in its growth a certain geographical unity in that its territories lay abreast the many tributary streams which drain down to the upper Rhine.

The growth of the Confederation may be briefly noted. It grew to a league of 'the eight ancient cantons' by 1353, at which time the following were members of the alliance: the Free Cities of Berne and Zurich and the Alpine cantons of Glarus and Zug. Their co-operation secured the defeat of the Habsburgs and by the year 1415 the possession, as subject territories, of their lands in the Aargau and Thurgau. A century later the Confederation had grown to comprise thirteen cantons by the accession of the shepherd community of Appenzell, and the urban republics of Fribourg, Soleure, Basle and Schaffhausen. In addition to these lands the Confederation held sway over territories gained in the south in the course of wars with the Burgundians and Italian states, notably Milan. These conquests included a part of eastern Savoy across the Rhône below Martigny, and important passage-way lands into Italy beyond the main Alpine watershed, viz., the Val. d'Ossola (part of the upper Toce valley), the Val. Levantina (upper Ticino), the Val. San Giacomo and the Valtelline (upper Adda valley). These intrusions southwards into warmer, more-favoured lands of essentially Romance speech left the Confederation in control of the main strategical points for an advance against the city state of Milan. Moreover, control of the Urseren valley, which led to the Furka pass, opened for them the way into the Valais. Finally, the Confederation was strengthened by alliances with the two large cantons of Valais and the Grisons. The former stretched across the axis of the Rhône above Lake Geneva between the summits of the Pennine and Bernese Alps; its population was German-speaking in the upper, and French-speaking in the lower, part of the Rhône basin; and its chief towns, notably Sion, stood along the banks of the Rhône. The Grisons, which in 1497 joined in perpetual league with the Confederation, was a republic of three component units and in its physical and social texture a miniature Switzerland on its own. The location of its lands astride the main headstreams of the Rhine and the Inn gave the Grisons strategical importance and encouraged them, hand in hand with the Confederation, to engage in wars of conquest with the Milanais and the Habsburgs.

The loosely knit confederation of Switzerland attained virtual independence by about 1500, but it was not until the peace of Westphalia in 1648 that its formal independence of the Empire and full state-hood was recognized. In territorial character it remained unchanged from this time until the French Revolution. The Reformation, in which Swiss city-states, especially Zurich and Geneva, took a leading part, introduced religious differentiation into a state already divided on the ground of language and physical geography. Nevertheless, the survival and permanence of the Swiss state, despite the dislocations which followed the French Revolution, testify to the fact that a nation-state can be built up out of apparently disintegrating elements.

Belgium and the Netherlands

The territories which comprise the present kingdoms of Belgium and the Netherlands provide a striking instance of the way in which the geography of a region can be completely transformed by human effort. The physical basis of the Dutch and Belgian states have, it is evident, remained far from stable throughout history: the coastal lands, which in Holland form to-day the richest and most populous part of the kingdom, have suffered from small but decisive changes in the relative level of land and sea, changes which had their source in either the subsidence of the land or, at other times, in the excessive storminess of the sea. A remote and desolate region on the frontier of the civilized world in the time of the Roman emperors, the lands of Belgium and of Holland, which may be collectively called the Netherlands or Low Countries, began to advance greatly in wealth and population in the course of the Middle Ages and have become finally at the present day one of the most densely settled parts of Europe. In its primitive condition and during many centuries of the Christian era the plain between the mouth of the Scheldt and that of the Ems was furrowed by the meandering channels of the Rhine and the Meuse, which in the final stage of their courses reached a coastland continually invaded by the sea. In fact, the alluvial belt along the littoral of Holland, which stands to-day beneath the level of high tide and is habitable only by an elaborate system of water control, must have stood in the early centuries A.D., as also did the maritime plain of Flanders,[1] largely beneath the sea. Eastwards from the coast of Holland the plain rises to a maximum of some 300 feet, but the advantage of this salutary elevation was offset considerably by the sterile character of its soils, by the excessive humidity of the climate and by the great burden of ill-drained waters. In fact, even to-day when capital and technique can be so effectively turned to the reclamation of land, some of this country consists of sandy heath, as in the Campine, or of water-logged flats, as in the broad and almost continuous belt which constitutes the eastern frontier zone of the kingdom of the Netherlands from the Bourtanger moor in the north to the marshes of Peel in the south.

Roman Phase

In their physical aspects no less than their human geography the Low Countries present markedly different features in the Roman period as compared with those of to-day. Parts of the islands which lie between the mouths of the Scheldt and the Meuse together with a thin strip of the ma inland farther to the north may be presumed to have lain, at least during high water, under the sea. Again, the Zuider Zee was then represented by the much smaller Lacus Flevo, which had a narrow outlet to the sea in the north. Moreover, the channels of the Rhine and Meuse had somewhat different courses which were already modified in some degree by Roman canal works. The Meuse then entered (near Boemel) the most southerly of the three Rhine channels, now represented by the Waal, so that it had no independent estuary. (The tradition of this junction of Rhine and Meuse, it may be noted, is reflected in the fact that the Waal at Rotterdam is still called the Old Meuse.) Finally, Drusus in 9 B.C. constructed a canal which led off from the Rhine near Arnheim, to the Yssel river, which drained northwards into the Lacus Flevo : in consequence, he was able by inland navigation for the most part, to lead a fleet against the Germanic tribes of the Frisian coastlands.

In their geographical position in relation to the chiet regions of population and culture the Low Countries were as ill favoured in the Roman period as they were fortunate in the modern world, since not only were the sea-ways to the Americas and the Far East unknown but also the neighbouring lands of the Baltic were 'barbarous' or undeveloped. Moreover, in the northeast across the Rhine stretched a marshy frontier zone which

[1] Cp. *infra*, Fig. 12, p. 69, and p. 330.

offered little attraction to settlers and natural obstacles to trade intercourse. On the other hand, the country south of the Old Rhine arm was incorporated into the Empire, and again, to the west of the Rhine–Meuse estuaries lay the Romanized, though relatively unimportant, province of Britain. In short, both within and without the Empire the Low Countries remained lands of backward civilization. They were occupied by Germanic tribes, Batavi and Frisii to the north of the Rhine, and Belgic Menapii and Morini to the south. The population was scanty and the settlements were small scattered hamlets; their chief resources were cattle, fish and water fowl. Along the Rhine stood a few small maritime cities: notably those which occupied the sites represented to-day by Leiden and Utrecht on the Old Rhine, and Nimègue, which stood on the Waal just above the confluence of the Meuse. The Roman name for Utrecht—Trajectum (= 'passage')—is suggestive of its geographical function: the town stood on the eastern edge of the alluvial belt of Holland and controlled a ford at a point where a route north-southwards could follow along higher, drier ground. There is little evidence to suggest that these Rhine cities enjoyed much commercial prosperity: there was some relation by river with the great cities of the middle Rhine, e.g., Cologne, and again some little contact by sea with the ports of south-eastern England: it is well to recall, however, the disinclination of the Romans for long passages across the tidal sea and their consequent preference for the great highway from Cologne to the ports of the Liane estuary at or near Boulogne and the sea route thence, where the Channel narrows (cp. Fig. 12).

The Salian Franks

The advent of the Salian Franks into the Low Countries, which has already been noted,[1] imposed a certain uniformity in language and nationality throughout the lowland belt between the Zuider Zee and the Yssel in the north and the plains of Flanders and Brabant in the south. Within this belt a distinctive form of Low German—Netherlandish—became characteristic, which is represented to-day by Flemish and Dutch. Certainly Germanic speech came to be prevalent with only local variation throughout almost the whole area later occupied by the seventeen provinces, except in the south-west, where the forest obstacle[2] had checked Frankish penetration and where Walloon or French speech prevailed: namely, in southern Flanders, in Hainaut, Artois and Namur. Except for the distribution of

[1] Cp. *supra*, Chapter III, pp. 66–70. [2] Cp. Fig. 12, p. 69.

Salian settlement through its western parts the Low Countries had no individuality during the early Middle Ages. They were absorbed within the Carolingian Empire, and on its disruption in the ninth century were divided along the line of the Scheldt between two neighbouring powers : the western part passed to the kingdom of the west Franks, which became France, the eastern part formed part first of the Middle Kingdom of Lothaire and later of the German kingdom. This division ignored the division between Frankish and other forms of speech—such differences were not then regarded as important. The Low Countries remained therefore for some centuries merely the border provinces of the kingdoms of France and of Germany, the latter forming part of the extensive Holy Roman Empire. With the development of feudalism they broke up into a number of separate fiefs, some of which like the county of Flanders owed allegiance to the kings of France, whilst others, like the duchy of Brabant and the county of Holland, owed allegiance to the Empire. In both cases these feudal territories exploited their borderland positions in order to secure a wide amount of independence. Further, some of them, notably Flanders and Brabant, thanks to their situation in relation to rivers and seaboard, built towns at river stations and at the heads of tidal creeks and flourished economically.

The Burgundian State

At the end of the fourteenth century the greater part of the territories now occupied by Belgium and Holland were united under a single princely house to form the so-called Burgundian State. The rise of this powerful state was certainly in no sense intrinsically inevitable. It was essentially the outcome of dynastic ambition and was achieved by means of diplomacy, inheritance, purchase and war. Its creators were the Valois dukes of Burgundy, who were related to, and vassals of, the French kings. The Burgundian princes held sway over regions other than the Netherlands, notably over the duchy of Burgundy (a French fief) and the county of Burgundy or Franche-Comté (an imperial fief), but there seems good reason for applying the term 'Burgundian State', as Professor Pirenne[1] suggests, to their provinces in the Low Countries alone. These provinces, fronting the North Sea, formed a large continuous territory which was detached from the Burgundian lands astride the Saône in the south ; in their density of population, cultural

[1] 'The Formation and Constitution of the Burgundian State', *A. H. R.*, XIV.

development and political importance the Low Countries as a whole, and the County of Flanders in particular, inevitably constituted the hub of the Burgundian realm and long survived the loss to France in the sixteenth century of the duchy and county of Burgundy. In 1463 the creation of a single states-general or council composed of the delegates from each of the assemblies of the Burgundian provinces in the Netherlands, symbolized their union as a distinct state, apart from the other Burgundian lands. Moreover, the incorporation, as a result of conquest in the mid-sixteenth century, of provinces in the north-east completed the union of the seventeen provinces of the Netherlands, which were grouped together in 1548 in a separate 'Circle'—the Circle of Burgundy—as one of the administrative divisions of the Holy Roman Empire.

The full story of the rise of Burgundian power cannot be summarized here: it must suffice to mark the main stages of their advance in the Low Countries and then to examine geographically the Burgundian State as it was constituted *c.* 1550 prior to the great revolt against Spain (Fig. 40).

The Burgundian princes acquired their first foothold in the Low Countries by the marriage in 1369 of Duke Philip with the heiress of Flanders and Artois. In 1430 the Burgundians won Brabant, and in 1428 the counties of Hainaut, Holland and Zeeland, and the lordship of West Friesland, whilst they further strengthened their position by establishing a protectorate over the bishops of Liège, Utrecht and Tournai. Moreover, this association under a common dynasty of the chief regions of the Low Countries had some basis in their existing economic inter-relationships. The great Flemish and Brabant towns exercised an attractive force on the Low Countries, promoted by agreements—such as the commercial agreement of 1339 which was made between Flanders, Brabant, Hainaut, Holland and Zeeland.

The vagaries of inheritance in the second decade of the sixteenth century united the Burgundian State in the Netherlands with Spain, the Empire and the other possession in the Old and the New Worlds which fell to the rule of the Emperor Charles V. Even so, the Low Countries formed a distinct unit within this miscellaneous realm, and one which Charles, himself a native of Brabant, was at pains politically to define. It was during his reign that the 'Easterners' or 'Overlanders', as were called the inhabitants of the north-eastern provinces of Gelders, Overyssel, Drenthe, Gröningen and Friesland, were absorbed by conquest, and that in consequence all of the seventeen provinces were bound together as an imperial 'circle' with a common states-

FIG. 40.—The Netherlands in the time of Charles V (after *Cam. Mod. Hist.* atla

The darker stipple shows the area of the Dutch Republic which won its independence from Spain. (Note its command of the Scheldt estuary.) The area left white within the boundary, together with the Church lands marked by the lighter stipple, remained united with Spain. By the Treaty of Münster (1648) Holland was ceded lands in north Brabant which joined up its Limburg territories

general. Nevertheless, it may well be asked to what extent the Burgundian State, thus constituted, possessed the real cohesive elements of statehood. In the first place the region occupied by the seventeen provinces had no clear-cut definition on the ground of physical geography. Certainly it was bounded to the west by the sea and a somewhat fluctuating zone of low plain which was largely reclaimed by dyking from the invasion of the tide. In every other direction, however, its frontiers lay along open plain, except in the south where they impinged on the Ardennes highlands, and were thus in easy contact with peoples of the same race and language in France and the Empire. Moreover, all the great rivers which drained their territories rose outside their frontiers. In fact, the cultural influences of the greater neighbouring states flowed into the Low Countries at each end. The 'Overlanders' had long been in touch with Westphalia and Germany generally, as the southern provinces of Flanders and Brabant had been invaded by French culture. The Low Countries, looked at as a whole, were actually divided along a north-south line into two distinct cultural belts. Holland proper and Zeeland, that is, the low alluvial plain between Helder and the Scheldt estuaries, were related culturally and economically with Flanders and Brabant, with which they shared in common original settlement by Salian Franks and Frankish speech. Moreover, in those four provinces maritime activity was chiefly concentrated and Romance culture was characteristic. On the other hand, the 'Overlanders' were largely Saxon in blood and their contacts were with Germany: thus Gelders and the other more northerly provinces long resisted inclusion within the Burgundian net, and the Burgundian rulers had to conquer these hinterland provinces of the county of Holland in order to safeguard the latter from attacks by land. It should be noted that the north-eastern frontier, as it was determined under Charles V, was a purely arbitrary one, although it did in fact coincide with a broad belt, from the Bourtanger moor to the Peel marshes, which owing to its natural character formed a separating zone of scanty settlement and restricted facilities for communication. Again, apart from its largely arbitrary framework, the Burgundian State, although predominantly Netherlandish in language, included in the south a population of Walloon speech. But this lack of homogeneity in language was not politically important, since language did not provide then a basis for political differentiation. Much stronger as a dividing force was the strength of provincial feeling. Citizens of the Burgundian State thought of themselves as primarily Brabanters, Flemings, Hollanders, according to the province of their birth, and it is suggestive that Erasmus, himself a Hollander, only late in his life (i.e. about

1550) styled himself a Netherlander, that is, a member of the united provinces. It was about the same time too that the word 'Netherland' was used in the songs of the Sea Beggars to denote the seventeen provinces as a whole. Thus the Netherlands came to form a well-defined though loosely knit political unit in which a distinctive national sentiment was forming. It should be emphasized that there was no political cleavage on the basis of language, and still more that there was nothing in 1550 to suggest the division of the Low Countries, as it was ultimately made, along east-west lines. Rather, as suggested above, the significant line of division ran north-south.

The United Provinces

The division of the Netherlands along an east-west axis was the unforeseen and unnatural result of their struggles with Spain, although it was related, also, to the physical conformation of the country. The chances of marriage and heredity having brought the Low Countries in 1516 into political union with Spain, they fell in 1555 under the rule of the Spanish monarch, Philip II. His persistent and lifelong attempt to establish royal despotism and to stamp out Protestant heresy in the Netherlands at the expense of their ancient urban and provincial liberties involved those lands in sporadic and continual rebellion for a generation. The revolt of the Netherlands in all its complications and fluctuations has recently been re-told,[1] and it is necessary here to note only two aspects. First, the striking part played by Holland and Zeeland in resisting Spanish power, and second, the resultant division of the Netherlands by 1609, at which time the seven most northerly provinces had made good their independence of Spain.

The rôle assumed by Holland and Zeeland as staunch and successful champions of the revolt was directly related to their geographical character and position. They occupied a strategical position astride the tidal waters of the Scheldt, Meuse, Rhine and Zuider Zee, and moreover quickly developed sea-power and thus the ability to control their sea entries. Further, whilst the province of Zeeland was made up of islands, that of Holland, owing to the low elevation of its polder lands, its many river estuaries, canals, and lakes as yet unreclaimed, was scarcely less insular. These water stretches, apart from floods deliberately made, imposed obstacles to the movements of troops, and safeguarded Holland and Zeeland particularly from the south and left them open to attack only from the east, especially from

[1] Geyl, *The Revolt of the Netherlands*, 1932.

Gelderland. It was the military need for security on their eastern borders which led the two maritime provinces to effect a union with the eastern provinces of Friesland, Gröningen, Drenthe, Overyssel and Gelderland—a union which was established largely by force. Moreover, it was an important factor that Holland and Zeeland, especially the former, were the richest and most populous of the northern provinces. What is more, they definitely prospered in the course of the wars, since their population and capital were reinforced by the inflow of skilled immigrants from the southern provinces and their command of the sea made commercial development possible. The territorial division of the Low Countries made in 1609, when a twelve-year truce was concluded with Spain, was a compromise 'determined by the interplay of force and counter-force, and these conformed not to the dispositions of the people, but to that of the soil'.[1] The line of division between the seven provinces of the United Netherlands (all of which had a maritime frontage) and those which remained under Spanish rule owed nothing to the distribution of either language or religion (Fig. 40). The arms of Spain, although they reconquered much of the southern Netherlands, had insufficient strength to push beyond the line of the lower Scheldt, since the great rivers involved them in serious transport difficulties and since, moreover, the Dutch held command of the sea. The United Netherlands, more popularly called Holland, as it stood in 1609 were uniformly Netherlandish (Dutch) in speech, but the southern or Spanish Netherlands contained people of both Netherlandish (Flemish) and of French (Walloon) speech. Further, in both the northern and southern provinces the population was divided in religion, and although the northern provinces became increasingly and emphatically Protestant whilst the southern remained essentially Roman Catholic, at the time of their escape from Spain their Protestant element formed still a small, though powerful, minority. The United Netherlands were left in control of the estuaries of the Scheldt, Meuse and Rhine. In industry and trade they had won for themselves the first position in the Low Countries, a position formerly held by Flanders and Brabant. Moreover, with a view to increasing their own trade and to preventing the revival of Antwerp, they used their controlling position at the estuary of the west Scheldt to prevent direct access between Antwerp and the sea. The formal independence of the Dutch republic was not recognized until 1648, at which time its frontiers underwent rectification. It lost a small part of south Gelders but gained territory on the

[1] Geyl, op. cit., p. 188.

left bank of the west Scheldt, which strengthened its hold on Antwerp and Brabant. About this time, too, it had become a great sea-state with considerable possessions oversea—in India and the Indies in the Far East, at the Cape of Good Hope, in North America and in the West Indies. It had, in fact, succeeded in part to the inheritance of Spain, which was declining in power, and of Portugal, which Spain had ruined.

The subsequent political geography of the Low Countries may be briefly noted. The attempt of the French king, Louis XIV, to conquer the Spanish Netherlands and Holland failed, but he secured permanently a considerable strip of Walloon country—Artois, Walloon Flanders and about a half of Hainaut, along his northern frontier. In 1713 the Spanish Netherlands passed to the rule of the Habsburg emperors. During the French Revolutionary wars the Low Countries in their entirety were conquered for the first and last time by France. The southern provinces were united with France, whilst the northern were organized at first as the Batavian Republic and then as a kingdom. The French official newspaper, the *Moniteur*, attempted in 1809 to justify on geographical ground the abolition of Holland as a kingdom and its absorption into France, since (it stated) 'la Hollande, en sa qualité d'alluvion des grandes artères françaises, le Rhin, la Meuse et l'Escaut, n'était réellement qu'une portion de la France'! Actually Holland was united to France in 1810, but with the downfall of Napoleon French rule in the Low Countries ended. In 1815 at the Congress of Vienna it was decided to unite the southern and the northern provinces and thus to create a single kingdom of the Netherlands. Even so, this territorial fabric, which had been the goal of many Netherlander leaders in the sixteenth century, proved unworkable in the nineteenth. In 1831 Belgium was constituted as a separate kingdom under a collective guarantee of the Great Powers, and in 1839 the Duchy of Luxemburg was made a separate state.

CHAPTER XIII

THE POLITICAL UNIFICATION OF THE GERMAN EMPIRE

THE German Empire was the creation of the Hohenzollern dynasty, the territories of which in the early seventeenth century consisted mainly of the electorate of Brandenburg and the duchy of East Prussia. That this house should have succeeded from a base in Brandenburg-Prussia in uniting within a single framework the bulk of the German peoples of Middle Europe is a remarkable fact, the explanation of which falls to the historian. It is relevant here merely to examine the geographical texture and growth of these principalities, and the territorial extension of the Hohenzollern lands in the course of several hundred years, which enabled them to play the leading rôle in Germany.

Brandenburg

Certainly the destiny of the Hohenzollern house was not implicit in the geographical character of its earliest possessions, and nothing is more outstanding in the history of Brandenburg-Prussia than the unremitting political effort of its rulers to make the best of scanty and unpromising natural resources. The history of Brandenburg precedes that of its Hohenzollern rulers, whose first possessions lay in the south about the upper Main. The area which came to be included in the electorate of Brandenburg was confined between the lower Elbe and Oder where these rivers stand closest together, and it consisted of a well-marked physical feature, namely the depressed zone, running east-west, which is drained by the river Havel and its tributary the Spree[1]. The first advance of the Germans into this region, then occupied by a scanty Slav population, was marked by the creation in the tenth century of the Nordmark which had for its eastern limit the Elbe and in which were built the fortified towns of Salzwedel, Stendal and Tangermünde. The Nordmark was established by

[1] This region in turn is part of the east-west depression of glaciated country designated by German geographers the region of the *Urstromtäler*. See Shackleton, *Europe,* 7th ed., pp. 282–4 and Fig. 40.

Henry I, king of the Germans and duke of Saxony, and it represented an outpost of Saxon territory which was designed not merely as a defensive marchland but also as a base from which German conquest, colonization and Christianity could be extended among the neighbouring pagan and non-German peoples—Wends, Lithuanians, and Prussians. This work was begun with the foundation of bishoprics at Havelberg in 946 and at Brandenburg in 949, but these foundations proved temporary, since the conquest and conversion of the Wends involved the Germans in a bitter and fluctuating struggle for two centuries. The Nordmark, or the Altmark as it came later to be called, was permanently extended beyond the Elbe and up the Havel valley only in the mid-twelfth century, when (in 1157) the Wend stronghold of Brannibor (Brandenburg) was finally captured and converted into a German fortress. With the accession of Albert the Bear, the first ruler of the Ascanian line, in 1133, the Nordmark entered upon two centuries of further expansion. The Mittelmark, which stretched eastwards to the Oder, was founded, whilst to the north of it, between the Elbe and Oder, the districts of Priegnitz (Vormark), Rupin and Ückermark were incorporated with the Nordmark which was created by the emperor in 1157 the margraviate of Brandenburg. It is worth noting that the capital of the march remained still on the left bank of the Elbe, at Tangermünde. Further, towards the end of the fourteenth century the Neumark was annexed beyond the Oder, and this, together with the Ückermark, formed a frontier outpost against the Slavs of Pomerania. Moreover, in the south by its possession of the districts of Lebus and Sternberg, which stood respectively on the left and right banks of the Oder, Brandenburg was able to keep guard on the Slav country of Lusatia.

Thus far Brandenburg had expanded to occupy a considerable area of continuous territory astride the lower waters of two important navigable waterways. That it had achieved some importance in the Holy Roman Empire was indicated in 1351, when it was created an electorate of the Empire, that is to say, it shared with six other principalities (three lay and three ecclesiastical), the privilege of electing emperors. Even so, its location made it essentially a march or frontier land, surrounded by alien peoples against whom it had to fight and conquer in order to survive. Much was done to strengthen and develop the Brandenburg lands by the encouragement of German settlement and the extension of agriculture. German immigrants—nobles, artisans and peasants—were brought in from Saxony, Flanders, Holland, Westphalia and Franconia, and the Wends were reduced to serfdom. Further, the founding of cities was undertaken. Berlin (the suffix 'in' marks its original Slav phase) had its beginnings as a German town about the year 1250, whilst at Frankfurt, seated on the left bank of the Oder, arose a military base from which the Neumark was conquered. But despite its successful beginnings the electorate in 1400 faced a precarious future. To the north of it the German duchies of Mecklenburg and Pomerania ruled the Slav population of the broad coastland belt ; eastwards of the Neumark stretched the Christian kingdom of Poland which had then already shown great power of growth ; farther to the south again Brandenburg impinged on Slav lands, in Silesia and Lusatia ; whilst elsewhere

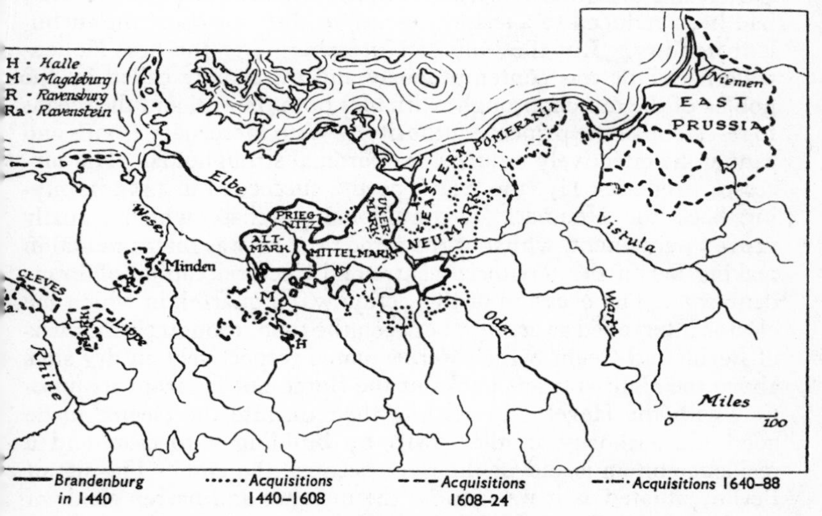

FIG. 41.—The Growth of Brandenburg-Prussia up to 1688

it was ringed around by German principalities large and small. Its peripheral location in some measure enabled it to avoid much of the civil war of medieval Europe, but broadly speaking the chances were either that it should be absorbed by its more powerful neighbours, above all by Poland, or that it should continue to grow, since the ill-defined limits and undeveloped character of this frontier region left ample room for expansion.

The political stability of the Brandenburg march was severely tested during the fourteenth century. Certainly, at the beginning of that century it had made considerable territorial advances, but the ensuing years brought internal disorders, political weakness and losses of land. In 1402 the elector actually pawned the

Neumark to the Teutonic Knights of Prussia, and in 1411 the elector Sigismund I, who had been elected emperor in the previous year, assigned the march of Brandenburg to Frederick of Hohenzollern, a scion of a minor Swabian house, which had its ancestral castle at Zollern in the Rauhe Alp, midway between the Neckar and the Danube. Frederick, who held the imperial office of burgrave of Nuremberg, actually became elector, ruling with full sovereignty by the year 1417. When he received it, however, Brandenburg had become much shrunken, since it included within its limits only the Altmark, the Mittelmark, the Sternberg district on the right bank of the Oder, and merely parcels of land in the Ücker and Priegnitz marches. Moreover, the electoral authority had been reduced to a shadow owing to the inroads of the turbulent nobility. But the 'toy of Nuremberg', as the first Hohenzollern elector was contemptuously and mistakenly called by the nobles of the march, brought with him both the will and the means to re-establish the princely authority. With mercenary troops and cannon he effectively reduced the baronial strongholds. His successor Frederick II, 'the Iron Tooth', succeeded in 1455 in buying back the Neumark, a conditional purchase which actually proved permanent, whilst at the same time he was instrumental in making Berlin the territorial centre and electoral capital of Brandenburg. The occasion of this action was a quarrel, in which the elector intervened as arbiter, between the twin, though rival, towns of Berlin and Coeln, which were situated respectively on dry sites above the right and left banks of the Spree not far from its junction with the Havel. In settling their dispute the elector made good his authority in the towns by building a fortress and a residence on an island in the river between the two. The site of Berlin, situated as it was amidst the marshes and barren sands of the Spree and Havel, had little to recommend it, but its position was by no means disadvantageous. Berlin was not only well placed for the navigation of the Spree and Havel, and thence to the Elbe, but it occupied an intermediate position between the Elbe and Oder. Its selection as capital in the thirteenth century was significant of the eastward extension of the Brandenburg march; its position midway between the Baltic and the Bohemian mountains was another geographical factor which offered possibilities for the future.

The fifteenth and sixteenth centuries testified to the statesmanship and ambition of the Hohenzollern dynasty of Brandenburg which effectively consolidated its hereditary position. By two political measures the electors prepared for the future. One was the law of 1473 which, contrary to the usual practice in Germany, made the territories of the march indivisible, and moreover fixed the succession by primogeniture. The second was an engagement between the three ruling branches of the Hohenzollern family, which so regulated the succession that their several lands should not pass out of the possession of their own family. Moreover, the electors devoted themselves with the industry and prudence which characterized their house to the exploitation of their lands which, despite their poor geographical endowment, made considerable economic advance under their firm and well-ordered rule.

Prussia

It was the united state of Brandenburg-Prussia which played the leading rôle in the creation of the German Empire, and the union of Brandenburg and East Prussia in 1618 is thus, in retrospect, a great historical landmark. In Prussia, as in Brandenburg, the accession of the Hohenzollern house was preceded by a long and chequered history of German military effort and colonization. At the accession of the first Hohenzollern elector of Brandenburg in 1411, Prussia had been for two hundred years a field of activity of the Order of Teutonic Knights. Prussia was a lowland country of numerous scattered marshes and lakes and of vast forests, which gave it its name ' the land of spruce '. It lay between the lower Vistula and the lower Pregel rivers, and was bounded northwards by a stretch of lagoons along the Baltic coast. It seemed likely that this desolate land and its Prussian population would be conquered either by the Poles or the Lithuanians, since the former held the plains of the middle and upper Vistula, and the latter occupied the lowlands to the south-east between the Niemen and the Bug. Actually, Prussia was conquered by invaders from the sea who sought the estuaries of its chief rivers, but not by the first-comers, the Danes, but by the Germans led by the Teutonic Order.

The conquest, which began in 1231, proved a bitter struggle which lasted some seventy-five years. The fourteenth century was, indeed, the golden age of the Teutonic Knights in Prussia. They succeeded in subduing the peninsular district of Sambia (Samland) which juts out westwards into the Baltic between the Frische Haff and the Kurische Haff. In result, by dint of piecemeal conquests, they brought under their rule a continuous territory which stretched from the last great bend of the Vistula (below Thorn) eastwards to beyond the lower Niemen and southwards from the two haffen (= lagoons) to the plateau of Masurianland, which was covered by lakes and marshes and formed the watershed between rivers draining to the Baltic and the Vistula.

Moreover, in 1309 they acquired, beyond the Vistula, the eastern part of Pomerania which was known as Pomerelia, the capital of which was Danzig. Danzig, formerly the Wend city of Gdansk, had already fallen under influences from the west: the Danes temporarily held it in the twelfth century, and for a time it had recognized the overlordship of Brandenburg. Its Slav population had already been converted to Christianity; German colonists and monks, e.g., at the Oliva monastery to the north-west of the town, had already settled near by. Further, Danzig was already developing as a port of commerce with the western Baltic. In 1402 the Teutonic Order assumed possession of the Neumark beyond the Oder, which the elector of Brandenburg, financially pressed, mortgaged; it acquired from the Knights of the Sword the lands which they had won and converted beyond the Niemen, namely Kurland, Semigalia and Livonia, whilst in 1347 it bought Estonia from Denmark. Finally, the Order secured in 1405 the maritime province of Samogitia which lay across the Niemen to the south of Kurland; this district was of strategical importance to the Order, in that it completed the territorial continuity of their widely extended Baltic lands.

The dominion of the Order assumed thus at the dawn of the fifteenth century formidable proportions: it constituted a great Baltic state which touched the Oder in the west and the Gulf of Finland in the north-east. In the midst of subject peoples of varied nationality the Knights introduced and settled free German peasants, who won new lands for the plough either from the forest or, as in the case of the fertile *Werders* of the lower Vistula, from the marsh. German colonists were established, too, in newly fortified towns: the Order built for its head-quarters in 1309 the fortress of Marienburg, which stands on one of the lowest channels of the Vistula. It built cities, which served as episcopal sees, at convenient centres in each of the conquered districts: at Kulm in Kulmerland; at Marienwerder in Pomerania; at Heilsberg in Ermeland; at Fischhausen in Sambia. But despite their great success in creating an ecclesiastical and military state in what had been formerly a land of distinct and scattered peoples and of backward culture, the Teutonic Knights were beset by grave difficulties at the end of the fourteenth century. In particular, there were internal sources of weakness in the discontent of the conquered peoples, both townsmen and serfs in the countryside; further, what was much more ominous was the persistent advance of the Polish kingdom on their southern frontier. For the Polish kingdom, comprising above all the greater part of the Vistula basin, had become a Christian state. In the fourteenth century it had its capital and university in the south at Cracow, whilst in the north Gnesen had long been a Metropolitan see. In 1386 the kingdom of Poland united with that of Lithuania under the house of Jagellon, and thus the Teutonic Knights were faced with a united Slav enemy whose advance was welcomed by their own subject population. The crushing Polish victory at Tannenburg in 1410 spelt disaster to the Order, but it escaped with the loss of Samogitia only, the possession of which by the Poles, however, divided its lands into two sectors. Finally, at the second peace of Thorn in 1466 Polish mastery was complete, and the territories of the Order were partitioned. The Order retained the lands beyond the Niemen which it had acquired from the Knights of the Sword, and, what is more important to note here, the land which with Königsberg as its new capital came to be known as East or Ducal Prussia. This territory, which the Order held as a fief of Poland, stretched from Memel (beyond the Niemen) westwards to Marienwerder where it fronted the Vistula for a few miles. Western Prussia, on the other hand, which stretched across the Vistula and contained many thriving cities along its banks from Toruǹ to Danzig, was incorporated with Poland, which thus secured its natural outlet to the sea. This region became known as ' Polish ' or ' royal ' Prussia. It was in the lands which remained under the Teutonic Order—East Prussia—that the interests of the house of Hohenzollern became involved, and it was there that they won an important addition to their territories.

In the sixteenth century East Prussia passed to the rule of a Grand Master of the Hohenzollern family who converted it into a protestant and hereditary duchy, although it remained formally a fief of the Polish kingdom. In result of the family compact made between ruling branches of the Hohenzollern family the duchy reverted to the elector of Brandenburg in 1618, who then found himself ruler of a state, the geographical basis of which embraced lands astride the Elbe, Oder, Vistula, Pregel and Niemen rivers. Further, the state made touch with the Baltic in Prussia at the ports of Memel and Pillau, which commanded the narrow entries into the Frisches and Kurisches haffen. It constituted, however, a discontinuous territory, since the broad belt of Slav lands within the Polish kingdom intervened between the Neumark and Marienwerder on the western border of East Prussia. Moreover, all the military energy of the electors was needed to establish their control over East Prussia, since the native nobility vigorously resisted their authority on the ground that they were aliens whose economic and religious interests ran counter to their own.

Brandenburg-Prussia in the Seventeenth and Eighteenth Centuries

The territorial gains of Brandenburg-Prussia in the seventeenth century served only to emphasize the two chief geographical features of that state, namely its discontinuity and its position athwart the great river valleys of Middle Europe. Within the Empire, as outside it in East Prussia, the state continued to grow. In 1618 was raised one of the many complicated 'succession questions' which continually beset European diplomacy, and in its ultimate solution Brandenburg was successful in securing small but important territories on the lower Rhine in Westphalia and on the middle Weser. The Cleves-Jülich inheritance, to which the elector had a strong claim, was characteristic of the dynastic, political groupings of contemporary Germany. It included a number of scattered duchies, counties and lordships which were of great value owing to their geographical position, wealth and population. In detail, the Cleves-Jülich lands comprised the duchy of Cleves, which lay across the lower Rhine where the Ruhr and Lippe rivers enter from Westphalia; the county of Mark, which was detached from Cleves and extended across the middle Ruhr northwards to reach the Lippe; the duchy of Berg, which stood on the right bank of the Rhine above Cologne; and finally, one other small area, the county of Ravensberg, which stretched westwards from the Weser just above Minden. Brandenburg secured only a share of this inheritance, nor did it fully secure it until 1666. Even so, this share, which included Cleves, Jülich and Ravensberg, was the lion's share, and it gave Brandenburg-Prussia a footing on the Rhine, Weser, Ruhr and Lippe. The potential importance of these lands can be gauged in relation to the traffic of the Rhine and to the resources of coal and iron, together with the industries already established, in the Ruhr-Lippe region. Certainly these Westphalian lands stood out even in seventeenth-century Germany as centres of industry and population.

During the Thirty Years War in Germany (1618–48) the march of Brandenburg suffered severely from the devastations of rival armies, since it lay across the main route-ways between the Baltic and the imperial territories in Silesia, Bohemia, Moravia and Austria. Even so, despite the great losses which it suffered in population and in cultivated lands, it emerged from the war with territorial gains. In 1637 the succession to the dukedom of Pomerania devolved upon the elector of Brandenburg. That duchy occupied the Baltic coastlands between the Recknitz river in the west and the Leba river in the east, and it included the mouth of the Oder, where stood the maritime towns of Stettin and Wollin, and the island of Rügen. In the south its somewhat indeterminate frontiers impinged on the electoral Ückermark and Neumark. Already by the fifteenth century its Slav inhabitants, despite their native rulers, had become largely Germanized. To Brandenburg its acquisition was strategically inviting, since it controlled the outlet from the Oder. The intervention of Sweden in the Thirty Years' War and its occupation of part of Pomerania including the port of Stralsund, prevented the electors, however, from securing the whole of their inheritance. At the peace of Westphalia in 1648 Brandenburg was assigned only eastern Pomerania, a region of sandy plain and arable fields bounded seawards by a harbourless coast (Fig. 41). Western Pomerania, including the Oder ports, remained in Swedish hands and was recovered in part by Brandenburg only in 1740. In compensation for the loss of western Pomerania the peace settlement of Westphalia ceded to Brandenburg four areas which had formerly comprised the archbishopric of Magdeburg and the bishoprics of Halberstadt, Minden and Cammin. The position of these lands and the important towns which they contained made them a valuable possession. The lands of Magdeburg and Halberstadt lay across the middle Elbe continuous to, and southwards of, the Altmark and the Mittelmark, and they continued south as far as the northern slopes of the Harz mountains. Cammin stood on the coast of Pomerania overlooking Wollin island at the mouth of the Oder. Finally, Minden on the middle Weser occupied a strategical position at the river crossing, whilst its appendant lands joined up westwards with the electoral territory in Ravensberg.

In effect, the territorial aggrandizement of Brandenburg-Prussia created in the north of Middle Europe a strong and growing German state, which held together in political union lands widely flung to the east and west, both within and outside the Holy Roman Empire. Within this ancient political structure, which was composed of a mosaic of principalities, the Habsburg emperor still remained the greatest power, since his dominions comprised Bohemia, Silesia, Moravia, Austria, Styria, Carinthia, the Tirol and, after 1699, the kingdom of Hungary. But thanks to the rule of 'the Great Elector' (1640–88) Brandenburg-Prussia assumed the dominant position among the many states into which northern Germany was divided. Moreover, its prestige was increased when in 1701 the elector secured the title of king *in* Prussia, that is, within the East Prussian lands which lay outside the bounds of the Empire. 'The frontiers of Prussia', it has been said, 'were its armies': it was only by effective military power wielded by its autocratic rulers that Brandenburg-Prussia maintained the political unity of its discontinuous, territorial fabric. It was the outstanding achievement of King Frederick William I (1713–40) that, realizing the need for military force, he built up a small but efficient army. What is more, by astute diplomacy rather than by war, he won accessions of territory which helped to round off and connect up his existing dominions. Thus at his death in 1740 *part* of western Pomerania with the Oder ports had been won; territory in northern Westphalia across the middle Ems river was incorporated; whilst farther west, between the Rhine and Meuse and contiguous to Cleves, a part of Gelders was added to the state. The territorial expansion of his reign served above all to consolidate the position of Brandenburg on the lower Oder.

The reign of Frederick II, 'the Great', marked an outstanding phase in the history of German unity, for thanks to his statesmanship Prussia became beyond question a first-rate power and the leading state in Germany. At his accession in 1740 Prussia was still, alike in area, population and resources, a small and secondary state. Its area was rather less than 50,000 square miles; its population about 2·5 millions. Around its nuclear area in Brandenburg it had built up one large compact region, but the geographical diffuseness of Frederick's territories almost justified Voltaire's derisive taunt that he was 'roi des lisières'. No one was more conscious than Frederick himself of the geographical short-comings of his inheritance. 'The greatest part of my territories', he wrote,[1] 'is dispersed or divided in such a manner, that they cannot mutually assist each other. I have no great rivers that run through my provinces; some border upon them, but few intersect them.' He inherited, however, a small but well-trained army, well-ordered finances, and an efficient bureaucratic machine, all of which he was quick to make subservient to his ambitious ends.

It is relevant here to note only the territorial effects of his remarkable career in diplomacy and war. The first of these effects was the acquisition of Silesia in 1742. The duchy of Silesia, comprising the upper basin of the Oder, was a large and fertile country which was one of the most populous lands of Middle Europe.[2] At the time of its conquest it was held by the Habsburg monarchy (Austria): originally the possession of Poland, it was Slav in population, having been but slightly affected by German penetration

[1] *The Confessions of Frederick the Great*, ed. Sladen, pp. 37–8.

[2] It may be added that the more populous and the richer part of Silesia lay in the north; the southern part, to-day outstanding in respect of its coal resources and industries, remained until the latter decades of the nineteenth century largely under forest. In the north loess soils were widely disposed.

and colonization. It had passed from Poland to the kingdom of Bohemia, of which it was the 'jewel of the crown', and in 1526, together with Bohemia, it had become absorbed into Habsburg state. The annexation of Silesia gave Prussia control of the Oder from its headstreams down to the sea; moreover, it added to Prussia nearly 14,000 square miles of territory and, what was more, 1·5 million subjects. The fact that it was not a Germanic country made its retention a matter of some doubt; actually, however, it was not only permanently retained but to a large extent Germanized by a policy of state-guided colonization. Even more remarkable than the annexation of Silesia was the incorporation into Prussia of vast areas of the Polish republic, which suffered a partial partition in 1772. By this act Prussia secured a large territory of great strategical value, since it was so placed as to link up geographically East Prussia beyond the Vistula and the Prussian lands in Pomerania, Brandenburg and Silesia (Fig. 42). Part of the lands filched from Poland had become largely Germanized, namely the provinces of West Prussia, East Pomerania, Culmerland, Ermeland and the Marienburg region around the lowest reaches of the Vistula. On the other hand, the southern part was purely Polish in population, occupying most of the basin of the Netze, which drains westwards to the Oder. The new acquisitions were incorporated as the province of West Prussia and the district of the Netze, whilst Ermeland was absorbed into East Prussia, within which, as an *enclave*, it stood. Collectively they constituted a valuable addition to Brandenburg-Prussia, since they contained good agricultural lands, mercantile towns and a relatively dense population. But it should be noted that Danzig and Thorn for the time being remained to Poland.

The state of Prussia at the death of Frederick the Great in 1786 was geographically transformed. In actual area 74,000 square miles, it had increased over 50 per cent. since 1740, whilst its population had more than doubled, since it now reached about 5·5 millions.[1] Not only had Frederick won new lands, but he had won lands of denser population and of greater resources than those which he inherited; moreover, he had created a really compact territorial framework. Only in the west in Westphalia and on the Rhine were Prussian lands detached. Further, Frederick's assumption of the title king *of* Prussia was significant of his ambition to promote the prestige of his state, which in the Empire formed only an electorate. Moreover, in 1786 the sovereign lands of Prussia, that is the lands which Frederick ruled as king, exceeded in area the lands which he ruled within the Empire. But despite

[1] Himly, *Formation Territoriale des Etats de l'Europe Centrale*, II, 83.

its rapid growth Prussia remained still, in comparison with the great European states like France, Austria and Russia, small alike in area, population and resources.

In the remaining decade of the eighteenth century the successors of Frederick won further additions of territory. In Franconia they acquired by right of succession the lands of the younger branch of the Hohenzollern family, namely the principality of Anspach between the Main and the Danube and that of Bayreuth situated about the upper waters of the Main, Eger and Saale. They were small in area—some 2,700 square miles, but well populated—400,000. Geographically they were detached from the other Prussian lands, and thus seemed to indicate a new field for Hohenzollern enterprise. Further, in the years 1793 and 1795 two further partitions effaced the republic of Poland from the map of Europe and added to Prussia over two million subjects and nearly 40,000 square miles of territory. Danzig and Thorn were thus united to West Prussia; and a vast stretch of land on the middle Vistula as far up as Warsaw and as far north as the middle Niemen passed under Hohenzollern rule. The eastern frontier of Prussia formed therefore in 1795 a long continuous zone aligned along the middle Niemen in the north and the Pilica tributary of the Vistula in the south. In result, the centre of gravity of Prussia was shifted eastwards, and its Germanic character much weakened. It had achieved formal compactness, but at the cost of a large proportion of population, which on grounds of race and religion were potentially hostile elements within the state. At about the same time East Frisia, with the port of Emden, passed by right of succession to Prussia, which thus secured its first foothold on the North Sea, and in 1802 Napoleon assigned to Prussia the territories of the bishoprics of Hildesheim and Paderborn and part of that of Munster in return for some much smaller areas on the left bank of the lower Rhine. These latter lands were of considerable value, since they stood in the zone intermediate between the Harz mountains and the Rhine and thus afforded an almost unbroken line of communication between Brandenburg and its duchy of Cleves.

Prussia in the Nineteenth Century

The wars of Napoleon produced drastic changes in the whole political order of Middle Europe, and although most of these changes proved only ephemeral, the political map had to be entirely re-drawn after the final defeat of the French in 1815. In 1807, as a result of Napoleon's victories at Jena and Auerstädt, Prussia was threatened with almost complete extinction and actually reduced by half in area and population (Fig. 42). The settlement made at Vienna in the years 1814–15 rehabilitated Prussia and moreover created the Germanic Confederation in the place of the Holy Roman Empire which Napoleon brought to an end in 1806. It is important to examine the character of Prussia in 1815 and its place in the new Confederation in order to understand the stages by which Prussia founded a united Germanic state in the empire of 1871.

The basis of the Vienna settlement for Prussia was that it gave up certain territories in exchange for equivalents elsewhere and that it was restored virtually to the position which it had held prior

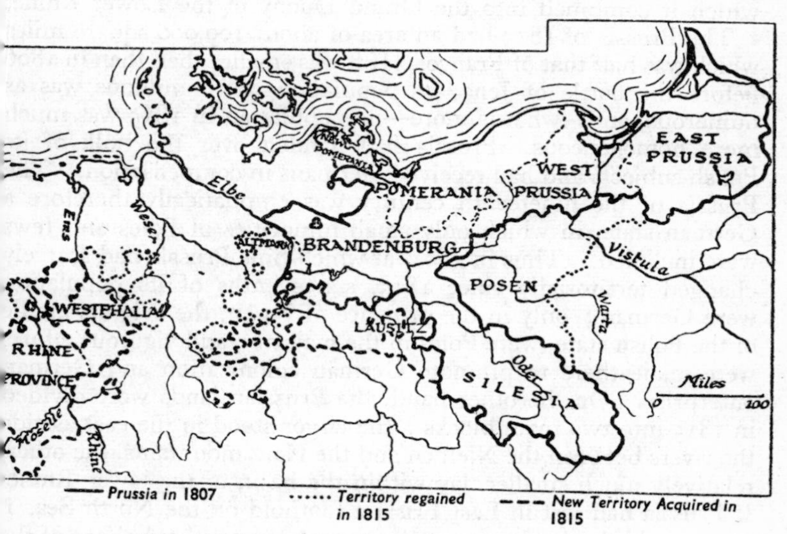

FIG. 42.—The Growth of Prussia, 1807–15

to the disaster of Jena. Of the country which it abandoned the most important was some two-thirds of that part of Poland which it had received at the two later partitions in 1793 and 1795. These extensive lands were assigned to the newly created kingdom of Poland, of which the Russian czar was made king. In effect, the eastern frontier of Prussia was withdrawn in the north from the upper Niemen to the old frontier of East Prussia, and in the south from the Pilica to the Prosna which drains north-west to the Warta. Prussia gave up, too, several scattered possessions in the west and south: Bayreuth and Anspach, East Frisia and part of Munster. In compensation for these Prussia was assigned lands in the Rhineland, on the Baltic and on its eastern margins. In the east it received back Danzig and Thorn, and the regions around Posen and Gnesen, which it formed into the Grand Duchy of Posen. In this way East Prussia and Silesia were brought into communication across Prussian territory. In the north Prussia received the western part of west Pomerania, which included the part of Stralsund and island of Rügen. Further, about one-half of the former electorate of Saxony passed to Prussia : this consisted of a belt of land which lay to the south of Brandenburg between the Saale to the Neisse. Finally, Prussia's chief gain was in the west where it was granted a multitude of what were formerly separate principalities on the Moselle, Rhine, Sieg and Ruhr, which it combined into the Grand Duchy of the Lower Rhine.

The Prussia of 1815 had an area of about 109,000 square miles which was half that of France. If it was smaller then than in 1806 before the battle of Jena, its population of 10 millions was as numerous, and—what is more—its population in 1815 was much more homogeneous. Prussia had handed over the bulk of its Polish subjects and had received Germans in compensation. The Prussia of the nineteenth century was emphatically therefore a German state, in which only small minorities of Poles and Jews were included. Thus in 1861, at which time Prussia had scarcely changed territorially since 1815, six-sevenths of its population were German ; only in the province of Posen, the original cradle of the Polish state, were Poles in the majority, and vigorous efforts were made there to promote German colonization and German enterprise. On the other hand, the Prussian lands were divided in 1815 into two main blocks : the larger stood in the east astride the rivers between the Niemen and the Harz mountains, the other, relatively much smaller, lay within the basin of the lower Rhine. If Prussia had lost in East Frisia a foothold on the North Sea, it clearly held the predominant position on the southern shore of the Baltic. It had become, in fact, the fifth Great Power of Europe, although considerably smaller in territory and man power than the other four. Moreover, its intermediate position in Europe left it exposed to these other states : its frontiers met those of Russia in the east, those of Austria in the south, and those of France in the west, whilst its Baltic seaboard was accessible to the fleets of Britain, the strongest naval power of the time.

The German Empire

Prussia succeeded during the fifty years which followed the Congress of Vienna in 1815 in entrenching itself effectively as the political, economic and cultural leader of Germany. Although its territories remained practically unchanged, its rapid growth in population, more rapid than that of any other state in continental Europe, strengthened its economic resources and man power and thus enabled it to increase its military power and diplomatic prestige. It was the greatest purely German state within the Confederation, and its frontiers impinged on those of nearly all the other smaller members. Austria, which held the presidency of the Confederation, was at a disadvantage in that it was essentially the negation of a nation state, being composed of many distinct nationalities. The only important minority in Prussia was that of the Slavs, who constituted about 13 per cent of the whole population in 1864. A quarter of the population of Silesia was Slavs ; there were Slavic Masurians in East Prussia and Wends in Brandenburg—but these were already largely Germanized. The greatest and most compact group of Slavs, and potentially the most restive minority element, was that of the Poles in the Grand Duchy of Posen. Even in that region, where Poles were in a marked majority, German immigration, which had grown stronger in the course of the nineteenth century, created islands of German settlement. In the towns of the Grand Duchy, with the exception of Posen itself, Germans began to predominate and it was Germans, too, who played the leading part as industrialists, traders and big landowners. For the rest, the other national minorities in Prussia were very small in numbers : Jews, widely scattered, formed a little more than 1 per cent of the population in 1864, whilst Letts and Lithuanians combined were scarcely as numerous as the Jews.

The final episodes in the history of German unification are concerned with diplomacy and above all with war. The ground was prepared by economic co-operation among most of the German states. Prussia took the lead in creating the *Zollverein* or customs union between the states of the Confederation, in order to remove tariff hindrances to the flow of trade. Almost all the states of the Confederation, excluding Austria, together with Luxemburg outside it, served their own and Prussian interests by joining the *Zollverein*. During the years 1864–6 the Schleswig-Holstein question was used by Bismarck to subserve his diplomacy, the chief end of which was the aggrandisement of Prussia. The duchies were occupied and eventually annexed to Prussia in 1865. The defeat of Austria in 1866 at Sadowa, near Königgratz, which stood on the upper Elbe on the direct route to Prague and Vienna, eliminated Austria from Germany and left Prussia in undisputed leadership. The sequel to this brief yet decisive war was the creation of the North German Confederation. The states north of the Main were united with Prussia in what was nominally a confederation but in reality an enlarged Prussian state.[1] The defeat of France in 1870 enabled Bismarck to complete his work, by the incorporation of the south German states into the northern confederation. The French, though German speaking, province of Alsace, together with part of Lorraine, was ceded to Prussia and in January 1871 King William I of Prussia proclaimed the German Empire.

The new German state, thus created, although in form still a confederation, was dominated by Prussia. It had a population of nearly 35 millions in 1871, almost equal to that of France. Its capital was Berlin, the capital of Prussia, a city of 825,000 inhabitants. Its maritime position was greatly improved by its control of a stretch of North Sea coast from Schleswig to East Frisia, including the estuary of the Elbe. In the south its frontiers pushed up against the Alps in Bavaria, and against the Bohemian, Erzgebirge and Sudetes mountains. As it was constituted in 1871 the German Empire did not correspond with the distribution of the German language, since beyond its frontiers, in Holland, Belgium, Switzerland and Austria populations of Germanic speech were independently organized. But language should not be identified with nationality, still less with statehood, and the small neighbouring states of Germany had developed their own distinctive nationalities and political interests. Within the German Empire itself it was less the spontaneous expression of national consciousness than the statecraft of Prussia which produced for the first time in Middle Europe a German state which was a highly organized and unified whole. And if it is true to say that the German national consciousness developed subsequently to the creation of the German Empire, it must be remembered that an element of coercion was present in the formation of many other European states.

[1] It should be noted that some of the states north of the Main (e.g., Hanover) were actually incorporated into Prussia, whilst many others were united within the North German Confederation.

CHAPTER XIV

SICILY

IN the preceding chapters it has been necessary, owing to the cramping limits of space, to concentrate attention on the human geography of different regions at single stages of time. The significance of historical geography is the more readily grasped, however, when it is possible to review side by side the geography of a whole series of historical periods. Sicily presents in miniature an excellent illustration of the changes in human geography which correspond to the vicissitudes of history: it is small enough to admit of summary treatment within one chapter; its remarkable geographical position exposed it to continual political and cultural changes; and its history and geography have been sufficiently well studied. The largest of the islands which constitute so typical a feature of the Mediterranean world, Sicily was exceptionally favoured by its geographical position, its size and its economic potentialities; and, although in some respects its history is unique, in many respects it is characteristic of the other islands of the Mediterranean sea. The central position which Sicily came to occupy in the Mediterranean from the time when, but only when, the civilization of the Phoenicians and Greeks had spread westwards, gave it both commercial and strategical importance: placed within one day's sail of the north African coast and much closer to the Italian peninsula, it at the same time separated and united the western and eastern halves of the sea. In area small enough to facilitate political unification yet also large enough to form a tempting prey, Sicily lay constantly at the mercy of the dominant sea-powers of the Mediterranean, the more so since its coasts were accessible and turned in every direction.

The history of Sicily reveals vividly the conditioning influence of its unique geographical position: it became a battlefield of contending races and religions, and of conflicting political and commercial interests. In part or as a whole, it was related politically at different times to Tunis, Greece, Italy, the Near East and Spain; it was a meeting-place of the nations and the cultures of the whole sea, and at one stage of its history its civilization was the most resplendent in the whole of Europe. The possession of the island was continually disputed by powers whose bases lay within the limits formerly attributed to Asia, Africa and Europe, and Professor Freeman [1] attached great importance to the problem to which of the continents it should belong. It may be noted, however, that this problem of Sicilian history, from the standpoint of modern geography, is quite trivial in importance and involves a mere play on words. Phoenicia, formerly ascribed to Asia, and Tunis, formerly ascribed to Africa, are now regarded merely as parts of the Mediterranean region, which in turn is included in the geographical conception of Europe. In short, the political destinies of Sicily were cast essentially in the Mediterranean, whether they were guided from Phoenicia, Tunis, Rome, Constantinople, Aragon or Naples. The insularity of Sicily proved the very antithesis to isolation : along the sea-ways came successive invaders, settlers, conquerors and rulers. 'The history of Sicily', wrote Freeman, 'is in all its stages a history of settlement, a history of men who found themselves new homes in a strange land', and with each group of immigrants came new cultural ideas and stimuli. In fact, the civilization of Sicily, alike in its material and its spiritual manifestations, underwent cyclical changes throughout its history. These changes are reflected in the numbers and distribution of population ; in the alternations of prosperity and depression in its economic life ; in the relative importance of commerce, agriculture and horticulture ; and in the varying fortunes of its cities. In short, the human geography of Sicily in the past is a changing pattern which was woven by its history on the face of its soil. With each set of immigrant rulers and in response to their efforts to adapt the island to their uses, the geography of Sicily was transformed. In other words, the physical geography of Sicily—the almost static basis of its civilization—was made to yield different human values at successive stages of time.

Sicily, which they called Trinakria,[2] was conceived by the Greeks as roughly triangular in shape, and Ptolemy's map, in eliminating its short western coast, depicts the island with three almost equal sides. More strictly there are four coasts, which are turned towards the four compass points as if to invite invaders from every direction. All four coasts were well provided throughout ancient and part of medieval times with harbours and sites for

[1] *The History of Sicily*, I, 1.

[2] The name is derived from the Homeric Thinakria, and did not arise out of the triangular shape of the island. This meaning was later attributed to the name. Freeman, op. cit., I, 53.

maritime cities, although physical changes as well as the increasing size of ships have much altered their usefulness in modern times. Even to-day Sicily can be reached by steamships at many points of its coast: at Palermo and Catania, which have artificially constructed ports, and at Trapani and Syracuse, where the natural harbourage is still adequate. Only small steamships, however, can find harbours on its southern coast, where stood formerly Phœnician and Greek havens. It is clear that many harbours which were both big and deep enough for early shipping have either shallowed or become entirely silted up. In some cases, as at Palermo, river alluvium has filled up old havens; in others, as at Motya, silt has been carried in by the sea, which is subject at times to strong inflowing currents induced by wind. In ancient times, the best harbours stood on the north, west and east coasts, which were not only well embayed but were furnished with jutting headlands and off-shore islands. In contrast to these coasts the southern coast was low, alluvial and unindented: nevertheless, a few of its river estuaries could be entered by ships even as late as the Middle Ages.

Sicily is almost entirely lacking in low and level land and is largely mountainous and hilly. The chief mountain chains lie in the north, where the Peloritani, Nebrodi and Madonie ranges form continuations of the Apennine system and rise to heights of over 5,000 feet. The highest rainfall occurs on these mountains and is distributed by many transverse rivers—for the most part irregular torrents or *fiumare*—which drain towards the north and the south-east. In the north and the north-east of Sicily there is scarcely any coastal plain, for the mountains descend to present high cliffs to the sea; westwards of Termini, however, the mountains are lower, the valleys wider, and the coastal plain, although still restricted, broadens out. In this part of the coast, between the mountains and the sea, lay the Conca d'Oro (the 'Golden Shell'), which provided Palermo with one of the richest though smallest plains of the world. At the north-eastern end of the island the volcanic Etna formed a dominant landmark and the highest point of the island. It is broad at its base and gentle in its slopes, and rises to nearly 10,000 feet: 'nurse of snow and fire', 'an awful yet bountiful lord'—so the ancients described it—Etna provided the conditions of the fertility which it periodically destroyed. For the lava which it erupted decomposed into soils rich in plant foods, whilst it sent down to its wooded and cultivable slopes abundant water. To the south of Etna stretches the largest area of lowland in the island. The Piana di Catania, or as it was known in Greek times, the Leontine fields, was as its shape suggests, an old gulf of the sea, which was filled up in Quaternary times ; through it passes the Simeto river, one of the few perennially flowing rivers of Sicily, which drains an extensive basin and is fed by a number of long tributaries. The periodical inundations of these rivers converted part of the Piana into pestilential marsh, so that it was avoided by settlers ; nevertheless some of it was early cultivated, for the Greeks remarked on its fertility, whilst they related, too, that wheat grew wild there. In the south-east of Sicily a broad limestone plateau, cut by deep gorges, descends to form a wide hilly plain behind the coast, but this country had little agricultural value owing to the porosity of the subsoil and the lowness of the rainfall. The southern coastlands of Sicily are less elevated than the northern, and are drained by several long rivers descending from the north or north-east. Although rather dry and exposed to the hot and violent sirocco winds usually from the south-west, the valleys, slopes and plains were well adapted to olive, vine and wheat cultivation, and the rivers provided water in summer for irrigation. Finally, at the narrow western end of Sicily the coast is fringed by low salt marshes, but the hinterland of hills and plains was covered with good impermeable soils, which were moderately well watered, since this part of Sicily lay in the track of the rain-bearing westerlies.

Thanks to its triangular shape, Sicily possessed not only a long stretch of coastline but also a continental area—a characteristic of its geography which was the more impressive to the ancient Greeks, who were used to small city-states and to an ubiquitous sea. In contrast to the littoral country and orientated seawards, lay (as in Brittany) the highlands of the interior, and this regional differentiation is expressed as clearly in the human as in the physical geography of the island. The continental area of Sicily consists of hills and valleys with little level land ; the elevation of the hills ranges broadly between 1,000 and 2,000 feet and thus ensured a moderate rainfall, whilst a typical feature of the inland topography consists of the many steep, isolated hills of resistant rock, upon which settlers could find defensible sites. The interior lands of Sicily were covered with impermeable soils—clays and loams—which were a distinct asset to a country of low rainfall. In contrast to Brittany, Sicily was well endowed by climate : although it shared the summer drought characteristic of the Mediterranean type of climate, it enjoyed great insolation and its rainfall was such that no part of the island, not even the arid south-east, was so subject to drought as interior parts of Spain, Greece, Algeria and Provence. The relatively high rainfall of the mountains and hills, although it exposed the lowlands to the devastations of floods and landslips, served nevertheless as a source of water which could be used in irrigation. Earthquakes and volcanic eruptions, it is true, formed part of the background of Sicilian life, but their incidence was infrequent and their effects much less serious than the destruction inflicted by human agency. In short, Sicily was a land of varied economic opportunity : its seas offered not only the tunny fish, coral, and an easy means of communication between its coast towns, but above all the routes of trade ; its rocks provided considerable mineral wealth—marble, alum, gypsum and sulphur ; whilst its soils were able to nourish many sub-tropical plants and cereals, even at high levels, which in the cooler, wetter lands of western Europe could bear only a few tree species.

Before the advent of the Phoenicians and Greeks to Sicily the island was settled by peoples whose culture has been traced back to the Neolithic and Bronze Ages. Greek historians distinguished three peoples in Sicily, namely the Sikans, the Elymians and the Sikels. Whether the Sikans and the Sikels were racially distinct and entered Sicily respectively from Spain and Italy are questions scarcely settled, since archaeology and tradition are at variance.[1] The settlements of these peoples were characteristically situated on the summits of hills and high up on the slopes of ravines and escarpments, aloof from the ill-drained valley bottoms, and surrounded by patches of cultivated land which had probably been cleared of forest. The settlements of the Elymians and the Sikels lay in the western part of Sicily : Eryx, which crowned Mount S. Giuliano, a conspicuous landmark by the sea, and Segesta, on a hill site further inland, were the chief Elymian stronghold cities. The Sikels, whose settlements in the Bronze Age are fairly well known, occupied the broad eastern half of the island. Some of their towns stood along the coast—between the present cities of Syracuse and Augusta, and to the east of Himera on the north coast. Others, situated to the west of Mount Etna, were perched on mountain-tops some 600 to 1,600 feet above neighbouring valley depths and were reached only by difficult, tortuous tracks. This group of sites is particularly interesting in that many are occupied even to-day by towns : notably Centuripa and Enna (Castrogiovanni) which stand respectively at 2,300 and 3,240 feet above sea-level. The upland villages and strongholds of these early peoples, together with their cultivated fields, formed islands

[1] Archaeology casts doubts on the racial distinctions of these three peoples, as also on the historical account of their original homes. It is suggested that they may well be racially united and have come mainly from Italy. See Peet, *The Stone and Bronze Ages in Italy and Sicily*, c. XVIII.

in what was probably a well-wooded land. The choice of site appears to have been dictated alike by the need of defence and the difficulty of clearing and of reclaiming floodable valley lands ; but it should be remembered that the rivers of Sicily, since they are largely torrential and unnavigable, deterred settlers and also that the Sicilian climate permitted cultivation and pastoral farming at high levels. In general it should be noted that the sea was rather a source of danger than of wealth at this time ; the Sikels were known to the Greeks as ' men of the mainland ', not of the coasts although they certainly had maritime settlements on the east coast Moreover, the presence of Mycaenean vases from Crete and copper probably from Cyprus, suggests that Sicily was reached already by sea routes from the eastern Mediterranean.

A new phase in the human geography of Sicily began when the Phoenician cities, notably Tyre and Sidon, extended their trade activities into the western part of the Mediterranean basin. Between the eleventh and ninth centuries B.C., subsequent to the foundation of Utica (in Tunis) and Cadiz, but prior to that of Carthage, the Phoenicians occupied islands and peninsulas around the Sicilian coasts, and traded with the Sikels. With a view to protecting their trade route to Gades (Cadiz) and Malaca (Malaga they established maritime stations in Sicily, as in Tunis, at point along the coast where the best natural harbours were available The neighbouring islands of Malta, Gozo, Pantelleria and Lampedusa were similarly occupied as trade stations at this time. Th advance of Greek colonists into the eastern coastlands in the earl eighth century B.C., caused the gradual withdrawal of the Phoenicians to the north-western part of the island, where they retaine the cities of Panormus (later known as Palermo), Motya and Solous which were well placed for short sailings to Carthage. Solous, o its low hill, formed an outpost which guarded Panormus to the east Motya on the west coast occupied the small island of S. Pantale which was joined to the mainland by a causeway and commande a deep harbour sheltered by a natural mole ; whilst Panormus– the Phoenician name is unknown and Panormus (= ' all haven ') Greek—was a peninsular city, on both sides of which narrow bay now occupied by dry land, provided excellent harbourage.

Motya was the most important of the Phoenician cities, but was destroyed by fire in 397 B.C. by the Syracusans. Its destruction by war, fire and plunder was so complete that it ceased to exi for many centuries, not only as a town but also it would seem an inhabited place. Even its name was forgotten ; its harbou shallowed in the course of time owing to the deposition of mu and sand carried in by the sea ; and Lilybaeum, on the mainlan to the south, now represented by Marsala, took its place as a Carthaginian city. In the third century B.C. Carthage strengthened its hold on western Sicily by creating the naval city of Drepanum (Trapani) at the foot of Mount Eryx. The importance of Panormus belongs to this later period of Carthaginian dominance of Phoenician Sicily, but there, as at Solous, all traces of the Phoenician city have disappeared—not a single building nor even a stone survives from this period.[1]

The first Greek colony in Sicily, Naxos, was founded in 735 B.C. on Cape Schiso at the foot of Mount Etna by immigrants from Chalcis in Euboea and from the island of Naxos. Syracuse, which was to become the greatest city and sea-port of Sicily, was founded a year later by a group of Corinthians. Other Greek colonies along the east coast were Catana (Catania) together with Megara and Taormina further south. Catania stood on a hill above its harbour on the northern edge of the Piana di Catania which forms the greatest area of plain in the whole island. It was already noted for its fertility, but it was avoided by settlers, and even to-day it lacks town sites although it has some scattered hamlets. A limestone plateau, however, dominates the plain from about 200 feet, and on this, a few miles from the sea, stood the colony of Leontini (Léntini). (The lake which lies near the town to-day, formerly described as unhealthy, did not exist in the classical period). To the north of Léntini the river Simeto, was actually navigable from the sea for laden ships [2]—a rare convenience in Sicily. Similarly, on both the north and south coasts the Greeks established themselves. Himera, situated on a headland between the estuaries of two rivers, was an advance post on the frontier against the Carthaginians, whilst Mylae (Milazzo) and Zankle (Messina), both of which stood on peninsulas and had good harbours of refuge, commanded the strait between Sicily and Italy. The south coast of Sicily, although it lacked islands, deep bays and small headlands, and although too it lay open to the prevailing south-westerly winds and later won a bad reputation for shipwrecks, nevertheless afforded at the mouths of rivers a number of harbour sites which were utilized by Greek colonists, notably at Gela (Terranova), Minoa and Selinous, with its port Mazara (Mazzara). In fact, the southern coastland of Sicily in Greek times was very populous: Gela commanded the Geloan fields, which were renowned for their fertility, and became an important town; and only a few miles inland one of the greatest

[1] Whitaker, *Motya*, p. 58.

[2] So Edrisi records at a later date (mid-twelfth century): *La Géographie d'Edrisi*, trans. Jaubert, II, 83.

Greek cities Agrigentum (Girgenti), which was founded by Gela in 580 B.C., actually challenged Syracuse itself. Agrigentum, like the older cities of Sicily, had an elevated site : it occupied a broad plateau, 800 feet above sea-level, some two and a half miles from the sea ; its haven stood where the two streams which encircled it joined, and it commanded a lowland region highly productive of wheat and fruit.

To the Phoenicians and the Greeks Sicily owed the establishment of maritime cities, the introduction of vine and olive cultivation, the development of industries, the forging of trade relations by sea and the increase in its population. The rise of Syracuse, its chief city and for a time the chief city of all the Greek world, epitomizes this prosperous period of Greek rule in Sicily.

Although archaeology shows that the site and neighbourhood of Syracuse were occupied in prehistoric times, the history of the city begins with its settlement by colonists who came there from Corinth in the year 734 B.C. In selecting this site for the second Greek colony in Sicily and in promising it great riches the Delphic oracle showed, not for the last time, the acuteness of its geographical knowledge and the reasonableness of its prophecy. The nucleus of Syracuse was the island of Ortygia which had its spring of Arethusa near the sea and commanded two deep, sheltered harbours, the Little Port to the north and, occupying a broad bay, the Great Port to the south (Fig. 43). As the town grew the island was joined to the mainland by a stone bridge and settlements on the limestone plateau of Achradina were absorbed and enclosed by a wall ; a little later it expanded to enclose other settlements on the Epipolai plateau.[1] On the southern slopes of Achradina quarries were dug for building stone, whilst the plain stretching beyond the town proved highly productive of cereals, vine and olive. Already in the early fifth century B.C. under its leader Gelon Syracuse had become the greatest Greek city of Sicily, although it was challenged in respect of wealth and population by Girgenti. It grew, records Strabo, 'both on account of the fertility of the soil and of the natural excellence of its harbours '. Its victory over the Carthaginians at the battle of Himera (480 B.C.) safeguarded Greek civilization in Sicily from the danger of Semitic predominance. In population it reached at least 200,000 and occupied an area of about seven square miles : its population subsequently declined steeply and only in recent years has exceeded that of Classical times.

Under the stimulus and impress of immigrants whose highly

[1] On the excavations at Greek Syracuse, see Randall-MacIver, *Greek Cities in Italy and Sicily*, chs. IX and X.

developed civilization made possible considerable adaptation of the geographical environment, Sicily reached one of the highest points in its chequered history. Strong, wealthy and populous cities girdled its coasts; the island entered boldly upon a career of maritime commerce; horticulture along the coastal belts made its beginnings; whilst advances were made in the agricultural development of the interior plateaux and in the exploitation of the

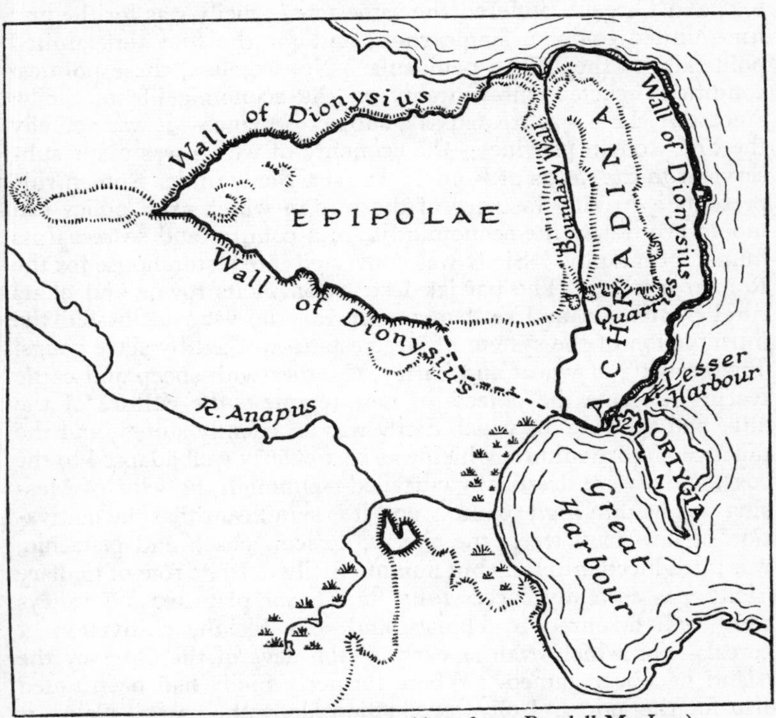

FIG. 43.—The site of Syracuse (data from Randall-MacIver)
The Fountain of Arethusa and the Castle of Dionysius are shown by figures 1 and 2 respectively.

natural resources—sulphur, marble, alum and building stone, with which the island was well supplied. Sufficient architectural evidences of Greek culture in Sicily have escaped the destruction of repeated warfare to attest its splendour and strength. Moreover, estimates which have made of the population of Sicily at this time when it formed part of Magna Graecia, at the western margins of the Greek world, suggest large numbers, which were reached again only in the Arab–Norman period and in the mid-nineteenth century.

The wars between the Carthaginians and the Greeks wrought destruction in Sicily, but greater evils followed when, during the first Carthaginian war (264–241 B.C.), the island became a battle-ground between Rome and Carthage. The whole island with the exception of the territories subject to Syracuse passed to Rome in 241 B.C. Greek Sicily, however, soon succumbed to Roman conquest : Syracuse was besieged and taken during the years 214–212 B.C., and Girgenti suffered the same fate. Sicily was for the first time united under a single ruler, and for the first time united politically to the Italian peninsula. Nevertheless, these political conditions reacted unfavourably on the economic life of Sicily, since the island was treated as a subject province—it was actually the first Roman province—the economy of which was made subservient to the needs of Rome. In fact, Sicily under Roman rule presents a striking instance of the way in which state policy can mould arbitrarily the economic life of a country and so recast its human geography. Sicily was converted into a storehouse for the Roman market. The partial destruction of its towns and of its rural population and settlements during the wars facilitated the introduction of the system of large estates worked by slave gangs. The growing of wheat and barley, together with sheep and cattle rearing, became the objects of new régime ; the culture of the olive and the vine for which Sicily was excellently suited, and the practice of horticulture, which was particularly well adapted to the coastlands, were drastically curtailed—although the wine of Messina was held in high repute ; and it is significant that the cultivation of new fruit trees, the cherry, apricot, peach and pistachio, was introduced into Italy but not into Sicily. In its rôle of granary Sicily was certainly successful ; its interior plateaux and valleys were well favoured by climate and soils for the cultivation of cereals—for which even as early as the days of the Odyssey the island had been famed. Where formerly Sicily had been noted also for the vine and olive production along the coastal plains, it became noted for the wheat grown in the Piana di Catania and in the high valleys around Enna and Centuripa in the interior. Roman policy and civil wars—there were several ' slave wars '—caused the continued decline and depopulation of the maritime cities. Strabo, who wrote about 7 B.C., describes the desolation of the southern coastlands of Sicily which were, owing to their position, particularly exposed to Carthaginian attacks ; neither Selinous nor Gela had settled populations and only Girgenti and Lilybaeum survived as large centres of population. Elsewhere along the coasts cities once famous for industry, horticulture and commerce had become mere agricultural towns. Under the empire some efforts were made to restore Sicilian cities. Thus Augustus rebuilt Catania and Centuripa ; moreover, he sent a colony to Syracuse and restored part of the old settlement. It is significant, however, that no attempt was made to fill out the whole circuit of the city, but only the Achradina plateau adjacent to the island of Ortygia. In short, Roman Sicily contrasts in its human geography with the more prosperous Sicily which it replaced. Its population had decreased ; its commerce had dwindled into an export to Italy of wheat, wool, hides, honey, saffron and fruit ; its coastal cities were sunk into relative insignificance, whilst in the interior the tendency towards the distribution of population in scattered villages on lowland sites was arrested, since the *latifundia* system of agriculture necessitated large central settlements.

When in A.D. 395 the Roman Empire was divided into two administrative parts, Sicily fell to the empire in the west. Its insularity did not protect it from the invasions of barbarians—Vandals from Tunis and Ostrogoths from Italy—but the immigrants were few in number and pillaged rather than overthrew its Romano-Greek civilization. The island continued to supply Italy with corn, and having become Christian in the first century A.D., became attached to the Roman Church, which held large estates in Sicily. In the year 535 Sicily was recovered by the Roman Empire in the east, of which it remained a part for over three centuries. It thus became orientated once again towards the Greek world of the Near East, and this political connexion greatly stimulated its economic development, since the Byzantine Empire was not only the most civilized but also the strongest sea-power of the time. Sicily became a *theme* of the empire, and in 733 was united to the Greek Orthodox Church. Commerce flourished and the cities of the coast revived, until in the eighth century the Mediterranean became a prey to Arab pirates. The Arabs, who had established themselves in Tunis, built up a powerful state there in the early ninth century : the fertile lands of Sicily had long tempted them, and the definitive conquest of the island was at length undertaken. Palermo fell to the invaders in 831 ; the 'Vale' of Mazzara in the west was conquered ten years later ; the 'impregnable' fortress of Enna fell in 858 ; Syracuse resisted capture until 878, and the conquest was completed only in 902 when Taormina yielded. Great destruction of life and much looting accompanied the conquest, but eventually under the rule of its victors Sicily entered on one of its most flourishing periods.

Arab rule injected new life into a country which had already much benefited by centuries of Byzantine influence. The Emirs of Sicily won their independence of the Caliphs of Afriqyia (Tunis) and devoted themselves to the development of the island's material resources. Moslem immigration from north Africa continuously and usefully reinforced a population which, compared with its numbers in the days of earlier Greek prosperity, had become depleted. The skill of the new Moslem landowners both in agriculture and horticulture, and in particular their aptitude in the practice of irrigation, were employed in Sicily, as in Spain, with remarkable success. Wheat-growing, it is true, dominated Sicilian agriculture, but in horticulture and in the cultivation of new plants the Arabs made their distinctive contribution. Irrigation was extensively practised, especially but not exclusively along the coastlands where, towards their estuaries, the rivers provided a sufficient volume of water for distribution. The cultivation of rice, cotton, the date palm and the orange were all introduced; the sugar-cane was introduced in all probability by the Arabs; whilst the mulberry tree, which had already entered Sicily with the Greeks, was more extensively grown in order to support the new industry of silk-worm rearing. The new subtropical plants —rice, cotton, sugar and the citrus fruits—were grown, above all, in the coastal plains where a sufficiency of water could be obtained by means of irrigation.

The rearing of asses, mules and goats and horses—the latter were already famous in Grecian times—formed a staple industry in the interior of Sicily. The island boasted eighteen cities and three hundred and twenty fortresses. In the towns many industries were practised, notably the manufacture of luxury goods, which must have owed something to Byzantine traditions; the silks and brocades of Palermo, cloth, worked leather, gold, silver and wood, were particularly characteristic. Moreover, Sicily was well placed in relation to the other parts of the Moslem world—Spain, Tunis, Egypt and Syria—for the exchange through trade of its surplus commodities.

It is a remarkable fact that Arab Sicily has not left any architectural monuments of its flourishing cities which were furnished with palaces, mosques and baths. Byzantine civilization in Sicily also lacks similar memorials. Nevertheless, full accounts survive, chiefly from the pens of Arabic writers, which depict Sicily under the rule of the Normans, who continued and perfected its Byzantine-Arabic culture. In the twelfth and early thirteenth century Sicily reached the highest cultural stage of its chequered history and became in fact the most prosperous and civilized state of Europe.

It was during the Arab period that Palermo, the old Phoenician city where the Arabs had secured their first foothold in the island, became a great capital and urban settlement. At its capture in 831 many of the inhabitants were slaughtered, but the city was repopulated by Moslem immigrants from Africa and Spain. It soon combined the functions of political capital, military headquarters and naval base. Already by the year 878 it is recorded that the town was growing beyond its walls ; the old town, which occupied a peninsula, consisted of two quarters—the Khalessa, where the Emir resided, and the Kassar hard by the chief port, which was a mercantile quarter. Ibn Haukal, an Arab traveller and a native of Baghdad who visited Sicily *c.* A.D. 960 or 970, has left a vivid picture of Palermo, the city of two hundred mosques. It is clear from his account that the two narrow gulfs which formed the original harbours of the town were already beginning to suffer from the deposit of river alluvium : of the two, that to the south was still big and deep enough to form the chief port, but the other to the north had partially filled up leaving only a basin used for an arsenal. Three new quarters had grown up outside the walls, in the largest of which, the Sacalibah, the many markets of the town—for oil, wheat, arms, copper goods, &c.—were concentrated. Papyrus, which was introduced in Grecian days from the Nile, grew in a marshy stretch within the town, and was used to make paper for the Emir and rope for ships : the marsh was later drained and built on and the papyrus plant has disappeared. An iron mine at Balhara, to the west of the town, provided metal for the fleet. There was abundant running water in the town, but inside the gates the houses supplied themselves with drinking water from their own wells. Outside the town, to the south, the River Abbas (Oreto) turned numerous mills and supplied canals which carried down water to fertilize gardens. On the basis of the number of butchers in the town, recorded by Ibn Haukal, Amari calculated,[1] ingeniously rather than convincingly, that its population reached some 300,000 ! In short, tenth-century Sicily, covered, as Ibn Haukal relates, with castles and fortresses, and inhabited and cultivated everywhere, presents a picture of material prosperity.

The Norman conquerors of Sicily, like those who conquered England at the same period, formed numerically a very small aristocracy of landowners who were largely ' French ' in culture. Sicily was conquered between the years 1061 and 1091 from bases in southern Italy which had been won from the Byzantine Empire. The ' kingdom of Sicily, Apulia and Calabria ' as it was consti-

[1] Ibn Haukal's *Description de Palermo au milieu du Xe Siècle*, trans. Amari, 1845.

tuted in 1130 formed a sizeable state: in area about four-fifths of England, its population was considerably greater than the latter's and so were its revenues.[1] The new-comers from the north, whose tall stature, fair hair and valour attracted the notice of southern writers, were very well fitted to promote the fortunes of their conquered lands, since their kings were strong, able and judiciously tolerant of the many races and creeds represented in their subjects. Their kingdom boasted a highly developed culture made up of Byzantine and Arab elements and even at the time of the conquest was rich in agricultural and commercial wealth. Apart from Sicily, the Campanian coastlands with the great seaports of Amalfi and Salerno, and the plain of Apulia, the principal outlet of which was Bari, had enjoyed considerable prosperity since *c.* A.D. 900, when they passed under the rule of the Byzantine emperors at Constantinople. These littoral lands were lavishly supplied with the products of the soil, of manufacture and of maritime trade: oil, wine, fruits and grain were grown along the coastal plains; timber was abundant in the interior mountains, where also cattle, horses and sheep were reared; whilst the manufacture of linen cloth, and the working of gold and silver were active in the coast towns. Southern Italy, cut off by the highland obstacle of the Abruzzi and linked politically and commercially with Constantinople, had developed an orientation distinct from that of northern Italy. Its political union with Sicily under the Normans represented a geographical association which had already appeared in Magna Graecia and which tended to remain almost permanent until the union of Italy in 1866.[2] In the Norman kingdom, however, Sicily formed the base with the capital at Palermo; at later periods the capital of the so-called kingdom of the two Sicilies shifted to the peninsula, to Naples.

During the twelfth and thirteenth centuries, thanks to the enlightened rule of its kings and to the revival of Christian commerce in the Mediterranean, Sicily advanced in population, wealth and culture, and became the envy and wonder of the world. With the rise in turn of Amalfi, Pisa and Genoa the Tyrrhenian Sea took again, as in the days of Rome, an important place in Mediterranean commerce. The ports of Sicily became essential stations on the

[1] The population of Sicily *alone* at the Norman Conquest has been estimated at about 2·7 millions; that of England at the same time is estimated by Carr-Saunders at about 1·5 millions. 'The income (*sc.* revenue) from Palermo alone was said to be greater than that which the king of England derived from his own kingdom': Haskins, *The Normans in European History*, p. 233.

[2] It is interesting that the cultural unity of Sicily and southern Italy is attested even in early Neolithic times. Cp. Peet, op. cit., p. 484.

routes pursued by the fleets not only of Genoa and Pisa but also of Venice ; through the Strait of Messina passed the usual route for ships from Pisa and Genoa bound for the Levant and Constantinople, whilst Venetian vessels called at Messina or Palermo *en route* for Africa and Spain. Sicily was thus able to derive revenue from tolls, and also to export with ease its surplus products : grain, skins, cotton—very inferior to that of the Levant but an important crop in the twelfth century—sugar, and silk fabrics from Palermo. The Arab geographer Edrisi, who came to reside at the court of King Roger II at Palermo about the year 1154 and was commissioned by him to prepare a scientific description of the earth, has left a succinct though glowing account of the human geography of the island. Its produce, the fertility of its soil and the amenities of its towns and dwellings made Sicily in his view—which in more prosaic terms historians have endorsed—' a pearl of the century '. Apart from villages and hamlets, the island possessed a hundred and thirty towns of which thirty-five stood on the coast ; a thousand years earlier, as Ptolemy records, there were only some sixty towns.

Along the north coast of the island, in the valleys or at the foot of the well-watered mountain chains, irrigated orchards, gardens and plantations formed the hinterlands of flourishing coastal cities. The Conca d'Oro plain behind Palermo presented a fine prospect of fertility : ' on all sides around the town ', wrote Edrisi, ' are found running water, springs and canals ; fruits are abundant and beautiful villas '. To the east of Palermo, at *Tarbi'at*, grain was ground by water-mills and a kind of macaroni was made in factories and exported. Eastwards around S. Marco stretched a vast well-watered plain ; violets, as well as fruits, were grown there ; silk was produced, and timber brought down to S. Marco from the mountains. The tunny was fished in the Bay of Termini. Milazzo, farther to the east, exported flax, whilst Messina was an outstanding city and port, a rendezvous of ships from all countries. Its port was deep enough to allow ships to unlade against the quay ; as a contemporary Ibn Jubair has it, ships could range themselves along the quay like horses attached to stakes in their stables. Iron and timber from the Peloritani mountains were utilized in the shipbuilding yards at Messina. The vine, chestnut, hazel-nut, pear, plum and other fruit trees were grown on the mountain-slopes, and Messina was still, as in Roman times, famed for its wine. Certainly the northern coastlands of Sicily, turned towards, and politically united, with Norman Italy, appear at this time the richest and most populous part of the island : at earlier periods the other coasts stood relatively higher. The east and south coasts held the greatest Greek cities, and the west coast held the chief Carthaginian strongholds. Even so, the remaining coasts and the interior plateaux and valleys alike shared in the prosperity of Norman Sicily. Catania was embellished with a cathedral and other great buildings, although in the year 1169, as again later in 1693, it was largely destroyed by an earthquake. Lentini, although a few miles from the sea, was a seaport, whilst ships entered the commodious ports of Syracuse to load up with wheat. In contrast to the general picture of fertility, the country between Noto and Cape Passaro in the south-east is described as 'entirely desert'—a condition which is attributable to the character of its rocks and its climate.[1] On the south coast Girgenti, which had been important enough to engage in conflicts with Palermo during the Arab period, still prospered: it derived much produce, especially wheat and fruits, from its immediate hinterland, so that the biggest ships could find cargoes there even in times of dearth. Finally, on the west coast the city of Trapani with its well-sheltered port engaged in tunny and coral fishing and in the preparation of salt from the marshes. Marsala (= 'the port of Allah') was the Arabic town which replaced the Carthaginian Lilybaeum destroyed by the Romans in the first Punic War; it was re-fortified by Roger I. In the interior of Sicily agriculture and stock rearing progressed, population increased and village settlements spread widely throughout the mountains and the valleys. The old hill-top towns still persisted, the most famous of which, the old Sikel site of Enna, was especially described by Edrisi. Enna, which already bore its present name Castrogiovanni, occupied a central position within the island and had played continually and inevitably an important part in its successive conquests. 'Although it is situated on a mountain', wrote Edrisi, 'nevertheless cultivated fields are found there, and running water; there is no need of art to spread this over the soil, which is excellent in quality. It is, moreover, a place difficult of access and so to speak impregnable.' The impregnability of Enna was a literary fiction which, though justly inspired by its remarkable site and difficulty of access, has no support in history. It was not, as its history shows, an impregnable city, and despite its difficulty of access and its military works it had trade, as well as industrial, activities.

Norman Palermo became a great cosmopolitan city, a place of industry, a port of call and the seat of government and pleasure. Its architecture typifies the blending of elements derived from Byzantine, Arab and Norman sources; its population was made

[1] See *supra*, p. 280.

up of Moslems, Greeks, Latins, Jews and Normans, who occupied separate quarters of the town. The official languages of the administration were Latin, Greek and Arabic alike, whilst the court, which was a great patron of science and of art, introduced the oriental splendour and ceremonial of Constantinople and the great Arab capitals ; the royal councillors and scholars were indifferently Greek, Arab and Norman, and the coinage imitated the gold coins of Byzantium, which contrasted with the silver currency of the Holy Roman Empire. The industries of Palermo embodied skill and artistry : fine cloths and silks, carved stone and metal work. Its luxuriant gardens abounded in exotic trees—the orange, lemon, fig, palm and pomegranate. Palermo, in short, impressed the traveller as did only the greatest cities of the medieval world, like Constantinople, Cordova and Baghdad : to Ibn Jubair it was 'a stupendous city, elegant, graceful and splendid, rising before one like a temptress'.

In the course of the thirteenth century Norman Sicily was absorbed into the Holy Roman Empire : even so it preserved its cultural pre-eminence, and the Emperor Frederick II, born in the south, chose to make his court and residence at Palermo. His fame and success as an enlightened patron of art and learning—he was known as 'stupor mundi'—are explicable against the Sicilian background, for in Sicily, it has already been noted, diverse nations and cultures met and fused. It was in the thirteenth century that Italian speech became predominant and characteristic in Sicily. Phoenician, Greek, Latin, Arabic and Norman French had all been spoken in the island ; Greek, its common language at the time of the Roman conquest, long remained dominant, since it was employed during the four centuries of Byzantine rule. The eventual dominance of Italian speech owed less, it would seem, to Roman rule than to the Norman period, when Sicily was bound closely by trade and political bonds with southern Italy. Moreover, in the thirteenth century, Frederick II encouraged the use of Italian and made it the official language. The belated establishment of Italian as the common speech of Sicilians explains the small dialect differences which exist to-day between Sicilian and north Italian speech : in France, in contrast, Provencal of the south and the French of Paris[1] became distinct languages, not dialects.

After *c.* 1300 followed a long period of retrogression in Sicily : the island became merely a possession of foreign princes, French and Spanish in turn. The power of the nobility increased ; heavy taxes and export dues, extortion and maladministration generally, much more than natural calamities like plagues and earthquakes,

[1] Cp. *En Sicile*, ed. Olivier, pp. 273–82.

undermined its prosperity. Sicily suffered, too, as did the Italian cities, from the geographical discoveries of the Renaissance which left the Mediterranean relatively a backwater. Population reached its lowest ebb since the days of the Greeks : it fell below the million mark, even so late as 1570 whereas, in contrast, the estimate for the Arab period is 2·7 millions. Only in the nineteenth century did population reach its former levels : by 1861 it had doubled at a little over 2 millions ; by 1921 it had once more doubled. Again, the decline of Sicilian prosperity is reflected in the decadence of its maritime cities : Turkish and Barbary pirates harried its coastlands, and rendered insecure, as in the early days of Arab expansion, the seaways of the Mediterranean on the trade of which Sicily to a large extent depended. The south coast in particular suffered, since the active trade relations which it had formerly maintained with Tunis largely ceased when that country passed under Turkish misrule. In agriculture there was also marked decline, followed by gradual recovery : the area of cultivated land contracted, and the cultivation of many plants which had required skill and irrigation tended to be abandoned : e.g., cotton, and sugar, of which in the sixteenth century Madeira became a great source of supply. The country was carved up into large estates which led to the disappearance of many small scattered villages and to the concentration of population in the large hill-top towns. Successful efforts, however, were made by the big landowners to check depopulation by the creation of new towns on new or old sites, in some cases at low levels ; thus it is estimated that, subsequently to 1500, some 224 new towns came into being, of which the majority date from the nineteenth century.[1] Finally, the wretched condition of the roads, on which internal communications in Sicily entirely depended, affords a striking commentary on the centuries of maladministration to which the country fell a victim. Many physical conditions adversely affected the maintenance of roads—the extent of clay, continual and severe floods and landslips, as well as the steep gradients—but even so, Sicily had a good road system during the Roman period, which was clearly maintained under Arab and Norman rule. In subsequent centuries the roads were almost entirely neglected and an official road map prepared in 1823 (Fig. 44), which distinguished between carriage roads and horse and mule tracks, graphically emphasizes Sicily's deficiency in roads and its consequent dependence on travel by horseback and transport by mules and asses. Palermo alone commanded carriage roads for

[1] Ahlmann, ' Etudes de Géographie Humaine sur l'Italie Subtropicale ', *Geog. Ann.*, 1925 and 1926.

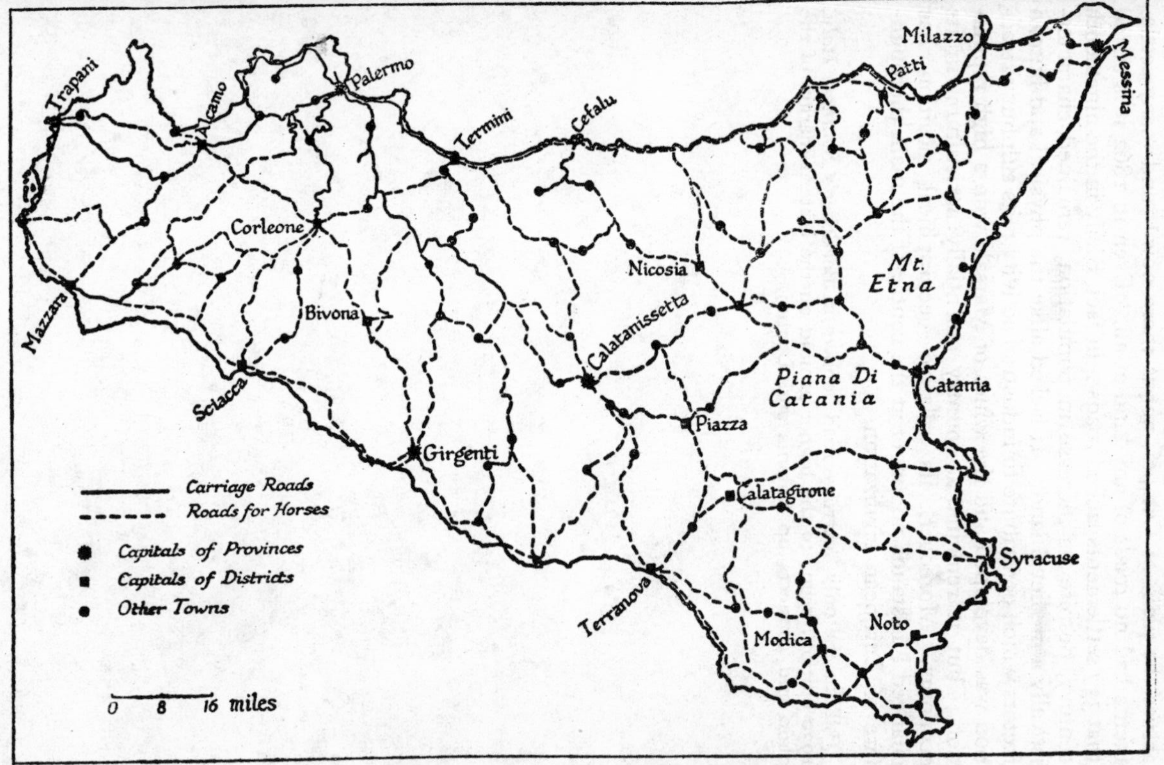

FIG. 44.—The Roads of Sicily in 1823

Note the very small mileage of carriage roads, leading to Palermo, Trapani and Mazzara

any distance ; bridges were generally lacking ; there was no road across the plain of Catania, nor is there now[1] ; and many settlements had no roads of any kind at all. Even in 1862 it is stated that 357 settlements lacked roads : in fact, Sicily in the nineteenth century, despite its increase in population, remained characteristically a medieval land. It lacked alike the physical and human factors which contribute to industrial activity ; its sulphur extraction was developed and the wines of Marsala won a high reputation ; but it remains a country essentially agricultural in its economy. Moreover, its relative geographical position has changed : it stands no longer at the centre of the main thoroughfare of European civilization.

[1] Thus the only ' carriage road ' shown in Baedeker's *Southern Italy*, 1930 edition, keeps to the higher ground on the eastern margin of the plain and connects up Catania and Lentini.

PART III

THE ECONOMIC GEOGRAPHY OF EUROPE

'The productions of vegetation have had a vast influence on the commerce of nations, and have been the great promoters of navigation, as may be seen in the articles of sugar, tea, tobacco, opium, ginseng, betel, paper, etc. As every climate has its peculiar produce, our natural wants bring on a mutual intercourse; so that by means of trade each distant part is supplied with the growth of every latitude, but, without the knowledge of plants and their culture, we must have been content with our hips and haws, without enjoying the delicate fruits of India and the salutiferous drugs of Peru.' GILBERT WHITE

CHAPTER XV

THE MEDITERRANEAN REGION IN THE MIDDLE AGES

THE geography of industry and commerce in the Mediterranean during the Middle Ages had its peculiar characteristics which distinguish it no less from that of the Roman Empire than from that of the present day. Certainly in medieval times, as under Roman hegemony, the Mediterranean held unimpaired its cardinal position in relation to the trade routes between Europe and the Far East : except for some short interruption its water-way continued to carry westwards oriental products from the terminal ports of the Black Sea and the Levant. On the other hand, there were some changes in the location and the relative importance of its chief maritime cities—in response rather to new human conditions than in result of physical changes. Moreover, although the Atlantic Ocean still formed an effective barrier frontier to Europe on the west, the Mediterranean ceased to be the only important route of European trade by sea. The increasing economic development of northern Europe is the characteristic feature of the economic geography of medieval Europe which makes a contrast with that of the Roman period. This economic advance is most marked in the basin of the Scheldt and the Rhine, to a lesser extent in England, while colonization pushing eastwards from the Rhinelands stimulated the rise of Baltic commerce. The creation of the Empire of Charles the Great in A.D. 800 marked an initial stage in the economic advance of north-western Europe, for the lower Rhine then formed the cultural and political axis of the empire. Succeeding centuries served only to indicate more clearly the importance of northern Europe in the industrial and commercial life of the Middle Ages. The rise of the Flemish cities ; the activity of the fairs of Champagne and Brie ; the rise of the Hanseatic cities—alike illustrate this fact. No less significant is the increase of population in France north of the Loire, and the greater importance of 'longitudinal' routes across Europe. In other words, the area of Europe which was both civilized and well populated had greatly expanded since the time of the Roman emperors, and the opportunities of the Mediterranean as a region of distribution and production were therefore enlarged. The route-ways across Russia from the Caspian and Black Seas to the Baltic seemed for a time to outflank the Mediterranean and to compete for its trade, just as did later and more effectively the direct sea route between Europe and the Far East. Nevertheless, this challenge fell short of success and the main north-south current of European trade ran across the Alps, until the Italians themselves opened up an alternative route by sea.

Three distinct periods may be noted as illustrative of the changes in the geography of Mediterranean commerce during the Middle Ages: the first between A.D. 476 and *c.* A.D. 750; the second from *c.* A.D. 750 to *c.* A.D. 1000; and finally the remaining five centuries of the Middle Ages. In the first period, which witnessed the collapse of the Roman Empire in the west and the state-building of the 'barbarian' immigrants, the Mediterranean continued as the centre alike of civilization and of commerce. The barbarians in their search for new and favoured settlement areas entered and conquered the peninsulas of Italy and Spain, while the Vandals crossed the Strait of Gibraltar and conquered Roman Africa and Sicily. The immigrants inherited rather than destroyed the existing culture, and—what is very important—the Roman Empire in the east maintained with its fleets some security for shipping. Many of the Roman seaport cities survived in the west, although Aquileia was destroyed and Ravenna began to silt up, but it seemed for a time that the empire might re-establish Roman rule in the western half of the Mediterranean: Spain, 'Africa', Sicily, south Italy and the Adriatic and Aegean coastlands, were conquered, conquests which conditioned Justinian's maritime supremacy. But although some of these lands were soon lost, Sicily and the littoral of south Italy were retained, so that the Adriatic 'lane' as well as the eastern Mediterranean remained Roman waters. Further, when it is recalled that Asia Minor, Syria and Egypt, the most civilized and densely populated parts of the medieval world, formed part of the empire, with its great cities of Constantinople, Antioch, Alexandria and Thessalonika, it is clear that favourable conditions for Mediterranean commerce still existed. Hence even in the western basin of the sea Carthage and the ports of Provence remained active at least until the early eighth century. Marseilles remained the chief port of Gaul, and Toulon, Fos, Arles, Sorgues, Valence, Vienne and Avignon were all trading cities associated with the Mediterranean.

Spices, fine textiles, and Egyptian papyrus were imported into Gaul; the chief export was probably slaves, Slav captives from the eastern frontier of the Frankish territories. In short, despite the political dislocations within the Mediterranean region, that sea continued to fulfil its geographical function as a highway of trade.

In the course of the eighth, ninth and tenth centuries, however, with the drastic change in political conditions brought about by the Mohammedan conquests, the Mediterranean became a region of conflict and, as Pirenne has emphasized,[1] trade routes were largely severed. As has been seen already, the Arabs dominated the sea from the seaports of their extensive coastlands and from their insular strongholds; piracy became rife; and from a base at what is now Garde Fresnet on the Provence coast they harried the whole of the Riviera and passes of the western Alps. From their own coasts they pushed into the inner waters of the Christian lands—into the Aegean where they sacked Thessalonika, and into the Tyrrhenian Sea where Genoa suffered a similar fate. They developed an extended coastwise trade between their own ports—Almeria, Denia, Tunis, Palermo, Medhia, Alexandria and the harbours of Syria. The strategical points on the former routes between the Levant, Gaul and Italy were in their hands; they held the entrepôt cities of the Levant—notably Antioch and Alexandria; the Strait of Messina was held by castles on both shores, while the arsenals of Tunis and Palermo held the other gate between the two basins of the sea. In the east Constantinople remained the only important Christian city from which intercourse between the Far East and western Europe continued, and almost alone of the great Christian ports in and around the Mediterranean basin it preserved some commercial activity by sea. In the west trade entirely vanished. Papyrus ceased to be used in Gaul after *c.* A.D. 737; Marseilles declined until the Crusading period, and the Carolingian Empire, founded in A.D. 800, became a truly continental state, isolated from Mediterranean influences. Markets and trading towns practically vanished, whilst the largely agricultural economy of the empire served less the purposes of exchange than the immediate needs of subsistence. Moreover, as will be seen, the earliest evidences of trade revival in the Carolingian Empire appear not in the Mediterranean coastlands but in certain Rhine and Channel ports.

Constantinople, thanks to its fleet, its political strength and the bad organization of its enemies, escaped the repeated assaults

[1] See *supra*, note 2, p. 201.

of the Arabs and retained a restricted Mediterranean frontage in Greece, Macedonia, Thrace, Asia Minor, and in the Adriatic. Moreover, the tenth century witnessed a revival of its naval power, which was marked by the recovery of Crete. In the Black Sea, the lands of which it shared with the Caliphate, it continued to trade, e.g., with Trebizond and the Chersonesus; it controlled the Straits into the Aegean, as well as the Aegean and the Adriatic seas. Thus during the centuries when commerce was breaking down in the Mediterranean, it preserved at least a localized trade within its home waters. Further, it established trade relations via the Black Sea and the Dnieper with the Russian state, which was organized in the ninth century by Swedes.[1] This trade is of interest in that it followed the only trade route across Europe frequented during the ninth and tenth centuries: Gaul and Italy alike no longer controlled trade routes into the continent, and the Hungarians were too uncivilized to admit the passage of merchants along the Danube.

Only in the remaining centuries of the Middle Ages, between *c.* A.D. 1000 and *c.* 1500, did the Mediterranean become the chief thoroughfare of European trade. The leadership in this revival fell to Italian cities, in which the Roman tradition of industry and trade survived the long period of barbarian immigration, settlement and conquest. The Moslem power at sea was successfully curtailed, and Crusading attacks which were launched against the Infidels in Syria, Egypt, Tunis and elsewhere were deeply tinged with the commercial ambitions of the Italian maritime states. The decline of the Byzantine Empire, particularly until the twelfth century, served only to advance the interests of the Italian cities, which were ready and strong enough to make capital out of its weakness; while religious antipathy towards the Moslems did not preclude the establishment, by means of treaties, of trading stations within their chief cities. The dominant feature of Mediterranean trade in the later Middle Ages was the transport and distribution of oriental wares which were bought in the Levant cities of Egypt and Syria: thus Venice, which had the biggest share in this maritime commerce, was called by Bishop Creighton 'a Joint-Stock Company for the exploitation of the East'. Nevertheless there were other regions of surplus commodities which entered importantly into trade. The Black Sea countries were sought for their cereals, skins, fish, alum, timber and slaves, whilst industry centred in the towns around the Mediterranean—notably at Constantinople, in Syria and in Italy—furnished manufactured

[1] Cp. *supra*, pp. 218–19.

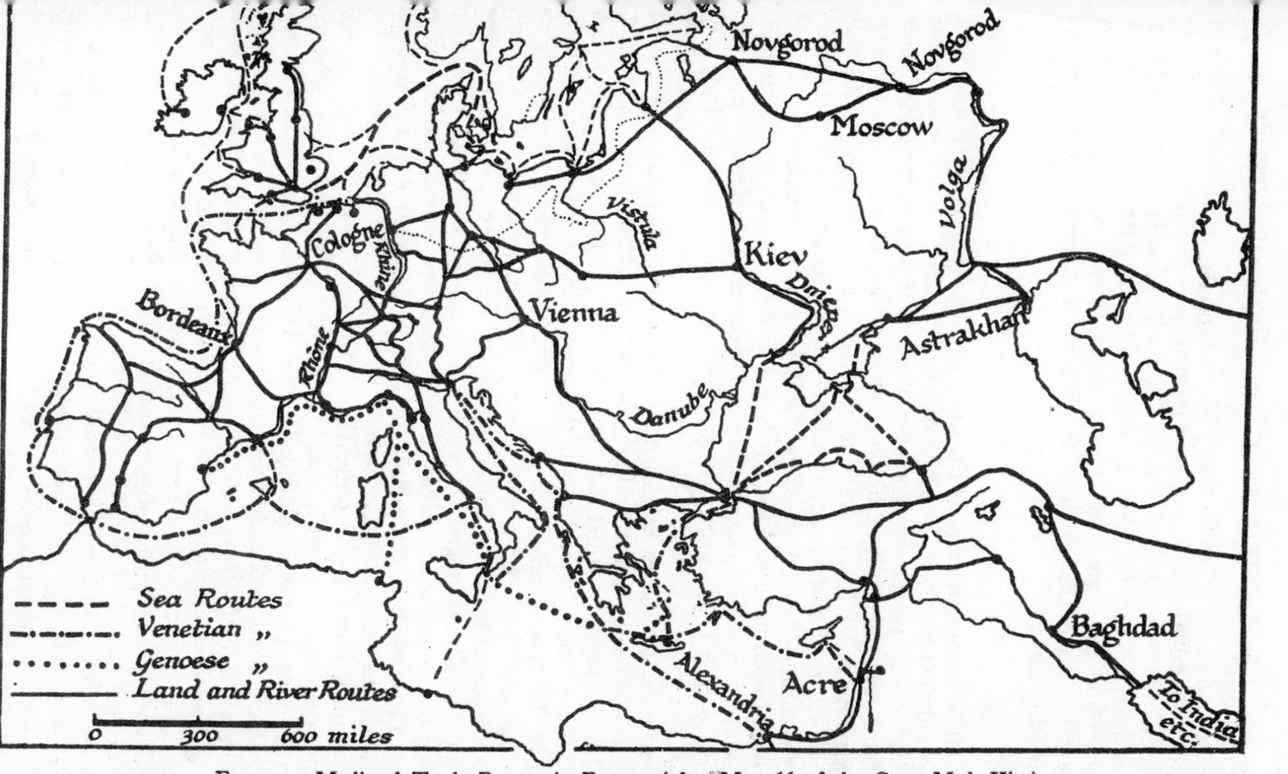

FIG. 45.—Medieval Trade Routes in Europe (after Map 66 of the *Cam. Med. Hist.*)

The faint dotted line indicates the southern limit of the region occupied by the Hanseatic towns. Note the trans-Russian routes which were opened in the ninth century; for the most part the routes shown were mainly used in the later Middle Ages. Novgorod on the Volga is usually distinguished as Nijni Novgorod from Novgorod or Great Novgorod, the Hanseatic trade depôt on Lake Ilmen.

commodities for exchange. Moreover, by means of overland routes and—in the fourteenth century—of direct sailings, the trade and industrial centres of Italy were closely related to those of interior and northern Europe. It is well therefore to focus attention here on some of the main towns and regions which entered so decisively into the medieval commercial life of the Mediterranean.

Venice

The lagoon islands at the head of the Adriatic offered meagre resources to their inhabitants: only small areas within the lagoons lay permanently above the sea; there was little cultivable land, and that badly drained; whilst drinking water was lacking. On the other hand, the lagoon islands were rendered habitable since a tidal rise of almost 3 feet[1]—a unique feature in the Mediterranean—flushed the lagoons daily; the maritime pine had established itself and fowl, fish and above all salt, were obtainable. Moreover, the islands occupied an excellent geographical position, since they stood near to the largest lowland region of Italy and at the point where the Mediterranean sea-ways penetrate farthest into the European continent. The commercial development of the lagoon islands was made possible by certain historical events, but it was not evident at first that the Rialto islands, in which Venice stood, should attain the predominant position. Between the Isonzo estuary and that of the Reno extend from east to west the five lagoons of Grado, Murano, Caorle, Veneta and Comachio, the last two of which are separated from each other by the alluvial marshes of the Po delta. The island townships or these lagoons received a large accession of population when the townsfolk of the mainland cities sought refuge in the lagoons from the ravages and conquests in turn of Visigoths, Ostrogoths, Franks, Huns and Lombards. The mainland cities of the old Roman Venetia which lay along the Via Postumia—Padua, Altinum, Heraclea, Concordia and Aquileia—as well as Oderzo, which stood to the north of this road, were attacked and sacked in some cases several times. The islands of the lagoons were peopled, as a rule, by refugees from the nearest mainland town. Thus Grado, which became the first archiepiscopal see in the lagoons, was settled by townsfolk from Aquileia; Caorle was settled from Concordia; Jesolo received inhabitants from Heraclea, and finally, Torcello and Malamocco which stood in the Veneta lagoon received fugitives from Altinum and Padua.

[1] An unwelcome rise of as much as 6 feet may occur if a S.E. gale is blowing.

The Venetian islands—e.g., Rialto, Olivolo and Giudicea—which formed part of the Rialto group within the Veneta lagoon, were the last to be settled in this way. When, *c.* 713, the first doge or duke was chosen as ruler over all the lagoon islands, the capital city was Heraclea on the mainland, but by *c.* 800 it was shifted to Malomocco, which stood near the estuary of the Po. It is only to the eighth century that the beginnings of Venice can be traced, when population overflowed from the Heraclea and Jesolo island groups into that of the Rialto and when (in 774) Jesolo was made a bishop's see.

The first activities of the lagoon dwellers were inspired by the character of their habitat. They had first to adapt their environment to their needs : they consolidated the soil by cutting channels and by building dikes of plaited osiers ; they built houses of wood and prepared harbours for ships ; they set about cultivating wheat and the vine, and collecting rain-water in cisterns. It is significant that as early as A.D. 536 the lagoon dwellers are described as salt-workers and sea-carriers. In the salt trade Venice came to secure a virtual monopoly, and the mainland cities became dependent on Venice for their supplies, for as Cassiodorus noted (in the early sixth century) 'men may live without gold or silver but not without salt'.[1] The use of the sea-ways, however, depended on the open water of the lagoons, and in the fifteenth century Venice had to expend efforts to prevent the silting up of its approaches. To this end the estuaries of the Brenta and Bacchiglione were diverted to the south, and that of the Sile to the north. The peculiarities of its setting governed likewise the political status of Venice. For the Byzantine Empire, thanks to its fleet, was able to retain its hold on the lagoons, after it had abandoned to the conquering Lombards its territories in the Italian peninsula. Thus Venice, as it grew, was a frontier outpost of the Greek world and until *c.* A.D. 1000 lay within the limits, though largely independent, of the Byzantine Empire—a political relationship which distinctly favoured its advance. In other words, their maritime setting and their maritime superiority, which made them difficult of access, protected the lagoons from conquest by the Lombards. Charlemagne conquered most of the islands, but only temporarily. Thus Venice was able largely to escape from the many feuds and entanglements of the peninsula, and in this respect enjoyed an advantage over Genoa. Finally, for the same reason, the geographical setting of the lagoon islands stimulated, notwithstanding jealousies and rivalries, the growth

[1] Cited by Horatio Brown, *Studies in the History of Venice*, I, 339.

of a community of interest, which found expression in the common rule of a Doge.

The fate of Ravenna, like that of Aquileia, was sealed both by barbarian attacks and by the accumulation of alluvium which cut it off from the sea. A prosperous and healthy city in the Roman period, Ravenna was nevertheless even then a lagoon city where houses were built on piles and where a well was worth more than a vineyard.[1] It served Rome as its naval headquarters in the Adriatic and as an imperial capital, protected by its marshes yet open to the sea; in the sixth century it admitted the fleets of the Byzantine Empire. When, however, the city passed from the rule of Constantinople to that of the Lombards, its maritime importance waned; in the twelfth century it was still a maritime city belonging to Venice, but its harbour and lagoon began to silt up and were transformed eventually into orchards, gardens, pine groves and desolate malarious marsh. The passing of Aquileia and Ravenna left Venice and its competitors free to exploit the commercial potentialities of their excellent geographical position. At the head of the Adriatic some three 'natural' routes converged: one was the Adriatic 'lane'; the second was marked by the valley of the Po; and the third came southwards by various easy Alpine passes from Germany, France and the Low Countries. Further, situated geographically about midway between the extremities of the Mediterranean basin and linked politically with the great commercial city of Constantinople, Venice was well placed to act as distributor throughout that sea. But 'natural' routes are not necessarily routes of trade, and it was incumbent upon Venice to overcome by continued effort the human obstacles which beset these routes and thus to secure them as channels of trade. To this end she succeeded in overcoming the towns of Chioggia and Comachio, her trade rivals, who profited by their greater proximity to the delta of the Po: already for some time the ships of Comachio had sailed up the Po and traded with Cremona. Then again, the Adriatic itself was by no means safe for shipping. Until the end of the eighth century the Byzantine Empire controlled the entry to the Adriatic from her coast cities of Durazzo and Brindisi; but the ravages of the Arabs in southern Italy threatened to block this passage, whilst at the same time the Dalmatian coast with its many sheltered bays, channels and islands formed a base for Slav pirates. Eventually, Venice won control of the sea by defeating the Arabs and by founding (*c.* A.D. 1000)

[1] Symonds, *Sketches and Studies in Italy and Greece*, 2nd series, new ed., p. 2.

a line of 'factories' along the Dalmatian coast at Zara, Veglia, Arbe, Trau and Spalato. Even so, the Normans captured Bari in 1071 and Palermo in the following year, and it seemed that the Adriatic entry might again be threatened; but once again the Venetians were successful in keeping the way clear.

Thus by the time of the First Crusade in 1096 Venice had sufficiently developed its maritime power to be able to furnish a large fleet for the transport of men, horses and supplies to the Holy Land. Moreover, it had already established trade relations with Alexandria and was well entrenched at Constantinople.

Its success in the Adriatic—'our gulf' it was proudly called and Edrisi called it the Sea of Venice—gave Venice not only access to the timber supplies brought down to the Dalmatian ports from the interior highlands, but also to the wheat and wine of southern Italy. Further, it had open access to wider commercial fields. In turn as vassal, ally and victor of the Byzantine Empire, Venice sought consistently trade advantages. Already in the tenth century it had established a dominant position at Constantinople over its Italian rivals, the cities of Amalfi and Bari; in 1082 it secured the right to trade without the payment of dues throughout the whole of the Byzantine Empire; whilst in 1204, turning the 4th Crusade to its own ends, it captured Constantinople itself, imposed there vassal rulers, and gained possession of three-quarters of the empire. Venice had no intention, however, of involving itself in the difficulties of ruling large land areas. The republic was dominated essentially by maritime and commercial ambitions, and its superior knowledge of geography indicated clearly the relative value of different lands.[1] Therefore it abandoned many of these territories in return for trade privileges within them, and retained in its own hands only those parts which would strengthen its commerce and which could be effectively held by sea-power. To enumerate the footholds (within the former Byzantine Empire) which were thus acquired is to indicate the stepping-stones and bases of the Venetian sea-state: Durazzo; in the Morea, Modon and Coron, ports of call for the galleys bound for Syria and Crete; the Ionian islands of Corfu, Cephalonia and Zante; Negropont in Euboea; the whole of the Cyclades island group in the Aegean; Lemnos; Gallipoli, and the Marmora ports of Panium, Rodosto and Heraclea; 'quarters' at Constantinople, and inland at

[1] As Dr. Miller remarks, with all the emphasis of understatement (*Essays on the Latin Orient*, p. 58), the action of Venice shows that 'an acquaintance with geography may sometimes be useful to politicians'.

Lüle-Burgas and Adrianople ; and finally, very important both for its own produce and as an outlying base at the junction of the routes from Syria and Egypt, the island of Crete. Some of these colonies, notably Durazzo and Corfu, were quickly lost; in 1261 Genoa usurped the dominant position at Constantinople ; but Crete was firmly held and was not abandoned in fact until the late eighteenth century.

FIG. 46.—The Territories of Venice *c.* A.D. 1360 (after Darby)

In pursuit of its commercial ambitions Venice built up an extensive empire, which (to repeat) consisted essentially of territories which could be of service to its commerce and could be held by sea-power (Fig. 46). The need for a local supply of foodstuffs and the desire to control passes on the trade routes explain the acquisition of mainland territory near Venice, but it is significant that this did not form a geographically compact area. Similarly, Venetian rule in Dalmatia was limited to the coastland, where it held all the chief seaports except Ragusa and from which it controlled the timber supplies of the adjoining mountains. Venice itself came to include a large urban population, estimated at 190,000 in 1423 and 110,000 in 1509. It was also a great industrial centre, having learnt from Constantinople many secrets of industrial technique. Rich-coloured silks, together with gold and silver work, formed Venetian specialities ; its glass industry goes back to *c.* 1090, and in the thirteenth century the ‘ glass houses ’, in which mirrors, table glass, mosaics, &c. were made, were concentrated at Murano ; the shipbuilding yards at Venice utilized the timber of the thick forests of northern Istria, Croatia and Dalmatia. In this particular industry the independent republic of Ragusa, in the last centuries of the Middle Ages, had a great reputation. It derived its timber from the forests, now largely destroyed, of Mount Sergio, Lagosta and Meleda, as well as from Bosnia.[1]

Pisa

The earliest settlement at Pisa stood on a headland between the mouths of the rivers Arno and Ausar, but owing to the accumulation of alluvium brought down by these rivers the town became separated from the sea, by some four miles in the tenth century and by over six miles to-day.[2] The Arno estuary, however, provided ample harbourage and space for shipbuilding yards in the Middle Ages, whilst the river flood kept open the approach from the sea ; even so, shallow water over the bar at the mouth of the river was liable to present difficulties for heavily laden ships. Landwards Pisa lay open and lacked the protection of a mountain rampart which made Genoa 'strategically an island', and the town was in fact confined by the growing territories of Lucca. Pisa therefore looked essentially seawards, and in the tenth century found there real opportunities for maritime enterprise. It was the only seaport on the Tyrrhenian Sea within the limits of Lombard Italy, and, further, Genoa offered at that time no competition, since the whole of the Ligurian coastland was suffering from the ravages of the Saracens. Nevertheless, the Arabs from the coasts of Tunis and Spain threatened (in the early eleventh century) to control and close the Tyrrhenian Sea : they were established at Palermo, they secured footholds on the Sardinian coast, and in 1004 sailed up the Arno and partially sacked Pisa. The Moslem threat united Pisa and Genoa in a vigorous and persistent effort to drive the Infidels from what they considered was *their* sea, and towards the end of the century they were launching their attacks against the chief strongholds of Arab power. They drove the Arabs from Sardinia where Pisa secured commercial privileges ; they attacked the Arab capital of Palermo which was then a great city and seaport with a population of 300,000 ; whilst they even sacked Mehdia in Tunis, which was probably the strongest city of the African littoral and had been turned into a pirates' nest. Successful within its home waters, Pisa extended its trade relations far afield : trade treaties were made with the Moslems of northern Africa and Spain ; in 1111 it was granted a 'quarter' at Constantinople with a quay on the Golden Horn ; it had stations at the same

[1] Cp. Turrill, *The Vegetation of the Balkan Peninsula*, p. 197.
[2] Heywood, *A History of Pisa*, p. 1.

time in Syria at Antioch, Laodicea, Sidon and elsewhere, and in Egypt at Alexandria and Cairo. The city became a market for oriental products; furs were prepared from skins brought from the Black Sea; whilst clothmaking became its chief industry. Wool reached Pisa from various sources—the best came from France and from Algarve in southern Portugal; other supplies came from Sardinia, whilst local wool of inferior quality was derived from sheep pastured on the winter herbage of the near-by *maremma* plain and of the meadows between the Arno and the Serchio estuaries. Water, which is essential in large quantities for the varied processes of the industry, was brought into the town by canals and aqueducts.

Pisa's successful activity incurred the hostility of neighbouring cities, especially Genoa, which sought supremacy within Tyrrhenian waters, and the inland cities of Lucca and Florence, which were jealous of the control of Pisa, at the maritime outlet of Tuscany. In its struggle with Genoa, although it had the earlier start, Pisa was much the weaker in the geographical factors which condition sea-power. Genoa had a better port, actually on the sea; it could draw upon the seamen of the whole littoral between Monaco and Porto Venere; it was better defended landwards, and had a larger territorial base. The city of Lucca harassed Pisa by land as Genoa assailed it by sea: the first had an important silk-weaving industry and stood on the Via Francigena, a route well frequented by merchants and pilgrims, which connected Villafranca and Rome. Lucca was at pains to prevent merchants and pilgrims from turning aside from the main highway in order to reach Pisa; moreover it threatened at times the route which ran between Florence and Pisa via Fuecchio, the main line of entry into Tuscany from the sea. Their common enmity towards Pisa united the cities of Genoa and Lucca in an alliance which was regarded as unnatural, in that Ligurians and Tuscans were sufficiently 'foreign' to each other and were as a rule mutually hostile. Certainly it proved disastrous to the Pisans, who tried to restore the balance of power in 1171 by an alliance with Florence which was then relatively less important and largely dominated by the fortresses of the feudal nobility in the surrounding countryside. This alliance gave Florence the right to use the port of Pisa on equal terms with the Pisans and in fact reduced that city to the rank of a vassal of the upper Arno town. Genoa succeeded in destroying the port and trade of Pisa in 1284 by sinking at the mouth of the Arno blocks of stone brought from the island of Capraria near by: a mole was thus formed which checked the all-important scour of the river water and caused the deposition of silt. But the port of Pisa was revived in some measure under the tutelage of Florence until it silted up *c.* 1406; and a little later, in 1421, Florence bought the town of Leghorn which, situated actually on the coast, succeeded as the port of Tuscany to the rôle of Pisa.

Genoa

The port of Genoa was neither the largest nor the best on the Ligurian coast, but it had incontestably the best situation. Genoa stands at the most northerly point on this coast; the Apennines, it is true, lie immediately behind the town and divide it off from the Po valley; but they afforded much protection landwards, an advantage which its rival Pisa lacked. Moreover, they are narrow and could be crossed by low passes at about 1,500 feet. In fact, a journey of roughly a hundred miles connected Genoa with both Milan and Turin. Along the coast an ancient route, the Via Francigena, linked the town with Provence and Tuscany, but the broad obstacle of the Alps, until the railway age, left it remote and detached from Germany. The deep water off the Ligurian coast was an advantage to Genoa in that the rivers were unable to build up a low marshy coastal plain, which, as in the case of the Tuscan *maremma*, might become malarious. The old taunt that Genoa possessed 'a sea without fish, mountains without wood, men without conscience and women without honour'[1] exaggerates at least its geographical deficiencies, for fishing was an active pursuit of the town in the early Middle Ages and timber for ships was brought down from the higher levels of the Apennines. The proximity of the mountains to the sea was in some respects an unfavourable factor: certainly they served to intensify the temperature of the coastlands, but they also rigidly limited the area of cultivable land. Thus, although a most varied cultivation was possible—wheat, olives, vines, the mulberry and orange were grown—the meagre territories of the Genoese republic, stretched out along the Ligurian Gulf, proved unable to produce an adequate supply of foodstuffs or of raw materials for industry. It was towards the open sea, therefore, that Genoa looked for economic opportunities, and there indeed that they were eventually found.

As has already been noted, the desolation of the Riviera coastlands at the hands of the Saracens handicapped the rise of Genoa and gave Pisa its chance. The part played by Genoa in the

[1] Cited by Bent, *Genoa*, p. 7.

First Crusade (1096–9) enabled it to establish a line of factories along the coast of Syria and Palestine, a trade asset of considerable importance, since it must be remembered how relatively populous and productive these lands were at this time. Genoese 'factories' or depôts were set up at Antioch, Tortosa, Arsuf, Caesarea, Acre, Apamea, Laodicea, Beirut, Tyre and Jaffa. Genoese trade relations by sea were first established in the eleventh century with their immediate neighbours: they traded with the ports of the Gulf of Lion from Marseilles to Barcelona, with Almeria in Moslem Spain, with Sicily, and with the Moslem ports of north Africa, especially Tunis, Bugia and Ceuta. In 1157, growing stronger in these 'home' waters, they overcame the remnants of Mohammedan power in Corsica, Sardinia and the Balearic islands, whilst in 1177 they courted trouble with Venice by winning a foothold in the trade of Alexandria. Further, a century later when Venetian rule at Constantinople was overthrown, they got control of the alum mines at Phokaia, an important source of a commodity indispensable to the dyeing industry of the Italian cities,[1] and secured a quarter and a quay at Galata, the suburb of Constantinople across the Golden Horn. They had colonies at the Aegean islands of Lemnos, Mytilene, Enos and Chios; they had the strongest position at Cyprus, whilst in the Black Sea, which became their distinctive sphere, they built up a colonial empire. Moreover, if, owing to the strength and jealousy of Milan, Genoese merchants were largely shut out from enterprise in Lombardy and Germany, they were quick to carry their trade over the western Alps to the fairs of Provence, Champagne and the Low Countries. Finally, about the year 1300 Genoa was the first of the Mediterranean cities to begin, by means of its galleys and by way of 'the Great Sea of Darkness', organized voyages with the Channel ports of Bruges and London.

Ports of Southern France and Catalonia

The ports of Provence, Languedoc and Catalonia, which had a subordinate share in Mediterranean trade, engaged in both coastwise sailings and even direct voyages to the Levant. In Low Languedoc, which had an active woollen industry, a number of ports which are now unapproachable from the sea, stood behind the then open water of the lagoons. Narbonne and Montpellier, with its outport of Lattes, were the chief ports; on the Rhône

[1] The chief supplies of alum came from the Levant: e.g., Syria, and Asia Minor. The alum of the Papal states was discovered near Civita Vecchia only in 1462.

delta Arles, St. Gilles and Aigues-Mortes, and in Provence Marseilles, above all, had direct relations by sea and were resorts of Italian traders. Politically, Languedoc and Provence lay outside the territories under the direct control of the French kings; hence a great international fair was created within the kingdom in the thirteenth century at Nîmes, the population of which grew 'as if by enchantment', and Louis IX established ports at St. Gilles and Aigues-Mortes. These cities sent ships to the Holy Land: Louis IX set off from Aigues-Mortes on his crusade, and it is interesting that he was reluctant, on his homeward journey, to land near Hyères in Provence (though he actually did so) because 'he would not,' he said, 'leave the ship until he reached Aigues-Mortes, which was in his own land'.[1]

The Catalonian port of Barcelona, like Genoa, cut off from the interior by mountains from which, however, it derived timber for shipbuilding, had active commercial relations with the Levant, especially after 1157 when it was united with the kingdom of Aragon. Barcelona itself was an active industrial centre (textiles and metal goods); it had easy relations by road with France via the Perthus pass, and an adequate port, the use of which, however, owing to its lack of depth, required expert pilotage. In the thirteenth and fourteenth centuries Barcelona established commercial relations throughout the Mediterranean, and its importance as a maritime city is reflected in two ways: in the general adoption of the Catalan Sea Laws and in the advances made in the production of efficient charts of the Mediterranean. The city of Narbonne, until its harbour sanded up in the late fourteenth century, was, unlike Barcelona, a trading port with some hinterland relations. To what extent did it serve as a starting-point for overland routes across the European isthmus between the Mediterranean and the Atlantic —the navigation of which was feared and largely avoided prior to *c.* 1300? The route from Narbonne was physically easy enough and involved no mountain passage as did that from Barcelona, but political conditions may have caused obstruction or difficulties, since the English dominated Gascony until 1453. There is some evidence of the transport of commodities along the route from Narbonne by way of Toulouse, thence by road or by the Garonne down to Bordeaux; but it was probably little used compared with that across the Alps or up the valley of the Rhône. An Arab geographer, Abulfeda, records the use of this route from Bordeaux in the thirteenth century for the carriage of English tin and copper destined for Alexandria:

[1] Joinville, *Saint Louis, King of France*, trans. Hutton, 7th ed., p. 193.

the metal was carried up the Garonne to Toulouse and thence by pack-animals to Narbonne whence it was shipped to Egypt.[1]

Cyprus

An important field for commercial exploitation in which the Genoese took the most prominent part, although Venetians, Florentines, Catalonians, Frenchmen and others also had a share, was the large, productive and conveniently placed island of Cyprus. Its position in relation to the seaports of Egypt, Syria and Asia Minor, and the many harbours along its broken coasts made it an important place of call for ships. In itself it provided a wide range of commodities eagerly sought by merchants from the west. It had rich supplies of salt on the borders of two lakes near to the maritime cities of Limassol and Larnaka; sugar was grown on the irrigated southern plains behind Limassol and Baffo; its wine was highly reputed; it made fine silks and brocades worked with gold thread; whilst it produced surpluses of wheat, varied fruits, cotton and indigo. Cyprus reached its greatest prosperity after 1291 when, with the fall of Acre, Christian rule in Syria and Palestine came to an end, and trade with the Saracen conquerors, prohibited by the Church, became possible only with great difficulty. Cyprus became known as 'the last Christian country' in the Levant, although Cilicia, known then as Little Armenia, survived as an important and wealthy Christian remnant on the mainland. The trade stations of the western cities in Syria were transferred to Cyprus, and that island became the chief emporium for the produce of the Far East, which was shipped across by Saracen merchants from the Syrian ports. The Genoese, who aimed at establishing a monopoly of the trade of Cyprus, did their best to canalize trade at its chief seaport, Famagusta, which faced towards Syria. They were not entirely successful and some of the other ports were able to maintain a small if specialized trade. Thus Larnaka shipped much salt, and Episcopi sugar. Nicosia, which stood well inland, was the capital of the island and had considerable textile industry. In return for the spices, sugar, salt, leather, silks, &c., which the western merchants shipped, they brought mainly woollen fabrics from France, Italy, Flanders and Spain, as well as tin and coral. The monopolistic exclusiveness of Genoa served to drive traders from Cyprus and they went back

[1] *La Géographie d'Aboulféda*, trans. Reinaud, II, 307. He derived this information from the writings of Ibn Saïd, who died in 1274.

eventually to the Syrian cities and to Alexandria. Cypriot prosperity dwindled, to reach its lowest ebb after its conquest in 1571 by the Ottoman Turks.

The Black Sea

The trade of the Black Sea had been at first the preserve largely of the Greek merchants of the Byzantine Empire, but as the empire weakened and as Venice and Genoa [1] established themselves firmly in Constantinople or its suburbs they secured increasingly the control of its trade. The control of the Bosporus channel, in fact, was the essential key to the control of the Black Sea trade, so that when, in 1261, the Genoese filched from the Venetians the supreme position at Constantinople they likewise succeeded in becoming the predominant commercial power in the Black Sea. The chief base of their trade was the Crimean peninsula which had many attractions to offer the merchant. Its southern coasts were well provided with natural harbours and with strong upland sites for cities; the southern half of the peninsula, again, is hilly and its climate is of the Mediterranean type, so that the olive and the vine, which had been introduced by the ancient Greeks, flourished. The mountain range inland afforded timber, whilst the low steppe, which formed the northern part of the Crimea, was good pasture country; finally, the Sea of Azov and the river Don abounded in fish. More important than these local assets was the positional advantage of the Crimean cities in relation to the caravan routes from Persia, the Far East and the plains to the north of the Black Sea coast. This advantage, too, was the more valuable in the late thirteenth and fourteenth centuries, since the Tartars, whose territories included the south Russian plain, the Crimea and Persia, maintained with considerable success the security of the roads.

The greatest trading colony of the Genoese was the city of Caffa (Theodosia) which the Tartars handed over to them about the year 1270. It stood on the south-eastern side of the peninsula, at the head of a broad bay, which was sheltered from the prevalent north winds. The chief Venetian station was to the west at Soldaja (Soudak), which the Genoese seized in 1365. At the mouth of the Don and situated on the left bank of the southern arm of the delta was the populous and busy Tartar town of Tana (Azov), in which the Genoese and the Venetians held, though precariously, trading quarters. Tana was very important as a

[1] Cp. Bratianu, *Recherches sur le Commerce Genoise dans la Mer Noire au XIIIe siècle* (with plates), 1931.

terminal of trade caravans which brought silk from China by way of Khareszan, Turkestan, Djungaria and Astrakhan; silk was brought also from Ghilan on the southern coast of the Caspian Sea; spices, &c. from India came by way of Kabul, Ourengj and Astrakhan, or across Persia to Asterabad, thence to Astrakhan by boat. In the interior of the Crimea the Tatar capital of Solgat (Crim) was also, like Tana, a mart for silk, spices, furs and leather. The Genoese at Caffa were able, therefore, not only to ship silks and spices but also those products which, ever since the days of the first Greek colonies, had been sought from the northern coast of the Black Sea: namely corn, salt, fish, slaves, skins and furs. Apart from their direct trade with Genoa, the Genoese at Caffa traded with Constantinople, the lower Danube, the Caucasus coast, the Tatar cities, Egypt and Syria. They succeeded in driving the Greeks from the commerce of the sea and in assuming their task of provisioning Constantinople—with salt fish and timber from the Crimea and wheat, which they shipped largely at Akkerman on the Dniester estuary and at Lykostomion on the Danube delta. How dependent the decadent Byzantine Empire had become on the victualling fleets of the Italians from the Crimea is suggested by the acute shortage of wheat and salt fish which it suffered in 1343 at a time when the Italians had been driven out of Tana and trade was dislocated. Another quarter of the Black Sea in which Genoese and Venetians had valuable trade connexions was Trebizond. This city had been an important trade outlet early in the Middle Ages, at a time when it stood on the frontier between the Byzantine and Arab territories. In the thirteenth century, moreover, like Little Armenia (Cilicia) to the south, it escaped the conquest of the Seljuk Turks, and it became an independent empire on the confines of the Turk and Tartar empires. Trebizond produced textile goods together with silver, alum and iron from its mountains, whilst it was a terminus for caravans which brought Indian spices, Chinese silk and Persian drugs.

The Genoese, in their attempt to establish commercial predominance in the Black Sea, showed geographical acumen in seizing the Bosporan forts of Roumili Hissari and Anatoli Hissari, which stood at the point where the broad channel from the Black Sea narrows for the first time. The Byzantine Empire had established forts and a custom house at the narrows, whilst a chain was stretched from bank to bank; and there likewise, in 1348, the Genoese established a naval base and a custom station. Incidentally, it may be noted that at this time the Italian fleets from the

Black Sea were the agent by which the Black Death was carried into Europe : having started in the Far East, the plague had spread among the Tatars, from whom it passed to the inhabitants of Caffa, which the Tatars were besieging in 1346 ; thence by sea it was carried to the maritime territories of Sicily, Tuscany, Genoa, Ragusa, Spalato and Venice.[1] The collapse of Black Sea trade was due to the conquering assaults of Mongols led by Tamerlane, at the end of the fourteenth century, and of the Ottoman Turks, half a century later. The Mongols, in contrast to the Tatar rulers, were a destructive force : their war bands cut the caravan links with the Far East by sacking the Tatar capital of Sarai and also Astrakhan, both Volga cities and caravan stations, and, moreover, they swept into the Crimea. The Turks, on the other hand, passed from Asia Minor into Thrace, and eventually captured Constantinople, and the Genoese forts at the Bosporus narrows. In command of the Bosporus 'bottle neck', the Turks had control of the Black Sea : Caffa itself fell to them in 1475, and the luckiest of its inhabitants suffered transportation to deserted areas at Constantinople. One of the terminals to trade routes from the Far East was thenceforth closed to western merchants.

Florence

The economic activity of Italy was by no means characteristic of its maritime cities alone, and in contrast to the trading sea-states of Pisa, Venice and Genoa were many inland cities which flourished alike in industry and trade. Florence in Tuscany like Milan in Lombardy, was an outstanding example of this class of city. Florence stood on the upper Arno in the midst of a broad upland basin which the river entered and left by way of rocky defiles. The Sieve and Ombrone headwaters of the Arno, which joined some distance above the town, brought down abundant water from the Apennines : thus Florence, in contrast to Siena on its hill-top perch, was plentifully supplied with water—an indispensable factor in the great cloth industry which was built up in the town. Moreover, the basin itself was highly productive of cereal foodstuffs, the vine and the olive, whilst the Tuscan hills provided pasture for sheep from which was derived part of the wool for the textile industry. Situated on a hill site and guarding its bridge across the Arno, Florence was well placed in relation to the main route-ways of central Italy in the Middle Ages, since with the rise of Milan the main

[1] Heyd, *Histoire du Commerce du Levant*, II, 196.

route northwards from Rome was deflected from the old Via Flaminia bound for Ravenna to pass through Florence *en route* for Milan. Florence also commanded a road westwards to Pisa via Lucca, and north-eastwards across the Apennines by the Futa pass to Bologna, to Ferrara at the crossing of the Po, and thence to Venice. The road to Rome ran along the depression of the Chiana, which was partially drained in the later Middle Ages, and through the town of Siena. Florence became to a remarkable degree a city of specialized industries, especially during the thirteenth century when Pisa had become virtually its vassal : both for its textile products and its finance it was famous throughout Europe. Every branch of the cloth industry, and in particular the art of dyeing, were practised with great skill. Wool was imported from Sardinia, Algarve in southern Portugal, Languedoc and elsewhere in France ; dyes and alum, both of which were essential to the cloth industry, reached Florence via Pisa or Genoa or were imported directly by Florentines themselves. (Dye-woods were an oriental product brought from the Levant ports, whilst alum was produced in several parts of the Mediterranean world, notably in Syria, in Tunis and at the mines of Phokaia in Asia Minor and at certain Black Sea places.) Oil, from which soap was prepared, was brought from Ancona and Gaeta. It was only after 1314 when Florence defeated and ruined Lucca, that it established a silk industry. The weaving of silk had been the chief industry of Lucca, and the production of raw silk, introduced from Sicily, had spread from Lucca around the Riviera coastland into southern France. Even so, the industry depended largely on silk imported via the Levant from the producing areas of Ghilan, on the southern shores of the Caspian Sea, from Persia, Asia Minor, Syria and China. Some measure of the rapid development of Florence as an industrial city is reflected in its population which increased from 45,000 in 1281 to 90,000 in 1331, and represents the size of a first-grade medieval town. Its merchants carried Florentine wares throughout western Europe and the Mediterranean, whilst some even carried fine cloth to China : they travelled overland from Azov to Pekin by means of wheeled vehicles, boats, camels and horses, the whole journey there and back occupying two years. The ambition of Florence to become the dominant city of Tuscany with a ' window ' on the sea involved it in conflicts with Pisa. The Arno afforded a way, but only for boats, up to Florence, it provided ample water to turn mills in the town throughout the year, and although it is suggested that, owing to the effect of then existing forests, the Arno had a greater volume of water in the Middle Ages than now, it could not be canalized so as to admit ships up to Florence.[1] Hence the struggle with Pisa was imperative if Florence was to extend its foreign commerce, and its success in controlling the seaport enabled Florence to build up a mercantile marine which traded alike in the Levant, and with the Channel ports of London, Bruges and Antwerp.

Lombardy and Piedmont

The economic development of Lombardy and Piedmont was fostered by the regulation of its watercourses. The measures of water control which had been effected by the Romans were neglected after the collapse of the empire, and the north Italian plain suffered in consequence from the abundance of water brought down by the Alpine tributaries of the Po, which inundated widely the valleys and plains. Thus, Lombardy is described in the tenth century as given over largely to forest, marsh and arid waste ; neither rice nor the mulberry tree was then cultivated ; and the country yielded little else of use to its inhabitants but cereals and flax and water meadow.[2] From the twelfth century onwards, however, the activities of monasteries and cities were directed to the regularization of the waterways with a view to reclaiming land for cultivation and in a lesser degree to using them for navigation. The river Po, with its enormous volume of water, proved not too serviceable for either purpose : its valley lay too low to allow the run-off of water for irrigation ; whilst despite its gentle gradient and sluggish flow, it was difficult for navigation owing to its numerous meanders and complicated channels, which spread over a wide flood plain. Nevertheless, it was a frequented way for ships and boats. Again, the right-bank tributaries of the Po, which came down from the Apennines, were of small service to irrigation, since they lacked water in summer, just when it was most required. On the other hand, the Alpine tributaries of the Po, although they were too swift for boats, were well adaptable to irrigation : not only, since they were snow-fed, did they flow abundantly in summer, but also, since their valleys stood high and were steeply graded, water could easily be led off to areas at a lower elevation. Thus both in Piedmont and in Lombardy west of the Adda, many irrigation works were carried out.

[1] Cp. Renard, *Histoire du Travail à Florence*, II, 331–4. The river in summer has to-day only a small flow of water in a large bed of sand and stone.

[2] Cp. Baird Smith, *Italian Irrigation*, I, 197.

Navigation

In the art of navigation the Mediterranean cities made marked advances during the later Middle Ages. Ships were built, especially at Venice and Genoa, which were capacious enough for the transport of bulk commodities, and of horses and men, while others, the galleys, driven by oars and a single sail, were of a smaller and lighter type designed for speed. The rudder was a medieval invention, whilst the compass, which seems to have originated among the Arabs of the Indian Ocean, was in use in the Mediterranean during the twelfth century. Moreover, a notable service to navigation was provided, from the end of the thirteenth century onwards, by the preparation of scientific sea charts or portolans, which were based on the observation and experience of seamen. The oldest extant sea chart is that of Pietro Visconte dated 1311, but it is known that Louis IX of France had charts aboard when he set sail from Aigues-Mortes for his Crusade in 1270.[1] The portolans originated among the maritime towns of Italy and Catalonia, and are drawn most usually on a scale of 1 : 6,000,000. They usually exaggerate the size of islands, bays and headlands, give the names of coastal settlements, mark shallows and indicate in red those ports where water and victuals could be got. Notwithstanding these aids to navigation, ships continued to hug the coasts and to break their voyages by calling at convenient ports situated on islands or on the mainland. The continual struggles between the maritime powers for the possession of the islands of the Mediterranean are an eloquent commentary on their usefulness, since they offered ports of refuge, naval bases, centres of information of interest to merchants and pilots, emporia for varied commodities and supplies of fresh water, wine and food. The Strait of Messina was a busy thoroughfare for vessels bound for the Levant from Marseilles, Genoa, Pisa and Amalfi : by this route the voyage was both shorter and safer than by the southern route around Sicily. The islands of Crete, Rhodes and Cyprus marked stages on the remainder of the journey : from Cyprus ships made for the many Syrian ports. It should be noted, too, that vessels sailed in organized fleets in order to defend themselves from piracy or from their enemies, since the sea, like frontier regions on land, was exposed to lawlessness at all times. Moreover, in winter, the period of winds and storms, sailings were almost entirely suspended.

The types of ship employed and the varied voyages made

[1] Nordenskiöld, *Periplus*, trans. Bather, p. 46 ; Stevenson, E. L., *Portolan Charts*, p. 2.

may be illustrated from the history of Genoa and Venice, which were easily the greatest sea-states in the last years of the Middle Ages. Three classes of ships were built at Genoa: the sailing ship proper, the galley, which was propelled by oars and auxiliary sails, and an intermediate type of ship, which had not only banks of oars but also a full set of sails on two masts.[1] This last type of ship was specially used for the transport of horses, bulk goods and food supplies, e.g., of the Crusaders. The greater part of Genoese commerce until *c.* 1300, was conducted by means of the sailing ship; the galley, which was swifter, less costly, easier to defend and smaller in cargo capacity, was used at first in local waters, but after *c.* 1300 it was sent to Flanders and to the Levant. A sailing ship of 600 tons is known to have been made at Genoa, but the largest ships were usually about 480 tons: these figures may be compared with those of Dutch and English merchantmen engaged in the trans-Atlantic passage in the seventeenth century, which were between 600 and 800 tons. Some four main voyages from Genoa may be noted: the first was a coastwise sailing between Barcelona and Sicily; the second was made to the Balearic islands, Ceuta, Bugia and Tunis; the third was bound for the Levant and Black Sea; and the last for the Channel ports. The fleets which set out for Tunis and the Levant left Genoa in spring, so that they could return in the autumn; alternatively they left in autumn and wintered abroad. At Venice in the fifteenth century two main types of ship were employed. The galleys, built by the state, were 'long' ships, and served both as warships and for the carriage of valuable cargoes of small bulk, above all spices. These ships undertook regular voyages to the Levant (e.g., Alexandria and Beirut), to Aigues-Mortes and the other ports of the Gulf of Lion, to the Barbary coast and finally to the English Channel, calling at Lisbon, London, Bruges and Antwerp. In contrast to the galleys were those privately built 'round' ships, which were intended to carry heavy cargoes, of salt, grain, wine and cotton. They carried cotton and alum from Syria; wine from Crete to England; slaves and grain from the Black Sea; and grain, oil and salt generally throughout the Mediterranean. Important developments in the rigging and arming of the round ship—it was provided with three masts and full rigging, was increased in size and armed with guns and muskets—made it safer, more manageable and superior for mercantile purposes to the galley.[2]

[1] Byrne, *Genoese Shipping*, p. 5.
[2] Lane, 'Venetian Shipping during the Commercial Revolution', *A.H.R.*, Jan. 1933.

At the end of the fifteenth century round ships usually of some 600, and even up to 2,400, tons were built at Venice and Ragusa, and galleys were less used. It is significant that at the very time when Venetian maritime prosperity was being utterly undermined the Republic was building its greatest ships; nevertheless, even its shipbuilding was threatened by the shortage of suitable and accessible supplies of Mediterranean timber.

CHAPTER XVI

THE BALTIC AND NORTH SEAS IN THE MIDDLE AGES

THE North Sea and, more particularly, the Baltic entered belatedly into the cultural and commercial life of Europe, since alike they lay aloof from the Mediterranean and its borderlands in which Graeco–Roman civilization had its base. It is significant that the Baltic Sea and Scandinavia were little known to Roman geographers, but although they lay entirely beyond the Roman frontier it must not be inferred that they lay outside the sphere of the Roman soldier and trader.

Actually Roman coins are found as far east as the Niemen and as far north as southern Sweden. Scandinavia was usually described as a group of islands, and even Ptolemy mapped it as a single large island. The frontier of Gaul stopped at the Old Rhine channel, and military excursions beyond it were confined to Westphalia; moreover, although Baltic amber reached Italy it followed a trans-continental route by way of the Vistula valley, and the Moravian Gate. The tidal North Sea was, of course, navigated by the Romans, but mainly at the Channel narrows: between the ports of the Lianne estuary at and near Boulogne, and London, Colchester, Richborough, Reculver and other south-east coast ports. There was contact between Britain and the Rhine ports of Leyden and Fectio, near Utrecht, but the Romans were somewhat loath to face the North Sea, which was uninviting by reason of its tides, storms, winds and Saxon pirates. It was considered a bold venture on the part of Drusus when in 9 B.C., having sailed from the Rhine into what is now the Zuider Zee, he passed along the Frisian coast to the mouth of the Elbe. But if the North Sea had political and even commercial importance to the Romans, intercourse with the Baltic and its coastlands was essentially a medieval development. It was only in the eleventh century that Adam of Bremen in his writings gives the Baltic its present name, demonstrates the peninsular character of Scandinavia, the rough shape and position of the sea and the nature of its maritime entries.

The Physical Conditions of Navigation and Commerce

It is important to envisage the physical conditions of the northern seas and their borderlands in relation to the culture of its population in the early Middle Ages. Physically the coastlands are essentially unchanged to-day, except that in Flanders old arms of the sea have been sanded up, whilst in the Baltic some harbours have shallowed, and spits of sand (nehrungen) have formed enclosing lagoons at the mouths of certain south Baltic rivers. Climate, although it has not drastically changed, certainly betrayed in the thirteenth and fourteenth centuries extreme conditions: severe winters which occasionally caused the freezing over of the Sound and the Belts, and stormy conditions which caused inundations in the Low Countries. But if the physical environment of northern Europe was much as it is to-day, the means of navigation were very rudimentary, and for this reason the geographical features of the coasts and of the sea, as aids or obstacles to shipping, had in the Middle Ages their own particular value.

The ships first used by the Frisians and the Vikings in the Baltic and North Seas did not differ markedly in type from those revealed in Stone Age cliff and cave drawings in southern Sweden. They were long, narrow, shallow-draught vessels, made of oak, steered by a rudder and driven by oars and a single sail. Seagoing vessels were about 100 feet long and had from twenty to thirty oarsmen each side. The Frisians made advances in shipbuilding by constructing larger ships with cargo capacity, which proved more seaworthy. Mariners found their way by the sun and the Pole star, whilst the shallowness of the North and Baltic Seas enabled them to take soundings easily. The compass in its practical and completed form, which was commonly used in the Mediterranean in the fourteenth century, was introduced into the north only in the following century; nevertheless, already in the twelfth century the principle of the compass was understood in the north and to some extent used on longer voyages, e.g., from England to Iceland.[1] Nor had the northern seas until the sixteenth century the advantage of charts, although pilot books giving sailing directions survive from the fifteenth century. Frisians and Vikings tended to move coastwise as far as possible, although it is well known how the Vikings ventured across the open sea to Iceland, Greenland and even

[1] A needle, magnetized by rubbing it with a lodestone, was mounted on a straw and floated on the water; by this means, when the Pilot Star was obscured from view, the north could be found.

North America. Outstanding coastal features—headlands, reefs and rocks—were useful as guides; favourable winds had to be awaited; sheltered bays, estuaries or lagoons afforded roadsteads or harbours of refuge; whilst islands, if conveniently situated, had a distinct value which in steamship days they have largely lost, since they helped both to mark out and to shorten sailing routes. Finally, mariners made use of surface currents, in particular, the anti-clockwise current which swings around the shores of the Baltic. In view of all this, it is easy to see why the sea gateways into the Baltic were little used before developments had taken place in the construction of sailing ships. Moreover, the unstable political, and backward social, conditions of the Baltic–Scandinavian countries scarcely favoured at first the growth of trade intercourse. Nor is it surprising that maritime relations by way of the difficult Scaw passage mark the second, and not the first, stage in the commerce between the North and Baltic seas. This commerce began in fact by land, by way of the short 'land bridge' at the base of the Danish peninsula.

The Baltic offered many facilities to medieval navigators which were lacking in the outer seas. An inland sea, free from tidal movements, it contained particularly in the west many deep bays and islands in close proximity. Moreover, its smallness and narrowness reduced sea passages, for it is only an enlarged Adriatic. The southern coastlands of the Baltic do, however, differ considerably in the possibilities which they afford for harbourage. East of the Oder estuary are stretches of coast in Pomerania, Samland and Kurland where low morainic hills front the sea. The coast has long been eroded here into a smooth, unindented line; no large rivers break through the cliffs and offer entries from the sea, whilst off-shore sand-dunes add to the inhospitable character of this coast. At the mouths of the great rivers, e.g., the Vistula and Niemen, which divide off the coasts of Pomerania, Samland and Kurland, sand spits enclosing lagoons gradually formed, since in the absence of tides alluvium carried down by the rivers was able to accumulate near their mouths. In the shelter of these spits harbour sites were available which, as will be shown, were early utilized. Further, in the eastern Baltic deeply penetrating gulfs give access to harbours well inland, whilst the sunken coast of Finland with its festoon of islands was also accessible from the sea. West of the Oder estuary, on the other hand, the coast features contrast with those of Pomerania, and between Rostock and Jutland the natural conditions for maritime commerce were excellent, since vessels found there abundant shelter, and could navigate well inland. Off the east coast of Jutland the sea is shallow and sheltered from the west winds, and the Tertiary rock which forms this low coastland has offered resistance to marine erosion: in consequence, the coast has not been smoothed out as in Pomerania but is actually deeply embayed. Moreover, in the western part of the Baltic, islands are concentrated: Rügen stands at the mouth of the Oder; Fünen and Zealand lie between Jutland and Sweden; and the islands of Bornholm and Gothland are so situated in relation to neighbouring coasts as to form useful maritime stations or trade centres. Again, the western coastlands of the Baltic had a signal advantage in their position, since they stood within short distance of the Rhineland and the Low Countries. They stood, that is to say, close to lands which had either been long developed or were about to become great centres of industry and trade. In short, in this small western sub-sector of the Baltic, between Jutland and the Oder, localized maritime life could develop between lands separated from each other by only short sea passages. There, in fact, lay the Aegean of the Baltic: and as the Aegean formed an early centre of Mediterranean civilization and commerce which had spread from the neighbouring lands of Egypt, Phoenicia and Crete, so in the western Baltic, maritime activity began in close relation—by land across Holstein—with the highly civilized and commercial Rhinelands.

The Baltic was approached from the North Sea by land routes across Schleswig and Holstein and also by three sea gates. The land routes were at first the more important. The first used of these was actually a short portage from the Eider river to the town of Schleswig which stood at the head of a long creek. Later, in the twelfth century, the chief land route ran from the Elbe to the Trave, from Hamburg to Lübeck, which became dominant cities of the Hanseatic League. This route was supplemented by the construction during the years 1390–8 of the Streknitz canal, between the Elbe above Hamburg and the Trave above Lübeck (Fig. 47). The sea entries to the Baltic consisted of three belts or sounds which were reached from the broad, tidal waters of the Skaggerak and Kattegat. Each of these sounds, which were politically controlled by Denmark, had its peculiar characteristics affecting navigation. They all had more than adequate depth of water for medieval shipping, and it is only to-day and by the biggest draught vessels that the shallowest of them, the Sound, would be avoided.[1] The most westerly

[1] The shallowest part of the channel through the Sound is the Drogden shallows which are only 23 feet deep.

channel, the Little Belt, owing to its position was better suited to local traffic than to ships making for Lübeck and eastwards thereof. The Great Belt presented certain difficulties: its entrance from the north was dangerous for small sailing ships because of its shoals; further, the channel from the Skaw into, and through, the Great Belt involved a zigzag course and constant changes of helm; and except for Aalborg, harbourage on the east Jutland coast was lacking for larger ships. The Sound,

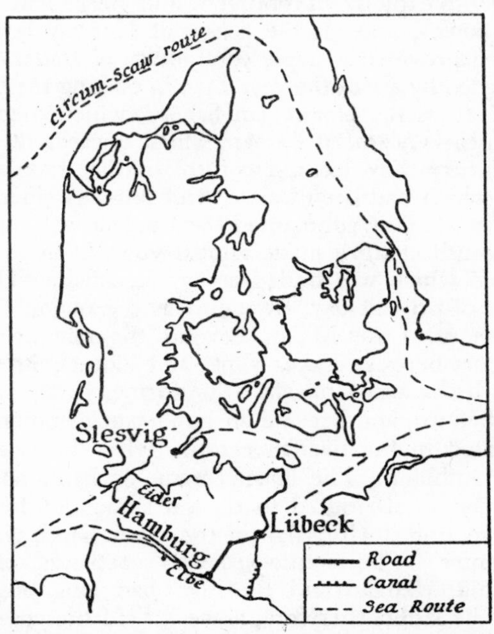

FIG. 47.—Medieval Routes between the North and Baltic Seas (after Reumert)
Note the striking positions occupied by Hamburg and Lübeck in relation to road and canal routes across the isthmus

on the other hand, presented distinct advantages which explain why it was marked out in the Middle Ages, as to-day, as the most favoured route. A straight SSE. course could be set from the Skaw and be pursued right through the Sound; there were many good harbours especially on the Scanian coast; and finally, the great importance of the herring fishery of the Sound stimulated the development of its commerce and its ports. Moreover, the Sound involved the shortest sailing for vessels bound for the ports eastwards of the Trave. From its outlet routes diverged to Lübeck at the head of its broad bay; to Stettin, in the lee of Rügen island; to Visby, the great port and mart in the island of Gothland, and thence to the more distant south Baltic ports.

The northern coastlands of the Baltic and the North Seas were drawn to some extent into the commerce of those seas. Both Norway and Sweden, which were bound politically to Denmark between 1397 and 1526, were relatively undeveloped and scantily populated countries, which the German merchants attempted commercially to exploit. Trondhjem and Bergen were the chief Norwegian towns, and off the coasts of Norway lay the shoals of cod which provided a staple commodity of trade. The Hansards succeeded by about the year 1410 in ousting the Norwegians and English from the Norwegian fishery, which they then controlled from their *kontor* at Bergen, whilst towards the end of the fifteenth century they secured control of the trade and fishing of Iceland, which had been united with Norway since 1262. In this field of trade they supplanted the English who had throughout the fifteenth century made annual voyages in the spring in search of cod which was traded as dry stockfish. The heart of medieval, as of present-day, Sweden was the region around, and to the south of, Lake Mälar, beyond the marshy depression which stretches between Lakes Vaner and Vätter; its two earliest towns were Birka and Uppsala. The former occupied an island site in Björköfiord, and became an important commercial centre, which declined in the twelfth century with the rise of Visby, in near-by Gothland. The Frisian name of Birka suggests that its origin may be attributed to the settlement of Frisians who came there to trade. Uppsala, on the other hand, was a pagan religious centre. The south-western coastlands of Sweden, namely Scania, Halland and Blekinge, had long been held by Denmark; the latter, therefore, since it held the coasts on both sides of the Sound was able effectively to control it.

The Baltic Sea, thanks to the harbourage which it provided and to its proximity to the North Sea coastlands, had, therefore, good commercial potentialities. Two other geographical advantages which it possessed should also be noted. The first was its fish resources, the second, the nature of, and the communications with, its hinterland. The presence of the herring shoals in the Sound off the coast of Scania is attested about the year A.D. 1060 by Adam of Bremen. Herrings were so numerous in autumn, he records, that nets were not necessary and they could be taken by hand. They formed, therefore, a real asset to Baltic merchants, until, as we shall see,[1] they ceased about the

[1] *Infra*, pp. 345–6.

year 1425 to frequent the Sound. Second, the Baltic, in contrast to the Mediterranean, was connected by long, navigable river-ways with an extensive hinterland ; not only was the northern plain of central Europe thus linked with the sea, but so also were the cities which lay along, and even within, the highland belt to the south. Moreover, some of these rivers, notably the Vistula, the Dwina, the Oder, the Elbe and the Rhine served as part of trans-continental routes which terminated on the shores of the Black and Mediterranean seas. Some of the Baltic rivers, notably the Vistula and the Oder, had provided valley routes since prehistoric times along which amber found in Samland (east Prussia) was carried southwards towards the Black Sea and the delta of the Po. Moreover, many of the Alpine passes, especially the Brenner and the St. Gotthard, carried medieval roads to the south. The ports of the North Sea and the Baltic were thus related to a widely flung hinterland from which was derived not only the products of the north European plain, but also Mediterranean products, and oriental commodities which were imported into the Mediterranean by way of Constantinople and later by the cities of northern Italy.

The Frisians and Vikings

The first stage in the opening up of the Baltic to trade was marked by the activities of the Frisians between the years A.D. 500 and 800. This German tribe was established in the islands and marshes of the coastland between the Rhine and Elbe and had for its neighbours the Franks to the west and the Slavs to the east. Near by in Jutland the Danes occupied the peninsula down to the Eider river and a belt of forest in Holstein which has since degraded into the heathland of the Sigeberger Heide. It was the achievement of the Frisians to establish trade relations not only within the North Sea—or the 'Frisian Sea' as it was then called—but also between that sea and the marginal lands of the western Baltic. The essential link in this trade was the land bridge of southern Jutland. Small ships with single sails sailed up the Eider river, and thence a short road journey led to Schleswig, which became an entrepôt for the distribution of the commodities of the two seas. The chief Frisian port was Dorestadt on the Waal channel of the Rhine, and from it were carried the manufactured goods—wine, metal ware, textiles, &c. —of the Moselle, the Rhinelands and the Frankish Low Countries. The Frisians were essentially intermediaries between the economically developed lands west of the Rhine and the backward, non-Romanized lands of the western Baltic. Frisians traded with the Swedes at Birka and also with the Slav stations of the southern Baltic: e.g., Old Lübeck on the Trave, with Jumna on either Wollin or Usedom island at the Oder mouth and with the town which preceded Danzig on the Vistula. The Baltic Sea presented one real obstacle to trade in that piracy formed a staple (and almost respectable) occupation of its bordering peoples. Of these the Vikings or Northmen, a term which includes Danes, Swedes and Norwegians, became most active in the ninth century, and exerted a powerful stimulus to the development of Baltic trade. Historians now emphasize the important part played by the Vikings, rovers and raiders though they were, in the revival of commerce in Europe. One aspect of this trade revival was the opening up of a trade route across Russia at a time when, owing to the advance of the Arabs, the Mediterranean Sea had almost ceased to act as a channel of trade. This route began by way of the Gulf of Finland to the city of Novgorod on Lake Ilmen, and eventually reached the Black Sea by way of the Dnieper and the Caspian by way of the Volga. Arab coins, minted in the eighth and ninth centuries at Samarcand and Baghdad, are found widely throughout the Baltic coastlands and testify to this trade intercourse. This is true particularly of the neighbourhood of Birka in south Sweden, and also of the island of Gothland which supplanted it as a convenient centre for Baltic trade. Similarly, the voyages made by the Vikings to Britain, Ireland, France, Iceland and elsewhere led to settlements and conquests which were destined to foster maritime trade.

The Southern Netherlands

'Flanders,' wrote Michelet, 'is the work of Man in despite of Nature.' Certainly physical forces played havoc with the coastlands of Flanders which were rendered serviceable as a stage for human activities only by strenuous and well-directed effort. It is true that the low, marshy maritime plain of Flanders was partially occupied by settlers both in prehistoric and Roman times, but the artefacts of these periods are found in a stratum of peat some two or three yards below the present surface. It appears that sands and clays of marine origin have been deposited over the Roman occupation level; in fact, a process, long and slowly operating, culminated, probably in the early fifth century A.D., in the submergence of maritime Flanders by the sea.[1] Hence the maritime plain was avoided by Frankish immigrants,

[1] See Des Marez, *Le Problème de la Colonisation Franque . . . en Belgique*, p. 61. Evidence of this late or post-Roman submergence is also forthcoming in parts of the south-eastern coastlands of England.

who moved and established themselves in interior Flanders to the south within the basins of the rivers which cut through the higher plateau districts of Brabant, Hainaut and Picardy, to the north of the Carbonnière Forest (Fig. 12). Maritime Flanders only slowly escaped from the domination of the sea. Not until the seventh century do future urban settlements, such as Bruges and St. Omer, appear to have been made on the southern margin of this belt. In the ninth century the sea definitely abandoned the plain : a line of sand-dunes was built up and behind this stretched an alluvial plain just below high-water mark, which by endiking could be reclaimed from the sea ; whilst the coastline itself was deeply indented by the estuaries of the rivers Aa, Yser, Zwin, &c., which at high tide became arms of the sea. The sea, though shallow towards the coast, was amply deep enough for medieval shipping, but silt was carried by marine currents into the sheltered bays and creeks. Unfortunately, the rivers were not powerful enough to scour away these deposits, which thus accumulated and served, towards the end of the Middle Ages, to obstruct the passage of ships to inland ports.

In southern Flanders to the south of the Carbonnière Forest, on the good soils which had already been worked under the Roman Empire, large feudal estates were created on the Roman pattern around the nucleated settlements founded by Frankish immigrants. To the north of the forest, except for the plains of the Scheldt and Lys, extended the 'terres incultes' of maritime Flanders, of the Campine sands and of North Brabant. These lands, because of their physical condition, contrasted markedly with the productive, light soils on the somewhat higher country to the south : they consisted of alluvium, heather moor and marsh. Lay and monastic lords had their estates mainly in the more Romanized south beyond the forest, and the Counts of Flanders themselves, who held the bulk of their lands on the Scheldt and its tributaries, resided until the late eleventh century chiefly at Lille, Arras and Douai. In the poorer lands to the north of the forest the typical settlement of the Frankish immigrants was the scattered hamlet, and the land was held by peasant freeholders in small holdings, as contrasted with the nucleated villages and large estates worked by serf labour to the south. The withdrawal of the sea stimulated remarkable activity in the maritime plain. Land which had sufficiently recovered from the sea to bear rich pasture grasses (schorres) was utilized for sheep grazing, whilst the practice of reclamation by building dams and cutting ditches was adopted with vigour by the counts, by monastic houses and by small freeholders. The result was the creation of ' polders ' or cultivable fields, and since the soils were light in texture and rich in carbonate of lime, they repaid in their productivity the capital outlay of reclamation. Even the vine was cultivated ; there was ample pasturage for sheep and cattle ; whilst salt was obtained from the marshes. Immigrants from southern Flanders settled as freeholders in the newly developing lands, and associations, known later as wateringues, were formed among the inhabitants of the polder lands with a view to regularizing drainage works.

It is clear, therefore, that during the tenth, eleventh and twelfth centuries, the agriculture of maritime Flanders rapidly advanced, many new villages and parishes were created, and population increased beyond the means of subsistence, so that emigrants left in order to settle in Britain and among the marshes and heaths of Holland, the lower Weser and the Elbe. More important still than this development was the rise of the industrial and commercial cities of Flanders. Its rivers, it is said, made Flanders. Endowed with a climate which tended to be too humid and with soils that tended to be either too sandy or too compact, devoid of mountain obstacles and favoured by numerous long navigable rivers, the country enjoyed unrivalled natural facilities for movement. Its rivers—the Aa, Yser, Lys, Scheldt, Dendre and Senne—flow in a general north-easterly or north-westerly direction, and were navigable far inland throughout the year—an invaluable asset at a time when road transport was difficult and costly. The chief drawback to these rivers were the floods which occurred, especially during the autumn, in their middle and lower courses, since there the gradient is very slight, whereas in their upper courses it is steep : hence, after long spells of rain, flooding lower down was inevitable, but this danger was met to some extent by the use of river gates and relief channels. Further, the estuaries of the rivers were in the tenth century long arms of the sea which reached well inland. Thus the estuary of the river Aa penetrated inland to Bergues ; that of the Yser to Dixmude ; St. Omer stood near the head of a creek ; whilst the Zwin, to become the most important of these creeks, reached inland to a little below Bruges. The rivers of Flanders, therefore, provided ideal medieval port sites : that is they stood well inland and were approachable by sea-going vessels, whilst boats could navigate far inland. The natural conditions thus favoured the development of trading cities, and already during the reign of Charles the Great, under the influence of stable political conditions, the manufacture of, and trade in, woollen textiles foreshadowed in the Low Countries their later importance. With the creation of the Empire of Charles the Great and its extension to the Elbe, the geographical position of the Low Countries was relatively changed and became highly favourable to trade. The lands about the lower Rhine, Meuse and Scheldt now occupied not a terminal or frontier position, as they had done under the Roman Empire, but a central position within the Carolingian Empire. Further, the greater part of the Emperor's estates lay between the Rhine, the Moselle and the Meuse, and the court, which resided principally at Aachen, provided a market, as also did the many bishopric and monastic centres which had developed in the Low Countries. The rivers Rhine, Moselle, Meuse and Scheldt were navigated, and the old Roman road from the archbishopric see at Cologne, thence to Aachen, Maestricht, Tongres and eventually to Boulogne, was also utilized. The plains of the Scheldt basin and along the Flanders' coast were well suited to sheep-rearing, and the old Gallo-Roman technique of the woollen industry survived. Hence, already in the early ninth century the so-called 'Frisian' cloth was made there in country farms, and marketed by sea, river and road, to England, Denmark and generally within the Carolingian Empire. The chief seaports at this time were Utrecht on the Old Rhine channel, Dorestat on the Waal Rhine to the south-west, and Quentovic, on the Channel, now represented by Etaples, at the estuary of the River Canche: all were destroyed by the invading Northmen by A.D. 857. Wine was carried down the Rhine and Moselle where monasteries of northern Flanders owned vineyards. The use of the excellent river-ways, which afforded deep southward penetration into the empire, fostered the development of certain towns as river stations and mercantile resorts: notably Valenciennes on the Scheldt and Maestricht on the Meuse at the crossing of the Roman east-west road from Cologne to Boulogne.

The precocious economic development of the Low Countries was arrested by the incursions of the Northmen and the collapse of Carolingian power. Its rivers, which facilitated trade, equally facilitated the ingress of the Northmen, who during the ninth century destroyed towns and carried their devastations southwards even into Artois and Picardy. The economic prosperity of the Low Countries, however, not only revived but advanced greatly. The revival was marked by the creation of towns which flourished to a remarkable degree. The germ or nucleus of the new industrial and trading cities was the stronghold built by monks, by lay-lords and by bishops. These walled settlements depended on agriculture and offered a refuge to the rural population in times of stress. Their situations, selected with an eye to topography, stood often on river routes and crossings. The transformation of these essentially agricultural centres into cities resulted from the settlement of merchants and citizens, who came and established themselves, often outside the walls but under the protection which their proximity afforded. Where the former feudal, ecclesiastical or monastic stronghold enjoyed good facilities for communication, there, above all, did trade and industry thrive. It should be recalled that in what is now Belgium and Holland Roman cities were almost lacking, since these lands owing to their very ex-centric position in relation to the chief trade routes of the Roman world were left largely undeveloped. Of the few Roman towns in the north there were one or two small Rhine stations, e.g., Fectio and Leyden, and a few small administrative centres, namely Tournai, Cassel, Maestricht and Tongres, which lie well southwards of the maritime plain. The medieval cities of the Low Countries were thus essentially new creations. They sprang up first in Flanders, and then in the twelfth century in Brabant; whilst the county of Holland became urbanized gradually from the thirteenth century onwards. Nowhere in medieval Europe was there such a localization of industrial and trading cities as in the County of Flanders, which was bounded eastwards by the Scheldt; this river, the principal artery of the country, was tidal up to Ghent (Fig. 48). In the thirteenth century the urban population of Flanders and Brabant equalled in number the purely rural population, and these lands became in fact—as they are still to-day—the densest settled area in Europe. The suburb of merchants and artisans which arose outside the walls of monastic and feudal centres was gradually absorbed into the earlier settlement and included within a single line of wall. Moreover, it is significant of this urban development that under the stimulus of commerce the towns of Flanders between the years 1100 and 1350 were continually extending their walls.

The cities which flourished—e.g., Ghent, Bruges, Lille, Ypres, Brussels, Louvain, Malines and Valenciennes—as well as Meuse cities like Huy, Dinant and Liège—were new settlements which enjoyed the advantage of well-chosen sites. Some cities, like Bruges and St. Omer, stood at the head of tidal estuaries; others were stations on land routes, like Ypres and Arras which lay on the road between Flanders and Paris; others again controlled river crossings near the head of navigation for boats, e.g., Brussels and Louvain which stood respectively on the Senne and Dyle rivers across which the main road between Cologne and Bruges

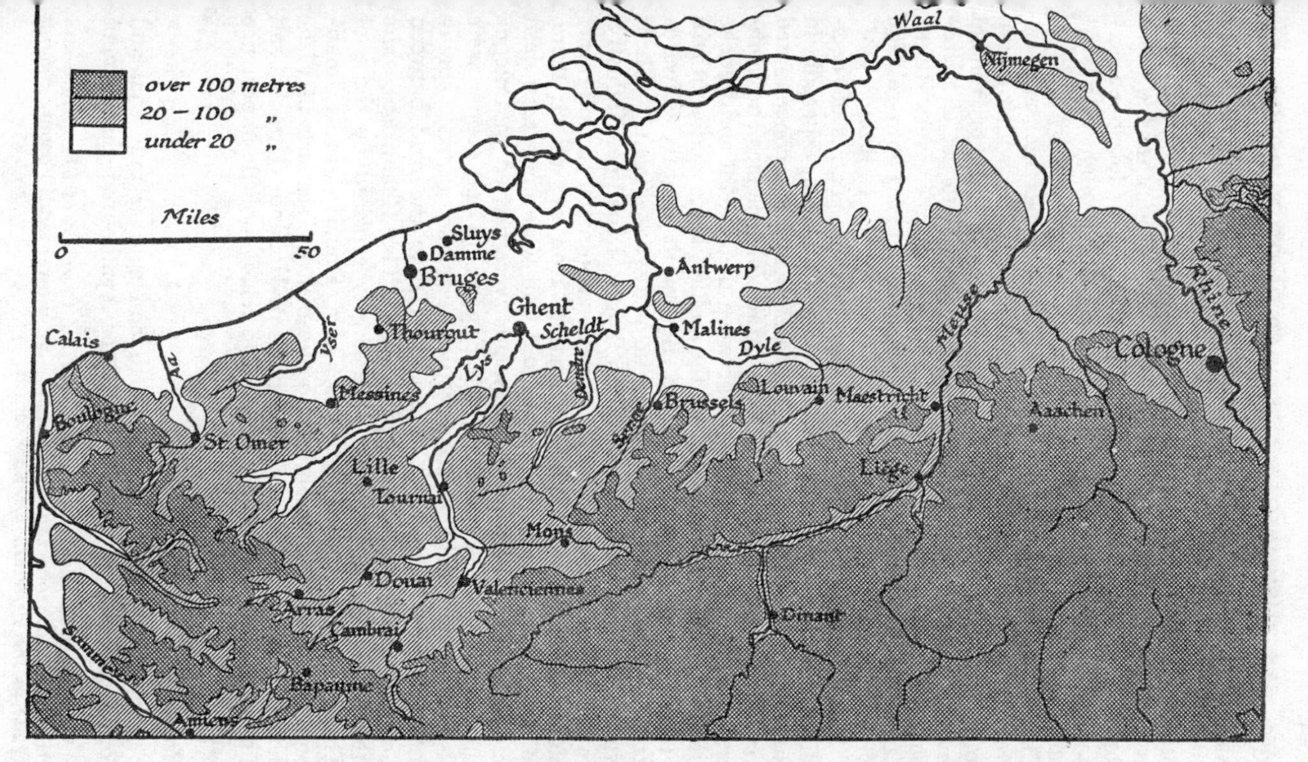

FIG. 48.—The Chief Towns of the southern Low Countries in the later Middle Ages

The present-day coastline is shown. Cp. Fig. 12, p. 69, for a reconstruction of the coastline in the fifth century

was carried. But apart from the local factor of their sites these cities as a whole owed much to their geographical position, which became as central under the conditions of medieval civilization as it had been remote in earlier times. England, after the Scandinavian settlement and the Norman conquest, developed economically; German colonization in the Baltic brought new lands into relation with the civilized west; at the near-by fairs of Champagne merchants from the Low Countries met and exchanged products with those from northern Italy; whilst at sea, until the rise of the sea-power of the Hanseatic cities, of Holland and of England, the Flemings had free scope to act as distributors throughout northern seas. Moreover, the rivers Rhine, Moselle and Scheldt brought the Low Countries into relation with southern Germany, Burgundy and the Paris Basin.

The towns of Flanders and Brabant became centres of specialized industry. Flax was grown and linen woven, especially in the basin of the Scheldt. The woollen industry was concentrated mainly in the towns of the Scheldt up to Valenciennes and Cambrai and also in those which lay between the Scheldt and Canche rivers. Some wool came from the polder lands and southern Flanders, but increasingly from the ninth century onwards English wool, which was superior in quality, was used.[1] Ghent was the chief centre of the woollen, Ypres of the linen, industry. In the upper Meuse mineral exploitation and metal-working were highly developed at Huy and Dinant. Iron was mined there, in the Ardennes, but tin, copper and lead were imported: lead and copper from the Harz mountains were carried to Cologne and thence to the Meuse; whilst English tin and copper were also utilized. Brabant, an agricultural region at first, sprang into industrial importance when about 1150 the road between Cologne and Bruges was opened up. The Champagne fairs which declined about 1250 were largely replaced by those of Thourout, Messines, Lille, Ypres and Douai. Finally, maritime commerce was essentially localized in the seaports of Flanders, especially at Bruges; the ports of Holland—Utrecht, and Tiel and Dordrecht on the Waal—had relatively little importance prior to the fifteenth century.

Bruges

Bruges, the Venice of the north and a great industrial and commercial city in the Middle Ages, symbolized the changes

[1] The best English wool came from the marches of Shropshire and Hereford and from the Cotswolds; cp. Power and Postan, *English Trade in the Fifteenth Century*, ch. 2.

which occurred in the economic geography of the plain of Flanders. The waters of a small stream, called the Reye at Bruges, flowed eastwards from Dixmude via Oudenburg, and were canalized at Bruges to encircle the new burg which was built in the ninth century to replace an earlier burg and to give greater security against the depredations of the Northmen. At this time and until about A.D. 1100 the sea came right up to Bruges by way of the Zwin, a broad arm of the sea into which the Reye flowed and which already in the eighth century was being embanked to facilitate its use by shipping. The building of dikes along the Zwin increased, however, the deposition of marine silt in the channel, since the silt could not be spread broadly on either bank and the river flood was quite inadequate to scour the channel. In consequence, about A.D. 1200 the tide no longer reached Bruges, and the port of Damme, a few miles below Bruges, was created at a point to which sea-going vessels could safely come ; whilst a lock was built there and a canal constructed thence to Bruges. By this means and, later in 1402, by a new Bruges–Damme canal, masted vessels did actually reach Bruges even in the fifteenth century : of this there is both written and pictorial evidence, which shows additionally that many stone bridges crossed the canal and had wooden leaves or 'traps' which could be opened to admit the passage of masts. Unremitting efforts were made to keep the waterways deep and clear by dredging, embanking and by canalizing river water. In 1378 the project of cutting a canal from the Lys above Ghent to Bruges seemed likely to serve three useful purposes : to relieve the Lys from flooding, to bring water to scour the Zwin, and to bring trade to Bruges. The project, however, failed owing to the vigorous opposition of Ghent which feared, not without reason, that some of its trade would be diverted to Bruges. In the early thirteenth century the outport of Sluys (= 'sluice') was founded at the mouth of the Zwin : it became above all the water junction of sea-going vessels and of barges and lighters which plied up the Zwin to Damme and Bruges, and as its name implies lock gates were built there to hold up tidal water. Ships could carry their cargoes directly up to Bruges or Damme on the tide and by the use of lock gates sail back with return cargoes on the falling tide.

Under the stimulus of trade and industry Bruges grew to the size and status of a first-rate town : its population of about 50,000 in the thirteenth and fourteenth centuries exceeded that of contemporary London.[1] *Mercatores*, traders and artisans

[1] The population of London about 1400, as estimated from Poll Tax records, was between 30,000 and 40,000.

alike, first settled outside the ninth-century burg, in a suburb to the south-west; a Waterhall, a covered dock, was built in the town across the river Reye, from which navigable canals with quays radiated throughout the town, and a Waterhouse was built on the outskirts of the town which raised and distributed water collected from streams at St. Bavay. Below the town, marshes were reclaimed for the cultivation of fruit, including even the vine, and for sheep pasture, but as the town grew—in common with other Flemish cities—it became dependent on imported wine, corn and fruit. At first Bruges was a considerable ship-owning port, but in its greatest years, from *c.* 1250 to *c.* 1450, its shipping declined: it did not become, therefore, a maritime power like Venice, but the shipping of the whole of Europe frequented its ports, thus following along the sea-ways which it had opened up formerly by its own fleets. The chief industry of the town was the manufacture of woollen fabrics which it exchanged with merchants from foreign parts; it was also a great entrepôt of goods brought along the many routes which converged on the Low Countries: England sent wool and lead; Gascony—which was under English rule between 1154 and 1453—sent wine and salt; spices, dye-woods and rich silk and metal goods were brought by merchants from Venice and Genoa, at first overland, until in 1314 regular sea services were established; corn, metals, dried fish, timber, furs and honey were brought from the Baltic by the merchants of the Hanseatic cities; Burgundy and France sent wine, as also did Lorraine from the vineyards of the Rhine and the Moselle; Spain and Greece sent fruits. Bruges reached its zenith in the fourteenth and early fifteenth centuries. Despite continual foreign wars and internal commotions the trade of the town prospered and the chief cause of its decline during the fifteenth century was the silting up of the approaches to the Zwin, which made it difficult of entry by ships, whilst even lighters had difficulties in passing up to Damme and Bruges. After 1350 big Spanish *nefs* would not venture above Sluys; a century later Sluys was almost abandoned; and in 1503 the Portuguese with their bigger ships avoided it and sailed for Antwerp which had deep open water. Subsequent efforts by Bruges to recapture its former trade, which included a canal to Ostend and Nieuport and the preparation of a map which deliberately exaggerated the breadth of its waterways, proved unavailing. Physical circumstances were too strong. Flanders could henceforth boast only small seaports which are to-day artificially constructed; it had not the natural facilities for the ocean-going shipping which then began to pass along its coasts; and the Zwin, finally endiked in the eighteenth and nineteenth centuries, provides now sheep pasture where formerly it provided a sea-lane.

The Hanseatic League

In the thirteenth century the commerce of the northern seas fell largely into the control of the Hanseatic League, a loose confederation of German cities which was organized under the leadership of Lübeck. The League arose out of the association of separate German cities which had already developed spheres of trade activity but which felt the imperative need to safeguard by concerted action the routes of trade. The earliest trade centres of Germany lay in the Rhineland, which formed the axis of German political and economic life. Cologne, the chief sea-port of Germany, without any rival down-stream, already in the early eleventh century traded with England, whilst in the Baltic in the twelfth and early thirteenth centuries the foundation of German cities along the coast from Lübeck to Riga fostered trading interests. Moreover, already in the twelfth century German merchants established a colony at Visby in the Swedish island of Gothland, which was excellently situated to exploit the sea-routes which the Vikings had opened up to trade: in particular Visby sought trade in the eastern Baltic at Riga, and set up a depôt at the old-established city of Novgorod. Further, Lübeck and Hamburg, situated at either side of the narrow land bridge between the two seas, had trade ambitions, and their co-operation with a view to protecting their commercial interests marked the initial stage in the development of the League. Both cities had advantages in that they were early created 'imperial' or 'free' cities (1226 and 1232): that is, they were free to manage their own affairs without the interference of local lords. The League eventually came into being, with its centre at Lübeck, about 1260–5, and at one time or another its membership included nearly a hundred cities. A condition of membership prescribed that cities should be situated on the sea-coast, at the estuaries of rivers or on the banks of navigable streams. The rule was not, however, stringently applied; but it is suggestive of the importance of water transport in the Hanseatic world that inland towns without effective waterway facilities often cut canals or improved their rivers. Thus both Brunswick and Hanover canalized their rivers to the Weser at Bremen. For the purposes of administration the territories of the League were divided into four 'circles' or regions. The Wendish circle, with Lübeck as its capital, included Mecklenburg and Pomerania, together with

Hamburg and the Wend (i.e., formerly Slav) cities of the coast from Vismar to Stettin. The Saxon circle, with Brunswick at its head, included many rich towns like Goslar, Hanover, Magdeburg and Minden, as well as new 'colonial' towns farther east, namely Berlin, Brandenburg, Leipzig, Frankfurt-on-Oder and Breslau. Prussia and Livonia, together with the island of Gothland, formed the third circle, in which stood the towns of Visby and those along the Baltic from Elbing to Reval. Finally, the fourth and latest administrative division comprised the oldest German towns in the lower Rhinelands, Westphalia and the Netherlands: its chief city was Cologne; it stretched as far east as Emden, as far west as Middelburg and as far south as Wiesbaden (Fig. 49).

Within the territories occupied by Hanseatic cities commerce conducted along the sea, river and land routes had therefore a considerable range, between Russia and the Low Countries in the one direction and between northern and central Germany and the Baltic ports in the other. Their extensive foreign commerce, which formed the characteristic feature of their activities, was organized at a number of *kontors* (or depôts) established in foreign parts. The chief of these were Novgorod, London, Bruges and Bergen, together with a number of subsidiary depôts; e.g., in England at Boston, Lynn, Yarmouth and Hull. Each of these cities was accessible by water, the Hanse merchants had their own warehouses, halls and even docks, and to their *kontors* were brought the commodities of wide hinterlands. Bruges was a great market for manufactured goods—woollen and linen textiles, metal goods, wine, &c.—as well as English wool; London was above all a market for wool, together with lead and tin, and, in the fourteenth and fifteenth centuries, cloth. The products collected at Bergen comprised salt fish, fish and whale oils, timber and timber products; whilst Novgorod was important for its supplies of flax, furs, honey, wax and (when the routes from south Russia lay open) silks, cottons, pearls and spices from Constantinople. It must not, however, be implied that the Hansards enjoyed at any particular time, and certainly not continuously, a complete trade monopoly within the area of their cities. In the later fourteenth century the English became large exporters of their wool, much of which went to the English staple town of Calais. Again, both English and Dutch merchants from about 1350 sailed directly into the Baltic, establishing trading relations particularly with Danzig, which was a great collecting centre for corn, timber, wax, pitch and tar. Further, in Iceland the Norwegian and English fishermen and merchants held the

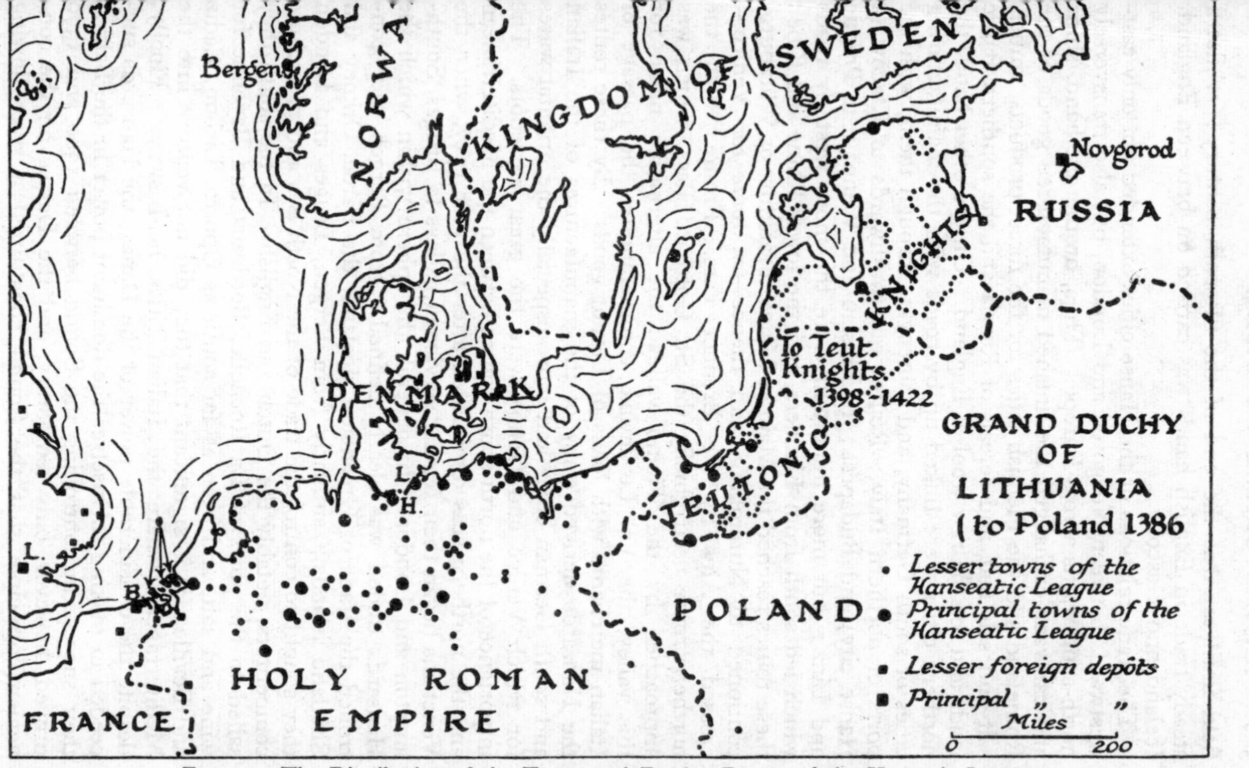

FIG. 49.—The Distribution of the Towns and Foreign Depôts of the Hanseatic League

Note the latitudinal character of the chief zone of Hanseatic activity. B is Bruges, L London which, together with Bergen and Novgorod, were the principal foreign depôts

field until towards the end of the fifteenth century; whilst a steady trade in English hands was carried on between England, Iceland and Gascony.

The trade relations of the Hanse cities extended not only east-westwards between Novgorod and London, but also transversely north-southwards across Europe. Thus, on the one hand, ships and caravans exchanged the finished manufactured goods of the Rhineland and the Flemish cities for the forest products, amber, salt and salt fish, and cereals of Russia and the southern Baltic lands and for the raw wool of England. On the other hand, the northern cities were linked up by roads with the manufacturing cities of south Germany, and moreover, through them, with the ports of northern Italy. Routes ran southwards to Cracow (a Hanse city) and Budapest; to Breslau and Vienna; to Prague and Linz; but more important were the more westerly roads which led south from Flanders, and the lower Rhine and Elbe: these routes reached the Main at Mainz, Frankfurt or Würzburg, continued to Nuremberg, and thence—*en route* for Venice—crossed the Alps by the Brenner Pass. From Milan the northern route used chiefly the St. Gotthard Pass, which was approached by the Ticino valley: the alternative name for this valley, the Val Levantina, commemorates the passage of Italian merchants with loads of Levant goods. By these routes the Hansards derived some of the manufactures of the Italian and south German cities and more especially the oriental wares for which Venice and Genoa were the great entrepôts. The importance of the north-south routes between the Mediterranean and the northern seas diminished after the year 1317, when the Venetians began their regular service of galleys to Bruges, Southampton and London. In general, the sphere within which the Hansards traded was clearly defined: from Bergen they controlled the trade of Greenland, Iceland, the Faroe, Orkney and Shetland islands; similarly from Bergen, Bruges and London they sought to control the trade of the North Sea and to exclude competitors, notably the Dutch and English. In the south they sailed to the ports of La Rochelle, Bordeaux and Bayonne for wine and salt, and even as far south as Oporto, Lisbon, Cadiz and Seville: it is significant that they did not venture into the Mediterranean where the Italian cities held sway. Finally, despite the considerable power of the Danes, the Hansards succeeded in making themselves the dominant power in the Baltic; their success in controlling the Sound between 1360 and 1370 proved, however, only temporary, and the Danes, on the convenient principle that the Sound constituted a river flowing through Danish territory, were able about the year 1430 to institute the payment of dues. The bulk of Baltic trade fell into the hands of the Hansards, although here again they were unable to exclude all competition : English, and more especially Dutch, increasingly sailed directly through the Sound *en route* for Baltic ports. After about 1350 English ships carried cloth to Danzig from which they brought back corn, timber, pitch and tar. The Hansards, especially Lübeck, monopolized the herring fishery of the Sound ; similarly, they had a large share in the fishery for cod, in the North Sea grounds, although in that ground the Dutch became successful rivals. The annual voyages of the Venetians to the English Channel and its ports deprived the Hansards of some of their distributing trade, and they tried to exclude the Venetian fleets from London and to restrict them to Southampton.

'The fate of Towns and Cities', wrote the English antiquarian Camden, 'is every jot as unstable as the state and happiness of Men': the history of the Hanseatic cities affords a commentary on this text. Not only has their importance as a whole completely changed, but so also has the relative importance of the individual cities. Lübeck, though challenged by Cologne, remained the first city of the League ; and Hamburg, so prominent to-day, claimed, and at best took, only third place. Within the known limits of the northern world the Baltic occupied a centrality, superior to that of the North Sea, and this fact is reflected in the somewhat greater importance of the Baltic ports. The Wend cities, in particular, such as Lübeck, Rostock and Colberg, have now only a local traffic (if any) where formerly they had real international significance. The small town of Visby in Gothland symbolizes to-day the rise and fall of the Hanseatic League: its medieval port is now covered by meadowland, and only ruined towers and fine old churches survive to recall the greatness which was cut short abruptly in the year 1361 by the assault of the Danes.

The commerce of the Hanse cities aptly illustrates what may be called 'the geographical theory of trade'. It has been already noted how the natural and manufactured products of different regions are somewhat sharply differentiated : the reflection, that is to say, of the way in which lands differently constituted in respect of climate, geology, soil, &c. have been variously adapted by man. Thus some regions were able to produce surpluses of foodstuffs, or mineral products, or manufactures or natural products, e.g., of the forest or of the sea. In this way certain regions were complementary in respect of the produce which they could interchange, and a basis was established—other conditions being favourable—for trade intercourse. Actually (despite the fact that they lay along the same belt of latitude and were not therefore too sharply distinguished in climate) the regions which were bound together by the trade of the Hanseatic League were to a very marked degree complementary. Moreover, they produced essential, not luxury, products. Thus the country west of the Rhine specialized in manufactured goods; woollen and linen textiles from the Flemish cities, and cloth from England, especially after about 1350; wine from the Rhine, Meuse and Moselle; iron and copper ware respectively from Liège and Dinant on the Meuse. It needed, on the other hand, both supplies of foodstuffs and of raw materials: the foodstuffs (rye and wheat, &c.) and flax could be supplied from the east Baltic plains via Danzig and Riga, whilst wool formed the chief export commodity of England. Again, to cite another instance, Norway welcomed, in exchange for its fish, furs and timber, the things which it could not produce, namely wheat and meal, salt, cloth, linen, flax and wine. In particular, it was difficult for climatic reasons to grow sufficient corn in Norway; as Edrisi records, the Norwegians harvested their grain still green and ripened it by the fire. Similarly, certain other commodities of considerable importance in the Middle Ages had limited areas of production. Thus honey [1] and wax—the one forming the common sweetening, above all in northern Europe, the other of service for light and for sealing documents—were forest products very abundant in Russia and the east Baltic (e.g., Lithuania); again, amber, which was made at Bruges into rosaries &c., was obtained on the coast of Samland in Livonia. Similarly, Germany possessed the chief supplies of silver in the Middle Ages; Swedish iron and copper were sought; and generally in naval stores—timber, pitch, sailcloth, hemp and rope—some of the Baltic countries and Norway had great local resources, which were completely lacking in some countries in which cities of the League stood, e.g., Holland. Finally, salt and fish, which had important places in the trade of the League, were localized products.

Salt has been probably at every stage of civilization a staple

[1] It is of interest that Herodotus, repeating what he had learnt from the Thracians, wrote of the Baltic countries as a region 'so densely filled by swarms of bees that it was impossible to penetrate'. Some sugar reached northern Europe from the Mediterranean where the Arabs had introduced its cultivation into Cyprus, Sicily and lower Egypt. Madeira became an important source of supply in the sixteenth century.

commodity of trade. In inland regions it is obtainable only where geographical conditions permit, but it was usually obtainable by evaporation of sea-water at the deltas or estuaries of rivers or along low marshy coasts. At all times an important article of human dietary, salt had an additional value in the Middle Ages as a preservative for fish. The early activities of Lübeck —even before A.D. 1200—were bound up in the exploitation of the salt deposits which occur in the rocks around Lüneburg and Halle. The salt was carried from these workings to the Trave and thence to Lübeck, where it served as a staple commodity of trade. Much of it was taken to the Sound where fishermen from Lübeck largely controlled the herring fishery. No less important as a localized area of salt production was the Bay of Bourgneuf in Brittany, where the town of Blaye was the chief centre of the trade, together with the islands of St. Martin and Oléron. The salt was prepared by evaporation, and was known (after the Bay of Bourgneuf) as 'Bay Salt'. Great fleets of Hanseatic or Dutch ships carried cargoes of salt direct to Bergen, to the Dutch fishing ports and generally throughout the Baltic. Salt was often carried as a convenient ballast cargo, and the exaction of part of the Sound dues in salt is suggestive of the value attached to this commodity. Lisbon, too, exported salt; and it was obtainable at some of the ports of south-eastern and north-eastern England.

In the Middle Ages, it has been suggested, the herring was 'a historical personage'. Certainly, the prescription of fish days by the Catholic Church and the lack of meat as a common foodstuff emphasized the importance of fish as an article of food and as a commodity of trade. It has already been noted how Lübeck with its salt resources early invaded the fishing grounds of the Sound where the herring shoaled every summer. Huts were built along the coasts of Scania and Schonen with the permission of the Danish kings; the herrings were fished by nets from flat-bottomed boats; and they were then transferred into large ships where they were salted. Nets and barrels were made on the coast, and foodstuffs were brought to support those engaged in these industries. Similarly, in Bergen the Hanseatic merchants supplanted the Norwegians and English in the fisheries off the Norwegian coast where cod was the chief fish caught. The supplies of salt fish—herring or 'stock-fish' (i.e., cod)—were traded not only in the Baltic and North Sea lands but in western France, Portugal and Spain. The years 1417 to 1425 witnessed the failure and disappearance of the summer herring shoals in the Sound: the herring, for reasons which have not yet been explained,[1] ceased to leave the North Sea for the Sound. But whatever the reason for this geographical change, it had certain marked effects, for what was a distinct loss to the Hanse cities and especially to Lübeck, was no less a signal gain to the Dutch.

In prosperity and power the Hanseatic League reached its zenith about the year 1400; despite continual political disturbances it prospered during the fifteenth century, and survived as a declining institution during the following century. The full story of its decline belongs to the historian, but two general points may be noted here. The discovery of America and the development of oceanic navigation altered adversely the relative position of the Baltic Sea in relation to the known world. Further, the national development of certain European countries, e.g., England and Sweden, induced a movement towards freedom from the commercial tutelage of the German cities. Finally, the decline of the Hanseatic League and the new orientation of world commerce are reflected in the rise of those lands about the Rhine delta which were to form later the Dutch Republic. Some of the towns of Holland were members, albeit humble ones, of the League, e.g., Amsterdam, but they had little importance at first as compared with the industrial cities of Flanders, the great towns of the Rhine between Cologne and Strasbourg, and the towns of Hamburg and Bremen. The process of endiking the maritime plains of the Netherlands, which had much suffered from marine inundation during the twelfth, thirteenth and fourteenth centuries, was a necessary prelude to the development of the Dutch lands. The failure of the herring fishery in the Sound gave a chance to the North Sea fishery which the Dutch were quick to exploit; the art of curing was learnt and applied; 'Bay Salt' was used for this purpose and also as an article of trade; and the port of Brille prospered. Similarly, the Dutch were to gain from the silting up of the channel to Bruges and its outports, since their coast offered in the Scheldt estuary an excellent deep water approach. In short, already in the heyday of the Hanseatic League the Dutch were building up a mercantile marine, and it is significant that the earliest records which were taken of the number of ships passing through the Sound show that Dutch shipping exceeded that of the League.[2]

[1] It is probable, as Professor Taylor suggests, that since Glacial Times the Baltic has become progressively fresher so that in the fifteenth century its waters became unsuitable for the spawning of the herring.

[2] That is, in the years 1497 and 1503. Moreover, between the years 1580–9, of an average of 4,892 vessels per year passing through the Sound, more than half were Dutch. Hill, *The Danish Sound Dues and the Commerce of the Sound*.

Moreover, as early as 1526 the Dutch had formed the idea (which, however, was not realized) of making Göteborg in south-western Sweden a great staple port, so that goods could be carried overland into the Baltic and the Sound dues could be evaded. In order to avoid payment of the toll dues they sought also the route along the coasts of Norway to the Arctic and White Sea ports of Russia.

CHAPTER XVII

WESTERN EUROPE DURING THE EARLY OCEANIC PHASE

DURING the sixteenth and seventeenth centuries the commercial and cultural relations of Europe became for the first time in history world-wide in extent. The Roman Empire and the medieval world had, it is true, by way of Egypt, Syria and Persia, established trade routes with the Far East—the land of tropical products and fine textile goods. During the period under review not only was a new sea route with the East brought into use, thanks to the discoveries of the Portuguese navigators, but further the discoveries of Columbus and the Cabots opened up parts of the American continent to European colonization, exploitation and trade. The Roman world had been focused on, and knit together by, the Mare Internum or Mediterranean Sea ; in the Middle Ages European commerce developed in the North and Baltic Seas new regions of activity which were bound up by land and sea routes with the centres of Mediterranean culture. In that age the flourishing cities of Venice, Alexandria, Constantinople, Bruges and Lübeck occupied sites which were strategically placed in relation to the contemporary routes of trade, whilst Egypt held pre-eminence as the best transit region for the Far Eastern trade. The discovery both of the new ocean route to the East and of the American continent and West Indian islands effected a re-orientation of European commerce and further, as a consequence, changed the geographical 'values' of European lands. The Baltic and the Mediterranean lost their former centrality and supremacy in European trade. In the new 'oceanic' world those states which had more westerly situations, with sea-boards fronting the Atlantic and the North Sea, enjoyed geographical advantages in relation to the sea routes to the Indies and the Americas.

It was a circumstance fortunate to some at least of these states that their new opportunities came at a time of political consolidation : certainly in Spain, Portugal and England the growth of royal power and national unity favoured economic advance. The seas which then became ex-centric and secluded, although they lost relative importance, nevertheless continued to play an active part in European commerce. The Mediterranean still distributed its own local products within and outside its own shores; whilst the Baltic continued to supply western Europe with essential raw materials, above all timber, with which to build its merchant marines. But Egypt and Alexandria declined in population and wealth, since not only were they outflanked by the new sea route to the east but also subjected to the misfortune of Turkish rule. Moreover, Venice ceased to rule in European commerce. In 1503 Lisbon received its first big cargo of eastern spices by way of the Cape, and Venice began to lose its entrepôt trade in these lucrative commodities; furthermore, her supply of accessible timber suitable for shipbuilding grew scarce—a scarcity which the whole Mediterranean region seems to have suffered in the course of the sixteenth century.[1] Thus although Venice long remained a vigorous maritime power and, in fact, built larger 'broad' ships in the sixteenth century than in her more flourishing days, she restricted her activities to the Mediterranean and even bought ships which had been built in Holland. The palm of Venice fell to those states of the west which had discovered the new routes and the New World, so that Lisbon, Seville and Cadiz, which had hitherto been merely ports of call for the Venetian galleys *en route* to Flanders, became entrepôt ports of international importance. Lisbon exploited the sea route to the east which her mariners had explored, notwithstanding the real difficulties which it presented. It was both long and slow; equatorial calms, storms around the Cape, the monsoons and Arab pirates demanded both courage and skill in navigation; the voyage to India occupied from seven to twelve months, and the journey there and back usually occupied some three years. Nevertheless, the oceanic route was utilized because it proved remunerative to do so, at first by the Portuguese alone and then later by their competitors the Dutch, the English and the French. Seville and its outport Cadiz, also exploited for a time Spanish conquests in the West Indian islands, Mexico and Peru. After 1545 Mexico and Peru sent large annual cargoes of silver, whilst the West Indian islands provided valuable sub-tropical commodities which could not be so successfully produced in the higher latitudes of Europe: above all sugar, rum, tobacco and cotton.

[1] Lane, 'Venetian Shipping during the Commercial Revolution', *A.H.R.*, XXXVIII, No. 2, 1931.

Spain and Portugal did not succeed in maintaining their initial advantage and in remaining ' the wagoners of the world ' which their position at the junction of Cape, Mediterranean and Atlantic routes seemed to indicate. The carrying and entrepôt trade of Europe passed to the Low Countries, the northern part of which became the republic of Holland, whilst the southern part passed from Spain to Austria in 1713. This latter region, it will be recalled, was a great workshop of the medieval world, with its industrial cities and its famous port and staple town of Bruges. Economic momentum, coupled with the fact that it remained well placed in the expanded modern world, made probable the maintenance of its medieval relative importance. Bruges, it is true, declined, since the new, large ocean-going vessels could not navigate its shallow channels, but during the first half of the sixteenth century Antwerp with ample, deep-water harbourage on the estuary of the Scheldt, usurped its commercial position. Ghent, which had long been famous for its cloth and linen industries, tried unsuccessfully to compete with Antwerp after 1550, when it gained direct access to the sea by opening up the Terneuzen channel. The wealthy and populous Low Countries, which included the present-day Belgium and Holland, formed Spanish possessions in the sixteenth century, and their revolt against Spain ruined Antwerp, since it suffered severely under the stress of war. The centre of international trade and finance was shifted north to Amsterdam, which was approached from the Zuider Zee, for it was only in the nineteenth century that a ship canal was cut to give a direct entry from the North Sea. The northern provinces of the Low Countries made good their independence of Spain, and established a republican state—the United Provinces of the Netherlands, which became known, after the chief of its seven provinces, as Holland.[1] On this basis the Dutch were able to build up and consolidate their maritime and commercial power; and during the seventeenth century they became the greatest, though not unchallenged, sea-state of Europe, whilst they excelled, too, in the practice of agriculture, in drainage technique, and in finance.

Spain

In the sixteenth century, thanks to the geographical discoveries, Spain became a land of great opportunities. In the past its prosperity had depended essentially on its well-favoured southern and eastern provinces and on its relations within the Mediterranean Sea. Linked to the rest of the Mediterranean world in the

[1] Cp. *supra*, Chapter XI.

days of Rome and of Moslem rule, it became in the south and east studded with wealthy and populous cities ; it had a good network of roads, it was productive alike of agricultural, mineral and industrial commodities, whilst the interior plateaux and steppe country supported horses and flocks of sheep which were famed for their wool. The expulsion of the Moors and Jews and the dynastic union of Castile and Aragon, all of which took place towards the close of the fifteenth century, brought to an end centuries of crusading wars and promised the benefits of united rule. The seaports of Spain looked out to both the Ocean and the inner sea: Barcelona faced towards Italy, in which Aragon had acquired both Sicily and Milan, whilst Ferrol and Corunna, and Seville and Cadiz were gates to the Atlantic and to imperialistic ambitions. The natural endowment of Spain, therefore, as Moslem industry had shown, was generous and varied. It could produce in the south and east much wheat, oil, silk, wine and fruit ; by means of irrigation many sub-tropical crops, like sugar, were cultivable ; the uplands yielded wool, which together with flax and silk, provided a basis for textile industry ; the country was noted for its wealth of metals, whilst in the mountains of the north and north-west timber was abundant. Moreover, under Moslem stimulus, Spain had developed numerous manufactures : silk and woollen fabrics, metal goods, leather, paper and steel. Finally, by their conquest of Mexico, Peru and the West Indian islands, the Spaniards won an Empire rich in precious metals and tropical products and secured a potential market for European manufactures. Thus sixteenth-century Spain was a favoured land : to what extent, however, did it exploit its new opportunities ?

Unfortunately Spain suffered from continental entanglements —not, as in the case of France, as a result of its peninsular character—but owing to the territorial acquisitions of its kings, who came to rule the Holy Roman Empire, the Low Countries, Franche-Comté and parts of Italy, in addition to lands oversea. The geographical diffuseness of the Habsburg dominions weakened Spain, since in order to establish the political cohesion of its far-flung possessions it needed to be predominant both by land and by sea, and this position, though continually sought, was not permanently won. The many wars fought in Europe wasted Spain of the treasure carried from Mexico and Peru ; moreover, it diverted the energies and wealth of Spain from the maintenance of sea-power on which rested the control of the most valuable of its imperial possessions, those in America and the Netherlands. In expelling the Moors and the Jews Spain deprived itself of its chief industrial and mercantile classes. Even so, Spain enjoyed for a time great prosperity. The city of Seville, which controlled the American trade, fostered many industries and grew in population to perhaps a quarter of a million. Ships from Antwerp, London, St. Malo, Nantes and La Rochelle called at Bilbao, Seville and other ports, whilst Barcelona had some share of the Mediterranean Levant trade. From its colonies in central America and the Caribbean Sea, Spain derived, in the later sixteenth century and onwards, not only silver and gold, but many tropical commodities. Sugar was brought from the Antilles islands, as also from the Canaries; dye-woods, hard woods, cochineal, indigo, cacao, vanilla, tobacco, emeralds, pearls, beaver and other skins—all these came, too, from the mainland or island territories of central America. Spain yielded up to trade, in addition to these colonial goods, its own varied products: leather from Cordova; cloth from Saragossa, Cuenca, Seville, Barcelona and Valencia; the wines of Malaga, Alicante and Xeres; the silk of Murcia, Valencia and Saragossa; paper and silk from Jaen; linen, silk and steel from Toledo; iron from the Biscayan ports; sugar, soap, olive oil, flax and wool. The merino fleeces of Spain were produced under the control of the powerful *Mesta* [1] organization, which united the sheep farmers of Spain: it enjoyed special privileges and organized the seasonal movement of sheep along specified 'sheep routes' from the summer pastures of Leon and Asturias in the north to the winter pastures of Estremadura and La Mancha in the south, a migration governed by the contrasting climatic conditions in the northern and southern parts of the Iberian plateau.

The city of Madrid and its fortunes provide some index of the greatness of Spain, and also of its subsequent decline. In origin a Moorish fortress, on the frontier zone of Andalos, Madrid owed its growth into a great town—as did Berlin—to political influences. It occupied a steeply-sided hill site, which was surrounded on two sides by the valley of the Manzares river. It had no river navigation, nor raw materials, and the near-by country was bare steppe; on the other hand, it had good water supplies and forest resources to the north-west. Its selection in the sixteenth century as a capital for united Spain gave recognition to its centrality of position. Its population, which stood at barely 25,000 in 1550, rose to 400,000 in the seventeenth century, but declined to some 150,000 by 1700.[2]

[1] Cp. Klein, *The Mesta*, passim. The sheep travelled enormous distances, which may help to explain why mutton was little eaten in Spain!

[2] Glunard and Monbeig, 'Madrid', *A. de G.*, Sept. 1932.

The prosperity achieved by Spain in the sixteenth century waned in the course of the subsequent century. The population of Spain, deprived of its productive Moslem and Jewish elements, weakened by war and emigration and also by its high proportion of economically unproductive elements (e.g., nobles, clergy), seemed unequal to play the great part which was offered it. In fact, the decline of Spain is abundantly evidenced. Augsburg merchants monopolized the raw materials—wool, timber and iron—which it proved too unenterprising to use industrially; French ships brought round to Seville and Cadiz textiles and other commodities for the American market, which Spain could not produce sufficiently itself [1]; attempts to re-settle with colonists from the north Granada and Valencia, from which the Moslems had been driven, failed, since the new settlers lacked the technique of irrigated agriculture practised in the south. The chief industries of Spain, first the woollen and later the silk, declined, whilst the Dutch and English intervened in the trade, and threatened the trade routes, between Spain and America. No less typical of the decline of Spain was the poor state of its roads which, despite the difficult relief of the country, had been adequate at earlier periods. Moreover, it actually imported iron goods from Milan despite the fact that good iron was mined in Asturias, and even failed to provide enough food for a population which had much declined by 1700; finally, like Venice, Spain had to import ships built in Holland.

It may be asked why Andalusia rather than the other Atlantic provinces of Spain provided the ports from which the American trade was conducted. It was from the ports of Andalusia, namely from Palos, Sanlucar and Cadiz, that Columbus set forth on his voyages to the west; this coastland, thanks to its proximity to that of southern Portugal, shared the activity in navigation which Prince Henry of Portugal had stimulated; moreover, Andalusia was a country rich in agricultural and manufactured commodities and therefore a good hinterland to its seaports. Certainly the royal policy of licensing shipping bound for America and also the practice of convoying merchant shipping made it convenient to concentrate the American trade at one port. Actually the city of Seville was selected for this purpose, although its outports Sanlucar, and Cadiz above all, gradually took an increasing share in the trade. At first, in the sixteenth and early seventeenth centuries, Seville largely and effectively controlled the American trade, but in the course of

[1] Girard, *Le Commerce Français à Séville et Cadix au temps des Habsbourgs*, passim.

the seventeenth century Cadiz usurped the first position in the trade. The bitter rivalry between Cadiz and Seville[1] and the eventual victory of the former is a striking instance of a common phenomenon in historical geography, namely, the competition of two ports on a tidal river, one of which stands near its tidal limit and at its lowest bridge, whilst the other stands at or near its estuary. Seville, which lay some sixty miles from the sea, was of the first type, whilst the port of Cadiz, which stood on an island near the mouth of the Guadalquivir, was of the other. In the sixteenth century, despite the fact that the river followed a tortuous course and that sand was liable to obstruct the channel, Seville was normally reached by the vessels engaged in the American trade. Two factors, however, militated against the usefulness of Seville as a seaport: one was a rocky bar at the entrance to the Guadalquivir, the other the need for big ships in the American trade and the consequent increase in their tonnage and draught. Unless the river was improved—and such works were not, in fact, undertaken—it was necessary to utilize more convenient ports situated near its mouth. Fortunately, good natural harbours were available both at Sanlucar and Cadiz. The former was a small town built around a hill-top castle on the left bank of the estuary where deep water reached the shore, but it also, like Seville, was inconvenienced by the bar at the estuary where only a few feet of water obtained; and it was Cadiz, which lay nearly twenty miles to the south-east, that became the more important. Cadiz during the Middle Ages had been merely a royal stronghold built on the northern end of a rocky off-shore island which presented an abrupt face to the sea. The island sheltered a broad bay and thus provided a useful roadstead accessible by a narrow entry to the north.

Holland

The second half of the sixteenth century witnessed the creation of the United Provinces of the Netherlands, which became generally known, after their most important member, as Holland. Their emergence as a state is treated elsewhere[2]; it is relevant here to examine only their remarkable economic development in the sixteenth and seventeenth centuries. Certainly the rise of the United Provinces provides a remarkable instance of the geographical changes which can be effected by human organization and enterprise. The geographical setting of the Dutch

[1] Girard, *La Rivalité Commerciale et Maritime entre Séville et Cadix*, passim.

[2] See *supra*, Chapter XII, pp. 258–60.

Republic, although it contained great potentialities for maritime commerce, was in many respects, as it remained for many centuries, unpromising. The naval historian Mahan emphasized the excellent geographical endowment which the Dutch were astute enough to exploit. 'The history of sea-board nations', he wrote,[1] 'has been less determined by the shrewdness and foresight of governments than by conditions of position, extent, configuration, number and character of their people—by what are called, in a word, natural conditions.' But it is easy to over-exaggerate the geographical advantages and to underestimate the historical and human factors. For it is clear, in the first place, that the geographical position of Holland only offered great opportunities in the modern period, not in the Roman, when the Baltic was scarcely explored and when routes by sea to the Far East and to the New World were unknown. Again, the physical conformation of Holland proper was such as to retard the growth of population and wealth, since it consisted largely of a low maritime plain, studded with lakes, and continually liable to inundation from the sea. Moreover, the low plains of Holland suffered much in the later Middle Ages from the excessively stormy conditions which created the Zuider Zee and flooded much good land.[2] Further, although the United Netherlands controlled the estuaries of three great navigable rivers—the Rhine, Meuse and Scheldt—and were well placed in relation to the Baltic and to the North Sea, in other respects it was the poorness of their natural equipment which struck contemporaries. Sir William Temple, who was ambassador at The Hague in 1668, summarized in his book [3] the geographical shortcomings of the Netherland state. It lacked the essential materials for ship-building—timber, iron and pitch; it produced insufficient supplies of food for its needs and had no goods for export, except butter, cheese and china-ware; nor even was it well supplied with good harbours. 'The best are Helversluys, which has no trade at all, and Flushing, which has little in comparison with the other Dutch towns.' Amsterdam, although it had secured much of the former trade of Antwerp and Lisbon, seemed (wrote Temple) 'the most incommodious Haven they have, being seated upon so shallow waters, that ordinary Ships cannot come up to

[1] *The Influence of Sea-Power on History*, p. 28.

[2] Thus in 1421 the populous and fertile Biesbosch region on the lower Meuse was inundated by the sea. On the severe climatic conditions in the later Middle Ages see Pettersson's article in *Q. J. M.*, XXXVIII.

[3] *Observations upon the United Provinces of the Netherlands*, 2nd ed., 1673, p. 210.

it without the advantage of Tides; nor great ones without unlading. The entrance of the Tessel (Texel) and passage over the Zudder-Sea, is more dangerous than a voyage from thence to Spain, lying all in blind and narrow Channels.' In short, Temple's conclusion that 'not a Haven that draws Trade, but Trade that fills a Haven and brings it in Vogue' testifies to the zeal and success of the Dutch in exploiting the opportunities which were presented to them in the later decades of the sixteenth century when the former economic pre-eminence of Flanders and Brabant had passed away owing to civil wars and when, too, new oversea commercial ventures became possible.

By their closure of the Scheldt the Dutch blocked the main entry into Brabant and Flanders, and since they had suffered much from the silting up of their tidal creeks the southern provinces became, compared with Holland, an almost land-locked country. In contrast, the Dutch provinces found their fortune on the seas. For Holland, as for Venice, fishing, coupled with the industry and trade in cured and salted fish, marked the original stage in its maritime and commercial career, since the shallow North Sea offered richer harvests than its ill-drained lowlands. The cultivation of its plains could not support a large population, and although it increased its productivity by the draining of land and by the study and application of agricultural science for which it became famous in the seventeenth century, a contemporary authority estimated that the soil of the United Netherlands could not support more than one-eighth of their inhabitants. In short, Holland sought and found its opportunities on the open sea, and it became not only, like medieval Bruges, an international focus of shipping and finance, but also, like Venice, a great ship-owning and naval power. At the end of the sixteenth century Spain and Portugal,[1] no less than Venice and the Hanseatic cities, were fast losing their trade as carriers by sea, and it was only in the latter half of the seventeenth century that England began to contest, though scarcely to overcome, the Dutch supremacy at sea.

Holland thus exploited to the full the opportunities presented by time and place. Amsterdam, built, it was said, on herring-bones, grew to a city of 300,000 inhabitants; its ships engaged not only in the local Baltic and North Sea trade, but also in the more distant Mediterranean, East Indian and American commerce; whilst it was linked with the Lek channel of the Rhine by way of the Zuider Zee, the Vecht river up to Utrecht, and

[1] The incorporation of Portugal into Spain, which lasted from 1580 to 1640, proved very damaging to Portuguese commerce.

thence by canal. The Baltic was the chief field of Dutch trade, but their fleets sought profit along all the other sea-ways. From Norway the Dutch carried much of the timber essential for their ship- and boat-building, which was remarkably specialized to serve the many different purposes for which vessels were required—freight, fishing, coaling, inland navigation—and for which they were justly renowned throughout Europe. From the plains of Prussia, Poland and even Russia they derived flax and above all the cereal foodstuffs on the importation of which they were dependent: for the most part these commodities were exported via Danzig, to which they were carried in hundreds of small carts and in great lighters along the Vistula. Dutch vessels carried homewards, too, coal from Newcastle, Sunderland and Blyth; wine from the Garonne and the Dordogne via Bordeaux, and wool from Spain, Germany and Ireland. The North Sea supplied them with herrings, which formed their chief commodity of trade; the Newfoundland banks were sought for their cod fishery, the waters off Greenland for whale hunting, which provided two valuable products, whalebone and train oil. Again, from the Far East Dutch merchantmen shipped cargoes of spices, cottons and silks, and from the New World sugar, rum and tobacco. In 1590 Dutch ships entered Mediterranean waters, and thus began to extend there the field of their activities. From Sweden Holland brought iron and copper: in fact, between the years 1600 and 1750, it was Dutch capital which financed and controlled the iron and copper mines of Sweden. With interior Europe Holland was linked up by the Meuse and the Rhine, which, together with its tributaries, opened up an important avenue into the heart of the Continent. Up these rivers were carried not only the luxury goods for which Amsterdam was the chief entrepôt, but also salted herrings, salt, flax and English cloth. On the Meuse and Rhine were employed large horse-drawn barges of 300 to 400 tons burden, called 'lurdinges', and they journeyed up the Rhine to Cologne and Frankfurt and up the Meuse into Luxemburg.[1] In one respect the use of the Rhine as a trade route had reversed since the Middle Ages when Oriental goods, brought across the Alps from Italian seaports, had been moved *down*-stream.

The United Provinces became, therefore, in the seventeenth century a wealthy and densely populated land, studded with active trading cities, and furrowed by a network of canals, which were easy to cut and serviceable both in the drainage of fields

[1] E. G. R. Taylor, *Late Tudor and Early Stuart Geography*, p. 102, citing Keymer's *A Description of Holland*.

and in the provision of waterways. Its towns tended to specialize in different branches of industry or commerce. Amsterdam was the chief mart for the East Indian trade; Flushing served the West Indian trade; Rotterdam dealt mainly with England and Scotland; and Middelburg and Dort imported French wines. Among the centres of industry that sprang up in Holland under the stimulus of immigrants from the southern provinces were Leyden which worked wool and silk; Haarlem which made linen; Delft was well known for its porcelain and beer; Surdam had big shipbuilding yards; Friesland had the whaling ports, whilst Enkhuizen and Mazlandsluys were the chief herring ports. Finally, The Hague was the political capital. Like England in the late eighteenth and nineteenth centuries, Holland depended on the outside world not only for corn but even for clothing and timber. In fact, the essence of its economy was its carrying trade, for the various branches of which it had specially designed vessels, and this trade included coastwise trading along the coasts of Spain, France and England. Freight in fact was its chief 'raw material': hence the dogged courage with which it fought England for the command of the seas, since thereon and in no other way could it maintain its greatness. But its very prosperity involved Holland in wars also by land. On its landward sides it was defended only partially by physical geography, which had in some other respects favourably conditioned its fortunes. Although it could flood its lands with ease and was difficult of approach for armies from the south because of the broad river estuaries, it lacked the excellent maritime frontiers such as those of Britain, which alone could effectively defend a sea-state against the great military power of France. Holland was most exposed, in fact, from the east, by way of Gelderland. The prolonged and costly war with France, while it weakened Holland, facilitated the development of English power at sea, and in the eighteenth century England ceased to occupy a subordinate position to Holland alike in commerce, finance and agriculture. In other words, the eighteenth century witnessed the continuance of the north-west shift of the centres of political and economic power; just as Seville, Cadiz, Lisbon, Antwerp and Amsterdam had challenged the commercial mastery of the Italian and Hanseatic cities, so England with its two leading ports of London and Bristol successfully challenged that of Holland.

France

The economic geography of France in the sixteenth and seventeenth centuries offers contrasts to that of its more typically maritime neighbours, Holland, England, Portugal and Spain. The wide range and genial character of its climate, the extent and diversity of its soils, made of France a land of varied and productive agricultural activity which was able to support a greater population than that of any other state in Europe. Thus in 1680 the population of France is estimated at nearly 19 millions, that of England and Wales at only $5\frac{1}{2}$ millions [1]; whilst it is significant how the relative importance of France in respect of numbers had greatly increased in the seventeenth century com-

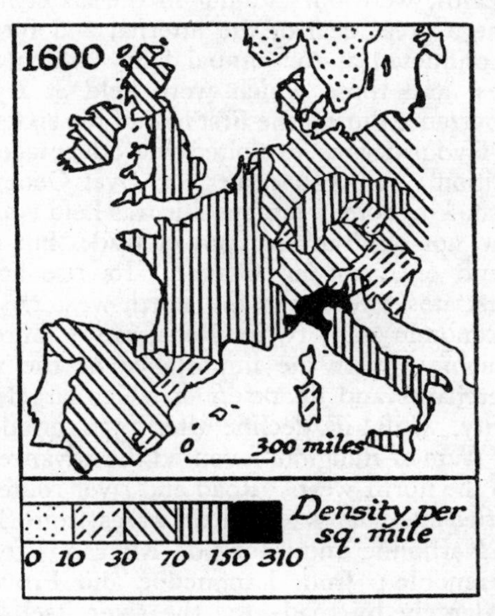

FIG. 50.—Population densities in western and central Europe *c.* A.D. 1600 (after Usher)

Cp. Figs. 2 and 15, and see the caption to Fig. 15 emphasizing the limitations of population maps of past periods. No density is shown for the areas left white

pared with the Roman period (Figs. 2 and 50). The position of France was such as to encourage both territorial and maritime ambitions, so that its political energies were divided. Peninsular France, in contrast to insular Britain, had extensive land frontiers —frontiers, moreover, which were in no sense clearly defined. Further, France possessed long coastlines well equipped with harbours and fronting two seas, so that it was offered two distinct fields of maritime activity. It was a disadvantage, however, for France that its Mediterranean and Atlantic coasts could be

[1] Willcox (ed.), *International Migrations*, vol. II, ch. I.

related seawards only by the long détour around the Iberian peninsula, a circumstance which discouraged coastwise navigation and also divided French naval power.[1] In fact, despite the efforts of Colbert in the seventeenth century to promote French maritime power and commerce, France tended in its economic relations to look within itself and towards its landward neighbours rather than towards the seas. Along its land frontiers France made contact with Spain, Italy, the Low Countries and Germany, and it should be noted that the first three of these, in respect of population and wealth, were outstanding in the sixteenth century.

At this time a great deal of the internal and foreign trade of France was conducted at the annual fairs, which were held in its chief cities, and those which were held at Lyons attained European importance during the first half of the sixteenth century. Under royal favour Lyons exploited the advantages of its geographical position: it began *c.* 1450 to rival Geneva, where, at the gate into the kingdom, a famous fair was held; and by *c.* 1500 Lyons became not only an entrepôt of trade, but also a centre of industry and of European finance. Its rise and brief pre-eminence illustrates effectively the north-westerly shift in the centres of economic activity in Renaissance Europe: Lyons inherited to some extent the importance of the north Italian cities, the merchants and financiers of which largely contributed to its prosperity, whilst its decline after 1550, amidst the welter of the French Wars of Religion, favoured the advance of Antwerp, still farther to the north-west. Road and river routes convergent on Lyons carried merchants and their wares from Spain by way of Toulouse, Narbonne and Mont de Marsan; from Italy via Geneva or Grenoble; from Languedoc and Provence up the Rhône valley largely by road—for the river itself was difficult to navigate up-stream because of its rapid current; from the Rhinelands and Burgundy by the Saône and Doubs; from Flanders by way of Nevers (on the Loire) or by Dijon and Villefranche; whilst, finally, the Loire, which was navigable below Roanne, connected Lyons with the Atlantic at the port of Nantes. Lyons thus collected the produce of France and its neighbours: cloth from Flanders, iron from Germany; silk, leather, wines, olive oil, whilst it derived raw materials—especially silk—for its manufactures. On the Rhône just above the delta Beaucaire was a busy resort of merchants who came from various parts of the Mediterranean region. For the rest, every province

[1] The Canal du Midi, constructed between 1666 and 1680, linked up the two seas, but it had numerous sluices and was only useful for boats. It ran from the Mediterranean, near Narbonne, to the Garonne, near Bordeaux.

of France had its own regional centres of trade: thus Dijon and Chalon served Burgundy, whilst Toulouse, Carcassonne and Nîmes served Languedoc.

In its rivers,[1] as Strabo had long ago noted, France possessed excellent natural ways, and of these the Loire was the most frequented. Except during floods, which tended to occur in summer, the Loire afforded a quick and safe means of transporting bulk goods and wine, whilst in the seventeenth century regular services of oar-driven boats were provided for passengers. Along the banks of the Loire stood some of the chief cities and royal residences of France: Orleans, Blois, Tours—where a bridge carried the road from Paris to Poitiers—and the seaport of Nantes, at the head of the estuary. The navigation of the Loire and its tributaries, of which the Vienne and the Cher were the most useful, suffered from the numerous toll stations, of which some two hundred are recorded in the sixteenth century. The Seine and its tributaries functioned in the transport of grain and other goods to the markets at Paris. Thanks to the efforts of Francis I in the first half of the sixteenth century, a new naval port, suitable for large ships, was built amidst the marshy alluvium of the Seine estuary, namely Le Havre, which came to usurp the position of the medieval port of Harfleur near by (Fig. 51). The Yonne was particularly serviceable in provisioning Paris with corn, vegetables, fruit, wine and salt, as well as wood fuel from the Morvan heights, which was floated down into the Yonne by way of the Cure. Paris derived grain from its relatively productive surrounding region between Chartres in Beauce to the west and Châlons and Vitré in the east: at the latter and at Bray, both river ports, the one on the Marne, and the other on the Seine, big grain markets were established.[2]

The roads of France, judged by Roman or by nineteenth-century standards, were in a bad condition; the Roman roads had been largely plundered for their stone and allowed to deteriorate, and although for economic and political reasons some minor improvements were made in the sixteenth and seventeenth centuries, scientific road construction awaited the succeeding century. Moreover, the use of the roads for the transport of commodities was impeded and restricted by a multiplicity of customs dues and other exactions, since prior to the French

[1] For a contemporary survey of French rivers see Coulon, *Les Rivières de France* (1644).

[2] Usher, *The History of the Grain Trade of France*. Despite its productivity in cereals famine sometimes occurred in the more unfertile regions of France, e.g., Limousin and Dauphiné, when recourse was had to herbs, acorns, chestnuts and roots to eke out insufficient corn. The big towns on the whole were well supplied.

Revolution, France in no sense constituted a single customs unit. Even so, it is clear that the roads of France (Fig. 37) were well used, notwithstanding the dangers to man and beast and the poor surface which tended to be worse during autumn rains and winter snows: merchants, ambassadors, couriers on foot and on horseback, clerics, pilgrims and other travellers frequented them continually. In 1553 appeared the *Guide des Chemins de France*, a small pocket-size volume, attributed to Estienne,[1] which is the first route-book of modern France: it shows the stages

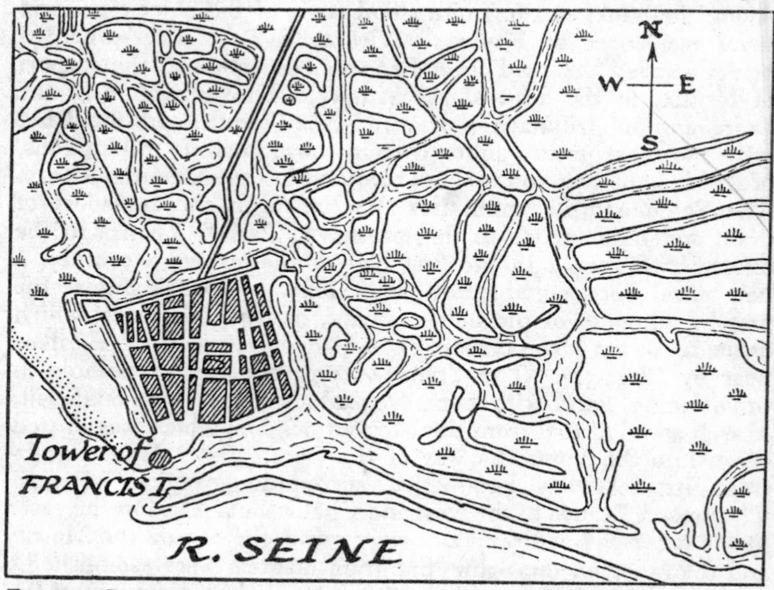

FIG. 51.—Le Havre in the sixteenth century (after Brunhes and Deffontaines). The town has since extended widely on the drained marshes around this nucleus

of travel town by town. As an illustration of a long journey across France may be instanced that of the Emperor Charles V who crossed France from Spain *en route* for the Spanish Netherlands in 1539: his route ran via Bayonne, Bordeaux, Poitiers, Loches, Blois, Orleans and Paris. In the south-east the favoured route across the Alps from Italy lay from Turin to Susa on the Doria Riparia, over the Mont Genèvre pass to Briançon, thence by the Lauteret pass to the Romanche river, and finally via Grenoble and the Isère valley to the Rhône and Lyons: this

[1] Estienne was 'Imprimeur du Roi' and probably the author of the *Guide*.

was the route used by couriers from Paris and from Madrid, and was supplied with stations at which horse relays were available.

Some idea of the speed of travel may be gained from the times taken by the post between France, Spain and Flanders which was organized about the year 1660.[1] Spanish couriers travelled from Cadiz and Madrid as far as the frontier station of Irun, from which point French couriers continued via Bordeaux, Poitiers and Orleans to Paris and Brussels. The journey from Irun to Paris took five to five and a half days in spring and summer, and a day longer in autumn and winter. The post between Madrid and Paris took about eleven days; that from Cadiz to Paris took between fifteen and twenty days; whilst Paris could communicate with Brussels in forty to forty-two hours in spring and summer, forty-eight to fifty hours in autumn and winter. At the same time coach services were run from Paris, e.g., to Brussels and to Bordeaux: they took about half as long again as the post. Normally, travelling by horse or by wagon was slow, but in cases of necessity express couriers performed remarkable feats: thus the news of the massacre of St. Bartholomew in Paris in 1572 reached Madrid in three days and three nights.[2] Military needs in the latter half of the seventeenth century were responsible for the construction of certain sections of roads, e.g., Louis XIV's road from Lorraine into Alsace via Pfalzburg. The needs of the salt industry in Vendée and Aunis in the west and also in Provence were met by the building of roads to market centres. Again, in order to facilitate the transport of salt from Briançon on the upper Durance to towns of the upper Po, the Mont Viso tunnel was cut in 1480 beneath the Traversette pass.

The chief industry of seventeenth-century France and the chief articles of export were 'toiles', that is fabrics of flax and hemp. These industries were localized mainly in the west—in Normandy, Brittany and Cambrésis. Flax was grown in Normandy on the plateaux of Lieuvin and Roumois, which are divided by the valley of the Risle, and the manufacture of linen was a winter occupation for the peasants. Fine linens were made around Louviers and Evreux, both of which were connected by river with Rouen, which served the industry as a market and a port of shipment. In Brittany, as in Normandy, the manufacture of linen—a traditional industry—made rapid strides in the sixteenth and seventeenth centuries. Hemp was grown in

[1] Cp. Bonnerot, '*Esquisse de la Vie des Routes au XVIe Siècle*', *R. des Q. H.*, 3rd series, XIX, 1931.

[2] Girard, *Le Commerce Français à Séville et Cadix*, pp. 534–5.

many parts of the coastal plain of Brittany, especially around Quimper, Vannes and Dol, as also in the country drained by the upper Vilaine and Cuesnon rivers, where stood the towns of Rennes, Vitré and Fougères. Flax was cultivated around Tréguier and also near Laval in what is now the department of Maine. A wide variety of fabrics was woven: sail-cloth, sack-cloth, canvas and many fine linens, the production of each of which was regionally localized. Thus sail-cloth, sack-cloth and canvas were made around Rennes, and fine linens south of St. Brieuc. At first many small ports served these industries, but of these Morlaix and St. Malo became the most important. Shipments were made chiefly to the ports of Spain, whence some of the textiles were carried to Spanish America,[1] whilst the Breton ports also supplied Holland with sack-cloth until the second half of the seventeenth century, when the manufacture was established in Holland itself. The woollen industry, although less important than those based on flax and hemp, was widely established in France and particularly in Picardy, Normandy, Champagne, Languedoc, Provence and, above all, in that part of Flanders which was united to France in 1668. It was in the sixteenth century that the silk industry became really established in France. Originally restricted to southern Spain and to Genoa, Venice, Lucca and some other Italian towns, the manufacture of silk had been established at Avignon by the Popes [2] as early as the fourteenth century, and it had passed thence up the Rhône valley to Valence and Lyons. Under royal patronage Italian silk-workers were established in certain French towns, and in the course of the sixteenth century Paris, Tours, Montpellier, Avignon and Lyons were engaged in the industry, which drew its supplies of raw silk from Provence and from Italy. In the seventeenth century first Tours, and then Lyons, won the primacy in this manufacture, and they exported silks, brocades and ribbons even to Spain. Silks from Lyons were sent chiefly via Marseilles, those from Tours by way of Nantes.

Among the exports of France and standing second to 'toiles' was wheat. The principal regions of production for export were situated along the coasts—in Provence, Languedoc, Labourd (between the lower Adour and the Pyrenees) and Brittany, and the explanation of this localization was clearly the relative cheap-

[1] Girard, *Le Commerce Français à Séville et Cadix*, pp. 534–5.

[2] During the so-called 'Babylonish Captivity', when there were rival claimants to the Papal see, Popes were resident at Avignon, and their presence, by creating economic demand, stimulated the industry and growth of the town.

ness of freight by sea as compared with carriage by land. An interesting instance of this trade was the shipment of wheat from Norman and Breton ports, especially from Rouen and Nantes, to Biscayan ports, to Guipuzcoa, Galicia and Portugal. This trade, which existed during the Middle Ages no less than in the sixteenth and seventeenth centuries, rested on sound geographical and economic bases, since the mountainous districts of northern Spain were deficient in wheat, the sea route was convenient, and return cargoes of iron, alum, wool and hides were available. Thanks to the development of the Newfoundland fishery in the seventeenth century, the ports of Brittany, which had long engaged in fishing and whaling, exported dried cod to Spain and to other Mediterranean countries.

The Mediterranean Sea

In the seventeenth century the French Mediterranean ports, and Marseilles in particular, won an important share in the commerce of that sea. If the old lucrative trade of the Mediterranean in carrying Oriental products to Europe had disappeared, nevertheless there remained an active coastwise traffic and also profitable business with the ports of the eastern basin of the sea, that is, in the Levant. These eastern ports were important for their supplies of raw materials, foodstuffs, drugs, and even some spices. From Smyrna ships brought back silk; from Sidon, the chief port of call in Syria, cotton; from Alexandria flax and leather; from Constantinople leather and skins; and from Acre soda. In the later years of the century coffee was brought from Egypt; whilst wheat from Salonika, and wheat and oil from Candia, the Morea and the Aegean islands were staple cargoes. In the sixteenth century, and even so late as 1650, French merchants bought spices at Cairo and Aleppo, but by the end of the seventeenth century the Levant cities themselves no longer received adequate supplies overland from the Far East and bought supplies from Dutch and English vessels. In the early seventeenth century a number of small ports along the Provence coast between Martigues and Antibes engaged in the Levant trade as well as in local coasting. Although Languedoc was a cloth-making region and its cloth was exported to the Levant, its old ports had ceased to function: Narbonne was cut off from the sea and had decayed, even by 1400; Aigues-Mortes had sanded up early, Montpellier had taken its place, but it too declined about 1400, largely as the result of the union of Provence to the French kingdom. At Frontignan, an outport of Montpellier on the edge of the sea, only a little coasting trade survived in the seventeenth century. Similarly, the port of Cette, which was deliberately selected *c.* 1660 to serve as a seaport to Languedoc, had no commercial relations with the Levant prior to 1715 : its site occupied the sandy base and lower slope of a limestone hill on the seaward side of the lagoon of Thau, and jetties were built to protect its harbour. In the latter decades of the seventeenth century Marseilles absorbed almost the whole of French trade in the Levant.[1] Toulon alone offered competition ; it was fortified by Vauban as a naval station, but its commerce failed to grow. Even so, it became for the first time a sizable town : its population of some 5,000 in 1550 grew to about 40,000 in 1675. Marseilles, however, became easily the greatest port and manufacturing centre on the Mediterranean coast of France. A new quay was built ; its harbour was dredged ; its near-by islands were used for quarantine stations and for the discharge of cargoes ; and its population increased to between 75,000 and 100,000 by 1700. It developed a number of industries on the basis of imported raw materials : soap was made with soda from Syria and olive oil from the Levant, since the supplies of Provence itself were insufficient. The soap industry had been formerly widely spread throughout Provence, but became increasingly concentrated at Marseilles and to a lesser extent at Toulon. Similarly, the hat industry was based on the wool, goat and rabbit skins of the Levant ; so also the cotton industry and sail-cloth manufacture, wax refining and tanning drew their raw materials therefrom. Finally two new industries were established at Marseilles about 1670, namely sugar-refining and the working of silk with gold and silver thread.

The ships which sailed from Marseilles differed from those of Holland and England which were adapted mainly to ocean sailing : those of Marseilles were smaller, lighter and faster than the Dutch ships with their larger cargo capacity. They set sail either for the Strait of Messina or, more usually, for the island of Malta ; thence they made for Crete *en route* for either Syria, Egypt, Asia Minor or Constantinople. Under favourable conditions, that is if winds were good and corsairs lacking, they reached Constantinople in between fifteen and twenty days, and Syria in less than thirty ; the return voyage took longer, since vessels were more heavily laden. The commodities which reached Marseilles were distributed both by land and by sea. French ships from St. Malo, Rouen and Le Havre sought cargoes there in return for their salt-fish and sugar ; so also did Dutch ships

[1] Masson, *Histoire du Commerce Français dans le Levant au 17e Siècle*, pp. 356–65.

which brought spices, ships' masts, rope and metals. On the other hand, silk, cotton, wool, drugs, and coffee were carried from Marseilles in mule-carts to Lyons and Geneva: often in order to escape the high dues claimed by Valence the carts avoided the highway along the lower Rhône valley and made north through Dauphiné and Savoy.

CHAPTER XVIII

THE DANUBE ROUTE-WAY[1]

THE part played by the rivers of Europe from the prehistoric period to the Railway Age has been so varied and so continual that it is easy to overestimate their importance in the human geography of the past. The risk, in fact, is not of ignoring but of exaggerating the rôle of rivers in historical geography, and it is probable enough, although statistical data are lacking, that the roads of Europe bore at all periods the greater part of the inland traffic. Even so, the larger European rivers, which were literally—if only down-stream—' les chemins qui marchent ', were continually used despite the many physical and human obstacles which hindered passage. It may be useful therefore to examine closely as a particular instance the function of one of the greater rivers at successive periods of time.

It is commonly stated that the Danube has afforded a great European ' corridor ' or ' natural route ' in the past to all kinds of human movement. Napoleon, who campaigned several times on the upper Danube above Pressburg, the present-day Bratislava, called it, although he knew well both the Rhine and the Nile, ' the King of Rivers ', and Talleyrand's assertion in 1815 that at the mouth of the Danube lay the centre of gravity of European politics rings oddly, until it is realized that he based it on political rather than economic considerations. In recent days it has been maintained that, owing to the physical conditions of the river and to the distribution of economic resources among the riverain states, the Danube as a waterway enjoys only a third-rate importance.[2] In view of the restricted use of the river to-day, although it has become an internationally supervised ' free ' waterway, it is the more desirable to discover its importance in the past. To what extent, it may be asked, has the Danube

[1] I am indebted to the editors of *Economica* for permission to reprint here in substantially the same form an article which bore the title: ' The Danube Route-Way in History '.

[2] H. Ormsby, ' The Danube as a Waterway ', *S.G.M.*, April 1923.

served men as a pathway, either along its channel or its valley, in migration, travel, trade and war? How far has the river actually provided a 'through' route-way from the Black Sea towards the upper Rhine? The answer to these questions must be sought in terms, not only of the actual physical conditions of the river—the régime of its waters, its shoals, its narrows, its cataracts and its seasonal ice, but also of the cultural conditions within the Danube basin—the political, economic and social ideas and organization of the bordering peoples. The physical conditions of the river have been markedly stable: it is clear, for example, that climatic conditions have changed very little in historical times, although there were periods when floods and freezing were exceptionally severe; and similarly the channels of the river remained in their natural state until the nineteenth century. Human conditions, in contrast, have continually changed throughout prehistoric and historical times, and this variable factor is of first-rate importance in any reconstruction of past geography: given the best possible natural route by land or by water, it will be utilized only when human circumstances are such as to impel men to engage in warfare, migration, commerce or travel.

The Physical Conditions of the Danube

It is necessary here merely to recall the more salient physical characteristics of the Danube, particularly those which have most evidently influenced communication. The river, which flows in a generally easterly direction from the Black Forest to the Black Sea, is navigable for some 1,500 miles, at least for barges of 200-ton load; the legal head of the river is Ulm, but even at Ratisbon and Passau the steamer service during the summer high-water season is sometimes discontinued. The Danube is an arterial way through Bavaria, Austria, Hungary and Yugoslavia, whilst it forms a boundary to Czechoslovakia, Rumania and Bulgaria. The river alternately winds its way through the plateaux or plains of Bavaria, lower Austria, Hungary and Rumania or flows in a confined valley through a series of defiles, notably between Passau and Krems, between Esztergom (Gran) and Budapest, and lower down, between Moldova and Turnu-Severin. In its originally unimproved condition, it occupied in certain of its reaches a broad and complicated network of channels within a flood plain marsh which was broadest in summer and was unsuitable alike for settlement and for roads. Marshy tracts extend above and below the Vienna gorge, between Bratislava and Comorn where the Waag enters, further south between Pek and the Drave confluence, and frequently in Rumania below the Iron Gate where the river flows below the high bank of the Bulgarian and Dobruja plateaux and spreads in varying width over the north bank *lunca* or flood plain. The plain of Hungary, the Bulgarian plateau and to a lesser extent the Wallachian plain, all of which have low rainfall, are covered with extensive deposits of light, porous soils which have been classified rather loosely under the term 'loess', the importance of which in the history of the movement and settlement of peoples in Europe has already been discussed.[1] Vidal de la Blache's generalized map [2] of the present distribution of woodland and loess in Europe indicates very clearly the broad but broken belts of loess which stretch diagonally across Europe, and which formed zones within which primitive and pastoral societies could freely roam. Loess is equally well distributed along many Danube tributaries—the Tisza (Theiss), the Temeş, the Drave, the lower Morava, and the March, whilst there are smaller patches in Bavaria; it occurs again in a belt between the Elbe and the Weser, in the Main valley, in the middle Rhine lands and in Belgium.

The waters of the Danube are derived from many and varied sources: the Black Forest and Bohemian *massifs*, the Swabian Jura, the Alps, the Yugoslav *karst* region, the Balkans and the Carpathians. Throughout the whole river water is highest in summer and reaches minimum depths in autumn or winter, when complete freezing or fast-moving ice may form a serious obstacle to navigation. Further, between Ulm and Bratislava the gradient of the river is at a maximum, and in consequence the current is very swift, so that up-stream movement is now costly of fuel, as it was formerly costly of labour. The steep-sided valley between Passau and Krems offered only a difficult and tortuous route by land along the heights on either bank. In Hungary, owing to the right-angled bend of the Danube above Budapest, the main 'through' route in historical times tended to run obliquely to the river, between Vienna and Belgrade, a route which avoided a Danube passage by crossing the Drave at Eszek. In Rumania, the broad flood plain did not provide a suitable emplacement for a road, and the main east-west routes followed either along the high Bulgarian bank or crossed the Wallachian plain well to the north of the river. The most difficult obstacles to movement both by river and by valley

[1] Cp. *supra*, Chapter III, pp. 54–5.

[2] *Tableau de la Géographie de la France*, p. 54. Cp. W. G. Ogg, Soil Map of Europe (1931), with text, for a newer and more scientific attempt to classify soils in Europe.

occur between Moldova and Turnu-Severin, where the river, forming a boundary between Rumania and Yugo-Slavia, effects a transverse passage through the Transylvanian Alps by way of a series of defiles and cataracts (Fig. 52). The valley sides are normally steep, and at times, e.g. at Kazan, precipitous ; there is scarcely a continuous ledge for settlements or for a road, particularly on the southern bank, where even to-day is found only a difficult track ; whilst to the north and south of the river the country forms a well-wooded plateau, lower in altitude than the neighbouring Balkans and Transylvanian Alps, but so deeply dissected by numerous north-south flowing rivers and their tributaries as to make communication east-westwards very diffi-

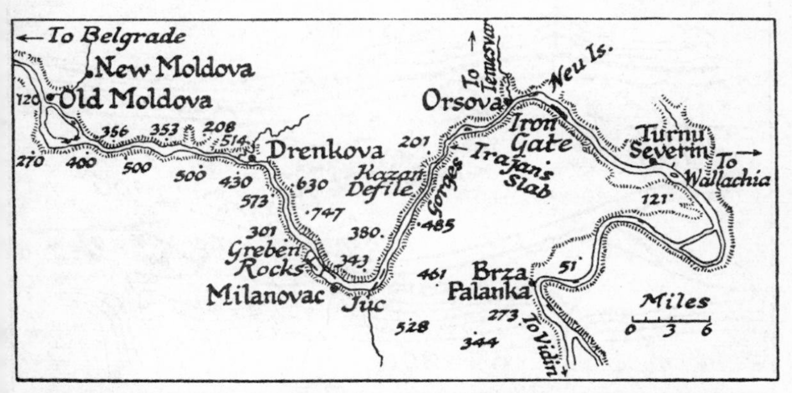

FIG. 52.—The gorge and cataract section of the Danube. Heights are shown in metres. Note the narrow channel past the Greben Rocks, the Juc cataract, the gorges at and below the Kazan Defile, and the Iron Gate.

cult. Passage by river was no less impeded by a series of obstacles. The Greben rocks formed a cataract and rigidly restricted the channel ; in the Klissura and Kazan gorges the winding river narrows to a minimum of 100 metres and is confined between high rocky walls ; it then broadens out to over 1,500 metres, but below Orşova, the former frontier town of Hungary, passes over the cataract of the Iron Gate, where a reef of hard rock lies across the river-bed through which, at low water, there was only a narrow passage near the southern bank (Figs. 52 and 53). On account of the confinement of the river in the gorges, and of the gradient of the valley, the current was extremely strong, especially during high water ; when water was low, in autumn and winter, great care was required in navigating the Greben and Iron Gate cataracts, whilst during January and February the river was liable to partial or complete freezing. It is clear, in view of all these physical factors, that the channel, above Turnu-Severin, formed almost a barrier to up-stream navigation in days before river improvement, steam power, and even tow-paths for haulage served partially to overcome these natural obstacles. It is worth noting that at the Iron Gate the Roman geographer Strabo divided the Danube into two sections, the *Danuvius* above and the *Ister* below.

The difficulties imposed by both the bed and valley of the Danube between Turnu-Severin and Moldova could, however, be avoided by routes to the north and south of the river. From

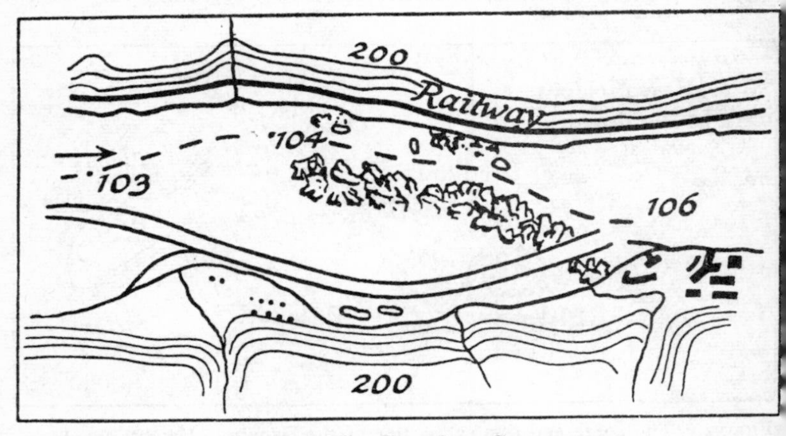

FIG. 53.—The Iron Gate Cataract

Note the reef of rocks and the artificial walled channel passing through it. The 200-metre contours are shown, and the broken line gives the distance in kilometres from Moldova. This provides a scale to the map.

Orşova on the north bank a valley route led across the Banat of Temesvar to the Temeş river, thence eastwards by the *pass* of the Iron Gate into Transylvania, or westwards to the Tisza valley. On the south bank the Timok valley from Vidin connected by way of the Straza pass with the Morava valley. These routes were local links subsidiary to the more important arterial routes which converged on Hungary via the Tisza valley from Transylvania and the Morava from Sofia or Nish.

Finally, below the Iron Gate, the Danube develops into a slowly moving stream ranging in breadth from 650 yards to a mile. It is generally navigable to flat-bottomed craft ; there were places where at low water the river was occasionally fordable [1] ;

[1] Pittard, *La Roumanie*, p. 102.

and it is liable to freeze over once in three years. It swings northwards and then eastwards again to avoid the Dobruja *massif* and reaches the sea by three main channels and seven mouths. This last reach of the river below Braïla had a special function, since it was commonly navigated by sea-going vessels : hence it is now characterized the ' maritime Danube ', as it was called the *Ister* by the Roman geographer Ptolemy.

The Danube in Prehistoric Times

The evidence of archaeology, although not yet complete, is sufficiently abundant to suggest inferences as to the routes along which peoples moved and cultures were interrelated during some three millennia B.C. Archaeologists continually refer to the Danube ' corridor '[1] which in prehistoric times, they suggest, possessed a twofold geographical significance. First, it afforded a relatively open, loess-floored path, particularly under the warm, moist conditions of climate in early Neolithic times, through regions of dense, virgin forest ; and second, the lower Danube lay near to the centres of prehistoric civilization in the Aegean basin, and the river and its affluents led westwards into the heart of continental Europe. Cultural influences, which flowed in both directions between the Aegean lands and the middle Danube plains, are clearly evidenced from Neolithic times onwards, and a common Neolithic civilization, derived from Aegean sources, was diffused from a base in Hungary as far as the Elbe, the Oder, the Rhine and the Meuse., There were riverside settlements, associated with fishing, on the lower and middle Danube in the Neolithic and Bronze Ages, the sites of which were located away from the marshy flood plain where loess hills or terraces reached the river. Even so, the extent to which the river route, by land or by water, was actually, as it is claimed, a ' corridor ' frequented by migrators and traders, may well be questioned, particularly as regards the lower river from the Black Sea, via the gorges and rapids up to Belgrade.[2] In fact, the Hungarian plain was reached by some three alternative routes, which seem to have superseded in importance that of the lower Danube valley. The Morava–Vardar route from the Aegean was opened up in the

[1] Childe, *The Danube in Prehistory*, p. 1.

[2] It seems highly questionable, on geographical ground, that prehistoric peoples succeeded in sailing *up* the Danube past the Iron Gate. The Greeks later did not do this. G. Childe writes (*Ant.*, vol. I, No. 1, p. 82) : ' At the moment the lower Danube has yielded only isolated clues. . . . Clear vestiges of the first settlement begin above the Iron Gate.' It may well be that evidence of continuous passage by river is not forthcoming.

third millennium B.C., and the south Danubian region was brought into the closest cultural association with Macedonia, Thessaly and the Aegean, with the result that Hungary and these southern lands mutually influenced each other. Further, the low passes of the eastern Alps admitted influences into Hungary from the eastern Mediterranean via the Adriatic, and finally two important links with south Russia and the Black Sea were provided by the Tisza and Maros valleys which run westwards from the Transylvanian plateau into Hungary. In the Bronze Age all of these routes, and that from north Italy in particular, were very important. The region between the Austrian Alps and Galicia and the Dobruja to the east formed a great culture province, the territorial base or centre of which was Transylvania with its abundant store of metals, and in the first centuries of the first millennium B.C. the characteristic feature of its civilization was its close connexion with the bronze ware of the Tyrol, of Etruria, and, above all, of the cities of Atteste and Villanova in north-eastern Italy.[1] The invasions of the Scyths from south Russia, *c.* 700 B.C., which abruptly ended the highly developed Bronze Age culture of the Carpatho-Danubian lands, illustrate the relative importance of the routes by land between Hungary and the south Russian steppe. Some of the Scyths reached the middle Danube from Galicia by way of the Tisza valley and the Jablonița and other passes of the Slovakian Carpathians ; others moved through Bessarabia, Moldavia and by way of the Oituz pass to the Maros and the upper Oltu ; the most intensive migration, however, which was towards the warm Mediterranean lands, crossed the Danube above the delta, passed through the Dobruja and thus into Bulgaria and Thrace. It is significant that, although the Wallachian plain was occupied, the passage of the Scyths through and beyond the Iron Gate cannot, on the present evidence, be proved.[2]

The Greek and Roman Phase

In historical times the Greeks, in the course of their exploration and colonization of the Black Sea coastlands, were the first people partially to frequent and to describe the lower Danube. They made their way through the winding Dardanelles and Bosporus, despite their strong currents, and entered the Black Sea, about the year 750 B.C., by taking advantage, it would seem, of the south-westerly winds which in spring replace the north-east trade winds in the Sea of Marmora. They established

[1] Pârvan, *Dacia*, pp. 1 and 19.
[2] Childe, op. cit., p. 394, footnote 9.

at the mouths of the great Russian rivers colonies which exploited the rich harvests of sturgeon and tunny and engaged in agriculture and commerce: notably *Tyras* (Cetatea Alba) on the Dniester and *Olbia* (Nicolayev) at the mouth of the Bug. Neither *Tyras* nor *Olbia* traded with the lower Danube, although the latter had trade relations with Hungary and Galicia by way of Transylvania. The colony most directly concerned with the Danube was Istria—it took its name from the *Ister*, the Greek word for the Danube—which was settled in the seventh century B.C. by Greeks from Miletus. Its site, which avoided the low, alluvial marsh about the delta, lay in the salt lake Halmyris (Lake Razim) just to the south of the delta, on an island which was then washed by the sea but has now become enclosed within a lagoon. Although the chief business of Istria was fishing in the waters of the delta, it developed also commercial relations. There is no literary evidence of Greek trade above the Iron Gate, and the presence of Greek bronze ware in Hungary is no proof of penetration through the Iron Gate, since there were alternative routes by land by way of Transylvania or Galicia.

The extent of Greek commercial penetration up the Danube and its tributaries is revealed by recent excavations at Istria and other sites in Moldavia and Wallachia. Istria, which flourished in the sixth century, at first controlled this trade from its fishing preserves in the delta, and later established a fishing and commercial station at Barboşi on the river Sereth near its confluence with the Danube.[1] By the third century B.C. other Greek cities engaged in trade with the lower Danube: notably *Tomi* (Constanţa) and *Calliatis* (Mangalia), situated on the Dobruja coast of the Black Sea, and the Aegean cities of Thasos, Cnidos and Rhodes. Merchants from the Greek cities brought dried fish, oil, wine and manufactured goods, and exchanged them for corn, skins, slaves and honey. In this trade the delta channels of the Danube afforded routes, and doubtless wine was carried along waterways rather than along roads in order to preserve its condition. An overland route to the Danube of about a day's journey for wagons linked Istria and Tomi respectively with *Carsium* (Harşova) and *Axiopolis* (Hinck). Already by the year 500 B.C. the Danube up to the Moldavian Sereth had become a Greek river, and during the following centuries Greek merchandise penetrated far up the Danube tributaries of Moldavia and of Wallachia east of, and including, the Oltu. Greek trading was

[1] Note 1, p. 374 and Pârvan, 'La Pénétration hellénique et hellénistique dans la vallée du Danube', *Bull. Hist. Sect. of Roumanian Academy*, vol. X (1923).

most intensive in the first century B.C. when Burebista had built up a vast Dacian kingdom which included the Black Sea cities from *Olbia* to *Apollonia* (St. Kyriacos); hitherto it had depended much on the caprice of the Scythian rulers of the lower Danubian hinterland.

Under the Roman Empire the Danube was for the first time fully explored from its headwaters in the Black Forest down to the Black Sea, and—what is specially significant here—for the first and the last time in history the whole river was brought within a single political organization. Even so the essential function of the Danube in the Empire was that of a political cultural and military frontier between the Empire and the barbarian world outside, although it should be observed that both on the upper and the lower river territories were incorporated which lay beyond the river: the Agri Decumates in the west, and the province of Dacia (Transylvania, the Banat and Wallachia) in the east. The geography of the Danube frontier zone has already been discussed, and the question which here arises is the effect which frontier conditions produced on the use of the Danube as a route by water or by road. It should be noted, then, that both the middle river above the gorges and the reaches below were navigated by flotillas, but it is clear that the cataracts imposed difficulties in the way of direct passage, difficulties which, it will be shown, Trajan tried to overcome. Middle Danube fleets were attached at different times to *Carnuntum* (Petronell above Bratislava), an important fortress guarding the approach to the Danube from the 'Moravian Gate', and also to *Sirmium* (Mitroviţa) and *Siscia* (Sisak), both of which stood on the road and river routes afforded by the Save valley. The Moesian fleet on the lower river was stationed at the fortress of *Ratiaria* (Arzer), and a detachment at Barbosi, the old Istrian mart, policed the river Sereth which flowed along the frontier between the Roman territories and the nomad, steppe country to the east. The craft employed on the middle river were mainly oar-driven, as indeed was still the case in the early nineteenth century, whilst sea-going vessels, furnished with a single sail as well as oars, entered the lower river. The function of the Danube flotillas was to carry military stores to the riverside garrisons, to transport troops across the river, to form pontoon bridges when required, and finally, to frustrate attempts of the barbarians to cross the frontier. In the course of the military organization of the Danubian frontier provinces roads were built which thus provided a continuous route by land from the mouth of the Rhine to that of the Danube, by way of *Vindonissa* (Windisch), which stands on the river Aar near its junction with the upper Rhine.[1] One road left *Vindonissa*, crossed the Rhine above Lake Constance, and continued north of the lake to reach the fortresses of Ratisbon and Passau. Another road—and this was the main east-west link—ran from *Vindonissa* via Augsburg, to the Danube at Vienna and continued via *Carnuntum*, Buda, and Belgrade to Kostolač, a route-centre (Fig. 54). In short, the Romans created a great military highway, and doubtless its

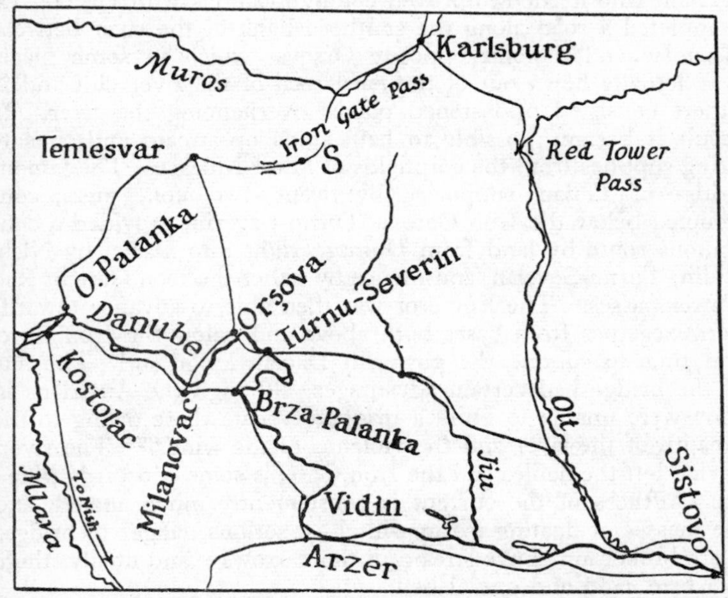

FIG. 54.—Roman roads along the gorge and cataract section of the Danube and into Dacia. The modern names are given.

S is Sarmizegetusa, the Dacian capital. (The precarious local route constructed by Trajan along the southern cliff of the river between Milanovač and a point opposite Orsova, is not shown.) (After K. Miller, *Itineraria Romana*.)

main traffic was that of armies and of transport wagons, which could move rapidly along short sections of the route as the exigences of frontier defence determined.

The difficulties of passage by road and by river between Moldova and Turnu-Severin before the roads described above were fully constructed are exemplified by the campaigns of Trajan against the Dacians, whose central stronghold was Sarmizegetusa, near Hatzeg in south-western Transylvania, to the west of Sibiu (Hermannstadt). Despite the nature of the valley,

[1] Miller, *Itineraria Romana*, pp. 259–68.

a whole series of small forts were built on both sides of the river at and just above the Iron Gate. During his Dacian wars (A.D. 101–6) Trajan used two arterial routes from Italy to the Danube: the one, by way of the Save, to Belgrade and to Kostolač; the other, from Durazzo and Nish, reached the river below the Gate at Vidin, whilst the middle Danube above Kostolač was used as a waterway. Improvements in road communication along the gorge and cataract section of the river were largely due to Trajan, who needed improved communications with Dacia. He completed a road along the southern bank of the river between Kostolač and a point opposite Orşova, which in some places was actually hewn out of the hard rock of the river cliff and in others consisted of fastened planks overhanging the river. In result it became possible to haul ships up-stream and thus to bring supplies from the cornfields of lower Moesia. The famous bridge of Trajan, supported by twenty-two stone piers, constructed below the Iron Gate at Turnu-Severin, provided a continuous route by land from Durazzo right into Dacia, by Nish, Vidin, Turnu-Severin, and thence by either the Iron Gate or Red Tower passes. The Emperor was then able to advance towards Sarmizegetusa from bases both above and below the Iron Gate, and thus to subdue the powerful Dacian kingdom.[1] The site of the bridge had certain advantages, although the Austrians in 1697 were unable to build a bridge of boats there owing to the breadth of the river and the violence of the winds.[2] The river, having left the defiles and the Iron Gate, is some 900 yards wide; the swiftness of the current is consequently much abated, and the masses of floating ice in winter—a serious danger to bridges—are broken up above stream in the narrows; and finally, there is a firm sand and gravel bed.

In short, the use of the Roman Danube as a route was essentially conditioned and restricted by its selection as a military frontier. Of necessity, the frontier zone of the Empire was peripheral in relation to the chief centres of population and wealth within it; and further, in this instance, the frontier lands were both lightly settled and little civilized in comparison with the Mediterranean coastlands. Hence it is possible to explain the paradox that, although the river appears to have enjoyed greater

[1] Henderson, *Five Roman Emperors*, ch. xi.

[2] Marsigli, *Description du Danube*, I, 25–32. They bridged a little higher up, using Banul island. The fate of Trajan's bridge is somewhat obscure: it is not certain that Hadrian destroyed it. Constantine in A.D. 330 bridged the Danube lower down at the Bulgarian town of Nicopolis.

advantages then than at any subsequent period, it failed to play an important commercial rôle in the Roman world. It was entirely under Roman control, whilst the Black Sea was a connecting waterway between the frontier regions of the Danube on the one hand, and the northern Black Sea coastlands and the Asiatic frontier along the upper Euphrates, on the other. Even so, it was the Mediterranean Sea which formed the highway of commerce with the Far East and linked up Rome with the entrepôt ports of Alexandria and Seleucia, the port of Antioch. The proverb is right: all roads did, during the Empire, lead to Rome. The Danube lay too distant to form an interior highway, and trade routes ran rather across than along the middle Danube, e.g. up the Maros into Temesvar and Dacia, or into Bohemia, the territory of the Marcomanni.

The Danube during the Barbarian Invasions

In the centuries which succeeded the breakdown of the Roman Empire in the west the middle Danubian lands were successively occupied by Germanic peoples or by nomad horsemen who were moving westwards from their homes in the Russian or Asiatic steppe. Clearly, there is no question here of movement up the Danube waterway, although when these peoples reached the river they continually raided across it by using simple boats of reeds or of hollowed tree-trunks. To what extent was ingress into the Pannonian (Hungarian) plain made along a direct Danube line? What seems in fact to have happened is that the lands of the old Dacian kingdom were occupied, and from this base Hungary was reached. Now Dacia originally comprised not only the Wallachian plain and the Moldavian and Banat plateaux, but also the Transylvanian basins of the Maros, the upper Tisza and the upper Oltu, which were girt around by the Carpathian mountains. In this latter region minerals, pasture, timber and arable lands were abundantly provided, and there were, additionally, numerous natural strongholds. Thus it would seem that Transylvania, as in prehistoric times, formed the nucleus of culture provinces, in this instance, of kingdoms formed in turn by the Visigoths, Huns, Avars and Magyars. This being so, it follows that the usual routes into Hungary followed the Tisza and the Maros valleys or passed along the Temeş valley of the Banat, rather than along the Roman roads to the north and south of the gorges, roads which could easily be blocked. Unfortunately, historical accounts of these migrations afford scanty evidence of the precise routes pursued. The Goths were the first to occupy Roman Dacia *c.* A.D. 250; in 270 the province was abandoned, and the lower Danube re-fortified as the frontier line; whilst by *c*. 350 the Goths had pushed their territories as far west as the lower Tisza. Their subsequent invasion of Gaul may have followed the Roman Danubian roads; it is known merely that they crossed the Rhine and captured Metz. Later the Avars pushed westwards from the Volga to the Danube, but, since their progress was arrested by the Gepids in Dacia and by the Eastern Roman Empire to the south of the Danube, some of them struck off north-westwards across the loess-covered Galician platform as far as the Elbe. Eventually, in co-operation with the Lombards in Pannonia, the Avars crushed the Gepids at a battle on an unknown site (A.D. 567) and were able to occupy Pannonia. Finally, at the end of the ninth century, after they had been repelled from the lower Danube, the Magyars (Hungarians) entered Pannonia from the north-east, where passes near the Tisza headwaters give access across the Carpathians from Galicia. In short, certain conclusions may be drawn as to the part played by the Danube in these successive migrations. It seems that the prairie and agricultural lands of Hungary were occupied by migrators who entered as a rule from Transylvania or Galicia rather than by a direct movement up the lower Danube; that the Danube waterway was not used as a route of invasion; and finally, that the new-comers were at least semi-nomadic, and both Pannonia and Dacia became so unstable politically as to preclude commercial activity along the Danube. It is difficult to believe, therefore, that either the middle or lower Danube formed an important waterway during these centuries.

The Danube during the Middle Ages

On the upper Danube below Ulm the river was used within the Empire of Charlemagne, who conceived the idea of constructing a canal which should run from Bamberg on the Main, via Nuremberg to the Danube at Kelheim, utilizing the rivers Altmühl and Regnitz. In his wars with the Avars, Charlemagne moved along the south side of the Danube valley using boats on the river, as far down as the Raab confluence. He hoped by means of the canal to move troops and stores more rapidly towards the theatre of war on the middle Danube. Had the canal been completed,[1] it would have carried only a localized traffic,

[1] Kretschmer, *Historische Geographie von Mitteleuropa*, p. 213. The project proved technically difficult because of incessant rains, and was therefore abandoned. The Ludwig canal is only deep enough for 150-ton barges, and it has no less than 100 locks: Gradmann, *Süd-Deutschland*, II, 247–8.

the function which it fulfilled when in 1845, as the Ludwig canal, it was eventually opened. There was no question in the time of Charles the Great of creating an effective waterway between the North Sea and the Black Sea.

Only at the end of the ninth century does commercial activity reappear on the lower Danube. In the Bulgarian Empire, it has been seen,[1] Great Preslav was a flourishing trading city, second only in wealth and size to Constantinople itself, whilst the port and fortress of Little Preslav was a centre of active trade in the tenth century with Greece, Russia, Hungary and Bohemia. Its commercial importance depended mainly on its relations with Russia, by way of the Dnieper to Kiev, and with Constantinople, by way of the Black Sea. Some trade relations with Hungary may have been carried on by river, but merchants from Constantinople were reaching Hungary by way of the Maritza-Morava land route. The Morava valley provided the essential artery of the Bulgarian state, and the lower Danube was a well-frequented waterway.

It may well be asked whether the Danube afforded a channel by which oriental silks and spices reached central and western Europe in the tenth and eleventh centuries. The lower river, it has been shown, was navigated by Black Sea shipping ; overland routes from China reached terminals on the northern shores of the Black Sea ; a market for exotic products had certainly developed in the west ; and, finally, the Mediterranean was virtually still a Mohammedan lake. All these factors, it might be thought, would have favoured a flow of traffic through the so-called Danube corridor, occupied as it was by Christian peoples. What, in fact, does history show ? It shows that the middle Danube lands were as yet so uncivilized and so disorganized politically as to exclude commercial intercourse. It was only in A.D. 955 that the Magyars were brought decisively to a halt by the western armies at the great battle on the Lech river, and the small-scale importation of eastern commodities into the lands of the upper Rhine, upper Danube and lower Main appears to have been made already from the Italian ports, over the Brenner pass and thence to Augsburg and Ratisbon, or over the Septimer pass to Lake Constance.[2] In other words, despite adverse conditions, the Mediterranean was fulfilling again its old Roman function as a link in the trade routes between the Far East and the western world. Only in the eleventh century, under the strong and able

[1] Cp. *Supra*, p. 177.

[2] Heyd, *Histoire du Commerce du Levant pendant le Moyen Age*, I, 84 and 903–7 ; and Tyler, *The Alpine Passes*, pp. 148–53.

rule of the Christian king, Stephen, were conditions at all suitable to commerce established in Hungary: an Hungarian church was actually built at Constantinople, not merely for merchants, however, but also for pilgrims travelling *en route* for Jerusalem.

It is well recognized that the Crusades, by establishing intercourse between the east and west, stimulated commercial activity, but their precise effect on the use of the Danube as a route is diversely interpreted.[1] Evidence available from the twelfth century shows that the river was used along certain sections rather than as a continuous 'through' route. Wine from Hungary was exchanged for salt from Wallachia by river, but the shipment of oriental commodities along the upper river (of which there is some record) is no indication that the Danube was the channel of importation from the east, since these commodities were carried overland from the Italian ports to Ulm, Ratisbon and Vienna. It is significant, too, that the people of Vienna expressed much surprise and interest when in the year 1278 a vessel left the town for the Black Sea.

The Crusaders used several routes in their journeys across Europe to the Holy Land.[2] In the first and second Crusades one of the routes ran overland from Ratisbon to Vienna, thence, leaving the Danube, to the Drave and Belgrade and by the Morava-Maritza route to Constantinople. This itinerary, it will be observed, used the old Roman routes, but not the Danube itself. The Emperor Barbarossa in the third Crusade sent supplies by river from Ratisbon down to Belgrade. But generally in the third and later Crusades the sea routes from Genoa, Marseilles and Venice were preferred, whilst in the first Crusade the Roman road along the Dalmatian coast was also taken to Durazzo, and thence by the *Via Egnatia* to Salonika. In other words, passage by road along the Danube was only one of several routes, and then only as far as Belgrade; in fact, for oriental commodities, as for pilgrims and crusaders, the most important route between western Europe and the Near East lay along the Mediterranean from the great Italian and lesser French ports.[3] In fact, trading on the Danube in medieval times was essentially localized in character. On the lower river from Braïla up to the Iron Gate, which formed the traditional frontier of Wallachia, foreign merchants, e.g.

[1] Hajnal, *Droit du Danube International* (1929), pp. 2–8. It is worthy of note that the author here revises the view of medieval Danube trade which he stated in his *Danube* (1920), pp. 110–11.

[2] Wright, *Geographical Lore of the Time of the Crusades*, pp. 307 and 317.

[3] Cp. Schaube, *Handelsgeschichte der römanischen Völker des Mittelmeergebiets*, &c. (1906).

Hungarians and Greeks, were permitted (in 1368 and 1413) to come and trade : the Genoese, in particular, had stations on the river as far up as Calafat, from which they shipped skins and grain by way of the Black Sea. Above the Iron Gate the legal right of passage along the river was shared by numerous feudal authorities and riverside towns. From Budapest up to Ulm 'staple' ports with boatmen's gilds claimed the right of transshipment of goods reaching their ports, and thus served to impede continuous traffic, whilst abuses of power by feudal lords who held up boats to ransom were not uncommon. Further, it appears that extreme climatic conditions, which must have hindered navigation, prevailed during part of the thirteenth and the whole of the fourteenth centuries : winter freezing and summer floods, exceptionally severe in character, together with years of drought, commonly occurred.[1] The prosperity of towns like Ulm and more particularly Ratisbon must be explained less in terms of short-distance Danube navigation than in terms of their position at points where trade routes between the Italian cities and northern Europe crossed the river.[2] In short, evidence of long-distance up- or down-stream traffic, either by river or road, seems lacking, and the inland sea, with fewer human and physical obstacles to overcome, despite its pirate coasts, continued to receive the main flow of commerce between the east and the west.

The Danube in Modern Times

In the sixteenth century the Danube below Comorn became a Turkish river. The Ottoman Turks, having conquered the Balkan peninsula, entered Hungary via Belgrade, an advance which affords one among many illustrations of the much greater importance of the route by way of the Morava from the Aegean than that by way of the lower Danube from the Black Sea. The Hungarian kingdom was shattered in 1526 by the battle at Mohacs on the Danube ; Vienna was besieged in 1529 and again in 1683 ; and Comorn became a fortified outpost of the Holy Roman Empire. In short, political and religious hostility lay across the Danube valley, and although trade treaties with the Turks were occasionally made, little intercourse except in

[1] Cp. Pettersson's article in the *Q.J.M.*, vol. XXXVIII, and Huntington and Visher, *Climatic Changes*, pp. 98–109. Pettersson argues that great tidal range produces severe stormy conditions, and shows that the tidal range passed from a minimum in A.D. 530 to a maximum in A.D. 1434.

[2] Cp. the map (8) of medieval roads and cities in south Germany in Gradmann, op. cit., vol. I.

time of war took place. During the sixteenth century a chain was drawn across the river at the Iron Gate. Turkish galleys, which sailed up as far as Budapest, passed over the Iron Gate at high water, but had at low water to unship their guns and anchors and send them by land.[1] The fact that by a treaty of 1535 the French were allowed to navigate on the lower river in armed ships indicates the insecurity of the conditions for trade, even when it was legally allowed. Moldavia and Wallachia were the 'Garden of Stamboul': their corn was requisitioned by the Turks whose ships collected it at Silistra, Braïla and Galatz and carried it to Constantinople. Vienna became a frontier city, a fortress ever ready for defence. Travellers in the sixteenth century avoided it, and it is significant that its bridges over what is now called the Danube canal were made of unfastened planks of timber which could be removed at short notice in case of attack. Travel through Hungary at this time was unsafe owing to brigands who ambushed travellers preoccupied in effecting passage over insecure wooden bridges. The conditions of travel are well illustrated by the journey of Count Busbecq, an imperial ambassador sent to Constantinople in 1554.[2] He travelled by coach from Vienna to Buda, where he shipped his family, horses and coaches into two small boats and a small pinnace which was drawn by a tug with twenty-four Turkish oarsmen. He moved down to Belgrade almost without a stop day and night along the continual meanders of the river, and not without difficulties in navigation owing to gales, to overhanging trees, and to water-mills which were placed in the channel. Even so, Busbecq considered this route safer than that by road, whilst it took only five days instead of twelve by land. From Belgrade he continued his journey overland by the Morava-Maritza route.

By a series of engagements fought at towns which commanded the few essential crossings on the Danube, the Tisza and the Drave, between Eszek (on the Drave), Mohacs and Belgrade (on the Danube), and Szeged (on the Tisza), the Austrians drove the Turks from Hungary and restricted them on the Danube in 1739 to fortified outposts at Semendria, Belgrade and Adah-Kaleh (Neu island, just above the Iron Gate). The whole of the Danube above Belgrade was therefore brought under the political control of Austria and Bavaria, and satisfactory conditions, it would seem, were created for the navigation of the river. What, in fact, occurred? A regular down-stream passenger service was started between Ulm, Vienna and Pressburg, the old Hungarian

[1] Marsigli, op. cit., II, 18.
[2] *The Life and Letters of . . . Busbecq*, ed. Forster and Daniell, I, 92–3.

capital. The journey from Ulm to Vienna took ten days, and from Vienna to Pressburg eight hours, but there was no up-stream passenger traffic, for against the current the journey from Vienna to Ratisbon took six weeks.[1] Further, the Danube water-way as a trade route between Austria and Hungary was scarcely utilized throughout the eighteenth century for reasons that were political and economic in character. Hungary at this time was merely a province of Austria which sought to promote its own industries and commerce at the expense of those of the dependent kingdom. Moreover, the Hungarian nobility, averse from Austria, desired isolation in which they could maintain their own power and privileges and enjoy the produce of the Hungarian soil, worked by serf labour. In consequence, when in the year 1782–3 for military reasons the Austrian Emperor ordered the improvement of the channel and tow-paths of the Hungarian Danube and its tributary streams, the local authorities resisted this order and, further, threw into the river the tree-trunks prepared for tow-paths.[2] Another difficulty to navigation was the numerous water-mills, of which there were over five hundred in the Hungarian Danube below Pressburg (Bratislava). The restricted export trade of Hungary in cattle, wool, salt and grain was carried overland to the port of Fiume, which was naturally well endowed, but badly connected landwards. Only during the later decades of the eighteenth century on the initiative of enlightened Austrian rulers were measures effectively take to open up Danube trade into the Black Sea, which had been permitted by a Turkish *Sened* of 1784. In 1786 two ships were sent from Vienna to the Black Sea, one of which was sunk by Turkish frontier guards, whilst in the following year three Hungarian ships carried grain down to the Black Sea. Although some successful efforts were thus made, many difficulties other than purely political ones still obstructed navigation. Up-stream carriage in oar-driven boats was both slow and expensive: it took one month, for instance, to take a load of grain from Pest to Vienna, with the aid of eight boatmen, forty horses and thirty drivers.[3] It is of interest that the Emperor Joseph II, in abolishing capital punishment, substituted as hard labour punishment the hauling of vessels up the Danube. Further, there was the necessity, unless the vessels drew five feet or less, of lightening them of cargoes above the cataracts and re-shipping lower down.

In the last phase of Danube navigation to be considered here

[1] Hajnal, *The Danube*, pp. 114–15.
[2] Marczali, *Hungary in the Eighteenth Century*, p. 83.
[3] Hajnal, *The Danube*, p. 118.

three important and promising innovations were made: in the first place, steamships were employed; in the second, the river was brought partially under international control; and lastly, engineering was slowly applied to remedy some of the physical defects of the waterway.

The formation of the Austrian Danube Steam Navigation Co. in 1830 captured the imagination of many enthusiasts who hoped that the Danube, so little known and so rarely used as a long-distance route, would justify in the future Napoleon's designation of it as the 'King of Rivers.' The operations of the Company were confined at first between Vienna and Pressburg, but were later extended to Belgrade and beyond. An English traveller in 1835 describes a steamship voyage from Vienna to Galatz [1]: the shoals, e.g., at Gönyö above Budapest, water-mills, and even the pillars of Trajan's bridge at low water gave trouble, but passage was easily effected through the bridges of boats which had long connected Buda with Pest, and lower down where the river contracts, Neusatz with the fortress of Peterwardein. Belgrade, with only a few Turkish fishing wherries on the river, was described as a city of the dead. Transhipment, both for passengers and for goods, still remained a normal feature above and below the cataracts, in fact, the journey from Vienna to Galatz involved three transhipments, at Pest, Moldova and Kladovo, which stood below the Iron Gate. Water was highest over the rapids during summer, but fell during the autumn, the best season for the grain trade. If they were unable, through lack of water, to steam past the Greben narrows and the Iron Gate reef, vessels transferred their passengers and goods into smaller steamers and barges at Drenkova (some twenty miles below Moldova), from which they were carried to Juc; there they were transferred again into larger steamers which conveyed them to Orşova; and the remainder of the journey to Turnu-Severin —where large steamers awaited—was made by boat or by land [2] (Fig. 52). Serious efforts to deepen and regularize the channel by blasting the rocky bed of the river were begun in 1832 by Hungarian engineers, but without success, although they forged a new land link by constructing a good but expensive highway between Moldova and Orşova. The Berlin Congress of 1878 authorized a tax on vessels passing through the Iron Gate with a view to financing new engineering works, which Austria-Hungary completed by 1899. It succeeded in providing a walled

[1] Quin, *A Steam Voyage Down the Danube*, two vols., *passim*.
[2] This was the practice described in 1857: Forrester, *The Danube and the Black Sea*, p. 156.

channel at the Gate suitable, according to seasonal conditions, for vessels drawing from five to eleven feet, but the rapidity of the current was actually increased to between seven and eleven miles per hour, and a 1,000-h.p. tug is required to tow up-stream through the channel a single 500-ton barge in one hour. Even so, the tonnage of goods which passed through the Gate in both directions had more than doubled in 1913 as compared with the average for 1901–5, and much the greater proportion went *up*-stream[1] (Fig. 53).

No less important than the partial removal of the obstruction below Orşova was the much-needed improvement of the channel at the Danube delta. On the lowest or maritime reach of the river, it has been seen that trade by means of sea-going vessels had always been a recurrent feature: Greeks, Romans, Bulgarians, Italians, and Greeks under the Turkish Empire, had successively entered the river to trade at ports above the delta. Early in the nineteenth century British ships were appearing at Galatz. In 1829, by the Treaty of Adrianople, Russia gained control of the Turkish principalities of Wallachia and Moldavia and also the branches of the delta. British and Austrian vessels seeking to enter the river to buy corn at Galatz or Braïla were held up by low water over the bars off the mouths of the Sulina and St. George channels. It would seem that, despite diplomatic representations and in order to favour the grain trade of their new port of Odessa, the Russians were unwilling to improve the approaches to the Danube. They refused, further, to re-employ a simple Turkish practice which had succeeded in maintaining an adequate depth of water over the bars: this was the attachment of an iron rake to all vessels leaving the river, with the result that the surface sand and mud of the bar were disturbed and carried away by the river current. It became normally necessary for ships to unload their cargoes into lighters in order to pass over the Sulina bar, and the dangers, expense and inconvenience of this operation, and the consequent high freight costs to Galatz, induced the Austrian Steamship Co. between 1840 and 1843 to employ an overland service from Cernavoda on the Danube above Braïla to Constanţa on the Black Sea coast, whilst for similar reasons in 1860 an English company built the first railway in Turkey, along the depression which marks this route. But the port of Constanţa was not adequately equipped to serve

[1] *A Handbook of Roumania*, p. 167. The traffic further increased during the Austro-German occupation in the Great War: see the figures for 1916 (p. 167). The chief up-stream cargo in 1912 and 1913 was cereals—especially maize—petroleum and salt.

the needs of this trade, and thus it became the more imperative to improve the channel of the delta. Incidentally, it is worth recalling how this short land bridge across the Dobruja was similarly used by the Greek colonies on the Black Sea coast, and how Roman Emperors fortified it with earthworks and a wall.

The Danube at length became a 'free' river by the Treaty of Paris of 1856, and a European Commission was empowered to control and improve the approaches to the river, at first up to Isatcha and later up to Braïla. Drastic improvements of one of the delta channels was necessary, whilst pilotage arrangements and rules for navigating the delta scarcely existed. Of the two chief channels, that of St. George was deeper, its approach more sheltered and its direction (ESE.) more convenient than the Sulina, which, on the other hand, was shorter and had deeper water over its bar.[1] In 1856, to quote an official report,[2] 'the entrance to the Sulina branch was a wild open sea-board, strewed with wrecks, the masts of which sticking out of the submerged sandbanks gave to the mariners the only guide where the deepest channel was to be found, while the banks of the river near its mouth were only indicated by clusters of wretched hovels built on piles, and by narrow patches of sand skirted by tall reeds, the only vegetable product of the vast swamps beyond'. Sulina was a small settlement of fishermen, lightermen, pilots and tavern-keepers, whose livelihood depended mainly on the difficulties to which vessels were subjected by the bar, which lay only half a mile from the Sulina entrance. In the course of some fifty years the European Commission effected real improvements at the delta. The Sulina channel, the one selected for improvement, was deepened and straightened up to Ismail by canalization and reduced in length from fifty-four to forty-two miles, whilst it was deepened to a minimum depth of 24 feet in 1902 compared with only 9·5 in 1857 (Fig. 55). Further, by a timely co-operation of nature with man, the bar was removed, since no sooner had engineers constructed two long piers into the sea at the Sulina mouth than a high river flood (in the year 1861) submerged the whole delta and swept away the bar: thus at the end of the century there was some 24 feet at the Sulina entry as against 8 feet in 1857, so that ocean-going vessels up to 6,000 tons could ascend with full cargoes to Galatz. Moreover, the approach to Braïla was improved by the removal, in 1895, of the Zeglina shoal, which stood just below the junction of the Sereth.

[1] Forrester, op. cit., Captain Spratt's Survey, cited pp. 22–8.
[2] *Parliamentary Papers* (1907), LXXXVII, Sir H. Trotter's Report.

What were the effects on the use of the Danube waterway of the application of steam power to ships, on the one hand, and of the application of engineering to river improvement, on the other? No attempt can be made here either to review the imperfect statistical data on the river's traffic available in the latter half of the nineteenth century, or to analyse the present traffic of the river, but a few general observations may be made. Commerce conducted along the Danube waterway undoubtedly grew to dimensions never before reached; but in 1911—a typical pre-war year—freight carried on the Danube was less than seven million tons, and the small relative importance of this figure can be gauged in comparison with that for the Rhine—fifty-seven and a half million tons on a waterway of about one-third the length.[1] There was not, and is not, any long-distance through traffic, e.g., from the Black Sea to the German ports of Passau and Ratisbon, and the German dream of a serviceable river and

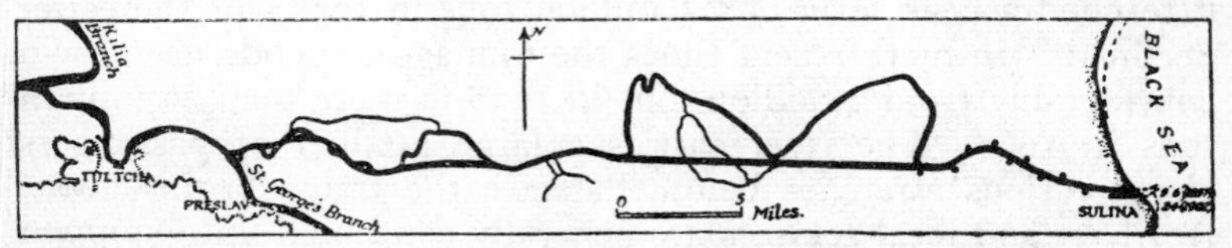

FIG. 55.—The Sulina Channel of the Danube Delta in 1857 and 1902

It may be seen how, between these dates, the channel was straightened out and lighthouses erected above Sulina. The water depths at the entry to the Sulina channel are given (in feet) for 1857 and 1902

canal-way from the North Sea to the Black Sea has long been postponed.[2] The Austrians certainly developed an active up- and down-stream trade, and even tried in the 1840's to open up trade with Persia by way of the Danube, the Black Sea and Trebizond. Their trade with Galatz and Braïla was carried on mainly via the Black Sea from Trieste and Fiume, whilst on the river itself their main business was derived from the up-and-down traffic between Budapest and Semlin and on the tortuous river Tisza up to Szeged. The cereal trade of Galatz and Braïla, ports at the junction of river and oceanic shipping, became

[1] Hines, *Report on Danube Navigation* (1925), p. 12.

[2] The Ludwig canal has locks at an average of one every two miles and can carry barges loaded with only 125 tons. Plans for the new Rhine-Danube canal, now under construction and to be completed in a few years' time, envisage boats carrying 1,000 tons of goods.

important, but in the inter-war years declined. Agricultural products, which form still the chief Danube cargo, were carried up- and down-stream, along different stretches of the river whilst down-stream Germany, Austria and Bohemia sent manufactured goods. Unfortunately the high cost of up-stream freight restricts the carriage of cereals, which are produced down-stream, in Hungary, Yugoslavia and Rumania, and are required up-stream, in the industrialized states of Austria, Czechoslovakia and Germany. After the 1914–18 war the creation of new states along the Danube, each with its own tariff restrictions, and the contraction of inter-Danubian trade, have adversely affected the use of the river, whilst the desired minimum depth of two metres at low water throughout the whole waterway—the depth required for barges of 650 to 700 tons capacity in use above the Iron Gate—has not been maintained. In 1923 and 1924 the freight carried on the river did not reach four million tons, although it reached a peak level of 7·5 million tons in 1936 but thereafter declined.[1] In more recent times the tonnage of goods has grown considerably from 7 million tons in 1950 to more than 23 million tons in 1960. The river carries a large number of passengers along various stretches below Passau: the traffic begins about April 1st and local services are generally continued until stopped by ice.

Résumé

The rôle of the Danube in history has scarcely been, therefore, that of a ' corridor ' or ' natural route ' for long-distance traffic, along its whole length, either from the west or from the east, either directly along its valley or along its waterway. Migrators from the east have constantly sought the loess-covered plains of Pannonia (Hungary), but they have reached them by diverse routes, the most important of which run obliquely to the Danube, namely those marked out by the valleys of the Tisza, the Maros and the Morava. Furthermore, the Danube never effectively challenged the Mediterranean Sea as a link in the trade route between the Far East and western and central Europe ; whilst the bulk of the grain from the lower Danube lands has always been carried seawards rather than up-stream. The Black Sea, especially after the opening up of the oceanic route to the east and the discovery of America, became an inland lake of small relative importance ; whilst, controlling the commercial activities

[1] Hines, op. cit. See also G. Kiss, "TVA on the Danube ?", *G.R.* XXXVII (1947).

of that sea, Constantinople ever attracted barbarian, pilgrim, soldier and merchant from the middle and lower Danube, and stood at the terminus of the trans-European overland route. The whole history of the Danube river shows not only how seldom human conditions have favoured the full utilization of the river and its valley as a route, but also how permanent, under the changing conditions of civilization, have been the limitations imposed by physical geography. No effort of man can remove the hindrances, expressing themselves in economic terms, which are imposed by seasonal changes of water-level, by swift-flowing currents, and by winter ice. Nor—and this is more important—can human effort furnish the Danubian lands with the productive coalfields which have revolutionized the commercial importance of the lower Rhine ports.

For some years after World War II international politics prevented the application to the Danube of schemes, comparable with that of the Tennessee Valley Authority, to exploit its great possibilities for better navigation, as for irrigation and hydro-electric power. Under the U.S.S.R.'s leadership, the Danube Convention of 1948 deprived the river of its international régime and virtually restricted its use to the Communist riparian states, which did not co-operate well with each other. However, with the relaxation of East-West tension and with the development of better relations between the Communist countries themselves, remarkable changes now promise new benefits to Danubian Europe. Austria has joined the Danube Commission and the Federal German Republic has been invited to join; representatives of E.E.C. and of the United Nations attend meetings of the Commission. The striking increase of traffic on the river includes shipping to and from Austria and Western Germany and use of the river by Italian, Greek and Lebanese ships. Moreover, the exploitation of the great hydro-electricity potential of the Danube is now taking place or is planned—in Austria, as in Communist countries downstream. These plans include the joint Yugoslav-Rumanian agreement in 1963 on a huge plant and navigation project at the Iron Gate.[1]

[1] For a recent account of developments on the Danube, see *International Rivers : Some Case Studies*, Occasional Publication I, Indiana University, Department of Geography, 1965.

CHAPTER XIX

EUROPE IN THE EIGHTEENTH CENTURY

THE population of Europe increased from about 100 millions in 1650 to 187 millions in 1800,[1] which suggests a rate of increase greater than at any earlier period. No complete explanation of this increase has been made, nor is a discussion of the underlying causes relevant here, although it may be noted that a decreasing death-rate is one factor in western Europe.

The growth of population was most marked in Great Britain, France, Prussia and Russia [2]—in the case of the last two countries territorial increases provide one of the explanatory factors. In contrast, in Spain and Italy the increase was relatively very small: in fact, the growth in the population of Europe was extra-Mediterranean. By 1800 European Russia outstripped France in the number of its population and on this basis stood first among all the states of Europe, but it should be noted that the density of population relative to unit area was much greater in France. In 1800 the population was still essentially and predominantly rural: England and Wales alone with 22·3 per cent of their population town dwellers show a tendency towards urban concentration, the result of the development of industry and trade. In Italy the urban population was fairly high, but the reason for this was essentially political—the fact that Italy was still organized in a number of small states. Elsewhere in Europe rural dwellers form 90 per cent or more of the total population: e.g., nearly 90 per cent in France and 96 per cent in Russia.

The large urban concentration of population was still rare, although in 1800 there were some twenty outstanding cities as compared with thirteen or fourteen in 1700.[3] London, an im-

[1] Compare the critical review of what is known of early population figures of the continents by Willcox, in *International Migrations*, vol. 2, ch. 1 (*Nat. Bur. of Econ. Res.*, N.Y., 1931).

[2] Woytinsky, *Die Welt in Zahlen* (1925), I, 24.

[3] For the figures given here see Woytinsky, op. cit., I, 132–5.

perial capital and the chief seaport of Britain, with a population bordering on the million mark (959,000) was the greatest European town, but no other city in Britain reached 100,000. Paris and Constantinople just exceeded half a million; Moscow, St. Petersburg, Vienna, Amsterdam and Naples reached over 200,000. There were further a number of large cities in Italy: Milan (170,000); Rome (153,000); Genoa (100,000), and Palermo in Sicily (140,000). In the Iberian peninsula only Madrid, Lisbon and Barcelona exceeded 100,000. For the rest the large towns with populations over or about 100,000 were few: e.g., Berlin (172,000); Brussels (150,000); Hamburg (130,000); Warsaw (100,000); Marseilles (111,000); Lyons (110,000) and Bordeaux (91,000). It will be noted that in almost every case these cities are either capitals or seaports or both. Moscow and Lyons had neither of these functions, although both had in the past served as capitals. Further, these large cities occupied excellent nodal positions in relation to land and water routes which favoured their growth as centres of industry and trade. Important regional cities in Europe had populations around 50,000 in 1800; so had seaports of the second grade and capitals of smaller states or subject states. Many cities already famous in the past and a few only important in recent times were included in this category: Liverpool and Birmingham, for example; Florence and Turin; Lille and Nantes; Cologne and Dresden; Prague, Budapest, Antwerp, Rotterdam, Ghent and Stockholm. No less significant of the small degree of urbanization achieved by 1800 and of the subsequent development in the nineteenth and early twentieth centuries are the figures for the following towns: Essen (4,000); Kiel (7,000); Chemnitz (14,000); Düsseldorf (10,000); Odessa (6,000); Cardiff (2,000); whilst the population of Alexandria—some 5,000—is a striking example of the changing fortunes of a town.[1]

France

France remained during the eighteenth century what it had always been—a country characterized by a predominantly agricultural economy and by rural settlements. If a rural, as distinct from an urban, settlement is held to be a population group of 2,500 or less, then 89 per cent of the population of France lived in villages in 1800; or again, it is estimated that at the same date scarcely 7 per cent of the population lived in towns of 20,000 or more inhabitants. It is evident, too, that although many processes of the textile industries were carried out in farms,

[1] Cp. *supra*, pp. 27, 199 and 349.

agriculture provided the main livelihood for the vast majority of Frenchmen. What is historically interesting about French agriculture at this time—as it appears in the masterly survey of Arthur Young—is its traditional and primitive character: in agricultural technique very little change had occurred since the later Middle Ages, whilst comparatively considered it was as backward as that of Holland, the Austrian Netherlands and England was scientific and progressive. What is of most interest to the geographer are indications of marked regional differences in agricultural production and practice, and the many intricate problems which arise out of these conditions, to the solution of which geography may contribute one ray of light.

In a general sense it is clear that the regional differentiation of France according to elevation, climate and position, soils and natural vegetation, is broadly reflected in a variety of regional differences in field systems and in the utilization of the soil. Thus the open-field system associated with nucleated villages was typical only in northern and north-eastern France (but not in French Flanders), roughly north of a line drawn from the eastern side of the Cotentin peninsula to Geneva.[1] The relationship thus shown between the open-field system and the arable plains of northern France is striking, and recalls the way in which in England the open-field system used to be typical of almost the whole of the English lowland but was lacking in the highlands of the west and north. That it was a system well adapted to cultivable lands rather than to pasture, marsh, heath and forest lands seems clear enough, but it seems no less to have established itself in the valleys and plateaux of Lorraine, and in the valleys of the Ardennes and Vosges. Both northwards and southwards of this open-field region conditions were different—particularly in western and southern France where the open-field system appeared only exceptionally. In the *Midi* agriculture had distinctive features related to its climate, soil and topography: the vine, olive and chestnut were grown, whilst small open fields of wheat did occur, and artificial grasses—clover, lucerne and sainfoin—were cultivated by irrigation. In contrast, again, in the mountainous regions of the Pyrenees, western Alps, Vosges and Jura communal forest bulked large, and pastoral farming was typical; the small areas of valley cultivation and meadow were enclosed and held by free peasants.

[1] Cp. Clapham, *The Economic Development of France and Germany*, 3rd ed., p. 7, and map 1.

The eighteenth century witnessed a development of the industries of France and also the beginnings of their concentration in factories inside the towns. Already some of the processes in the textile industry were carried on in the towns. Many varied manufactures, of which the linen, woollen and silk textiles were outstanding, were widely distributed throughout France, and there was as yet little sign of that marked localization which became characteristic towards the end of the nineteenth century. The growth of manufacture, not only of textiles, but also of such products as iron, hardware, glass, salt, and metal goods increased the demand for wood fuel, and, since wood was almost alone used as fuel both in manufacturing processes and for domestic purposes, France began to suffer from a real scarcity of timber, which became one of the most serious and continual complaints of contemporary industrialists, statesmen and other publicists.[1] It is in fact remarkable that all through the eighteenth century, despite some small attempts at the planting of limes and Italian poplars—both fast-growing trees—the supply of wood grew scarce not only in the big towns like Paris and Lyons and in districts like Languedoc where forests were traditionally restricted by reason of the climate, but also in those regions, like Franche-Comté, Dauphiné, Vivarais, Quercy and Périgord, which were formerly among the most forested regions of France. Indeed many of the famous forests of France, such as the Morvan, had become either bare of trees or at most reduced to mere remnants.

The use of coal, which might have remedied the deficiency of timber, was only slowly understood and applied, and when towards the end of the century industrialists increasingly sought its use, they found it for various reasons difficult to obtain. It is a remarkable fact that, despite its wealth in coal measures, in Lorraine, in southern Hainaut on the north-western flank of the Ardennes, in the St. Etienne district and elsewhere, France was quite unable to meet its own needs. There are several reasons to account for this paradox. In the first place coal-mining consisted for the most part of petty, scattered workings in private hands which only 'scratched' the Coal Measures. There were, it is true, in the latter half of the century, a number of undertakings by big companies especially at St. Etienne, and at Anzin in the north, which used steam-engines to pump the

[1] See the excellent monograph of Rouff, *Les Mines de Charbon en France au XVIIIe Siècle*, ch. III. It may be recalled that already in the seventeenth century Colbert prophesied that France would perish through lack of timber.

mines and sank shafts up to some 900 feet. But above all, in addition to its shortcomings in quality and in quantity, French coal suffered severely from the high cost and inefficiency of inland transport. On the one hand, a multiplicity of internal customs and dues of various kinds had to be paid at points along the roads and rivers; on the other, the provincial roads were bad and carriage by pack animals and wagons was slow and costly. Even the rivers and canals were burdened by tolls, and by the exactions of organized boatmen; moreover, they were rendered difficult owing to the seasonal variations in their régimes. In fact, so obstructed was river navigation that more coal was carried by road than by river, and this was true even at Paris despite its striking position near the convergence of several navigable streams.[1] In a few cases canals were constructed to give access from the mines to the rivers: for example, the Givors canal, opened in 1780, linked up the Rive-de-Gier mines near St. Etienne with the Rhône and thus with Lyons, whilst many canals were cut to serve the northern coal-fields around the upper Scheldt. Even so, it proved impossible to compete successfully against sea-borne British coal. Thus on account of the excessive costs of inland transport and despite the duties imposed on foreign coal, Bordeaux found it more economic to import Welsh coal rather than that from the mines at De Solages and Carmaux in the region of the upper Tarn, and so also Normandy purchased British coal rather than that from the mines of southern Hainaut. Such in fact were the conditions in France that industrial leaders urged the removal of restrictions on the entry of coal from Britain and the Austrian Netherlands on the valid ground that restrictions on their import imperilled the industries of France.

The Scandinavian States

The Baltic coastlands produced, as in the past, a surplus of essential commodities: foodstuffs, naval stores and raw materials. Their timber, iron, copper, sail-cloth, flax, tar and hemp were in demand in the western maritime countries, especially in Great Britain, Holland and France; the cereals from the south-eastern Baltic ports had a market in Holland, Sweden and, increasingly towards the end of the eighteenth century, in Great Britain. The naval stores of the Baltic and of Norway found their chief market in Great Britain: they formed in fact an indispensable basis to British naval and commercial power,

[1] Rouff, op. cit., p. 380.

since timber of the quality and types required for warships was deficient in England, whilst that of New England was held in disrepute.[1] The great importance to Great Britain of the Baltic naval stores is illustrated by the vigour with which the Sound was kept open to trade[2]: in the light of this—to cite only one instance—Nelson's action in 1800 in bombarding Copenhagen and destroying the Danish fleet becomes as intelligible as it was violent. On the other hand, the Baltic states were backward in manufacture (for example, of woollen and cotton textiles), and were unable in their northern climate to produce effectively, if at all, certain goods for which Britain and Holland were carriers. Thus English and Flemish textiles, French and German wines, and varied sub-tropical products from the East and from the West Indies were in steady demand in the Baltic. Even so, this demand was small in scale whilst Baltic products were bulk goods, so that many ships reached their ports in ballast.

Denmark and Norway, its dependent province, though contrasted in area, vegetation and physical character, were alike in the smallness of their populations and in their lack of important industries. Norway produced insufficient grain, salt, iron and copper for its own needs but received these commodities in return for its products, namely timber (firs) and fish, chiefly cod and herrings. Its fishing suffered to some extent towards the end of the eighteenth century, since the herrings 'very transitory in their resorts' migrated from Norwegian waters to Marstrand in the Kattegat. Bergen, the Norwegian capital and largest town, numbered in population only some 10,000 in the year 1800. Denmark exported on a small scale horses, other livestock and dairy produce, and had a small transit trade with Sweden, via Zealand, and with Germany via Schleswig or Holstein. The capital city of Copenhagen, which had one of the best harbours in northern Europe, had a population of 100,000 in 1800. Denmark's chief geographical asset was its position commanding the Baltic entries, and Sound dues were collected at Elsinore.

In 1784 the Rendsburg or Holstein canal was opened: it was cut from a point north of Kiel to Rendsburg on the Eider river, whence by tide or wind ships drawing up to 9 feet could reach the North Sea at Tönning. This waterway greatly reduced the

[1] Albion, *Forests and Sea Power*, pp. 24–5.

[2] Between the years 1658 and 1814 British fleets were sent about twenty times to maintain the 'freedom' of the Sound. Cp. Hill, *The Sound Dues and the Command of the Baltic*, p. 165.

distance involved in the dangerous navigation round the Skaw; at first it was used mainly by local traffic, especially between Prussia, Emden and Holland; but when during the Napoleonic Wars the Elbe and Weser were closed to shipping, British vessels took cargoes to Tönning, sailed 'light' through the canal, loaded a Baltic cargo and returned through the Sound. In fact, between 1808 and 1814 the coasts of Schleswig and Holstein came to possess a fortuitous importance, since the French ruled nearly the whole sea-board between the Adriatic and the Elbe with the notable exception of Portugal. The English packet service for passengers and mails, which normally sailed to Calais, Ostend, Helvsetsluys and Cuxhaven, was suspended in 1805, and the packet from Harwich made for Husum in Schleswig, although its small river harbour was both inadequate and difficult of entry. The peculiar conditions created by war, however, made Husum temporarily useful as a place of debarkation for Hamburg, Lübeck and Berlin, to which passengers and goods were moved over bad roads in carriages or wagons.

In contrast to the south Baltic lands Sweden was unable in the eighteenth century to produce sufficient corn to meet the requirements of its scanty population. Not only was the country covered by extensive forests of beech and oak in the south and of fir elsewhere but also it was endowed with a climate uncongenial to cereal agriculture: thus an eighteenth-century writer records that during a period of ten years the crops fully ripened only in two or three years and were definitely bad for two or three years. This deficiency in foodstuffs might have been made good by the importation of wheat from Swedish Pomerania; instead, however, rye, which formed the staple breadstuff in Sweden, was imported from Russia by way of Riga. Again, although varied small-scale industries were carried on at Stockholm, Sweden's limited need of manufactured goods was satisfied by imports from Holland and England. In fact, the products of Sweden were derived essentially from its mines, its forests and its fisheries. Of its minerals iron, noted for its quality and its purity, was steadily in demand especially in England, Holland and France, although in the latter half of the century Russian iron entered into competition. The iron ores occur both in central Sweden and also in the far north, in the old province of Norrland, but these latter fields owing to their remoteness and relatively bad communications were scarcely worked in this century, and the workings lay in the south, the chief being at Dannemora. The ore was smelted into pig by means of charcoal and forged into malleable bar iron, in which form it was exported.[1] The forests of Sweden, on both sides of the Gulf of Bothnia, yielded abundant timber and the derived products, pitch and tar. Swedish fishermen sought the Marstrand shoals in the Kattegat where the herrings were fished both in spring and autumn: as in Norway, they were either salted or smoked and traded in the Baltic, France and the Mediterranean.

The foreign trade of Sweden was exclusively in the hands of a number of staple towns, of which Stockholm and Göteborg were by far the most important. The former was built on a number of islands and peninsulas in Lake Mälar, and possessed good deep harbourage, although careful pilotage was necessary to effect entry. Göteborg commanded the maritime terminal of the central plain of Sweden in the west as did Stockholm in the east. It stood at the head of the estuary of the Göta which drains into the Kattegat, but vessels could not reach the town and had to discharge their cargoes into lighters. Göteborg imported grain and salt; it was the chief port for the herring fishing and for the Greenland whale hunting; it exported iron, fish, and oil extracted from whale blubber and from herrings. In the transport of the bulk products of Sweden internal and external trade waterways played an important and increasing part. The many large lakes of central Sweden were linked up by river and canal ways: thus the Strömsholm canal, facilitated the carriage of iron and copper from Dalecarnia to Stockholm, whilst the capital was also linked with Orebro by way of Lakes Hjelmar and Väner and auxiliary rivers or canals. The project of a continuous waterway between Stockholm and Göteborg was eventually carried out in 1800, by the cutting of a rocky bed for a canal past the Trolhätten cataracts on the Göta river, just below the point where it leaves the Väner lake: prior to 1800 a short portage was necessary at this section of the river. The Trolhätten canal allowed passage to ships of 9 feet draught; it served above all a regional purpose as an outlet for iron and wood from Vermland.

Middle Europe

Middle Europe during the eighteenth century was politically a much-divided land. Within the Holy Roman Empire, which covered a large part of the region, there were about three

[1] It is estimated that in 1730 some 36 per cent of the malleable iron supplies of Europe came from Sweden; iron formed the bulk of Swedish export by value—75 per cent; most of it went to England, whose imported iron came very largely from Sweden, though decreasingly so as the century went on. See the *Econ. H.R.*, Oct. 1932.

hundred principalities of varying sizes, which were practically independent states. The largest of these were Prussia[1] and Austria, both of which ruled further territories outside the Holy Roman Empire. The Prussian state occupied a broad but discontinuous belt in the northern half of Middle Europe, since it reached the Niemen and the middle Vistula in the east and the Ems, Rhine and Meuse in the west. On its eastern margins it impinged on Russian territory, for the republic of Poland, which had occupied broadly the basins of Vistula and the Warta, had been partitioned between Russia, Prussia and Austria in the years 1772, 1793 and 1795. The territories of the Austrian house of Habsburg, which held the imperial title, formed an association of kingdoms, duchies, counties, &c., which were contained essentially within the basin of the middle Danube. In the south the frontiers of Austria stretched to the Alps, the lower Save and the Transylvanian Alps; in the north they extended beyond the Carpathians to include Polish Galicia, the Bohemian kingdom in the upper basin of the Elbe, and the margraviate of Moravia. On the western margins of the empire stood a number of small states, notably Denmark, the Netherlands, and Switzerland. It is important to bear in mind the patchwork political pattern of Middle Europe in reviewing its economic geography, since the multiplicity of frontiers and tariff obstacles affected the flow of trade, and since, too, the many rulers had great opportunities, which they utilized in varying measure, of developing the economic resources of their states.

The population of the Austrian Empire, which suffered severely from the impact and effects of the Thirty Years' War (1618–48), increased steadily during the century and half which followed. No accurate censuses of population are available for the eighteenth century, except in Sweden and the Austrian territories, where a census was taken by the Empress Maria Theresa. Even so, it seems reasonably clear that the number and distribution of population scarcely changed between the early seventeenth and the late eighteenth centuries. The areas of densest population were still the middle Rhineland, the Neckar basin, the Prussian lands in Westphalia, and those of electoral Saxony within the basins of the middle Elbe and Oder. The distribution of population was related to the exploitation of economic resources—to the degree of industry and trade and above all to the productivity of agriculture. In a country where agriculture was the predominant economic activity the fertility of soils was an important

[1] See *supra*, Chapter XIII, for the political development of Brandenburg-Prussia.

factor in governing the density of population. But no less important were the energy and enterprise of individual princes, some of whom were often at pains to encourage immigration and settlement and also to undertake the reclamation of land for the plough.

Middle Europe in the eighteenth century was essentially a land of rural settlement based on agriculture, the original features of which had long been defined. The open-field system and a simple rotation of crops and fallow were still general in the arable regions. Serfdom was still characteristic except in a few areas, notably in Austria and in the polder lands of the north-west. Landholding tended to conform to two distinct types and to a broad geographical distribution. Small peasant holdings were typical west of the Elbe, whilst to the east, in the region of later German conquest and colonization, great estates held by the nobility were prevalent. In the methods of agriculture and the variety of crops small but important changes were introduced in the course of the eighteenth century. Red clover, which was grown in northern Italy and in Brabant as early as the sixteenth century, came into general use in Germany, as a useful fodder and rotation crop, in the latter half of the eighteenth century. In addition, potatoes were grown as a foodstuff. Although they had been introduced into Europe from Central America at the end of the sixteenth century, their cultivation in Europe was only slowly undertaken. They were grown, however, in the Rhenish Palatinate about 1700, and some twenty years later in Brandenburg ; only after 1750, however, did they become a general field crop in Germany, where the northern plain was well suited in soil and climate to their cultivation. Already at the end of the seventeenth century tobacco was grown in many parts of Germany, not only in more southerly areas like the Palatinate and Franconia, but also in electoral Saxony and the Altmark of Brandenburg. Further, in pastoral farming some progress was made : horse-breeding was stimulated by the needs of war, and the use of clover as a winter fodder was an aid in the breeding of cattle and sheep.

The forest cover of Middle Europe, the most striking feature of its vegetation at the dawn of history, had become considerably curtailed by the end of the eighteenth century. Despite the reversion of much arable land to woodland during the Thirty Years' War, the forests diminished in area before the persistent inroads of colonists who made clearings for agriculture, of cattle which ate the young trees, and of owners of forests, who cut trees to meet the demand for timber for building, for blast furnaces and for the export trade. In some regions, as in the sand spit of the Frische Nehrung in East Prussia and in the Ems basin, the clearing of forests on sandy soil had disastrous effects, since the soil, no longer held together by the tree roots, became loose and shifting. Certainly, many governments took measures to preserve the forests by curtailing clearing and even by new planting, but the demands of the export trade entailed much destruction of woodland. In particular, the export to Holland caused much cutting in the upper Rhineland, timber being felled in the Black Forest and elsewhere and floated down the Rhine. Again, the use of charcoal in blast furnaces, e.g., around Solingen in Westphalia, took toll of the forests, and there was even division of opinion among contemporaries as to whether or not it was worth developing mineral resources at the expense of the forests. Where new plantations were made, oak was the species preferred ; coniferous trees, however, were also planted, as in the Harz at the end of the seventeenth century.

The observant traveller in Middle Europe at the end of the eighteenth century would have detected, notwithstanding a certain uniformity, many regional contrasts in the utilization of the soil, which reflected as much the varying degree of human enterprise as the varieties of natural conditions. He would have noticed, above all, as did Arthur Young [1] in the late 1780's, that northern Italy provided some of the most striking examples of 'advanced' farming. On the rich soil of Lombardy, above all, agriculture was highly developed ; moreover, in the Lombard and Venetian plains generally cultivated lands were enclosed. Manuring was understood and applied, there was little or no fallow, and turnips were grown as a winter fodder crop. Meadows were rich and the corn of good quality in the states of northern Italy. The vine and olive, the mulberry, hemp and flax and maize were all widely grown. In general, as Arthur Young records, it was the agricultural population of north Italy—Tuscany, Piedmont, Lombardy, Venice and the other smaller states, which fostered the development of its towns.

In more northerly latitudes of Middle Europe, in lands less favoured by climate and soils than northern Italy, some economic advance was made by the large-scale settlement of emigrants who often brought new land into use. Not only were forests curtailed to serve the needs of agriculture, but so also were marshy wastes reclaimed. Where the peasantry were freeholders, as in the polder lands of the Netherlands and thence north-eastwards to the estuary of the Elbe, agriculture and cattle-raising

[1] *Voyages en Italie et Espagne*, trans. Lesage, chs. I–IV.

made great progress, which was the result of both the tenurial conditions and the great natural fertility of the land. By a process of diking against the inroads of the tidal waters much good land was won for the cultivation of corn, oil seeds and for meadow, and dairy farming became the chief occupation of these maritime lowlands. Elsewhere, even where serfdom and high taxation depressed the economic activity of the countryside, the land was made to yield some return. On the poorer soils of Prussian Westphalia—in the middle Ems basin and in the Vecht valley—where flax had been introduced, it became almost the exclusive crop, and Bielefeld was important for the manufacture of linen. Farther south, in Hesse, as in the middle Rhineland generally and in the valley of the Moselle, fruit and flax were cultivated and wine was manufactured. In the lower Rhineland below Coblenz corn was grown and exported to Holland. In the north German plain between the Oder and the Ems, where there was still much marsh and heath and poor sandy country, agriculture had an uphill fight, and the peasants found in spinning an auxiliary occupation to farming. Mecklenburg, where large estates were typical, was noted for horse-breeding and dairy farming. Electoral Saxony, which occupied the foothill country north of the Erzgebirge and Riesengebirge, developed textile industries which reacted favourably upon farming, and sheep-rearing was thus the most profitable occupation, whilst fruit cultivation also prospered. Prussian Silesia, like Saxony, had the advantage of broad loess-covered tracts, and benefited by the proximity and prosperity of Saxony. Silesia sent thither wool and madder, whilst wheat from lower Silesia was carried down the Oder and exported from the port of Stettin. Southern Germany, more favoured than the north in respect of soils and climate, recovered more rapidly from the dislocations and devastations of the Thirty Years' War. In the Rhenish Palatinate—the fertile plain around the cities of Spires and Worms—corn, fruit and wine were produced, and much corn was grown in the Rhenish plain of Baden. In Franconia, which occupied most of the basin of the Main, hops and fruit were the chief crops. In the lower and more favoured parts of Swabia fruit, flax and wine were produced. The Bavarian lands to the south of the upper Danube were relatively backward; one-third of the best arable lands, wasted during the Thirty Years' War, remained uncultivated at the beginning of the eighteenth century, whilst the Danube ceased to be an important trade highway. On the other hand, the valley of the Inn made some agricultural progress, and part of the Danube marshes was drained. In the

Austrian dominions agricultural conditions were fairly favourable. Austria itself escaped the ravages of the Thirty Years' War but lost many Protestant subjects through emigration, whilst in 1683 Vienna itself had been threatened by the advance of the Turks. During the reign of Maria Theresa (1740–80) a small agricultural advance was made in Austria, Styria and Carinthia by the introduction of clover and mulberry trees and by improvements in cattle-breeding. In 1699 Austria received back from the Turks the kingdom of Hungary which produced much cattle, wine, wool and corn, but many restrictions were imposed on Hungarian trade in order to defend Austrian interests.[1] In Bohemia and Moravia, although much arable land had reverted to forest during the Thirty Years' War, agriculture was moderately prosperous under a system of large landholding and serf labour.

Within the extensive northern lands of the Prussian state, thanks to the application of much human effort and capital, agriculture made considerable progress. At the death of Frederick the Great in 1786, the Prussian kingdom stretched from the Niemen and Netze rivers in the east westwards beyond the middle Elbe, and included, further, detached parcels of land as far westwards as the Rhine and Moselle. The state was organized by its kings as a large estate which aimed at self-sufficiency; except in a few areas, for example in Westphalia and Silesia, it was thinly populated. A great deal of the Prussian lands was covered with sandy soils and marshy wastes, whilst rather more than one-quarter of their area was under forest. Frederick the Great himself summed up realistically the geographical content of his kingdom at the time of his accession in 1740: 'A third at least of my dominions lies in waste; another third is in woods, waters, or marshes. The third, which is cultivated, produces nor wine, nor olives, nor mulberry trees. No fruits nor garden-stuff come to anything, without great care, and very few to the true point of perfection. I have only a few parts in which the wheat and barley have some reputation.'[2] Prussia was a land of village settlement, and its Hohenzollern rulers, above all Frederick the Great, were at pains to develop its agricultural resources. It is estimated that a million immigrants, notably Huguenots from France, were settled in various parts of Prussia during the period 1640–1786, and at least one-fifth of these were established with special privileges on the land. Some 900 villages were founded during the reign of Frederick the Great alone, whose greatest achievement in peace was his work in reclamation: marshland

[1] Cp. *supra*, Chapter XVIII, p. 385.
[2] *The Confessions of Frederick the Great*, ed. Sladen, p. 38.

was reclaimed in East Prussia, in the Warta valley, at the Oder estuary, and in Brandenburg, where the draining of the Oderbruch was a large-scale undertaking. Clover and tobacco were cultivated ; lupins were grown on sandy soil and then ploughed in to fertilize it, whilst even mulberry trees and sericulture were introduced, although this latter innovation was eventually frustrated by the northern climate. To Frederick the Great 'men were dearer than wood', but although he cleared forest land for cultivation, he also passed laws to preserve the forests. Moreover, the geographical location of forests determined very largely the purpose of clearing : where they stood near rivers or large towns, they were cut for timber ; where they were distant from waterways, they were cleared for agriculture.

The city of Berlin, which, like Madrid, owed its importance to its selection as a political capital, was extended and rebuilt by Frederick the Great as his chief residence and seat of government. Unlike Madrid, Berlin enjoyed good waterways, since it was connected with the Elbe by the Spree and Havel rivers and with the Oder by a canal. Prussia's best seaport, Stralsund in western Pomerania, had the least trade, since it lacked river communications such as Stettin commanded at the head of the Oder estuary. Actually the busiest trading port of Prussia was Memel, which stood at the entry to the shallow Kurisches Haff.

One of the chief food crops of Prussia in the latter half of the eighteenth century was potatoes, and beer was the common drink. Prussia proper, Pomerania, and Posen, which was added to Prussia in 1795, yielded a surplus of cereals—especially rye, barley and oats—which supplied Berlin and Brandenburg generally and were also exported via Danzig. Berlin, which had a population of 172,000 in 1800, developed a number of small industries—linen, china-ware and printing. Its nearest port, Stettin, supplied the capital with Rhenish wine, fish and colonial produce.

Already in the Middle Ages Germany had played the leading part in Europe in the exploitation of mineral resources, and many of its miners, who were loosely called Saxon, had migrated to, and settled in, many parts of the Continent where they could apply their technical skill, notably in Transylvania, in Bohemia and in Hungary. In the Middle Ages silver, iron and salt were the chief minerals produced in Germany, but in the eighteenth century, in addition to these, coal was increasingly sought. In Germany the first coal workings were started around Aachen and Zwickau, although near Liége mining began as early as the twelfth century. In the eighteenth century coal was needed to supplement or replace charcoal in the preparation of salt and in the manufacture of glass. Thus the coal district of Saarbrücken gained in importance with the improvement of the Lorraine salt works. In the Ruhr coal workings began *c.* 1734, and developed particularly towards the end of the century when the Ruhr was made navigable down to the Rhine. In upper Silesia, although a beginning was made, very little coal was actually produced in the district between Beuthen and Tarnowitz. The manufacture of salt was carried on widely in many parts of Germany, although only a few places produced it on a large scale. When Schönebeck and Halle became Prussian (*c.* 1720) foreign salt was prohibited, and the former place supplied the whole of Prussia. Elsewhere in Germany there were many local supplies : for example, Hal in Swabia ; around Münden ; at Dürrenberg near Merseburg ; and at Brockenhausen in the duchy of Mark. Many other metals, notably iron, silver, tin and copper, were mined, in many of the highland regions of Germany. Iron was extracted in the Fichtelgebirge especially near Wunsiedel ; in the Harz around Freiburg ; around Bayreuth ; and in the Henneberg district.

It is important to emphasize the small scale and the diffusion of the mineral workings in eighteenth-century Europe : neither the demand for coal and iron nor the technique of their production on a large scale yet existed. The trade of Middle Europe, like its industries, was almost entirely local in character and petty in scale. The reasons for this were largely political : the success of the Dutch and British in maritime commerce and their power at sea made it impossible for the north German towns to play the important part in European trade which had been theirs in the sixteenth century. Further, no efforts were made in the eighteenth century to provide suitably constructed roads for internal transport. And finally, the remarkable subdivision of Middle Europe into some three hundred distinct states involved the continual crossing of frontiers and the payment of customs. Under these conditions the movement of goods was costly : thus it is estimated that wood for fuel could be economically carried by road for a distance of about 12 miles only, and it is said that Bavarian peasants, who owed wood to their landlords in the towns, preferred to buy it there rather than to carry it from their own lands. Since the roads were so bad recourse was made where possible to the waterways, especially for bulk goods like cereals and timber. The Vistula and the Rhine above all were useful in the carriage of these commodities. The former carried large quantities of grain down to the port and market of Danzig, whilst the latter carried—among many things—much timber from the Black Forest *en route* for Holland. Even so, the river-ways of Middle Europe presented many difficulties and impediments to the trader. To cite one instance: on the Weser between Minden and Elsfleth there were no less than 32 toll gates, and of these twelve fell in Hanover, four in Prussia, three in Hesse, and one each in Paderborn, Brunswick, Wolfenbüttel, Lippe and Oldenburg! The use of the excellent river-ways of Middle Europe was thus drastically restricted by political conditions. Nevertheless, some attempts were made to improve inland communications by the construction of several canals. Thus the Plaue canal, which was constructed during the years 1743–5, connected the Havel with the Elbe below Magdeburg and served in the transport of salt from Schönebeck to Brandenburg and Pomerania; in the Ückermark the Templin and Fehrbelin canals were opened respectively in 1745 and 1766; finally, in 1772 the Bromberg canal linked up the Netze river with the Brahe and the Vistula.

Russia.

In territory, population and trade European Russia made marked advances during the eighteenth century. Already by 1780 its estimated population of nearly 27 millions just exceeded that of France and was the greatest of all the European states [1]: by reason of its vast area, however, Russia stood among the least densely populated states of Europe. In 1700 its place in Baltic trade was insignificant and the only maritime outlets within its own territory were the ports of the White Sea, notably Archangel, which was open to ships for only six or seven months of the year.

The foreign policy of Russia in the eighteenth century, as initiated by Peter the Great, aimed consistently at expansion towards the coastlands of the Baltic and Black seas. In the north by his successes over the Swedes Peter was able to secure on the Gulf of Finland Russia's first Baltic outlet, whilst in the south Catherine the Great in the latter half of the eighteenth century defeated the Cossack horsemen of the steppe and gained control of the Crimean peninsula,[2] the Sea of Azov and the Black

[1] Woytinsky, op. cit., I, 24.

[2] Russia thus secured in the southern part of the Crimea a small area of Mediterranean climate and products. The geographical contrasts within the Crimea were clearly noted by a contemporary writer. 'The northern division is flat, poor and only fit for pasturage. In the southern parts the valleys are astonishingly productive, and the climate

Sea coast between the Dniester and the Don, whilst Russian power was extended even beyond the Caucasus to the town of Tiflis on the river Kur. The agricultural development of the Black Earth zone and the rise of the Black Sea ports are essentially nineteenth-century phenomena, although Catherine began to distribute large and potentially valuable estates in the Black Earth region to politicians, generals and favourites. The small flow of Russian trade in the eighteenth century was above all to the Baltic. The foundation of Peter the Great's capital city at the head of the Gulf of Finland signalized the advent of Russia as a Baltic power and deflected trade from the port of Archangel. Founded in 1721, St. Petersburg was built on piles amidst the marshes of the Neva estuary, near the junction of the sea-way from the Gulf of Finland and the inland waterway from Lake Ilmen, the Volkhov, Lake Ladoga and the Neva. Unfortunately, owing to a bar of sand at the mouth of the Neva, vessels could not reach the town from the sea ; in consequence, Baltic vessels had to tranship goods into barges at the port of Cronstadt, which stood on an island off the Neva mouth—an operation which greatly increased freight charges to St. Petersburg and involved long delays.[1] This difficulty was not overcome until the Poutiloff canal was opened in 1884 between the town and Cronstadt, which then enabled St. Petersburg to serve as the first port of Russia. Riga, which had the advantages of a more westerly situation and good river communications, was easily second in importance.

It was only after 1774, when by a treaty with the Turks it was granted the right to navigate the Black Sea and the straits of the Bosporus and the Dardanelles, that Russia was enabled to utilize its recently acquired sea-board on the Black and Azov seas. In the 1790's Taganrog, which lies westwards of the Don estuary, was the chief Black Sea outlet : it derived goods—especially iron and wheat—not only from the basin of the Don, but also from the Volga with which the Don was connected at first by a short land portage and eventually *c.* 1800 by the Kamüshinski canal. In addition, smaller ports like Kherson and Otchakoff commanded the trade of other great Russian rivers. Odessa was opened up as a port only in 1795, and by 1805 it

extremely mild, from the exclusion of these violent winds by which the northern division is frequently incommoded.' Ellis, G., *Notes on a Map of the Caucasus* (1788), p. 8.

[1] Jeans, *Waterways and Water Transport*, p. 177. Thus Newcastle coal sometimes took as long in transit between Cronstadt and St. Petersburg as between Newcastle and Cronstadt !

had already a population of 15,000. In 1804, too, Sebastopol with its excellent harbourage was selected as an exclusively naval port. Odessa had certain geographical advantages which favoured its commercial advance. Situated on the sea-coast between the estuaries of the Dniester and the Dnieper, it stood much nearer to the Bosporus than did either Kherson or Taganrog; it was open all the year whereas Taganrog was closed by ice between November and the end of March; and finally, it had deep-water access, so that there was no need of lading and unlading ships in the roadstead of the port, as was necessary at Kherson. Odessa served the wide hinterland of the Ukraine, which was potentially very productive, especially in wheat and flax, and also that of the Dnieper, itself a trade route, which was connected by short canals with both Riga and St. Petersburg. Even so, the trade of Odessa and indeed of all of the Black Sea ports, was very small before 1800, even in comparison with that of the White Sea, and was almost negligible compared with that of the Baltic. Their trade was largely in the hands of the Greek merchant marine of the Turkish Empire, which carried goods to and from Constantinople and Smyrna. From the standpoint of the chief trading states of western Europe, the Black Sea lay very distant; Russian goods could be shipped much more quickly and cheaply by way of the Baltic. Moreover, the passage through the Dardanelles and Bosporus was very difficult for sailing ships: a strong surface current flows out from the Black Sea; the straits were both tortuous and strewn with rocks and islands, and in summer the easterly wind made sailing through the narrow waters dangerous. Nevertheless, the end of the eighteenth century saw the appearance of Austrian and British ships at the Russian Black Sea ports and also at Galatz in Moldavia, above the delta of the Danube.

The surplus commodities of Russia were, for the most part, those which had figured in its medieval trade: timber, furs, honey, hemp, tar, linen, sail-cloth and flax, to which were now added cereals, especially rye and wheat, and—from about 1750—iron. The iron workings were located mainly in the southern Urals, and also in the Altaian and Nertschinskian mountains. Despite the great distances involved, and thanks to winter sledge-ways and river navigation in spring and summer, transport within Russia was relatively easy and inexpensive. The Russian rivers were navigable over such long distances, and their courses were so related to each other that it was easy, by the construction of a number of short canals, to replace old land portages between rivers: thus the Caspian and Baltic seas were linked up by a canal between the upper Volga and the Volkhov ; further, the Baltic and Black seas were united by canals, and the Don was joined to the Dnieper. Moreover, a long summer route of some 2,000 miles, chiefly by river navigation, reached St. Petersburg from Siberia and even from China.[1]

[1] The line of this route was as follows : by the Selenga river to Lake Baikal ; by the Angara river to the Yenisei : overland to the Ket, thence by the Ob, Irtysh and Tobol rivers ; overland to the Chusovaia river and thence to the Kama and upper Volga. See Oddy, *European Commerce* (1805), pp. 67–8.

CHAPTER XX

EUROPE IN THE RAILWAY AGE (*c.* 1870)

THE revolution in industry and transport, which had its origin in Great Britain in the eighteenth and nineteenth centuries, effected drastic changes in the human geography not only of that country but also of continental Europe. By the year 1870 Britain had long borne the impress of this transformation. Its population had grown greatly and had altered markedly in its distribution. Its major industries had undergone a remarkable regional localization. Finally, by the construction of canals, roads and above all railways, a new route network and new means of transport had been created. It would be misleading to infer, however, that similar conditions were established generally on the continent, even in its western parts. On the contrary, many of the distinguishing features of Britain in the age of coal and iron were barely perceptible on the continent in 1870, and made their appearance belatedly and sporadically at the end of, and subsequently to, the nineteenth century. Thus the development of big urban groups and the regional concentration of industries and population had not advanced there to a degree comparable with that in Great Britain. On the other hand, the revolution in transport had made considerable way on the continent by 1870, since with only small exceptions a system of main railway routes had been established in the several states. Thus although the traveller on the continent in 1870 was able to move more rapidly and more safely than at any earlier period, and although too he could observe many remarkable instances of changes in the distribution of industry and population, even so he must have been continually struck by the many unchanging features of its ancient and traditional life.

In the following pages an attempt is made to review broadly the economic geography of continental Europe about 1870, and it will be necessary to make use of the statistical material which then becomes available.

Population

The population of Europe in 1871 is estimated at 293

millions[1]: it had approximately doubled in the course of a century and, further, it had increased more rapidly than at any earlier period. Even so, Europe was increasing in numbers less rapidly than the other continents: whereas its population constituted about 26 per cent of that of the whole world in 1810, its proportion was barely 22 per cent in 1874. This change in relative world position on the basis of population numbers was chiefly due to the colonization of lands in the Americas, notably in the U.S.A., and also to natural increases in Asia. It should be noted, moreover, that during the nineteenth century emigration from Europe came to assume large proportions. In fact, it is estimated that between 1816 and 1888 some 23 millions emigrated from Europe, above all from the United Kingdom and Germany, and of these about three-fifths settled in the U.S.A.

The population of Europe about the year 1870 was very unevenly distributed both politically and regionally. Actually, the Great Powers of the time in the political sense of the term were those states with the greatest aggregate populations, which were approximately as follows:

		Millions
British Empire (1871)		234
United Kingdom	31·6	
Colonies	11·6	
India	191	
Russian Empire (*c.* 1871)		86
European Russia	74·1	
Asiatic Russia	12·1	
German Empire (1871)		41
France (1866)		38*
Austria-Hungary (1869)		36

Although the relative importance of the Great Powers in diplomacy and war was not directly proportionate to their population numbers or man-power, it is none the less significant that in this respect they easily surpassed the other European states. The second grade of these was occupied by states like Italy (about 27 millions) and Spain (about 16 millions). For the rest the states of Europe had small populations ranging from that of Belgium (5·1 millions) to those of Denmark, Norway and Greece, all of which stood below 2 millions.

An important change was taking place about the year 1870 in the relative distribution of man-power between the Great Powers,

[1] An estimate for 1762 gives 130 millions, for 1778 150 millions. Mulhall, *The Dictionary of Statistics*, p. 441.

* In 1876 the population of France was only 36·9 millions, but its territory had been reduced by the loss of Alsace and part of Lorraine in 1871.

which was the threefold result of the constitution of the German Empire in 1871, its acquisition of Alsace and part of Lorraine from France, and finally, the differential growth of the French and German populations. This change can be readily grasped if the man-power figures for the chief European states in 1860 and 1890 are examined:

GREAT POWERS IN ORDER OF MAN-POWER (i.e. MALE POPULATION BETWEEN THE AGES OF 15 AND 55)

	1860. Millions	1890. Millions
Russian Empire	17·7	25·2
France	10·9	10·8
German Empire	10·6†	12·5
Austrian Empire	9·1	10·4
United Kingdom	7·5	9·7

Thus in 1860 France had a small numerical advantage in man-power over Germany, an advantage which was the more real in that Germany was then a loose confederation of states. From 1871 onwards the new and highly organized German Empire won an increasing lead in man-power. It is significant, too, that already in 1860 the lands later united within the German Empire supported a greater number of men of military age than did Austria, which had long been the greatest state of Middle Europe.

The geographical significance of these aggregate figures is more fully revealed if the relative densities of population in the different states is examined. Thus it will be seen from the table below that great inequalities obtained in the average density of population per square mile, the figures ranging between 12 and 425.

APPROXIMATE POPULATION DENSITIES PER SQ. MILE IN OR ABOUT 1870

Belgium (1866)	425	Denmark	121
Holland	285	Portugal (1864)	112
United Kingdom (1871)	261	Rumania	99
Italy (1871)	242	Spain (1860)	80
German Empire (1871)	205	Bulgaria	80
France (1866)	182	Greece	58
Austria	176	‡Russia in Europe	35
Switzerland	173	Sweden	23
Hungary	125	Norway	14
Poland	123	Finland	12

† i.e. in the territories, excluding Alsace and part of Lorraine, which were included in the German Empire in 1871.

‡ In Asiatic Russia the density was 2 per sq. mile, and for the Russian Empire as a whole 10 per sq. mile.

A study of these figures suggests that population was densest in western and Middle Europe and thinned out particularly in the north (in the Scandinavian states), to lesser extent in the east (in European Russia), and finally, to a still lesser extent in the south-east and south-west (in the Iberian and Balkan peninsulas). Further, although they indicate relatively high densities in the more industrialized countries of western Europe, it should be noted that in the case of Italy a high density was maintained under an essentially agricultural economy.

Again, within the several states of Europe, the distribution of population as between town and country showed considerable variations, and showed further, particularly in the west of Europe, an increasing concentration of population in the towns. It may be recalled that the essence of urban development is economic specialization—the grouping together of people who are engaged primarily in industry and trade and are dependent for their supplies of food on the agricultural countryside or on importation. The application to industrial production of steam power derived from coal, which was one of the most important features of the Industrial Revolution, led, at first in Britain and later on the continent, to a concentration of industry in towns which were situated on or near to coal-fields. Hence it is not surprising that Britain had become urbanized to a considerable degree by 1870, as the figures below eloquently show. On the statistical basis that towns are settlements of 2,000 or more inhabitants, the distribution of population between town and country in England and Wales was as follows:

1821 . . 50 per cent of the total population lived in towns
1871 . . 61·8 " " " " " "

In contrast, no continental state had reached so high a degree of urban development. In Germany and France the process of rapid city growth was still in its infancy. Only 36·1 per cent of the total population of the German Empire lived in towns in 1871,[1] and in France only 31·1 per cent in 1872. This sharp disparity in urbanization between southern Britain and the continental states emphasized the fact that in the latter the bulk of the population still lived in rural settlements and engaged above all in agricultural pursuits. Outside Germany, France, Belgium and Holland, in which the new methods of industrial organization and the construction of railways had first spread

[1] The revolutionary change in the German Empire after 1871 is illustrated by later figures: thus in 1900—60 per cent of the population lived in towns, since when the proportion has continually increased.

from England, rural settlement was even more preponderant. Thus in the Russian Empire about 89 per cent of the population were living in the country, and in Sweden 87 per cent—a figure roughly true for Norway and Denmark. In contrast the proportion of the population occupying rural settlements in Italy is somewhat lower; this, however, was not the result of new industrial developments, but rather an indication of its traditional social and political organization in cities.

In short, the concentration of population and industry in the towns of western Europe, which is so striking to-day, had scarcely begun in 1870. If capital cities are excepted, there were sixteen towns in the United Kingdom with over 100,000 inhabitants in 1871; in Germany only eight; in France only eight and in Russia only six. Elsewhere, except in Italy, the big town existed rarely, apart from the capitals of states. These cities, however, tended generally to grow at a faster rate than others and thus to concentrate an increasing proportion of the total population. The following figures [1] give the populations of the chief European capitals in 1850 and 1880, and it will be seen that Berlin grew most rapidly during these decades:

POPULATION IN THOUSANDS

	1850	1880
London	2,363	3,830
Paris	1,053	2,269
St. Petersburg	485	877
Vienna	444	726
Berlin	419	1,122
Rome	175	300

In general, outside Britain the great towns of 1870 were rather old cities, seaports, provincial and state capitals than new industrial growths. Thus in Germany state capitals like Munich and old medieval cities like Cologne, although they grew less fast than new industrial centres like Essen, Chemnitz, Duisburg and Düsseldorf, much exceeded them in numbers. Thus:

	1800	1850	1880	1920
Munich	30,000	110,000	230,000	631,000
Cologne	50,000	97,000	145,000	634,000
Essen	4,000	9,000	57,000	439,000
Chemnitz	14,000	32,000	95,000	304,000
Düsseldorf	10,000	27,000	95,000	407,000
Duisburg	—	—	41,000	244,000

It should be emphasized, therefore, that many of the great industrial cities of the continent are largely post-1870 phenomena.

[1] Woytinsky, *Die Welt in Zahlen*, I, 132–5.

Agriculture

It has already been noted that outside Great Britain rural settlement remained predominant throughout Europe, and it was agriculture which formed the basis of European economy in 1870. The grain lands of southern Russia and the U.S.A. were only just beginning to supply large quantities of cereals for export and the increasing needs of Europe had to be satisfied from its own soil, partly by an extension of cultivation but above all by more intensive methods. Actually the acreage under crops increased markedly in the course of the century as a result of the utilization of land formerly under forest, pasture, marsh or heath. The following figures [1] indicate approximately this advance in cultivation :

ACREAGE UNDER CROPS IN EUROPE [2] (IN MILLIONS)

1820	1840	1860	1880
364	427	471	546

No less striking was the increased yield of grain per acre, notably in Germany and western Europe generally, a change which was consequent on many factors : the abandonment of the open-field system, agricultural improvements in the rotation of crops and in the preparation of the soil, and the use of fertilizers. The production of grain in Europe, in result, was more than proportional to the increase of cultivated land.

GRAIN PRODUCTION IN EUROPE IN MILLIONS OF BUSHELS

1820	1840	1860	1880
2,800	3,300	4,200	5,040

Actually, up till about 1880, Europe produced sufficient grain for its own needs and slightly more per head of the population in 1880 than in 1820. Meat and wine, in contrast, despite great increases in production, did not quite keep pace with the growth of population. On the other hand, the cultivation of potatoes on a large scale, an almost entirely nineteenth-century innovation on the continent, produced an increasing supply of food, particularly in France, Prussia and Austria proper :

POTATO PRODUCTION IN EUROPE IN MILLIONS OF TONS

1820	1840	1860	1880
20	40	50	60

Another new crop which was grown increasingly on the better

[1] Mulhall, op. cit., p. 7.
[2] ' Europe ' in these tables includes the United Kingdom.

soils, especially in France and Germany, was the sugar beet. Its cultivation began about 1806, when a great part of Europe, under the control of Napoleon, was cut off by the British blockade from the sea and thus deprived of supplies of imported sugar from the West and East Indies. Among the variety of cereal crops grown should be noted maize, which was cultivated in more southerly parts of the continent, e.g., in Italy and Hungary. Further, it is noteworthy that the yield of cereals varied markedly in different parts of the continent. Denmark had the highest yield, both in wheat and rye, whilst that of Russia was very low: thus Denmark produced 31·8 bushels per acre, Russia only 5·5.[1] In barley and oats Holland showed the highest yield. Finally, it should be noted that the forest resources of Europe had become, despite some small efforts at afforestation and as a result of the extension of agriculture and the demand for timber, greatly depleted by the late nineteenth century. Available figures for the years between 1870 and 1877 indicate broadly that proportion of the areas of European states which were officially described as 'forests and woods'.

PROPORTION OF THE AREA OF CERTAIN STATES UNDER 'FORESTS AND WOODS' ABOUT 1870

	Per cent		Per cent
European Russia (1872)	42	Switzerland (1877)	19
Sweden (1875)	41	France (1874)	16
Austria proper (1875)	30	Holland (1875)	6
Prussia (1876)	23	Denmark (1876)	4
Norway (1870)	22		

In fact, only a few countries, notably Russia, Sweden and Norway, had surplus quantities of timber for export.

Industry

The Industrial Revolution above all in Great Britain and to a much lesser extent on the continent gave Europe in 1870 the leading position in the world in the exploitation of mineral resources and in other branches of industry, notably the textiles. Europe was fortunate in the possession of large reserves of coal and iron, both of which became of essential and increasing importance under the changing conditions of industry and transport. The use of coal as a source of power and the manifold uses to which iron, and later steel, were put in the manufacture of machinery, railways, ships, &c., stimulated their production on an ever-growing scale. Although its resources in coal were not potentially so great as those of the U.S.A. or of China, it appears

[1] These figures relate to years between 1870 and 1876.

that soon after 1870 Europe was producing more than two-thirds of the coal output of the world. Similarly, it was producing more than three-quarters of the world's pig iron. The relative importance of the chief producing countries is shown in the following table:

COAL PRODUCTION, INCLUDING ANTHRACITE, ASPHALT AND BITUMEN, IN MILLIONS OF TONS
(Annual Average 1870–4)

United Kingdom	120·7
U.S.A.	43·1
German Empire	31·8
France	15·1
Belgium (1871)	13·7
Austria proper (1870)	6·4

PIG IRON PRODUCTION IN MILLIONS OF TONS
(Annual Average 1870–4)

United Kingdom	6·4
U.S.A.	2·2
Germany	1·8
France	1·2

The strong position occupied by Germany in the course of the 1860's in the production of coal and iron and its superiority therein to France recall the dictum of Keynes that 'the German Empire was built more truly on coal and iron than on blood and iron'.

Foreign Trade

The commodities exchanged by the different states of Europe will be noted later, but it is interesting here to examine a statistical table [1] which indicates for many of the continental states the extent to which imported and exported merchandize was carried by land and river on the one hand, and by sea, on the other. It should be noted that these percentages relate to the value, not to the weight, of goods moved.

PERCENTAGE BY VALUE OF TOTAL IMPORTS AND EXPORTS INTO AND FROM COUNTRIES IN 1875 BY LAND AND RIVER, AND BY SEA

Countries	Imports		Exports	
	By land and river	By sea	By land and river	By sea
Russia in Europe	48·4	51·6	28·8	71·2
Denmark	6·2	93·8	15·1	84·9
Holland	57·8	42·2	73·3	26·7
Belgium	63	37	69·4	30·6
France	35·1	64·9	33·3	66·7
Italy	37	63	49·2	50·8
Austria	82·2	17·8	84·6	15·4
Spain (1873)	22	78	9·4	90·6

[1] *Statistical Abstracts for . . . Foreign Countries*, 1860–75, p. 96.

Thus of the countries listed above those which imported and exported more by inland routes than by sea were Austria, Holland and Belgium. Further, those which imported goods mainly by sea were Denmark, Spain, Italy and France, whilst these states, together with Russia, exported mainly by sea. It is noteworthy in the case of the latter that whereas imports entered equally by land and by sea, exports went for the greater part by sea. Further, it is striking how small a proportion of Spanish trade was carried over the Pyrenees.

Communication and Transport

Certainly the means of transport in continental Europe were revolutionized by about the middle of the nineteenth century as a result of the establishment of railways. 'Effective distance', that is, the time occupied per unit distance in the movement of persons and goods was, in result, drastically curtailed for the first time in history. In fact, thanks both to the railway, and to the telegraph which by 1870 connected not only the main cities of Europe but also the oceans and the narrow seas, and also to the steamship which already played some part in maritime communications, a beginning was made in that annihilation of distance which still continues to this day.

Railway construction, which began in England, was undertaken generally on the continent, first in Belgium, rather later in Germany, and later still in France, but even in Scandinavian and Mediterranean Europe a system of trunk lines had been for the most part completed by 1870. The mileage of railways built and the pace at which building took place varied considerably in different parts of the continent. Railway construction needed not only large capital sums, supplies of coal and steel, and technical skill, but also an effective demand for the carriage of goods and passengers. Thus the development of railway construction was governed by a number of factors: in particular, the economic condition and population density of the different states. Among these many factors were purely geographical ones: the actual distances to be covered, the relative position of the state and the physical difficulties presented by the lie of the land. In other words, a country like Belgium was well adapted for, as it was quick to undertake, railway construction: it possessed iron and coal, although the latter lay deep and was difficult to exploit; it was small in actual area and densely settled; its heavy industries promised useful freight; and finally, it occupied a strategical position at one of the chief north-western entries into the continent. In contrast, in southern, eastern and northern Europe generally, where the population was essentially rural, scattered and low in density, and further, where large-scale industries and capital were largely lacking, there were both less need and less ability to embark upon large-scale railway programmes. Moreover, in certain countries the relief of the land presented further obstacles to the railroad: thus in Italy the continuous and centrally placed Apennine mountains and in Spain the steep-edged interior tableland increased the engineering and economic difficulties.

In general, almost every European state had built by 1870 a network of main railway routes, which afforded access between its chief cities and in a number of cases provided also long-distance

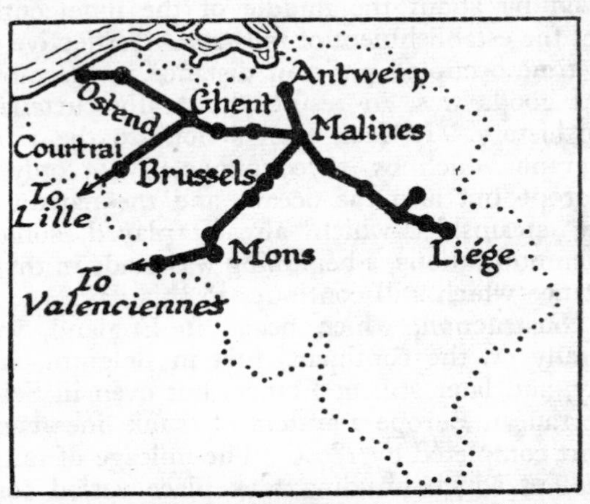

Fig. 56.—Belgian Railways in 1842 (after Jouffroy)

trans-continental routes, e.g., between Calais and Marseilles and between Hamburg and Trieste. In the Balkan peninsula railway construction was the most belated: Serbia had no lines at all; Greece opened its first line in 1869, between Athens and Piraeus; in northern Turkey, in the region which became Rumania, a line was built as early as 1860, to connect up Cernavoda on the Danube with the Black Sea port of Constanţa.[1] Thus trans-continental routes were not completed between western Europe and Constantinople; in 1878 the line ended at Bazias on the Danube between Belgrade and the Iron Gate. Nor did the Russian railroads allow of continuous passage in 1880 farther eastwards than Nijni Novgorod. In the west of Europe, in contrast, many railways were open even in the 'forties.

[1] Cp. *supra*, p. 387.

Already by 1842 the Belgium state had built a good network of lines (Fig. 56), so that it was then possible to travel from Antwerp via Brussels and Mons towards the French frontier, or from Antwerp or Ostend by way of Malines to Liége, whence a few years later lines were extended to the German frontier and Cologne. In Germany railway building began in the various constituent states of the Confederation, but even so it proceeded fast particularly from the 'forties onwards and resulted in the creation of a number of long-distance lines (Fig. 57). Although in the north there was a tendency at first to build east-west railway lines subsidiary to the north-south river routes, nevertheless Germany, together with Austria,

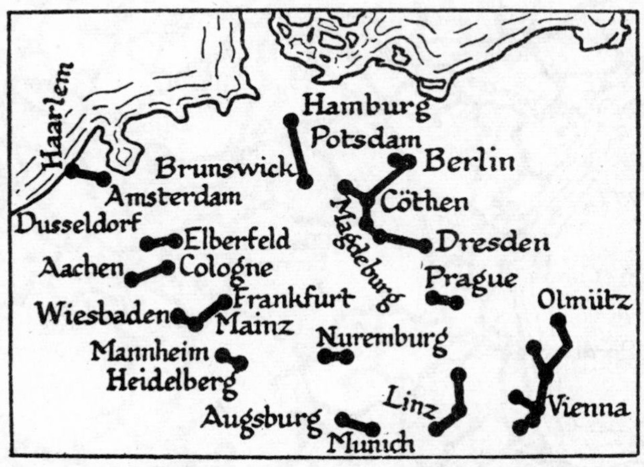

FIG. 57.—Railways in Middle Europe in 1841 (after Jouffroy)

was the first country to complete a continuous north-south transcontinental railroad. This achievement made itself effective in a striking manner when in 1851 the British Indian mail, formerly carried across France, was sent overland between Trieste and Hamburg with the result that news reached London some forty hours earlier than Paris, which lacked complete rail communications with Marseilles until 1855 (Fig. 58). In fact French railway construction lagged behind that in Belgium and Germany, but in 1842 the state conceived and defined the geographical plan to which its railroads were to conform. Paris was made the essential focus of the railway system, which was designed not only to connect the capital with the chief peripheral cities—Marseilles, Calais, Brest, Strasbourg and Bordeaux, but also to exploit the great opportunities of France as a gateway to the continent and as an isthmian passage-way between the North Sea and the Mediterranean. In result, by 1870 the Pyrenees had been turned at each end and a tunnel had been pierced

FIG. 58.—Railway Development in France up to 1870 (after Brunhes and Deffontaines)
Note the early development in Belgium

through the Alps beneath the Mont Cenis pass. Finally, in Russia, which enjoyed extensive, though seasonal, waterway facilities, but included an enormous area, railway routes had not advanced far by 1870, although the arterial line between St. Petersburg and the Black Sea ports was open. Little, in fact, was done before 1857, except the line between Moscow and

St. Petersburg, which was remarkable since, in accordance with the will of the autocratic Czar, it followed a directly straight course.

The effects of the revolution in inland transport produced by the use of the steam locomotive must not be exaggerated. Even in 1870 the mileage of railways built, scarcely, except in Great Britain, approached one-third of the present length; further there were vast regions in eastern, southern and northern Europe which lacked effective railroads, and many districts within each state which stood remote from the constructed lines. Thus about 1870 a contemporary wrote of Russia: 'In this country, so rich in corn, there were until recently no good roads; the means of communications were so few as to cause scarcity and even famine in a number of provinces, while others enjoyed a superfluity', although even so, sufficient railways had been built by 1868 to facilitate considerable increases in the export of corn as compared with 1847. Again, it must not be inferred that the waterways were abandoned under the competition of railways. On the contrary they continued to carry a fair proportion of the inland freight and certainly a greater volume of goods than in earlier periods. Thus it is estimated [1] that in 1875 21 per cent of all the goods carried in Germany were conveyed along the inland waterways. Moreover, from 1870 onwards, the rivers became increasingly more serviceable than hitherto. In the first place, obstructive tolls had been largely abolished, and further, the principle of free passage along international rivers had been applied, notably to the Rhine and the Danube. In the second place, many engineering works had been begun, if not as yet successfully completed, to improve the navigability of the great European rivers, by embanking and thus confining the channel in low-lying sections of their valleys, and by widening and deepening the channels at difficult points, as in the case of the Rhine at the rocky Bingen reef and in that of the Danube at and above the Iron Gate.[2] In particular, the traffic of the Rhine greatly expanded owing to its position adjacent to the rapidly developing Westphalian region which exported coal in large quantities and imported iron. Mainz lost its transfer rights in 1831 and thanks also to river improvements the head of navigation was advanced to Mannheim whence the railway was built to Basle in 1846. Again, the canals as an adjunct to river navigation had been considerably extended, especially in Holland, Germany and France, and for the carriage of heavy

[1] Clapham, *The Economic Development of France and Germany*, p. 354.
[2] Cp. *supra*, Chapter XVIII, p. 386, and Fig. 53.

goods they remained important. Finally, considerable advances were made in the construction of main highways on scientific lines, so that much was done to remedy the road conditions, e.g., in the Prussian Rhineland, since, except in France, roads had been deplorable in the early nineteenth century.

On the high seas, the inner seas and the greater rivers steam power had already for a few decades definitely established its practical utility. Even so, it played a small part as compared with wind power in the navigation of 1870. Thus, in maritime commerce the sailing ship was still by far the chief carrier. In the case of the United Kingdom, which led the way in the construction of iron and steel ships and in the use of steam, some 20 per cent of the tonnage of the merchant marine in 1870 was steam driven ; the figure for France was 14 per cent, for Germany 8 per cent, for Holland 5 per cent and for Norway as low as 2 per cent. In the carriage of passengers, too, steamship services had in a number of cases been established. Regular services by steamship between Europe and North America were in operation, and the European traveller had already a choice of points of embarkation. He might leave from Liverpool or Bristol ; from Cherbourg where a rather intermittent service began in 1847 ; or from Hamburg or Bremen which transported numerous immigrants to North America. The Hamburg-America Line, as it was ultimately called, began steamship services as early as 1856, which started weekly crossings to New York in 1872. Bremen instituted weekly passages in 1866.

In the carriage of messages no less than in that of passengers and freight revolutionary changes had been effected by 1870. The telegraph by land lines and by sea cables spanned the world which shrank in consequence into a single market. By land the telegraph replaced the system of semaphore signalling from poles which had been used in France and Prussia. In 1851 Dover and Calais were united by cable, and in the '50's the other narrow seas of Europe were similarly united. In the '60's, further, the first trans-Atlantic cables were laid.[1]

France

France in the nineteenth century benefited greatly from the effects of the Revolution of 1789, which abolished serfdom, removed the internal customs, and increased the number of peasant proprietorships. In 1870 rather more than half of the population of France still derived its livelihood from agriculture, and, what is more, more than half of those who worked the

[1] Clapham, op. cit., p. 363.

land were small freeholders. The effect of peasant ownership of small compact holdings, instead of scattered strips in the open field, was expressed in the improvement of agricultural methods and in the increasing yield of the soil. It is estimated that in 1877 cereals were grown on 30 per cent of the total area of France but even so, despite its large production of cereals, France had to import small quantities of grain. Potatoes, which had formerly been disdained in France, were produced with greatly increasing yields between 1850 and 1875. Further, in the cultivation of sugar beet and of the vine France held the first place not only in Europe but in the world. It is estimated that one-twentieth of the whole area of France was covered with vineyards in 1872, and although production was greatest in the south there were only nine departments in which the vine was not grown. In industry France stood high among the European states. If its coal resources were scarcely comparable with those of Great Britain, the U.S.A. and Germany, they enabled it to satisfy three-quarters of its consumption in 1870. The chief mines were located in the northern field around Valenciennes, in the upper Loire basin around St. Etienne and Rive de Gier, in Burgundy around Le Creusot, and finally around Alès in the south-west. The chief iron workings, after the loss in 1871 of the Lorraine mines, stood in the three departments of the Nord, of Meurthe and Moselle, and of Saône and Loire. In the textile industries France occupied an important place on the continent: cottons, woollens, linens and silk fabrics were manufactured. The imports of France included raw materials for its textile industries, coal and coke, coffee, grain and animals. Among its exports the chief were silks, woollens and to a lesser extent cottons, wines, spirits, apparel, and 'millinery and small fancy wares'.

Belgium

Belgium was one of the smallest of the European states, but it was easily the most densely populated, a characteristic of the region already in the later Middle Ages.[1] Its population was almost equally divided into Walloon (French) and Flemish (Germanic) speaking groups. Less than a quarter of its area, that is, the Ardennes region above all, was classified as 'woods and forests'; almost the whole of the remainder was divided between meadow and pasture and arable land, on which cereals, potatoes, flax and beet were cultivated. The agriculture of Belgium was, and had long been, practised on the best scientific lines. In the mining of coal Belgium stood fourth among the

[1] Cp. *supra*, Chapter XVI, p. 334.

European states, notwithstanding that the coal lay deep and was difficult to obtain. Hainaut was the chief field, the mines of the province of Liège standing second. The abundance of coal, the early development of railways and a long tradition of industrial activity all served to foster manufacturing to a high degree. Iron smelting and steel production, based only partially on local ores, glass making and linen weaving were the chief industries. Among the exports iron in various forms, linen, and machinery stood first; among the imports grain, flax and hemp, manures, cotton, oil seeds and iron ore may be noted. Belgian trade relations were mainly with northern Europe, but extended also to the Americas. Of its great medieval cities Ghent maintained some of its former relative importance, being included among the four largest towns, Brussels, Liège and Antwerp being the other three. Antwerp, since the opening of the Scheldt in 1795, had become one of the chief maritime gates of Europe.

Holland

Holland was a considerable imperial state: its colonies occupied about fifty-five times the area of the homeland and were nearly seven times as populous. Commerce remained the chief element in Dutch economy, the bulk of it being carried on with the North Sea and Baltic lands and also with the Far Eastern colonies, whence tropical products, e.g., coffee, cocoa and rice, were brought. The agriculture of Holland was well developed, and made to yield large supplies of cereals and potatoes. Its greatest city, Amsterdam, which had a population of about a quarter of a million in 1870, made continual efforts to improve its access to the sea. In the eighteenth century, owing to the merging of two islands at the mouth of the Zuider Zee and the consequent shallowing of that sea and owing also to the growing draught of ships, it had created an outport on the North Sea at Nieuwe Deep, from which a canal was cut to Amsterdam. In 1876 the convenience of the town and port was much increased by the construction of a direct, deep-water canal, which reached the sea at Ijmuiden. Further, Rotterdam, although it had only about half the population of Amsterdam, was growing fast as one of the principal gates of the Rhineland.

Denmark

Denmark in 1870 in many respects lacked the distinguishing features of its present economic geography. Cereal production —particularly barley, rye and oats—then played the most important part in its agricultural economy. The best-cultivated lands were those of the big estates, on which record yields were obtained, but five-sixths of the country was held by free-holding peasants. The butter of the peasants was disdained in 1870 both in the towns and abroad, and the only butter fit for export was that of the great landowners. The revolution in the agricultural economy of Denmark which made it an important producer of bacon, butter and eggs for export began only towards 1890, when the competition of American cereals carried to Europe by steamship led to increased attention to dairy farming.

Germany

The remarkable economic development of Germany in the latter half of the nineteenth century transformed the human geography of a country which, it has been seen,[1] was an economically stagnant region in the previous century. Political conditions for a long time arrested its economic progress. In 1815 the loosely organized German Confederation consisted of thirty-nine states, and although this marked an advance on the conditions of 1789 when over three hundred states existed, its political organization was still such as to obstruct its internal and external relations. Not only did each state in 1815 have its own customs system but some of them had tariff obstacles within their own territories: thus there were sixty tariffs within the Prussian state. Moreover, the fact that state territories were often discontinuous further increased the complications for traders. Further, many different systems of coinage, measurements and postal systems obtained, and many different legal codes governing commerce and finance. Germany long remained, in fact, a predominantly agricultural land which satisfied almost completely its own needs. In 1850 industry was still essentially a rural occupation, and despite the creation of peasant proprietorships, open-field villages were still to be found. The economic advance of Germany began under the stimulus of railway construction, of the Zollverein movement, of the extension of educational facilities, and finally, of the political unification, achieved by Prussia, in 1871.[2] Moreover, it was conditioned by the great potentialities which Germany possessed in its coal, lignite and iron resources. The Zollverein or customs union, which was created under the leadership of Prussia, substituted from 1832 onwards a broadening area of absolute free trade for a muddle of intersecting customs units, and only low tariffs were set up

[1] Cp. *supra*, Chapter XIX, p. 406.
[2] Cp. *supra*, Chapter XIII, pp 274–6.

against foreign goods in the early 1870's. Further, the great international rivers, the Rhine, Elbe and Danube, were improved and freed from tolls.

Already by 1870 there were clear signs of those drastic changes in the scale and localization of industry and in the growth of towns which occurred for the most part after 1870. In 1871 the most densely settled parts of the empire were the old Free cities of Lübeck, Hamburg and Bremen, and the region between the middle Elbe and Oder, which prior to 1871 formed the kingdom of Saxony. This concentration of population[1] reflected the industrial importance of the region: lignite was mined in shallow pit and open workings, whilst textiles—cloth, cottons, stockings and lace—were the chief industry. Except in the case of the cotton industry, which was relatively new, the textiles were made in the countryside and steam power was not yet employed. Another region of outstanding development in industry and population numbers about 1870 was the Ruhr or Westphalian coalfield. Since 1840 coal had been effectively mined in the southern part of the field in the Ruhr and Roer valleys, as also in the Saar basin; similarly, the lignite beds along the lower Weser and Rhine were also being exploited. Textile industry, utilizing the soft water of the Wupper valley, and iron and steel working, based at first on local ore, were also established in the Ruhr region: thus silk manufacture at Crefeld, woollens and cottons at Elberfeld-Barmen, and steel at Solingen, were becoming increasingly important. By its acquisition of Alsace and eastern Lorraine in 1871 Germany strengthened its industrial position, since the former had a well-developed cotton industry and the latter formed almost the whole of what was the largest ironfield in Europe, although its value was restricted until after 1880 when it became possible to convert its phosphoric ores into steel by means of the Gilchrist-Thomas basic process. In contrast to the actively developing Saxon and Westphalian coalfields, that of upper Silesia began large-scale exploitation only in the 1870's.

Austria-Hungary

The Austro-Hungarian Empire, embracing extensive territories astride the middle Danube and fronting the Adriatic in Istria and Dalmatia, constituted in 1870 not only one of the major states of Europe but also, with the exception of Dalmatia, a single customs unit. In the varieties of its nationalities,

[1] The density per square mile in Saxony was 477 in 1871, the average for the whole empire being 202.

languages, customs, religions and cultural levels, it was a Europe in miniature. There were only four large cities of over 100,000 inhabitants, namely Vienna, Budapest, Prague and Trieste. The land of the empire was almost equally divided between forest, pasture and arable. The rearing of horses, cattle and sheep was important, especially in Hungary, which was characterized by large villages of 10,000 and even 20,000 people. Austria-Hungary produced large supplies of grain of all kinds and a surplus for export; in viticulture it had a place second only to France among European states; whilst in the '70's it produced sufficient sugar from the beet to meet its own needs and even for export. But agricultural methods were unscientific in many parts, for example in Hungary, where large estates were typical, the yield was low and manuring not generally understood. A variety of minerals were exploited, and sufficient coal and lignite raised for Austrian purposes. The cotton industry had established itself in the towns of Bohemia and to a lesser extent in those of Lower Austria. Trieste, the port of Austria, developed an industry in the milling of corn brought from the Black Sea; Fiume, a smaller town with an excellent harbour, served increasingly as the port of Hungary, with which it was linked by rail. Steamers on the Danube formed a convenient link between Austria and Hungary for the carriage of passengers and goods. Finally, the trade of Austria-Hungary was of an essentially miscellaneous character: goods of the same designation were both imported and exported—a typical feature in the late nineteenth century, which expresses the increased fluidity of exchange. The item 'Fancy wares including jewellery' is interesting as one of the exports in 1870.

Russia in Europe

Russia in Europe, including Finland and the kingdom of Poland, formed only a small part, about a quarter, of the area of the whole Russian Empire, but it was essentially its heartland, containing some six-sevenths of its total population. If Russia was the most populous state in continental Europe, it was nevertheless scantily populated per unit of area and in many respects the least developed economically and culturally. Rather more than two-fifths of its area was described in 1870 as under 'woods and forests', which produced much surplus timber for export. In fact, Russia in Europe consisted very broadly of two regions defined by a line between lat. 50° N. in the west and lat. 56° N. in the east: the northern half of the country was largely forest and marsh with sporadic patches of cultivation; the southern half, which included the Black Earth belt, contained wide expanses of arable land together with patches of sandy waste and forest. European Russia was thus a land of great potentialities as a producer of cereals, flax and hemp, whilst it had considerable resources of coal, iron, petroleum, as well as timber. In other words, it included a variety of economically complementary regions, since these enjoyed a variety of climatic conditions and of natural products. Actually, however, owing to its low cultural level and to its inadequate communications by rail, road and river, internal and external trade was very small in relation to its population numbers, its area and its potentialities. Up to 1850 the Russian population, differentiated sharply in race and language, was made up almost entirely of an unfree peasantry. Agriculture was of a primitive type, and the country supplied its additional needs by means of home industries, a few state factories, and a few others established on the estates of large proprietors. The manufacture of cotton goods, the only industry which was then organized on capitalistic lines, was carried on around Moscow and also in Poland around Lodz. The Moscow region derived its raw cotton from Persia and the Levant, by way of the summer fair of Nijni Novgorod, to which it was carried up the Volga. There were few other industries in 1870 which had achieved any scale or marked localization : in 1871 a start was made at Ekaterinoslav in the working of iron and the production of steel. The scale of Russian foreign trade may be gauged by the fact that it was less than a third by value of that of Belgium. Export was mainly by sea, and for the greater part by way of the Black Sea ports. Imports came overland as well as by sea. Among these was tea, which was brought overland and by sea from China and formed, together with rye bread, a staple element in the Russian dietary. Among the exports of Russia that of wheat increased rapidly in the '60's and supplanted flax in the first place ; other exports in 1870 were a variety of cereals, flax, hemp and linseed, timber and bristles. Among the imports stood coal, raw cotton, machinery, wrought iron and rails, tea, raw wool and textiles. Great Britain and Germany were the chief customers of Russia.

Rumania

To the north of the lower Danube the principality of Rumania, which was created by the political union of the former Turkish principalities of Wallachia and Moldavia, showed already in 1870, despite its relatively backward cultural condition, considerable economic potentialities. It possessed timber and mineral resources in the mountain zone of the Carpathians and the Transylvanian Alps ; oil wells, vineyards and orchards in the foothill belt below ; and broad stretches of plain which were well favoured in soils and climate for cereal production. Rumania held a seaport, Constanţa, on the Dobruja coast of the Black Sea ; its chief surplus commodity, cereals, were being exported on an increasing scale, especially from its Danubian port of Galatz, although the condition of the channels through the Danube delta made shipment difficult.[1] Its chief customers, both of which traded by sea, were Austria and Great Britain. Essentially, as it proudly claimed, a Danubian and not a Balkan state, Rumania had an area about a quarter that of France and a population of about 5 millions.

The Mediterranean States

Although it had long ceased to be the main axis of European culture and the chief thoroughfare of its international trade, the Mediterranean still played an important part in European navigation and commerce, and, moreover, one which was becoming more markedly so, thanks to the development of the grain production of south Russia and to the opening of the Suez canal. The first place in Mediterranean trade was held by Great Britain, which held strategical bases at Gibraltar and Malta, and in 1878, at Cyprus. Among the Mediterranean states proper, all of which engaged characteristically in maritime trade and in coastwise navigation, Italy owned the greatest tonnage of shipping and shared with France the chief trade of the sea. The use of the steamship, which then formed a small part of the total shipping, involved direct voyages and the avoidance of a number of formerly essential stations, notably at Crete, Cyprus and Cyrenaïca, although it made other stations, e.g., Gibraltar and Malta, necessary for coaling. The leading seaports of the Mediterranean were in many cases those which had flourished in the medieval period, but their relative positions were changed and other cities had entered the field. In Spain, Barcelona and in France, Marseilles were still pre-eminent ; in Italy, Genoa and Palermo as formerly, together with Naples and Leghorn, shared the bulk of the trade ; in Turkey, Constantinople and Smyrna, in Egypt Alexandria, and in Palestine Jaffa, retained their traditional importance. Among the ports of more recent development were Algiers, the link between France and its Algerian territories ; Trieste, the Austrian outlet at the head of the Adriatic ; and Port Said, at the entry to the Suez canal, the foundations of which were laid only in 1859.

[1] See *supra*, Chapter XVIII, pp. 387–8.

The Suez canal, the long-cherished project of the French, had just been opened in 1870. It was only in the years 1846–7 that French engineers established the fact that the levels of the Red Sea and the Mediterranean were approximately the same, and thus disposed of a bogey which had helped hitherto to discourage the canal scheme.[1] Great Britain, needlessly suspicious of French aims in the Levant, consistently opposed the canal project, and urged as an alternative the construction of a railway between Alexandria, Cairo and Suez, to facilitate the passage of merchants and mails. Actually this was completed in 1858. The geographical changes produced locally by the construction of the canal were small: the canal itself was a deep channel some 90 miles long across a desert isthmus; a fresh-water canal, essential to settlement along the canal banks, was carried from the Nile at Cairo to Suez; and finally Port Said and Suez grew up at the terminals of the canal. From its first years of operation the figures show that the canal was predominantly used by British vessels, above all those bound for India: thus 72 per cent of the total tonnage which passed through the canal during the years 1870–4 was British owned. Finally, the opening of the canal promised stimulus to the development of those Mediterranean ports which offered rapid rail systems across the continent: e.g., Trieste and Marseilles, and later Genoa and Brindisi. On the other hand, it reduced the overland traffic passing through the Turkish cities of Aleppo and Damascus.

Italy

Italy, prior to its union in 1866 under the royal house of Savoy, was divided into seven states, some at least of which were notoriously misgoverned. It was essentially a land of agricultural economy, despite the number and size of its cities and its high density of population, but it produced insufficient grain for its large population. Although there were local industries in Italy there was no large-scale Italian industry, whilst internal tariffs obstructed trade. After the union the customs tariff of Piedmont, where the new dynasty formerly ruled, was adopted for the whole country, except for the small area in Rome where the Papal state still survived. Railway construction had begun in the separate states, but after the union attempts were made to complete a network for the whole country. The limited raw materials of Italy, notably silk and hemp, were utilized in industry the development of which, however, was greatly handicapped by lack of capital, coal and industrial technique.

[1] Cp. *supra*, Chapter IX, p. 196.

Even so, the trade of Italy increased rapidly after the union, its principal customers being France, England and Austria. In 1870 cotton and cotton goods, coal, grain and sugar were imported, whilst amongst the exports silk, especially raw silk, and wine in casks, stood easily first and second respectively.

Spain

Although it was about 75 per cent greater in area than Italy, Spain had a population not much more than half as large. About one-fifth of the country lay under forests ; there were considerable stretches of poor, unsettled steppe ; stock-raising, which included sheep, cattle, horses, mules and even camels, together with agriculture, formed the main livelihood of the population. A great part of the country was held in badly managed, large estates by the nobility, and, even in 1880, it is estimated that about 14 per cent of the country, though capable of cultivation, lay fallow. The rich endowment of Spain in coal and minerals was as yet but little exploited. The coal mined was insufficient to meet the small local needs, and iron was exploited only on a very small scale. The chief mineral product of Spain was lead, which was mined in Alpujarras and in the Sierras of Gador and Lujar. In consequence of these latter workings, a writer [1] in 1880 notes : 'The kingdom (*sc.* province) of Granada seems as if transformed. People who had lived . . . in the deepest misery found their lot suddenly improved and their labour richly paid.' There were only a few small-scale industries, of which the cotton, woollen and silk manufactures were, in that order, the most important in the '70's. Foreign and colonial trade was small in scale : the chief imports in 1870 were cotton, sugar, coal and fish ; the chief exports, wine, dried fruits, cork, lead and esparto grass. In short, Spain, which still held remnants of its once extensive empire, signally failed to exploit its economic possibilities, largely because of its maladministration. Communications, in particular, were bad, so that 'the greatest abundance often exists in one province, while in the next, which lies 10, 15 or 20 miles distant, the other side of a mountain range, famine may prevail'.

Greece

Greece, a political creation of the nineteenth century, was backward economically as it was ill-favoured geographically. Its area, including the Ionian islands, was half as great again as that of Holland, but its population in 1870, less than 2 millions,

[1] Kolb, *The Condition of Nations*, 1880 ed., pp. 704 and 707.

was only half as great as Holland's. About one-half of Greece was mountain and rock; about one-sixth was under forest, and of the rest only a small part was cultivated. Its chief city and capital, Athens, had only about 40,000 inhabitants. The lead and zinc mines of Laurium in Attica were being worked, but there were scarcely any industries. The chief export was currants. In fact, carrying and trading by sea formed the chief resource of the Greek state.

EPILOGUE

' All Europe is essentially of one spirit ' (but) . . . . ' we are dealing in the case of Europe, with an outstandingly manifold, outstandingly riven structure ; the Balkans constitute its truest prototype.' COUNT H. KEYSERLING, *Europe* (1928).

EPILOGUE

EUROPE IN THE TWENTIETH CENTURY

WHILE events and processes long operative in the past contributed much to Europe's present-day map, alike in its political, social and economic aspects, much too that happened during the last fifty years has helped to characterize it. It was in Europe that the two world wars of this century started, as the results not only of its own internal divisions and tensions but also of its ascendancy, as yet unchallenged, in world affairs, and of the degree to which so many parts of the world had become associated with it. These wars wrought changes in the social and political organization of the Continent as they produced changes in its relative stature in the world. Events outside it, notably the remarkable growth in the demographic, economic and military strength of the United States and the Soviet Union, both of which originally drew their civilization from European sources, drastically altered Europe's relative position. It ceased to hold in its hands a virtual leadership of the world which it had won by its activities in the fields of imperialism, finance, manufacture and commerce ; nevertheless it retains substantial economic importance as it retains also geopolitical interest as an international theatre of dangerous tensions. But Europe since the end of World War II has lost something which it possessed in the nineteenth century, the sense of being a community which shared certain basic cultural ideas and regulated its relationships — and differences — by diplomatic methods broadly acceptable to all. To those many differences which traditionally marked it, but had not always seemed politically significant—differences of language, nationality, religion, and levels of material culture—are now added another, which cuts deep, being based on fundamentally opposed ideologies. Indeed the division of the Continent, above all but not quite so simply, into two opposed parts, recalls the situation sixteen hundred years ago when the weakening Roman Empire found itself beset by vigorous so-called ' barbarian ' peoples eager to inherit its wealth and civilization.

The Dynamics of Population

The population of Europe more than doubled since 1871, from about 293 millions to around 600 millions in 1965, despite losses by emigration, especially before 1914. While the birth rate remains fairly high, and indeed recovered in western countries during and after World War II from the low levels of the 'thirties, it remains unequal regionally, being as high as 25·8 per thousand in Iceland, 23·4 in Portugal, 22·5 in the U.S.S.R., over 20 in Ireland, Spain and the Netherlands, but as low as 19·1 in Italy, 18·2 in France, 18·5 in Western Germany, 18·3 in the United Kingdom and 13·1 in Hungary.[1] A remarkable demographic change has come in this century with increased life expectancy, with 'death control' so-called, thanks to the lowering of mortality rates, in particular those of infants. Low infant mortality rates are now achieved in western and northern Europe above all, but also elsewhere, notably in the U.S.S.R. : amongst the lowest (per thousand) are those of the United Kingdom (22·4), Iceland (17·0), the Netherlands (15·8) and Sweden (15·0). High infant mortality rates persist however in parts of southern and east-central Europe : thus for Portugal the figure is 78·6 (per thousand), for Yugoslavia 77·5, for Poland 49·1, for Hungary 42·6, and for Bulgaria 35·3.

Emigration tends still to reduce Europe's population increase, which at 0·9[2] per cent per year is the lowest of the continents. Although emigration after World War I faced stiff obstacles from the receiving countries, notably the United States, it has continued though at a lower rate, when, for example, Russians and Ukrainians move across the Urals to settle in the rapidly developing lands of Siberia and Kazakhstan and British leave the United Kingdom or Maltese leave Malta to find new homes in Canada, Australia and elsewhere. Thus despite the large absolute increase in its numbers, Europe now claims a smaller share of the world's population, rather less than one-fifth in 1965, as compared with an estimated quarter in 1800. This smaller share of the world's man-power marks at the same time Europe's declining status and the rise of the continents more recently opened up to settlement and economic development.

However, as a result more of differential rates of natural increase than of migration, population growth is unequal in the different major parts and the different countries of the Continent, although less so as birth and death rates continue to fall, sometimes sharply, almost everywhere. Eastern and parts of east-

[1] *Demographic Yearbook 1963*, New York 1964.

[2] This figure relates to Europe, including Turkey, but excluding the U.S.S.R.

central Europe, notably the U.S.S.R.,[1] Yugoslavia and Poland, have still high (though decreasing) rates of natural increase : this means that they have higher proportions of the able-bodied age-groups (i.e. more military and economic man-power) than those parts of the Continent where natural increase is lower. This applies particularly to northern, western and central Europe which have both lower birth rates and longer life-expectancy, so that countries there have an increasing proportion of elderly people and thus a relatively smaller share of able-bodied. However, the trend, so well marked in northern and western Europe, towards the lowering of both birth and death rates is being increasingly shown in other countries, notably in Communist Czechoslovakia, Hungary, Rumania, Eastern Germany and Bulgaria. Even so, the U.S.S.R.'s annual rate of natural increase remains high—1·5 per cent, although it has fallen from 1·7 per cent in 1959. The former figure compares with 1·0 per cent for northern and western Europe and with only 0·8 per cent for southern Europe. There, despite the ruling high birth rates, the rate of natural increase is reduced by high death rates and by emigration.

Although the demographic dominance of Communist Europe remains evident, there are clear signs that it is reducing somewhat. In relation to international politics, the population of Europe divides not so unequally. If the populations of European U.S.S.R. and its partners in the Warsaw Pact are totalled, a figure of about 260 millions is reached, which is rather less than that for the European members (Turkey included) of the North Atlantic Treaty Organization. The remaining 75 millions of Europe's population includes those of five microstates and of seven countries which are either neutral in status or otherwise uncommitted to either bloc—Switzerland, Sweden, Austria, Ireland, Finland, Yugoslavia and Spain.

The events of World War II and after, by inducing large-scale transfers of population, have much simplified Europe's map of nationalities. The mass murder of European Jews under Hitler's Germany, together with the emigration of Jews to Israel both before and after this war, have largely obliterated the Jewish population of what had become known as the 'Hebrew Pale' (Fig. 59), following a Regulation of tsarist Russia in 1835.[2] The

[1] In the provisional results of its Census of January, 1959, the U.S.S.R. claimed that its mortality rate was only 7·5 per thousand and was the lowest in the world.

[2] The Hebrew Pale comprised areas of western Russia, Poland, Lithuania and Bessarabia, all of which lay within the Russian Empire before 1914. Within it restrictions were imposed on the residence and owning of property by Jews. Jews originally entered this region via the

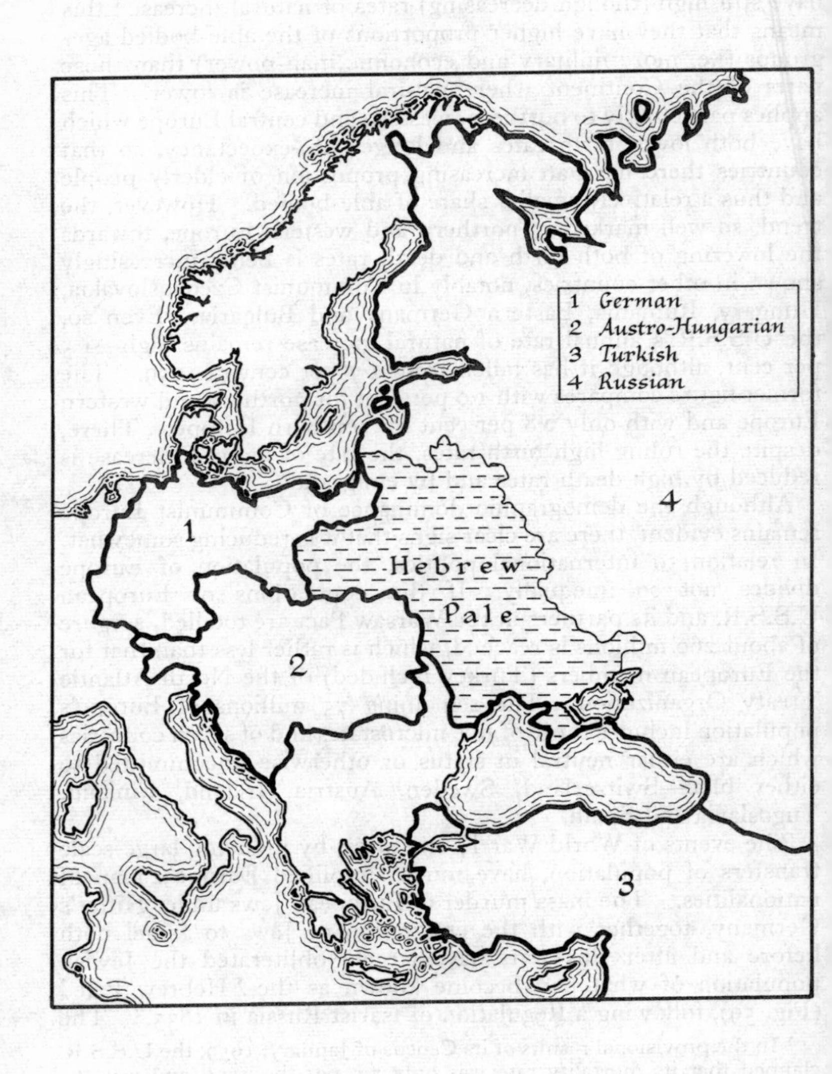

FIG. 59.—The extent of the Hebrew Pale as delimited in 1835, and of the empires of Central and Eastern Europe in 1914

main movements within the Continent were of Germans who, in the course of centuries, by invitation and colonial effort, had become widely distributed, as outliers within the territories of other nations, forming the ' minority groups ' so-called and giving rise to ' minority problems ' during the inter-war years 1919–39. Most of these Germans were repatriated, but the drift has been steadily from Eastern Germany (The German Democratic Republic) to Western Germany (The Federal German Republic), to the economic advantage of the latter, thus in receipt of an ever increasing labour force. The effect of these and other such changes in a continent where nationalist feeling still runs high, may be rated salutary, in that a recurrent source of international disagreement and tension has been largely removed.

Another feature of Europe's geography of population, of which early signs were noted above (pp. 414–15), is the higher degree of urbanization which has followed industrial expansion and the consequent attraction of country folk to the towns. Thus, while it is difficult exactly to compare the figures for urban populations in the different countries, there is no doubt of the increased preference everywhere for city-dwelling.[1] The highest figures are for the United Kingdom (81 per cent), the Federal German Republic (71 per cent), and Iceland (72 per cent) ; while countries, where the population was traditionally rural, have large and rising urban populations : thus the figure for the U.S.S.R. as a whole reached 48 per cent in 1959, and those for Poland, Hungary, Rumania, Bulgaria are given respectively as 36, 35, 23, and 25 per cent for 1952. The metropolitan city, too, has become more and more characteristic, and those areas of virtually continuous urban growth called ' conurbations ' are clearly evident or appearing above all, but not exclusively, in Britain, where they began, and in Western Germany. Yet it is again a sign of changes going on throughout the world that, although Europe had in the 1950s about a third of over eighty outsize cities with populations exceeding the million-mark, it has a smaller proportion of these now than in the past.[2]

Caucasus and the Crimea and their numbers were greatly increased when, in the fourteenth century, owing to religious persecution in Germany and western Europe generally, they found a haven of refuge in Poland. Being culturally advanced, they were welcomed, the more so since Polish cities had suffered much from the Tatar invasions. Turkey, too, displaying rough tolerance lacking in most of the Christian world, was equally a home for the Jews. The Jewish population, above all of Poland, was decimated under Nazi rule, 1939–44. The Jewish population of the U.S.S.R., reported at only 2.27 millions in 1959, had decreased from the 3 millions numbered in 1939.

[1] See W. G. East and A. E. Moodie (eds.) *The Changing World*, 1956, p. 39.

[2] See A. M. Lambert, 'Millionaire Cities, 1955', *Economic Geography*, vol. 32, 1956, pp. 283–93.

Economic Progress

Natural resources are not the gift of nature but the creation of man—and certainly the people of Europe have shown in this century, by scientific and technological advances, by the acquisition of skills, and by the use of their growing labour force—how high levels alike in agriculture, manufacture and in trade may be achieved.

For Europe as a whole economic progress, measured by the scale of production and world commerce, is impressive. Some of the highest yields of crops are registered in countries of western and central Europe. The total production of basic foodstuffs amounts of sizeable shares of world output : thus Europe produces a third of the world wheat, 70 per cent of its potatoes, and 29 per cent of its meat. Agriculture is widely mechanized and the range of crops is considerable—bread and fodder grains, flax and hemp, oilseeds, sugar beet, and other root crops, the vine and a range of fruits and vegetables. Yet despite the high efficiency of farming in many parts of the Continent and despite the scale of output, some countries, notably Britain, Western Germany, Norway, Switzerland and Greece, have to import a large part of their requirements, although this fraction has decreased over the last twenty years, while other countries which formerly offered surpluses of food, like Hungary, on occasion need to import additional supplies. Similarly, to meet the needs of its large-scale industry, European countries have to import many agricultural raw materials—natural fibres, oilseeds, cane sugar, raw rubber, and inter-tropical fruits and drinkstuffs. But, total production apart, the Continent reveals remarkable regional contrasts in farming—in its organization, in the size of farm units, in crop specialization and yields, and in economic efficiency generally, not to mention the varying local provision of soils, landforms and climate. Thus in some of the countries of east-central Europe, e.g. Czechoslovakia, the Soviet system of collective farming reigns ; in the Scandinavian countries a different form of co-operative organization is effectively applied to farming ; in the United Kingdom, France and elsewhere farming is for the individual farmer. In the south of European U.S.S.R. farming is 'mixed' but cultivation is extensive and highly mechanized, giving low yields per acre, and broadly comparable to that practised on the prairies of North America. Yields too are low in southern Europe. In contrast, cultivation in Denmark, Britain, Western Germany and north Italy is highly intensive and highly capitalized ; yields are accordingly high. In western and central Europe agriculture is subsidized, as in France and the United Kingdom. In southern Europe, notably in northern Italy and in southern France and Spain, irrigated crops are grown on small areas—rice, citrus fruits, fodder, vegetables and flowers. But there are considerable areas, alike in southern and east-central Europe, where agricultural backwardness persists, marked by low crop yields, under-employment of too-large farm populations, deficiency of capital and fertilizers and unscientific rotations.

In part explanation of these disparities in agricultural efficiency, it should be recalled that the agricultural revolution of the eighteenth and nineteenth centuries took place in England, inspired it is true by the earlier achievements in the Low Countries, and stimulated by the growth of industry and towns which presented an ever growing market. Until it suffered in the 1870s from the competition of the grain lands of the United States, England had reached highest levels of farming in the world. Thus it became a centre of diffusion of 'the new husbandry' from which ideas and practices made their way slowly in the Continent. But many obstacles, such as poverty and ignorance, maladministration, and outworn forms of organization long impeded progress in eastern and southern Europe. The break-up of large estates and the establishment of peasant holdings, one of the results, achieved by stages, of the two world wars offered new possibilities. In east-central Europe, the establishment of the collective-farm system, which involves the provision by the State of tractors, farm equipment and technical knowledge, should make for substantial improvements. In parts of southern Europe, especially in Spain, agricultural practices improve but slowly.

Although European agriculture remains in good heart and still engages the activities of most of the people, it is the industrial and commercial advance of this century which most focuses attention. As noted above (pp. 417–18), the new way opened up to industry by the Industrial Revolution was adopted by stages, first in western and central Europe and last in eastern and southern Europe. The development of railway systems illustrates the pace of the changes : for example, the Russian railway system, linking its European and Asiatic territories was completed only by the beginning of the twentieth century, and in 1914 its total mileage was only that of the United Kingdom and about half of that existing in the U.S.S.R. today. Even as recently as 1914, what has been called 'technical' or 'industrial' Europe reached from the west only as far as Bohemia, Upper Silesia and a few cities further east in Russia and the Ukraine. The advent of the U.S.S.R., with its vigorous policy of industrialization, especially since 1928, started large-scale developments in eastern Europe. As a result, modern industry, centred in the towns, now increasingly characterizes this major fraction of the Continent, no less than the earlier industrialized countries of the west. And because this part of Europe was late to start acquiring industrial skills and exploiting its resources, it now progresses at a faster rate, stimulated alike no doubt by Soviet planning and by the applications of the newest techniques.

Notwithstanding the great destruction of material resources and dislocations caused by two world wars, the countries of the Continent restored their economies with remarkable speed. After the second world war this process in the west owed much to the timely help afforded under the Marshall Plan ; in eastern Europe the response came from the rigorous mobilization of state resources under centralized Soviet plans supplemented by heavy reparations from former enemy countries. In both areas success has come with the change-over from war to peace-time industries and with adaptations required by changing conditions—in technique, in the creation and use of new materials, and to changing markets. Although coal remains the prime source of mechanical energy, the use of petroleum, now mainly refined in the countries of importation, has much increased, while, in European U.S.S.R., France, Switzerland and elsewhere hydro-electricity supplies have been expanded. The iron and steel industry has continued to grow, as also the heavy industries—machine tools, automobiles and tractors, farm and mine equipment and the rest. The chemical industries with their ever widening range from fertilizers and plastics to artificial rubber and fibres, dyestuffs and drugs have grown in response to new discoveries and thus widening opportunities. And at the other extreme the whole range of consumer goods which include necessities like foodstuffs and textile fabrics and luxury goods like the products of the fashion houses of Paris, Milan and London have regrown in scale.

Europe's industrial stature rests on a generous allotment of coal reserves and of labour, much of which is skilled, and on scientific and technological enterprise. Heavy industries, and with them dense populations, mainly urban, have become concentrated on the coalfields which extend discontinuously across Europe from Britain to the Ukraine. Considerable industrial developments have however been achieved on the basis of hydro-electric energy in countries deficient in coal—notably France, Italy, Switzerland and Sweden, while a number of metropolitan cities, situated off the coalfields, have become very important industrial areas : London, Paris, Berlin, Leningrad among them. The industries of the several countries are to a considerable degree dependent on

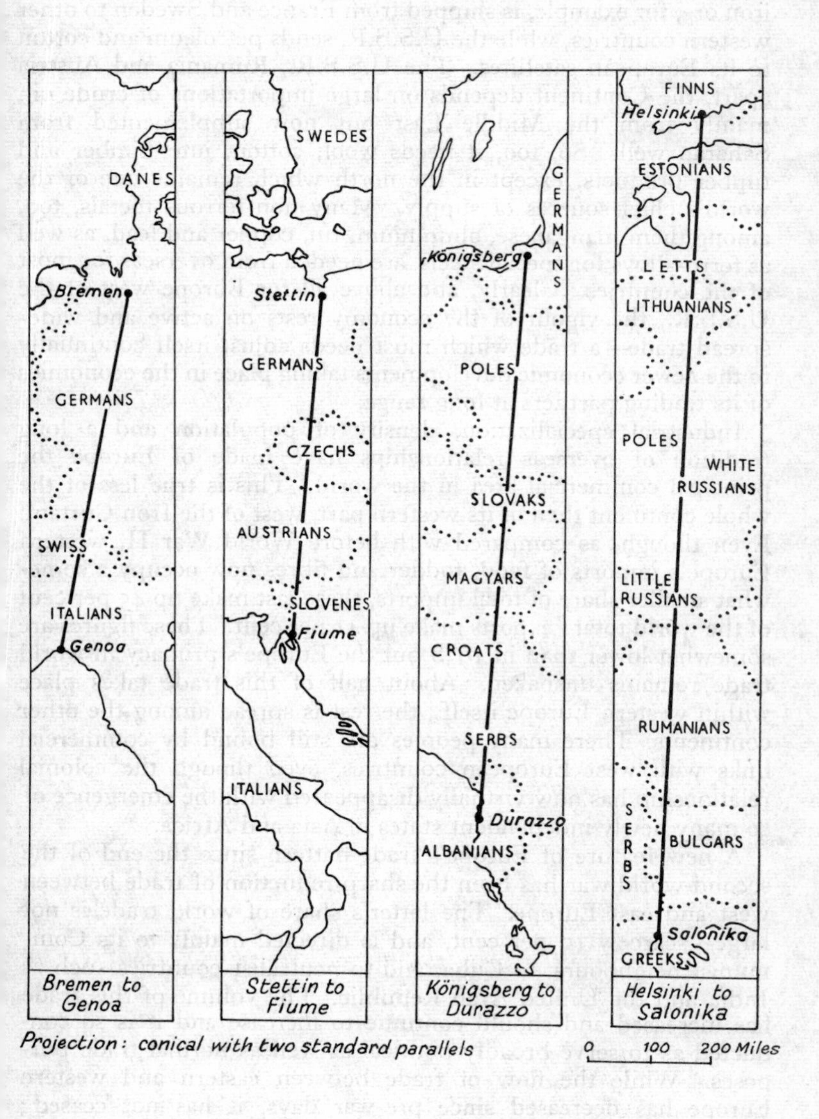

FIG. 60—The Generalized Nationalities Pattern of Europe before World War I

inter-European exchanges and overseas supplies of goods. Thus iron ore, for example, is shipped from France and Sweden to other western countries, while the U.S.S.R. sends petroleum and cotton to its European satellites. The U.S.S.R., Rumania and Austria apart, the Continent depends on large importations of crude oil, mainly from the Middle East but now supplemented from Saharan wells. So, too, it needs wool, cotton, jute, timber and timber products, except in the north which remains one of the world's chief sources of supply. Many non-ferrous metals, too, among them manganese, aluminium, tin, copper and lead, as well as ferro-alloys for special steels, are needed from overseas for most of the countries. Clearly, and above all for Europe west of the U.S.S.R., the vigour of the economy rests on active and widespread trade—a trade which must needs adjust itself continually to the newer economic developments taking place in the economies of its trading partners at long range.

Industrial specialization, density of population and a long tradition of overseas relationships have made of Europe the principal commercial area in the world. This is true less of the whole continent than of its western part, west of the Iron Curtain. Even though, as compared with before World War II, western Europe's imports of food, fodder and fibres now occupy a somewhat smaller share of total imports, these last make up 45 per cent of the world total ; exports make up 41 per cent. These figures are somewhat lower than in 1938 but the Europe's primacy in world trade remains unshaken. About half of this trade takes place within western Europe itself ; the rest is spread among the other continents. There many peoples are still bound by commercial links with west European countries, even though the colonial relationship has now virtually disappeared with the emergence of so many newly independent states in Asia and Africa.

A new feature of Europe's trade pattern since the end of the second world war has been the sharp reduction of trade between west and east Europe. The latter's share of world trade is not large—scarcely 10 per cent, and is directed mainly to its Communist neighbours, to Cuba, and to neutralist countries such as India and the United Arab Republic. The volume of this trade has increased and should continue to increase and it is so conducted as to serve broadly political as well as normal trade purposes. While the flow of trade between eastern and western Europe has decreased since pre-war days, it has not ceased ; indeed it has grown steadily since 1950. Even so, trade within the European Soviet bloc remains the main objective, so that these countries are tied ever more closely to each other and to the

U.S.S.R. Yugoslavia occupies an anomalous position among the Communist countries of eastern Europe in that it trades freely with the West. In respect of trade therefore political division is reflected in the broad pattern of commerce : two trading areas stand largely aloof from each other. The one, led by Moscow, trades outside the Soviet bloc as may seem from time to time politically expedient and will be able to seek more than its present small share of world trade. The other, which is made up of several trading groups, enjoys an ascendancy in world trade.

The Changing Political Patterns

Europe has achieved a high density of population, supported by highly developed and specialized agriculture, industry and trade, notwithstanding its remarkable political disunity. Its surface, which occupies only one-twelfth of the inhabited Earth, is divided into some thirty-four independent states, about a quarter of the world total. Ironically the number of states has increased since 1914, when there were twenty-six, during that precise phase of its history when improved means of communication and transport facilitated the administration of large territories. The independent states of Europe today range in extent from the immensity of the U.S.S.R., which accounts for two-fifths of the Continent, to the relative minuteness of five micro-states and of the international exclave of West Berlin, and include also eight land-locked states.[1] Europe is easily the most politically divided of the continents, so that it has the greatest length of boundary per unit area in the world. The sharp contrast between its political pattern and those of the other continents is self-evident and the opprobrious term ' Balkanization ' has been applied to it.

It is easier to explain in general terms how Europe has become so politically comparted than to understand why it has proved so reluctant to abandon its divisions. Its fragmentation results from a long and chequered history. It results from the development of nationalism, the creed of the nations which took shape there, each within a loosely defined habitat during the centuries which followed the barbarian invasions of Europe. This Continent, we have seen, has had much, and a too-much remembered history ; nor has it lacked that variety and diversity of physical geography which earlier fostered separatist cultural development. Its many national groups (Fig. 60), long attached to specified homelands,

[1] On these, see W. Gordon East, 'The geography of landlocked states', The Institute of British Geographers *Transactions and Papers 1960*, vol. 28, 1960, pp. 1–22.

FIG. 61—Mackinder's proposed Middle Tier of States in East-Central Europe

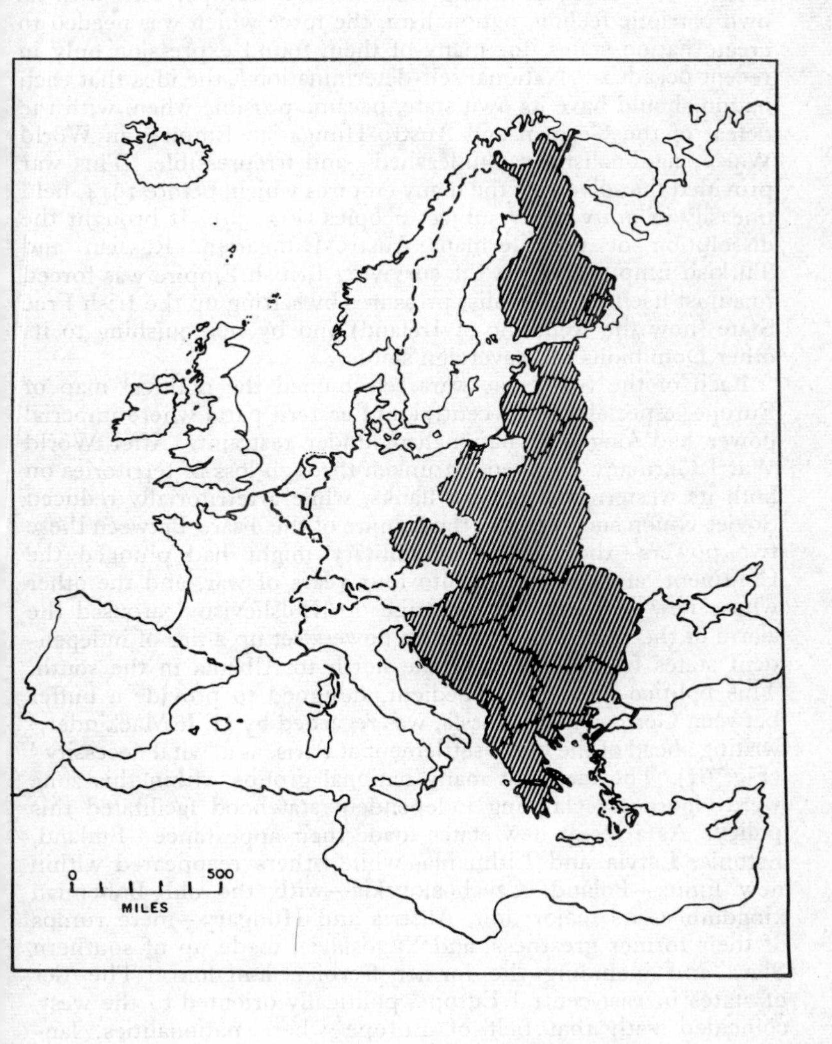

FIG. 62—Unstead's Belt of Political Change in Europe

developed those different languages which in large measure distinguish and separate them. But it should be emphasized that while nationalities have long characterized Europe, each with its own patriotic feeling, nationalism, the force which was needed to create nation states, for many of them found expression only in recent decades. ' National self-determination ', the idea that each nation should have its own state, became possible when, with the defeat of the German and Austro-Hungarian Empires in World War I, nationalism was unleashed—and irrepressible. This war provided the solvent of the many empires which, before 1914, held uneasily in unity many subject peoples (Fig. 59). It brought the dissolution of the German, Austro-Hungarian, Russian and Turkish Empires, whilst the surviving British Empire was forced to adjust itself to nationalist pressures by setting up the Irish Free State (now the Republic of Ireland) and by relinquishing to its other Dominions full sovereign status.

Each of the two great wars refashioned the political map of Europe, especially in its central and eastern parts where imperial power had long held nationalism under restraint. After World War I Germany emerged, shrunken through loss of territories on both its western and eastern flanks, while a territorially reduced Soviet Union succeeded to the Empire of the Tsar. Between these two powers—the one whose military might had plunged the Continent, and the world, into four years of war, and the other whose new revolutionary doctrine of ' Bolshevism ' aroused the alarm of the west—the victorious powers set up a tier of independent states from Finland in the north to Albania in the south. This politico-territorial expedient, designed to provide a buffer between Germany and Russia, was regarded by H. J. Mackinder,[1] writing ahead of the peace settlement at Paris, as a ' vital necessity ' (Fig. 61). The fact that many national groups within this zone were vigorously claiming independent statehood facilitated this policy. As a result new states made their appearance—Finland, Estonia, Latvia and Lithuania, while others reappeared within new limits—Poland, Czechoslovakia—with the old Bohemian kingdom as its major unit, Austria and Hungary—mere rumps of their former greatness, and Yugoslavia, made up of southern Slavs and including the former Serbian kingdom. The tier of states in east-central Europe, politically oriented to the west, coincided with that belt of Europe where nationalities, languages and cultures presented their most complicated patterns

[1] H. J. Mackinder, M.P., *Democratic Ideals and Reality*, London, Constable & Co., 1919, pp. 196 and 200.

(Fig. 60). Designed as an effective buffer between two would-be strong military powers and as a *cordon sanitaire* against the revolutionary dangers from Russia, this tier of states proved disappointing to its architects. This 'belt of political change in Europe', as J. F. Unstead called it, later to be known as 'The Shatter Zone',[1] suffered from many serious and weakening difficulties (Fig. 62). Most of these states contained sizeable alien groups, raising 'minority problems' so-called; except for Czechoslovakia, they were unripe for democratic government; nationalism, involving contempt for, and enmity towards neighbours, and finding expression in restrictive economic practices, helped to generate international tension; and not least poverty and backwardness and, in some cases, outmoded social structures and agrarian systems persisted. It is not surprising, therefore, that the tier of buffer states proved only a pack of cards when Hitler attacked in turn Austria, Czechoslovakia and Poland, Mussolini invaded Albania, and Stalin, under the Russo-German Pact of 1939, moved his army forward to recover areas formerly part of the Russian Empire.

Few of the states of Europe escaped participation in, or enemy occupation during the second world war and once again the political map was remade. Once more the distinction was emphasized between the stable territorial patterns of the nation states of northern and western Europe, including Iberia, where most of them had deep roots in time, and those of the belt of political change in east-central Europe. The hopes of western statesmen and publicists that the settlement there, while respecting national cultures, should establish democratic institutions and find, by means of federalism, an escape from the small rigidly defined and separatist sovereign state, have had no hopes of realization since 1945. The advance of the Red Army brought Russian power westwards to the Oder and the Elbe: the historic struggle of Teuton and Slav entered upon another phase, marked by the ascendency of the U.S.S.R., heir to Pan-Slav Russia. Not only did the U.S.S.R. enlarge its own territories in Europe by the incorporation of Estonia, Latvia and Lithuania, and by gains from Finland, Germany, Poland, Czechoslovakia and Rumania, but it succeeded in turning the former tier of buffer states to its own advantage into a tier of Communist-organized dependencies. The symmetry of the pattern is marred for the U.S.S.R. by the western

[1] See W. Gordon East 'The concept and political status of the Shatter Zone', *Geographical Essays on Eastern Europe,* ed. N. J. G. Pounds, Indiana University Press, 1961.

form of democracy which persists in Finland, although this country is tightly linked to the U.S.S.R. by trade bonds, as also by the deviation from Moscow's ' line ' of Yugoslavia, under President Tito, who has been able to maintain his own variety of national Communism. This Russian solution in east-central Europe, with its denial of the freedoms enjoyed in the west, leaves much to be desired. It has achieved something however in mitigating inter-nation frictions, in reducing the importance of boundaries between the countries of the zone, and in resolving some of the minority difficulties which remained, despite the large refugee movements to the west.[1] Substantial economic changes, too, promise material improvement, following the agrarian reforms which broke up remaining large estates and redistributed them to the peasants.

The territorial settlement of Europe after World War II has produced a politically, economically and culturally divided continent, made up, above all, of two blocs, the one led and supported by the U.S.S.R. and the other by the United States. In addition there remain a number of states which are formally neutral, like Switzerland, Sweden and Austria, and others uncommitted to either bloc, namely the Republic of Ireland, Yugoslavia, Spain and Finland, although of the last two, the first has United States military bases and the second has only limited freedom of action in foreign affairs. The division of the Continent is epitomized in that of Germany, with the Federal German Republic allied to the West and the Democratic German Republic clearly dependent on the U.S.S.R., and with Berlin, of which the greater part, under western control, forms unenviably an international exclave within Communist Europe.

How sharply the political pattern of Europe has changed can be recognized when it is remembered that the former ' power centre ' of Europe—*Mitteleuropa*—which Germany sought to organize, has utterly disappeared, that the former buffer zone between Germany and the U.S.S.R. has become an insulating border to the latter, and that the Iron Curtain now bisects the Continent from the Baltic to the Adriatic Sea. Whereas in 1914 six of the Great Powers of the world—the British Empire, France, Germany, Italy, Austro-Hungary and Russia—lay in Europe and some of them were strengthened by their overseas dependencies, the position since 1945 has been that the only two remaining Great

[1] Thus the problem of the large Magyar settlement in the south-eastern Transylvanian region of Rumania may have been eased by the creation of the Hungarian Autonomous Region in 1952.

Powers lie respectively in North America and Eurasia and find in Europe their principal zone of contact. The old system of alliances, which sought to achieve a 'balance of power', while it succeeded in overthrowing the would-be masters of Europe in two world wars, facilitated the rise of another—the U.S.S.R. The political decline of Europe in the world, the consequence of divisions intensified by nationalism, is laid bare by its dependence on two countries whose territories lie either wholly or in large measure outside its conventional limits.

Trends towards Economic and Political Integration

E Pluribus Unum, the phrase which appears on American coins and single-dollar bills, testifies to a remarkable achievement of modern history—the union through federation of no less than fifty states. In contrast, and at a late stage of its history, Europe finds itself still divided and indeed has never advanced beyond the unity achieved by the legions of the Roman Empire. It has vigorously resisted the attempts made successively by Napoleon, the Kaiser Wilhelm II and Hitler to effect unity by force. Certainly no short cuts to unity by federation offer any hope of success in view of the acute differences that exist. Yet, alike in the political as in the economic field, trends towards regional unity are evident, the result, no doubt, of many pressures as also of constructive thought. Clearly the United States has encouraged unity in western Europe as a means of increasing its defensive strength; clearly too fear of the Soviet Union has emphasized the insecurity of states which stand alone; and lastly, economic considerations indicated the advantage of larger units for the betterment of production, trade and living standards.

The creation of the Organization for European Economic Co-operation (O.E.E.C.) was one of the fruitful achievements which followed Marshall Plan aid to western Europe in 1947. As O.E.C.D., its membership now includes (in addition to the U.S.A. and Canada) eighteen European countries including neutrals—and also Spain, although none of the Communist countries is a member. It was left to three small countries—Belgium, the Netherlands and Luxembourg—to move further by establishing a Customs union in 1947. Benelux developed by stages, overcoming difficulties and national fears; by reducing tariffs between each other, they stimulated the flow of trade, although they established too a common tariff to countries outside. The creation of the European Coal and Steel Community, by associating western Germany, France and Italy with the three Benelux countries, marked a leap forwards. The objective was to provide a single large area for industries which are particularly inter-dependent. E.C.S.C. controls considerable resources including the coal of the Ruhr and the iron ore of Lorraine. It has sufficient powers to reorganize these heavy industries, arrange for uniform freight rates, rationalize the location of plants, and stimulate labour movements from one country to another. E.C.S.C. was launched in 1952 at a time of expanding markets but it has successfully weathered the difficulties caused by a fall in demand during 1958–9. Moreover, from the political standpoint, E.C.S.C. was remarkably successful in bringing France and Western Germany into close and friendly relationship and in thus ending a long period of Franco-German hostility. What is more, it lays a foundation for possible political integration at a later state. As yet however it is only an inter-governmental, not a supra-governmental organization.

In 1958 the six countries of E.C.S.C. created the Common Market (or European Economic Community) with the aim of establishing, by stages, free trade within its limits and a common external tariff (Fig. 63). Machinery has been, or will be set up to effect the purposes of the Community, of which the overriding one is an increase of material welfare. Certainly the Community controls powerful resources : a population of 175 millions, a hard-coal production of 250 million tons, and a steel output of over 75 million tons. As such these considerably exceed the industrial resources of the United Kingdom and make some approach to the scale of those of the Soviet Union. It should not be imagined that E.E.C. does not face serious and continuing difficulties, for the lowering of internal tariffs reacts sharply on the vested interests of the several countries where, for example, agriculture is subsidized unequally and where too social services are at quite different levels.

The successful approaches towards regional unity in western Europe have unfortunately checked the wider unity within it which seemed the ultimate promise of O.E.E.C. The United Kingdom, in particular, never quite sure how far it is part of Europe and ever mindful of its position as the senior partner of a maritime Commonwealth, was unwilling to join the Six on the terms set out in the Treaty of Rome which came into force on 1 January 1958. The United Kingdom had to consider its special relations with Commonwealth countries, with which it does the bulk of its trade : these enjoy free entry for certain goods into its market and trade under a system of preferences. Further, the United Kingdom did not feel able to subscribe to the objective of eventual political integration. Accordingly, in order to safeguard its position against the new powerful trade bloc, it succeeded (in 1960) in creating the European Free Trade Association (E.F.T.A.), popularly known as The Outer Seven (Fig. 63). It was able to enlist six of its smaller trade partners of western Europe, while Finland became an associate, thus increasing the membership to eight. E.F.T.A. is a much less ambitious project than E.E.C. It has no idea of seeking political integration nor of forming a community ; and it does not aim at a common external tariff. More modestly it seeks the removal of tariffs, quotas and similar restrictions to trade between the Seven, and accepts the position that agricultural subsidies may persist and that labour movements between the members will not be free. Relations between E.E.C. and E.F.T.A. have remained good ; actually Britain and others came to wish, but have so far failed, to effect entry to the Common Market.

In their halting efforts towards integration the leading countries of western Europe have achieved modest success only by creating further divisions, for the eighteen countries of O.E.E.C. are now split into the Six, the Seven and the rest, a few of which may attach themselves to either group. On the defensive side, too, something was achieved by the North Atlantic Treaty Organization, which binds together thirteen European states with the United States and Canada (Fig. 64). This grand alliance for defence, created in 1949, has at least preserved the peace by the stationing of United States forces in Britain, Western Germany and the Mediterranean Basin and thus made possible first economic recovery and then progress. Its wider purposes—the strengthening of free institutions and the formation of a broadly based multinational community—have had little success : witness the failure of democratic government in some of the N.A.T.O. states and their continual differences in foreign policy.

Trends towards military and economic integration are no less evident in eastern Europe where, behind the Iron Curtain, the U.S.S.R. has been at pains to organize its empire. The Warsaw Pact of 1955, the Soviet reply to N.A.T.O., associates for defence Eastern Germany, Poland, Czechoslovakia, Hungary, Rumania and Bulgaria with the U.S.S.R. (Fig. 64). Only the deviation of Yugoslavia breaks the territorial continuity of this pattern and, by its defection, Albania has deprived the U.S.S.R. of its foothold on the Mediterranean where the American Sixth Fleet and other N.A.T.O. forces rule.

On the economic side the U.S.S.R. has organized its realm through C.M.E.A., the Council for Mutual Economic Aid, set up in 1949. The initial policy of Stalin which exacted large-scale reparations from ex-enemy states and sought industrialization of

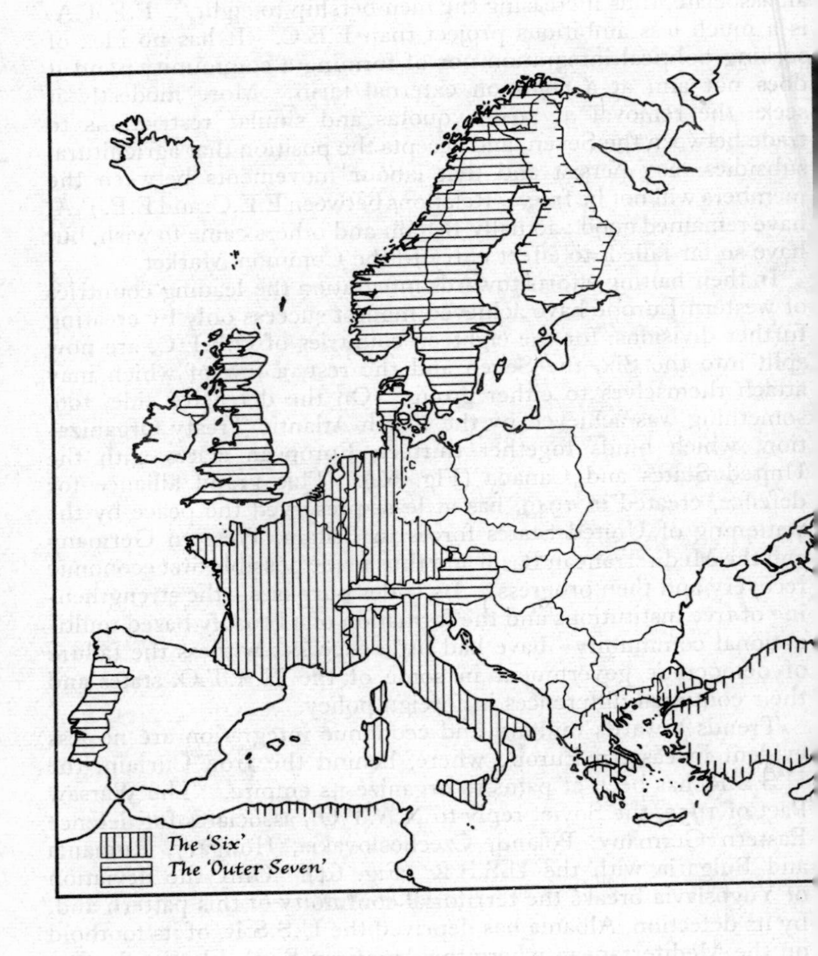

FIG. 63—The pattern of the Common Market (E.E.C.) and E.F.T.A. Greece, Turkey, and Algeria – as well as many other African states – are associate members of E.E.C., while Finland is an associate of E.F.T.A.

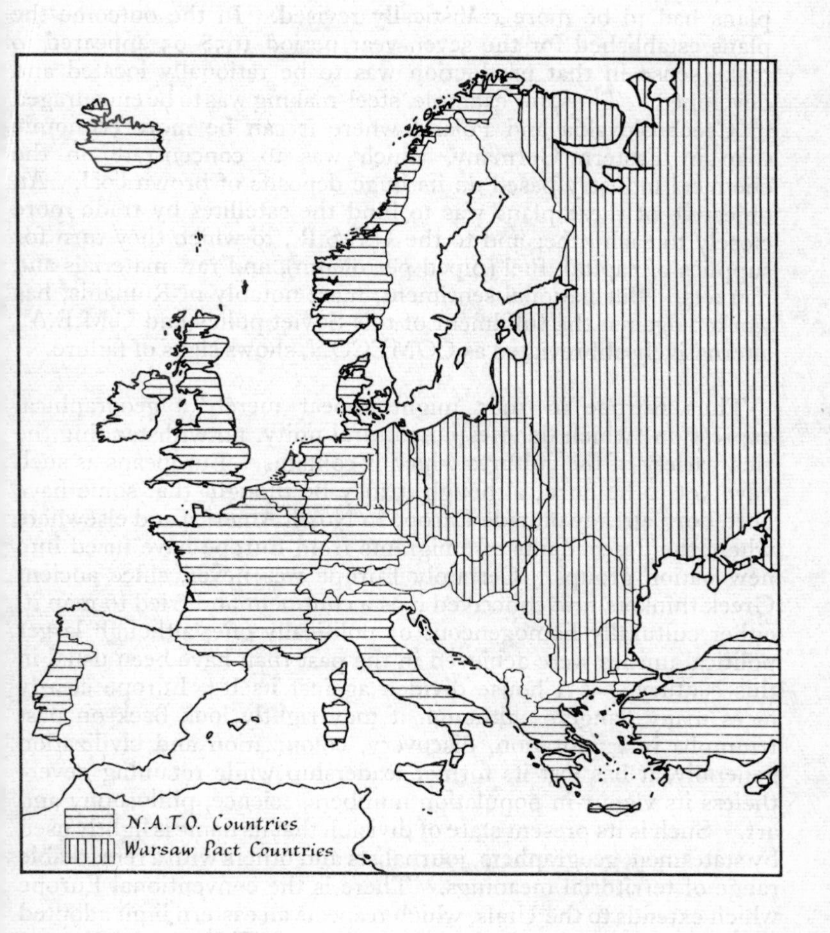

FIG. 64—The Territorial pattern of the two Defence Organizations in Europe

the satellite countries at all costs, was only partially successful, although success was achieved in establishing one-party (Communist) régimes. Economic difficulties lay behind the revolts in Hungary, Eastern Germany and Poland and existing economic plans had to be more realistically revised. In the outcome the plans established for the seven-year period 1958–65 appeared to make sense in that production was to be rationally located and developed. Thus, for example, steel-making was to be encouraged in Czechoslovakia and Poland where it can be more economic than in Eastern Germany, which was to concentrate on the chemical industry based on its huge deposits of brown coal. An objective of these plans was to bind the satellites by trade more closely to each other and to the U.S.S.R., to which they turn for supplies of capital, fuel (piped petroleum), and raw materials and markets. But national sentiment, most notably in Rumania, has worked against the fulfilment of this Soviet policy and C.M.E.A., alternatively abbreviated as COMECON, shows signs of failure.

Thus Europe in 1965 might appear merely a geographical expression[1] which denotes no cultural unity, notwithstanding the rich variety of the cultures which it contains. Europeans as such have yet to be born, although it may be thought that some have been born already outside Europe in North America and elsewhere where the descendants of emigrants from Europe have fused into new nation groups. Certainly Europe was never, since ancient Greek thinkers first conceived it as a continent and tried to map it, either culturally homogeneous or politically one, although larger political unities were achieved in the past than have been usual in this century. 'A house divided against itself', Europe clearly faces many dangers; although it may rightly look back on past triumphs in exploration, discovery, colonization and civilization generally, it has lost its former leadership while retaining nevertheless its vigour in population numbers, science, philosophy and art. Such is its present state of division that its name is lightly used by statesmen, geographers, journalists and others with a remarkable range of territorial meanings. There is the conventional Europe which extends to the Urals, which respects an eastern limit adopted only since 1833 when Volger first used it. There is the Europe which lies west of the Iron Curtain, and that, somewhat smaller, which is made up of the eighteen countries of O.E.C.D. There is also 'Little Europe'—the six countries of the Common Market.

[1] On this see 'Europe—A Geographical Expression', in *A Geography of Europe*, ed. G. W. Hoffman, 2nd ed. 1961.

And it has always seemed true, as Dostoevsky believed, that Russia, which bestrides Eurasia, was (as it remains) a world apart. Thus there are presently several Europes and unity—meaning by that political integration—lies away off. Federation promises no easily and quickly won solution of Europe's disunity because federation needs for its success a community spirit which does not yet exist. Rather the prospect is that Europe may crystallize into two parts, with a few small states sitting uneasily between the two; and the Iron Curtain, no flimsy fabric, may long persist and thus preserve the uneasy peace.

SELECTED BIBLIOGRAPHY

THE bibliography includes for the greater part works which have been consulted in the writing of this book. It was not thought necessary to include standard works on the present-day geography of Europe, notably the volumes of the *Géographie Universelle* and of Methuen's *Advanced Geographies*, including G. W. Hoffman's *A Geography of Europe* (1953) 2nd ed. 1961. Similarly, the large-scale topographical maps available in the European states have not been listed, since these are noted in the present-day geographies mentioned above.

Among the many available historical atlases may be noted:

Putzgers, F. W., *Historische Schul-Atlas*, Bilefeld and Leipzig, 1929. (A useful small atlas.)
Philip's *Historical Atlas, Medieval and Modern*, 6th ed., 1927.
Shepherd, W. R., *Historical Atlas*, 7th ed. revised and enlarged, 1930.
Vidal de la Blache, P., *Atlas Général Historique et Géographique*, 1926.
Schrader, F., and Gallouédec, L., *Atlas Classique de Géographie Ancienne et Moderne*, 1925.

In addition may be noted the atlas volumes of the *Cam. Med. Hist.*, *Cam. Mod. Hist.* and those of Sprüner and Lane-Poole.

LIST OF ABBREVIATIONS USED IN FOOTNOTES AND BIBLIOGRAPHY

A.	Antiquity.
Ac. des I. et B.-L.	Académie des Inscriptions et Belles-Lettres.
A. de G.	Annales de Géographie.
A.H.A.	American Historical Association.
A.H.R.	American Historical Review.
A.H.E. & S.	Annales d'histoire économique et sociale.
Arch.	Archaeologia.
Bul. Int. Com. Hist. Sc.	Bulletin of the International Committee of Historical Sciences.
Bul. Rum. Acad.	Bulletin of the Rumanian Academy.
Cam. Anc. Hist.	Cambridge Ancient History.
Cam. Med. Hist.	Cambridge Medieval History.
C.J.	The Classical Journal.
E.H.R.	The English Historical Review.
Econ. H.R.	The Economic History Review.
G.	Geography.
Geog. Ann.	Geografiska Annaler.
G.J.	The Geographical Journal.
G.R.	The Geographical Review.

H.	History.
Hak. Soc.	The Hakluyt Society.
J.A.	Journal Asiatique.
J.A.G.S.	Journal of the American Geographical Society.
J.E.A.	The Journal of Egyptian Archaeology.
J.H.S.	Journal of Hellenic Studies.
J.R.A.S.	Journal of the Royal Asiatic Society.
J.R.S.	Journal of Roman Studies.
La G.	La Géographie.
Mem. Geog.	Memorie Geografiche.
Pol. Sc. Qu.	The Political Science Quarterly.
P.R.I.	Proceedings of the Royal Institution of Great Britain.
Q.J.E.	The Quarterly Journal of Economics.
Q.J.M.	The Quarterly Journal of Meteorology.
R. des Q.H.	Revue des Questions Historiques.
R.d'E.P.	Revue d'Economie Politique.
Rev. des Soc. Sav. . .	Revue des Sociétés Savantes.
R.G.It.	Rivista Geografica Italiana.
Rev. Hist.	Revue Historique.
S.G.M.	The Scottish Geographical Magazine.
Soc. Asiat.	Société Asiatique.
S.R.	The Sociological Review.
Trans. R.H.S.	Transactions of the Royal Historical Society.

CHAPTER I

THE MEDITERRANEAN LANDS OF THE ROMAN EMPIRE

No attempt is made here to list the original texts of Greek and Roman geographers, but the following recent editions of particular importance may be noted: *The Geography of Claudius Ptolemy* was edited and translated by J. Fischer in 1931 (a work of great scholarship) and also by E. L. Stevenson in 1932. The *Geography* of Ptolemy was written some time between A.D. 141 and 168. The *Geography* of Strabo, who lived from *c.* 64 B.C. to A.D. 20, is available in the Loeb edition (Greek text and English translation). It is edited and translated by H. L. Jones; 8 vols., 1917–32.

General Studies

Mommsen, *The Provinces of the Roman Empire from Caesar to Diocletian*, 2 vols., 1909 (needs to be supplemented by results of recent archaeological studies).

Rostovtzev, *The Social and Economic History of the Roman Empire*, 1926 (extensive bibliographies).

Semple, *The Geography of the Mediterranean: its relation to Ancient History*, English ed., 1931.

Newbigin, *The Mediterranean Lands*, 1928.

Philippson, *Das Mittelmeergebiet*, 4th ed., 1931.

Bunbury, *A History of Ancient Geography*, 2 vols., 2nd ed., 1883.

Jones, H. S., *Companion to Roman History*, 1912.

The Mediterranean Pilot (Admiralty Publication).

Louis, *Le Travail dans le monde romain*, 1913.

Cam. Anc. Hist., vols. 7–10, 1928–34.

Holland Rose, *The Mediterranean in the Ancient World*, 1933.
Myers, J. L., ' Ancient Geography in Modern Education ', *S.G.M.*, Sept. 1928.
Cagnat and Chapot, *Manuel d'archéologie romaine*, 2 vols., 1920.
Tarn, W. W., *Hellenistic Civilisation*, 2nd ed., 1930.
Juster, *Les Juifs dans l'Empire romain*, 2 vols., 1914.
Cary and Warmington, *The Ancient Explorers*, 1929.
Rostovtzev, ' The Decay of the Ancient World . . .', *Econ. H.R.*, Jan. 1930.

Population

Beloch, *Die Bevölkerung der grieschischen-römischen Welt*, 1886.
Cavaignac, E., *Population et capital dans le monde Mediterranéen antique*, 1923.
Usher, ' The History of Population and Settlement in Eurasia ' (with maps), *G.R.*, Jan. 1930.
Collingwood, ' Town and Country in Roman Britain ', *A.*, Sept. 1929.

Commerce and Routes

Charlesworth, *Trade Routes and Commerce of the Roman Empire*, 2nd ed. revised, 1926 (map).
Warmington, *The Commerce between the Roman Empire and India*, 1928 (map).
Miller, K., *Itineraria Romana*, 1916. (Roads in the second century A.D.)
Cartellieri, *Die römischen Alpenstrassen*, 1926.
Ormerod, *Piracy in the Roman World*, 1924.
Ewbanks, ' Navigation on the Tiber ', *C.J.*, 1929 and 1930.
Vidal de la Blache, ' Voies de Commerce dans la Géographie de Ptolemée ', *Ac. des. I. et B.-L.*, 4th series, 1896.

Italy

Homo, *Primitive Italy and the Beginnings of Roman Imperialism*, trans., 1927.
Ashby, *The Classical Topography of the Roman Campagna*, 1902.
Frank, T., *An Economic History of Rome*, 2nd ed., 1927.
Rome and Italy of the Republic, 1933, vol. I of An Economic Survey of the Roman World.
Frothingham, *Roman Cities in Northern Italy and Dalmatia*, 1910.
Randall-MacIver, *Greek Cities in Italy and Sicily*, 1931.
The Etruscans, 1927.
Arturo Solari, *Vita Publica e Privata degli Etruschi*, 1931.
Almagia, ' The Repopulation of the Roman Campagna ', *G.R.*, Oct. 1929.

Spain

Bouchier, *Spain under the Roman Empire*, 1914.
West, L. C., *Imperial and Roman Spain*, 1929.
Mélida, *Monumentos Romanos de España*, 1925 (plates and map).
Goury de Roslan, J., *Essai sur l'histoire économique de l'Espagne*, 1887.

Gaul

Desjardins, *Géographie historique et administrative de la Gaule romaine*, 2 vols., 1884 (maps).
Bérard, ' Les conditions des établissements maritimes sur la côte de Provence dans l'Antiquité ', *A. de G.*, Sept. 1927.

Clerc, M., *Massilia. Histoire de Marseille dans l'antiquité . . . 476 A.D.*, 1927.
Aquæ Sextiæ. Histoire d'Aix en Provence dans l'antiquité, 1916.
Constans, *Arles antique*, 1921.
Bonnard, *La Navigation Intérieure de la Gaule à l'époque Gallo-Romaine*, 1913.
Jullian, C., *Histoire de la Gaule*, 8 vols., 6th ed., 1920–9.

Africa

Gsell, *Histoire ancienne de l'Afrique du Nord*, 8 vols., 1920–8 (the standard work).
Albertini, M., *Roman Africa*, trans. 1927 (with plates and map).
Toutain, *Les Cités romaines de la Tunisie*, 1896.
Cagnat, *Carthage, Timgad, Tébessa*, 1927 (well illustrated).
Ventre, *Les Ports de Carthage*, 1913.
Comte Byron Khun de Prorok, 'Recent Researches on the Peninsula of Carthage', *G.J.*, Mar. 1924.
Warmington, B. H., *The North African Province from Diocletian to the End of the Vandal Conquest*, 1954.

Syria

Bouchier, *Syria as a Roman Province*, 1916.
Dussaud and others, *La Syrie antique et mediévale*, 1931 (contains photographs and archaeological data).
Dussaud, *Topographie historique de la Syrie antique et mediévale*, 1927 (maps).
Rostovtzev, *Caravan Cities*, 1932 (with plans).
Dobias, *Histoire de la Province romaine de Syrie*, 1924. (French resumé, trans. in 4 vols., in preparation.)
Carle, 'De l'alimentation en eau de Palmyre dans les temps actuels et anciens', *La G.*, XL (1923).

Asia Minor

Ramsay, 'Historical Geography of Asia Minor', *G.J. Supplt.*, vol. 4, 1890.
Hogarth, 'Roman Routes in Asia Minor', *G.J. Supplt.*, vol. 3, pt. 5.
Anatolean Studies presented to Sir Wm. Ramsay, Manchester, 1923.
Chapot, *La Frontière de l'Euphrate de Pompée à la conquête Arabe*, 1907.

Egypt

Histoire de la Nation Egyptienne, ed. Hanotaux: vol. III, by Chapot, *L'Egypte Romaine*, 1933.
Kammerer, A., *La Mer Rouge, L'Abyssinie et l'Arabie depuis l'antiquité*, vol. I, 1929. *Soc. Roy. de Géog. d'Egypte*, vol. 15 (contains many reproductions of old maps and plans).
Hall, H. R. H., *The Ancient History of the Near East*, 8th ed., 1932.
West, L. C., 'Roman Egypt' (commercial life), *J.R.S.*, vii (1917).
Murray, 'The Roman Roads and Stations in the Eastern Desert of Egypt', *J.E.A.*, Oct. 1925.

Balkan Peninsula

Childe, V. G., 'New Views on the relations between the Aegean and North Balkans', *J.H.S.*, L., 1930.
Evans, A. J., 'Antiquarian Researches in Illyricum', *Arch.*, XLVIII and XLIX, 1885.
Cvijic, *La Péninsule Balkanique*, 1918.

Jackson, Sir T. H., *Dalmatia*, 3 vols., 1887.
Miller, W., *Essays on the Latin Orient*, ch. I, 1921.
Jardé, A., *Les Céréales dans l'Antiquité Grecque*, 1925.
Zimmern, *The Greek Commonwealth*, 5th ed., 1931, part I.
Glover, T. R., *Greek Byways*, 1932.

Agriculture

Billiard, *La Vigne dans l'antiquité*, 1913.
Roman Agriculture, 1928.
Hehn, *La Vigne et le Vin chez les Romains*, 1903.
Hehn and Stallybrass, *The Wanderings of Plants and Animals*, 1888.
Jardé (see above).

Malaria

Jones, W. H. S., *Malaria : A Neglected Factor in the History of Greece and Rome*, 1907.
Angelo Celli, *Storia della malaria nell' Agro Romano* (i.e. Campagna), 1925.
Simkhovitch, *Toward the Understanding of Jesus and other Historical Studies*, 1921.

Mineral Exploitation

Rickard, *Man and Metals*, 1932, vol. I (with bibliographies).

Maps

Some provisional sheets of the 1 : 1,000,000 map of the Roman Empire have already been issued, namely, the Edinburgh, Rome, and Aberdeen sheets. For the maps of Ptolemy, see the works edited by Fischer and Stevenson, noted above.

CHAPTER II

THE EUROPEAN FRONTIER REGIONS OF THE ROMAN EMPIRE

General Studies

Lapradelle, *La Frontière*, 1928 (introductory chapters).
Febvre, L., *La Terre et l'Evolution Humaine*, 1922, part IV (English edition, *A Geographical Introduction to History*, 1925).
Fawcett, *Frontiers*, 1924.
Articles in *Bul. Int. Com. Hist. Sc.*, July 1933.
Cagnat, article on 'Limes imperii' in Daremberg and Saglio, *Dict. des Ant.*, 5 vols., 1873–1919.
Haushofer, *Grenzen*, 1927, ch. XVI.
Mommsen, *The Provinces of the Roman Empire, etc.*, 2 vols., 1909.
Pelham, H. F., 'A Chapter in Roman Frontier History', *Trans. R.H.S.*, New Ser., 1906, vol. XX.
Miller, K., *Itineraria Romana*, 1916 (with numerous maps of second-century roads).
Tourneur-Aumont, *Etudes de Cartographie Historique sur l'Alemanie*, 1918.

The Rhine Frontier

(Exhaustive archaeological investigation of the Roman frontier region in south-western Germany is still in progress, the results being published by the Reichs-Limes Kommission.)
Olwen Brogan, 'An Introduction to the Roman Land Frontier in Germany', *Greece and Rome*, Oct. 1933 (with map and photographs).
Schumacher, *Siedelungs und Kulturgeschichte der Rheinlande*, vols. I and II, 1921–3.
Norlind, *Die geographische Entwicklung des Rheindeltas bis um das J.* 1500, 1912 (with map of embanking in South Holland in 1300).
Jullian, C., *Histoire de la Gaule*, 6th ed., 1920–9, vol. VIII.
Desjardins, *Géographie historique et administrative de la Gaule romaine*, 2 vols., 1884.
Fabricius, article on the '*Limes*' in Pauly-Wissowa's *Real-Encyclopädie*, vol. XIII, 1926.
Germania Romana, ein Bilder-Atlas, 2nd ed., 1924–30.
Pelham, 'The Roman Frontier in Germany' in *Essays*, ed. Haverfield, 1911.
Babelon, *Le Rhin*, 2 vols., 1909.
Blanchet, *Les Enceintes Romaines de la Gaule*, 1907.
Koepp, *Die Römer in Deutschland*, 1903 (with maps and illustrations).
Cumont, *Comment la Belgique fut romanisée*, 2nd ed., 1919.
Holmes, T. R. E., *Caesar's Conquest of Gaul*, 2nd ed., 1911.
Holwerda, *Die Römer in Holland*, 1910.
Demarteau, J. E. de, *L'Ardenne Belgo-Romaine*, 3rd ed., 1911 (with a map showing Roman settlement).
West, L. C., *Roman Gaul*, 1935.
Pârvan, *Dacia*, 1928 (sketches prehistoric and Roman culture, with map).
'Le Limes Dacique', *Bul. Rum. Acad.* (Hist. section), 1929.
Marsigli, L. F., *Description du Danube*, 6 vols., 1744 (contains much archaeological data).
Gradmann, *Süd-Deutschland*, 2 vols., 1931 (a learned and comprehensive study).
Hertlein, Gessler and Paret, *Die Römer in Württemberg*, 1928–32 (three volumes have appeared; well illustrated).
Iorga, *Formes byzantines et réalites balkaniques*, 1922.
Relations entre l'Orient et l'Occident au moyen âge, 1923.

The Danube Frontier

CHAPTER III

THE BARBARIAN INVASIONS AND SETTLEMENT

Clapham, J. H. and Power, E. E., *The Cambridge Economic History of Europe*, vol. I, *The Agrarian Life of the Middle Ages*, 1941.
Dopsch, A., *Wirtschaftliche und soziale Grundlagen der europäischen Kulturentwicklung aus der Zeit von Cäsar bis auf Karl den Grossen*, 2 vols., 2nd ed., 1923–4. [English translation (abridged). *The Economic and Social Foundations of European Civilization*, 1937.]
Bury, *The Invasion of Europe by the Barbarians*, 1926.
The Later Roman Empire, 2 vols., 1923.
Halphen, *Les Barbares*, 1926.
Lefebvre, *Germains et Slaves*, 1903.
Fleure, *The Peoples of Europe*, 1925.
Giles, 'The Peoples of Europe', *Cam. Anc. Hist.* (1926), II, ii.
Haddon, *The Wanderings of Peoples*, revised ed., 1927.

Myres, J. L., ' Neolithic and Bronze Age Cultures ' (with maps), ch. II of *Cam. Anc. Hist.*, vol. I, 1928.

Evans, ' The Barbarian Invasions ', *Journ. Royal Anthropological Soc.*, 1913 (with series of small-scale maps).

Novarro, J. D. de, ' Prehistoric Routes . . .' (of amber trade in Europe), *G.J.*, Dec. 1925.

Huntington, ' The Evolution of Climate in North-Western Europe ' (a review of studies by Dr. C. E. P. Brooks), *G.R.*, Jan. 1922.

Dill, *Roman Society in the last century of the western Empire*, 2nd ed., 1899.

Hoffmann, A. von, *Das deutsche Land und die deutsche Geschichte*, 1923.
Das Land Italien und seine Geschichte, 1921.

Miller, K., *Itineraria Romana*, 1916 (contains maps of roads of the second century A.D.).

Hodgkin, T., *Italy and her Invaders*, 4 vols., 2nd ed., 1892, re-issued 1930.

Leeds, *The Archaeology of the Anglo-Saxon Settlement*, 1913.

Bloch, *Les Caractères Originaux de l'Histoire Rurale Française*, 1931.

Schumacher, C., *Siedelungs- und Kulturgeschichte der Rheinlande* . . . 1921, &c., vol. II. (Extensive bibliography in vol. III.)
Materialen zur Besiedelungs-Geschichte, vol. V of catalogue of Mainz Central Museum.

Des Marez, G., *Le Problème de la colonisation Franque et du régime agraire en Belgique*, 1926.

Elsaas Lothringischer Atlas, ed. Wolfram and Gley, Frankfurt, 1931 (contains maps of early archaeological and settlement distributions).

Blanchard, R., *La Flandre*, 1906.

Tourneur-Aumont, *Etudes de Cartographie Historique sur l'Alemanie*, 1918.

Schlüter, O., ' Die Besiedelungsfläche in Deutschland um 500 n. Christ ' (in Hoops, *Reallexikon* . . ., 1913).
Die Siedelungen im nordöstlichen Thüringen, 1903 (six maps).

Blanchet, *Les Trésors de monnaies romaines et les invasions germaniques en Gaule*, 1900.

Gradmann, *Süd-Deutschland*, 2 vols., 1931.
Das ländliche Siedlungswesen des Königreichs Württemberg, 1913.

Martiny, *Hof und Dorf in Altwestfalen*, 1926.

Loth, J., *L'Emigration Bretonne en Armorique*, 1883.

Schütte, *Our Forefathers : the Gothonic Nations*, 2 vols., 1929 and 1933 (a learned study of the ethnology of the German and Scandinavian peoples).

Maury, *Histoire des grandes forêts de la Gaule et de l'ancienne France*, &c., 1850.
Les Forêts de la France dans l'Antiquité et au Moyen Age, 1866.
Les Forêts de la Gaule et de l'ancienne France, 1867.

Hoops, *Waldbäume und Kulturpflanzen im germanischen Altertum*, 1905 (deals mainly with prehistoric periods but includes also chapters on plants of Roman Germany, Anglo-Saxon England, and northern Germany in the early Middle Ages).

Clouzot, ' Anciennes forêts de la France ', *La G.*, xvii, 1908.

Hehn and Stallybrass, *The Wanderings of Plants and Animals*, 1888.

Hubert, H., *The Rise of the Celts*, and
The Greatness and Decline of the Celts, English editions, 1934 (with maps).

Childe, V. G., 'Races, Peoples and Cultures in Prehistoric Europe', *H.*, Oct. 1933.
'The Danube Thoroughfare and the Beginnings of Civilisation in Europe', *A.*, Mar. 1927 (with map).
Fleure, H. J., 'The Life of Europe', *G.*, Sept. 1934.
Tulippe, O., *Considérations sur la Géographie du Peuplement*, Liége, 1932.

CHAPTERS IV AND V

RURAL SETTLEMENT AND AGRICULTURE IN WESTERN AND CENTRAL EUROPE IN THE MIDDLE AGES

General Studies

Clapham, J. H. and Power, E. E., *The Cambridge Economic History of Europe*, vol. I, *The Agrarian Life of the Middle Ages*, 1941.
Halphen, L., *L'Essor de l'Europe XIe-XIIIe Siècles* (1932).
Reports of the Commission on Rural Types of Settlement, published by the Union Géographique International, part I, 1928, part II, 1930 (contains regional studies of European settlement and gives many references to other local studies).
Comptes Rendus du Congrés International de Géographie, Paris, 1931, vol. III, L'Habitat Rural (studies of settlement in many areas of Europe).
Power, E., 'Peasant Life and Rural Conditions (*c.* 1100 to *c.* 1500)', *Cam. Med. Hist.*, vol. VII, 1932.
Boissonnade, *Life and Work in Medieval Europe*, English trans., 1927.
Thompson, J. W., *An Economic and Social History of Europe*, 2 vols., 1928 and 1931 (a full and useful text-book well illustrated with maps).
Meitzen, *Siedelungen und Agrarwesen*, &c., 3 vols. and atlas volume, 1895 (the pioneer work on settlement in western Europe, the facts and theses of which are now much challenged).
Ahlmann, 'The Geographical Study of Settlements', *G.R.*, Jan. 1928.
Coulton, *The Medieval Village*, 1925.
Simkhovitch, 'Hay and History', *Pol. Sc. Qu.*, Sept. 1913.
Curschmann, *Hungersnöte im Mittelalter*, 1900.
Hehn and Stallybrass, *The Wanderings of Plants and Animals*, 1888.

Regional Studies

1. *France and the Low Countries*

Foville, A. de, *Enquête sur les conditions de l'habitation en France*, vol. II, 1899 (historical introduction by Flach, J.).
Longnon, *Les Noms de Lieu de la France*, 1920–9.
Bloch, *Les Caractères Originaux de l'Histoire Rurale Française*, 1931 (a synthesis of economic history based on an understanding of regional geography).
Furth, *La Frontière Linguistique en Belgique*, &c., 1896.
Sclafert, *Le Haut-Dauphiné au Moyen Age*, 1926.
'A propos du déboisement des Alpes du Sud', *A. de G.*, May and June 1933.
Tourneur-Aumont, *Etudes de Cartographie Historique sur l'Alemanie*, 1918.
Deffontaines, *Les Hommes et leurs Travaux . . . Moyenne Garonne*, 1932.
Pirenne, *Histoire de Belgique*, 7 vols., 3rd ed., 1909–22.

Blanchard, R., *La Flandre*, 1906.
Lefèvre, M. A., *L'habitat rural en Belgique*, 1925.
Blanchard, R., *Les Alpes françaises*, 1925.
Dienne, *Histoire du déssèchement des lacs et des marais avant 1789*, 1891.
Maury and others, on French forests : see bibliography to Chapter III.
Halkin, *La Culture de la Vigne en Belgique*, 1896.
Lamprecht, *L'État economique de la France pendent la première partie au moyen âge*, trans. Marignan, 1889.

2. *Middle Europe*

Kretschmer, *Historische Geographie von Mitteleuropa*, 1904.
Hoffmann, A. von, *Das deutsche Land und die deutsche Geschichte*, 1923.
Knüll, *Historische Geographie Deutschlands im Mittelalter*, 1903.
Schumacher, *Siedelungs- und Kulturgeschichte der Rheinlande*, vol. 3, 1925.
Schlüter, O., *Wald, Sumpf und Siedelungsland im Altpreussen vor der Ordenzeit*, 1921 (with map of forest, marsh and settlement land).
Thompson, J. W., *Feudal Germany*, 1928.
'East German Colonisation', *A.H.A.*, 1915.
Gradmann, *Süd-Deutschland*, 2 vols., 1931.
Hoops and others, on forests : see bibliography to Chapter III.
Borchgrave, E. de, *Histoire des Colonies Belges en Allemagne* . . ., 1865.

3. *Mediterranean Region*

Marinelli (A Note on settlement in Italy), in *G.T.*, Autumn, 1925.
Harris, 'Some Notes on Field Systems in Mediterranean Lands', &c., *S.R.*, July 1928.
Philippson, *Der Peloponnesos*, 1892.
Ahlmann, on Sicily and South Italy : see bibliography to Chapter XIV.
Klute, F. (ed.), *Die ländlichen Siedlungen in verschiedenen Klimazonen*, 1933 : chs. on Albania, Bulgaria, Crete and Italy.

4. *Northern Europe*

Klute (ed.) (see above), ch. I by Rudolph, on Norwegian settlements.
Hallendorff and Schück, *History of Sweden*, 1929.
Olsen, M., *Farms and Fanes in Ancient Norway*, trans. 1928.

CHAPTER VI

MEDIEVAL TOWNS AND ROUTES IN WESTERN AND CENTRAL EUROPE

(See also bibliographies to Chapters XV and XVI)

Towns

Pirenne, *Medieval Cities*, 1923.
Bücher's *Industrial Evolution*, trans. and ed. S. M. Wickett, 1901.
Foville, A. de, *Enquête sur les conditions de l'habitation en France*, vol. II, 1899 (section by Flach).
Stephenson, C., 'Investigations into the Origins of Towns', *H.*, April 1932.
Fleure, H. J. 'City Morphology in Europe', *P.R.I.*, XXVII, part I, 1931.
Pirenne, Cohen and Focillon, *La Civilisation Occidentale du XIIe siècle, à la fin du XVe siècle*, 1933.
Püschel, *Das Anwachsen der deutschen Städte in der Zeit der mittelalterlichen Kolonialbewegung*, 1910 (many plans).

Wolf, G., *Die Norddeutsche Stadt*, 1928.
Sander, P., *Geschichte des deutschen Städtewesens*, 1922.
Schmoller, *Deutsches Städtewesen in älterer Zeit*, 1922.
Gantner, J., *Die Europaïsche Stadt*, 1928.
Gradmann, *Süd-Deutschland*, 2 vols., 1931 (contains many studies of German towns).
Sée, *Louis XI et les Villes*, 1892.
Lenthéric, *Les Villes Mortes du Golfe de Lion*, 1876.
Keussen, *Köln im Mittelalter*, 1918.
Rörig, F., and Vogel, W., *Lübeck*,
Keutgen, F., *Urkunden zur städtischen Verfassungsgeschichte*, 2 parts, 1899.
Alengry, *Les Foires de Champagne*, 1915.
Allix, ' Les Foires ', *La G.*, May 1923.
Deffontaines, *Les Hommes et leurs Travaux . . . Moyenne Garonne*, 1932.
Dickinson, R. E., ' The Development and Distribution of the Medieval German Town ', *G.*, vol. 27 (1942) and ' The Morphology of the Medieval German Town ', *G.R.*, vol. 35 (1945).
Articles in the *Town Planning Review* (on the spacial development of important European cities).
Abercromby, P., *Town and Country Planning*, 1933 (Home Univ. Ser.).
Lavedan, P., *L'Histoire de l'Urbanisme*, vol. I, *Antiquité et Moyen Age* (1926).
Lavedan, P., *Géographie des Villes* (1936).

Routes

Coolidge, W. A. B., *The Alps in Nature and History*, 1908.
***Alpine Studies*, 1912.**
Tyler, J. E., *The Alpine Passes : the Middle Ages*, 1930.
Bonnerot, *Les Routes de France*, 1921.
Rauers, on German roads, and Newton (ed.) on medieval travel : see bibliography to Chapter XVI.

CHAPTER VII

EARLY STATE-BUILDING IN WESTERN AND CENTRAL EUROPE

Freeman, E. A., *The Historical Geography of Europe*, 2 vols., 3rd ed., by Bury, 1903.
Western Europe in the Eighth Century, 1904.
Longnon, *Atlas de la Géographie de la France*, 2 parts, 1912 (the first part is a volume of text explanatory of the maps which cover the period from Caesar to 1380).
Géographie de la Gaule au sixième siècle, 1878.
Jacobs, A., *Géographie de Grégoire de Tours, de Frégidaire et de leurs continuateurs*, 2nd ed., 1861.
Kretschmer, *Historische Geographie von Mitteleuropa*, 1904.
Hoffmann, *Das deutsche Land und die deutsche Geschichte*, 1923.
Knüll, *Historische Geographie Deutschlands im Mittelalter*, 1903.
Mirot, *Manuel de Géographie Historique de la France*, 1930.
Bury, *The Invasion of Europe by the Barbarians*, 1928.
Halphen, *Les Barbares*, 1926.
Lefebvre, *Les Germains et les Slaves*, 1903.
Loth, *L'Emigration Bretonne en Armorique*, 1883.

Chaume, M., *Les Origines du duché de Bourgogne*, part I, Histoire Politique (1925); part II, Géographie Historique (1927) (with useful maps).
Cartellieri, A., *Die Weltstellung des deutsches Reiches 911–1047*, 1932.
Lot, Pfister and Ganshof, *Les destinées de l'Empire en Occident de 395 à 888*, 1933.

CHAPTER VIII

THE BYZANTINE EMPIRE

The Alexiad of Anne Comnena, trans. Dawes, 1928 (written in the early twelfth century, it describes events of the preceding century and contains some topographical information).
La Géographie d'Édrisi, trans. Jaubert, 2 vols., 1840 (written in the mid-twelfth century).
Cam. Med. Hist., vol. IV, 1923.
Stein, *Geschichte des spätrömischen Reiches*, 1928.
Bury, *The Later Roman Empire*, 2 vols., 1923.
Vasil'ev, *History of the Byzantine Empire*, Eng. trans., 2 vols., 1928.
Rambaud, *L'Empire Grec au Xme siècle*, 1870.
Runciman, J., *Byzantine Civilisation*, 1933.
The History of the First Bulgarian Empire, 1930.
Diehl, *Byzance*, 1924.
Justinian et la Civilisation Byzantine au 6me siècle, 1901.
Baynes, *Byzantine Empire*, 1925.
Freeman, *The Historical Geography of Europe*, 3rd ed. by Bury, 2 vols., 1903.
Zlatarski, *Geschichte der Bulgaren*, 1918 (maps).
Anderson, 'The Road System of Eastern Asia Minor', *J.H.S.*, XVII, 1897.
Jireček, *Die Heerstrasse von Belgrad nach Constantinopel*, 1877.
Die Handelstrassen und Bergwerke von Serbien, 1879.
La Civilisation serbe au moyen âge, 1920.
Gravier, *Les Frontières historiques de la Serbie*, 1919.
Temperley, H. W. V., *A History of Serbia*, 1917.
Heyd, *Histoire du Commerce du Levant au moyen âge*, 2 vols., new impression, 1923.
Mordtmann, *Esquisse Topographique de Constantinople*, 1892 (with large-scale contoured plan).
Millingen, A. van, *Byzantine Constantinople*, 1899.
Ebersolt, *Constantinople byzantine et les voyageurs du Levant*, 1918.
Beylié, *L'Habitation byzantine*, 1902 (Byzantine architecture).
Myres, J. L., 'The Marmora Region', *S.G.M.*, XXVI, 1910.
Miller, W., *Essays on the Latin Orient*, 1921.
The Latins in the Levant, 1908.
Darby, H. C., 'The Medieval Sea-State', *S.G.M.*, July 1932.
Tafrali, O., *Topographie de Thessalonique*, 1913.
Thessalonique au XIVme siècle, 1913.
Gregorovius, *Geschichte der Stadt Athen im Mittelalter*, 2 vols., 1889.
Hudson, G. F., *Europe and China*, 1931 (a survey of their relations up to 1800).
Tozer, H. F., *The Islands of the Aegean*, 1890.
Casson, *Macedonia, Thrace and Illyria*, 1926 (mainly prehistory).

Turrill, *The Plant Life of the Balkan Peninsula*, 1929 (Chapter X deals with the effect of Man in modifying the natural vegetation).
Regnault, 'The Rôle of depopulation, deforestation and malaria in the decadence of certain nations', *Ann. Report of the Smithsonian Institution*, 1914, 593 (1915).
Cvijic, *La Péninsule Balkanique*, 1918.
Newbigin, *Geographical Aspects of Balkan Problems*, 2nd ed., 1919.
Ramsay, 'The Historical Geography of Asia Minor', *G.J. Suppt. Papers*, vol. 4, 1890.
Diehl, 'L'Egypte Chrétienne et Byzantine', 1933: vol. 3 of *Histoire de la Nation Egyptienne*, ed. Hanotaux.
Diehl, *L'Afrique byzantine*, 1896.
Salonique, 1920.
Hogarth, *The Nearer East*, 1902.
'Modern and Ancient Roads in Eastern Asia Minor', *G.J. Suppt. Papers*, vol. 3, part 5, 1890.
Andréadès, A., 'De la population de Constantinople sous les empereurs byzantins', *Metron.*, vol. I, no. 2 (1920).
Laurent, *L'Arménie entre Byzance et l'Islam*, 1919.
Le Strange, *The Lands of the Eastern Caliphate*, 2nd ed., 1931.
Pears, Sir E., *The Destruction of the Greek Empire*, 1903 (maps).

CHAPTER IX

ARAB EUROPE IN THE MIDDLE AGES

Contemporary Arabic Sources in Translation

Edrisi, *Description de l'Afrique et de l'Espagne*, trans. by Dozy and Goeje, 1866; Spanish trans. by Blasquet, 1901.
Géographie d'Édrisi, trans. Jaubert, 2 vols., 1836–40.
La Géographie d'Aboulféda, trans. Reinaud and Guyard, 2 vols., 1848.
Al Bekri, *Description de l'Afrique septentrionale*, trans. Slane, 2nd ed., 1913.
Ibn-Al-Awam, *Livre d'Agriculture*, trans. Clément-Mullet, 1864.
The Travels of Benjamin of Tudela, ed. Komroff, 1928 (twelfth-century travels).
Blochet, ed., *Histoire d'Egypte de Makrizi*, 1908.
Ibn Batutah's Voyages, trans. Defremery and Sanguinetti, *S.A.*, 4 vols. (relate to the fourteenth century).
Ibn Khaldun, *Histoire des Berbères*, trans. Slane, 1925.
Goeje, M. J., ed., *Bibliotheca Geographorum Arabicorum*, 8 parts, 1870–94. (The texts are in Arabic, the prefaces in Latin. Part VI, however, contains a French translation of Ibn Khurdādbah's *Livre des routes et des provinces*, written *c.* A.D. 850.)
Makkari, Al, *History of the Mohammedan Dynasties in Spain*, trans. and ed. Gayangos, 2 vols., 1840.
Ibn Haukal, 'Description de l'Afrique septentrionale', trans. Slane, *J.A.*, 5th ser., XII—XIV.

Secondary Works

General

Le Strange, *The Lands of the Eastern Caliphate*, 2nd ed., 1931.
Kremer, A. von, *Kulturgeschichte des Orients unter den Chalifen*, 2 vols., 1875–7 (English trans. of part, 1920).

Levy, R., *An Introduction to the Sociology of Islam*, 2 vols., 1931 and 1934.
Patzelt, *Die fränkische Kultur und der Islam*, 1932.
Sten de Geer, 'The Sub-Tropical Belt of Old Empires', *Geog. Ann.*, No. 3, 1928.
Carra de Vaux, *Les Penseurs de l'Islam*, 5 vols., 1921–6.
Nordenskiöld, *Periplus*, trans. Bather, 1897.
Stevenson, E. L., *Portolan Charts*, 1911.
Schaube, *Handelsgeschichte der romanischen Völker . . .*, 1906.
Semple, *The Geography of the Mediterranean Region*, 1931.
Pirenne, *Medieval Cities*, 1923.

Syria and Palestine

Gaudefroy-Demombynes, *La Syrie à l'époque des Mamelouks d'après les Auteurs Arabes*, 1923.
Smith, G. A., *The Historical Geography of the Holy Land*, 25th ed., 1931.
Dussaud, *Topographie historique de la Syrie antique et mediéval*, 1927 (maps).
Dussaud and others, *La Syrie antique et médiévale illustrée*, 1931.
Le Strange, *Palestine under the Moslems*, 1890.
Huntington, *Palestine and its Transformation*, 1911.
Butler, 'Desert Syria', *G.R.*, Feb. 1920.
Rey, E. G., *Recherches géographiques et historiques sur la domination des Latins en Orient*, 1877.

Egypt

La Géographie de la Nation Égyptienne, ed. Hanotaux, vol. I by Roncière, 1930.
Butler, A. J., *The Arab Conquest of Egypt*, 1902.
Lane-Poole, S., *A History of Egypt in the Middle Ages*, 1901.
Maspéro and Wiet, *Matériaux pour servir à la géographie de l'Égypte*, 1914, etc.
Quatremère, *Mémoires géographiques et historiques sur l'Égypte*, 2 vols., 1811.
Kammerer, A., 'La Mer Rouge, l'Abyssinie et l'Arabie depuis l'antiquité', vol. I, 1929: *Soc. Roy. de Géog. d'Egypte*, vol. 15.
New Atlas of Egypt, Gaza, 1928.

Africa

Diehl, *L'Afrique byzantine*, 1896.
Gsell, *Histoire ancienne de l'Afrique du Nord*, 8 vols., 1920–8.
Caudel, *Les Premiers Invasions Arabes dans l'Afrique du Nord*, 1900.
Desmolins, E., *Comment la route crée le type social*, 2 vols., Paris, n.d.
Gautier, *Les Siècles obscures du Maghreb*, 1927.

Spain

Lévi-Provençal, *L'Espagne Mussulmane au Xe Siècle*, 1932.
Dozy, *Histoire des Mussulmans de l'Espagne*, 3 vols., new ed., by Lévi-Provençal, 1931.
Recherches sur l'histoire politique et littéraire de l'Espagne, 3rd ed., 2 vols., 1881.
Stokes, *Spanish Islam*, 1913 (English abridgement of Dozy's *Histoire*).
Whishaw, B. and E., *Arabic Spain*, 1912.

Albornoz, ' L'Espagne et l'Islam ', *Rev. Hist.*, March 1932.
Reinaud, J. T., *Les Invasion Sarrazins en France* . . ., 1836.
Altamira, *A History of Spanish Civilisation*, 1930.
Williams, Leonard, *The Arts and Crafts of Older Spain*, 3 vols., 1907.
Chaytor, *A History of Aragon and Catalonia*, 1933 (mainly political).
Castejon y Martinez de Arizala, *Cordoba Califal* (illustrated), 1930.

Sicily (see bibliography to Chapter XIV).

CHAPTER X

THE RUSSIAN STATE

' The Chronicle of Novgorod, 1016–1471 ' (*Camden Soc.*, 3rd ser., vol. xxv, 1914).
Ibn Dasta, *Book of Precious Treasures* (compiled in the first half of the tenth century from earlier sources which were accounts of Arab travellers in Russia). Russian trans. only.
Newton, A. P., ed., *Travel and Travellers in the Middle Ages*, 1926.
Hakluyt, *The Discovery of Muscovy*, Cassell's ed., 1889.
Giles Fletcher, *Russe Commonwealth*, 1598 (Hak. Soc., 1856).
Pares, *A History of Russia*, 1926.
Pokrovsky, *History of Russia*, n.d. (London) (an authoritative work).
Klyuchevsky, *A History of Russia*, trans. Hogarth, 5 vols., 1911–31.
Thomsen, V., *The Relations between ancient Russia and Scandinavia and the Origin of the Russian State*, 1877.
Keller, ' Distribution of Vegetation on the Plains of Russia ', *Journal of Ecology*, XV, No. 2, Aug. 1927.
Minns, E. H., *Scythians and Greeks in South Russia*, 1913.
Rostovtzev, *Iranians and Greeks in South Russia*, 1922.
' The Origin of the Russian State on the Dnieper ', *Ann. Rep. of A.H.A.*, 1925.
Gillett, ' A Sketch of the Historical Geography of the Black Earth Region of Central Russia ', *S.G.M.*, Jan. 1922.
Beazley, Forbes and Birkett, G. A., *Russia from the Varangians to the Bolsheviks*, 1922.
Vaughan Cornish, *The Great Capitals*, 1923, Chapter VI.
Jacobs, G., *Arab Trade in the Baltic*, 1887.
Fleming, Essay on Russia in *Studies in Regional Consciousness and Environment*, ed. Peate, 1930.
Milioukov and others, *A History of Russia*, 3 vols., 1932.
Captain John Smith, the Travels and Adventures of, 2 vols., ed. 1819.
Skrine, F. H., *The Expansion of Russia, 1815–1900*, new ed., 1915.
Cam. Med. Hist., vol. IV, 1923, ch. VII.
Sumner, B. H., *Survey of Russian History*, 1944.

CHAPTER XI

THE POLITICAL UNIFICATION OF FRANCE

Longnon, *La Formation de l'Unité Française*, 1922.
Atlas historique de la France, 2 vols., 1912.
Flach, *Les Origines de l'Ancienne France*, 3 vols., 1886–1904.
Powicke, ' The Origins of France ', *H.*, vols. xi and xii (a critique of Flach's work).

Mortillet, G. de, *Formation de la Nation Française*, 1897.
Richer, *Histoire de la France* (888–995), 1930, vol. I of series edited by R. Latouche.
Freeman, E. A., *The Historical Geography of Europe*, 3rd ed., 2 vols., 1903.
The Franks and the Gauls, Historical Essays, 1st ser., 1871.
France and Gaul, Historical Essays, 3rd ser., 1871.
Mirot, *Manuel de la Géographie Historique de la France*, 1930.
Lavallée, *Les Frontières de la France*, 1864.
Brette, *Les limites et les divisions territoriales de la France en 1789*, 1907.
Jullian, C., *De la Gaule à la France*, 1922.
Le Paris des Romains.
Halphen, *Paris sous les premiers Capétiens*, 1909.
Poète, *Une Vie de Cité : Paris de sa naissance à nos jours*, 3 vols. and album, 1924–31.
Articles in the *A. de G.*, e.g. ‘ La Cité ’, vol. xl ; ‘ Paris ’, vol. ix.
Bonnerot, J., *Les Routes de France*, 1921.
Lodge, ‘ The Relations between England and Gascony ’, *H.*, Sept. 1934.
Berthaut, *Les Ingénieurs géographes militaires*, 1624–1831, 2 vols., 1902.
Brunhes and Deffontaines, *Géographie Politique et Géographie du Travail*, 1926 (vol. II, Part 2 of series ed. by Hanotaux, G.).
Sorel, *L'Europe et la Révolution Française*, 2nd ed., 1908–11, part iv, ‘ Les Limites Naturelles ’.
Boiteau, *État de la France en 1789*, 1861.
Halévy, D., *Vauban, Builder of Fortresses*, English trans. 1924.
Weil, *Napoléon Ier géographe*, 1927 (vol. in series ed. Brunhes and de Martonne).

CHAPTER XII

THE CREATION OF SWITZERLAND, BELGIUM AND THE NETHERLANDS

A Manual of Belgium and the Adjoining Territories (with separate atlas), Stationery Office, n.d.
Pirenne, *Histoire de Belgique*, 3 vols., 3rd ed. 1909–22.
‘ The Formation and Constitution of the Burgundian State ’, *A.H.R.*, vol. xiv.
Himly, *La Formation Territoriale des États de l'Europe Central*, vol. II, 1876.
Geyl, P., *The Netherlands Divided*, 1609–1648 (1936).
Edmundson, G., *History of Holland*, 1922.
Cumont, *Comment la Belgique fut romanisée*, 2nd ed., 1919.
Wieder, *Monumenta Cartographica*, 1925–
Brants, *La Belgique au XVIIe siècle*, 1907.
Cammaerts, *Belgium from the Roman Invasion to the Present Day*, 1921 (maps).
Martin, W., *A History of Switzerland*, 1931
Coolidge, *The Alps in Nature and History*, 1908.
Alpine Studies, 1912.
Oechsli, *History of Switzerland*, 1499–1914, 1922.
Robertson, J. M., *The Evolution of States*, 1912, part V.
Merian, *Topographia Helvetica*, 1642. Facsimile, Basle, 1927.

CHAPTER XIII

THE POLITICAL UNIFICATION OF GERMANY

Himly, *La Formation Territoriale des États de l'Europe Centrale*, 2 vols., 1876.
Marriott and Robertson, *The Expansion of Prussia*, 1915.
Dawson, W. H., *The Evolution of Modern Germany*, new ed., 1919.
Barker, J. E., *Modern Germany*, 5th ed., 1915.
Reddaway, W. F., *Frederick the Great*, 1904.
Robertson, Sir C. H., *Bismarck*, 1918.
Dawson, W. H., *The German Empire 1867–1914*, 2 vols., 1919.
Pinnow, H., *History of Germany*, Eng. trans., 1933.
Henderson, E. F., *A Short History of Germany*, 2 vols., 1927.
Ward, A. W., *Germany, 1815–90*, 3 vols., 1916–18.
Barraclough, G., *The Origins of Modern Germany* (1946).

CHAPTER XIV

SICILY

Strabo, *Geography*, Loeb ed., 8 vols., 1917–32.
Geography of Claudius Ptolemy, trans. and maps, ed. Stevenson, 1932.
La Géographie d'Édrisi, trans. Jaubert, 1836–40, vol. II.
Ibn Haukal, *Description de Palermo au milieu du Xme siècle*, trans. Amari, 1845.
Extrait du Voyage d'Ibn Djobeir (Jubair), trans., 1884.
Ahlmann, 'Études de Géographie Humaine sur l'Italie Subtropicale' (two excellent studies in *Geog. Ann.*, 1925 and 1926).
Peet, *The Stone and Bronze Ages in Italy and Sicily*, 1909.
Freeman, E. A., *The History of Sicily from the earliest times*, 4 vols., 1891–4 (these volumes cover the history of Sicily up to 330 B.C. and contain much topographical information).
The Normans at Palermo, Historical Essays, 3rd ser., 1871–92.
Randall-MacIver, *Greek Cities in Italy and Sicily*, 1931 (deals with the archaeology of Syracuse, Enna and other sites).
Gregorovius, *Siciliana, Sketches of Naples and Sicily in the Nineteenth Century*, trans., 1914.
Lenormant, *La Grande-Grèce*, 1881–4.
Fischer, *Die Sizilische Frage*, 1913.
Wermert, *Die Insel Sicilien*, &c., 1905.
Hoffmann, A. von, *Das Land Italien und seine Geschichte*, 1921 (gives a brief review).
Maggiore-Perni, *La Popolazione di Sicilia e di Palermo del X° al XVIII° secoli*, 1889.
Mori, 'La distribuzione della popolazione in Sicilia e le sue variazioni negli ultimi quattro secolì', *Mem. Geog.*, XII, 1918, p. 125.
'Sulla formazione di nuovì centri abitati in Sicilia negli ultimi quattro secoli', *R.G.It.*, XXVII, 1920.
Olivier, *En Sicile* (contains short articles by experts on many aspects of Sicilian civilization), 1910.
Diehl, *Palerme et Syracuse*, 1907 (well illustrated).
Whitaker, *Motya, a study in Phoenician colonisation*, 1921.
Giovanni, V. de, *La Topografia antica de Palermo dal secolo X° al XV°*, 2 vols., 1889–90 (plans).

Amari, *Storia dei Musulmani di Sicilia*, 3 vols., 1854–72.
Gay, *L'Italie méridoniale et l'Empire Byzantin*, 867–1071, 1904 (mainly political).
Haskins, C. H., *The Normans in European History*, 1916 (chapters 7 and 8).
Delarc, *Les Normands en Italie*, 1883.
Chalandon, *Histoire de la Domination Normande en Italie et en Sicile*, 2 vols., 1907 (mainly political history).
Schaube, *Handelsgeschichte der romanischen Völker des Mittelmeergebiets*, 1906 (deals with the place of Sicily in medieval commerce).
Lévesque de Burigny, *Histoire générale de Sicile . . .* (until 1734), 2 vols., 1745.
Renan, J. E., *Mélanges d'Histoire et de Voyages*, 1878.

Large Scale Topographical Maps

1 : 100,000 Instituto topografico militare, 1880.
1 : 500,000 Instituto geografico militare, ed. 1898.

CHAPTER XV

THE MEDITERRANEAN REGION IN THE MIDDLE AGES

(See also bibliographies to Chapters IX and XIV)

Schulte, A., *Geschichte des Mittelalterlichen Handels*, 2 vols., 1910.
Schaube, A., *Handelsgeschichte der romanischen Völker des Mittelmeergebiets*, 1906.
Heyd, *Histoire du Commerce du Levant au Moyen Age*, 2 vols., 1923.
Thompson, J. W., *An Economic and Social History of the Middle Ages*, 2 vols., 1928 and 1931.
Beazley, *The Dawn of Modern Geography*, 3 vols., 1897–1906.
Boissonnade (trans. by Power), *Life and Work in Medieval Europe*, 1927.
Hoffmann, A. von, *Das Land Italien und seine Geschichte*, 1921.
Pirenne, *Medieval Cities*, 1923.
Patzelt, *Die fränkische Kultur und der Islam*, 1932.
Fleure, H. J., 'Cities of the Po Basin', *G.R.*, July 1924.
Brown, H. F., *Venice, an historical sketch of the Republic* (maps), 1893.
Studies in the History of Venice, 2 vols., 1907.
Chapter XIII in *Cam. Med. Hist.*, vol. IV, 1923.
Okey, *Venice and its Story*, 4th ed., 1930.
Hodgson, F. C., *Venice in the Thirteenth and Fourteenth Centuries*, 1910.
Diehl, *Venise*, 1915.
Ravenne, 1903.
Lane, F. C., *Venetian Ships and Ship-Owners of the Renaissance*, 1934.
Renard, *Histoire du Travail à Florence*, 2 vols., 1913.
Byrne, E. H., *Genoese Shipping in the 11th and 12th Centuries*, 1930.
Heywood, *A History of Pisa*, 1921.
Symonds, *Sketches and Studies in Italy and Greece*, new ed., 3 vols., 1898.
Hutchinson, 'The Oriental Trade and the Rise of the Lombard Communes', *Q.J.E.*, XVI.
Baird Smith, *Italian Irrigation*, 2 vols., 1852 (with volume of maps).
Lenthéric, *Les Villes Mortes du Golfe de Lion*, 1876.

Miller, W., *The Latins in the Levant*, 1908.
Essays on the Latin Orient, 1921.
Kammerer, A., *La Mer Rouge, l'Abyssinie et l'Arabie depuis l'antiquité*, vol. I, 1929.
Nordenskiöld, *Periplus*, trans. Bather, 1897.
Stevenson, E. L., *Portolan Charts : their origin and characteristics*, 1911.
Bratianu, G. I., *Recherches sur le Commerce Génois dans la Mer Noire au XIIIe siècle*, 1929 (with plates).
Iorga, 'Une Ville " Romane " Devenue Slave' (Ragusa), *Bul. Rum. Acad.* (Hist. Sect.), vol. XVIII (1931).
Reichenheim, 'Die wirtschaftliche Bedeutung von Barcelona', *Instituts für Meereskunde*, new ser., B, No. 8, March 1933 (Berlin).

CHAPTER XVI

THE BALTIC AND NORTH SEAS IN THE MIDDLE AGES

Thompson, J. W., *Economic and Social History of the Middle Ages*, 2 vols., 1928 and 1931.
Power and Postan, *Studies in English Trade in the Fifteenth Century*, 1933.
Cam. Med. Hist., vol. VII, A. Weiner, 'The Hansa'.
Nordenskiöld, *Periplus*, trans. Bather, 1897.
Reumert, J., *The Commercial-Geographic Importance of the situation of Copenhagen*, 1929 (contains useful maps).
Koppe, W., *Lübeck-Stockholmer Handelsgeschichte im 14 J.H.*, 1933 (vol. 2 of series ed. by Rörig and Vogel).
Vogel, *Geschichte der deutschen Seeschiffahrt*, vol. 1, 1915.
Kendrick, *The Vikings*, 1930.
Montelius, *The Civilisation of Sweden in Heathen Times*, trans. F. H. Woods, 1888.
The Baltic Pilot : The North Sea Pilot (Admiralty Publications).
Waghenhaer, *The Mariners' Mirror*, English ed., 1588.
Werdenhagen, *De Rebuspublicis Hanseaticis Tractatus, cum Urbium earum Iconismis, Descriptionibus, Tabulis Geographicis et Nauticis*, 1641, 2nd ed. Frankfurt (contains 191 engraved views of towns, maps and sailing charts of all European coasts with the compass lines and sailing routes marked).
Hill, C. E., *The Danish Sound Dues and the Command of the Baltic*, 1926.
Admiralty Handbooks : *The North Sea ; The Baltic Sea.*
Saxo Grammaticus, *The Nine Books of the Danish History*, trans. O. Elton, 1894.
Schmeidler, B., *Hamburg-Bremen und Nordosteuropa vom 9–11 Jahrhundert*, 1918 (critical researches on the Ecclesiastical History of Hamburg by Adam of Bremen written in the twelfth century).
Die Chronik Arnolds von Lübeck . . . übersetzt von Dr. Laurent, forword by Lappenberg, 1853.
Seeger, *Westfalens Handel und Gewerbe v. 9 bis 14 J.H.*, 1926.
Jeffries Davis, article on fifteenth-century London, in *Tudor Studies*, ed. Seton-Watson, 1924.
Letts, *Bruges and its Past*, 2nd ed., 1926 (illustrated).
Pirenne, *Histoire de Belgique*, 7 vols. : vol. I, 3rd ed., 1909, and vol. II, 3rd ed., 1922.

Newton, A. P., ed., *Travel and Travellers in the Middle Ages*, 1926.
Beazley, *The Dawn of Modern Geography*, 3 vols., 1897–1906
Boissonnade, *Life and Work in Medieval Europe* (trans., 1927).
Rauers, *Zur Geschichte der alten Handelsstrassen in Deutschland* (with large-scale road maps), 1907.
Olins, *The Teutonic Knights in Latvia*, 1928.
Keary, *The Vikings*, 1891.
Schulz, F., *Die Hanse und England v. Eduards III*, 1911.
Hallendorf and Schück, *History of Sweden*, 1929.
Cammaerts, *Belgium from the Roman invasion to the present day*, 1921.
Semple, 'The Development of the Hanse Towns in relation to their Geographic Environment', *J.A.G.S.*, XXXI, 1899.
Darby, 'The Medieval Sea-State', *S.G.M.*, May 1932.
Fawcett, 'The Nordic Region', *S.G.M.*, March 1932.
Pettersson, article on late medieval climate in Europe, *Q.J.M.*, XXXVIII.
Wiener, 'Early Anglo-German Trade', *Economica*, No. 5.
Fifteenth-Century Pilot Books, *Hak. Soc.*, No. 79 (1889).
Wertheim, Hans, (ed.), *Imago Mundi* (1936).
Pirenne, H., *Histoire de l'Europe des Invasions au XVIe Siècle*, 5th ed., 1936.

CHAPTER XVII
WESTERN EUROPE DURING THE EARLY OCEANIC PHASE

General Studies

Braudel, F., *La Méditerranée et le Monde Méditerranéen à l'Epoque de Philippe II*, Paris, 1949.
Renard and Weulersse, *Life and Work in Modern Europe*, trans., 1926.
Clark, G. N., *The Seventeenth Century*, 1929.
Ogg, D., *Europe in the Seventeenth Century*, 2nd ed., 1931.
Heawood, E., *A History of Geographical Discovery in the Seventeenth and Eighteenth Centuries*, 1912.
Newton, A. P., *The European Nations in the West Indies, 1493–1688*, 1933.
ed. *The Great Age of Discovery*, 1932.
Taylor, E. G. R., *Tudor Geography*, 1930.
Late Tudor and Early Stuart Geography, 1934.
ed., *A Brief Summe of Geographie*, by Roger Barlow, *Hak. Soc.*, 1932.
Botero, Giovanni, *The Causes of the Magnificence and Greatness of Cities*, trans. R. Peterson, 1606.
Mundy, Peter, *A brief relation of certain Journies, etc., 1628–34*, printed 1914.
Hughes, C., *Shakespeare's Europe* (a selection from Fynes Moryson's Itinerary), 1903.
Williamson, *Maritime Enterprise, 1485–1558*, 1913.
Marguet, *Histoire Générale de la Navigation du Xme au XXe siècle*, 1931.
Fordham, 'Les Guides Routières, Itinéraires et Cartes-Routières de l'Europe, 1500–1800', *Bul. Soc. Arch. hist. et art.*, 1926.
Gallois, *Les Géographes Allemandes de la Renaissance*, 1890.
Bellet, *La Grande Pêche de la Morue à Terre-Neuve*, 2nd ed., 1902.
Selden, J., *Of the Dominion, or the Ownership of the Sea*, trans., 1652.
Fulton, T. W., *The Sovereignty of the Sea*, 1911.
Lybyer, 'The Ottoman Turks and the Routes of Oriental Trade', *E.H.R.*, Oct. 1915.
Corbett, J. S., *England in the Mediterranean*, 1603–1713, 2 vols., 1917.

Pollard, *Factors in Modern History*, 3rd ed., 1932 (Chapter III on changes in world trade routes).
Godart, *L'Ouvrier en Soie*, 1899, part I.
Baker, J. N. L., *A History of Geographical Discovery and Exploration*, 1931 (maps).
Woytinsky, *Die Welt in Zahlen*, vol. I, 1925.
Robertson, J. M., *The Evolution of States*, 1912, part V.

Spain and Portugal

Altamira, *Historia general de España y de la civilizaceon española*, 4 vols., 1911.
Haring, *Trade and Navigation between Spain and the Indies in the time of the Habsburgs*, 1918.
Girard, *La Rivalité Commerciale et Maritime entre Séville et Cadix*, 1932.
Le Commerce Français à Séville et Cadix au temps des Habsbourgs, 1932.
St. Simon, *Mémoires*, vol. xviii, p. 415 (on Spanish roads).
Glunard and Monbeig, ' Madrid ', *A. de G.*, Sept. 1932 (maps and plans).
Reichenheim, ' Die wirtschaftliche Bedeutung von Barcelona ', *Instituts für Meereskunde*, new ser., B, No. 8, Mar. 1933.
Klein, J., *The Mesta* (a study in Spanish economic history, 1273–1836), 1920 (with map of sheep routes).
Bensaude, *Histoire de la Science Nautique Portugaise*, 1917.
Keymer, John, *A Description of ye wealth and fruitfulnes of ye Kingdome of Portugall* (MS. n.d. at British Museum).

France

Coulon, *Les Rivières de France*, 1644.
Merian, *Topographia Galliae*, 1654.
Hanotaux, *La France en 1614*, 1913.
Masson, *Histoire du Commerce Français dans le Levant au 17e siècle*, 1896.
Martin, G., *Histoire économique et sociale*, 1927.
Bresard, *Les Foires de Lyon aux 15e siècle*, 1892.
De Gourcy, *La Foire de Beaucaire . . .*, 1911.
Estienne, *Guide des Chemins de France*, 1553 (new ed. by Bonnerot in preparation).
Fordham, Sir G., ' Une carte-routière de France du XVIIe siècle ', *La G.*, Sept.–Oct. 1926.
Roads on English and French Maps at the end of the seventeenth century, 1926.
Bonnerot, J., *Les Routes de France*, 1921.
' Esquisse de la Vie des Routes au XVIe siècle ', *R. des Q.H.*, 3rd ser., vol. xix, 1931.
Belloc, A., *Les Postes Françaises*, 1886.
Dienne, *Histoire du dessèchement des lacs et marais en France avant 1789*, 1891.
Usher, *The History of the Grain Trade in France*, 1913 (map).

The Low Countries

(See also bibliography to Chapters XII and XVI)

Coornaert, ' Les Routes commerciale d'Anvers en Italie au XVIe siècle ', *A. de G.*, March 1927.

Keymer, John, *A Description of Holland* . . . (gives a full account of Dutch Trade, written about 1600, MS. at the B.M.).
Wegg, *Antwerp 1477–1559*, 1916.

Historical Maps, Plans and Charts

Werdenhagen, *De Rebuspublicis* . . . (1641) (see bibliography to Chapter XVI).
Atlas des Villes de la Belgique au XVIe siècle, 2 vols., n.d.
Waghenhaer, *The Mariners Mirror*, English ed., 1588 (contains port charts and sailing directions).
Ortelius' Theatrum Orbis Terrarum, 1579.
Braun and Hagenburg, *Civitates Orbis Terrarum*, part I (first German ed., 1574).
Sanson, *Nouvelle Introduction à la géographie*, 1695.
Wieder, *Monumenta Cartographica*, 1925– (Reproductions of rare maps, plans and views, together with cartographical monographs).

CHAPTER XVIII

THE DANUBE ROUTE-WAY

Schweiger-Lerchenfeld, *Die Donau als Völkerweg, Grossschiffahrtstrasse u. Reiseroute*, 1896.
Hajnal, *The Danube*, 1920.
Droit du Danube International, 1929.
Childe, V. G., *The Danube in Prehistory*, 1930.
Fluss, M., *Donaufahrten und Donauhandel im Mittelalter*, 1920.
Ormsby, 'The Danube as a Waterway', *S.G.M.*, April 1923.
Pârvan, *Dacia*, 1928 (a study of prehistoric culture).
Marsigli, *Description du Danube*, 1744, 6 vols. (contains much archaeological material).
Quin, *A Steam Voyage down the Danube*, 2 vols., 1835.
Bright, R., *Travels from Vienna through Lower Hungary*, 1818.
Forrester, T., *The Danube and the Black Sea*, 1857.
Suppan, *Die Donau und ihre Schiffahrt*, 1917.
Baiconianu, *Le Danube*, 1917.
Sturdza, D. A., *La Question des Portes de Fer*, &c., 1899.
Smith, H., *The Economic Functions of International Rivers*, 1931.
Hines, W. D., *Report on Danube Navigation*, 2 parts, 1925.
La Commission Européenne du Danube et son œuvre de 1856 à 1931, Paris, 1931 (contains many maps).
Chamberlain, *The Régime of the International Rivers: Danube and Rhine*, 1923.
Sasek, *The Danube* (1936).

CHAPTER XIX

EUROPE IN THE EIGHTEENTH CENTURY

Clapham, J. H., *The Economic Development of France and Germany, 1815–1914*, 4th ed., 1936.
Sée, *La France économique et sociale au XVIIIe siècle*, 1925.

Young, Arthur, *Voyages en France en 1787, 1788 et 1789*, ed. Sée, 3 vols., 1931 (this is the first *complete* edition of the *Travels in France* since 1794).
Voyages en Italie et Espagne (in 1787 and 1789), trans. Lesage, 1860.
The Travels of Arthur Young in France and Italy : selections therefrom are conveniently printed in the Everyman's Library.
Maxwell, C., *The English Traveller in France*, 1932.
Hauser, article on French economic development 1600–1800, *Econ. H.R.*, Oct. 1933.
Kretschmer, *Historische Geographie von Mitteleuropa*, 1904.
Ogg, *Economic Development of Modern Europe*, 1918.
Albion, *Forests and Sea Power*, 1926 (Harvard Econ. Studies).
Martin, G., *La Grande Industrie en France sous le Règne de Louis XV*, 1900.
Usher, *The History of the Grain Trade in France*, 1913 (map).
Masson, *Histoire du Commerce Français dans le Levant au XVIIIe siècle*, 1911.
Rouff, *Les Mines de Charbon en France au XVIIIe siècle*, 1922.
De Raymond, *Tableau de l'Empire de Russie*, 2 vols., 1812.
Oddy, *European Commerce*, 1805 (contains a map of canals and navigable rivers).
Fernow, B. E., *A Brief History of Forestry in Europe, the U.S.A. and other countries*, revised ed., 1911.
Heckscher, ' The Place of Sweden in Modern Economic History ', *Econ. H.R.*, Oct. 1932.
Blanchard, M., *Les Routes des Alpes . . . 1796–1815*, 1920.
Beer, G. de, *Early Travellers in the Alps*, 1930.
Jeans, J. S., *Waterways and Water Transport*, 1890.
Cahen, article on eighteenth-century traffic on the Seine between Rouen and Paris, *A.H.E. and S.*, Oct. 1931.
Macpherson, *Annals of Commerce, Manufactures, Fisheries and Navigation*, 4 vols., 1805.
Haliczer, ' The Population of Europe, 1720, 1820, 1930 ', *G.*, Dec. 1934 (includes ' dot maps ' showing the distribution at these dates).

Maps

Cassini de Thury, Maps of France 1720–89, and Ferraris's *Carte Chorographique de la Belgique* (69 sheets), 1797 (these are among the first large-scale maps which begin to become available towards the end of the eighteenth century).

CHAPTER XX

EUROPE IN THE RAILWAY AGE (*c.* 1870)

British and Foreign Trade and Industry (1854–1908), Stationery Office, 1909.
Statistical Abstract for the Principal and other Foreign Countries from 1860 to 1875–6, Stationery Office, 1877.
Kolb, *The Conditions of Nations, Social and Political*, new ed. and trans., 1880.
Mulhall, *The Dictionary of Statistics*, 1892.
Woytinsky, *Die Welt in Zahlen*, 1925, vol. I.

Clapham, J. H., *The Economic Development of France and Germany, 1815–1914*, 4th ed., 1936.

Reclus, E., *Nouvelle Géographie Universelle*, vols. I–V, 1878–9.

Ogg, *The Economic Development of Modern Europe*, 1918.

Knowles, *The Economic Development of Europe in the Nineteenth Century*, 1932.

Day, *A History of Commerce*, new ed., 1922.

Gonnard, *L'Émigration Européenne au XIXe siècle*, 1906.

Levasseur, E., *La Population Française*, vol. I, 1889.

Worms, *L'Allemagne Économique*, 1874 (a history of the German Zollverein).

M'Culloch, J. R., *A Dictionary, Practical, Theoretical and Historical, of Commerce and Commercial Navigation*, new ed., 1882.

McPherson, G., *Transportation in Europe*, 1910.

Colin, A., *La Navigation commerciale au XIXe siècle*, 1901.

Fry, H., *The History of North Atlantic Steam Navigation . . .*, 1896.

Hallberg, *The Suez Canal*, 1931.

Jeans, *Waterways and Water Transport in different countries*, 1890.

Le Chatelier, *Chemins de Fer de l'Allemagne*, 1845.

Jouffroy, ' Aperçu du Développement du Réseau Ferré en Europe à 1848 ', *A. de G.*, XL (with maps).

Marlio, *L'Allemagne et la Navigation interieure*, 1907.

Wallace, D. M., *Russia*, 1877 ; revised ed. 1907.

Laveleye, E., *The Balkan Peninsula*, trans. and ed. by Thorpe, 1887.
Essai sur l'économie rurale de la Belgique, 2nd ed., 1875.

Webster, W., *Spain*, 1882.

Weber, A. F., *The Growth of Cities in the Nineteenth Century*, 1899.

Bowen, F. C., *A Century of Atlantic Travel*, 1932.

Schulte, A., *Tausend Jahre*, 1925 (German history and culture on the Rhine).

Demangeon, A., and Febvre, L., *Le Rhin : Problèmes d'Histoire et d'Economie*, 1935.

Kovalevsky, *La Russie à la fin du XIXe siècle*, 1900.

Drachmann, *The Industrial Development and Commercial Policies of the three Scandinavian Countries*, 1915.

Morgan, O. S. (ed.), *Agricultural Systems of Middle Europe : a symposium*, 1933 (this collection of papers shows how medieval features still survive in parts of east-central Europe).

Brown, J. C., *Pine Plantations in France*, 1878.
Reboisement in France (in Alps, Cevennes and Pyrenees), 1876.

Henderson, W. O., *The Zollverein* (1939).

Weber, Adna F., *The Growth of Cities in the Nineteenth Century: A Study in Statistics*, New York, 1899.

Wrigley, E. A., *Industrial Growth and Population Change : a Regional Study of the Coalfields of North-west Europe in the later Nineteenth Century*, 1961.

INDEX